THE ORIGINS OF VIOLENCE

Anatol Rapoport

THE ORIGINS OF VIOLENCE

Approaches to the Study of Conflict

With a New Introduction by the Author

Transaction Publishers
New Brunswick (U.S.A) and London (U.K.)

Second printing 1997

New material this edition copyright © 1995 by Transaction Publishers, New Brunswick, New Jersey 08903. Originally published in 1989 by Paragon House.

Library of Congress Catalog Number: 94-12483
ISBN: 1-56000-783-4
Printed in the United States of America

Library of Congress Cataloging-in-Publication Data

Rapoport, Anatol, 1911–
    The origins of violence : approaches to the study of conflict / Anatol Rapoport ; with a new introduction by the author.
        p. cm.
    Originally published: New York : Paragon House, 1989.
    Includes bibliographical references and index.
    ISBN 1-56000-783-4
    1. War. 2. Peace. 3. Conflict management. 4. Arms control. 5. Disarmament. I. Title.
U21.2.R37   1994
303.6—dc20   94-12483
                                                                          CIP

To Gwen

Contents

Introduction to the Transaction Edition *ix*
Preface *xvii*
Introduction *xxi*

PART I. THE PSYCHOLOGICAL APPROACH
 1. On So-Called Aggression 3
 2. The Evolutionary Perspective 14
 3. The Behavioral Perspective 33
 4. The Attitudinal Perspective: We and They 53
 5. Uses and Limitations of the Psychological Approach 73

PART II. THE IDEOLOGICAL APPROACH
 6. Ideology: The Substrate of Thought 97
 7. The Ideal of Individual Freedom and the Cult of Property 116
 8. The Ideal of Collective Freedom and the Cult of Struggle 135
 9. Addiction to Power 152
 10. The Cult of Violence 176
 11. Ideological Issues of the Cold War 196
 12. The End of Ideology 223

PART III. THE STRATEGIC APPROACH
  13. The Strategic Mode of Thought   247
  14. Limits of Individual Rationality   276
  15. Cooperative Games and Strategic Bargaining   304
  16. The Intellectualization of War   325

PART IV. THE SYSTEMIC APPROACH
  17. The Systemic View of the World   347
  18. Arms Races   366
  19. Indices, Parameters, and Trends   393
  20. The War System   414

PART V. IN QUEST OF PEACE
  21. Pacifism   443
  22. Conceptions of a World Order   489
  23. Conflict Resolution and Conciliation   510
  24. Problems of Peace Research   537
  25. Problems of Peace Education   569
  26. Concluding Remarks: Can There Be a Science of   585
      Peace?
      Bibliography   *593*
      Name Index   *605*
      Subject Index   *611*

Introduction to the Transaction Edition

This book had been in print six months when the Berlin Wall came down. During the months of euphoria that followed I started to write what I thought would be a sequel, *Peace, an Idea Whose Time has Come*. Ideas, I wrote, lie dormant until their social environment provides the nourishment for their germination and growth. So it was with the steam engine, which was first demonstrated by Hero of Alexandria in 130 B.C. Not until the beginning of the Industrial Revolution in eighteenth-century England could the idea come to fruition and usher in a new age.

The same can be said of the atomic theory of matter, formulated in the fifth century B.C. by Democritus and "awakened" by Dalton in 1803. The idea of universal peace was planted by the prophet Isaiah twenty-eight centuries ago. It seemed to me when I was writing *Peace, an Idea Whose Time has Come* that the institution of war could no longer adapt to the social climate. And I ventured to assume that this time came when the Cold War bubble burst.

Like any other type of organized system the institution of war continues to exist by virtue of adaptation to a range of environments. It emerged in the earliest civilizations when division of labor and permanent settlements gave birth to the military profession. It developed mightily in the age of empire building. It was adapted to the dynastic ambitions of European monarchs, and when absolute hereditary monarchy declined, it became adapted to patriotic sentiments nurtured by the mass media in incipient democracies. In some countries like Germany it thrived on aristocratic militarism. In the Soviet Union the military establishment became an object of veneration as the defender of the nation against ruthless invaders. In the United States, which had never been invaded and where no militaristic traditions existed, the war system remarkably became successfully adapted to "technolatry," the worship of technology, and to the addictive anti-depression "fix" of a perpetual war economy.

In short, I envisaged the demise of the war system as a consequence of "running out of adaptations," when accumulated historical experience, effectively disseminated through vastly improved communication facilities and increasing interdependence of populations, would reveal its essentially parasitic role in modern societies. This was the rationale of viewing peace as an idea whose time had come. For a few months it seemed that the revolution of 1989, which triggered the demise of totalitarian Communism, would usher in a united, peaceful Europe, which would resume its role as the fountainhead of enlightenment, the process blocked by the burgeoning growth of mechanized violence throughout our century.

My brightest hopes were rekindled by the immediate consequences of *glasnost*—the dismantling of restrictions on reading and writing in the Soviet Union, especially the euphoric proclamations of the dismantling process, which made the disavowal of thought control irreversible. *Glasnost* was in effect an emancipation proclamation. The works of the "enemies of the people," of heretics and of dissidents, which had been kept in *spetzkhranienie* (restricted sections of libraries) were put on public display. "Unpersons" became celebrities. Immediate publications of proscribed works were promised. I recall the exhilarating shock of the announcement that Orwell's *Animal Farm* and *Nineteen Eighty-Four* would soon be published in Russian translations. I read avidly and savored literate Russian, which replaced numbing officialese. I witnessed a process that the Germans called *Vergangenheitsbewältigung* (overcoming the past), which went farther and deeper in Russia.

All the more bitter was the disillusionment. There was no spurt of productivity in the Soviet Union as there had been in Poland in 1956 in the wake of a de-Stalinization wave (the Polish "October"). On the contrary, the economy faltered and came to the brink of collapse. Morale plummeted. And, of course, the most severe blow to my hopes was the explosion of hatred and violence rooted in ancient vicious passions and manifested in we-they dichotomies supposedly long discredited in Europe—ethnic and religious. Blood flowed in Tadjikistan, Armenia, the Azerbaidjan, Moldova, Georgia.

The former Soviet Union was by no means the only theater of explosive violence that ushered in what had been heralded as The New Order. Moreover, not all the explosions could be seen as consequences of collapsed centralized power as in the Soviet Union and in Yugoslavia. The chronic violence in the Third World continued unabated. A war against helpless civilians, rationalized as "punishing aggression" was unleashed by the United States in the Middle East.

It seems at first thought that *Peace, an Idea Whose Time has Come,* conceived as a sequel to *The Origins of Violence,* is in greater need of "updating" (not to speak of retraction) than the present book. This is not so, however. The title of the sequel was not meant to imply that peace is about to replace war as a normal state of human affairs. It was meant to reflect the *now prevalent* rejection of war as a normal phase in the relations between states and the *now prevalent* (nearly universal) idea that war is an evil without redeeming features, that it must be rooted out as an institution by common effort.

Some time ago the Baha'i community in Toronto advertised a slogan on subway cars: "Peace is inevitable." Speaking to those groups I pointed out that a more realistic slogan would be "Peace is possible." The implication was that it was now more than ever necessary to *work* for peace, that for the first time in human history it seems as if such work would bring results. The time to work for peace in expectation of results has indeed come.

So I will stand by everything I said in *Peace, an Idea Whose Time has Come.* But all the more, *The Origins of Violence* is in need of revision. Its main shortcoming is the heavy emphasis on the Cold War as the principal obstacle to peace.

Without doubt the Cold War was the most likely source of the most devastating violence to be perpetrated on the human race by human beings. In a previous book (*The Big Two*) I wrote that in both the Soviet Union and in the United States absolute power of life and death over all men, women, and children was vested in "a few individuals at the controls of vast military machines, which, once set in motion, can obliterate hundreds of millions of lives in a few hours."

This situation persisted throughout the four decades of the Cold War. Perhaps its most important but rarely recognized characteristic was the weak or altogether lacking connection between the most obvious sources of violence, such as hatred, rage, cruelty, etc. and its manifestations and effects in war. I was fond of pointing out that nowadays you don't have to hate anyone in order to kill everyone. A laboratory where scientists work on ways to "improve" poison gases may look no different from one where they are searching for cures of deadly diseases. The offices of the Pentagon look no different from those of an insurance company or of any other management nerve center. The war between the United States and the Soviet Union was not pictured (at least not by its planners) as a sequence of battles in which men stick bayonets into each other or as charges by gallant horsemen brandishing sabers but primarily as exchanges of devastating blows against entire populations launched by technicians sitting at consoles deep underground. None of the traditional martial virtues are relevant for this sort of devastation. Physical strength is not needed: there are no heavy weapons to wield. Bravery is not needed: there is no enemy to come face-to-face with. Above all, hatred is not needed, as it was in conventional battles, where inhibitions against killing one's own kind (our mammalian heritage) had to be overcome.

For this reason psychological roots of violence were de-emphasized in the analysis of war and of its evolution. War itself was depicted primarily as a struggle between states not peoples. States were viewed as analogues of organisms in the hierarchy of "living systems"—cells, organs, individuals, groups, social classes, states, the international system. These "organisms" were pictured not simply as collections of individuals any more than individuals are simply collections of cells or organs. Just as human individuals were endowed with consciousness, goal-directedness, etc., which their constituents (cells, tissues, etc.) did not possess, so states were assumed to have "psychologies" that did not necessarily resemble psychologies of individual human beings.

From this perspective it was possible to assume that human individuals may be "by nature" peaceful rather than aggressive (as is commonly assumed when explanations are offered for the persistence of war among humans). If this is so, then the traditional efforts of pacifists to discredit war by denying its supposed biological determinants appear as attempts to break into an open door.

Of limited effectiveness also appeared some of the remedies offered for diffusing the hostility between the populations of the Big Two, assumed to be among the important instigating factors of World War III. Among the proposed remedies were "people-to-people" programs. For instance, a proposal was made to exchange a hundred thousand children between the United States and the Soviet Union (to be rotated yearly), which supposedly would be an inhibiting factor against a genocidal attack, as the start of World War III was usually imagined. The assumption behind the proposal was that its implication would be analogous to an "exchange of hostages," widely used in antiquity as a guarantee of good faith between enemies attempting to resolve their conflict.

From the point of view dominant in *The Origins of Violence* people-to-people contacts were not likely to diffuse the time bomb threatening total destruction, because the sort of violence represented by World War III was not rooted in psychological makeups or states of minds of human individuals but in something else. The threat of total destruction was assumed to be rooted in the dynamics of a *system* endowed with an ability to survive, grow, and develop in a particular environment. The system was the institution of war. The environment, particularly in the United States, was the permanent war economy, to which a large sector of American business became addicted. It was the creation of a war economy that quickly and effectively put an end to the depression of the 1930s. The Cold War ensured its continued growth. It provided a sort of paradise for business: an assured growing market, elimination of risk, elimination of the constant pressure to reduce costs, since cost-plus contracts made *maximization* of costs the most profitable policy. Evidence of addiction is still clearly manifested in energetic resistance against reduction of the military sector of the economy and its supporting adjuncts. The sources of resistance are by no means limited to the military establishment and its business adjuncts. Workers are anxious to protect jobs, scientific and technical professionals careers, politicians pork barrel contracts in their turfs.

Much more relevant than "aggressiveness" as a psychological feature or "hatred" as a psychological state underlying the robustness of war mentality in the United States seemed to me to be the habits of thought induced by business practice in the business community and by supposed imperatives of rationality among the intellectuals of the self-styled "defense community." As an example of the former I cited in *The Origins of Violence* an attempt to apportion expenditures on nuclear weapons by cost-benefit accounting, where costs were expressed in budgeted dollars and "benefits" in the value to the opponent of targets destroyed. As an example of pretense to austere, fearless "rationality" I cited Herman Kahn's detailed analysis of "escalation" governing U.S.-U.S.S.R. hostility. The framework of his analysis is a 44-rung ladder beginning with "pre-play" maneuvers and ending with the total ejaculation of the nuclear arsenal (at one time called the "wargasm"). Nuclear exchanges start already on the twelfth rung of the ladder. The implication was that anti-war activists, blinded by fear and repugnance, failed to appreciate the formidable intricacies of problems spawned by the Cold War and the opportunities it offered for advances in sophisticated strategic thinking.

Elsewhere in this book, as an example of another mind-set, I cited a passage from Treischke's *Politics*:

> It is war which furthers the political idealism which the materialist rejects. What a disaster for civilization it would be if mankind blotted its heroes from memory! The heroes of a nation are the fighters which rejoice and inspire the spirit of its youth and, the writers whose words ring like trumpet blasts become the idols of our boyhood and early manhood.

Referring to this passage Lord Balfour wrote in his preface to the English translation of Treischke's work:

> Political theories from those of Aristotle downward have been related, either by harmony or contrast, to the political practice of their day, but of no theories is this more glaringly true than of those expounded in this volume. They could not have been written before 1870. Nothing quite like them will be written after 1917.

Had I foreseen the impending end of the Cold War when I was writing *The Origins of Violence,* I might have written of Herman Kahn's *On Escalation.*

Metaphors and Scenarios: "Nothing like this could have been written before 1945 nor can be written after 1989." Like Lord Balfour's comment, this one would have expressed a belief in a progressive disestablishment of war in human affairs.

I still believe in the ultimate demise of war as an institution. My belief was expressed implicitly in *The Origins of Violence* and explicitly in *Peace, an Idea Whose Time has Come*. What I need to re-examine critically is the tendency to emphasize a focal point, that is, the supposedly most important source of the most extended violence. Lord Balfour implicitly identified imperial Germany and its militaristic ideology as such a focal point (note the reference to 1870 as the year of the birth of German hyper-militarism and 1917, as he supposed, the year of its death as a consequence of defeat). Had I written something similar in the final years of the Cold War, I would have identified American "technolatry" and Soviet totalitarianism as the most important sources of the most extended violence and would have prophesied the end of the Cold War as a fatal blow to these ideologies, in consequence of which the writings of the American civilian strategists (Albert Wohlstetter, Herman Kahn, Colin Gray) would become permanently obsolete.

Those writings, like those of Treischke, indeed became obsolete, but the dissipation of their rationales or glorification of violence was not accompanied by a recession of the level of global violence. There is no dearth of explanations of why the dissipation of the superpower confrontation did not move the world closer to global peace, and they might well be the content of the "updated" introduction to this book. But such ex-post-facto explanations would not have served my original purpose in writing the book, nor in taking the opportunity of justifying its re-issue.

My original purpose was to contribute to the growing prominence of peace education, potentially a vehicle of enlightenment, the prerequisite of the demise of war as an institution. From this point of view peace education is seen not as an attempt to make people more peace loving, tolerant, cooperative or whatnot nor as a set of remedies (invariably doomed to become obsolete) for the war disease but as an attempt to induce *awareness* of the ever-broadening and cumulative processes that have brought humanity to the present precarious state. This requires emphasis on the historical perspective, often neglected in increasingly positivist social sciences. The late Kenneth Boulding summarized this emphasis in an apparently inane but really profound aphorism: "Things are as they are because they got that way."

The positivist (predominantly a-historical) methods in the social sciences stem from tendencies to imitate the methods of the natural sciences, in which the positivist paradigm has been phenomenally successful. Their limitation stems from a fundamental difference between the natural phenomena and the sort of events and processes that are central in human affairs. The reality studied in the natural sciences is independent of what people write, say, or think of it. Whatever I choose to think, say, or write about the moon has no effect on the moon. But whatever I say, write, or even think about human behavior may, depending on the extent of dissemination of my ideas, influence human behavior. This is the well-known self-reinforcing (or, at times, self-inhibiting) property of assumptions or predictions made by humans.

Moreover, what humans write, say, or think about social reality *is* part of social reality. For this reason education in the social sciences (which includes peace education) differs from that in the natural sciences. To understand physics, it is not necessary to read Aristotle, in fact may lead to confusion, since he was often grossly in error. But to understand the nature of human societies reading Hobbes or Rousseau or Kant or Lenin or Hitler can be of great help, not because those thinkers were right in their observations (most of them were widely off the mark) but because their writings are themselves raw data of social processes reflecting the social and ideational climate in which those authors lived.

It is in this spirit that I hope *The Origins of Violence* will be read. The book is a record of ideas and preoccupations of someone, the second half of whose life coincided with the second half of the twentieth century. I remember vividly the aftermath of the First World War. For the first time in history the idea that war is a social disease made inroads on the mainstream idea that war is a normal phase in relations among states. For the first time the psychological roots and the social effects of patriotism, nationalism, and martial virtues were subjected to critical scrutiny. Remarque's novel *All Quiet on the Western Front* was the most eloquent expression of this radical change of perspective.

It was not so easy to attribute World War II to nationalistic hysteria, or, as from a Marxist perspective, to the dynamics of the capitalist system. Much stronger cases could be made for self-defense; a clash of incompatible ideologies made much more sense than in World War I. But even here it was not easy to separate genuine conviction from rationalizing rhetoric. In *The Origins of Violence* I attributed the principal driving force of total destruction not to a clash of incompatible value systems (the mainstream explanation at least in America) but to the self-propelling dynamics of war as a global institution. In these dynamics I saw the principal threat of World War III.

The threat has receded but not the level of violence if this level is assessed in terms of intensity of effect rather than extent of destruction. To be sure the Gulf War could be seen as a brief episode of World War III: disappearance of the traditional battle field, massive and indiscriminate killing of civilians, state of the art super-technology of destruction, almost total impotence of defense, hence total immunity of attacking personnel.

But the focus of violence has shifted radically. Confined largely to the Third World, violence is now perpetrated predominantly by people on people caught in whirlpools of hatred, retribution, and sadistic orgies. "What are the principal fountainheads of this (traditional) sort of violence?" is a fair question. Should we re-examine the old conviction shared by many—both by the ill informed and by sophisticated thinkers (Freud, contemporary sociobiologists)—that violence or evil in general (as Calvinist theologians would have it) is inherent in "human nature," and that therefore no secular enlightenment or institutional reforms will exorcise this incubus?

I have never denied the possibility that aggressive tendencies in humans may stem from a biological heritage. I have only refused to view this heritage as a *principal* origin of violence among humans. In view of the events of the past five years, I attach more significance to this origin, but regard this change of view as a stimulus of further and deeper investigations, namely, of the *extent* of this predilection and of the conditions under which it becomes widely and destructively manifested.

All in all we need to recognize that the sources of violence are constantly changing. If anything is to be learned from recent dismal lessons of history is that we need to learn to anticipate these changes. It has been said of generals that they are always planning to fight the preceding war. It can be said with equal irony of peace activists that they are usually trying to prevent the preceding war.

It does seem, however, that the demise of the bipolar world has turned the attention of the peace researchers, peace educators, and peace activists to the three cardinal global problems, global in the sense that they can yield (if at all) only to global solutions: the eradication of all organized violence, the protection of a life-sustaining environment, and the universal application of principles of social justice (including an equitable distribution of resources). None of these three problems can be solved separately. They are all totally intertwined. Without eradication of war and of the mentality that breeds it (primacy of "national interests," and their geopolitical implications) attention cannot be seriously turned to the other two problems. On the other hand, failure to arrest the degradation of the environment and to alleviate the gross inequities produced by unfettered market forces and the autonomy of capital will inevitably create sources of conflict, which, although of ancient origin, are essentially new in our age: conflicts over land and water, for example (rather than the familiar ones over markets, spheres of influence, ideology, national identity, or world hegemony). This development was not anticipated in the present book. I feel compelled to point this out and urge the readers to give it serious thought.

Preface

This book embodies the material of an introductory course in a four-year peace and conflict studies program at the University of Toronto. At the time the program was established, there was just one similar program in Canada at the University of Waterloo; in the United States there are anywhere from 60 to 200 programs of this kind, depending on which are regarded to be of comparable scope.

Although the book grew out of a course taught in Canada, the preponderance of material in it deals with American politics and with the American scene generally. The fact that I spent most of my adult life in the United States partially accounts for this emphasis. In addition, the large amount of attention devoted to what goes on in the United States is justified by the very special role the U.S. is playing in contemporary world affairs. Only one other country plays a comparable role—the Soviet Union. These roles are clearly determined by the "superpower" status of the two countries. The term superpower has a quite concrete meaning: It refers to the ability of the governing groups of either country literally to destroy everything we call civilization within a few hours. Perhaps they have the ability to destroy all human life on this planet *at will*. One hesitates to ascribe any such intent to any group of human beings. However, the phrase "at will" need not refer to action by design. It refers to the *ability* to initiate a chain of events, perhaps not even consciously or specifically intended, which will in fact lead to such a catastrophe. The situation has no precedents, nothing remotely similar in human history.

The danger is widely recognized and freely discussed. Seemingly reasonable proposals have been made for what should be done about the danger. Their impact on superpower decision-makers seems practically nil, though certain changes in public attitudes are discernible. If historical analogies are relevant, we must assume that it is just such changes of attitudes—gradual and cumulative—that eventually can lead to radical transformations of human societies and, with them, of the human condition.

Some of these changes have been for the better, some for the worse. Among the changes for the better, in my estimation, have been those that have emancipated large portions of humanity from drudgery, have improved the general level of health, have to some extent induced more widespread respect for the dignity of the individual, have broadened areas in which human beings can cooperate, and have reduced ruthless exploitation of human beings by other human beings. All these changes were consequences of the spread of science as an organized social activity in two ways. One, easily recognized, has been by application of reliable knowledge about the world to the design of technology. The other way, less widely appreciated, has been via emancipating human beings from delusions and superstitions. It is this emancipation that I call enlightenment.

I take the stance that the predicament in which humanity now finds itself stems from a lag in the enlightenment process initiated by the natural sciences. Thinking about matters pertaining to the role of conflict in human affairs, particularly large-scale conflicts involving organized violence, is still circumscribed by frameworks and paradigms that are no longer adequate. Can one hope that a science of conflict (or its obverse side, a science of peace) can emancipate our thinking from these binds and clear the way for a new way of thinking, which Einstein once declared to be a precondition for avoiding an irreversible catastrophe?

A science is developed in a framework of a discipline. Does the area usually designated as "peace and conflict studies" deserve to be subsumed under "disciplines"? Kenneth E. Boulding (1978) mentions "three tests of a discipline: does it have a bibliography? can you give courses in it? and can you give an examination of it?" To these he adds a possible fourth: "does it have any specialized journals?" The last criterion is easily satisfied for peace and conflict studies. The *Journal of Conflict Resolution* in the U.S., the *Journal of Peace Research* and the *Bulletin of Peace Proposals* in Norway, the *Yearbooks* of the Stockholm International Peace Research Institute in Sweden, the *Peace Research Reviews* in Canada (to name a few) are well established and widely read periodicals devoted entirely to conflict and conflict resolution.

The references at the end of this book answer the first of the questions posed by Boulding. The opening sentence of this preface answers the second. A meaningful answer to the third ("Can you give an examination in it?") depends on how skillfully the large literature, unquestionably relevant to the study of conflict, can be focused, so that passing an examination can be regarded as evidence of well-organized knowledge. Knowledge of what? Presumably knowledge of how people through the ages, from Heraclitus to Hitler, from Isaiah to Gandhi, thought and felt about conflict and conflict resolution, war and peace. An immersion in peace and conflict studies should induce the student to wonder how the same age could have produced an Erasmus and a Machiavelli or a Treitschke and a Tolstoy. Appreciation of how those people thought and especially of how those thoughts are interrelated, how they complement each other, or why they clash with one another, constitutes *self-knowledge* writ large—knowledge transcending one's individual self, self-knowledge on the level of humanity. This is the sort of knowledge that a science of conflict (or a science of peace) is supposed to generate. It differs from the knowledge imparted by the natural sciences, but is no less important as a component of enlightenment.

Two books have to a considerable extent shaped my thinking about the subject treated here. One is Quincy Wright's monumental work, *A Study of War* (1942), in which this most pervasive and most important form of conflict is conceived both as a type of event and a type of institution, and a formidable effort of scholarship and analysis is brought to bear on both these aspects of war. The other book, *The Science of Conflict* by J.A. Schellenberg, was written, I believe, in the same spirit as the present volume. This author devotes considerable space to the thoughts of Adam Smith, Charles Darwin, and Karl Marx, surely because of the powerful impact that those thinkers have had on the ideological framework of the Western world. Familiarity with this framework is a prerequisite for the sort of self-knowledge that a science of conflict is supposed to impart.

In this book, the writings of thinkers who have made significant contributions to the predominant ideational framework of our civilization are described and evaluated. While I have tried to be objective in my *analyses* of the various contributions to the study of conflict, I have not been morally neutral, as the reader will readily perceive.

The "sewing together" of the very diverse strands in the different approaches to the study of conflict discussed here has been my principal task. The frequent cross-references strewn throughout the pages in the form of (cf. chapter ——) are meant to call the reader's attention to the interconnections. If the book is used for studying, following these cross-references is recommended.

Originally the book was intended to serve as a text of a year's course at a university. It can, however, be used as a reference work. If each of the five parts is supplemented by a thorough discussion of the relevant references, several courses can be easily constructed on the basis of the indicated material, which, I am sure, will continue to grow.

I take pleasure in expressing my thanks to Professors World Peace Academy for encouraging me to write this book; to Professor J.A. Schellenberg and Seymour Kurtz, my wife Gwen, and my son Anthony for perceptive comments on early drafts and many helpful suggestions. Whatever shortcomings or errors have remained are, of course, my own.

ANATOL RAPOPORT
Toronto

Introduction

In introducing the theme of their book, *Games and Decisions*, R. Duncan Luce and Howard Raiffa (1957) remark that more has been written on conflict than on any other subject save two: love and God. How accurate this estimate is cannot be ascertained without actually examining everything that has been written or at least large representative samples of it. But the estimate seems plausible. Aside from feelings associated with excruciating pain, which is, as a rule, of mercifully short duration, the most intense feelings experienced by human beings are probably those engendered by conflict and by love. These are "chronic" conditions. They remain in the field of consciousness for long stretches of time, inducing thought about their genesis, nature, and effects. The third theme, God, also frequently recurring in what people write (and presumably think) about, probably reflects a concern with one's ultimate fate and, on a higher level, with the fate of all of us.

This book is about conflict. A vast variety of events, conditions, and processes is subsumed under that label. It will be our task to inquire about what all these have in common, if anything. Our discussion will also be concerned with the other two themes mentioned by Luce and Raiffa, which have a bearing on conflict, usually in various guises.

There are ways of categorizing conflicts according to the number of people involved. We can speak of *intra*-personal conflict going on within an individual—for instance, the state of mind induced by conflicting loyalties, identity crises, ambivalent relations to others, or doubts. There are *interpersonal* conflicts between pairs or among small numbers of persons, *intergroup* conflicts, involving distinguishable categories of persons, e.g., ethnic groups, adherents of different systems of beliefs, religions, or political parties. And there are *wars*.

The events of the past decades have left no doubt that war is by far the most important form of conflict among human beings. It has become commonplace to say that today an outbreak of a major war between the superpowers, the United States and the Soviet Union, threatens the human race with extinction. It would seem, then, that if a study were to devote amounts of space to various forms of conflict in proportion to the importance of their consequences, war, as a theme, would completely overshadow all others. But this would be a poor way of allotting to war the amount of attention it deserves. Only by relating war to other forms of conflict and even to other areas of human activity can we get a measure of understanding of this phenomenon; and understand it we must, if we want a chance of escaping what it threatens.

The threatened war between the superpowers and the ramifications of this threat have come to occupy a central position in contemporary thought because this danger is not merely a bigger danger in the sense of portending more destruction and more suffering than other wars, but is an entirely different kind of danger, altogether unprecedented in human history. In trying to get an understanding of this danger and ideas on how best to avoid it, we have no historical experience and no reliable theory to go by. All we can be reasonably sure of is that if an all-out war between the superpowers occurs, it will turn out to be "a war to end war," but not in the sense in which World War I or World War II were to have been.

To study war under the threat of annihilation, we must get as broad an overview of conflict as possible, yet within manageable bounds, since there is no time to devote many years of study to it. We want to be objective, because objectivity in pursuit of knowledge is the best guarantee of getting reliable knowledge. Yet we cannot afford to lose sight of the urgency of the situation.

In our study of conflict, we will follow four different approaches: the psychological, the ideological, the strategic, and the systemic.

Most people conceive of conflict as generated by the psychological states of individuals—their attitudes toward other individuals or categories of individuals, their "character," their reactions toward actions or attitudes of others and so forth. There is a widespread notion that a predilection for "aggression" is embedded in human nature and that conflicts are consequences of manifestations of aggressive impulses driven by this trait. We will consider these notions under the psychological dimension of conflict and will examine evidence for or against various psychological theories as well as the relevance of these theories to the study of conflict on different levels.

The ideological dimension is the psychological "writ large." An ideology can be regarded as the psychological makeup of a culture or society, a substrate of collective thought, as it were. In this approach, not the individual but the cultural environment will be at the center of attention. To a large extent, attitudes of persons toward others and toward different aspects of social life are shaped by the repertoire of ideas, beliefs, prejudices, conceptions of good and evil, and of the nature of the human condition dominant or prevalent in their culture. Normally, people internalize these views and attitudes in the process of being socialized.

It may well be that psychological makeup is a factor in the extent to which persons can see the world in ways other than those prevalent in their cultures. But by and large, the stamp of their own culture is impressed on most individuals growing up in it. We will examine the role that ideology has played, plays, or can play as an instigator of large-scale conflicts. This is an important question that relates significantly to the relation between the superpowers. It is maintained (and many believe) that the main obstacle to the establishment of normal relations between the United States and the Soviet Union is the incompatibility of "Communist" (or "totalitarian") and "Capitalist" (or "democratic") ideologies. Chronic enmity and lack of trust are supposed to be consequences of the ideological chasm that separates the two cultures. This idea will be examined, its origins traced, and an opinion will be offered on its validity.

The next aspect of conflict to be examined will be the strategic. Here theories of *decision* in conflict situations will be formulated and examined. Some such theories indicate ways of determining *optimal* or *rational* courses of action when the outcomes of one's actions are determined not only by these but also by actions of one or more others who are also choosing courses of action in accordance with certain principles of rationality or optimality. The term "strategic" refers to plans of action in situations of this sort—in particular, to long-term planning or military operations.

War, including preparations for war, will be presented as it appears to the professional. This "professional" need not be someone who is actually in military service. The planning and the conduct of war engages vast numbers of people, some with highly specialized skills who, while not categorized as military personnel, nevertheless have made activities related to war their principal occupation. It will be instructive to see war as they see it. In particular, we will see why certain vitally important questions about war may not readily occur to the professional—for example, to what extent war and activities related to it can be conducted "rationally," where the usual distinction betweeen rationality and ethics is preserved. Next, the question will be raised whether it is possible to make this distinction in all instances. It is in this approach to the theory of conflict that the most searching questions about the present status of war as an organized human activity will be posed.

Finally, the systemic approach will deal with those aspects of large-scale conflicts that are not subject to deliberate human control. From the systemic point of view, large-scale conflicts are regarded as massive phenomena governed by analogues of forces, somewhat in the same way as the weather or the evolution of ecological systems is determined. It is possible to look at such phenomena through an instrument of "low-resolving power," so to speak, whereby the complex details of their inner dynamics are ignored and only the gross global trends remain in our field of vision. One ignores the trees in order to see the forest. One tries to see the massive behavior of humankind through the eyes of the proverbial Martian, who is ignorant of motivations, strategies, and rationalizations, and who sees only the gross effects. On the basis of these low-resolving power observations, such an observer might get the impression that humankind is making elaborate preparations to commit suicide. Rational decisions and deliberate choices of action play no part in the systemic models of conflict. In a way, therefore, the systemic approach is a complementary opposite to the strategic approach.

In the last part of the book, we shall be concerned with the problem of achieving peace through conflict resolution, through the impact of ideologies countervailing the presently dominant ones (which put obstacles in the way of peacemaking), through applying results of scientific research, and through education.

Our categorization of the approaches to the study of conflict should not be regarded as reflecting some sort of objective reality. Reality is far too complex to be captured by categories that we impose on it. Thus, it is futile to argue about whether racial prejudice should be subsumed under the "psychological" or the "ideological" dimension of conflict, or whether a critique of the theory of balance of power belongs to the strategic or the systemic approach. We treat those aspects separately in the interest of organizing our exposition. If the reader wishes to see a mode of conflict from a perspective different from ours or from more than one perspective, we would regard this rethinking as an indication that we have achieved our goal—to stimulate thinking about conflicts from various points of view.

A word is in order concerning the attitudinal stance in this book. We believe that in writing about matters where human affairs play a crucial role, and especially where human fate is in the balance, neutrality is impossible, and calling a stance "neutral" is irresponsible. At the same time, we believe that all science, including social science (in the light of which we have tried to conduct this study) is and ought to be at all times *objective*.

Objectivity is by no means identical with moral neutrality. Objectivity demands open-mindedness, an ability to see evidence that does not support one's point of view, and to understand arguments that one does not agree with sufficiently to present them fairly. It is quite possible to adhere to these principles and yet wholly accept one set of values and categorically reject another. The physician does not pretend to be neutral with regard to the life-and-death struggle between the patient and the disease. He is unequivocally on the side of the patient. This does not prevent the physician from being objective in the sense that he does not permit his judgment to be influenced by hopes or fears or distorted by selecting evidence in favor of preconceived ideas in preference to evidence that refutes them. By the same token, we take a stand condemning the institution of war as unequivocally and uncompromisingly as the abolitionists of a century and a half ago condemned the institution of slavery.

This stance will at times make it difficult for us to develop our arguments. Some decisions of governments, particularly of the superpowers, can be clearly seen in retrospect to have been irrational from the point of view of the interests of those governments. For instance, the U.S. attack on Cuba in April 1961 was a military fiasco and in addition damaged the image of the U.S. in the eyes of the Third World. Likewise, the Soviet attack on Czechoslovakia in August 1968 was counterproductive in the sense that it killed the traditional pro-Russian orientation of the Czechs, the best friends the Soviet Union had in Eastern Europe. Besides, the intervention severely damaged the image of the Soviet Union among the left-wing intellectuals in the West and strengthened the anti-Soviet stance of the NATO allies. We agree with the critics of the American and Soviet regimes that these actions were counterproductive. But we cannot stress this pragmatic argument, since we wish to avoid giving the impression that, had the results been different, the actions would have been justified. For instance, the Bay of Pigs operation might have been successful and might have led to the overthrow of Castro. In this case, the policy of overthrowing unfriendly governments by force would have been justified on pragmatic grounds. Or the Russians might have succeeded in crushing resistance in Afghanistan within a few weeks instead of being bogged down there for years. Then the "Brezhnev Doctrine" would have appeared successful. Since, however, we condemn power politics as a matter of principle, we cannot wholeheartedly join the pragmatists in condemning specific interventions on the basis of their failure to achieve their goals.

The above is just one example of the difficulties we had to face in trying to combine objectivity, as it is usually understood in scientific discourse, and partisanship, unavoidable in a sincere treatment of the present theme. Other difficulties arose from the necessity of striking a balance between technical exposition and a readable style. Some of our arguments stem from considerations that can be explained only in technical language—for instance, the language of formal decision theory. Even if drastically simplified, these explanations may tax the patience of a technically uninitiated reader. We have not been able to solve this problem in the past, and have not solved it here.

The impossibility of preserving a stance of neutrality and detachment in the present context has been mentioned. We hope that the unprecedented immensity of the issues involved will be seen as sufficient justification for breaking out of the traditional constraints of academic discourse.

THE
ORIGINS OF
VIOLENCE

PART

THE PSYCHOLOGICAL APPROACH

1

On So-Called Aggression

For the first time in the history of humanity, collective violence has made us an endangered species. Perhaps it is true that every age, not just ours, has been dominated by conflict between human beings. And it is true that previous premonitions of doom did not materialize. But our age *is* different. The prescience conferred on human beings by science, unlike the visions of seers of earlier ages, has proved to be astonishingly reliable with regard to certain kinds of events. These are the events governed by physical laws that have become known to humanity only within the last few centuries. Predictions based on inferences derived from those laws come true. The planets move in their prescribed orbits. Their positions can be predicted centuries in advance. Chemical reactions proceed as predicted. Machines normally work as they have been designed to work, and when they don't we know the reason why.

It is on the basis of those well-nigh perfectly reliable laws that dire predictions are made concerning the consequences of a major nuclear war—that civilization almost certainly cannot, and humanity quite probably cannot, survive such a war. This warning is not to be mistaken for just another doomsday prophecy like those common in earlier ages, but must be taken seriously.

The warning is indeed taken seriously by many who have given thought to this matter. Thus, the present observation that our age is dominated by conflict has acquired a new, unprecedented, and ominous meaning. Conflict among humans is now no longer seen as a normal aspect of the human condition, nor as a driving force improving human life through competition, but as a malady or a source of evil, in the sense of being a threat to the very existence of humanity.

So-Called Evil

The wide attention attracted by Konrad Lorenz's book, *On Aggression* (Lorenz 1966) can be ascribed to the vividness with which he described a vast variety of behavior patterns observed in a vast variety of animals. In spite of their differences, they bear a striking, immediately recognizable resemblance to our own behavior in situations involving conflict. Therein lies the reason for the book's wide readership.

The original title of Lorenz's book, "Das sogenannte Böse," makes the connotation of evil in conflict manifest. "Das Böse" is a German noun derived from an adjective meaning evil, wicked, mischievous, malevolent. The modifier "sogenannte" ("so-called"), unfortunately omitted in translation, also conveys something about Lorenz's message. It cautions the reader against anthropomorphic interpretations of animal behavior.

Lorenz is a biologist. His creative life is immersed in the rich world of living nature—in particular, the world of animals, some of which resemble us in striking ways. Biologists regard man as part of that living world, unique in some ways, but on the whole sharing many features with other creatures, certainly physical features and perhaps also mental and emotional ones. It is now established as firmly as anything can be established by criteria of validity acceptable to scientists that man and many other animals share common ancestors. Some of these may be remote, others not so remote. Our common heritage includes not only limbs, stomachs, and lungs but also some mechanisms of neural activity that underlie the formation of habits. We may be justified in assuming a common ancestry of mental and emotional characteristics.

Yet Lorenz by his qualifying phrase "so-called" bids us be wary of facile anthropomorphic interpretations of animal behavior. Before the advent of modern science, philosophers ascribed wisdom to the owl, diligence to the ant and the bee, innocence to the dove, courage to the lion. These Aesopian notions obviously stemmed from certain superficial resemblances—the expression on the face of the owl, the busy scampering of the ant, the meek appearance and gentle cooing of the dove, and so forth. We can never get inside an animal and experience its "thoughts" and "feelings," if any. We can't even get inside the skins of our fellow human beings and *directly* experience their thoughts and feelings. We are, nevertheless, convinced that our fellow human beings think and feel as we do. It is our remarkable language that "binds our consciousnesses." Because we "almost" experience the thoughts and feelings of our fellow human beings when they tell us about them, we tend to project our own thoughts and feelings on them and, by extension, on other fellow creatures. Even biologists can't help "anthropomorphizing" whenever they try to learn something about humans by careful, thorough, and systematic study of other animals.

The layman draws parallels between nonhuman and human behavior by intuitively "recognizing" similarities. Dogs fight. Their movements, the sounds they make—even the "expressions" on their faces—lead us to believe that they feel rage as we do when we fight or want to fight. We call such behavior "aggressive." So when two tropical fishes in an aquarium position themselves face-to-face and go through certain motions until one of them turns around and swims away, we attribute "aggressive" behavior to these fishes. From this inference it is only a step to postulating a principle governing such behavior and designating it by a name—"aggressiveness."

Questions now arise. Is this the same principle that governs the behavior of two children when one grabs one end of a toy held by the other and pulls? Is it the same principle that is manifested when children quarrel without fighting? When one person insults another? When men shoot at each other in a duel? When nations go to war?

Single Word Explanations

We often think we understand something when it has been named. Indeed, understanding is akin to recognition, as when something apparently unfamiliar turns out to be familiar. It sometimes becomes familiar simply by being named, just as a person becomes familiar when his name becomes known. We are all too readily satisfied with explanations that amount to no more than giving a name to a presumed cause of an event to be explained. A character in a comedy by Molière "explains" why opium induces sleep: "Because it has a dormative property."

It is commonplace to ascribe certain patterns of human behavior to "instincts." People are assumed to like making money because of an "acquisitive instinct." They conceal certain parts of their bodies because of the "instinct of modesty," come together because they are instinctively gregarious or avoid each other because of a distance-keeping instinct.

Single word (or short phrase) explanations, like dormative property, instinct, human nature, or the will of God are vacuous. They are like the answer "because" that an adult, impatient with a child's curiosity, gives to its persistent questions beginning with "why." Answers of this sort are meant to choke off further questions, not to explain. For if to explain means anything, it means to show that something that does not seem to fit into one's ideas of what is expected turns out to fit once attention is turned to circumstances of which one had not been aware.

As the range of observations of human behavior broadened and ideas about human nature became less parochial, more attention was devoted to environmental (cultural) determinants. At one time, psychologists denied the existence of instincts in humans. The work of ethologists (biologists studying behavior of animals) restored respectability to the concept. Instead of "instinct" being a catchall term serving as a one-word explanation, the word acquired a technical meaning with a demonstrable range of applicability. If man was to be regarded as part of the living world, kin to all life, it was difficult to keep insisting that this particular creature had been divested of instincts which his ancestors must have possessed.

In the light of Lorenz's work, the question as to what extent man's aggressive behavior could be regarded as a manifestation of an instinct becomes a respectable question. And it becomes all too clear *why* this question has come to the forefront of attention in our age of ever more destructive conflicts and threats of annihilation. Is violence in human life inevitable because an "instinct of aggression" is an immutable component of the human psyche?

Instinctive Behavior

Criteria that justify labeling a form of behavior "instinctive" are fairly clear. First, there must be good evidence that such behavior is not learned. Using the jargon of modern information technology, we would say that the organism has been "programmed" to behave as it does. Second, the behavior must be manifested by almost every member of the species. That this must be so can be seen to be a consequence of being "genetically programmed," because all members of a species are supposed to be endowed with very similar genetic profiles. Third, because instinctive behavior is independent of the organism's experience, it is expected to be fairly uniform throughout the species. It is allowed that some learned features could be superimposed, introducing individual differences. But we ought to be able to infer an *underlying* common pattern that satisfies the criterion of uniformity of instinctive behavior. The same uniformity applies to instances of the behavior observed at various times.

Organisms of limited learning capacity exhibit the clearest forms of instinctive behavior—apparently unlearned, uniform throughout the species, and remarkably rigid, even though often exceedingly complex. The behavior of the digger wasp providing for her brood is a striking example. First she digs a hole. Then she looks for a species-characteristic prey, for instance, a tarantula of a certain species. (No other species will do.) She stings the tarantula in a certain spot, paralyzing it, and drags it to the edge of the hole. Leaving her prey on the edge, she enters the hole as if to see that everything is as it should be, emerges, and drags the tarantula in. Then she lays her eggs on the body of the victim. The still-living body will serve as food for the offspring when they hatch.

This pattern seems to satisfy all the criteria of instinctive behavior. The rigidity of the pattern is especially impressive. If, during the time the wasp inspects the hole, the tarantula is removed some inches away, the wasp will drag it back to the edge, then enter the hole again as if to inspect it, in spite of the fact that she has done this just a few moments before. Evidently the sequence "drag, leave on edge, inspect, drag into hole, lay eggs" must be preserved just so. The components of the sequence cannot be separated from each other. If during the inspection the tarantula is again moved, the whole process will be repeated no matter how many times the chain is broken.

Drives

In animals with capacity to learn, such rigidity is seldom observed. Therefore if we wish to speak of instinctive behavior of such animals, we must loosen our definition. We may want to include forms of behavior that vary from individual to individual, provided we can assume a genetically determined basic pattern underlying the variations. We know, for example, that all living creatures ingest nutrients and eliminate wastes, and that all perform actions to insure reproduction of their kind. Since these actions are performed in a vast variety of ways and yet *all* living beings, not just members of some species, do them, we are justified in postulating *something* that underlies these forms of behavior. The usual name for this "something" is "drive."

In a way, drive can be regarded as a one-word explanation, like instinct. Psychologists of certain schools of thought, in the first instance behaviorists, keep warning of the delusions that are easily induced by the habit of proposing explanations that verge on tautologies (like appealing to the dormative property of opium). Nevertheless the concept of drive has its uses. Reference to it need not be taken as attempted explanation of why organisms behave as they do. The reference can be understood simply as calling attention to the *generality* of a certain form of behavior. To say that there is a hunger drive is simply to say that all animals eat. To say that there is a reproductive drive is to call attention to the fact that all living things reproduce.

The term "drive" can be imbued with somewhat stronger theoretical significance. One can understand drive as something that induces an animal to behave in a certain way independent of the presence of particular external stimuli to induce the behavior. A drive can be understood as that which underlies *spontaneous* behavior motivated from the inside. Take hunger. Hungry animals can be observed *actively* searching for food. This is not the same as reacting to the presence of food by eating it. Also, an animal can be observed becoming restless and actively searching for a mate, not just reacting to the presence of one. It is this apparent spontaneity of some forms of behavior, i.e., independence from external stimuli, that has led some psychologists and ethologists to postulate the existence of drives.

In his book *On Aggression*, Konrad Lorenz suggests that underlying the behavior of at least the vertebrates are four great drives: hunger, sex, fear, and aggression. We have mentioned hunger and sex. That activities presumably instigated by these drives are necessary for continued survival of any species cannot be denied. A case can also be made for fear. This drive can be assumed to instigate various forms of escape behavior, which removes the animal from the vicinity of danger. Thus, fear is conducive to survival. However, spontaneity of behavior instigated by fear is difficult to establish. Escape behavior seems invariably to be triggered by some external stimuli.

Is Aggression Part of Being Human?

It is the last postulated drive—aggression—that is most directly related to the theme of this book. Of the greatest interest is the question whether aggression is a basic drive in human beings and, if so, whether, like the need to eat or the need to mate, a need to "aggress" is present in human beings regardless of the presence of appropriate stimuli.

Lorenz offered evidence of the spontaneity of aggression in coral fishes. He observed a population of some 100 tropical fish represented by some 25 species. As expected, fights began to occur soon after this colony was established. It is generally known that such fights take place predominantly between members of the same species (intra-specific aggression) rather than between members of different species (inter-specific aggression). This was fully corroborated in Lorenz's fish population. On the basis of chance alone only about 3% of the bites were expected to be inflicted on members of own species. Actually about 85% of the bites were so inflicted.

The spontaneity of aggression hypothesis was supported by the observation that the bites inflicted on members of other species came predominantly from fish that were the only representatives of their species. It appeared as if their aggression, seeking an outlet, was directed against otherwise inappropriate targets for lack of appropriate ones.

Other observations on cichlids (a species of tropical fish) yielded even more dramatic results. These fish were observed to kill even their mates when other targets of aggression were not available. Let us see the implications of the idea that the aggressive drive resides in human beings, that is, seeks an outlet even in the absence of stimuli that might elicit aggression.

It is almost a folk saying that there will always be wars because human beings are aggressive by nature. There is no lack of evidence of "man's inhumanity to man." Reading some accounts of human events, we can easily get the impression that murder and massacre, torture and enslavement, robbery and rape are the principal activities of human beings. It is hardly worth mentioning that this evidence by itself does not warrant the conclusion that the dominant ingredient of "human nature" is violence. Another list could be compiled of instances of altruism and cooperation, passionate quests for knowledge and wisdom, celebrations of love and friendship. In spite of the seemingly ubiquitous propensity of boys to fight, the very young human child seems to be a gentle creature, readily reaching out to other small living creatures, human and nonhuman, with gestures of affection rather than with threats of violence.

What Can Be Said About Human Nature?

Diametrically opposite doctrines about human nature are found in religions. The doctrine of the original sin in Christian theology implies that man is essentially evil. In its extreme form, as in the teaching of Calvin, the human being is pictured as depraved from birth. Moreover, according to this teaching, man can do nothing to increase his chances of salvation. His fate (to be saved or damned) is supposed to be decided from the beginning of time. In contrast, nothing of the sort can be inferred from the teaching of the presumed founder of Christianity as his teaching is recorded in the Gospels. On the contrary, the view that human beings are fundamentally good and compassionate is more in agreement with what Jesus is supposed to have taught. Two incidents related in the New Testament support this view. One is Jesus' encounter with children. "The Kingdom of God belongs to such as these," he said (Luke 18:16). This can be taken to mean that human beings in their primitive (i.e., childlike) state are good. And surely Jesus' conception of goodness coincides with complete absence of aggressiveness.

The other incident is related in the scene where Jesus invites the person without sin to cast the first stone at the adulteress (John 8:7). The fact that no one does suggests that compassion, triggered by the realization of own unworthiness, overrides the aggressive impulse, even when an attack appears justified. The implication is that compassion is a dominant affect in the psyche of the human individual, i.e., that human beings are fundamentally good.

In Leo Tolstoy's version of Christianity, the belief in the inherent goodness of human beings is evident in numerous stories and essays. On the other hand, Jonathan Swift in his *Gulliver's Travels* (especially in Book IV) eloquently represents human nature as utterly evil.

Among psychologists, the complete spectrum is represented at one end by Freud's abject pessimism and at the other by Abraham Maslow's guarded optimism.

Freud's Death-Wish Hypothesis

In his theory of neurosis, Sigmund Freud at first attributed aggressive impulses to frustration generated by the inhibition of a child's sexuality directed toward the parent of the opposite sex—the so-called Oedipus complex (Brill 1938, pp. 906–909). Later, however, Freud suggested another source of aggression—the so-called death wish, the longing of every living being to revert to its original state of nonbeing. Since, however, this supposed drive to self-destruction is opposed by the opposite instinct of self-preservation, it is turned outward and manifests itself in a tendency to wreak destruction on others. Possibly the trauma of World War I inspired this idea. We who live in the last decades of the violent twentieth century may not appreciate the profound shock experienced by thoughtful Europeans as a result of that war. The faith in "progress," in steady maturation of civilization with its commitment to civility and its abhorrence of savagery, was shattered by four years of senseless carnage. The outbreak was consistent with the idea of a dormant destructive drive suddenly released.

In *Civilization and Its Discontents*, Freud pictured the human psyche as a battleground on which the drive to live and create (Eros) and the drive to die and destroy (Thanatos) contend for supremacy, and he attributes the failure of man to achieve a harmonious existence (what he calls "civilization") to the latter.

> . . . I adopt the standpoint that the inclination to aggression is an original, self-subsisting instinctual disposition in man and . . . that it constitutes the greatest impediment to civilization . . . [C]ivilization is a process in the service

of Eros, whose purpose is to combine single human individuals, and after that families, then races, peoples and nations, into one great unity, the unity of mankind. . . . But man's natural aggressive instinct, the hostility of each against all and of all against each, opposes this program of civilization. This aggressive instinct is the derivative of the death instinct which we have found alongside of Eros and which shares world dominion with it. And now, I think the meaning of the evolution of civilization is no longer obscure to us. It must present the struggle between Eros and Death, between the instinct of life and the instinct of destruction, as it works itself out in the human species. (Freud, 1930/1961, p. 69.)

Maslow's List of Human Needs

Central to Abraham Maslow's theory of human personality is the concept of self-actualization, which he regards as a fundamental human need. In Maslow's view, human beings strive to fulfill this need once the primal physiological needs and the need for safety (keenly felt by children) are satisfied. The self-actualization needs comprise:

The need to belong. Every normal human being wants to belong to some group of human beings, mostly to the group that helped rear him or her.

The need to love. Every normal human being wants to love someone and to be loved.

The need for self-esteem. Every normal human being wants to feel that he or she is worthwhile. This feeling is usually satisfied if a person feels that he or she has some control over the environment. Possessing skills helps to actualize this need.

The need for growth. Every normal human being wants to understand not only self but the world around, wants to grow mentally and spiritually, to expand his or her potential for meeting intellectual challenge and appreciating beauty, for autonomous and creative activity. (Maslow, 1943).

Human Potentiality

A view fundamentally opposed to the views regarding the "essence of human nature" invokes the image of a *tabula rasa*—a blank page on which anything can be inscribed. Proponents of the *tabula rasa* model assume that whatever a person turns out to be is a consequence of his or her experiences. Initially, when the stock of experiences is empty, the person is completely "neutral," that is, ready to go in any direction.

Clearly, the idea of instinct is incompatible with the *tabula rasa* model.

It is equally clear that the model goes too far if it implies that anyone can be taught to do anything and be anything. Obviously, some actions or abilities are beyond any human being no matter how intensively trained. This is surely the case with regard to physical capabilities. No human individual can be taught to fly or to run as fast as a cheetah. There is a limit to human memory, although this limit is probably far above the memory capacity that human beings normally utilize. It is also an open question whether it is equally easy to impose any values, appetites, or inclinations on any human being. It may very well be that some values or appetites are in more, others in less, harmony with what is "normal" for human beings.

It would probably be accurate to say that there is an enormous store of varied potentialities within every human being. *Which* will be brought out by the milieu in which the person lives or by deliberate training depends on circumstances. The critical events in one's life, the accidental impulses in one direction or another, the responses that the environment happens to make to different actions on different occasions may be crucial, but not at all easy to identify.

An example of built-in potentiality for which there is good evidence is the capability of learning to speak and understand a human language. I agree with Noam Chomsky (1968, p. 27) when he insists that this capability is part of being human. Given any normal social environment, i.e., contact with speakers, practically every child will, within a few years after birth, learn to speak his native tongue. Moreover, he will learn to speak it grammatically without any formal instruction in grammar. However, *which* language the child learns depends *entirely* on the speech community in which it grows. Thus, in the case of language, the nature-versus-nurture question is answered both ways. *That* the child will learn to speak and understand is probably genetically predetermined. *Which* language will be learned has nothing to do with its genetic profile.

The potential for learning human (i.e., grammatical) language must be just one of a very great number of such built-in potentials. So instead of saying that human nature is essentially this or that, or that "there is no such thing as human nature," it would seem more accurate to say that human nature is potentially very rich, but not infinitely rich. This extreme richness, the full extent of which we do not know, suggests that we are not far wrong if we answer "yes" to all questions about the "nature of human nature."

"Are human beings naturally cruel and destructive?"

"Change 'naturally' to 'potentially,' and the answer is 'yes.' "

"Are they kind, competitive, cooperative, brave, cowardly, gregarious, autonomy-seeking, lazy, industrious, noble, mean, greedy, generous . . . ?"

"Yes, yes, yes, . . . yes—potentially."

The answer "yes" to all questions does not express acceptance of the *tabula rasa* model. It may be much easier to bring out some features of human nature than others. Attempts to mold human beings into one type may be associated with much greater psychic costs than attempts to shape them otherwise.

In this view, generalizations about human nature from observations are both correct and wrong. All of us have preconceived ideas about practically everything. If we have preconceived ideas about what human nature is like, we will (usually unconsciously) tend to select observations tending to corroborate these ideas and to ignore or relegate to the role of exceptions observations tending to refute them. We can assume with some confidence that people who insist that human beings are predominantly aggressive are reinforced in their views by selecting (mostly unconsciously) just those instances of human behavior that can be called "aggressive." In contrast, people who hold the opposite view select the instances that tend to confirm a picture of the human as a basically benevolent, compassionate, cooperative being.

What About Lorenz?

Lorenz is a scientist well aware of the dangers of self-deception via selective attention. Did he include "aggression" and not, say, "compassion" in his four basic drives because he, like many laymen, had a preconceived idea of human nature and paid more attention to evidence that supported it? Not at all. He came to his conclusion by examining the role that the aggressive drive ("das Böse") has played in making a great variety of animals what they are, i.e., successful survivors of the evolutionary process. He went on to assume that similar processes must have made the human being what he has become. He looked at aggression from the evolutionary perspective. In the next chapter we will follow his example.

2

The Evolutionary Perspective

Static and Dynamic Views of the World

Adapting to one's world entails classification. Recognizing *kinds* of things, qualities, or events is probably a built-in capability in every animal with a nervous system. It would be impossible for an organism to respond differentially and consistently to every one of a virtually infinite variety of stimuli impinging on it. Appropriate responses must be made to stimuli that are recognized as instances of *categories*. A category may be a range of smells, a range of sounds or shapes, or a set of similar configurations of stimuli. The important thing is that small differences should not confuse the organism as to what is being perceived. The *meaning* of the impinging stimulus must be grasped, be it a sign that food or a mate or an enemy is present.

In humans categorizations are characteristically accompanied by the affixing of verbal labels. Once the categories are fixated in our consciousnesses by being named, it is to names that we then respond.

Categorization tends to perpetuate a "static" view of the world. In this view, things are what they are because that's the way they are. In contrast, a dynamic view of the world asserts that (to quote an apparently inane but actually profound quip of K.E. Boulding) things are what they are because they got that way.

The contrast between the static and the dynamic outlooks has been clearly manifested in the dispute between the creationist and the evolu-

14

tionist views of the living world. The creationist view is, of course, evident in the biblical account of creation. To this day the proponents of this view insist that all species are what they are because they were created that way. Each species, they maintain, was endowed with anatomical, physiological, and behavioral characteristics, and it has retained them to the present day.

The evolutionist view explains the divergence of living organisms by assuming that each species came to be what it is today by a process of gradual changes and that these changes came for the most part as adaptations to the environment in which the species was living.

That organisms are adapted to their environments means that sufficient numbers of them can survive at least to the age when they reproduce themselves in sufficient numbers to keep the species going, even though all individuals die. So much is recognized by both the creationists and the evolutionists. They part company in the way they account for the adaptedness of living organisms. The creationists, for the most part, give credence to some providential principle, some agency that has "seen to it" that creatures are equipped with proper mechanisms of survival—the hunters with sharp teeth and claws, their prey with fleet feet and keen senses. Thus, the creationists see what *is* as being a result of a one-time purposeful action by a goal-seeking being. Evolutionists insist that the adaptive features of living creatures developed gradually over many generations.

Natural Selection

Here again there is (or once was) a divergence of views. An older school of evolutionists (now practically extinct) supposed that adaptations developed in the course of "strivings" of the evolving creatures. For example, the giraffe got to be what it is because for many generations giraffes stretched their necks in trying to reach the leaves on tall trees. The necks got a little longer in each generation, and these increments were supposedly passed on cumulatively to the next generation.

If this explanation were correct, this would mean that characteristics acquired during an organism's lifetime could be transmitted to its descendants. Since there is no evidence (except in the case of artificial genetic modification) for the transmission of acquired characteristics, this "teleological" (goal-guided) model of evolution was eventually abandoned. It was replaced by the natural selection model, which is now accepted with some variance in details by practically all contemporary biologists.

As is generally known, the natural selection theory of adaptation is the core of Darwin's theory of evolution. It was inspired, as Darwin himself related (1859/1964, p. 63), by the writings of Thomas Malthus (1798/1966) on population. Malthus argued that there was a natural limit to how much a population could grow. He wrote about human populations, but Darwin extended Malthus's idea to the population of any living organism. Malthus's point of departure was that if the population increased by a certain constant per capita rate, then the growth of the population would be a geometric progression. The absolute size of the population would grow at an increasing (not a constant) rate. On the other hand, the food supply can increase only in an arithmetic progression, that is, at most by constant amounts in successive periods of time. These different rates of increase guarantee that eventually any population will outgrow the available food supply. It will then be checked by starvation.

The form of Malthus's mathematical argument did not matter to Darwin. To him the essential idea was that more individuals are born in a population than can survive to reproducing age. Consequently, a competition ensues for available resources, such as food. This is the meaning of the "struggle for existence" part of the slogan emblazoned on the banner of Darwinism. Who wins? Clearly, the victory goes to those who are somehow better adapted to the conditions in which they live. This is the meaning of the other part of the slogan that represents the theory of natural selection: survival of the fittest.

According to the theory of natural selection, the differences giving the more fit more chances to survive and to reproduce are induced by accidental variations in their genetic makeup. It is these random fluctuations in the genetic profiles of individuals that are passed on to succeeding generations. The struggle for existence continues. Again, those that survive are those that are advantageously different. Thus, the differences accumulate across generations. This is the way evolutionary modifications occur. Since different populations live in different environments, evolutionary changes tend to be divergent. Eventually, populations split into different species that can no longer interbreed. This is the way Darwin viewed the origin of species.

Vulgar Darwinism

The publication of *The Origin of Species* in 1859 created a storm of controversy. The biblical account of creation was still taken seriously; to challenge this account meant to challenge the word of God. Yet in certain circles the idea of a "struggle for existence, survival of the fittest" had a powerful appeal. The idea suggested that competition was a "natural law," providing ample justification for the pursuit of self-interest.

For those who interpret the "struggle for existence" as a ubiquitous competition of all against all, it is easy to form an idea that well-adaptedness is synonymous with success in combat—strength, cunning, fierceness, ruthlessness. Further, it is easy for the more powerful and ruthless members of a society to identify their own success with virtue, since victory in the struggle for existence insures the maintenance of a high level of vigor in a population of competing individuals.

The grim acceptance of the "law of the jungle" easily evokes an image of nature "red in tooth and claw." We may decry the cruelty and selfishness of the victors. But their victory appears to be all to the good. They won because they deserved to win. Their victory made the world a better place because the unworthy were eliminated.

The philosophy of ruthlessness of Friedrich Nietzsche (1887/1909) with its contempt for compassion can be traced to the same source. Among nationalists a sort of vulgar Darwinism stands out as a rationalization of war. F. von Bernhardi in his book, *Germany and the Next War*, writes:

> The struggle for existence is the life of Nature, the basis of all healthy development. All existing things show themselves to be the result of contending forces. So it is in the life of man. The struggle is not merely the destructive but the life-giving principle. (Bernhardi 1914, p. 18).

Bernhardi goes on to cite Claus Wagner, author of a book entitled *Der Krieg als schaffendes Weltprinzip (War as a Creative Universal Principle)*:

> The natural law to which all laws of Nature can be reduced is the law of struggle. All intrasocial property, all thoughts, inventions, and institutions, as indeed in the social system itself, are a result of the intrasocial struggle, in which one survives and another is cast out. The extra-social, the supersocial struggle which guides the existence and development of societies, nations, and races, is war. The internal development of the intrasocial struggle is man's daily work—the struggle of thought, wishes, sciences, activities. The outward development, the supersocial struggle is the sanguinary struggle of nations— war. In what does the creative power of the struggle consist? In growth and decay, in the victory of the one factor and the defeat of the other. The struggle is the creator since it eliminates.

The above excerpts reflect a mentality that glorifies aggression, identifies with the aggressor, sees aggression as the prime mover of progress. In a corrupted version of Darwin's theory of evolution, interpreted to bolster their own commitment to violence, the political theorists of imperial Germany found an authoritative rationale for their philosophy of life.

Greatly disturbed by what he believed to be a deeply rooted predilection for violence in the human psyche, Derek Freeman (1964) called attention to the australopithecus, our supposed direct primate ancestor, who lived about three million years ago. This creature abandoned life in the trees for life on the ground and changed his diet from a vegetarian to a flesh-eating one, thereby becoming a hunter. Since hunting necessitates killing, so Freeman's argument goes, aggression came to be part of the australopithecus's psychological makeup, as handed down to us.

In this picture our ancestor appears as a fierce beast, stalking or chasing his prey, catching it, killing it with his hands, and devouring the bloody flesh. The imagery suggests cruelty, and cruelty suggests aggression.

What Freeman has described is *predation*, which ought to be distinguished from aggression. The evolution of aggression and of predation may have followed entirely different paths and may have depended on entirely different bases of adaptation. Let us examine the psychological underpinnings of aggression on the one hand and of predation on the other.

First, let us compare intent. The aim of the aggressive act is in one way or another to do harm or damage to another—a person, an animal, at times even a thing. This is not the aim of an act of predation, which is defined as killing for some utilitarian end other than inflicting harm on the prey, i.e., to obtain food. A lioness kills an antelope; a fisherman catches a fish; a frog captures a fly. All these are instances of predation, not aggression. It is rash to ascribe human affects to nonhumans, but if we nevertheless wish to do so, we should not imagine that a lioness is moved by "malevolence" against the antelope, any more than the fisherman against the fish, least of all the frog against the fly. Affects resembling those characteristic of aggression may be *grafted* onto predation, but they are not necessary components of it. In contrast, affects of hostility in one form or another are necessary components of human aggression.

Let us agree to reserve the term "aggression" to denote hostile actions directed against members of own species. At times what appears to be aggression is observed to be directed at members of another species, suggesting a distinction between *intra*-specific and *inter*-specific aggression. The latter form of aggression is beyond the scope of this book. We will turn our attention to intra-specific aggression as seen in evolutionary perspective.

Reproductive Success

In the natural selection theory of evolution, no features are regarded *a priori* as contributing to well-adaptedness. Well-adaptedness is inferred only *a posteriori*, exclusively in terms of relative reproductive success, that is, the number of offspring of individuals characterized by a certain genetic profile that survive to reproduction age relative to the numbers of offspring of individuals characterized by other genetic profiles. It is obvious that if this survival and reproductive difference persists over generations, eventually the types enjoying greater reproductive success will become increasingly more numerous relative to the others and, perhaps, will eventually supplant them altogether.

Reproductive success can be conferred by *any* anatomical, physiological, or behavioral characteristic. Let us see why aggressive behavior has been assumed to have been selected for in the process of evolution.

The most common situations in which intraspecific aggression takes place are observed in fights over mates or territory. The former usually involve males, the victor taking possession of a female. The latter result in conquest of territory, for instance a nesting site from which intruders are excluded. Both kinds of combat are assumed to enhance reproductive advantage of the *type of organism* engaging in such contests. It is usually the stronger or the more aggressive male that wins the female. If his strength or aggressiveness is determined genetically, the corresponding genes are thereby transmitted to offspring in greater numbers than the genes of the losers (who are less likely to find females). Consequently the frequency of stronger or more aggressive males in the population increases, since the winners of fights over females inseminate more females.

Seen in this way, intraspecific aggressive behavior is just one of innumerable forms of behavior that in certain contexts in certain species has proved itself to be an "adaptation." That is, certain *kinds* of aggressive behavior turned out to confer reproductive advantage. There is, however, a great deal more to be said on the subject than that rewards in the form of adaptation go to the strong, the fierce, and the brave. From another vantage point it appears that not fierceness but, on the contrary, restraint in fighting confers adaptive success. Intraspecific fighting in most species is seldom fatal. There is good reason to suppose that fighting with no holds barred would be maladaptive. Severe injuries could incapacitate the winners as well as the losers. The "weapons" that males of certain mammalian species use in intraspecific combats seem to be designed to minimize severe injuries. The backward curved horns of certain goat and antelope species, the antlers of deer, conducive to "locking horns" rather than goring, are well-known examples. Among the carnivores, possessors of lethal weapons such as sharp teeth or claws, certain postures inhibit the infliction of severe injury or death. When wolves fight, the loser assumes a posture as if inviting the victor to kill him (exposing his neck), and this gesture seems to stop the fight.[1]

If aggressive behavior can be seen as the product of "survival of the fittest," inhibition of aggression can legitimately be interpreted in the same way. There are innumerable examples of intraspecific *cooperation*, which can equally reasonably be regarded as a product of evolutionarily determined adaptation. The nurturing and cooperative features of family life among birds and mammals and the complex patterns of cooperation among social insects are well known. Wolves hunt in packs. Animals that are prey rather than predators have been observed to protect themselves from predators by various cooperative strategies.[2]

There are other less well known but truly dramatic instances of cooperation between individual animals that are neither family members nor members of a social group. An example is the exchange of protective shells that takes place between hermit crabs (Hazlett 1983). These creatures have soft, unprotected hindquarters. A hermit crab protects his behind by putting it inside an empty snail shell. Apparently these snail shells are a comparatively scarce resource, because many of these crabs are seen wearing shells that are either too large or too small for them, suggesting that they use what they can find. Now and then a pair of these creatures meet and exchange their shells. The exchange takes place after the two go through certain motions as if arranging a deal. The interesting thing about these exchanges is that they mostly result in each crab's acquiring a better-fitting shell.

Interspecific cooperation is as common as cooperation within species. Insects and flowers "help" each other: plants by providing food for the insects, insects by pollinating the flowers. Plants use carbon dioxide in their metabolism to release oxygen which is indispensable to animals. An ecological system consisting perhaps of thousands of species can be regarded as a huge cooperative enterprise. It must be so regarded, because unless the species were somehow adapted to each other's lifestyles, the system could not persist in a more or less steady state. Of course, the complex food chains include predation. Some species eat other species. But we should not impose our human-centered notions on our interpretations of these processes. Some aspects of predation are cooperative as well as competitive. Carnivores preying on ungulates generally pick off the weakest or ill members of the herd. This culling may contribute to rather than detract from the viability of the herd.

Aggression or Cooperation?

Where does one draw the line between aggression and cooperation? Ethologists have described encounters between members of the same species that can be interpreted as "aggression" only because "victory" seems to go to one or the other. The "loser" leaves the field; the "winner" retains the prize, usually a mate or a staked-out territory. But in many of these encounters, there is no physical contact between the "'combatants." The contest consists only of postures. Some of these can be interpreted as "threatening," if we persist in drawing analogies with apparently similar postures in animals we understand. But these postures could also be interpreted as signals, establishing a form of cooperation, for example in apportioning territories in such a way that adequate food supply is assured for more members of the species than if they were crowded. When in a waiting room someone intends to sit down next to me in a seat temporarily vacated by my traveling companion, I say, "Sorry, this place is occupied." Was this an instance of "intraspecific aggression" or an invitation to cooperate by adhering to established social courtesies?

In assessing some behavior pattern as "aggressive" or "cooperative," we must keep in mind that making this distinction is a carry-over of the static outlook—the habit of describing the world in terms of fixed categories. The most striking feature of evolution is that characteristics of living things, whether structural, physiological, or behavioral, are constantly changing—transformed into something quite different from what they once were. In particular, *functions* can undergo radical changes, while their evolutionary history clearly points to their underlying "identity," that is, their common origin. These commonalities are called homologies.[3] The wing of a bird, the foreleg of a horse, and the hand of a human are illustrations of this principle. Their functions (flying, running, grasping) are widely different, but they are all features of an anatomical scheme that underlies the design of all vertebrates, birds, and mammals alike, ungulates and primates alike.

In light of this observation, the conjecture concerning the genesis of human aggression, specifically its supposed roots in our ancestral shift to a predatory way of life, appears dubious. We have already suggested that the evolutionary history of aggression and predation may have been quite separate. Aside from this, even if the psychological underpinnings of the two forms of behavior are related, the frequent transformations of function in the process of evolution throw doubt on the origins of human aggression based on biological heritage. Yes, the australopithecus may have used his well-developed hand to strangle prey, but the human uses it also to play the violin or to caress a child.

In terms of the extent of destruction wreaked, modern war is surely the most extreme form of aggression and marks *homo sapiens* as by far the most aggressive creature that has ever inhabited this planet, aggressive not only within his own species but against all other species, plant and animal. Yet the same features of the human psyche that make the devastation possible underlie the most encompassing forms of cooperation. The meshing of the components of a vast war machine is accomplished by the same mechanisms of behavior as the meshing of the components of any other cooperative enterprise, including those engaged in the production and distribution of the essentials of life, such as protection of populations from epidemics. It is for this reason that seeking the roots of human aggression in our biological heritage may be a misguided effort. Nevertheless, let us examine the genetic approach to human aggression in its current sophisticated version, presented in the works of the sociobiologists.

Sociobiological Theory of Human Aggression

The publication of the seminal work on sociobiology (Wilson 1975) occasioned lively, sometimes acerbic, controversy reminiscent of the controversy about evolution and particularly about the descent of man that raged in Europe in the decades following the publication of Darwin's work. At that time, the main issue appeared to be the challenge to religious views on the origin of life and especially of man. By implication, the issue involved also the question about the "nature" of man, whether he is essentially different from animals, being a possessor of a "soul," having awareness of moral values, and the like.

Today the authority of religious teachings is no longer a central issue, but the "nature of man" is. It is interesting to note that the political implications of the various views of man have changed. In the nineteenth century, it was the politically conservative who mostly sided with the Church in ascribing to man a unique status in the scheme of creation, while the liberals and the radicals, more inclined toward agnosticism or atheism, maintained that the transition from nonhumans to *homo sapiens* was a gradual one. In the twentieth century, the controversy shifted to the question of whether "heredity" or "environment" was primarily responsible for molding the human psyche. The political right championed the heredity factor; the left, environmental determinants of attitudes and behavior. The extremes of the political spectrum corresponded to the one or the other all-or-none view—racism in Nazi Germany, economic determinism among the Marxists.

R. Ardrey, in his book *The Territorial Imperative* (1967), recalls the Theatre of Social Protest in the 1930s. The message in Sidney Kingsley's play *Dead End* was that poverty was responsible for crime; in Lillian Hellman's *The Little Foxes*, that money was the root of all evil; in Irwin Shaw's *Bury the Dead*, that, but for propaganda, there would be no wars. From the point of view of liberal social critics, it was all right to attribute the behavior of animals to genetic determinants, but not that of humans.

It was scandalous to insinuate that the poor were poor because they were genetically inferior. It was an article of faith that humans, once enlightened, would learn to control their own destiny, would leave the realm of necessity to enter the realm of freedom.

The position of the sociobiologists represents a swing of the pendulum in the opposite direction. In fairness it must be said that although the emphasis on biological determinants may seem congenial to conservatives, there is not much evidence that this turnabout reflects a political shift to the right. Rather it appears to have been spurred by enthusiasm for recent impressive advances in ethology, the systematic study of innate patterns of animal behavior. It was especially the rich evidence shedding light on the evolutionary development of these patterns, quite analogous to the development of anatomic and physiologic features, that stimulated keen interest in instincts. "Instinct" became a respectable and fruitful theoretical construct in biology. If to view man as a member in good standing of the animal kingdom was to remain consistent with accepting the heritage of Darwinism, then to deny categorically the existence of instincts in man's psyche was to hold on to an untenable position, to insist on a discontinuity between *homo sapiens* and the rest of the living world. The instincts in man may have become concealed under thick layers of cultural superstructure, but many must have remained, perhaps deep in the subconscious. To uncover them appeared to sociobiologists a scientific duty to be discharged regardless of how disturbing these discoveries might be to conventional liberal ideology.

It is one thing to postulate the existence of instincts in man in a general sense and quite another to insist on the existence of a specific instinct or drive to account for some form of human behavior. Ardrey does this. He accords to "territoriality" a status comparable to that of Lorenz's fundamental drives—hunger, sex, fear, and aggression. In fact, Ardrey seems to attribute even greater importance in some cases to the drive to acquire or protect a territory than to the sex drive. The female of the Uganda kob (an antelope), he notes, is sexually unresponsive to any male who has not succeeded in securing a patch of grazing land as his own. Thus, Ardrey concludes, ". . . males compete for real estate, never for females. . . . When the female arrives in a territory, she becomes the sole, if momentary, property of the male whose grass she crops." (Ardrey 1967, p. 51.)

Evidently the temptation to translate these findings into explanations of familiar human behavior is irresistible:

> And it may come to us as the strangest of thoughts that the bond between a man and the soil he walks on should be more powerful than his bond with the woman he sleeps with. Even so, in a rough preliminary way we may test

the supposition with a single question: "How many men have you known in your lifetime who died for their country? And how many for a woman?" (pp. 6–7.)

It is hardly necessary to point out that the vast majority of men who "died for their country" died not in consequence of satisfying a drive, but in consequence of obeying orders. We see here an instance of freewheeling speculation by word association:

1. Killing in war is a by-product of "fighting for one's country."
2. Country means territory.
3. Many instances of territoriality are found among animals.
4. Therefore the origins of war can be traced to a deep-seated instinct for aggression in human beings.

This tme the "instinct for aggression" is not purely for aggression's sake, as it appears in some of Freud's speculations, but is a means of acquiring or protecting "real estate."

In citing "fighting for one's country" as an instance of territoriality, Ardrey unwittingly advances the *cultural* determinant (which he demoted in his exposition to secondary importance) rather than the biological determinant of aggression (which he presented as primary). For certainly it cannot be established that the men who "died for their country" enjoyed a procreative advantage over those who did not. Yet the sociobiological theory of cultural evolution stands or falls with the applicability of the concept of procreative advantage in all relevant contexts. Only in this way can the sociobiological approach justify the claim that it is an extension of the Darwinian idea to behavioral evolution and a challenge to the "dogma" of cultural determinism.

Ardrey wrote from the point of view of an amateur biologist. His principal professional preoccupation was with the theater and film. Although his speculations about territoriality as a fundamental drive in human beings may be interesting in their own right, we need not expect from him scientifically rigorous arguments in support of his position. We can, however, expect from professional sociobiologists the same degree of rigor in their discussion of the biological basis of cultural evolution as we find in their meticulous studies of animal behavior and their reasoning concerning its genetic underpinnings. Here our expectations are not borne out. A case in point is the attempt to derive "social success" from Darwinian principles. The derivation stands or falls with the answer to the question of whether "social success" confers a reproductive advantage and whether it is genetically transmissible. The sociobiologists would have a case if the socially

Table 2–1.

Surviving children per married couple where wife's age exceeds 45 years, classified by social status, 1911, England and Wales. Source: England and Wales, Register General, Census of England and Wales: 1911, Vol. XIII, "Fertility and Marriage." Cited in Vining, 1985.

Social Class	Surviving children per married couple
Professional and higher white collar	2.94
Lower white collar, commercial	3.38
Skilled manual	3.79
Unskilled	3.88
Textiles	3.11
Coal mining	4.45
Agricultural laborers	4.57

successful could be seen to have larger families or at least more children surviving to adulthood. For then, supposing the genes making for social success exist, the socially successful would have a differential reproductive advantage.

The criterion of larger-than-average families is crucial for the argument, since the sociobiologists do not make the error of defining superior adaptedness on *a priori* grounds, e.g., as a property of aggressiveness, acquisitiveness, or the like. They adhere to an *a posteriori* definition of adaptedness—empirically demonstrable differential reproductive success. It behooves us, therefore, in assessing the sociobiologists' arguments, to examine the relative fertility of the "socially successful" and others. Unfortunately for these arguments, rather the opposite is observed. An example of such observations is shown in Table 2–1.

In a comprehensive work on fertility differentials, D. Wrong (1980) has shown that the inverse relationship (lower fertility rates in the upper social strata), as exemplified in Table 2–1, was a typical concomitant of the overall decline in birth rates in the West. There seem to have been instances of a direct relationship between higher social strata and higher fertility in Europe, e.g., in pre-industrial rural Germany. The weight of the evidence, however, sheds strong doubt on the conjecture that the rich have, by and large, enjoyed relatively greater reproductive success in the West. Without conclusive evidence of "fitness" in the Darwinian sense, the sociobiological hypothesis about the genetic basis of social success becomes untenable.

Equally dubious are the arguments of the sociobiologists to the effect that aggression in human beings is rooted in biological fitness. E.O. Wilson writes:

> Throughout recorded history the conduct of war has been common among tribes and nearly universal among chiefdoms and states. The spread of genes has always been of paramount importance. For example, after the conquest of the Midianites, Moses gave instructions identical in result to the aggression and genetic occupation by male langur monkeys. Combinations of genes able to confer superior fitness in contention with genocidal aggression would be those that produce either a more effective technique of aggression or else the capacity to prevent genocide by some form of pacific maneuvering. (Wilson 1975, pp. 572–573.)

Let us now consult the source of this remarkable idea.

> And they warred against Midian, as the Lord commanded Moses, and they slew every male . . . and the children of Israel took captive the women of Midian and their little ones.
> And Moses was wroth with the officers of the host, who came from the service of the war. And Moses said unto them . . . "Have you saved all the women alive? . . . Now therefore kill every male among the little ones, and kill every woman that hath known man by lying with him, but all the woman children that have not known man by lying with him, keep alive for yourselves." (Numbers 31:7, 14, 17–18.)

If spreading the genes of the Israelites were the aim of the war against Midian, then Moses' insistence on slaughtering the male children would make sense. Of course, Moses need not have been conscious of this aim. The case for biological determinism does not need to be supported by evidence that organisms know what they are doing when they do what is likely to promote the spread of their own genes. And surely the gene itself has no "goal" in "mind." The strength of the position taken by the sociobiologists is that the survival of the fittest is, in the last analysis, a tautology: precisely *those* genes become predominant that have reproductive advantage over others—*whatever* confers this reproductive advantage.

It seems that Moses, believing that he was fulfilling some plan of Jehovah's, was actually stacking the cards in favor of Israelite genes competing with Midianite genes. The Israelites, as they were slaughtering the Midianite male children, may have experienced various emotions, but regardless of what they were experiencing, they, too, were acting in the service of their genes, not necessarily in the service of their god, and not because the genocidal genes were giving orders, but because these genes, by making killing pleasant or by making it appear imperative, enjoyed reproductive advantage. In this way (so the sociobiologists would argue) propensity for committing genocide would be transmitted to succeeding generations.

The trouble with this explanation is that it focuses on just those aspects of the situation that seem to support it and ignores other aspects. Selective genocide (killing only males) is consistent with efficiency of spreading own genes, since a male can inseminate several women in a short time. But what is the genetic advantage of killing all female non-virgins and sparing virgins? After the alien males are killed off, all alien women can become recipients of own genes, whether they are virgins or not. (There may have been some sense in killing pregnant captive women.) Further, how does the genetic basis of genocide shed light on innumerable wars in which genocide was *not* practiced?

Evolution Independent of Genes

The outstanding weakness of the sociobiologists' approach to the genesis of human behavior patterns is their insistence on seeking a genetic basis of every evolutionary process of the living world. It may well be that all such processes in the *nonhuman* living world are traceable to genetic factors. But human cultural evolution seems to be a glaring exception. Reluctant as we may be to hold on to views that resemble earlier insistence on man's exceptional status in creation, we cannot ignore the uniqueness of the cultural dimension in the evolution of human behavior.

There are forms of large-scale secular changes in the history of humanity that bear a striking resemblance to biological evolution, but there is no evidence that there is in any way a connection. One clearly seen stream is the evolution of languages; the other is the evolution of artifacts.

Languages can be grouped into categories obviously analogous to biological species, even to subspecies, genera, or classes. For instance, French, Italian, and Spanish belong to the Romance group; English, Danish, and German to the Germanic group; Russian, Ukranian, and Polish to the Slavic group. If these languages are regarded as "species," their dialects can be regarded as varieties or subspecies; larger groupings, such as the Indo-European or the Sino-Tibetan can be defined as "phyla" in the taxonomy of languages.

Clearly related languages have proximal "common ancestors"; more distantly related ones, more remote ancestors. Thus, a "family tree" of languages can be constructed having the same kind of structure as the "tree of life," showing the birth of new species as instances of divergence from common ancestors and also extinction of species (dead languages) as the tips of branches.

As in biological evolution, strong evidence pointing to the ancestry of a language is the presence of "vestigial parts." Consider the silent k's and gh's in English spelling. In speech, being silent, they perform no function. They are carry-overs from Germanic languages, where they did and still do have phonetic significance. The silent k in "knight" is evidence that "knight" is a cognate of the German word *Knecht*. So is the silent gh. The silent gh's in "night" and "through" point to the pedigree of these words reflected in their German cognates, *Nacht* and *durch*.

Similar vestiges can be observed in artifacts. The ancestor of the modern automobile was the "horseless carriage," which entirely justified its name. It was, in fact, a carriage without a horse. It even had a stand for a whip. The early cars were tall like carriages and had running boards. Later, as the cars were reduced in size, the running boards disappeared. But just before they disappeared completely, their vestige remained in the form of a very thin (and completely useless) projection below the doors.

The cuff buttons on our shirts are still functional, but the cuff buttons on our jackets are vestiges. They were once functional but are no longer. These examples can be multiplied endlessly.

If there is an "aggressive drive" in humans, it may well be a vestige, having lost its original adaptive value. The conjecture is all the more reasonable, because an entirely new dimension has been added to the "evolution" of human beings, which, it seems, has completely overshadowed the mechanism of biological evolution. This is cultural evolution. The evolution of languages and artifacts is the clearest manifestation of cultural evolution, and there is not a shred of evidence that the mechanism of this evolution is in any way related to, much less determined by the mechanisms of biological evolution, except in the sense to be mentioned below.

Let us look at a possible analogue of natural selection in at least some aspects of cultural evolution. The first question that comes to mind concerns the units on which such selection pressure operates. In the case of the evolution of languages, we know that these units cannot be the languages themselves. Although the divergence of languages can with some stretch of imagination be likened to reproduction (like asexual reproduction by fission in unicellular organisms), there are not enough languages to make an analogue of natural selection in this context credible.

It is, however, possible to regard individual *utterances* of words as analogues of individual organisms and the subsequent utterances of the same words by other speakers as the analogue of reproduction. The repeated utterances may differ slightly from each other, suggesting analogues of mutations. Most of these "mutations" do not stick. They are not incorporated in subsequent utterances but rather "corrected." These are the mutations that are "selected against." Occasionally, however, a slightly different variant of a word seems to be better adapted, say, because it is easier to pronounce without detracting from comprehension. Then it will be imitated and will enjoy enhanced "reproductive success," eventually displacing the original pronunciation. The same processes can be imagined to govern the evolution of grammatical and semantic features of a language.

In this view, a language is seen as a "population" of utterances embedded in an environment. This environment consists of the speakers of the language—a speech community. It is to the speech community that the language becomes adapted, just as a biological species becomes adapted to its environment.

The environment of a biological species always contains other species, so that the species must itself be regarded as part of the environment of other species. Thus the evolution of biological species involves also the evolution of their environment. We should therefore speak of the co-evolution of species.

In the same way a language evolves together with its environment, the speech community in which it is embedded. There is no reason to attribute the evolution of the speech community to changes in its genetic profile. The evolution of the speech community is part of cultural evolution, and as such may well be connected to the evolution of the language that defines the speech community—if not significantly in its phonetic or grammatical aspects, perhaps significantly in its semantic aspects.

Like a language, a technology is embedded in a human population. The reproduction of artifacts bears a more obvious resemblance to the reproduction of biological organisms than does the reproduction of utterances. As we have seen, artifacts undergo mutations and evolve, even bearing traces of their ancestry in their vestigial parts.

What is the analogue of selection pressure in this process? Clearly, selection of artifacts to be further reproduced is made by human beings. Even more clearly than in the evolution of a language and its speech community we can observe the coevolution of a technology and the society or culture in which it is embedded. A strong case for influence in both directions can be made in the context of this coevolution, a circumstance of utmost relevance to the study of war and peace, as we shall show in Part IV of this book.

Now we return to the question of a connection, if any, between cultural and biological evolution. The existence of such a connection is emphatically affirmed by sociobiologists whose arguments we will examine in a moment. In our view, some aspects of cultural evolution may perhaps exert some influence on the direction of human biological evolution, but the influence of the latter on the former is not likely to be of significance.

Possible influences of cultural evolution on the biological are via *inter-*

ference with the natural selection processes. Medical control of diseases provides survival and reproduction opportunities to genetic types which otherwise may have been systematically eliminated by natural selection. Also, voluntary control of family size has eliminated the reproductive success of superior natural fertility. Indeed, the artifacts of civilization may turn us into a species that would be very poorly adapted to its physical environment if it were deprived of these artifacts. The human has become a domestic animal whose chances of survival in the wild may be practically nil.

Implications of Cultural Evolution and Transformation of Functions

We humans can live in any climate, although our bodies are adapted only to the tropics. We wear clothes. Our children could survive even if the maternal instinct were to disappear completely because we have an infrastructure of institutions for taking care of them. The blind, deaf, and crippled among us can lead almost normal lives, thanks to the ingenious prosthetic devices and other assistance rendered to them in civilized societies. And there are good prospects that even more ingenious devices and better assistance could be made available if higher priorities were assigned to these goals.

Now look at the obverse side. It is possible that whatever has remained of the aggressive instinct, which ages ago may have conferred a survival advantage on us, exists only as a vestige in our species. However, this instinct *is no longer necessary* as an instigator and a driving force of violence. With the advent of weapons of total destruction it is no longer necessary to hate anyone in order to kill everyone.

There is no way to account for this development by reference to natural selection. The method of sociobiology is sterile in the context of cultural evolution. Can the mechanisms of cultural evolution, in particular of technological evolution, tell us anything?

Along with these mechanisms their coevolving psychological concomitants may be of prime importance. In particular, the transformation of function, which, as we have seen, has played a most prominent role in biological evolution, may be at work also in cultural evolution. The ecstacy of the mystic may be a homologue of the paranoia of the mass murderer. The self-discipline of the ascetic may be a manifestation of the same sort of compulsion that underlies the amorality of the scientist engaged in weapons research. The ingenuity of the innovators in the field of war technology may be just a variant of artistic creativity. The satisfactions experienced by those who have added to the richness of human life and by those who have contributed to the threat of our extinction may be quite similar. This closeness of opposites is reminiscent of the principle underlying the effectiveness of antibiotics. These substances resemble nutrients on which pathogenic organisms feed. The bacteria attach themselves to the antibiotic units. These occupy sites that otherwise would have been occupied by nutrients, and the bacteria die of starvation.

Human traits that are considered to provide psychological satisfactions include courage, self-control, camaraderie, codes of honor, social cohesion, loyalty, and creativity. When these are added up in the context of the war system, they spell not a richer life but ignominious death.

We see a fundamental difference between the way transformation of function works in the context of biological evolution and in the context of cultural evolution. In the former, transformation of function is always a result of adaptation. Forelegs became wings for the reptiles and their descendants, the birds, who took to the air. They became hands when some primates adapted to their environment by learning to grasp. The brain, which in some animals is chiefly a processor of smells, became an organ of thought in the course of man's peculiar adaptation to his environment.

Transformation of function in the context of cultural evolution works both ways—adaptively and maladaptively. The aggressive drive (if it exists) can be "sublimated," that is, transformed into creative energy. But the creative urge can also be degraded into the development of megadeath technology. Organization of effort using the new communication and information-processing technology has made possible vast cooperative enterprises, binding total strangers into symbiotic networks. The same psychological state that underlies these networks also underlies the organization of the war machine. It, too, is a vast cooperative enterprise binding people into symbiotic networks.

Once again we are reminded of the principle that makes antibiotics effective. As the substances that simulate food deprive bacteria of nourishment, so a cultural environment that simulates a fertile soil for creativity and collegiality—the war system—deprives human beings of healthy spiritual nourishment and stunts their growth.

Notes

1. Some ethologists have pointed out that the wolf's surrender gesture acts not as a stimulus inhibiting aggression, but rather a withdrawal of a stimulus that evokes aggression, namely turning away the muzzle. In the light of this expla-

nation, restraint in combat need not be ascribed to anthropomorphic concepts like compassion.

2.. Birds have been known to "mob" birds of prey, e.g., owls, and to attack cuckoos whose young, hatched in other birds' nests, kill their "foster siblings" by pushing them out of the nest. These are some of rather rare instances of interspecific aggression (as distinguished from predation).

3. The difference between an analogy and a homology, as these terms are used in evolutionary theory, is that an analogy is a manifestation of similarity of function, while a homology is a manifestation of a common origin. Thus, the wing of a bee and the wing of a bird are instances of analogy: both are used for flying. But their phylogenic histories are quite different. An example of a homology is given in the text.

3

The Behavioral Perspective

The advent of the experimental method as a way of obtaining knowledge marked a parting of the ways between speculative philosophy and science. While the paradigm of philosophical inquiry could be embodied in the question "What is the nature (or essence) of . . . ?" the paradigm of experimental science can be encapsulated in the question, "What will happen if . . . ?" Accordingly, the typical format of a scientific assertion became "If . . . then . . ." This format had already been established in mathematics, representing the general framework of a *theorem*, that is, a piece of knowledge obtained by logical deduction. Now it was extended to knowledge obtained by induction, i.e., generalization from observations.

In particular, the shift of attention away from inquiries about the "nature of things" toward the causes of events led psychologists to formulate so-called "reactive" theories of aggression, specifying conditions under which aggression can be expected to be observed. The search for such conditions is not the same as amassing evidence that the human is (or is not) "by nature" aggressive. Reactive theories could not conveniently accommodate spontaneity of aggression, i.e., the idea that aggression can be triggered by a "drive" independently of aggression-releasing stimuli.

Frustration and Aggression

A specifically formulated reactive theory of aggression was advanced by J. Dollard and his collaborators in their seminal work, *Frustration and*

Aggression (1939). The "If . . . then . . ." format of the theory is expressed on page 1 of that book: "This study takes as its point of departure the conception that aggression is always a consequence of frustration."

The link between frustration and aggression also underlies Freud's theory of aggression. One of the tenets of Freud's theory is that small children develop "protosexual" (Oedipal) drives toward parents of the opposite sex. Suppression of these drives, accompanied by jealousy directed against the parent of the same sex, is supposed to constitute frustration, which is manifested in aggressive impulses.

On the face of it, Freud's theory appears to be a reactive theory inasmuch as it links aggressive actions to underlying "causes" rather than to spontaneous manifestations of an inherent drive. This conclusion is unwarranted since the theory contains the assumption that *everyone* experiences Oedipal frustration in early childhood. If this is so, then the theory is not really an "If . . . then . . ." theory, because the "if" part (presence or absence of frustration) cannot represent different conditions and cannot be manipulated. No test can be designed to refute Freud's theory. A theory that is consistent with all conceivable observations seems to explain everything. But a theory that explains everything actually explains nothing.

Unlike Freud's theory of aggression, the theory proposed by Dollard and his collaborators seeks to discover linkages between specific frustrating experiences and specific acts of aggression. It seems to provide reasonable explanations of increased frequency and intensity of aggressive actions in certain phases of life. For instance, expressions of hostility, such as temper tantrums and the like (interpreted as instances of aggression), have been noted at an age when a child's wants, likes, and dislikes seem to have become more complex than the child can express in language. Another phase, usually thought to be associated with increase in aggression, is at the onset of puberty, when presumably the aroused sexual urge is frustrated by socially imposed taboos.

Strictly speaking, however, a frustration-aggression theory so formulated could be dismissed, like Freud's, as impervious to being proved wrong. Surely every human being has experienced some frustration at some time. Thus, any aggressive action can always be referred to some antecedent frustrating incident. And surely every human being has at some time or other acted aggressively. Therefore, it could be claimed that every frustrating experience must have led to an aggressive act at some later time. Nevertheless, this weakness of the general formulation of the frustration-aggression theory need not mean that it is worthless. A way out of the "unfalsifiability dilemma" is to design experiments where a frustrating experience is introduced under proper controls and an aggressive act is predicted under specified conditions. In this way, the hypothesis linking frustration to aggression can be made falsifiable and so can acquire some theoretical leverage.

Frustration-Aggression Experiments

In the usual frustration-aggression experiment, a person is subjected to a presumably frustrating experience and later given an opportunity to commit an act of aggression. To reinforce the significance of a positive result, a control experiment must be performed. That is, it must be shown that if a person is *not* subjected to frustration, while other conditions remain the same, then when an opportunity to commit aggression is presented, no aggression or, at any rate, less aggression will be observed.

There are standard rules to be followed in investigating matters of concern to psychologists via observing behavior under controlled conditions, and these apply especially to testing the frustration-aggression hypothesis, which is a carry-over from earlier psychological speculations.

To begin with, concepts like frustration and aggression have to be *operationalized*. Since a test involves predictions of what will be observed under specified conditions, both the conditions and the expected observations have to be carefully described in sufficient detail so that there can be no ambiguity about what is controlled and what is expected to be observed. "Frustration" can be imagined as a consequence of a variety of experiences, such as being unable to satisfy a need, being insulted, or being unable to solve a problem. Likewise, aggression can be assumed in a large variety of actions: physical assault, verbal insult, and so on. In each case, the experimenter must select from these supposedly frustrating experiences and supposedly aggressive actions those that will serve as the independent and the dependent variables in the experiment.

Next comes the problem of making a subject undergo a frustrating experience. If according to a chosen hypothesis suggested by the frustration-aggression theory, the aggression is expected to be directed against the source of frustration, the person who "frustrates" the subject must be instructed to do so. This necessity of carefully arranging the conditions in a social-psychological experiment is most frequently met by using a "stooge," i.e., a confederate of the experimenter, who carries out the latter's instructions without arousing the subject's suspicions that the set-up is all pretense. The stooge usually poses as another subject in the experiment.

These arrangements amount to a deception perpetrated on the subject. An ethical code governing experimentation on human beings prescribes a "debriefing" procedure following an experiment, whereby the deception is revealed. Among other things, the subject learns that the purpose of the experiment was not what he had been told it was. Aside from questions that these procedures raise about the possible psychological effects of the disclosure on the subject, routine use of deception may throw doubt on the significance of the results in future experiments. The great majority of laboratory experiments in social psychology use students as subjects. As increasing numbers of students become "veterans" of these experiments, others hear about the ruses used. Thus, the population from which subjects are recruited may become "polluted" by suspicions about the experimental setup. Assuming that the "naiveté" of the subjects in social psychological experiments is a desideratum (somewhat analogous to the purity of genetic strains in biological experiments), one can see how the continued use of deception can create serious methodological problems.

For these reasons the value of social psychological experiments designed to test the frustration-aggression hypothesis varies widely. Well known to the people in this field of research is the trade-off between the "realism" of the experimental setting and the tractability and significance of the data. Significance of the data is enhanced by their volume and by the rigidity of controls. However, attempts to make the experimental situation resemble situations encountered in real life may involve elaborate deception and lengthy experimental sessions. Deception may jeopardize control, as when the subject suspects the true purpose of the experiment. Long-lasting sessions put limitations on the volume of data that can be gathered in the allotted time. These restrictions create problems in obtaining significant results if the effects produced by varied experimental conditions are slight.

With these reservations, we turn our attention to some experiments that seem to shed some light on possible linkage between frustration and aggression.

Experimental Evidence for the
Frustration-Aggression Theory

A clear demonstration of a direct linkage between a frustrating experience and aggressive behavior was seen in an experiment performed by R. Barker, T. Dembo, and Kurt Lewin on young children (1941). One group of children was shown a roomful of attractive toys seen through a wire screen inducing an expectation that they would be allowed to play with them, which they finally were, but only after a long wait. Another group of children was permitted to play with the toys immediately. The difference in behavior between the two groups was striking. The children who did not have to wait played with the toys happily without showing any evidence of aggressiveness. The children who were made to wait were destructive. Many smashed the toys, threw them against walls, etc.

One is reminded of the Arabian Nights tale of the genie imprisoned in a bottle. For centuries he planned to shower rich rewards on whoever liberated him from his prison. But as the centuries went by and no rescue came, his intended gratitude turned to rage against the liberator, in which state the hero of the story found him.

Many social psychological experiments do no more than confirm expectations suggested by conventional wisdom. Thus, persons familiar with the way people act surely knew of the linkage between frustration and aggression long before social psychologists started to do their experiments. However, the existence of such common knowledge does not necessarily render experiments superfluous. To begin with, "common knowledge" does not always turn out to be reliable. Moreover, when observations are sometimes consistent and sometimes inconsistent with "common knowledge," more systematic observations may reveal more about distinct conditions under which different events will be observed. Finally, common knowledge may be refined or sharpened by properly designed experiments. In addition to knowing under what conditions frustration may lead to aggression, we may be able to establish quantitative relations between the degree of frustration and the degree of aggression.

One measure of the degree of frustration is the nearness of the goal at the time that the attainment of the goal is thwarted. An experiment by M.B. Harris (1974) showed that aggression is more intense if blocking the attainment of the goal occurs when the goal is almost within the grasp than when it is still far off. Harris's subjects were people standing in line at checkout counters in a store. Her confederates tried to cut into the line. The intensity of aggression expressed against these apparently rude people was considerably greater when the cutting-in occurred in front of the second person in line than when it occurred in front of the twelfth person.

This result throws some light on the observations that violent social protest frequently occurs not among the most downtrodden in a society but among those who are somewhat better off. Thus, the riots in the U.S. during the sixties exploded not in the most depressed areas of the country but in Watts (a section of Los Angeles, California) and in Detroit, Michigan, where living standards were by no means the lowest. The explanation of this phenomenon is given in terms of frustrated *rising expectations*. It is not the people without hope who feel themselves most frustrated (severe deprivation is not synonymous with frustration), but people who have made some headway, who are led to expect more, and whose hopes have been disappointed. Also, the fact that severe riots occurred in the U.S. during the 1960s, a period of considerable improvement in the economic and social

position of Blacks, supports the idea that a partial but inadequate fulfillment of expectations may be a more intensely felt frustration and hence
a more powerful instigator of aggression than no fulfillment at all.

In the light of this knowledge, the adamancy of despotic regimes in
refusing to grant minimal liberties to their oppressed populations becomes
understandable.

Catharsis

If frustration leads to aggression, and if the aggressive impulses are, in
turn, frustrated, say by an authority figure (parent, teacher) or by social
taboos, we can suppose that *this* frustration will create even more pressure
to commit aggression. This reasoning leads to the notion that allowing a
frustrated person to "let off steam," i.e., to somehow satisfy his aggressive
urge, will attenuate this urge. Thus, if the aggressive impulses stimulated
by the original frustration could be diverted into harmless channels, socially
undesirable conflicts might be avoided. Such defusing of aggressive urges
by providing alternative outlets is called the *catharsis effect*.

The result of an experiment performed by S. Feschbach (1955) was
interpreted as evidence supporting the catharsis effect of imagined aggression. The experimenter presumably induced a feeling of frustration in a
group of students by insulting them. Then one-half of the insulted subjects
were given an opportunity to write imaginative stories about aggression
while the other half did not have this opportunity. A control group of
subjects was not insulted. All three groups were then given a questionnaire
on which they could express hostility toward the experimenter or displeasure with the experiment. Both insulted groups expressed more hostility
and displeasure than the control group. Those who had the opportunity
to write the stories expressed somewhat less hostility than those who did
not. The former result can be interpreted as evidence in favor of the
frustration-aggression theory; the latter in favor of the catharsis theory.

In another similar experiment, J. Hokanson and H. Burgess (1962) obtained results which showed that engaging in aggression fantasy reduced
subsequent aggression considerably less than acts of direct aggression
against the insulting person.

The results of both experiments can be interpreted in a way that minimizes the specific effect of catharsis. It is possible that deflecting attention
of the subjects by asking them to perform a task (which they may have
found interesting) simply made the insult less salient in their memory.
More convincing support for the catharsis effect would have been obtained
if subjects, given an opportunity to write stories *without* aggressive content,

showed *less reduction* of aggressive tendency afterward than those given the opportunity to write stories with aggressive content. Unfortunately this additional control was not introduced. It might, as a matter of fact, have provided evidence *against* the catharsis theory if writing stories without aggressive content produced more attenuation of aggression than writing stories with aggressive content. As for the Hokanson-Burgess experiment, it can be interpreted to mean that the important thing about catharsis is the chance to get even.

The most interesting questions arising in connection with the catharsis hypothesis concern the possibilities of deflecting aggressive urges into harmless activities. The finding that getting even may allay anger does not really bear on this problem. If getting even provides some comfort to the person who got his revenge, the question arises about what this does to the person on the receiving end. Does he also feel that the score has been settled; or, on the contrary, that now the roles of the "creditor" and "debtor" have merely been reversed?

When we examine the ongoing vendettas in societies or subcultures where avenging murder by murder is regarded as a duty, or the escalation of terrorist activity following punishment meted out to terrorists by governments, we cannot help having serious misgivings about the uses to which catharsis effects (if they exist) can be put.

The illusion of a catharsis effect can be produced also by displacing aggression generated by frustration. This is sometimes done deliberately by governments faced with intense discontent. In such cases, pointing to a conspicuous and helpless scapegoat, e.g., a minority group, deflects the fury of the populace. Aggression against the power elite is thereby forestalled, but this sort of "catharsis" cannot be said to be a means for defusing violence. Violence is merely shifted onto another target. Moreover, the impunity with which violence against a scapegoat can usually be perpetrated may contribute to aggravation rather than attenuation of aggression on subsequent occasions.

Disentangling Frustration, Aggression, and Catharsis

Experiments performed by L. Berkowitz and E. Rawlings (1963) and L. Berkowitz and R. Green (1966) were addressed to a number of questions related to the frustration-aggression and the catharsis hypotheses. The design and execution of these experiments were rather elegant, and some of the results are extremely interesting. We will therefore examine them in some detail.

Each experimental session involved two persons, one a bona fide subject, the other a stooge. The stooge, posing as subject, was introduced to the other subject either as a "boxer," a "speech major," "Kirk Anderson," or "James Anderson" (see below). The ostensible purpose of the experiment was to observe physiological effects associated with various tasks. To induce credence, blood pressure of the subjects was ostensibly taken in the course of the sessions.

In the first phase of the sessions, the subject and the stooge worked on a simple intelligence test. While they worked, the stooge either insulted or did not insult the subject. The insults consisted of remarks like "You're certainly taking a long time with this" or references to "cow college," a derisive nickname for the subject's university.

In the next phase, the subjects watched an excerpt of a film, *The Champion*, in which the protagonist is subjected to a severe beating in a prizefight. Presumably to facilitate their understanding of what is going on, the experimenter gave the subject a synopsis of the story that culminated in the boxing scene. In one version, the protagonist (who took the beating) was portrayed as a despicable fellow who, one would presume, "deserved" the beating. In the other version, the protagonist was portrayed as a basically decent person, who had behaved badly because he had been victimized when he was young. This story was supposed to induce empathy for the protagonist and presumably a feeling that he did not "deserve" the beating.

The independent variables were the eight experimental conditions involving all combinations of "insulted or not insulted," "speech major or boxer," and "deserved beating or did not deserve beating."

In the final phase of the experiment, the subjects were given an opportunity to punish their "tormentor." They were asked to judge the "creativeness" of an apartment floor plan, supposedly designed by the stooge. All subjects saw the same very conventional floor plan of a three-bedroom apartment, to which it was probably difficult to give high marks on "creativity." The "mark" given by the subject for the floor plan was to be in the form of one or more (fictitious) electric shocks: one, if the plan was deemed to be good; more than one, if it was judged to be poor. The subjects could make the supposed shocks (which they thought were real) of different durations. Thus, the severity of the "punishment" could be assessed on two dimensions: duration and number. These measures, interpreted as "amount of aggression," were the dependent variables of the experiment.

On the basis of this measure, the following questions could be answered relative to the experimental conditions:

1. *Does frustration trigger aggression? Do the insulted subjects administer more or longer shocks than the not-insulted ones?*
Answer: Yes.

2. *Is more aggression manifested against a presumed boxer than against a presumed speech major?*

Answer: Yes.

3. *Is more aggression manifested after viewing violence that seems justified than after seeing violence that seems unjustified?*

This question has a bearing on the catharsis hypothesis. We might suppose that in viewing "justified" violence, the subjects could more easily identify with the boxer administering the beating than in viewing "unjustified" violence. Consequently, we might expect a stronger catharsis effect in the former than in the latter condition. It turned out, however, that the average number of shocks administered by the subjects who viewed "justified" violence was 29, while the average number administered by those who viewed "unjustified" violence was 17. On the duration scale, the average duration of shocks in the "justified violence" condition was 302 milliseconds; in the "unjustified violence" condition 125. It seems, then, that the experiment exhibited an "anti-catharsis" effect. Experiencing aggression vicariously (by identifying with the aggressor) *increased* rather than reduced the amount of aggression vented against the presumed source of frustration.

To account for this result, as well as for other inconsistencies sometimes observed in frustration-aggression experiments, Berkowitz suggested a reactive model somewhat more complex than the simple frustration-aggression model. He assumes that frustration induces a general "arousal," that is, a heightened readiness to react to stimuli. What sort of behavior is triggered depends on many factors. For instance: What sorts of "targets" are available for aggression? Is the sort of aggression to be vented socially approved in the given situation? According to Berkowitz, effects attributed to catharsis may be more convincingly explained by the various kinds of social learning—in particular, by social learning previously internalized.

With regard to some results that seem to support the catharsis hypothesis Berkowitz writes:

> [Catharsis], of course, is not the only explanation of the results. The men who saw the filmed violence could have become uneasy about their own aggressive tendencies. Watching someone being hurt may have made them think that aggressive behaviour was wrong: as a result, they have inhibited their hostile responses. Clearly, there was scope for further experimentation, particularly studies varying the attitude of the subjects toward the filmed aggression. (Berkowitz 1964, p. 35.)

This is what Berkowitz and his collaborators set out to do. The study brought out the importance of social learning as a determinant of behavior. Whether and under what circumstances frustration will lead to aggression, at whom aggression will be directed, and what form it will take—these are the important questions to which the paradigm from earlier (particularly Freudian) speculations does not address itself but which *are* addressed in more recent theories of social learning. A case in point is the unexpected finding that the stooge introduced as a "boxer" was subjected to more punishment than the stooge introduced as a "speech major." Like the "anticatharsis" effect, this also may have been a result of identifying with the boxer in the film, which led to imitating what was seen on the screen. Or the difference may have been induced by certain internalized social norms: it is all right to hurt a boxer, who is in a position to hurt back. But it is not all right to hurt someone engaged in more intellectual pursuits (who often wears glasses).

What's in a Name?

An even more interesting finding was that the *name* by which the stooge was introduced made a difference in the amount of punishment he got (Berkowitz and Green 1966). In one scenario, the stooge was introduced as Kirk Anderson, in another as James Anderson. The name of the actor who played the protagonist in *The Champion* was Kirk Douglas. It turned out that the stooge whose name was given as Kirk got more punishment than the one whose name was given as James.

Recall the mobbing of Cinna in Shakespeare's *Julius Caesar* (Act III, Scene 3). A crowd of Roman citizens meet Cinna, a poet, and bombard him with such questions as: "What is thy name?" "Whither art thou going?"

Cinna: What is my name? Whither am I going? Where do I dwell? . . .
    Truly, my name is Cinna.
First Citizen: Tear him to pieces; he's a conspirator.
Cinna: I am Cinna the poet. I am Cinna the poet.
Fourth Citizen: Tear him for his bad verses, tear him for his bad verses.

Identifying things, persons, conditions, and events with their names is, perhaps, the most important component of the process we call social learning. It seems that this manner of learning is unique to our species. As we shall see in Chapter 5, this crucial role of language in shaping human behavior sheds much light on the genesis and dynamics of human conflict.

Conditioning and Imitation

That animals can learn—that is, can acquire new behavior patterns or lose old ones—is known to anyone who has even superficially observed animals. Studies of learning by animals under controlled conditions were stimulated by the classical experiments of I. Pavlov (1903/1928), to whom psychology owes the theoretically powerful concept of *conditioned response*. In Pavlov's experiments behavior of animals was modified by introducing a *conditioning* stimulus before eliciting a natural response—for instance, the sound of a bell shortly before presentation of food to a dog. Eventually, the dog's natural response to the food (salivating) was transferred to the bell. The bell seemed to have acquired a "meaning," e.g., "food is coming," and started the response originally associated with food.

In this sort of conditioning, now called "classical" or "Pavlovian," the conditioning stimulus elicits the response conditioned to it by simply preceding the stimulus that naturally elicits the response. Later, another form of conditioning was developed in learning experiments, namely, *instrumental* conditioning. In this procedure, the subject (usually an animal) has a choice of responding in more than one way to a stimulus to which initially no response is naturally conditioned. As the animal responds, initially apparently at random, one way or another, some of the responses may be punished, others (usually a particular one) rewarded. Gradually, the relative frequency of the "correct" response increases and eventually becomes fixated as "learned."

Besides classical and instrumental conditioning, there is still another form of learning. If cats are raised from birth in the company of rats and never see cats kill rats, they almost never kill rats when they grow up (Kuo 1961, p. 24). That exceptions are observed suggests that the tendency to kill small animals may well be incorporated in feline nature. But the fact that this tendency can be practically eradicated points to the importance of learning in acquiring patterns of behavior.

Let us see how a cat learns *not* to kill rats. If it were punished for killing and rewarded for not killing, the learning would be an instance of instrumental conditioning. However, no extrinsic rewards or punishments were involved in the experiments. The only difference between the non-killer cat and the "normal" killer cat is that the latter saw a cat kill a rat and the former did not. We have here evidence of learning by *imitation*. The fact that a kitten that has never seen a cat kill a rat does not kill rats when it grows up suggests that cats that *do* kill rats have learned to do so by imitating other cats. We also see that the supposed inherent tendency in cats to kill rats is not by itself sufficient to induce rat-killing. It must be supplemented by an example set by other cats. Imitation can be regarded as a primitive form of social learning.

Experiments on Social Learning

The subjects in experiments in social learning are frequently children. The tendency of children to imitate adults is well known. In view of the frequently observed imitative behavior of other animals, especially of primates (cf. "monkey see, monkey do"), we can assume that this tendency is innate in children, perhaps part of our heritage from evolving ancestors.

Instrumental conditioning superimposed on imitation is part of the child's socialization process. Imitation of socially approved behavior patterns is rewarded and thereby incorporated into habits. Already quite early in life a child's tendency to imitate an adult model varies with the attitude of the adult toward the child and with the nature of the model's behavior.

An experiment by M.R. Yarrow and P.M. Scott (1972) is especially instructive in this respect. The different experimental conditions involved the attitude of the model toward the child subject—nurturant in one condition, cold in the other. Also the behavior of the adult model varied in the two conditions—positive in one, negative in the other. It was found that the children tended to imitate positive behavior of the nurturant model but not her negative behavior. However they tended to imitate the cold model's negative behavior but not her positive behavior. This suggests that imitative behavior of even very young children involves not just mechanical aping but deeper perceptions. It seems the child tends to imitate not merely the actions of the model, whatever they are. The results of the experiment suggest that the child forms an impression of the "kind of person" the model is and then imitates *that character*.

Socialization and Moral Development

The type of performance involved in the Yarrow-Scott experiment has a bearing on children's acquisition of values by social learning. J. Piaget, whose researches on the development of the child's cognitive faculties were particularly illuminating, advanced also a theory of the child's moral development (Piaget 1932/1966). Conspicuous in Piaget's model of development is a shift at a certain age from so-called "objective" to "subjective" value judgments about actions.

Perhaps the terms "objective" and "subjective" are not quite fortunate in this context. Ordinarily we associate maturation with a growing ability to make "objective" judgments—that is, judgments arrived at by taking into account realities independent of one's wishes, hopes, or fears, which do influence "subjective" judgments. In Piaget's theory of the child's moral development, on the contrary, "objective" judgments are the more primitive, and "subjective" ones more mature.

To illustrate, suppose a young child is asked to make a comparative judgment about which of two boys was "naughtier." One tried to help his mother put away the dishes after a party, stumbled, and fell, breaking fifteen cups. The other climbed up to steal jam from the cupboard and dropped one cup. Up to a certain age, according to Piaget's theory, the child judges the first boy to be "naughtier." It applies an "objective" measure of naughtiness, namely, the amount of damage. Older children take subjective factors into account, in this case the intentions of the one boy and of the other. The intention of the first was "good," that of the second "bad." So the second was the "naughtier."

Piaget's theory of cognitive and moral development stresses the dependence of these faculties on the state of development attained rather than on learning. The theory can be interpreted to imply that a child can be guided to its judgment by "subjective" criteria only after it has reached the "subjective" stage of moral development. Moreover, once that stage is reached, the child will be relatively immune to attempts to bring it back to the more primitive stage by ordinary conditioning processes.

An experiment by A. Bandura and F.J. McDonald (1963) was designed to challenge that interpretation by showing that social learning (by imitation) can "overrule" the type of moral judgment associated with one of Piaget's "stages." The subjects in that experiment were "subjective" children, i.e., children who normally evaluated actions by the subjective criterion. In one condition, the child was given an opportunity to imitate an adult model who evaluated an action by an *objective* criterion and was reinforced when it imitated the model. In another condition, opportunity to imitate was present but the child was not reinforced for imitating. In the third (control) condition, the child was reinforced for making "objective" judgments but opportunity to imitate was not present. The results, shown in Figure 3–1, suggest that imitation alone and reinforced imitation were about equally effective in eliciting an "objective" evaluation in "subjective" children. Reinforcement alone had a considerably weaker effect. We note also that the shift to objective judgment persisted at least two weeks after the experiment.

The results of the Bandura-McDonald experiment suggest that social learning can effect a shift to a lower stage of "moral development" as these stages were defined by Piaget. Of even greater interest is the question of whether social learning can effect a shift to a higher stage, that is, from

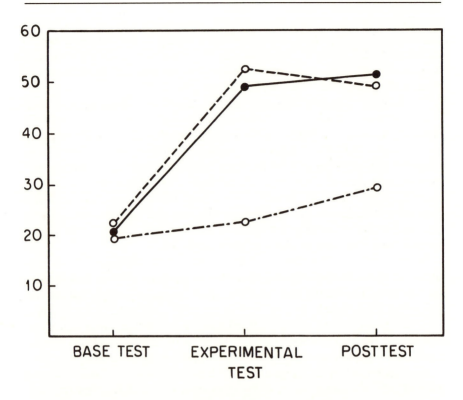

Figure 3.1. After Bandura and McDonald, 1963. Percentages of moral judgments based on the "objective" criterion by children in the "subjective" stage. Experimental test: after exposure to model making "objective" judgments; Post test: two weeks later. Solid line: model and child reinforced. Broken line: model reinforced; child not reinforced. Dots and dashes: no model present; child reinforced.

the "objective" to the "subjective" stage. In this connection, another interesting question arises. "Objective" and "subjective" criteria can be used in evaluating not only morality of actions but also ability or competence. The question of interest is whether a shift from "objective" to "subjective" evaluation can be transferred from "non-moral" to "moral" situations.

P.M. Crowley (1968) performed an experiment on children in which reinforcements and/or discussion were used in attempts to effect a shift from the objective to the subjective evaluation. There were thus four training conditions. In one, stories involving moral questions were presented to the children. The child who identified the "naughtier" child "correctly" (i.e., by the "subjective" criterion) was reinforced. In the

Table 3–1 (after Crowley, 1968)
Mean number of stories out of 12 evaluated by a "subjective" criterion by predominantly "objective" children.

Training received	Mean
Non-moral stories with correction only	4.4
Non-moral stories with correction and discussion	3.3
Moral stories with correction only	11.0
Moral stories with correction and discussion	10.9
Control	1.5

second condition, discussion was added in which the intention of the action was emphasized (the attempt to effect a shift via social learning). In the third condition the children were presented with non-moral story pairs. For example, one hunter killed a deer because he was a good shot; another because he was lucky. Who was the better hunter? In the fourth condition, non-moral stories were coupled with a discussion in which the children's attention was called to competence. Children in the fifth (control) group were tested and retested without either reinforcement or discussion. The results are shown in Table 3–1.

The data suggest that there is little transfer of induced subjective orientation from judgments in non-moral situations to judgments in moral situations. Further, training in the use of subjective criteria results in considerable shifts in that direction whether the training consists of reinforcements only or reinforcements and discussion. The latter result is of special interest because, as we have seen, reinforcement is relatively ineffective in producing shifts to a more primitive stage of moral evaluation (cf. Figure 3–1).

L. Kohlberg (1963, 1968), extending Piaget's theory of moral development, postulated three levels, each consisting of two stages. He called the first two stages "preconventional," the next two "conventional," the last two "post-conventional." The designations suggest that in the middle stages moral judgments are most dependent on conformity to the social environment. The levels and stages are shown in Table 3–2.

Strictly speaking, a moral sense, as we usually understand it, does not yet appear in the first two stages. For the very young child, "bad" is simply what is punished. Relations to people other than those empowered to mete

Table 3–2
Kohlberg's stages of moral development

Level	Stage	Characteristic
Preconventional	1. Punishment and obedience	Authoritative concern for sanctions
	2. Instrumental, relativistic	Comparison of costs and benefits
Conventional	3. Interpersonal concordance	Good intentions; meet others' expectations
	4. Law and order	Doing duty; maintaining social order
Post-conventional	5. Social-contract legalistic	Changing law through democratic procedures to improve society
	6. Universal ethical principles	Principles above social norms

out rewards and punishments do not yet exist. The same egocentrism characterizes the second stage. Actions are now evaluated by a "cost-benefit analysis": "Is the forbidden thing worth a spanking if caught?" Morality in the sense of concern for the welfare, comfort, or feelings of others is still absent. Of course, the identification of "good" and "bad" with profits and losses characterizes many areas of adult activities. However, in the perspective of Kohlberg's evaluation scheme, this merely means that these activities (for example, economic activities) are carried out on a primitive level of moral development.

Concern for others, better said for others' opinion of self, becomes a factor in the third stage. The standards of the peer group become paramount in distinctions between "good" and "bad." But larger social concerns are still beyond the horizon of awareness. These enter in the fourth "law and order" stage. The standards of a narrow in-group are replaced by the standards imposed by the society as a whole, expressed in laws. From the dictate of laws, there is no appeal. Unquestioning obedience of authority embodied in the law-enforcing agencies becomes the essence of morality in this stage.

On the post-conventional level, conceptions of morality begin to transcend established conventions and the dictates of authority. The "good" is now seen to be embodied in principles to which the standards of a just society are supposed to adhere instead of being defined by existing social standards. However, in the fifth stage obedience to existing laws is still imperative. The only recourse against social injustice is changing the law. Therefore, while criticism of the law is not a violation of morality, breaking the law is.

Finally, the highest stage in the development of the moral sense, according to Kohlberg, is the recognition of absolute principles of justice that take precedence over obedience to law. Imperatives of morality may now involve conscientious objection, civil disobedience, and so on.

It should be clear that Kohlberg's model is open to serious criticism. The standards of a particular social philosophy, usually called liberal humanism, or something similar, shine through all too clearly. This is especially evident in Kohlberg's conception of the "highest stage" of moral development. No doubt he had in mind the heroic and principled actions of persons who defied laws regarded as unjust from the point of view of a liberal humanist. Deliberate violations of statutory laws that sparked the civil rights movements in the U.S. in the 1960s and the various forms of resistance to military conscription on grounds of conscience come to mind. The difficulty with this conception of the "highest level" of moral development is that vigilante actions and organized crime can also be subsumed under disregard of law on "moral grounds." Who is to say that terrorists of any ideological persuasion are not acting out entirely sincere convictions of the "rightness" of their cause? Or that racketeers do not have their own moral code that transcends statutory laws?

However, the general or limited validity of Kohlberg's model of moral development need not be an issue in this discussion. We are interested not so much in the rank order of the several conceptions of morality as in the degree of importance of social learning in the inculcation of attitudes to the extent that these can be inferred from behavior. Kohlberg's scheme can be a convenient point of departure in this inquiry. Once the stages of moral development have been defined, children who "normally" exhibit moral judgments characteristic of one stage can be subjected to training (reinforcement, discussion, and the like) aimed at influencing their judgment to ascend to a "higher" stage or descend to a "lower" one. The effects of such training can then be assessed.

Experiments on Obedience to Authority

Experiments that have shed light on the role of indoctrination in aggressive behavior were carried out by S. Milgram (1963). The object of the experiments was to see to what extent people will obey orders to hurt an innocent human being. Clearly, situations of this sort came to the forefront of public attention in connection with war atrocities, for which perpetrators disclaimed responsibility by claiming that they had no choice but to obey orders of superiors.

Milgram's subjects were drawn from a broad cross section of American life ranging from businessmen to professionals, from blue to white collar occupations. They were told that the experiment in which they were to participate was on the effects of punishment on learning. Two men participated in each session. One was a bona fide subject, the other a stooge. The roles of "teacher" and "learner" were ostensibly assigned by lot, but actually the real subject was always the "teacher."

The learning task consisted of associating nonsense syllables. The stooge (in the role of "learner") was instructed to make mistakes. The real subject (the "teacher") was instructed to punish the mistakes by electric shocks. These were fictitious, but the subjects apparently did not suspect this.

The strength of the shocks was graduated from 15 volts (quite mild), increasing over 15 volt intervals to 300 volts (very severe) and beyond. The strongest were labeled only XXX, meant to cause anxiety in the person ordered to administer these shocks.

At the start of the session, the supposed "learner" was strapped to a chair and had "electrodes" placed on his body, an obvious allusion to an electric chair execution. The subject, seated in another room, was instructed to provide the stimulus syllables, to which the "learner" was to respond with syllables that he had to learn to associate with them. Each mistake was to be punished by a progressively more severe shock. The question to be answered was how far the subject would go in administering the steadily increasing shocks if he had evidence that they caused severe pain. If the subject hesitated, he was urged by the experimenter to go on.

To create the impression that the shocks were really painful, the "learner" would knock on the wall separating the rooms, then would complain more and more urgently that he could not stand the shocks any longer. The experimenter would urge the subject to go on by saying, "You must continue," "You have no choice," and the like.

The subjects showed evidence of extreme anxiety as they continued to administer supposedly dangerous shocks. In fact, 35% of them refused to go on beyond a certain point. As significant, however, is the fact that fully 65% of the subjects did go on to the end into the region ominously marked XXX, a symbol vaguely suggesting serious danger.

How can the results be interpreted and what is their significance? As pointed out, the experiment was intended to demonstrate the strength of social learning, which supposedly overrules inhibitions against inflicting bodily harm on innocent human beings. An intent of the experiments may also have been to show that the compulsion to "obey orders" is not confined to people brainwashed by military discipline or to people indoctrinated with ideologies fostered in totalitarian states. The "learner" in Milgram's experiments was not represented as a "subhuman" the way, say, the Germans were taught to regard members of "inferior races." Nevertheless, orders to inflict pain and possibly serious damage on fellow human beings were obeyed by a large majority of subjects.

One must conclude that it was not the habit of "blind obedience" that the subjects learned in the process of being socialized. Such indoctrination is not characteristic of the American scene. And of course the subjects were not threatened with punishment if they refused to obey. It must have been the "setting" that was compelling. The orders were given by a "scientist"—a respected figure—in surroundings that suggested civilized procedures (a laboratory of Yale University) in a voice that carried authority. Probably the assumption that the "scientist" knew what he was doing and that it was unthinkable that a subject in an experiment would be seriously hurt played a key role in inducing obedience. This conjecture is reinforced by the finding that when the same experiment was conducted in another setting, the results were different. The other setting was in a run-down commercial building in the downtown shopping area of the industrial city of Bridgeport, Connecticut. There was no indication that the "laboratory" was in any way connected with a university. In this setting, only 48% of the subjects went all the way, providing additional evidence that the operation of moral imperatives is strongly situation-oriented.

The question arises as to the effect of milieus on personnel in charge of the control levers that can unleash a nuclear war. How conducive are these milieus to eliciting unconditional obedience? That there is good reason to fear the worst follows from the circumstance that the operations to be performed are thoroughly rehearsed. Those levers must have been pressed (or whatever one does with them) innumerable times in drills to condition the people to go through the motions when the appropriate signals or orders are received. These rehearsals are meant to assure the "real" operations if and when they are ordered. Provisions have also been made to forestall the "failure" of the performance, say by a sudden full realization of what the performance means. If some people cannot get themselves to go through the motions, others stand ready to take their place. Possibly the operations are duplicated and triplicated, so that the probability of all of them "failing" simultaneously is practically nil.

This hypothetical, but by no means unthinkable, prospect is mentioned here in order to make an essential point. Predisposition to aggression, whether genetically determined or induced by specific experiences (e.g., frustration) is in no way a precondition for the release of violence beyond our capacity to imagine. Social learning suffices to elicit practically any form of behavior that a human being can perform physically in pre-learned situations. If one can speak of inherent predilections in human beings, perhaps the readiness to acquire behavior patterns through social learning is the strongest. It is this *generalized* predilection rather than specific predilections to specific forms of behavior or acquisition of specific attitudes that can turn people into compassionate human beings or brutal murderers, into independent thinkers or automatons responding to command signals with preprogrammed actions ranging from the simplest reflexes to highly complex operations.

Are Different Forms of Moral Behavior Correlated?

One important finding in experiments seeking answers to questions about moral behavior is that correlations between one type of moral (or immoral) behavior and another are weak. Initially, a very large study (Hartshorne and May 1928) involving over 10,000 schoolchildren, revealed no correlation between frequencies of transgressions of different kinds reported by the children. The transgressions seemed to be entirely situation-bound. Later, more refined statistical techniques revealed some evidence of a predisposition in some children to honesty independent of the situation. Nevertheless, the relative weakness of these correlations points once more to the greater importance of social learning relative to inherent predispositions. People who would not think of cheating at cards cheat on their income tax returns. People who are kind and considerate to their colleagues are not infrequently cruel to members of their families. The kindest of parents are often despotic bosses. Members of criminal syndicates may be scrupulously honest and loyal to each other and to their organizations.

Formation of Attitudes

All these observations in field studies and in the laboratory are evidence of the prime importance of social learning in the formation of attitudes. The most important of these observations is that attitudes underlying moral judgments and behavior revealing conceptions of morality are typically situation-specific, as one would expect if these attitudes are induced by social learning. Parents, teachers, and clergymen may preach generalized kindness and generalized honesty. But whether people learn to be kind or cruel, honest or dishonest will, in general, depend on the social situation in which they find themselves; for it is in such situations that they learn to behave in one way or another. This is what the behavioral perspective shows with impressive clarity.

4

The Attitudinal Perspective: We and They

A high official of the empire of Lilliput, briefing Gulliver on the affairs of the country, relates the origin of the long war between Lilliput and the neighboring empire of Blefuscu:

It began on the following occasion: It is allowed on all hands that the primitive way of breaking eggs, before we eat them, was upon the larger end; but the present majesty's grandfather, while he was a boy, going to eat an egg, and breaking it according to the ancient practice, happened to cut one of his fingers; whereupon the emperor his father published an edict, commanding all his subjects, upon great penalties, to break the smaller end of their eggs. The people so highly resented this law that our histories tell us that there have been six rebellions raised on that account; wherein one emperor lost his life and another his crown. These civil commotions were constantly fomented by the monarchs of Blefuscu; and when they were quelled the exiles always fled for refuge to that empire. It is computed that eleven thousand persons have at several times suffered death rather than submit to break their eggs at the smaller end. Many hundred large volumes have been published upon this controversy; but the books of the Big-endians have been forbidden, and the whole party rendered incapable by law of holding employments. During the course of these troubles, the emperors of Blefuscu did frequently expostulate by their ambassadors, accusing us of making a schism in religion by offending against a fundamental doctrine of our great prophet Lustrog, in the fifty-fourth chapter of the Blundercal . . . This, however, is thought to be a mere strain upon the text; for the words are these: that all true believers shall break their eggs at the convenient end. And which is the convenient end seems, in my humble opinion, to be left to every man's conscience, or at least in the power of the chief magistrate to determine. Now, the Big-endian exiles have found so much credit in the Emperor of Blefuscu's court, and so much private assistance and encouragement from their party here at home, that a bloody war hath been carried on between the two empires for thirty-six moons. . . .

A painting by V.I. Surikov, a Russian master, depicts a woman in a sledge holding up her index and middle fingers to a watching crowd. She is a noble woman, a *boyarinia* being taken to be interrogated. The two fingers are a gesture of defiance. The boyarinia is an Old Believer. This sect insists that the proper way of making the sign of the cross is with two fingers.

The Russian Orthodox Church had decreed that the sign of the cross is to be made with index finger, middle finger, and thumb, symbolizing the Trinity. Disobedience constituted a political offense, punishable by banishment from public life. (The boyarinia was banished to a nunnery.)

The Lilliputian official's suggestion that the decision about which end of the egg is the convenient end be left to each person's conscience misses the point. The method of breaking the egg is not the issue, any more than the way of making the sign of the cross is the issue. The way one breaks an egg or the way one makes the sign of the cross *marks* one as being one of "us" or one of "them." *That* is the issue.

Everywhere in human social life, we find this division into "us" and "them": friends and strangers, allies and enemies, teammates and rivals, partners and competitors. Are conflicts between such groups, including wars, just extensions of conflicts between individuals, husbands and wives, plaintiffs against defendants? If so, then the insights into the human psyche might provide us with clues about the genesis and dynamics of all conflicts. But there are strong indications that this is not so, that conflicts between "us" and "them" are of a different order from those between "me" and "thee."

We have seen how the sociobiologists attempted to explain enmity between unrelated groups on the basis of adaptations conferring reproductive advantage on carriers of "aggressive genes." In extreme cases, the aggressiveness manifests itself in equivalents of genocide. Recall Wilson's reference to the massacres perpetrated on males of an alien group by langur monkeys as a way of perpetuating one's own genes and his conjecture that the massacre perpetrated by the Israelites on the males of the Midianites served the same purpose (cf. Chapter 2).

This sort of struggle for existence suggests that distinctions between "kin" and "non-kin" would have been selected for and so incorporated in the human psyche. Indeed, the earliest distinctions between "us" and "them" may well have been along lines of kinship. Since the earliest human groups were probably families, carriers of similar genetic complexes, recognition of kin did not depend on sensitivity to the other's genetic make-up. His being one of the group was sufficient to identify him as "kin."

The advent of the Industrial Revolution and its attendant changes undermined kinship as a basis of social organization. Thereafter the dichotomy "we–they" acquired meanings totally unrelated to kinship. Other distinctions have taken their place reflecting the complex network of relationships in political, military, bureaucratic, business, and academic life. Names of professions and occupations number in the thousands. Instead of belonging to a kinship clan, people belong to organizations where their basic role is determined, not by who they are, but by what they do or, frequently, by how they think.

Top Dog Versus Underdog

Social philosophers who see the class structure of a society as a primary source of intergroup conflict trace the origin of classes to the division of labor. They also see the existence of classes as a necessary and sufficient condition of *exploitation*, the social analogue of parasitism, a process that enables members of one class to appropriate the fruits of labor of another. It is this exploitative relationship, a consequence of the class structure of a society, that is seen by some social philosophers as the source of all social strife. Moreover, they see in social strife a prime mover of historical change. As is well known, Karl Marx was the most prominent exponent of this view. His theories reach into both economics and sociology and, especially in his early works, into psychology.

The identification of the source of social classes in the division of labor has earned credibility. A society can be defined as an assemblage of people interacting with each other in a variety of cooperative activities, whereby individuals act in some well-defined roles related to those activities. Societies arose most probably in consequence of the establishment of agriculture as a way of life. People who tilled the soil did not wander. A settled life gave rise to communities with large populations that made division of labor efficient. Improved technology of agriculture in providing food made it possible for some people to be freed from the necessity of tilling the soil. The roles of soldier, priest, medicine man, merchant, and others freed from physical labor became firmly entrenched in early agricultural societies.

The settled way of life put a premium on superior arable land. Clashes for possession of such land led to permanent military establishments and, with these, the institution of war. The booty of victory was frequently not only land but also slaves to till it and to do other work for masters, who came to regard the slaves as their property. Out of this structuring came the sharp division of human societies into top dogs and underdogs.

The attitudes of underdogs vary over a tremendous range. There is little in common between a member of a modern guerrilla group (usually an underdog who has taken up armed struggle) and a follower of the late Martin Luther King, leader of a nonviolent underdog movement, or between a plantation slave and a member of a persecuted religious sect. Studies designed to tap attitudes of underdogs reveal not so much psychological predilections associated with a subjugated social position as adjustments to the position characteristic of a particular culture or a particular society. These adjustments differ vastly over historical periods and from one social milieu to another.

Equally great differences have characterized the attitudes of top dogs toward underdogs, ranging from complete indifference, as when slaves were identified with cattle or with beasts of burden, to starkly sadistic blood thirst, usually evoked by perceived or imagined attempts of the underdogs to challenge their masters or exploiters. Counterrevolutionary terror, lynchings, etc., are examples of reactions of this sort.

Rationalization of exploitation and dominance is often reflected in patronizing attitudes toward the underdogs, who are regarded as childishly irresponsible or mentally inferior. Here dominance is interpreted as a custodial responsibility, as in "White Man's Burden."

A vivid example of a completely placid attitude toward slaves, devoid of either disdain or rancor precisely because the slave was regarded as a farm animal can be found in the famous work of Cato the Censor (234–149 B.C.) on farming (Cato 1933).

Advising on adjusting the inventory at the end of the year, Cato wrote

> If anything is needed for the year's supply, it should be bought; if there is a surplus of anything, it should be sold. . . . Let him sell the old work oxen, the blemished cattle, the blemished sheep, the wool, the skins, the old wagon, the worn-out iron tools, the aged slave, the slave that is diseased, and everything else that he does not need. (pp. 7–8.)

It is noteworthy that the slave was a very special type of underdog. Typically, he was an outsider. In this way slavery differed from other types of bondage, such as clientage or helotage. Probably an actual member of a slave-owning society could not be turned into a genuine slave. Ancient Roman law, for example, provided that if a Roman citizen was enslaved as a punishment for a crime, he had to be sold abroad (Levy-Bruhl 1931/ 1960).

Aside from revealing passages in Cato's work, surprisingly little is known about the attitudes of Roman masters to slaves. If the pretense that slaves were beasts could not be kept up (which, perhaps, it could not), possibly the masters were brutalized in consequence of cognitive dissonance (cf. below). Easy access to slave women must have shaped attitudes toward sex. Aside from these conjectures, we have little to go by. Evidently slaves were not regarded as an important subject.

Even less is known about the atitudes of the slaves toward their masters. Understandably, slaves did not write or, at any rate, did not publish. Throughout classical antiquity only three large-scale slave revolts, involving over 100,000 slaves each, have been recorded, all in a short span (135–70 B.C.). In all cases, these were associated with severe breakdowns of the social order as well as with large concentrations of slaves with a common language (additional evidence of the primacy of the social milieu as a determinant of attitudes).

Peasant revolts in sixteenth-century Europe were also associated with the social upheavals attending the Reformation. The revolt of peasants, certain Central Asian tribes, and cossacks led by Emelian Pugachev in Russia in the 1770s swelled into a full-scale military campaign. Here, too, however, next to nothing is known about how those underdogs "felt." One might surmise from the intensity of the violence (massacres, pillage) that they were incensed with hatred. But such projections are rarely reliable. Hatred is something one feels toward human beings. We cannot be sure that the rebelling underdogs regarded their masters or oppressors as human beings any more than the latter regarded them as such.

Characteristic of underdog versus top dog conflicts has been persistent expression of empathy for the plight of the underdog by members of the upper social strata. It is difficult to establish the earliest manifestatons of this attitude. The explicit protests of the biblical prophets against social injustice may not qualify since these persons may themselves have been of the lower strata. We do find examples of conscience-inspired criticism of the prevalent attitude toward slaves already in antiquity. Plutarch (A.D. 46–120) comments on Cato's advice to sell aged slaves:

> For my part, I cannot but charge this using his servants like so many beasts of burden, and turning them off, or selling them when they grow old, to the account of a mean and ungenerous spirit . . . I would not sell even an old ox that had laboured for me; much less would I remove for the sake of a little money a man grown old in my service from his usual place and diet. (Plutarch 1841.)

With the advent of accelerating social change, protests against exploitation of human beings became common. The protesters, were, however, still predominantly members of the dominant social strata. The most eloquent indictment of slavery in the United States was voiced by white abolitionists. The most eloquent indictment of serfdom in Russia can be found in the work of I.S. Turgeniev,[1] a member of the land-owning gentry. Idealized images of peasants as amalgams of earthiness and saintliness appear in the works of L.N. Tolstoy,[2] a titled Russian landowner. The imminent overthrow of the capitalist system by its underdogs (the proletariat) was announced by a son of a lawyer (Karl Marx) and the son of a factory owner (Friedrich Engels).

Only in recent times do we have firsthand accounts of the underdogs' inner experiences. A rich source of these is found in the writings of American Blacks, some former slaves or children of slaves.

> A white policeman yelled, "Hey, boy. Come here!" Somewhat bothered, I retorted: "I'm no boy." He then rushed me, inflamed, and stood towering over me, snorting, "What d'ja say, boy?" Quickly he frisked me and demanded, "What's your name, boy?" Frightened, I replied, "Dr. Poussaint. I'm a physician." He angrily chuckled and hissed, "What's your first name, boy?" When I hesitated he assumed a threatening stance and clenched his fists. As my heart palpitated, I muttered in profound humiliation, "Alvin."
>
> He continued his psychological brutality, bellowing, "Alvin, the next time I call you, you come right away, you hear? You hear?" I hesitated. "You hear me, boy?" (Poussaint 1971).

Conflicts between underdogs and top dogs are frequently quiescent. At times this calm may be real, as when social stratification is stable and the underdogs seem to take their subjugated status for granted. At other times, however, the absence of overt conflict may be misleading. Pressures may be building toward an explosion.

J. Galtung has advanced a "structural theory of aggression." His point of departure is a criticism of the frustration-aggression theory. A more reliable instigator of conflict, according to Galtung, is the position of the underdog "that gives a view to a better life situation and resources. . . . A theory of aggression should combine the idea of frustration with the idea of perceiving aggression as a possible way out of the frustrating situation." (Galtung 1964, p. 96.)

Galtung denotes social status by a vector; that is, a multidimensional measure. If we assume only two levels, T (top dog) and U (underdog), then n dimensions of social status will give rise to 2^n possible positions. For example, in a two-dimensional social system, where income and educational status are the two dimensions of status, we can, in principle, have four social positions: UU, UT, TU, and TT. The same structural description can be assigned to nations (cf. below).

Galtung argues that multiplicity of criteria provides the top dogs with opportunities to oppose the frustrated underdogs by bestowing on them a higher status on dimensions that do not weaken their own dominance. Promises of rewards in the afterlife have been a well known ploy. However, Galtung points out, these ploys can backfire:

> Thus, to institute mass education and give knowledge to the masses with the idea that "this will satisfy them, they will think less of getting property" is both unpsychological and unsociological. Not much time will pass before the UT, high on education, starts wondering why he should be less well off than the TT, not to mention TU—he may find comfort in his top position for a while, and then start worrying about his low position. (Galtung 1964, p. 111.)

These considerations introduce Galtung's theory of revolution (overt conflict between underdogs and top dogs) as a consequence of inconsistent status discrepancies on different dimensions. The theory is clearly related to that of revolutions based on rising expectations that remain unrealized. Among the conditions conducive to revolution in our era, Galtung specifies the following:

1. Creation of large groups of intellectuals who feel that in their high level of education they have a key not only to their own well-being but also to the well-being of the whole society.
2. Making few positions available at the top, so that access of the well-educated to positions of influence is limited.
3. Making mass education accessible, so that autodidactic rather than formally trained leaders can arise. These are likely to be imbued with the spirit of self-righteousness, which may turn into revolutionary fervor. Revolutionary leadership is most likely to come from their ranks.
4. Blocking all other changes, so that the rise of education is not accompanied by a rise in power.

In a later chapter, we will see how revolutionary potential has been reduced by providing the well educated access to power under certain conditions.

Speakers Versus Non-Speakers

Language as a binding force in human groups became crucial when people banded into aggregates larger than clans united by kinship ties. The biblical legend of the Tower of Babel attests to the realization of the crucial role of common language in a cooperative enterprise. Sometimes this crucial role is reflected in language itself. The word "Slav" is related to the Slavic word for "word" (*slovo* in Russian). The implication is that the Slavs regarded other Slavs as people with whom one could speak. On the other hand, the Russian word "niemets" (and similar words in some other Slavic languages), meaning "mute," was originally used by Slavs to designate people who did not speak Slavic languages. Today the word means "German," suggesting that the Germans were the predominant non-Slavic-speaking people with whom the ancient Slavs could not speak.

Surely the ability to communicate with someone is a most important criterion in identifying him as a potential friend, partner, or collaborator. Given the propensity of humans to think in dichotomies, it is easy to understand that people with whom one could not communicate were classed with enemies. At any rate, resolution of conflicts by appeal to common values, by discussing the merits of a case, by striking deals, and so forth, becomes all but impossible without a common language. In fact, contact between people speaking mutually unintelligible languages must have induced apprehension that easily led to hostility. The process must have been self-enhancing.

Some people, dedicated to reduction of international violence, see the institutionalization of a world language as a contribution to world peace. L.L. Zamenhof (1859–1917), the inventor of Esperanto, was among them. This synthesized language was created at a time when nationalism was seen by many as a principal source of war danger. The political climate in Europe at that time made this idea credible. Interestingly, the grammar of Esperanto is essentially a simplified form of the grammars of European (and only European) languages, and its vocabulary was composed of most easily recognizable cognates of words in European languages. Thinking about problems of war in those days was entirely "Eurocentric." If, however, communication or the lack of it were really the principal factor in determining attitudes conducive to war or peace, the situation in Europe in the nineteenth century could not have been problematic. Persons who, through shaping the foreign policies of their respective countries, determined trends toward war or away from it hardly had any difficulty communicating with their foreign colleagues. Besides being members of the educated classes and therefore fluent at least in French, the diplomatic language of the time, they also shared a common outlook on the tasks of diplomacy, common conceptions of "national interest," and the like. Clearly, the chronic hostilities and frequent wars among the European states of that period could not be ascribed to a lack of a common language. The role of language as a determinant of positive or negative attitudes in modern societies must be sought elsewhere.

In some societies, people divide into distinctive linguistic groups even if they supposedly speak the same language. For languages have dialects in vocabulary and pronunciation. Our contemporary meaning of the word *shibboleth* derives from the use of this word as a test to ferret out fugitives in the war of the Gileadites against the Ephraimites.

> And the Gileadites took the fords of the Jordan against the Ephraimites; and it was so, that when any of the fugitives of Ephraim said: "Let me go over," the men of Gilead said unto him: "Art thou an Ephraimite?" If he said: "Nay"; then said they unto him" "Say now Shibboleth"; and he said "Sibboleth"; for he could not frame to pronounce it right; then they laid hold on him and slew him. . . . (Judges 7 : 5–6.)

One's dialect often betrays one's place on the social scale. Bernard Shaw's play *Pygmalion* revolves around this theme. In a Viennese production of *My Fair Lady*, a musical comedy based on the play, Eliza, who in the original speaks Cockney, spoke German with a pronounced Viennese accent ("Wienerisch"), while Professor Higgins and his entourage spoke cultured German. The unmistakable class distinction, as revealed through accent, was just as evident in the translation as in the original.

During the perseecution of the Jews in Nazi Germany before the mass exterminations, intense hatred against them was kindled by aping Jewish accents in inflammatory speeches and even by simulating it in print. This ploy was especially effective, because Yiddish, the language spoken by East European Jews, is close to German and so could be portrayed as a "caricature" of German.

In sum, language functions in accentuating the "we–they" dichotomy, not only by separating the "speakers" from the "non-speakers" but also by inducing intense positive or negative affects by the way it is spoken.

Believers Versus Non-Believers

The next dichotomy we will examine—between "believers" and "non-believers"—is not based on immediately perceived differences of appearance or intelligibility. It becomes apparent only in consequence of prior indoctrination and is totally dependent on it.

One of the most severe wars in European history in terms of human suffering was the Thirty Years War (1618–1648), usually classified as a war of religion because the opposing sides, with one exception, were Catholics and Protestants. The participation of that one exception, France, a Catholic state aiding the Protestant coalition, throws some doubt on the genuineness of the religious issue and suggests that some more mundane political considerations were involved. There is little doubt, however, that hatred of the enemy among the rank and file participants of this conflict was genuine and intense. Often this hostility, however induced, has been utilized by contending power elites, whose war aims had little to do with religious beliefs.

The origin of the word "religion" (Latin *re*, back + *ligare*, to bind) points to the social function—binding a society by shared beliefs. Agreeing on what is true acts like a bond between people if only because there are more opportunities of accepting others' statements as true. Saying "yes" (as well as saying "no") can be habit-forming. Agreeing on what is good provides an even stronger bond. One can trust others to be on one's side in disputes, conflicts, and hostile encounters. Above all, commonly held beliefs, especially if they contradict others' commonly held beliefs, provide conceptually clear criteria for distinguishing "us" from "them." The distinction is strengthened by participation in communal activities connected with religion, worship, rituals, festivals, and so on.

In seventeenth century Ukraine, cossacks lived in self-governing military communities, engaging mostly in marauding and plundering regions ruled by the Poles and the Turks. In his novel about these people, *Taras Bulba*, N.V. Gogol (1809–1852) describes the procedure of accepting new members into the community. The interrogation is simple.

"You believe in Christ?"
"Yes."
"And in the Holy Trinity?"
"Yes!"
"Go to church?"
"I do."
"Let's see you make a sign of the cross."

If this is done properly, the young man is welcomed into the band.

The obverse side of accepting cobelievers as friends and allies is the cruelty with which infidels of all kinds are persecuted. When this occurs, the religious issue is often no more than an excuse for plunder. The revocation of the Edict of Nantes by Louis XIV and the persecution of the Huguenots that followed were surely motivated by prospects of booty in the form of confiscated property. The first holy war waged by the followers of Mohammed was surely primarily a war of conquest. The role of religious fervor in this conquest was an energizing one. If any inhibition existed against killing, raping, and robbing, the conviction that these atrocities were carried out to glorify God dispelled them. The same can be said about persecution of adherents of different faiths on one's own soil. Frequently, the property of the victims was expropriated. Torture and burning at the stake were rationalized as being for the heretic's own good, since they expiated his guilt and saved his immortal soul.

Hatred of heretics who departed from orthodox beliefs in often trivial details has frequently been more intense than hatred of infidels professing remote faiths. This could simply be a consequence of the fact that heretics were conveniently close. However, two other explanations suggest themselves. First, the small difference between the heretic and the orthodox believer might make it easier for the former to seduce the latter; this probably made the heretic seem more dangerous. Second, heretics are usually more helpless than infidels, who may live in other countries and have armies of their own. Tormentors often experience more intense hatred of those they mistreat than do their victims for them.

The mistreatment of the "deviationists" in the Soviet Union, especially in the late 1930s, resembled closely the practices of the Inquisition. The psychological content of both persecutions may well have been similar.

Racism

Aside from language, the notion of race generates the most conspicuous criteria for distinguishing between "us" and "them." This is so despite the findings of anthropologists that race is an extremely fuzzy concept, by no means easy to define in a way that permits an unambiguous classification of human individuals on grounds of objective criteria. Here we are speaking not of "race" but of the *notion* of race, which is a very different thing.

People of different ancestry may differ in several physical features such as skin color, texture of hair, proportions of limbs, etc. These differences gave rise to the early notions of race. For a long time white schoolchildren were told that there were three "races": white, black, and yellow; or else four, if American Indians were counted as a separate "red" race. All this is nonsense. The Australian black-skinned aborigine is as far removed from the African black as he is from the pale-skinned European. But none of this matters if people *want* to distinguish "races" without bothering about ambiguities and contradictions.

In the United States, during the slavery era and for several generations afterward, "Negro" was a juridical, not an anthropological term. One was legally a "Negro" if one was so labeled. Definitions were offered in terms of the number of direct ancestors who were "Negroes." But since those were also "Negroes" by virtue of being so labeled, the definition had no objective content.

In Germany, during the Nazi regime, the same rules applied with regard to Jews. This situation was even more arbitrary, since no reliable physical tests were known that would establish a person's Jewish parentage. Thus, the important thing in distinguishing people of different "races" is consensus on how to do it, which usually involves consulting documents or hearing testimony of witnesses rather than referring to criteria related to genetics.

Although distinctions on the basis of "race" have been associated with the most intense emotions, usually involving severe hostility, there have been no important wars between "races," at least no important wars in which "race" was emphasized as the division between friends and enemies.

The matter looks quite different if the underdogs of a society are identified as racially distinct. *Structural violence* is the name given by Johann Galtung (1969/1971) to designate the domination of one group by another by possession of the *potential* for violence, against which the latter has little or no defense. Galtung advanced this concept in order to call attention to a crucial distinction between a situation characterized by absence of overt violence and genuine social peace. According to Galtung, the distinction is important, for ignoring it may lead to the illusion that the absence of overt warfare between the countries of the impoverished Third World and the affluent industrialized world is a state of "peace." Of course, one is free to offer a definition of peace as simply the absence of war. But lumping all instances of "absence of war" into one category may lead to seriously mistaken conclusions or expectations.

If we accept structural violence as a category of conflict, we can say that racial conflicts have been common in history, again reminding the reader that "racial" must often be interpreted in the vulgar rather than scientific sense of the word.

Institutionalized slavery is the crassest example of structural violence. The physical distinction between people of African and European descent helped slavery to become entrenched in the United States, where for about a half-century the use of slave labor on cotton plantations was exceedingly profitable. The physical distinctiveness of Blacks made rationalization of slavery easy. Racism, the notion that people of one ancestry are superior or inferior to those of another, has its roots, at least in America, in slavery and its aftermath.

In contrast to American racism, which was rooted in a rationalization of (structural) violence already perpetrated on the slaves, German racism was an instrument of *instigating* violence. Also, unlike American racism, justifications for which were often cited from the bible, German racists enlisted the services of university professors, possibly because of the long-standing German tradition of holding scholarship in respect. Accordingly, a rich pseudo-science proliferated in the Third Reich. It had all the trappings of a scientific discipline. Learned papers were written on "indices," largely involving skull structure, thus providing a quantitative basis for racial criteria. Much was written also about the "spiritual" characteristics (or lack thereof) of various "races." Race hatred was incorporated into the educational system of the Third Reich.

At the roots of this program of indoctrination was a deeply entrenched superstition about blood. Blood appears in the most ancient texts as an object of worship in sacrificial rites usually involving slaughter of animals, in some cases of humans. Since the spilling of blood of others reinforces the feeling of power over them, one's own vulnerability becomes associated with one's own blood. To bleed means to lose the substance of life, hence to succumb.

On the next level of abstraction is the notion of the "purity" of the blood. Not only must one's blood be kept from spilling; it must be protected from "pollution." And if we extend the notion of self to one's line of descent (a throwback to the possibly genetically determined kin versus non-kin dichotomy), blood "pollution" becomes identified with miscegenation. Dread of miscegenation became central in Nazi race mystique.

> The importance of the blood value of a people . . . only becomes totally effective when this value is recognized by a people, properly valued and appreciated. People who do not understand this value or who no longer have a feeling for it or lack a natural instinct, thereby immediately also begin to lose it. Blood-mixing and lowering of the race are then the consequences which, to be sure, at the beginning are not seldom introduced through a so-called predilection for things foreign, which in reality is an underestimation of one's own cultural values against those of alien peoples. . . . For this reason international-mindedness is to be regarded as a mortal enemy of these values. (Hitler quoted in Blackburn 1985, p. 139.)

Indeed, all life and all culture were declared by the Nazis to be based on race. The highest human values were the creation of the superior "Aryan" race. If the term "Aryan" means anything at all, it is a synonym of "Indo-European," which refers to a family of languages, a categorization that is in no way related to genetics. But of course the reduction of "Aryan" superiority to absurdity could not dispel the myth of racial superiority.

Once the Germans were identified as "Aryans" and "Aryans" were declared to be superior, the most alluring wish fantasies and the most numbing fears fell into place. The roads to salvation and damnation were clearly delineated. The world became understandable, and one's own rightful position in it was assured. Beliefs of this sort are all too easily entrenched and cannot be easily discarded.

The Nazis declared all worthwhile culture to have been created by the "Aryan" race. Some races on the intermediate level of the hierarchy were said to be able to preserve culture but not to create it. At the other end was the Jew.

The Jew could only destroy culture. And he did it with sadistic lust, because once culture was destroyed, the way would be clear for the Jew's dominance of the world. Here we discern an echo of the Nibelung saga, especially as it was adapted by Richard Wagner in his musical masterpiece, *The Ring of the Nibelungen*. The archvillain of this epic is the dwarf Alberich, who forswears love in order to achieve power to rule the world by reducing everyone to slavery.

The Jews were portrayed in the schoolbooks of the Third Reich as "onerous parasites in the living space of our people . . ." The life of the Jews was described as "roaming, plundering nomadism" . . . a "barren ode to desolation" for the "host" population on which the parasitic Jew preyed. (Christoffel 1944, p. 37, quoted in Blackburn 1985, p. 140.)

In portraying the Jew as rapacious and destructive, the Nazis made wide use of biblical sources. German schoolchildren read lurid accounts of the massacres of the Canaanites by the ancient Hebrews. If one accepts the racist dictum of genetic determinism of national characteristics and if one identifies the modern Jews as descendants of the ancient Hebrews, then the primary sources of the Old Testament leave nothing to be desired as vivid evidence of the destructiveness and rapaciousness of the Jews.

> . . . but thou shalt utterly destroy them, namely, the Hittites, the Amorites, the Canaanites, and the Perizzites, the Hivites, and the Jebusites; as the Lord thy God hath commanded thee. (Deuteronomy 20 : 17.)
> So Joshua smote all the country of the hills, and of the South, and of the vale, and of the springs, and all their kings; he left none remaining, but utterly destroyed all that breathed, as the Lord God of Israel commanded. (Joshua 10 : 40.)
> And thou shalt consume all the people which the Lord thy God shall deliver thee: thine eye shall have no pity upon them: neither shalt thou serve their gods; for that will be a snare unto thee. (Deuteronomy 7 : 16.)

No less damning are the reasons given in the Old Testament for this genocidal policy.

For thou art an holy people unto the Lord thy God: the Lord thy God hath chosen thee to be a special people unto himself, above all people that are upon the face of the earth. (Deuteronomy 7 : 6.)

In racist propaganda stereotypes of inferiority of a persecuted population are often mixed with stereotypes of "superiority," especially if such "superiority" presents a threat. Thus, American racists often ascribe superhuman sexual potency to Blacks. Similarly, anti-Semites mix contempt with grudging admiration of Jewish shrewdness and vitality as a cohesive group. Here, too, the Nazis were able to base their portrayal of Jews on evidence "out of their mouths," as it were.

The following passage attributed to Benjamin Disraeli explaining the survival of Jews in history was incorporated in a book of readings for the studying of English.

Do you think that you can crush those who have successfully baffled the pharaohs, Nebuchadnezzar, Rome, and the feudal ages? The fact is you cannot destroy a pure race of the Caucasian organization. It is a physiological fact: a single law of nature, which has baffled Egyptian and Assyrian kings, Roman emperors, and Christian inquisitors. No penal laws, no physical tortures, can effect that a superior race should be absorbed in an inferior, or be destroyed by it. The mixed persecuting races disappear; the persecuted race remains. And at this moment in spite of centuries, of tens of centuries, of degradation, the Jewish mind exercises a vast influence on the affairs of Europe. I speak not of their laws, which you obey; or their literature with which your minds are saturated but of the living Hebrew intellect.[3]

The same source provides "evidence" of the Jewish "conspiracy."

You never observe a great intellectual movement in Europe in which the Jews do not greatly participate. The first Jesuits were Jews; that mysterious Russian diplomacy which so alarms western Europe is organized and principally carried on by Jews; that mighty revolution which is at this moment preparing in Germany, and which will be in fact a second and greater Reformation, and which so little is as yet known in England, is entirely developing under the auspices of Jews, who almost monopolize the professional chairs in Germany. . . . So you see that the world is governed by very different personages to what is imagined by those who are behind the scenes.[4]

Here, indeed, the dictum, "Lord preserve us from our friends," applies.[5]

Nationalism

Nationalism refers to a set of attitudes that reflect admiration of or loyalty to the culture, the inhabitants, or the institutions of one's own country, often accompanied by hostility or disdain for the culture, institutions, or populations of other countries. Frequently nationalism, especially in discussions of its role in war-proneness, refers primarily to the latter (negative) aspects, while the former (positive) aspects are called "patriotism."

By "country" we understand here a nation-state, that is, a politically unified region, whose inhabitants share certain characteristics, in the first instance a common language and usually also common knowledge about the history of the region, especially of events that reflect a common fate of the inhabitants, for example, struggles against invaders or foreign rulers.

The concept of nationalism so defined is a comparatively recent notion. It originated in Europe following the decline of the feudal system and of the power of the Church. The Treaty of Westphalia at the end of the Thirty Years War (1618–1648) left to the rulers of domains the power to prescribe the religious affiliation of their subjects. At that time, this meant primarily affiliation either with the Roman Catholic Church or with one of the Protestant sects that arose during the Reformation. Thus, the power of the secular princes was greatly increased and their domains were more firmly welded into integrated political units. The modern international system with states as autonomous units can be said to have emerged at that time.

However, it is not until the nearly absolute power of the princes was challenged by the French Revolution that nationalism emerged as a major force in European history. In many instances nationalist sentiments had strong admixtures of democratic notions, promulgated throughout Europe during the French Revolutionary Wars and their aftermath. This mixture was especially conspicuous in countries ruled by foreign elites, e.g., Hungary, Italy, and Poland. The struggles led by patriots of those countries against foreign domination mark the high tide of so-called "progressive" nationalism. As a result of those struggles, Italy became an independent nation-state, and Hungary, although incorporated into the Austro-Hungarian empire, was granted considerable autonomy. The Polish revolts against Russia in 1830 and 1863 failed, but Polish nationalism retained its vigor until independence was finally achieved at the end of World War I.

It is interesting to note that in Germany, where the pressure for unification was coupled with the quite mild democratic ideas of 1848 (e.g., a demand for a constitution), this movement was regarded by the power elites of the many German states as revolutionary and was suppressed. It seems that at that time, any basis of loyalty other than to the *person* of the sovereign was viewed by the power elites with darkest suspicion.

During the second half of the nineteenth century, the nature of nationalism in Europe changed. It was now divested of democratic sentiments and became more nearly the expression of the political Right. The reason for the change seems to have been the growing prominence of class antagonisms in the wake of the Industrial Revolution and the growth of an industrial working class, a proletariat. Strongly influenced by the ideas of Karl Marx, the ideological commitments of the workers stressed international solidarity, diluting commitments to national loyalties. The "we" of the class struggle appeared now to be incompatible with the "we" of the nation. In Germany, especially, the principal activity of the labor movement, the organization of trade unions, was equated by the upper and middle classes with disloyalty to the state, which these classes regarded as the embodiment of the nation and all its values. In sum, nationalism of the late nineteenth century reflected a vehement rejection of social change that would somehow curtail the privileges of the upper social strata.

At about the same time, this extreme form of conservative nationalism appeared in Russia. There, however, the emphasis was less on preserving the prerogatives of the nobility and the gentry than on a mystique of a "Russian soul." This soul was seen partly in the conspicuous piety of the Russian masses, partly in the idealized "Russian character," which was pictured as broad, spontaneous, passionate, above all generous, contemptuous of "materialist" values, fiercely loyal to friends, and equally fierce in reacting to anything that resembled "betrayal." Believers in this mystique were the adherents of the "slavophile" (anti-Western) wing of the Russian intelligentsia. A famous exponent of this outlook was Fyodor Dostoyevsky.

In his youth, Dostoyevsky was close to revolutionary circles. At the age of 28 he was condemned to death. Commutation of the sentence was announced as he was being taken to his execution. He spent several years in Siberian banishment, where he began his literary career. There he evidently underwent a complete "conversion." Perhaps this reversal was an instance of a victim identifying with his tormentors, a phenomenon observed in connection with brainwashing. At any rate, Dostoyevsky became a reactionary nationalist of the Russian variety, consumed with vitriolic hatred of Jews and of all foreigners, especially Poles. How the creator of Alyosha Karamazov and of Prince Myshkin, embodiments of Christian charity and compassion, could write the diatribes that Dostoyevsky directed against non-Russians is hard to understand. We are constantly reminded of the complexity of the human psyche. It is phenomena of this sort that suggest the answer "Yes" to all questions concerning the nature of human nature (cf. Chapter 1).

Nationalism is commonly listed among the principal contributory causes of World War I. To what extent this is true is an open question. "Causes" of historical events are not easy to discern if one thinks of such "causes" as analogous to causes of natural events. There is no doubt, however, that the events leading up to the outbreak of World War I and its early phases can be regarded as manifestations of nationalism. The instigating event was the assassination of Crown Prince Ferdinand of Austria by a young Serbian. At that time, the Balkans were a scene of intense rivalry between Russia and Austria-Hungary. Both monarchies strove to broaden their respective spheres of influence in the region, which for centuries had been dominated by the Turkish empire. As in the course of the nineteenth century Turkish power declined, the nationalist aspirations of the Slavic peoples, the Serbs, the Bulgarians, the Montenegrins, etc., became vociferous. Russia assumed the role of a "protector" of these people who were bound to Russia not only by proximally related languages but also by adherence to the Greek Orthodox faith. Encouraged in these aspirations, nationalist organizations, particularly in Serbia, became increasingly militant and hostile to Austria and her expansionist policies. The assassination of the Austrian Crown Prince took place a few years after Austria's annexation of Bosnia and Herzegovina, provinces with predominantly Slavic populations, previously wrested from Turkey.

The passions kindled during the weeks following the assassination culminated in mass hysteria when war was finally declared. In Paris and in Berlin, in Vienna and in St. Petersburg, strangers embraced each other on the street. Crowds lined the main thoroughfares of the cities, cheering recruits marching off to railroad stations to be taken to the front. In the first weeks, before the severe bloodletting began in earnest, the war was portrayed in the press, in speeches, and in prayers as a challenge and an opportunity: a challenge to test the nation's virtues and mettle in the awesome crucible of battles and an opportunity to prove the nation worthy of unflinching loyalty and love.

It is likely that in the reality of war, which in those days was experienced not only in the ordeal of battle but also in the frustrations of sessile trench life, the romantic image induced and self-induced in those young soldiers may have faded. But the "we–they" dichotomy, the most essential feature of the image, remained. The "we" and the "they" were distinguished not by imagined virtues credited to "us" and the imagined vices ascribed to "them" but by the all-too-real circumstance that one's own life depended on every one of "us" and was jeopardized by every one of "them." No other dichotomy could be so stable. When one left the relative, precarious safety of the trench and went "over the top" to attack "them," it was one's own artillery comrades who pinned "them" down. From "them" one could expect only death.

Here, then, is an instance of mutually reinforcing and continually inter-changeable causes and effects. German and French nationalism may have induced and nurtured chronic hostility between Germans and Frenchmen. Conceivably, this hatred might have been eventually attenuated in the course of a protracted period of peaceful coexistence, if the two states engaged in trade, scientific collaboration, cultural exchanges, and the like. But once this hostility led to legitimized mass violence, the stark battlefield reality of "us" versus "them" obscured everything else. Only with the onset of extreme war weariness did resentment against one's own power elites begin to replace the hatred of the "enemy."

Americans and Russians now find themselves in a similar situation. Many years of propaganda, propped up by images induced by ideological com-mitments, have produced a "we versus they" gulf between the two nations. In circles seriously dedicated to the cause of peace, e.g., many church groups, grass roots peace movements, etc., it is taken for granted that this artificially induced hostility is the greatest source of danger, a potential cause of World War III. Consequently, the remedy for the present pre-carious situation appears, against the background of this image, to be a dissipation of hostility. All sorts of people-to-people contacts and ex-changes are proposed to enhance tolerance, mutual understanding, and similar positive attitudes toward the people on the other side of the chasm.

Even though the ultimate value of such programs for promoting durable peace may be considerable, they are not likely to attenuate the present danger because the focus of hostility has shifted. Although Russians and Americans never met as enemies on a battlefield, the "we versus they" paradigm based on a *pure* military adversarial relationship is now firmly established. "They" are feared—and mostly hated (since hatred is often a close companion of fear), not necessarily because their values differ, not necessarily because they entertain different beliefs, and not necessarily because they lack virtues we admire or possess vices we despise. No, the reason "they" are the enemy is because they are perceived to be the "enemy." They are perceived as standing poised to destroy us. It is taken for granted that they would do it if they could or thought they could get away with it. This is the image of "them" produced by propagandists of both countries. The usual propaganda picturing the others as depraved or evil, although occasionally indulged in, is no longer essential to induce acceptance of the prospect of war.

In pure military thought, the question *why* an adversary is an adversary makes no more sense than the question why Black is the adversary of White in a game of chess. That is to say, in pure military thought, the adversary is simply *given*, like an axiom in a mathematically formulated theory. It makes no more sense to ask whether an adversary is really an adversary than to ask whether a meter is "really" a meter. It is a meter by definition. So is the adversary an adversary by definition. The significant problems revolve about the question of how to deal with him.

In this context, hostility as an emotion may play no part. Hostility induced in a population helps, because it provides support for the preparation of war. These preparations need no longer be justified on the grounds that "they" are wicked, depraved, against God, or what not (although these images can help). The most credible rationale for preparing for war is that the "we versus they" dichotomy poses the question about who shall survive.

This shift of focus from emotions generated by our imagined virtues and their imagined vices to an even more primitive "kill or be killed" posture reflects a decline of nationalism as an effective lever for manipulating populations. Already at the outbreak of World War II, the mood of Europe was quite different from what it was in the heady summer of 1914. In 1939 there were no parades, no cheering crowds. The predominant mood was one of resignation rather than of enthusiasm, even in Germany, in spite of a tremendous resurgence of nationalism in the immediately preceding years. Perhaps memories of World War I exerted a damping influence. However, the German victories in the spring and summer of 1940 brought out a nationalist euphoria in full force. This was probably the pinnacle of that mood in Europe.

Notes

1. See especially his *Papers of a Sportsman*, scenes and episodes from the life of Russian serfs described with exquisite sensitivity and profound psychological insight.
2. Toward the end of his life, Tolstoy abandoned the literary genre for which he is famous—the panoramic novel—and devoted himself to writing simple tales in artless folk idiom, accessible to the unlettered. The stories all carry the message of Christian teaching.
3. Cited in Blackburn 1985, p. 146 from Fischer, H. 1943, p. 99.
4. Ibid.
5. The passage is falsely attributed to Disraeli. Actually, it is spoken as a eulogy to Jews by a character in one of Disraeli's novels (*Coningsdy*, Boston: L. C. Page and Company, 1904, pp. 303, 305). The character seems to have been modeled after Lionel Nathan de Rotschild. The passage has often been quoted in anti-Semitic tracts.

5

Uses and Limitations of the Psychological Approach

Is War a Manifestation of Aggression?

As war technology developed to the extent that killing at a distance became possible, the importance of aggressiveness as a prime mover of behavior in battle, though still considerable, must have diminished simply because, as the distance between the attacker and the target became greater, the attacker could act with greater deliberation. Striking a blow with a club or a sword required a higher level of adrenalin (the hormone enhancing aggressive behavior) than aiming an arrow.

This progressive devaluation of aggressiveness as a prime mover of war continued in the wake of developing war technology and complex social organization. The rifleman still had to see a target; the artilleryman no longer did. Moreover, the battle ceased to be the only significant event of war. Elaborate preparations for war centering on production, the working out of logistics, the design of strategies, and so forth, related not only to active fighting but also to policies, and diplomacy, and eventually equaled or even surpassed in importance the efforts related directly to fighting. There is no reason to suppose that all that supporting activity is guided or aided by aggressiveness. Surely, no relationship can be discerned between the intensity of that activity and the intensity of the aggressive drive that is supposed to generate it.

Consider the present situation. A nuclear war between the superpowers, which in most people's estimation (as well as in the estimation of the political leaders of the superpowers) could be unleashed at any time, would surpass by several orders of magnitude any outburst of violence that has yet occurred on this planet. Yet it would be foolhardy to ascribe to people who are currently preparing such a holocaust a degree of aggressiveness commensurate with the magnitude of that outburst. We can easily conjecture that present-day Americans or Russians are, on the whole, considerably less aggressive in their demeanor or in their psychological makeup (to the extent that we can infer it from their behavior) than, say, the Vikings of the tenth century or the Mongols of the thirteenth.

The unprecedented violence of a nuclear war must be attributed to the destructive power of modern weapons. The aggressiveness of *persons* may well have little or nothing to do with it. As an entirely credible scenario of a nuclear war that may destroy civilization and, perhaps, the human race, we can envisage exchanges of most devastating blows without any human being actually meeting another human being in face-to-face combat. It is not necessary to hate anyone in order to kill everyone. Once this is recognized, the genesis of war appears in an entirely new light.

If Not Aggressiveness, What?

According to estimates based on reliable knowledge of physical and chemical laws, extinction of human life on this planet can easily come about if only a fraction of existing nuclear warheads are exploded over cities. These explosions may raise enough smoke to blot out enough sunlight so as to usher in a climatic catastrophe called "nuclear winter." Briefly, the temperatures on the surface of the earth would be drastically lowered for several months. As a consequence, all crops and animals would be destroyed. Survivors of blasts and radiation fallout would surely die of exposure and hunger. The total disruption of social organization, on which civilized human beings now completely depend for their lives, would compound the physical disaster.

These quite probable consequences of "nuclear exchanges" are well known, and no serious attempts are made to deny them. Nevertheless, as this is being written, the concerns that override all others in the minds of the decision makers are concerns with something called "national security" or "military balance," not how to eliminate the possibility of total destruction. It is taken for granted by the decision makers of both superpowers that a necessary and sufficient condition for safeguarding "national security" is to be at least as "strong" as, and preferably stronger than, the adversary. "Strength" is defined in the same way it was defined by European statesmen and generals in the eighteenth and nineteenth centuries.

So is "balance of power." At that time, the numbers of divisions and battleships, plus command of certain geographically strategic sites, the tonnage of warships, sizes of populations, etc., all were factors in "national security" and entered calculations of the "balance of power." The indices and measures have changed as the components of military potential have changed, but the identification of "national security" with destructive power has remained intact.

In the pre-nuclear age, when victories and defeats were decided by confrontations of armies on battlefields, these indices could still be regarded as relevant to "national security." They made sense inasmuch as the outcomes of land and sea battles determined the "winners" and the "losers" of a war. These were clearly differentiated. The "winners" got to have their way in the drafting of peace treaties after the cessation of hostilities. The terms of the treaties were deemed to be more or less advantageous to one side or the other. Hence concern with "national security" meant concern with the possible advantages expected to be gained or disadvantages expected to be suffered following successes or failures in battles. In this way, military strength was linked by a long chain of hypothetical circumstances to "national security."

We will assume (for the sake of argument) that "national security" can be defined in terms of the advantages or disadvantages accruing to states, e.g., trade treaties, conquest of new territories, formation or dissolution of alliances, acquisition of colonies in lands where people do not possess enough military power or lack the sort of social organization that would have enabled them to resist colonization, etc. Note that all these advantages or disadvantages were the most frequent prizes or punishments associated with outcomes of eighteenth and nineteenth century wars.

None of these "classical" war aims can be meaningfully realized as prizes to accrue to a "victor" in a nuclear war. In fact, declarations to the effect that there can be no winners of a nuclear war have been made by political leaders of nuclear states. (Statements that can be interpreted as maintaining the contrary will be examined in Chapter 16.) We note nevertheless that each superpower shows symptoms of acute anxiety—fear of being attacked by the other. All war preparations are still justified in the name of "national security" but the usual advantages traditionally associated with "national security" are nowhere mentioned. Indeed, it would be ludicrous to speak of the outcome of a nuclear war in terms of conquered provinces, advantageous trade treaties, or acquired naval bases.

Only one rationale for continuing the accumulation of destructive potential has retained currency, namely, "defense." On closer examination, however, this rationale also reduces to an absurdity, since nuclear weapons cannot defend anything or anybody. They can only destroy everything and everybody. When pressed on this point, the nuclear weapons enthusiast plays his last trump, namely, deterrence. The possession of nuclear weapons is supposed to deter another possessor of nuclear weapons from using them by inducing fear of retaliation. This reliance on the "balance of terror" as a stabilizing influence in global politics is the contemporary version of the "balance of power" doctrine.

What this amounts to is that the predominant state of mind that is supposed to govern the present precarious relations between the superpowers poised for each other's destruction is not aggressiveness but fear. But there is no evidence that this is the dominant psychological state of the leaders on whose decisions the fate of the earth hinges. Fear, as it is usually understood, is accompanied by well-known physiological states. The behavior triggered by rage (the supposed psychological concomitant of aggression) is attack; that triggered by fear is flight. If both rage and fear are present, one or the other form of behavior will result, but not both simultaneously, since one is conducive to "fight," the other to "flight." Nor do the two cancel each other, resulting in a neutral state, i.e., calm. Instead, sudden transitions are observed, as when a cowering animal suddenly attacks, or when an animal, apparently poised for fighting, suddenly flees.

Neither the physiological state associated with rage nor that associated with fear can persist in an individual animal for more than a short time. But the state of fear, in terms of which the present postures of the superpowers can be most reasonably explained, has persisted practically unabated for over forty years. Therefore it cannot be the state of any individual. In fact, if one observes the political leaders of the superpowers as they go about their daily business, one finds them neither in a state of fear nor in a state of rage. Their emotional state is probably indistinguishable from that of any person going about his business day in, day out. How then can maintaining the persistent state of the world on the brink of disaster be attributed to an emotional state?

This paradox throws some doubt on the sort of thinking that seeks explanations of large-scale violence, such as war, in terms of psychological states similar to those associated with violence perpetrated by individuals. If the psychological dimension is to be at all relevant to the study of conflict, it should direct our attention to other psychological concomitants of conflict behavior.

Diversity of Psychological States Associated with Conflict

As we have seen, one of the most striking features of evolution is transformation of function in the process of adaptation. To cite George Simpson's (1950) felicitous comparison, evolution is "opportunistic" rather than original. The flying reptiles and birds did not "invent" wings; they put limbs to a new use—flying. Man did not "invent" articulate speech; he put the organs used in eating and breathing (tongue, teeth, lips, lungs) to new uses.

The ritualization of aggression, often entailing complete elimination of bodily contact, hence of bodily harm, appears to be the evolutionary analogue of what is called *sublimation* of aggression in human beings. Psychologists who hold tenaciously to the belief in an ineradicable aggressive drive in humans explain superior intellectual and artistic achievement by sublimation, that is, redirecting the aggressive drive into activities that seem to have something in common with aggression but do not lead to destructive results.

The satisfaction provided by creative activity is, for the most part, a feeling of mastery. Now mastery over other living things may well be related to the fulfillment of aggressive tendencies, but drawing a parallel between this sort of mastery (subjugation) and mastery over a lump of clay (the artist's mastery) or over one's own body (the athlete's mastery) seems farfetched. In fact, the ascetic may derive intense satisfaction from mastering (i.e., suppressing) his own appetites. Believers in the ubiquitous aggressive drive regard sadistic and masochistic satisfactions as two sides of the same coin. But there is no hard evidence that the motivations of the conqueror and those of the saint, of the boxer and of the poet, stem from the same source. Insistence on this interpretation amounts to making the theory of the aggressive drive unfalsifiable and therefore sterile. It is this insight, namely, that the concept of aggressive drive *dissolves* when we follow all its suggested implications, that has been the most valuable contribution of the theory of aggression to the theory of human conflict.

In what follows, we will examine several situations depicted in personal accounts, field studies, poetry, and fiction that will give an idea of the immense diversity of attitudes and psychological states associated with war.

Ecstasy

We have examined the biblical account of a war involving a massacre supposedly ordained by God and several passages where such orders are explicitly cited (cf. Chapters 2, 4). Apparently exalted reverence alternating or combined with the bloodthirstiness of sacrifice rituals was a dominant war mood of the ancient Hebrews. The sentiment is eloquently expressed in biblical poetry.

Hear, O ye kings, give ear, O ye princes
I unto the Lord will sing. . . .

Lord, when Thou shouldst go forth out of Seit
When Thou didst march out of the field of Edom
The earth trembled, the heavens also dropped
Yea, the clouds dropped water
They quaked at the presence of the Lord
Even you Sinai at the presence of the Lord and God of Israel.

These verses are attributed to a woman (Judges 5 : 2–5). Some may see in them an expression of feminine sadism, possibly rooted in a sexual attraction to men of great strength, most conspicuous in violence.

A Businesslike Attitude

Tribal warfare is not always orgiastic. We follow an account by M. Meggitt of the way the Mae Enge tribesmen of Papua New Guinea wage war. Military instruction given to boys is matter-of-fact and practical, devoid of romanticizing or heroics:

> Never waste arrows on a difficult target, such as your enemy's head; always aim at his body. . . .
> Do not start to dodge until your adversary has drawn his bow to the point of release, for then he will have difficulty in aiming anew; if you move too soon, he can easily follow you. . . .
> If you can see the pale shaft of your enemy's arrow in flight, remain still, for that arrow will miss you, but if you see only the point approaching you "like a black insect," duck or dodge! (Meggitt 1971, p. 62.)

Of the 71 campaigns examined, 61 could be traced to just three types of events: disputes over land, theft of pigs, and avenging homicide. The decisions to go to war were made at council meetings. These sessions were marked by extremely careful and reasoned deliberations. Preparations, e.g., assembling weapons and supplies, were also carried out in a businesslike manner. Actual fighting was done with tactical skill comparable to that of today's seasoned professionals.

Idealism

The noble and heroic theme persists through the centuries. Here is an excerpt from the musings of a warrior king, Frederick II of Prussia:

> War opens the most fruitful field of all virtues for every moment: constancy, pity, magnanimity, heroism, and mercy shine forth in it, every moment offers

an opportunity to exercise one of the virtues . . . (Quoted in Bernhardi 1914, p. 27.)

And here is an excerpt from the writings of a noted German historian:

It is war which fosters the political idealism which the materialist rejects. What a disaster for civilization it would be if mankind blotted its heroes from memory. The heroes of a nation are the fighters which rejoice and inspire the spirit of its youth, and the writers whose words ring like trumpet blasts become the idols of our boyhood and our early manhood. (Treitschke 1897–1898/1916, Vol. 1, p. 67.)

Abhorrence

Erasmus of Rotterdam, regarded by some as the most erudite scholar of the Renaissance, wrote this about war:

If thou abhor theft, war doth teach it. If thou detest parricide, that is learnt in war. For how shall he fear being moved to slay one, that, hired for so light a stipend, doth slay and murder many? If the neglecting of the laws be most present pestilence of a common weal, the laws in the time of war shall keep silence. If thou esteem adultery, incest, and filthier things than those, . . . war is the master instigator of all these things. If impiety and the neglecting of religion be the spring of all evils, these things, i.e., piety and religion, by the tempests of war are overthrown. (Erasmus 1517/1946, p. 49.)[1]

Hero Worship

Next consider the psychological state of the most fervent of Napoleon's troops as depicted in the following passage from Tolstoy's *War and Peace*:

They were commanded to look for a fording place to cross to the other side. The colonel of the Polish Uhlans, a handsome old man, flushing red and stammering from excitement, asked the adjutant whether he would be permitted to swim across the river with his men instead of seeking for a ford. In obvious dread of refusal, like a boy asking permission to get on a horse, he asked to be allowed to swim across the river before the Emperor's eyes. The adjutant replied that probably the Emperor would not be displeased at this excess of zeal.

No sooner had the adjutant said this than the old whiskered officer, with happy face and sparkling eyes, brandished his sabre in the air shouting "Vive l'Empereur!" and commanding his men to follow him, he thrust to his horse, that floundered under him, and plunged into the water, making for the most rapid part of the current. Hundreds of Uhlans galloped in after him. It was cold and dangerous in the middle of the rapid current. The Uhlans clung to one another, falling off their horses. Some of the horses were drowned, some, too, of the men. . . .

The Hero Worshipped

Then Tolstoy turns the spotlight on Napoleon:

> . . . sitting on the log and not even looking . . . When the adjutant, on going back, chose a favorable moment and ventured to call the Emperor's attention to the devotion of the Poles to his person, the little man in the grey overcoat got up, and summoning Berthier began walking up and down the bank with him, giving him instructions and casting now and then a glance of displeasure at the drowning Uhlans who had interrupted his thoughts.

Joy

Here is an autobiographical description of the feelings of a young man going into combat:

> And then came a damp cold night in Flanders, through which we marched in silence, and when the day began to emerge from the mists, suddenly an iron greeting came whizzing at us over our heads, and with a sharp report sent the little pellets flying between our ranks, ripping up the wet ground, but even before the little cloud passed, from two hundred throats the first hurrah rose to meet the first messenger of death. Then a crackling and a roaring and a howling began, and with feverish eyes each one of us was drawn, faster and faster, until suddenly past turnip fields and hedges the fight began, the fight of man against man. And from the distance, the strains of a song rended our ears, coming closer and closer, leaping from company to company, and just as Death plunged a busy hand into our ranks, the song reached us too, and we passed it along: *Deutschland über alles, über alles in der Welt.*
>
> Four days later we came back. Even our step had changed. Seventeen-year-old boys now looked like men. (Hitler 1925/1943, pp. 164–165.)

Apathy

In his novel, *All Quiet on the Western Front*, E.M. Remarque describes the feelings of a young man returning from combat:

> An hour later we reach our lorries and climb in. There is more room now than there was.
>
> The rain becomes heavier. We take out waterproof sheets and spread them over our heads. The rain rattles down, and flows off at the sides in streams.

The lorries bump through the holes, and we rock to and fro in half-sleep.

Two men in the front of the lorry have long forked poles. They watch for telephone wires which hang crosswise over the road so densely that they might easily pull our heads off. The two fellows take them at the right moment on their poles and lift them over behind us. We hear their call "Mind—wire—," dip the knee in a half sleep and straighten up again.

Monotonously the lorries sway, monotonously come the calls, monotonously falls the rain. It falls on our heads and on the heads of the dead up in the line, on the body of the little recruit with the wound that is so much too big for his hips. . . . it falls on our hearts.

An explosion sounds somewhere. We wince, our eyes become tense, our hands are ready to vault over the side of the lorry into the ditch by the road.

It goes no further—only the monotonous cry: "Mind—wire,"—our knees bend—we are again half asleep.

At the Pinnacle of Power

On the day the Allies landed in Normandy, June 6, 1945, Winston Churchill addressed Parliament:

> An immense Armada of upwards of 4,000 ships, together with several thousand smaller craft crossed the channel. Massed airborne landings have been successfully effected behind enemy lines, and landings on the beaches are proceeding at various points at the present time. The fire of shore batteries has been largely quelled. The obstacles that were constructed in the sea have not proved so difficult as apprehended. The Anglo-American Allies are sustained by about 11,000 first line aircraft, which can be drawn upon as may be needed for the purpose of the battle. . . . Reports are arriving in rapid succession. So far the commanders who are engaged report that everything is proceeding according to plan. And what a plan! The vast operation is undoubtedly the most complicated and difficult that has ever taken place. (Churchill 1953, pp. 5–6.)

The predominant mood here is one of exaltation induced by pride of accomplishment and a sense of power. The vast machine that took years to build has at last been activated. Superb organization of men and machines has borne fruit. A mighty blow is about to be struck in the cause of freedom. Part of the satisfaction is surely the conviction of being on the side of decency and justice. But part is also intrinsic to the feeling of power itself. This aspect of power addiction can be seen more clearly in a passage from Robert Kennedy's account of the U.S. preparations to launch a preemptive strike against Cuba in October 1962:

President Kennedy was impressed with the effort and dedicated manner in which the military responded—the Navy deploying its vessels into the Caribbean; the Air Force going on continuous alert; the Army and the Marines moving their soldiers and equipment into the southeastern part of the U.S.; all of them alert and ready for combat. (Kennedy 1969, p. 118.)

Self-righteousness could not have been as strong in Kennedy's feeling of "satisfaction." An attack by Cuba on the United States was not expected. Nor would the missiles installed in Cuba make much difference in the outcome of "nuclear exchanges" between the superpowers. The installation of the missiles was most likely a gesture of defiance: "You've got them aimed at us in Turkey and Greece; we can do the same to you." Alternately, the missiles might have been meant to serve as a deterrent against the repetition of the Bay of Pigs invasion. (If so, no better example can be found of a "deterrence" that backfired.) Thus, to all intents and purposes, the blow at Cuba was going to be a "Pearl Harbor"-type unprovoked attack. It may have given rise to considerable feelings of guilt. Nevertheless, Kennedy's pride in the "dedicated manner" in which the war machine was being primed for action must have been as intense as Churchill's or, for that matter, Moltke's (cf. below), whose organizing genius made it possible for a military train to cross the Rhine every ten minutes transporting millions of men to the fields of carnage.

Among the Victims

The following is an eyewitness account of the sinking of a ship evacuating women and children from Okinawa when Americans invaded that island in 1944:

We heard children crying our names from various directions. Ten of them swam to our raft and got on, but their weight sank it; and they were forced to cling to whatever they found floating. . . .
On our raft were my wife, my daughter, and I. . . .
On the third night, my daughter began to complain. She wanted to go home. She wanted water. My heart ached because I could do nothing for her. At about midnight, my wife, who had been holding her, said that our child had stopped moving. I took her in my arms. With her last strength she clung to my neck and then died of cold and exposure. (Dana 1978.)

The Leaders' Concern for the Victims

It would be wrong to attribute to the managers of war utter callousness toward those whom war destroys. Evidence of concern can be seen in

Robert Kennedy's description of his brother's feelings during the Cuban missile crisis:

> It was not only for Americans that he was concerned or primarily the older generation of any land. The thought that disturbed him most and that made the prospect of war much more fearful than it would otherwise have been, was the specter of the death of the children of this country and all over the world—the young people who had no role, who had no say, who knew nothing even of the confrontation, but whose lives would be snuffed out like everyone else's. They would never have a chance to make a decision, to vote in an election, to run for office, to lead a revolution, to determine their own destiny. (Kennedy 1969, p. 106.)

The fate of humanity hung in the balance when Kennedy got from Khrushchev a letter, the tone of which Kennedy did not like. Instead of capitulating to the American ultimatum, Khrushchev proposed a deal: the Soviets would remove the missiles from Cuba; the Americans would remove the missiles from Greece and Turkey. Actually, Kennedy had already planned to remove those obsolete missiles. But to accede to Khrushchev's proposals was, in Kennedy's estimation, unthinkable. The United States would never yield to pressure. The preparations for a "surgical strike" went on. Only when the next letter came from Khrushchev, in which no mention was made about the missiles in Greece and Turkey, was Kennedy "let off the hook" and able to write a conciliatory reply, which defused the crisis.

Evidently concern about the deaths of innocent children who "would never be able to vote" was weighed against the prestige of the United States. The prestige turned out to weigh more. It was unthinkable for Kennedy to do anything that would impair the image of the United States as never yielding to pressure.

We have listed a large variety of (admittedly inferred) psychological states, all associated in one way or another with conflict, aggression, and violence. What, if anything, do all these states have in common? For Deborah of the Old Testament, war was an ecstatic experience. Some modern psychologists might conjecture that this ecstasy is somehow related to female sexual experience. This sounds reasonable, but how do we know?

Hitler described the feelings of young men marching into battle. Possibly the description, as far as it went, was accurate. Remarque described the feelings of young men returning from battle, possibly also accurately. What happened in the meantime to transform elation into apathetic despair? Surely, the battle experience, but how?

Churchill and Kennedy were both immensely proud of the war machines at their disposal. Churchill was convinced that his war machine was a necessary tool to rid the world of a regime gone berserk. Although the Allied victory of 1945 accomplished this, the world did not get a chance to breathe a sigh of relief and settle down to the business of living.

Kennedy could not possibly have had the same faith in what his war machine could accomplish. He was well aware that if it were activated, civilization would collapse. Why, in spite of the enormous difference between what was at stake, were Kennedy's feelings so similar to Churchill's?

As we shall see, the value of psychology in suggesting answers to some of these questions depends crucially on how psychological concepts and theories are linked with other approaches to human behavior, where the point of departure is not the human individual but larger systems, or where only the structure of human thinking processes remains within the sphere of attention. These approaches will be developed in succeeding chapters. We will close this part with a brief review of some branches of psychology that have in some degree contributed and may contribute more to our in-depth study of conflict.

Some Psychological Approaches

Personality Theory

Bypassing the question of whether Kohlberg's stages of moral development (cf. Chapter 3) can be regarded as levels of maturity, we can regard them as descriptions of personality types. There have been attempts to construct a typology of attitudinal sets that could be related to different political outlooks, in particular to attitudes toward violence and war. The so-called "authoritarian personality" was at one time supposed to be strongly associated with a "fascist" outlook, characteristic of the extreme political Right, comprising, for example, sympathies for fascism and related ideologies (cf. Adorno et al. 1950). One of the outstanding traits of persons who rated high on the so-called F-scale was supposed to be an extreme intolerance of outlooks or opinions disagreeing with a set of rigid beliefs held by the "authoritarian" person. Pronounced racial or ethnic prejudices were also supposed to be strongly correlated with high F-scores. It was found later that persons sympathetic with the far Left of the political spectrum also frequently scored high on the F-scale; so that a monotone relationship between this scale and the position on the political spectrum could not be supported by evidence.

More recently, William Eckhardt (1972) proposed another spectrum of personality related to political attitudes, in particular to attitudes on war and peace. Eckhardt called his scale the compassion–compulsion dimension. In his studies persons near the compulsive end of the spectrum were found to be oriented positively to coercive means of social and political control. Like the persons rating high on the F-scale, they tended to be prejudiced against racial and ethnic minorities and jealous of the prerogatives of power. Persons near the compassion end leaned toward a more charitable view of human nature, placed hopes on the realization of democratic ideals and, above all, rejected violence as a means of social control or of pursuit of interests.

Investigations of this sort might be of some importance in the study of war and peace if it could be established that personalities of leaders or the model personality characteristic of a nation are important factors in a nation's war-proneness. Arguments to that effect have been advanced. Much has been made of the authoritarian attitudes of the Germans, for example, which, in turn, were assumed to reflect childhood experiences in harshly authoritarian family life. Whether nations can be rated on a scale of war-proneness is a question that can be significantly answered by reference to appropriate data. We will examine some such data in Chapter 19.

The most important findings in this area of personality studies have been confirmed by fairly reliable statistical data to the effect that the intuitively conjectured "complexes" of attitudes and activities do in fact exist and that persons on both ends of the compulsion–compassion scale are concentrated in certain identifiable social groups and are likely to engage in distinguishable types of activities.

As expected, persons on the compulsive end tend to support outspokenly "hawkish" postures of the government (at least in the U.S., where the studies were conducted); those on the compassion end tend to be critical of them. The former more than the latter have a dominant father figure in their background; the latter tend to support permissive childhood discipline. The former tend to be bureaucratically, the latter democratically oriented. It is unlikely that the personality type is an important factor in determining occupation, orientation, or lifestyle. More likely, the social milieu shapes the personality types. At least this is the conclusion suggested by theories of social learning.

Cognitive Dissonance

This theory, most cogently formulated by Leon Festinger (1957), has been well supported by systematic and controlled observations. It provides a far-reaching explanation of many facets of human behavior. In particular, it illuminates some fundamental aspects of conflict both on the interpersonal and intergroup level.

The basic assumption of cognitive dissonance theory is that we feel uncomfortable when we have to face what appears to be a contradiction. Possibly intolerance of apparent contradictions is part of our biological heritage and therefore a result of adaptation. For the unfamiliar can be regarded as a "contradiction" of sorts: "I am supposed to be familiar with my surroundings, but here is something I have never seen before." Feeling a pressure to do something about the unfamiliar in order to remove the discomfort (e.g., to fight it, flee from it, examine it more closely) may well have survival value.

The form of cognitive dissonance of special interest in the study of conflict is that associated with keen emotional states. When we are compelled to entertain two apparently incompatible ideas at the same time, we let one of them "win" in a mentally conducted contest in order to reduce the tension. Which of the ideas we will help to "win" may depend on many factors, and it is these that are of special interest to the social psychologist.

Many instances of *rationalization* can be explained as attempts to reduce cognitive dissonance by inventing reasons why the decision that was made (and can't be reversed) was the right decision after all. For instance, Mr. X, after lengthy deliberation, having decided to buy a car of type A rather than of type B, may experience cognitive dissonance. Obviously B had *some* advantages over A; otherwise, no lengthy deliberations would have been necessary. Having bought A, Mr. X deprived himself of B. Frequently, such cognitive dissonance can be reduced by convincing oneself that A is really greatly superior to B, i.e., by playing up the advantages of A and playing down those of B. In this way, one comes to feel that one has made the right decision.

The fox in Aesop's fable felt a contradiction between wish and reality: "I want those grapes; I can't reach them." He reduced the resulting cognitive dissonance by convincing himself that the grapes were sour and that he did not really want them.

An experiment by Leon Festinger and J. M. Carlsmith (1959) turned out to be a dramatic demonstration of a cognitive dissonance effect. The subjects were required to perform a long and boring task, then to rate it on a scale indicating how interesting it was. Afterward they were induced under some pretext to tell the person who was supposedly the next subject in the experiment that the task was quite interesting and enjoyable. For this deception (as the subjects perceived it to be) they were paid either one dollar (in one condition) or twenty dollars (in another condition). Finally, the subjects were again asked to evaluate the task on a scale ranging from "very boring" to "very interesting."

The principal finding of this experiment was that the second evaluation of the subjects who were paid *one* dollar shifted more toward the "interesting" end of the scale than that of the subjects who were paid *twenty* dollars.

The theory of cognitive dissonance suggests the following explanation of this at-first-sight surprising finding. The subjects, in telling others that the task was interesting and enjoyable may have experienced cognitive dissonance embodied in the contradiction, "I am a truthful person. But here I am deceiving someone." The subjects who were paid $20 (a substantial sum in 1959 when the experiment was performed) could tell themselves that they perpetrated the deception for the money. This may not have reduced their guilt feelings (if they had such), but at least they could feel that they had a sufficient reason for acting the way they did. Those who were paid only $1 did not have a satisfactory rationalization of their action. But cognitive dissonance could be reduced if the subjects could convince *themselves* that the task was not quite so boring after all; hence, the deception was less of a deception. This would explain the more favorable evaluation of the task by the students who were paid less.

Observations from everyday life provide additional instances of apparently irrational behavior that becomes understandable in the light of the cognitive dissonance theory. Frequently people who order a meal in a restaurant and find it distasteful nevertheless force themselves to eat it all. The usual rationalization involving reference to starvation in poor countries makes little sense, since the hungry cannot possibly be satiated by food eaten by someone else. A hungry person could conceivably be fed if the meal were *not* eaten, so that it could be given to the hungry person. This is an argument *against* eating the food one does not want. But this argument, too, is fallacious, because in all likelihood the uneaten food would go into the garbage can, not to the hungry. A common explanation of the compulsion to eat what one has bought is in terms of early childhood training (insistence on leaving a clean plate). Cognitive dissonance provides another, perhaps more far-reaching explanation. The contradiction now is: "I paid for this meal. But I don't want to eat it. I don't like to waste money. But I wasted it." Assuming that it is impossible (or embarrassing) to get the money back, one way of reducing cognitive dissonance is to convince oneself that the meal is not distasteful or that one is hungry enough to eat it. That one is in fact eating it becomes "evidence" that this is so.

Cognitive dissonance sheds light on the harsh treatment of minorities and other underdogs by dominant groups. Assuming that a member of a dominant group thinks of himself as a decent person, he may experience cognitive dissonance induced by the contradiction, "I am a decent person. But I am being cruel to these people." This dissonance can be reduced by convincing oneself that the humble or the oppressed *deserve* to be treated harshly, because they are wicked, lazy, irresponsible, carriers of an ancient curse, a horrible disease, or the like. In extreme cases, the oppressed can be regarded as nonhumans. Such dehumanization of persons upon whom cruelties or injustice have been perpetrated is typical in societies with sharp divisions between elites and underdogs. In many instances, such dehumanization has led to massacres, such as the Holocaust of the 1940s, which was mass extermination of human beings in specially constructed slaughterhouses.

In the light of cognitive dissonance theory, it is understandable why victims of mistreatment are often most brutally treated when they are guiltless and helpless. When no other rationalization of mistreatment occurs, the victims are dehumanized. The more brutally they are treated, the greater becomes the need to justify brutality. The justification is accomplished by the brutality itself: if they are treated this way, they *must* deserve it. The argument is analogous to the rationalization, "Since I am eating this repulsive food, I *must* be hungry."

Dostoyevsky's intense hatred of Poles and Jews is especially well illuminated by the theory of cognitive dissonance. The Poles were subjected to particularly cruel repressions following the revolt of 1863. The persecution of the Jews became sharply intensified shortly thereafter. Dostoyevsky, converted to the mystique of the Russian People as God-seekers and preservers of Christian virtues amid the corruption of materialist Western civilization, must have experienced a contradiction: "Russians are generous, charitable, kind. But Poles, aspiring to political and cultural autonomy, were subjected to harsh repressive measures, and the Jews are ruthlessly persecuted." Abandoning the veneration of the Russian people and therefore of Russia as the embodiment of the "Russian soul" was for Dostoyevsky out of the question. Therefore the Poles, and especially the Jews, had to represent to him everything that was vile and inimical to what Russia presumably stood for.

Cognitive dissonance suggests a plausible explanation of the well known tendency to select from the environment just those inputs that support one's preformed images and attitudes. This selection *forestalls* cognitive dissonance by excluding clashes with accustomed ways of thinking and feeling. Intensity of prejudice is both a cause and a consequence of just such selection. Everything favorable about a disliked person or group is ignored, dismissed as "exceptional," or explained away. Everything unfavorable is readily accepted, reinforcing the prejudice. Paranoid delusions reflect an extreme pathological form of this process, because they cannot be refuted no matter how compelling the evidence against them may seem to a normal person.

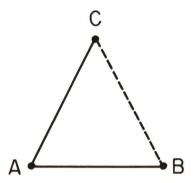

Figure 5.1. An unbalanced triangle.

Theory of Attitudinal Balance

A model of interpersonal relations proposed by F. Heider (1958) shows how attraction and repulsion complement each other. Assume for simplicity that any two persons are related either "positively" or "negatively" to each other. The positive relationship is friendly, the negative one hostile. Consider now any three individuals, and let them be represented by a triangle whose sides are either solid or dotted lines. Figure 5–1 is an example.

The persons are labeled A, B, and C. Here A and B and A and C are friends, but B and C are enemies.

In any such triangle, the number of dotted lines may be none, 1, 2, or 3. If this number is even (i.e., 0 or 2), the triangle is said to be *balanced*; if odd, *unbalanced*. The theory of attitudinal balance asserts that triangles depicting relationships among triples of persons tend to become balanced. Let us see possible reasons why this may be so.

The triangle ABC in Figure 1 is not balanced, since there is only one dotted line in it. This line represents hostility between B and C. The two solid lines represent friendly relations between A and B and between A and C. It is reasonable to assume that certain strains can develop in this situation. For instance, C may resent A's friendly feelings toward B, whom C regards as his enemy. Or else, A, who likes both B and C, may regret their animosity toward each other and may try to reconcile them. If any of the relationships change from positive to negative or vice versa so that the number of positive relationships becomes even, the triangle will become balanced.

It is easy to verify that a balanced triangle satisfies the following four relations:

The friend of my friend is my friend.
The enemy of my friend is my enemy.
The friend of my enemy is my enemy.
The enemy of my enemy is my friend.

Consider now a population with any number of individuals, where each pair is connected either by a positive or a negative relationship. A network of this sort is called a *sociogram*. It can be shown that if the above four principles are satisfied in a sociogram, every triangle in it will be balanced.

The notion of balance can be extended to polygons with any number of sides. A balanced polygon is one with an even number of negative links. It has been shown (Harary, Norman, and Cartwright 1965) that if every triangle of a sociogram is balanced, every polygon in it is also balanced. We can then say that the sociogram as a whole is balanced. The final conclusion of this (so far) purely mathematical reasoning is that a balanced sociogram can be partitioned into two subpopulations (one of which may contain no members) such that between any two members belonging to the same subpopulation the relationship is positive, while the relationship between any two members belonging to different subpopulations is negative. The sociogram is then said to be *polarized*. It can be said to consist of two camps hostile to each other. Within each camp, the members are bound by ties of friendship. Thus, the same "force" embodied in the four principles governing friendly and hostile relationships generate both friendship and enmity.

In the special case where one of the two subpopulations is "empty" (contains no members) there are no negative links. Consequently, in such a sociogram, everyone is bound by ties of friendship to every one else.

In international relations positive links are called *alliances*. Trends toward polarization of the international system (i.e., partition into two hostile blocs) have been frequently observed and are consistent with attitudinal balance. However, an international system in which every state is allied with every other is also balanced. It is interesting to note that the European international system was in that state for five years of its history, 1815–1820 (the "Accord of Europe," cf. below).

It is easy to see connections between the theory of attitudinal balance and the theory of cognitive dissonance. The tendency toward a balanced sociogram reflects an intolerance of ambiguity, specifically a tendency to recognize just two kinds of people: friends and enemies—us and them. This tendency is an instance of the so-called *two-valued orientation*. We will examine this aspect of human psychology in the context of the relationship between language and behavior.

Language and Behavior

In his book *Signs, Language and Behavior*, Charles Morris (1946) subdivided semiotics (theory of signs) into three disciplines: *syntactics*, *semantics*, and *pragmatics*. Syntactics is concerned with the relations of the smallest units of language (phonemes, morphemes, etc.) to each other without reference to meanings. Semantics is concerned with the relations between words and their referents (what the words stand for). Pragmatics is concerned with the relations between language and the users of language. Psychologists interested in the role of language in cognition call their discipline *psycholinguistics*. Those who were influenced by the ideas of Alfred Korzybski (1870–1950) use his designation of a similar area of inquiry—*general semantics*.

There is strong overlap between the contents of pragmatics, psycholinguistics, and general semantics. They differ somewhat in emphasis and are addressed to different publics. Pragmatics is a branch of language science and intersects with philosophy. Psycholinguistics is in part a branch of experimental psychology. General semantics has been widely popularized and has found an audience in many sectors of the general public, particularly in the United States.

The main emphasis in general semantics is on the circumstance that our knowledge about the world around us is *mediated* by language. We do not experience reality directly. Rather we "read" what is on a "screen" interposed between us and reality. This screen is language. To put it in another way, our perception of reality is shaped by what others and, most important, we ourselves *tell* us about reality.

The units of human language, in contrast to units of "languages" used by other animals, have no necessary connection to what is actually "out there." Other animals use *signals* to communicate about what is *here and now* and only that, e.g., about the presence of food or enemies, about readiness to mate, warnings against encroaching on one's territory. Humans, on the other hand, can speak and think about the past and the future, including a past that never was and several hypothetical futures. The units of human language are not signals: they are *symbols* whose meanings cannot be inferred from the way they sound or from the circumstances in which they are uttered. The meanings of words are known only in consequence of social learning.

Human language has vastly increased man's power of abstraction and his power of imagination. Imagination enables man to learn by ways other than by direct trial and error. It enables him to transmit knowledge accumulated by experiences to future generations. With the advent of writing, human beings acquired practically unlimited memory capacity. Knowledge accumulated over many generations became the collective heritage of humankind. Of all animals, only man has *culture*. And, of course, science and technology are by-products of abstract language.

Korzybski's main idea was that human language is a mixed blessing. On the one hand, it is the uniquely human survival mechanism which has emancipated our species from the tyranny of the environment, making it unnecessary to develop specific adaptations to specific habitats. It was language that has co-evolved with the human brain and so enabled man to create a technology that confers a formidable power of control over nature. On the other hand, this very nature of human language, its abstractedness, permits a complete rupture between language and reality, hence between the mental images we concoct with the aid of language and our actual environment.

Korzybski went so far as to identify the degree of correspondence between words and their referents with the degree of sanity of the person using or affected by words. In his book, *Science and Sanity* (1933), he defines the degree of sanity on a scale where complete sanity is at one end and insanity at the other. The degree of sanity corresponds to the reality content of the language used. "Sane" use of language, according to Korzybski, is exemplified by mature science, where the correspondence between symbols and referents, between theoretical formulations and observations are subjected to continual checking and revision, thus preserving and improving the correspondence. At the other end is the language of psychosis, free-floating, self-stimulating, chaotic, compulsive.

But the language of psychotics is not the only example of language cut off from its moorings in the real world. Much of traditional philosophy, having been generated entirely by internal mental processes not subjected to the discipline of reality-testing, also belongs, according to Korzybski, at the "unsane" end of the scale ("unsanity" being not quite "insanity" but not far from it).

Korzybski listed a number of features characteristic of "unsane" language:

False-to-fact identification—confusing words with what words stand for. "The word is not the thing" was his favorite maxim; "The map is not the territory." This sounds like a truism, but it is one thing to voice agreement with it and quite another to be aware of the distinction at all times. In fact, we identify a thing, an event, or an action with the word that designates it every time we make a classification. And this is precisely what our abstract language does for us: makes classifications. We will readily admit that every chair, beetle, or child is different from every other chair, beetle, or child. But we still behave as if we believed that a chair is a chair, a beetle a beetle, and a child a child. Our language does our thinking for us.

The consequences are far-reaching. We classify persons according to characteristics that are most salient in our social milieu. It is not difficult to see the connection between the particular way our accustomed designations "slice our world" for us and various sources of social conflict rooted in prejudices, tribal loyalties, and taboos.

Allness—tacitly assuming that some thing, event, condition, or property can be *completely* described by words. Just as no map can represent a territory in all details, so no verbal description of anything can be complete. Losing sight of this fact leads to *closure*—becoming impervious to revision of one's views in the light of new evidence.

Elementalism—the tendency to separate aspects of reality that are actually inseparable, because language separates them. In Newtonian metaphysics, the structure of space was falsely regarded as absolutely independent of the structure of time. We tend to think of "causes" and "effects" as qualitatively distinct categories, of "heredity" and "environment" as independently acting factors of development, of "facts" and "values" as components of cognition and attitude respectively hermetically separated from each other.

Two-valued orientation—the tendency to think in dichotomies: good versus evil, love versus hate, intellect versus emotion, democracy versus tyranny, seeing the world in terms of blacks and whites with no intermediate shades of grey.

Stuart Chase (1938), who popularized Korzybski's ideas, coined the phrase "tyranny of words," a picturesque designation of the deeply ingrained habit of imagining that something exists just because it has been named. Actually, this habit characterized much of the thinking in traditional philosophy. In Goethe's *Faust* (Part I, Scene 4), Mephistopheles makes fun of philosophers' predilection for reification in his conversation with a student.

STUDENT:	Yet in the word must some idea be.
MEPHISTOPHELES:	Of course! But only shun too over-sharp a tension,
	For just where fails the comprehension,
	A word steps promptly in as deputy.

Discussions of reified abstraction comprise much of the content of Plato's *Dialogues*. But we need not delve in antiquity to find examples of promiscuous reification. In a book published in 1948, Richard Weaver writes:

I should urge examining in all seriousness the ancient belief that a divine element is present in language. The feeling that to have power of language is to have control over things is deeply imbedded in the human mind. We see this in the way men gifted in speech are feared or admired, we see it in the potency ascribed to incantations, interdictions, and curses . . . knowledge of the prime reality comes to man through the word; the word is a sort of deliverance from the shifting world of appearances. The central teaching of the New Testament is that those who accept the word acquire wisdom and at the same time some identification with the eternal.

Identifying words with reality underlies not only the obfuscations that comprise the content of much traditional philosophy and theology. It also provides fertile soil for superstitions, especially word magic. Above all, it gives demagogy its vast power over the mass mind. It is not surprising that one of the most telling characteristics of totalitarian regimes is a monopoly of information and communication, that is to say, of the public functions of language.

Demagogy is skillful use of language to elicit immediate and reliable reactions from a population. These reactions are analogous to conditioned responses "grafted" on an animal's psyche through training. Brainwashing is a form of such training applied to humans.

We need not confine our attention to conspicuous examples in Hitler's Germany and Mussolini's Italy. The same immediate responses to words characterize attitudes in large sectors of the public even in democratic countries. For instance, massive political support given by the people of the United States to the continuation and escalation of the arms race can be traced to the imagery elicited by words that paralyze critical thought. It is practically impossible to block measures that are justified by the needs of "defense" or "national security." Intellectuals working for the self-styled "defense community" have created a whole vocabulary designed to elicit images to which conditioned responses will be made: missile gap, window of vulnerability, deterrence, civil defense, and the like. The imagery evoked by these words, some calculated to trigger alarm, some reassurance, preempts, as it were, the "mental space" of people, leaving no room for ideas that could lead to reality-testing.

In sum, the contributions of psychology to systematic and disciplined study of conflict, its genesis, its dynamics, and its consequences are considerable. Above all, connections have to be established between the psychological approach (largely centered on the mental life and behavior of human individuals) and other approaches, where large aggregates of human individuals or the structure of inferential thinking are at the center of attention.

Notes

1. The English translation by Thomas Paynell cited here was published in 1559.

PART

THE IDEOLOGICAL APPROACH

6

Ideology: The Substrate of Thought

An individual's behavior can sometimes be explained satisfactorily by analyzing his thought processes which reveal how his perceptions, conceptions, and actions interact with each other. Can we gain an understanding about the behavior of large aggregates of individuals by analyzing their *collective* thought processes and tracing their determinants? The method of investigation used in the attempt to gain such understanding has been called "sociology of knowledge."

In the opening sentence of his book, *Ideology and Utopia*, Karl Mannheim (1949) writes: "This book is concerned with the problem of how men actually think. . . . There are modes of thought that cannot be adequately understood as long as their social origins are obscured." Uncovering the connections between modes of thought and their social origins is the task of the sociology of knowledge.

A central conception underlying this method is that people's ways of thinking are always rooted in some particular "soil," as it were. Different soils give rise to different modes of thought and, for the most part, people are not aware that their modes of thought are shaped by the soil from which they sprang and in which they are rooted. These different soils are called "ideologies."

We have used the term "ideology" in the plural. Karl Marx, who among the social philosophers of the nineteenth century was most intensively concerned with the social origins of collective thinking, used the term in the singular for reasons that we shall see in a moment.

In Karl Marx's social philosophy "ideology" has a rather pejorative connotation. It often refers to outlooks generated by viewing the world through the prisms of special interests. In this context, an ideology can be thought of as a system of rationalizations. Specific rationalizations of social institutions and policies can often be traced to what Marx called *class interests*. For instance, in the United States slavery was sometimes justified on the ground that Negroes were descendants of Noah's son Ham, who had been disrespectful to his father, thereby displeasing Jehovah. It is not surprising that this and similar biblical allusions were much more common in the slave states, where the prosperity of slave owners derived from slave labor, than in the industrialized north, where slavery was not profitable. In our day, social welfare programs are often decried by those who resent paying taxes to support them, on the ground that these services undermine the character of their beneficiaries.

Ideology normally refers not so much to specific rationalizations as to a broad worldview that encompasses a whole paradigm of rationalizations. Thinking along some channels is compatible with such a paradigm, while along other channels it is not, and therefore tends to be blocked. What one supposes to determine the paradigm of rationalization depends on what one supposes to be the primary determinant of values. Karl Marx took economic interests to be such primary determinants and other values to be derivative of these. Supporting this point of view is the observation that the generally positive attitudes toward the natural sciences in the Western world went hand-in-hand with the rise of a new dominant class, which derived its prosperity and power from a mode of production increasingly based on machinery run by harnessed energy. This mode of production with its attendant social changes became possible only in consequence of the rapid development of the natural sciences. Thereby the prestige of science was enhanced and the scientific view of the material world became more acceptable than it had been earlier.

The pejorative aspect of ideology in the Marxist formulation of sociology of knowledge appears in what Marx saw as the subordination of cognitive and moral frameworks of thought to class interests, in particular to the economic interests of the dominant and therefore exploiting class. For example, during the potato famine in Ireland, there was powerful opposition in England to shipping grain to the stricken land on the grounds that such shipments would interfere with the natural forces of the free market.

More generally, in the realm of social philosophy the ideologues of capitalism seemed to be unable to grasp the long-term implications of the capitalist mode of production, perhaps because their class interests imposed on them a rigid framework of thought impossible to transcend. Criteria of truth, of justice, even of beauty are, from the Marxist point of view, rationales supporting the social system (and therefore the dominance relations) in which they prevail.

In Marxist philosophy ideology appeared as something to be *emancipated* from, since it tended to obscure social realities. In particular, the world view adopted by the "bourgeoisie" during its ascendance and entrenchment as the dominant class was said to have been imposed on the whole society. Marx envisaged the emancipation of the proletariat (the propertyless class) from its oppressed position as a consequence of acquiring a "class consciousness" and with it a percepton of social reality "as it really is" (not as it appears through the prism of bourgeois ideology). Thereby the proletariat would, Marx argued, attain the power to overthrow the bourgeoisie and to establish a society in accordance with its own class interests. Since, however, Marx identified the class interests of the proletariat with the interests of humanity as a whole, he imagined that the society to be established by the proletariat would no longer be a class society. Exploitation would disappear, and there would no longer be any need to mask the nature of social reality. For this reason, Marx did not apply the term "ideology" to the ways of thinking of the *emancipated* proletariat. Only in a class society, according to this view, does ideology, in the singular, determine the mode of thought imposed by the dominant class, whose interest it serves, by masking the exploitative nature of existing social relations.

In this way, the Marxist conception of emancipation seems to anticipate the basic therapeutic idea of psychoanalysis. Neuroses, acording to the psychoanalytic view, stem from suppressed drives or early traumatic experiences, submerged in the unconscious mind. The neurotic is seen as not free, being subjected to either compulsions or crippling inhibitions. His therapy is based upon allowing the suppressed drives or trauma to emerge into the conscious mind. Then their sources can be seen for what they are and can be dealt with. Thereby the person's ego (the conscious rational component of the mind) attains the capacity to guide the person's behavior into constructive channels.

We could say that Marx envisaged the attainment of class consciousness by the proletariat (and with it the perception of "true" social reality) as a sort of successful psychoanalysis on a mass scale.

As has been said, Marx would not have ascribed an "ideology" to the emancipated proletariat. Mannheim, while acknowledging Marx's significant contribution to the sociology of knowledge, went further. He pointed out that no society and no sector of society, identified through some sort of communality of outlook, can be regarded as free of ideology. For it is precisely ideology that (by definition) holds the society or any portion thereof together.

The Scope of the Term "Ideology"

Today the term "ideology" is used in a broader sense to denote any conceptual medium in which thinking about the "nature of the world" is immersed. The question arises as to how general or how fundamental or pervasive a mode of thought must be in order to deserve being identified as an ideology. Faced with a set of beliefs, one may seek to uncover a substrate that underlies all of them and call it an ideology. But one can go further. Beliefs in different realms of experience may be based on different cognitive foundations, but these foundations may themselves have a common underlying substrate, which should properly be called an underlying ideology.

An ideology, as Mannhein uses that term, refers to a way of thinking about social reality, about the human condition, about the meaning of history, matters clearly related to value orientations. It is worth noting that in the realm of physical science, where value orientations are usually expected to be excluded, analogues of ideologies are found. These modes of thought have been called *paradigms*, with changes of paradigms referred to as *scientific revolutions* (cf. Kuhn 1962). In contrast to violent conflicts that at times marked clashes of value-oriented ideologies, scientific revolutions have been peaceful affairs. It will be instructive to see why.

Two far-reaching scientific revolutions were ushered in almost simultaneously at the beginning of this century. One was in the physics of the very large; the other in the physics of the very small. Both required a radical overhaul of the very fundamental notions of physical reality, which had been so firmly entrenched in the thinking of physicists that it was only with great effort that they were able to discard the old paradigm. In the case of relativity theory, the harbinger of the revolution in the physics of the cosmos, what had to be abandoned was the conception of an absolute framework of space and of time flowing at a constant rate, the same for all observers. In the new framework, time and space were combined into a single four-dimensional continuum. The concept of time "flowing at a constant rate, the same for all observers" became untenable. In the case of quantum mechanics, dealing with the world inside the atom, the notion of deterministic causality, one of the metaphysical pillars of classical physics, had to be abandoned.

So much is known to most persons who take an interest in these matters. Less known is the fact that the shift of paradigm could not have occurred had not the "scientific mind" internalized a particular mode of thought of its own, namely, the primacy of empirical evidence over preconceived notions, no matter how entrenched. For it was empirical evidence that induced physicists to embrace the theory of relativity and quantum mechanics, even though this acceptance required a drastic change in thinking about the primeval categories of physical science: space, time, and causality.

Here we have an example of two incompatible modes of thought, one underlying classical physics, the other the new physics, but both united by a deeper paradigm, namely, a mode of thought that *requires* a revision of even the most deeply rooted metaphysical conceptions if theories constructed within their frameworks fail to be corroborated by empirical evidence. This is, of course, the distinguishing feature of the scientific mode of thought, which can also be called an ideology. We will now examine this mode of thought more closely.

Rationalism and Empiricism

Rejection of the primacy of empirical evidence as a final arbiter of truth has had a long history. Plato was openly contemptuous of the "evidence of the senses," which he thought gave a distorted, "corrupt" image of reality. The real truth, he insisted, was attainable only by looking within oneself and exercising one's reason. The gift of reason, Plato argued through his spokesman Socrates, is given to every human being, even the humblest.[1]

In the realm of mathematics, empirical evidence is neither necessary nor sufficient to establish the truth of a proposition. A mathematical truth can be established only by deduction, where the point of departure is a set of unproved and unprovable propositions (postulates) expressed in undefined and undefinable terms. Plato, who held mathematics in greatest esteem, believed that only deductive reasoning—arguing from general principles to particular cases—can lead to true knowledge. This theory of knowledge is called *rationalism.*

Outstanding philosophers who were rationalists include Descartes, Spinoza, and Kant. Descartes was one of the earliest of the modern philosophers of science. His invention of analytic geometry was a fundamentally important contribution to mathematics. Spinoza attempted to derive ethical principles by deductive reasoning following the method used by Euclid in systematizing geometry. Kant taught that the great achievements of eighteenth century science were essentially creations of the human mind, in which *a priori* knowledge of physical reality (space, time, and causality) is embedded. These important contributions to modern thought are mentioned as examples of intellectual achievements of rationalism, achievements no less remarkable in spite of the fact that an essential ingredient of modern scientific thinking (recognition of the primacy of empirical evidence) was excluded from that paradigm.

The theory of knowledge that emphasizes the primacy of sensory data is called *empiricism*. It may seem obvious to us that all scientific knowledge about the "real" world should in the last analysis be based on the evidence of the senses. As we have seen, however, this view has not always been dominant. The primacy of sense data was explicitly argued by Francis Bacon (1561–1626), who insisted that acquisition of knowledge resulted from putting questions "directly to nature," i.e., ascertaining what *is* rather than believing in what *ought* to be—that which was deduced by formal reasoning.

Galileo Galilei, who is usually credited with introducing the experimental method in the study of motion, was more of a rationalist than an empiricist. It was not enough for him simply to record the quantitative features of falling bodies or a swinging pendulum. He felt that he had to deduce these features by mathematical reasoning. On at least one occasion he gave more credence to the mathematical deduction than to an empirical fact that contradicted it. He had deduced (erroneously) that the period of the pendulum is independent of amplitude. This is *approximately* true for small amplitudes but not for large ones. When another scientist reported the experimentally observed discrepancy, Galileo simply ignored this finding.

However, before we dismiss Galileo's prejudice in favor of rationally deduced results even if they contradict observations, we should imagine what would have happened if Galileo had been a pure empiricist. Then he would have chosen for his falling bodies the most numerous things that fall near the surface of the earth, namely, leaves and raindrops. With leaves he would have gotten nowhere since their fall, perturbed by air currents, is erratic. As for raindrops, measuring their rate of fall would have brought Galileo to Aristotle's mistaken law of falling bodies, the very law Galileo disproved in laying the foundations of modern mechanics.[2]

Although, as we have said, modern science recognizes the primacy of empirical data as the "final court of appeal" between contending theories, its mode of cognition is actually an amalgam of rationalism and empiricism.

Outside of science, a gulf still exists between those who accept as true only what they think ought to be true because it is deduced from "self-evident" principles and those who dismiss all theorizing and pay attention only to what they believe to be incontrovertible evidence of the senses. Rationalism carried to extremes degenerates into dogma, not infrequently entrenched in an officially sanctioned ideology. Examples are by no means confined to the sterile speculations of the medieval scholastics. We will examine a contemporary instance in Chapter 8. Empiricism can also degenerate into a caricature of itself. An example can be seen in the arguments advanced by Alexander Bryan Johnson. The writings of this amateur American philosopher would not merit serious attention except for the fact that they represent an extreme form of pragmatism, about which we shall have more to say in Chapter 11.

In his book *A Treatise on Language* (1836/1946), in which Johnson anticipates the principal ideas of Korzybski, he comments on a report of a traveler returning from some South Sea island. In the report the traveler states that the tides on that island occur not fifty minutes later each day, as everywhere else, but always at the same time of day. Understandably, this report aroused considerable interest and most likely considerable skepticism, because, if true, the events described would be incompatible with the theory of tides derived from Newton's law of universal gravitation.

Johnson, however, refused to see any difficulty engendered by the report if it turned out to be true. If the observations were not in accord with Newton's theory, Johnson argued, the theory should be discarded. To him, reality consisted of facts, not theories.

With equal emphasis, Johnson rejected the results of mathematical deduction if they failed to conform to physical "facts." He saw no difficulty in the ancient paradox of Achilles and the Tortoise, not because he understood its resolution by a rigorous mathematical argument but because he refused to recognize the validity of mathematics uncoupled from the evidence of the senses.

The Achilles paradox was posed by the Eleatic philosophers. They argued that in a race between the athlete Achilles and a tortoise, in which Achilles runs ten times faster than the Tortoise, who had been given a head start, Achilles can never catch up with the Tortoise. For by the time Achilles has traversed the Tortoise's head start, the Tortoise will have moved ahead by one-tenth of that distance; by the time Achilles passes *that* distance, the Tortoise will have moved one-tenth of that distance, and so on. The flaw in this argument is the false assumption that the sum of an infinite number of intervals is necessarily infinite. In this case, the sum of all the times that Achilles takes to traverse the diminishing distances between him and the Tortoise equals $1\frac{1}{9}$ of the time it took him to pass the original handicap. This is the time it takes to catch up with the Tortoise.

But this is not the way Johnson refutes the Eleatics' argument. He simply declares that an interval too small to be perceived by the senses is nonexistent *because* it cannot be perceived by the senses. Thereby he assigns no value whatsoever to logical deduction and by implication to all "theory."[3]

A half-century later, Thomas A. Edison, the genius of technological invention, indicated the sort of qualification he expected from young men whom he hired to work in his laboratory: knowledge of facts. He preferred a young man who could tell offhand what the speed of sound is to one who could discourse learnedly about "theory." This sort of anti-intellectualism has been endemic in American life. It is well exemplified by a remark attributed to Henry Ford, another "practical" genius: "History is bunk." Only with the advent of technologies directly inspired by abstruse physical and mathematical theories was this traditional anti-intellectualism overcome, regrettably, however, primarily in areas related to preparations for war.

The Scientific Outlook

Like all human activities, science changes in content and method. However, as a *mode of cognition* it remains rooted in two mental processes: deduction and induction. Deduction proceeds from general assumption to particular conclusions; induction infers general principles from particular observations. The so-called "scientific method" is often described in textbooks as a cycle. On the basis of observations, a hypothesis is formulated about some general "law" (induction). Logically following consequences are deduced from the hypothesis in the form of predictions of what else will be observed (deduction). Further observations either corroborate or contradict these predictions. In the former case, the hypothesis is confirmed; in the latter case disconfirmed. A disconfirmed hypothesis is modified or replaced by another and the cycle is repeated. Several hypotheses that fall into a logically coherent pattern constitute a *theory*.

Actually no scientist follows this regime. Workaday scientific activity is more like running a maze, stumbling in and out of blind alleys, following hunches, making bold guesses, or hedging against criticisms of colleagues; wondering which statistical tool is appropriate in assessing the significance of the results; assessing the work of others in relation to one's own; seeking out promising "lines" of investigation both with respect to expected "payoffs" in the form of publishable results and in terms of opportunities of getting support. Nevertheless, the inductive-deductive cycle is a statement about the "rules of the game" and a display of the only legitimate basis on which an assertion can claim the status of a scientific proposition. Either it is a logically valid consequence of some antecedent assertions assumed to be true (a product of deduction) or it is a summary of properly carried out observations (a product of induction). This definition of a scientific assertion is more important for what it excludes than for what it includes. It *denies* scientific status to assertions not generated in this way—for example, to assertions reflecting one's personal impressions, guesses, or evaluations; assertions in which the terms are not sufficiently precisely defined to permit testing what is asserted; above all, assertions supported by some-one's personal authority or regarded as true simply because they are widely believed to be true.

The scientific outlook is an ideology in the sense that it provides a framework of thought for distinguishing truth from falsehood. On this point there is general agreement. A more controversial question concerns the extent to which the scientific outlook provides also a framework for dis-tinguishing good from evil. According to our definition above, an ideology must include such a framework. There is a widespread notion that science can or ought to be concerned only with questions pertaining to truth or falsehood (questions about what *is*), that it is not competent to deal with questions pertaining to good and evil (questions about what ought or ought not to be). We do not agree with this position. Although it may not be possible to *prescribe* values on the basis of scientific cognition, at least one value is implicitly inherent in the nature of scientific activity itself; namely, a devotion to truth, without which scientific activity would be meaningless. Once this is admitted, much more follows.

Truth can be effectively pursued only in certain social milieus; for in-stance, those in which freedom of inquiry is encouraged or at least not inhibited, and those in which no authority is recognized as the final arbiter of truth. One can even say that egalitarian rather than hierarchical forms of social structure ought to be preferred by someone committed to the scientific outlook, since in matters on which science can make judgments, the *source* of assertions, whether they come from someone high or low in the social hierarchy, should carry no weight. Above all, since science is essentially a cooperative enterprise, freedom of information and commu-nication, which entails also freedom of association unhampered by bound-aries imposed by political, religious, ethnic, or other classification of people, ought to be highly prized in the value system generated by the scientific outlook.

In this way, the scientific outlook can be regarded as an *integrative* ideology. Not only are rationalism (emphasis on deduction) and empiricism (emphasis on induction) synthesized in it, but also pursuit of knowledge and, unless deliberately denied, a commitment to certain values that are in accord with ethos embodied in religions emphasizing the dignity of the human individual and the essential unity of humanity.

Static and Dynamic Views of the World

Partition of modes of thought into types can be made along several di-mensions. One important partition is between a predominantly static and a predominantly dynamic view of the world. The former emphasizes constancy, the latter change. Since ideologies usually involve commitments to value systems, it is often difficult to say whether an ideology is reflecting a view of the world as the bearers of the ideology think the world *is* or as they think it *ought* to be. Thus, an ideology that emphasizes change may reflect also an attitude toward change: whether change is welcomed or decried.

Heraclitus was, perhaps, the first to express a worldview in which change was explicitly at the focus. "You can't step into the same river twice" and "War is the father of all things" are well known aphorisms of his. What Heraclitus' attitude toward continual, relentless change was is hard to say. In contrast, Plato's attitude toward change was outspokenly negative. He imagined a Golden Age in the distant past, which became increasingly corrupted through cumulative changes, all for the worse. So convinced was Plato that all change is corruption that he attributed knowledge of everything to babies who, he imagined, forgot what they knew as they grew up.

Diametrically opposed to the pessimistic attitude toward change was the faith in "progress" that characterized nineteenth century thought in the Western world, especially among the comfortably situated. The following sample may serve as an illustration of this almost childlike faith:

> . . . the teachings of history are to the effect that practices and institutions, which at the time seem to be necessary conditions of social and political conditions of all people, and yet stand condemned as counter to principles of morality, justice, and political expedience, vanish in an almost inconceivably short space of time, and become so far obsolete as to be with difficulty revived, even in imagination. (Amos 1880, pp. 6–7.)

In particular, the author sees war as an institution on the way to becoming obsolete. He conjectures that before this institution disappears altogether, its harmful effects will be attenuated. War, in other words, will become progressively more humane:

> . . . the modes of conducting Wars between such civilized States have been steadily undergoing changes in one continuous direction, the object of these changes being the diminution of miseries inherent in warfare, the limitation of its area, and the alleviation of the evils incidentally occasioned by it to the Neutral States. (pp. 15–16.)

One need only apply control guided by knowledge in order to abolish war altogether:

... even if there are those who regard all hopes for a time of permanent Peace utopian, it is not denied in any quarter that there are general causes that produce both Peace and War and that these causes can, to some extent, be controlled so as to foster the one and not the other. (p. 230.)

Static views of society are represented by so-called "organismic" models in which society appears as a sort of analogue of an organism. The observed features and institutions of a society are seen as necessary to maintain its organic unity on which its survival depends. Medieval social philosophers pictured the social order as something ordained by God and the different social strata as performing functions assigned to them by the Creator. The human social order was a sort of reflection of the heavenly order, which, like the human order, was hierarchical. The rank-ordering of the Christian princes by Pope Julius II reproduces the flavor of that mode of thought (cf. below).

In view of the conspicuous continual flux and change that pervades modern industrial societies, it is difficult to conceive of them as "organic wholes." Nevertheless, the organismic view of human society has been prominent in the thinking of cultural anthropologists who study the cultures of pre-literate people. This orientation may be due in part to the necessity of making descriptions of these societies make sense. Accordingly, the various customs, beliefs, and networks of social relations of these societies are often pictured as something like vital organs. In particular, interventions by invaders, colonists, missionaries, and the like, have been pictured as harmful no matter how well intentioned, because they disrupted the functional organization of the society, which supposedly reflected an effective adaptation to the environment.

Margaret Mead wrote of the Manus that they did succeed in changing their way of life to adapt to the new ways imposed upon them by Americans. But before this happened, they went through a period of great stress.

... their only poor memory is for the period of the nineteen-thirties, when they were sharing little bits and pieces of Christian civilization, a little literacy with nothing to read, Christian valuation of human life but no modern preventive medicine to keep it going, money but no economic system which made money function efficiently, aspirations to be civilized which were blocked by the fact that the white men they met both refused to treat them as equals, as human beings, and to believe that they were capable of sharing in the white men's superior civilization.

This story seems to have a happy ending of sorts. The Manus, it seems, pulled themselves up by their bootstraps and entered the modern world. They could do this, according to Mead, because they changed *everything*,

discarded the old culture in toto, instead of trying to graft parts of the
white man's culture onto theirs.

> For here we have another part of the secret of felicitous change. The people
> . . . all changed together as a unit—parents, grandparents and children—so
> that the old mesh of human relations could be rewoven into a new pattern
> from which no thread was missing. As living individuals remembering their
> old ways and their old relationships, they could move into a new kind of
> village, live in new kinds of houses, participate in a new form of democracy,
> with no man's hand against another, no child alienated from the self or from
> others. (Mead 1956, pp. 451–452.)

Note that the organismic view of society can embody both a conservative
and a radical ideology. Viewing a society or a culture as an organism and
empathizing with it (as one can empathize with an organism) makes one
look askance at "tampering" with the culture, introducing changes that
will produce discord. Reforms appear dangerous. Either leave an organismically integrated culture alone (the conservative view) or make it possible for it to be completely restructured (the radical view).

Materialism and Idealism

The dichotomy between "materialism" and "idealism" has been a constantly recurring theme in philosophical and political discussions in the
Soviet Union, always with special emphasis on the class struggle. It is non-
Soviets who regard both materialism and idealism as "ideologies." In Soviet
polemics, only idealism is so designated. Recall that in Marxist philosophy
"ideology" carries a pejorative connotation. Materialism, especially in its
sophisticated "dialectical" form, is supposed to reflect emancipation from
idealism, the ideology of the bourgeoisie.
   Materialism is an image of reality comprising the totality of interactions
between material particles. Idealism is an image of reality viewed as an
interaction of "minds," or, perhaps, as the product of a supreme Mind.[4]
It is clear that materialism is more in accord with atheistic positions, while
idealism makes room for a deity and for a notion that the universe was
created with some goal in mind.
   Othodox Marxists see idealism as primarily a world view influenced by
religious doctrines. During the early struggles of industrial workers for
higher wages, better working conditions, the right to organize, and so forth,
the church authorities frequently sided with the opponents of such reforms,
thus encouraging the spread of antireligious attitudes among the activists

of the labor movement. The juxtaposition of materialism and idealism as a class struggle confrontation has its origins in that phase of European social history.

Another source of confrontation between the two world views for Marxists was Marx's reinterpretation of Hegel's philosophy of history. Marxists, while acknowledging Marx's intellectual debt to Hegel, are fond of pointing out that Marx turned Hegel's philosophy of history upside down or rather right side up to make it stand on its feet instead of on its head. Hegel's philosophy of history was a reflection of a dynamic ideology par excellence. The central concept was that of the Idea which, in contemplating (or perhaps creating) reality, alternates between a "thesis" and its denial, an "antithesis." This confrontation of opposites is resolved by a "synthesis," which embodies both, and as a result, reveals a more advanced view of reality.

This conception of intellectual progress is not as farfetched as it may seem when it is described in the sometimes pompous language of German philosophy. It can be illustrated by a homely example. If A maintains that a certain house is on the right side of the street (thesis), while B maintains that it is on the left side (antithesis), the two apparently contradictory statements can be integrated in another encompassing both, namely, that the house is on the *east* side of the street (synthesis). Thereby the relative meanings of "right" and "left" are revealed.

The thesis-antithesis-synthesis principle is embodied in modern philosophy of science. Any hypothesis is a thesis. Empirical evidence contradicting the hypothesis is an antithesis. A synthesis occurs if a theory is constructed which encompasses *both* the successes and the failures of the hypothesis from a new perspective. For instance, classical mechanics accounted very well for motions of bodies subjected to forces, and classical optics accounted for most of the phenomena involving light. However, the result of an experiment indicating that the velocity of light with respect to observers in motion relative to each other was the same for all observers was incompatible with classical mechanics and classical optics. On the other hand, the theory of relativity, which entailed a radical revision of our most fundamental assumptions concerning space and time, could account for both the successes of the classical theory and for the apparently anomalous result of the Michelson-Morley experiment.[5]

Hegel applied his thesis-antithesis-synthesis paradigm to a theory of the historical process. The Idea, in passing through these stages, was supposed to drive history forward, presumably to fulfillment of a goal embodying the epitome of progress. As such, the model was dynamic (oriented to change), progressive (accepting change as both necessary and desirable), and in harmony with the new idea of evolution. This paradigm was em-

braced by many young Germans who had been "infected" with the progressive ideas of the Enlightenment. Many of them regarded themselves
as enemies of the established order rationalized as a manifestation of the
will of God. Karl Marx was among these.

Although accepting the "dialectic" of the Hegelian system (essentially
the dynamics and emphasis on juxtaposition of opposites), Marx rejected
the idealist mode of thought. In a way, Marx's "dialectical materialism"
was itself a synthesis of Hegel's dialectics with the older static materialist
view of the world. For the confrontation of contradictory ideas, Marx
substituted the class struggle, i.e., a process consisting not of disembodied
thoughts but of concrete events. The interests of one class became the
thesis, those of another, the antithesis. The clash of class interests was
thought to bring about social revolutions in which the erstwhile lower class
would emerge victorious. But even as it became the upper class, a new
lower class would challenge it, and so on.

Seen in this way, Marx's model of history seems to be a materialist
interpretation of Hegel's idealist model. Calling the one a "thesis," the
other an "antithesis" might suggest that a "synthesis" of idealism and
materialism could be effected. As we shall see, however, (cf. Chapter 8)
the idealism-materialism dichotomy became a "gut issue," above all in the
Soviet Union, with some temporarily disastrous consequences even for
Soviet science—a dramatic example of the far-reaching and, for the most
part, debilitating effects of ideological conflict.

Orientations Toward the Past, the Present, and the Future

Another way of typing ideologies is by their orientation toward the past,
as reflected in the idea of the Golden Age; toward the present, as reflected
in pragmatically oriented world views; or toward the future.

Veneration of the past appears frequently to be a symptom of inability
to cope with the stresses of change. At times nostalgia contributes to
romanticizing "the good old days." The past was when one was young.
Filtered through selective memory, it tends to appear as a time of happiness. The Nazis, in their demagogic appeals to the masses, glorified the
virtues of the ancient Germans. Calling the new order in Germany "The
Third Reich" was an allusion to the heroic past. The Second Reich (1871–
1918) was the empire welded by Bismarck after Prussia's victory over
France. The First Reich (800–1806) was supposed to have been a restored
Roman Empire.[6] The Third Reich, like the First, was supposed to last a
thousand years. (It lasted 12.)

In religion, fundamentalism carries a strong admixture of a longing to return to the simple faith of the forefathers. In the U.S. the political version of fundamentalism was emblazoned on the banner of Barry Goldwater, presidential candidate in 1964. He called upon Americans to revive the traditional American virtues: unbounded optimism, self-reliance, and competitive energy, which, he maintained, were diluted by welfare state policies; and, above all, "the will to win," which, he repeated, was undermined by a timid foreign policy—"soft on Communism," as the homily went. Recalling the fervor with which the U.S. entered World War II, he wrote:

> Overnight we became a nation totally committed to the winning of the war . . . and we began right then an all-out drive to produce the equipment and the men to get the job done as quickly as possible.
> Three words were entered in the long list of time-honored and patriotic slogans which had moved Americans to supreme efforts and their finest hours. "Remember Pearl Harbor" became the rallying cry which would rank with those old sayings of the past such as "Remember the Maine," "Fifty-four forty or Fight," "Make the World Safe for Democracy!"[7] (Goldwater 1970, p. 76.)

The following message expresses most clearly the attempt to deny to oneself and others the loss of the Golden Age:

> That America still represents a beacon of freedom to the oppressed peoples of the world is a view so widely accepted that it can be had from any place on the compass. Much the same can be said for the old but cherished cliché that America is the land of opportunity, that to the needy, she is the land of plenty; to the statesman, the land of noble experiment, to the free and would-be free throughout the world, always and everywhere a friend. (Goldwater 1976, p. 9.)

Social philosophies oriented toward the present tend to be conservative in the sense that they accept the premises on which existing social systems are based. They may include positive attitudes toward "reforms," but the very concept of "reform" implies improvement within the framework of an existing system. The goal of reforms is to make the system work better. In politics, conservatism is often contrasted with liberalism, but to the extent that liberalism espouses change within existing social systems, it can be regarded as a variant of conservatism.

As its name implies, conservatism places high value on preserving existing arrangements. This attitude stems from a conviction that a paramount virtue of a social order is that it *is* an *order*. Preservation of an order entails not only respect for established rules of behavior but also, in the case of traditional conservatism, respect for the authority of persons occupying high positions in the social hierarchy. Conservatives in this sense, who also have some sense of social justice, tend to couple this commitment to social inequality with a recognition of the responsibilities of the elites.

The outstanding exponent of these views was the British statesman Edmund Burke (1719–1797). His social philosophy can be summarized in the following principles:

1. Social order is of divine origin, being part of the cosmic order created by God. Therefore stability and tranquility of a society (prime virtues) are consequences of obedience to authority, which, in turn, is a manifestation of reverence for God.
2. There is a hierarchical structure of social organization. Families are organized into classes, classes into nations. Each component has its proper functions. The highest form of social organization is the nation.
3. A nation represents unity of purpose of its inhabitants. It embodies traditions and rules of behavior. Traditions, especially ancient ones, must be revered.
4. Inequality is inherent in any social organization. Leadership belongs to traditional leading strata, in the case of Britain to a hereditary aristocracy. Because of the privileges accorded to the aristocracy, the aristocrat has developed a sense of honor, devotion to public service, and identification of public interest with his own. (Auerbach 1968.)

The content (as distinguished from the fundamental assumptions) of the conservative's view of the "good society" differs in different historical and geographical milieus. For instance, the American statesman John C. Calhoun (1782–1850) can also be designated as a typical conservative. His concern, however, was not with preserving the privileges of a hereditary aristocracy, which the United States did not have, but with preserving "states' rights" against the encroachment of the federal government. (Incidentally, "states' rights" in Calhoun's time were a bulwark against the erosion of the institution of slavery.) From this point of view, which defines the conservative ideology as one in which preservation of the existing order or of traditional values is central, the content of what is preserved is not important.

In Western Europe and in America, liberalism has been associated with a commitment to "equality" rather than to a hierarchical order. However, to the extent that liberals differ from radicals in rejecting fundamental structural changes in existing societies, they, too, can be regarded as committed to preservation and therefore can be called conservatives. The important criterion of conservatism, according to the present classification, is accepting the existing framework of social organization rather than idealizing the past or envisaging the distant future.

Ideologies oriented toward the future have had a long history. Several varieties are associated with utopian ideas. Mannheim reserved the term "utopias" for world views in which the existing social order was attacked. What he called "ideologies" were world views defending the existing social orders. From this point of view, the defense of the capitalist system would be associated with an "ideology," while an attack on it from socialist positions would be associated with a "utopia." Marxists would accept the former conclusion but not the latter. They would see a fundamental difference between "utopian" and "scientific" socialism. Characteristic of utopian socialism are vivid descriptions of a future classless society based on cooperation rather than exploitation. A Marxist would regard a question about the kind of society he envisages for the future as an "undialectical" question. Action undertaken with the view of overthrowing capitalism would *itself* change the view of the future society in a way that could not be foreseen prior to an effort to bring this future society about.

This is, perhaps, the most important insight contributed by Marx into the nature of social reality; namely, that this reality changes as a result of our getting to know it and especially as a result of actions undertaken to make an impact on it. The corresponding idea in modern sociology goes under the name of "self-fulfilling assumptions." Whatever sufficiently many or sufficiently influential people assume about social reality becomes a part of that reality. In other words, there is no "external observer" of social reality, such as can be at least imagined in relation to the physical world.

We cannot emphasize too strongly that the above classification of ideologies is just one of many possible ones. Ideologies are exceedingly complex interlacings of thinking, knowing, and feeling. They cannot possibly be described "objectively" and classified in terms of readily recognizable criteria, in the way that animals, minerals, languages, or postage stamps can be put into well-defined categories. The main reason, of course, is that whoever tries to describe or classify ideologies is himself an adherent of some ideology, which will determine what he regards as important.

In what follows, we will be examining several systems of thoughts, beliefs, and evaluations that appear to us to deserve being called ideologies. Others may disagree. Still others may wonder why we did not include much-publicized ideologies like "racism," "communism," "totalitarianism," or "humanism." There is no limit to the "isms" that can be subsumed under ideologies—but they all crisscross each other. None is pure. In fact, we did speak of "racism," but we subsumed it under the psychological dimension of conflict. We shall have occasion to speak of racism again, but this time as a component of a broader ideology. We shall also have occasion to discuss modern Communism at length in the context of a broader ideology.

The distinguishing feature of each of the ideologies we will be examining in the next three chapters is a commitment to a central value, for instance the primacy of the individual in a "good society" (Chapter 7) or the primacy of a collective energized by a common purpose (Chapter 8) or the primacy of power as the most important good to possess or to aspire to possess (Chapter 9). In each case, these commitments will be examined also in their extreme form where they have developed into something akin to obsessions. We will argue that it is these obsessions that underlie so-called ideological conflicts.

Notes

1. In *Meno* Socrates provides a demonstration by guiding a young slave through a proof of a simple version of the Pythagorean Theorem (Plato 1875).
2. According to Aristotle, the speed of falling bodies was supposed to be proportional to their weight. It turns out that spherical bodies falling through a resisting medium, such as raindrops through air, attain a terminal velocity proportional to their mass.
3. This stance can be said to be the polar opposite of pure rationalism reflected in Plato's theory of knowledge.
4. This view, most clearly expressed by Bishop George Berkeley (1685–1753), was satirized in the following double limerick.

> Please solve me this riddle, dear God.
> I find it exceedingly odd
> That the sycamore tree
> Simply ceases to be
> When there's no one around in the quad.
>
> Your perplexity strikes me as odd.
> *I'm* always around in the quad.
> That's why the tree
> Never ceases to be.
> Yours very sincerely, God.

5. This experiment, performed in 1881, was designed to determine the "absolute" velocity of the earth in space, which was conceived as the velocity with respect to the "ether," supposed to pervade all space and to constitute a framework of a coordinate system with respect to which the "true" velocities of all bodies should be established. The results of the experiment were entirely negative.

The velocity of light, well within the margin of experimental error, turned out to be the same in all directions.

6. Charlemagne's coronation in Rome as "Emperor" in A.D. 800 was conceived as the restoration of the Roman Empire. The "Empire" broke up after Charlemagne's death and was reconstituted as the "Holy Roman Empire of the German Nation" under Otto I in 962. It was dissolved after Napoleon crowned himself "Emperor." The fact that, loosely interpreted, the "Empire" lasted about a thousand years may have inspired Hitler to proclaim that the Third Reich would last as long.

7. The American battleship *Maine* was blown up in the harbor of Havana on February 15, 1898. The cause of the explosion was never discovered, but the incident was used to incite a war against Spain. The slogan "Fifty-four Forty or Fight" was used to incite a war against Britain in 1844 over a territorial dispute. "Make the World Safe for Democracy" was used as justification for America's entry in World War I.

7

The Ideal of Individual Freedom and the Cult of Property

In a book about Washington, D.C., by a Soviet writer we read:

> Since the United States was founded to this day (and forever after, as the presidents tell the people), the pinnacle of all progress is the sacred institution of private property. All other forms of social organization are heresy." (Iakovlev 1983, p. 10.)

In the publisher's blurb on the back cover we read:

> . . . This sheds a bright light on the essence of American democracy. . . . And to the extent that the possession of property is identified in the understanding of Americans with "freedom," its defense by any means is the highest duty of the Property Owner."

Relevant to our discussion is the charge that in America freedom is identified with property. How accurate is this charge? Is it indeed the case that a "nation conceived in liberty and dedicated to the proposition that all men are equal" has adopted the worship of property as its social creed, has made it a de facto official religion?

A Ritual of Self-Praise

That the U.S. form of social organization is the epitome of perfection is certainly asserted in many presidents' inaugural addresses (House Document 93–208, 1974). It is noteworthy that so much emphasis is placed on the incomparable virtue of the American political and economic system. At times, it is asserted that the system was ordained by God, an echo of the medieval conception of social organization.

> *Washington:* "Every step by which they [the people of the United States] have advanced to the character of the independent nation seems to have been distinguished by some token of providential agency. . . ." (1789)

> *Monroe:* "And if we look to the condition of individuals, what a proud spectacle does it exhibit! On whom has oppression fallen in any quarter of the Union? Who has been deprived of any right of person or property? . . . If we look to the history of other nations, ancient or modern, we find no example of a growth so rapid, so gigantic, of a people so prosperous and happy . . . the heart of every citizen must expand with joy when he reflects how near our Government has approached perfection." (1817)

> *Benjamin Harrison:* "No other people have a government more worthy of their respect and love and a land so magnificent in extent, so pleasant to look upon, and so full of generous suggestion to enterprise and labor." (1889)

> *Warren Harding:* "Surely there must have been God's intent in the making of his new-world Republic." (1921)

American presidents tell the American people that theirs is the most perfect system of government and social organization that ever existed on this planet. In this respect, the American people are told exactly what the Soviet people were told until recently about their government and their social organization, not only in speeches on ceremonial occasions but daily through all mass media, in schools, universities, and at all public functions, without exception.

Identification of personal freedom with property in American creed is not as explicit as the Soviet writer makes it out to be. A case in point is the silence of early American rulers about the fact that the institution of slavery put black people into the category of property. Monroe's rhetorical question, "Who has been deprived of any right of person or property?" can only be understood as applying only to white persons.

To take another example, not even many Americans know that part of Abraham Lincoln's first inaugural address was devoted to reassurances that the institution of slavery, where it existed at the time, would remain inviolable. In support of this reassurance, Lincoln quotes the Constitution:

> No person held in service or labor in one state under the laws thereof, escaping into another, shall in consequence of any law or regulation therein be discharged from such service or labor, but shall be delivered up on claim of the party to whom such service or labor be due. (Article IV, Section 2.)[1]

Lincoln continues:

> It is scarcely questioned that this provision was intended by those who made it for the reclaiming of what we call fugitive slaves; and the intention of the lawgiver is the law. All members of Congress swear their support to the whole Constitution—to this provision as much as to any other. To the proposition, then, that slaves whose cases come within the terms of this clause "shall be delivered up" their oaths are unanimous. Now, if they would make the effort in good temper, could they not with nearly equal unanimity frame and pass a law by means of which to keep good that unanimity? (1861)

The "sacred right of property" is not literally mentioned, but the impression is unavoidable that certain persons *were* property in the eyes of the American law, and no "natural rights" were accorded the persons who constituted this property.

The "natural rights" listed in the American Declaration of Independence are "life, liberty, and the pursuit of happiness." In the older version of John Locke (1690/1966) they are "life, liberty, and property."[2] R. Morris, professor of history at Columbia University, conjectured that Jefferson substituted "pursuit of happiness" for "property" because it was a more inspiring slogan. Nevertheless, Morris calls attention to the circumstance that " . . . the American Dream has been tied over the course of time to individual enterprise and the capitalist system. So that anybody who favors some type of collectivism is apparently opposed to the American Way." (Quoted by Margot Hornblower 1975.)

Similar thoughts are expressed by E. Friedenberg:

> The Founding Fathers adopted their familiar reference to "life, liberty, and the pursuit of happiness" from John Locke's phrase, "life, liberty, and property" . . . And there could have been little doubt in the minds of the Founding Fathers that the possession of ample means made a successful pursuit of happiness far more likely. Liberty and property go well together, each enhances the other. . . . (Friedenberg 1975, p. 41.)

The Idea of Freedom

To get some perspective on the relation between freedom and property in the American creed, we will examine the idea of freedom in its various versions and ask whether a hypertrophy of one of the aspects of freedom has indeed created a "cult of property" and, if so, how pervasive this cult is and what are the implications of its robustness.

In our day the most frequent rationalization of mass violence, either in the past, presently going on, or projected into the future, is the reference to the struggle for freedom. Clearly, if both sides of a violent struggle claim to be fighting for freedom, one of two conclusions is suggested. Either each side is interested in winning freedom only for itself (whatever freedom means to it) by denying it to the other side, or else each side has a different conception of freedom.

In the first instance, the contention that the conflict is for freedom is specious. In the second case, the matter is more complex. Indeed, it is the wide disparities in the conception of freedom that lend substance to the argument that present-day tensions between the superpowers are generated by a clash of ideologies.

Mortimer Adler, a philosopher who delved deeply into the history of ideas, examined the writings of theologians, philosophers, social scientists, and statesmen. From the mass of writings about freedom, Adler singled out three versions in which the focus is the freedom of the human individual (Adler 1958):

Circumstantial freedom of self-realization. In this conception, freedom consists essentially in the ability, under favorable circumstances, to act in accordance with one's own wishes for one's own good, as one sees it.

Acquired freedom of self-perfection. In this conception, freedom is pictured as a reward of sorts for efforts directed at making oneself a better person—more virtuous or moral, wiser, etc.

Natural freedom of self-determination. This freedom is assumed to be possessed by all human beings. It is identified with the *potential* supposedly incorporated in human nature which makes it possible for an individual to decide for himself what he shall do or shall become.

Circumstantial freedom of self-realization is perhaps the most primitive conception of freedom. In identifying with the ability to do as one pleases, it recognizes only external constraints on this ability. The qualification "circumstantial" refers to "favorable circumstances," which means simply the absence of constraints. Children seem to conceive freedom essentially in this way. However, this conception is not limited to children. It is also embodied in the philosophy of Thomas Hobbes, as is evident from the following passage:

> Liberty or freedom signifieth (properly) the absence of opposition (by opposition I mean external impediments of motion), and may be applied no less to irrational and inanimate creatures, than to rational. For whatsoever is so tied, or environed, as cannot move but within a certain space, which space is determined by opposition of some external body, we say it hath not liberty to go further.
>
> And according to this proper and generally received meaning of the word, a free-man is he that in those things that by his strength and wit he is able to do, is not hindered to do what he has a will to do. But when the words *free* and *liberty* are applied to anything but *bodies*, they are abused, for that which is not subject to motion, is not subject to impediment. (Hobbes 1651/1929, Part II, p. 161.)

Most remarkable is Hobbes' restriction of the meaning of constraints ("impediments") to physical constraints. He says this explicitly in another passage:

> . . . liberty . . . is nothing else but an absence of the lets and hindrances of motion . . . all *servants* and subjects are free who are not fettered and imprisoned.[3] (Molesworth 1939–1945, Vol. II, p. 120.)

Any *internal* constraints, e.g., fear of punishment, let alone dictates of conscience, are explicitly excluded from what Hobbes regards as impediments to freedom. This orientation suggests an image of "ultimate reality" as consisting of moving bodies. A body is "free to move" as long as it does not bump into another body. Further evidence for the primacy of this image is Hobbes' contention that the idea of freedom is applicable to "irrational and inanimate creatures" no less than to persons.

Almost diametrically opposed to this mechanical conception of freedom is that of Acquired Freedom of Self-Perfection. In contrast to the notion of Circumstantial Freedom, which is immediately perceivable by anyone who has ever been constrained from satisfying current desires, Freedom of Self-Perfection cannot be understood, much less appreciated, by anyone who has not internalized several other notions to the extent of regarding their meanings as self-evident, for example, "virtue," "wisdom," or "human nature."

Clearly, Freedom of Self-Perfection can be ascribed only to human beings and, as a rule, only to exceptional human beings. Note that this conception of freedom, more than any of the others, is independent of external constraints. Presumably it can be acquired by anyone regardless of the circumstances in which he finds himself. The Buddhist ideal of emancipation from desires is clearly related to the Acquired Freedom of Self-Perfection. As the qualification "acquired" implies, it must be striven for. Since striving may require self-imposed discipline (e.g., curbing appetites or passions), we have in this notion an allusion to the paradox that acquisition of "freedom" may be predicated on restriction of "freedom." Of course the two meanings of "freedom" differ in this formulation. However, philosophers or theologians, who take seriously the existence of categories like "freedom," "virtue," and the like, independent of conceptions of them by humans, do not resolve the paradox in this way. Rather, they distinguish between "real" freedom and "illusory" freedom. The same applies to "moral law" in terms of which Acquired Freedom of Self-Perfection is sometimes defined. St. Paul says that "moral law" is something "spiritual"

> . . . but I am carnal, sold under sin . . . I see another law in my members [meaning carnal desires—A.R.] warring against the law of my soul, and bringing me into captivity to the law of sin which is in my members." (Romans 7: 14, 23.)

In other words, "true freedom" in this conception is only freedom to do good, or, as is sometimes asserted, "true freedom" is the freedom to obey the will of God.

The next conception of freedom is, in a way, like that of Circumstantial Freedom, also opposite to the preceding one. Whereas in Freedom of Self-Perfection the emphasis is on effort in acquiring a state (perfection), the emphasis in the notion of Freedom of Self-Determination is on its being possessed by everyone. In contrast to the present-day rhetorical claim to freedom as a "right," Freedom of Self-Determination is thought of as a *given*. This conception probably has a direct bearing on the free will-determinism controversy among Christian theologians.

The concept of freedom as the *potential* for self-determination underlies Maslow's model of human nature, in which the needs for affiliation and growth are presumably embodied. It also underlies the doctrine of "natural rights," in which the dignity of the individual is identified with his autonomy.

The Philosophy of Laissez-Faire

The ideal of individual freedom is embodied in the political philosophy of liberalism. Its home is indisputably England. English social philosophers from Locke to Spencer identified good government with least restrictive government. The standard criterion that justifies the restriction of an individual's freedom, according to this view, is the protection of another individual's freedom. For example, a government is justified in prohibiting murder, because murder deprives the victim of the freedom to live. This emphasis on the government as the principal agency restricting freedom is coupled with the view that the way of guaranteeing freedom of individuals is by restricting the authority of governments. In the sphere of political economy, this view has been called "laissez-faire." It can be regarded as the ideological foundation of liberalism.

"Every one," wrote Adam Smith, "as long as he does not violate the laws of justice, is left perfectly free to pursue his own interest in his own way and to bring forth both his industry and capital into competition with those of every other man or order of men." (Smith 1776/1910, Vol. 1, p. 400.)

Note that this conception of freedom resembles Freedom of Self-Realization, except that it refers to a specific context in which this freedom is to be exercised, namely, the sphere of economic activity. This context is developed at great length in Adam Smith's magnum opus, *An Inquiry into the Nature and Causes of the Wealth of Nations*.

The Wealth of Nations is generally regarded as the work that laid the foundations of "classical" economics. It contains an idealized account of the activities of individuals free to produce commodities in any quantities within their capability and to engage in trade with one another. This trade takes place in a "market," where the farmer, the hunter, the artisan—in short, producers of all possible goods—come together. Each has a surplus of goods that he himself has produced and lacks goods produced by others. Hence all benefit by exchanges. The rates at which these exchanges take place are determined by the "laws of supply and demand." When the supply of some commodity increases, the rate of exchange it commands relative to other commodities must fall, because the producers of that commodity must compete for customers. When the demand for a commodity increases, the rate of exchange rises, since now more customers compete for the commodity. These fluctuations tend to drive the rates of exchange (essentially the market prices of commodities) to a steady state. Increases in production drive the prices down; but the decreases in price increase demand, which brings the prices back up. Thus, any deviation from the steady state brings forces into play that act opposite to the deviation, restoring the balance.

So far, we have presented only a descriptive theory of how a "free market" operates. Coupled with a belief that a society in which economic activities are based on the operation of such a market is a *good* society, the theory becomes normative, that is, comprises a value content and so reflects an ideology.

As has been said, an ideology embodies some basic assumptions about how the world is and how it ought to be. Often these assumptions remain unstated either because they are regarded as self-evident or because they have been so deeply internalized that they are no longer in the field of consciousness. A fundamental assumption of free enterprise ideology is that the behavior of a human being engaged in economic activity can be more or less accurately described by a model of a being that has come to be called *homo economicus*. In pursuing economic activities, this creature is faced with recurring decision problems, namely, how much to produce, how much of the product to offer for sale, how high a price to ask, how high a price to agree to pay for other commodities, and so on. The model is based on the assumption that at all times, these decisions will be governed by attempts to maximize gains and/or minimize losses. Assuming money to be a universal medium of exchange, the principle amounts to acting in a way that will maximize the flow of money toward self. *Homo economicus* is assumed to have no other concerns.

How closely do ordinary human beings resemble *homo economicus*? Even a cursory perusal of literature, both fiction and nonfiction, in which values are expressed or reflected will make clear that the *homo economicus* has by no means been commonly portrayed as an admirable model of a human being. On the contrary, activities directed solely toward increasing monetary gains have often been emphatically or implicitly depicted in an altogether unfavorable light. In fact, prohibition of usury in the Middle Ages was incorporated into the ethos of Christianity. The Shylocks, the Scrooges, the Karamazovs of world literature were portrayed as terrible examples of greed, ruthlessness, and general moral degradation.

In contrast to this portrayal in the literature of social criticism, the *homo economicus* of classical economics was supposed to provide a refutation of the belief that pursuit of economic gain is necessarily immoral or worthy of contempt. On the contrary, the amorality of *homo economicus* was supposed to demonstrate a principle that has since gained much credence in modern science, namely, that systemic properties emerging from interactions of large numbers of elements may have no resemblance to the properties of the elements themselves. Thus, *homo economicus* may be acting entirely selfishly, guided exclusively by tropisms toward where most money can be made. But the sum total of all these activities, the steady state of a market economy, approached or preserved in consequence of the laws of supply and demand and of free competition, represents, according to the proponents of a free market economy, the concrete realization of a social ethos espoused by Jeremy Bentham (1780/1948): "The greatest good for the greatest number."

Adam Smith compared the dynamics of the market to an "invisible hand." Not the decree of some benevolent potentate but something analogous to a natural law increases the well-being of a population, if only the law is allowed to operate without interference. The obvious advantage of such an arrangement is that the beneficial regulation does not depend on the good will or the social wisdom of any individual or group of individuals and so is immune to deterioration of the character or the replacement of a "good" ruler by a "bad" one.

> It is not from the benevolence of the butcher, the brewer, and the baker that we expect our dinner, but from their regard to their own interest. We address ourselves not to their humanity but to their self-love and never talk to them of our own necessities but of their advantages. Nobody but a beggar chooses to depend chiefly on the benevolence of his fellow citizens. (Smith 1776/1910, Vol. 1, p. 13.)

We would do Adam Smith an injustice if we concluded that his view of human society was identical to that of Hobbes (cf. below), whose men "in the state of nature" were engaged in perpetual warfare of everyone against everyone. In his only other full-length book, *The Theory of Moral Sentiments* (1759/1966), Smith discusses at length the socialization of the individual as a result of interactions in which each is a "spectator" of the behavior of others and also of his own ("the man within your breast"). In these interactions, the attitudes of people toward each other are shaped by a desire to win the approval not only of others but also of one's self. "Conscience" is thus understood as the desire to be praiseworthy. It is only in the sphere of economic activity that the individual (as *homo economicus*) is guided not by conscience and not by desire for approval of others but by self-interest.

We note further that in Smith's model of the free market, the central figure, the individual free to come and go, to buy and sell, to produce or not to produce is a *common* individual, a farmer or an artisan or a merchant, one of a great multitude. He is not a potentate who, by commanding, instigates large-scale historical events, or a lawgiver who prescribes rules of conduct. Adam Smith's free individual does not wield power. It is only the sum total of such individuals' activities that determine the operation of an economy. The idea of democracy was nurtured by that model. From then on, this idea remained linked in the minds of influential social philosophers of the Western world with the doctrine of free enterprise.

In Adam Smith's time the laissez-faire philosophy was a radical one, precisely because it seemed to be in accord with the ideals of political democracy. It was only after laissez-faire economics and the conception of freedom linked to this mode of thought were energetically challenged in the nineteenth century by the exponents of socialism that laissez-faire became identified with a conservative world view.

What the Philosophy of Laissez-Faire Replaced

In the heyday of European colonial expansion during the voyages of discovery, the economic theory underlying the conservative world view was the so-called *mercantile* theory. Its main thesis was that the wealth of a country is measured by the amount of gold and silver it possesses. At that time, money was practically synonymous with gold and silver. It followed that the more a country sold and the less it bought, the richer it got, because in this way its supply of precious metals was increased. The insatiable thirst for gold of the Spanish conquering marauders was a vivid reflection of this mode of thought.

The simplemindedness of this theory is clear to anyone who understands that the great value of gold is not intrinsic in the metal but derives from its comparative scarcity. The streets of heaven are sometimes pictured as being paved with gold. It stands to reason that the inhabitants on these streets cannot possibly be rich on that account alone. Emancipation from poverty (i.e., satisfaction of needs) can be assured only if appropriate goods and services are available. And no amount of gold can make goods and services available unless people are willing to perform the services and to produce the goods. And this they are not likely to do if money (i.e., gold) can be picked off the streets. The inhabitants of cities paved with gold, if they thought that the gold made them rich and so made work unnecessary, would starve to death.

Elementary as this reasoning is, it can be inaccessible to people unable to grasp the purely relative value of money. This idea is especially difficult to grasp if one tacitly assumes that the total amount of both money and goods available remain constant and the principal way to obtain goods is by buying them. In that case, the amount of money in one's possession is indeed a measure of one's wealth.

Thus, it is not hard to see why the demise of the mercantile theory followed in the wake of rapidly increasing production capacity. In fact, if the basic idea of the "new economics" were to be expressed in a few words, it is that the wealth of nations is measured by their productive capacities and by trade volumes. Given full access to markets and a large production capacity, everyone could be richer if enough were produced and distributed through free trade.

The new economics rode the crest of the wave of the future. England bet on this future, while the established "great powers," Spain and Portugal, persisted in the old mode of thought. The upshot was that world power passed from the old empires to a new empire better adapted to the consequences of the Industrial Revolution, which itself was a product of the new mode of thought.

Critique of Laissez-Faire and of the Capitalist System

Let us now see how well Adam Smith's free market model fit into the economic system that arose in consequence of the Industrial Revolution. The producers, trading in the primitive free market, owned not only what they produced but also the tools with which they worked. The cobbler owned his awl, the bricklayer his trowel. With the advent of machines (which is what the Industrial Revolution was about), the means of production could be acquired as property only by those who had sufficient capital, since machines were much more expensive than artisans' tools. By virtue of owning the new means of production, the "capitalists," as these entrepreneurs came to be called, acquired also ownership of the product. And since the commodities produced by machines could be sold much more cheaply than those produced by hand labor, the artisan could not compete with the machine. To gain access to the new means of production, hence to a means of making a living, the erstwhile free artisan had to become a hired worker, a "proletarian" without property. This separation of the producer from his tools, hence from the product of his labor, brought about profound changes in social relations. It was these new social relations that became the target of Marx's critique of the capitalist system.

Marx's analysis begins with the so-called theory of value formulated earlier by David Ricardo (Sraffa 1951–1955). This theory asserts that the exchange value of an item is determined by the "average amount of socially necessary labor" invested to produce it. If a coat is worth, say, ten bushels of wheat, then, according to the theory, this ratio reflects the ratio of the amount of labor that has gone into making a coat to the amount that went into producing a bushel of wheat. For the moment we bypass the question of how this "average amount of labor" is to be determined. We note only that conceiving exchange value in this way amounts to conceiving labor as the universal medium of exchange, a role usually assigned to money.

If money consists of pieces of gold, silver, or copper (as it did before various symbols of these substances replaced them), then "labor" is seen to be a more fundamental medium of exchange. For the exchange value of gold itself depends on its comparative scarcity and this, in turn, means that it takes a great deal more work to produce a certain amount of gold than a comparable quantity of many other things.

If the labor theory of value were offered as a descriptive theory, one might draw testable conclusions about rates of exchange between various items offered on the market, or variations of these rates associated with technological changes (which affect the amounts of "socially necessary labor"). Then some means of measuring these average "socially necessary amounts of labor" would have to be found. If such means could not be found, the theory, not being testable, could not be a descriptive theory. Marx, however, turned the labor theory of value to other uses, namely, to construct a conceptual scheme within which exploitation of some people by others could be seen as a necessary feature of the capitalist system.

As we have seen, the capitalist system arose in consequence of replacing the artisan by the factory worker in the new mode of production introduced by the Industrial Revolution. Now how much was the labor of the hired worker worth in the market? According to the labor theory of value, the worker's worth (exchange rate of work) is determined by how much labor was required to "reproduce" the worker's ability to work. That is to say, his labor was worth the amount of labor it took to enable the worker to reproduce his own body (to raise a family). Since, however, the worker, in transforming raw materials into a finished product, *puts labor into the process*, this finished product acquires value in excess of what it took to keep the worker going. Marx called this added value *surplus value* (Mehrwert).

It seemed natural to equate the entrepreneur's profit to this surplus value. Moreover, since the amount of profit (i.e., the capitalist's income) depended not only on the amount of work expended by him but essentially on the magnitude of his enterprise, it followed that the rate of accumulation of *capital* (wealth to be invested to produce more wealth) was directly related to the amount of capital already accumulated.

Marx's social philosophy was based on conclusions drawn from his model of a society based on private ownership of means of production. Two of these conclusions are directly related to our discussion of freedom. One is that the "steady state" model of the free market implied in Adam Smith's picture of an economy is not tenable. In a capitalist system, as depicted by Marx, wealth would inevitably become concentrated in fewer and fewer hands, while the mass of the workers (the "proletariat") would become progressively impoverished. Technological advances would accelerate this process. As machinery became more complex, the market value of labor would drop (because of the increased supply of "hands" competing for employment). It would be difficult to ascribe to this process the action of a benevolent "invisible hand" that in the long run assured the "greatest good for the greatest number" without restraining anyone's "freedom."

Another casualty of Marx's analysis of the capitalist system was the notion of freedom as a blessing in the social environment of laissez-faire economics. For the context in which this concept would be most frequently invoked would be the freedom of the worker and of the employer to enter a contract, whereby the worker would be given access to the means of production (machinery) in return for his labor and therefore the product of his labor. It is easy to see that this freedom is illusory as far as the worker is concerned, since if he wants to live and to provide for his family, he has no choice but to agree to the terms of the contract. And if, as has been argued, the value of labor is determined by what it takes to keep the worker's body and soul together (allowing for the opportunity to produce the next generation of workers), then this is just what the worker will get. This is what Ricardo called the "Iron Law of Wages." It is this discrepancy between the respective positions of the proprietors and the proletarians that cast a shadow of doubt on the meaning of "freedom" in a society based on a free enterprise economy. And it is this discrepancy and the consequent clash of the "haves" and "have nots" that constitutes the content of the class struggle, the centerpiece of Marxist social philosophy (cf. Marx and Engels 1848/1955).

The Class Struggle

The social history of nineteenth-century Europe indeed appears to be dominated by a struggle between the "working class" and the forces defending the privileges of the propertied classes which, for the most part, were supported by the power and authority of the governments. The struggle took on different forms in several European countries, depending on their political systems.

In Germany, where the style of government throughout the nineteenth century remained frankly authoritarian, repression of workers' movements was at first severe. Toward the end of the century Bismarck, the chancellor of the newly created German Empire, sought to reduce the revolutionary ardor of the workers by initiating some social security measures. Ironically, imperial Germany, ruled by an arrogant elite and uncompromisingly hostile to democratic ideas, had the most advanced system of social security in Europe at that time.

In Austria, the Catholic Church remained the bulwark of conservatism. Attempts to immunize workers against the "Marxist virus" were conspicuous and persistent. They did not abate, and, indeed, were intensified after the collapse of the monarchy in 1918, leading to the sharp polarization of Austrian politics between "Christian" and "socialist" parties.

In England the workers' movement was focused on the formation of strong labor unions. In contrast to Germany, where the ideological influence of Marxism was strongest, the English workers thought along more pragmatic lines, concentrating on wresting economic concessions from employers on *ad hoc* bases rather than on thoughts of a proletarian revolution. Toward the end of the nineteenth century, the intellectual leaders of the British socialist movement for the most part abandoned the central idea of Marxist doctrine—the class struggle—emphasizing the inevitable *evolutionary* transition to socialism.

In Russia, an absolute monarchy, conditions for a massive revolutionary workers' movement did not exist, not only in view of the harshly repressive measures available to the regime, but also because of the low level of industrialization. Industrial workers were only a minuscule fraction of the Russian propertyless masses. The great majority were peasants only recently emancipated from serfdom and overwhelmingly illiterate. To be sure, during serfdom, peasant revolts were not unknown. But these were sporadic events, triggered by despair, often led by adventurers, totally unlike the revolutionary workers' movements envisaged by Marx. Marxism penetrated Russia only in the last decades of the nineteenth century. The leadership of the revolutionary movement inspired by it was wholly confined to intellectuals. The rank and file consisted of small numbers of workers, largely in the very few industrial centers.

In one respect, however, all these workers' movements were similar. The distinction between a worker and a "bourgeois" (the latter category often comprising all who did not work with their hands) was clear. The worker looked different. He did not wear a business suit. His hands were rough. In some countries (e.g., England), his speech differed markedly from that of the bourgeois (or "gentleman" in England).

Class membership was largely hereditary. Sons of workers could not realistically aspire to rise to higher strata. For this reason, the sharp differentiation between the workers and the bourgeoisie remained prominent in nineteenth-century Europe. It was reflected in the structure of mass politics. Parties with socialist or near-socialist programs became a major political force wherever they could operate in the open.

Freedom, Opportunity, and Pursuit of Property

In the United States, the class struggle was attenuated by two circumstances. During the first century or so of its existence, the United States was expanding rapidly by occupying a practically empty continent. Whatever resistance was offered by indigenous populations was easily crushed by superior war technology. The proletarization of the masses that marked the social change attendant on the Industrial Revolution in Europe (transformation of farmers and artisans into industrial workers) had no counterpart in America. The truly downtrodden were the slaves, for whom resistance in the form of a class struggle was out of the question.

The other circumstance was that in the last decades of the nineteenth century, i.e., in the time of the most rapid industrialization in America, industrial labor was recruited very largely from recent immigrants. Organization of this genuine proletariat was difficult because of language and cultural differences, which were sometimes deliberately exacerbated by farsighted employers to inhibit the formation of labor unions. There is no question that opportunities, virtually nonexistent in the "Old Country," did open up for energetic immigrants. For example, the almost total transformation of the Jewish population in the United States from predominantly workers (especially in the New York garment industries) to business and professional occupations is clear evidence that the "land of opportunity" image of the United States, at least during the decades of mass immigration, was anything but a myth.

The widespread view, especially among Europeans, of American culture as being dominated by preoccupation with money is superficial. Compulsive concern with wealth has traditionally pervaded the middle and upper strata of European societies as well. There are differences, however. The preoccupation of the French and British middle and upper strata was with *possession* of wealth, evidenced by the attention devoted to matters related to inheritance and to profitable marriages. In America, the strongest preoccupation was with the active *acquisition* of wealth. The so-called American Dream, a vision of ubiquitous prosperity, is the large scale version of the individual "rags to riches" story. Wealth in the American ethos is not a privilege of the well-born but a reward for ability, vision, and energy. There is no stigma on the *nouveau riche*. On the contrary, millionaires are often proud of their humble origins. The well-publicized encouragements given by the rich to the poor to become rich like them and evidence that this is possible have contributed much to defusing the class struggle in the United States.

It is this link between absence of restrictions, seizing opportunities, and becoming rich that connects the ideal of freedom with the love of and respect for property in the dominant American ideology.

The absence of a politically unified labor movement and the total adherence to laissez-faire policies by the American government before 1933 created the most favorable conditions for unimpeded concentration of economic power in giant corporations. It is worth noting that this complete domination of economic and political life in America by business could persist even under conditions of extensive political freedom. To be sure, franchise was not guaranteed to women until the passage of the Nineteenth Amendment to the Constitution in 1920, and Blacks were virtually disfranchised in the southern states until the 1960s. Still, the level of formal political liberty in the United States in the period of rapid industrialization could compare favorably with that in many European countries. This circumstance on the one hand puts in question the Marxist thesis that in a class society, the State must necessarily be an instrument of oppression, and on the other hand lends credence to the Marxist thesis that political liberty in a bourgeois state does not mean much.

A serious ideological challenge to the hegemony of business in the United States came with the advent of the Great Depression in 1930. An almost complete absence of social security arrangements (which had been long established in several European countries) vastly aggravated the plight of the unemployed. Lines at soup kitchens and people scrounging in garbage cans became a common sight. The absurdity of starving amid plenty could not fail to suggest disturbing questions about the viability of an economic system that had evidently failed so dismally. The production capacity was still all there. People willing to work, even for a pittance, were still there. But the machines remained idle. Worse, food was deliberately destroyed as people went hungry. Wheat was used as fuel to bolster its price on the world market. Why did the system not work as it was supposed to work according to the immutable laws of supply and demand, which were supposed to insure "the greatest good for the greatest number?"

The so-called New Deal launched by Franklin D. Roosevelt's administration was a considerable break with the laissez-faire philosophy. For the first time in American history, the government took a dominant role in the economic life of the country, which inevitably entailed some regulation of private business activity. In particular, the right of collective bargaining was ceded to workers together with some protection against intimidation by employers. The new policies quickly became a major political issue, supplanting the traditional issues related to the government's role in economic life, such as protective tariffs or the free coinage of silver. It did not take long to recognize that this new role assumed by the government, so at variance with laissez-faire policy, would have far-reaching and possibly irreversible social implications.

Opposition to New Deal policies centered in the Republican Party. For some years, it appeared as if the class struggle had at last found a political voice. Throughout the Roosevelt years the workers and generally all low income groups, ethnic minorities, and Blacks constituted a formidable political coalition that assured large majorities in the federal legislature supporting the programs of the New Deal.

What now seemed especially anomalous from a Marxist point of view was that the State, in addition to tolerating political liberties extended to the propertyless, went so far as to pass measures supported by the under-privileged against the opposition of the supposedly ruling class. Acting in this manner, the State seemed to be not only neglecting its historical func-tion of protecting the privileges of the ruling class against challenges by the oppressed class but actually to be abrogating it by actively championing the interests of the lower strata. Indeed representatives of business interests conceived of themselves as victims of oppression.

It was in these circumstances that "liberty" became the catchword of militant business as it launched a counteroffensive against the New Deal. The attack was concentrated on one issue: government interference in the economic process was declared to be tantamount to the subversion of freedom. Characteristically, the organization of business groups most fer-vently opposed to New Deal measures called itself "The Liberty League."

Throughout the 1930s, the anti-New Deal forces could not gather enough support to defeat the coalition of the low-income groups. During the war, the debate on economic policy was virtually suspended. After World War II, however, the scene was quite different, and in the changed circumstances the conservatives were able to seize the political initiative.

Already in the 1930s the conservatives raised the "communist" issue in elective politics. Government "interference" in business, let alone engaging in business (e.g., launching the Tennessee Valley Authority project) was often portrayed by the conservative opposition as "creeping socialism." "Socialism" and "Communism" were not usually distinguished. Both were dubbed as inimical to "liberty." Unlike the Europeans, most Americans react negatively to the word "socialism," and it was possible to draw some political capital from this attitude. Nevertheless, the distrust of Big Business (on which many blamed the economic fiasco of the Great Depression) was still profound. Attitudes toward the Soviet Union were not yet as uniformly dominated by fear and repugnance as they were to become later. The totalitarian regimes of Germany and Japan appeared as greater dangers, especially after these states embarked on a rampage of aggression and conquest. To some extent, the staunch condemnation of these adventures by the Soviet Union predisposed some sectors of the working class and of the intelligentsia toward the Soviet regime. These sympathies, however, were fragile and were subsquently eroded or shattered by the postwar actions of the Soviet regime. Nevertheless, before World War II the Amer-ican image of world politics was not yet dominated by a fixation on the Soviet Union as the number one enemy of everything that America was supposed to stand for.

The situation after World War II became fundamentally different. The expected postwar depression did not materialize (thanks to the backlog of demand for commodities in short supply during the war). The quasi-class struggle mentality that played a fairly significant part in the political mood of the 1930s was not revived after having been suspended during the war. The unions were now establishments rather than militant organizations struggling for recognition. What appeared as encroachments by the Soviet Union on the political freedoms that were expected to be established in the liberated countries of Eastern Europe produced strong anti-Soviet moods in the general American public. What was perhaps an ordinary power struggle in the now strongly bureaucratized labor unions became transformed into a purge of the Communists, who, because of their energetic organizing activity during the 1930s, had achieved a measure of influence in the labor movement. As often happens, resentments were developed toward the victims of the purges. Finally, the Korean war, depicted to the public as an ideological war "against Communist aggression" led to the crystallization of "anti-Communism" as a basic tenet of American ideology. A tone of pugnacity appeared in the inaugural addresses of American presidents:

> Kennedy: "We dare not forget. We are heirs to the first revolution . . . We are proud of our ancient heritage and will not permit ourselves to be witnesses of its slow extinction." (1961)

The self-congratulatory tone continued unabated:

> Nixon (in his first inauguration): "No other country in history was ever as near to achieving a good society of plenty. . . ." (1969)

> Nixon (in his second inauguration): "Let us be proud that our system has given more liberty and prosperity than any other. . . ." (1973)

Is this ritual rhetoric obligatory like toasts at a banquet? Yes and no. The clichés are surely dictated by ritual, but the speeches are not without content. The substantive theme is the affirmation of faith in the *system*. The allusions are to the trappings of political freedoms, but the most significant content of freedom, as well as its foundation, is revealed in a passage from R. Hofstadter's book, *American Political Traditions*:

> The sanctity of private property, the right of the individual to dispose of and invest it, the value of opportunity, and the natural evolution of self-interest and self-assertion, within broad legal limits, into a beneficent social order have been staple tenets of the central faith in American political ideologies; these conceptions have been shared in large part by men as diverse as Jefferson, Jackson, Lincoln, Cleveland, Bryan, Wilson, and Hoover. The business of

politics—so the creed runs—is to protect the competitive world, to foster it on occasion, to patch up its incidental abuses, but not to cripple it with a plan for common collective action. American traditions also show a strong bias in favor of equalitarian democracy, but it has been a democracy in cupidity rather than a democracy of fraternity. (Hofstadter 1962, p. viii.)

The identification of the main component of freedom with freedom to make money has remained deeply embedded in the mainstream of American ideology. The identification is revealed in the definition of "inalienable rights" in the American Declaration of Independence: "Life, liberty, and the pursuit of happiness." The identification of property with happiness was natural in the era when the fruits of freedom were most clearly related to the triumph of individualism and most visibly manifested in the energy of private enterprise released from restrictions carried over from the era of absolute monarchies. The self-congratulatory oratory of the inaugural ceremony was originally entirely sincere. The American elite actually believed that America was a model to be emulated by the rest of the world.

It was only after the foundations of laissez-faire were challenged that the oratory became increasingly defensive and spiked with pugnacity (recall Goldwater's anguish about the erosion of the "will to win," which reached its peak in the ominous threats of the Reagan Administration. This was the transformation of a faith into a cult, of what was originally an important concrete realization of freedom (release of pent-up energies) into a fetish. Dramatic evidence of this deification of property is seen in the bizarre behavior of the so-called "survivalists," a cult spawned by the threat of nuclear war. Their preparations for the holocaust included burying paper securities in metal casings deep underground evidently in the expectation that after the nuclear devastation they will dig them up and claim what is rightfully theirs.

8

The Ideal of Collective Freedom and the Cult of Struggle

The President of the United States calls the opposite side an "empire of evil" assuming the U.S. as an "empire of good" and expresses in this way the idea of separation of good and evil. On the other side of the Iron Curtain, Soviet leaders declare a principle of "peaceful coexistence" of countries with different political and economic regimes, that is, they praise a combination of good (socialism) and evil (capitalism). So each side behaves according to the principles of the ethical systems concerning the combination of good and evil elements. When the relationships are personified, American representatives urgently try to establish personal collaboration with Soviet representatives, demonstrating in this way their sacrificial willingness for compromise (as it is supposed in the first ethical system). But Soviet representatives behave diffferently, they try to expand and dramatize any conflict demonstrating sacrificial uncompromising behavior (in complete accord with the principles of the second ethical system. (Lefebvre 1987.)

In the article from which the above citation was taken, Vladimir Lefebvre is concerned with "reflexion," roughly defined as a multileveled mechanism of cognition, perception, and judgment. A person may perceive the world (have an image of the world inside him) and may also perceive his perception, that is have an image of his image. Or else he may form a conception of someone else's image of the world, or even of someone else's conception of his own image, and so on. The same multilevel system of judgments can be applied to values attached to persons and to relations between persons. For instance, a person can say, "I disapprove of X's approval of Y, but I am disturbed by this attitude of mine," as in "My daughter is in love with this young man, and I don't like it, but I feel guilty about my rejection of him."

In the domain of ethical concerns Lefebvre postulates two types of attitudes toward "good" and "evil." Here "good" and "evil" are understood in their completely abstract meanings, devoid of content. One attitude approves of a "combination of good and evil," another disapproves of it. "Approval" and "disapproval" are also understood in a completely abstract sense. In Lefebvre's mathematical model, they are represented simply by"1" (good) and by "0" (bad), respectively. Nonetheless, this disembodied approval or disapproval can also be interpreted in terms familiar to discussions of ethics. Apparently, "combination of good and evil" can be interpreted as using bad means to attain good ends (accepting "the end justifies the means" principle.) Disapproving the combination of good and evil can be interpreted as rejecting the "end justifies the means" philosophy.

Lefebvre invented a mathematical formalism (closely related to Boolean algebra),[1] in terms of which reflexion is pictured in the form of expressions involving multitiered exponents (Lefebvre 1982). Operations on the expressions lead to rigorous deductions involving judgments of persons represented by the bases of the exponential expressions (the lowest tier). Of interest to us is the following, at first sight somewhat paradoxical, result: a person who has internalized what Lefebvre calls "the first ethical system" (i.e., one who regards as inadmissible compromise between good and evil) *in the abstract*, can view compromise between *persons* who hold views opposite to his own positively and so can seek a compromise with them. In contrast, a person who has internalized Lefebvre's "second ethical system," i.e., one who has a positive attitude toward compromise between good and evil (again in the abstract), will eschew compromise with persons who hold views opposite to his own. Instead, he will spare no effort to emerge victorious in conflicts with them.

These results were deduced formally from Lefebvre's models of the two types of actors—adherents to the one or the other of the two ethical systems. In the light of the interpretation of these deduced results in concrete situations, Lefebvre offers explanations of the large difference in attitudes manifested by most Americans on the one hand and persons who lived until recently in the Soviet Union on the other.

To demonstrate these differences in certain attitudes, Lefebvre conducted a study in which respondents to a questionnaire were asked to indicate their judgments of certain situations. One group of respondents was recruited from a wide cross section of the American public; the other from recent immigrants from the Soviet Union to the United States.[2] Table

Table 8–1 (After Lefebvre 1987)
**Responses of Americans and of Soviet immigrants
to questions involving moral judgments**

Question	Proportion of American respondents answering "yes"	Proportion of Soviet-born respondents answering "yes"
Should a doctor conceal from a patient that he has cancer in order to diminish his suffering?	.08	.89
Should a malefactor be punished more severely than the law requires, if this may serve as a deterrent to others?	.11	.84
May one give false evidence in order to help an innocent person avoid jail?	.20	.65
May one send a cheat sheet during a competitive examination to a close friend?	.08	.62
Would a good person seek a compromise with an insolent person in a conflict situation?	.76	.30
Two terrorists are hijacking a small plane. There is a possibily of killing them without injury to the passengers. Another possibility is to start negotitions first and try to persuade them to surrender. The head of the rescue group made the decision not to negotiate with the criminals. Did he act correctly?	.25	.58

8–1 shows the proportions of respondents in both groups answering "yes" or "no" to the questions presented.

The differences in the proportions answering "yes" and "no" in the two populations were offered as evidence for the hypothesis that attitudes in harmony with the first ethical system (prohibiting the use of evil means in pursuit of good ends) are reflected in the responses of Americans, while attitudes in harmony with the second ethical system (permitting the use of evil means in the pursuit of good ends) are reflected in the responses of the Soviet emigrés. Lefebvre interprets the answers to the first four questions in this way: Lying to the patient in order to reduce his anguish, punishing a malefactor more severely than the law requires in order to deter others, giving false evidence to help an innocent person avoid jail, helping someone cheat to enable him to pass an examination—all these seem to entail using evil means to attain worthy ends. Americans predominantly disapproved of such actions; Soviet emigrés predominantly approved them.

Answers to the last questions supposedly reflect contrasting attitudes toward seeking a confrontation with an adversary and seeking a compromise. Apparently Soviet emigrés lean toward confrontation, Americans toward compromise.

The answers to the last two questions seem to confirm Lefebvre's hypothesis concerning American and Soviet attitudes toward confrontation and compromise. With regard to the first four questions, however, the matter is less clear.

Consider the doctor who conceals from the patient that he has cancer. The doctor appears to be using evil means (lying) to achieve a good end (reduce the patient's suffering). Suppose, however, the doctor acted in the opposite way: told the patient the truth even though this would cause him suffering. Could we not conclude with equal justification that in acting so, the doctor is still using "evil means to serve good ends," namely, fails to alleviate the suffering of the patient in order to tell the truth (which may be regarded as an imperative of his profession in the particular cultural milieu)? If both answers can be interpreted as confirmations of the hypothesis, the hypothesis appears to be unfalsifiable and therefore devoid of theoretical leverage. The same considerations apply to the questions on giving false evidence and supplying a cheat sheet to a friend.

Let us now take a second look at the last two questions from which it appears that persons brought up in the Soviet Union tend to disdain compromise with an adversary, while those brought up in the United States tend to seek such compromise. The answer given by the majority of Soviet emigrés to the question relating to the hijacking is of particular interest. Almost all recent Soviet immigrants to the United States are of Jewish origin, since only members of that ethnic group have been allowed to emigrate in significant numbers. The fact that they have emigrated is strong indication that their attitudes toward the Soviet state are predominantly negative. Further, because of their Jewish origin, they could be expected to be admirers of Israel, especially when the relations between the Soviet Union and Israel are bad. Admiration of Israel may have in large measure determined their attitude toward terrorist hijackers, since the adamant position of Israel with regard to terrorists of all varieties is well known. In other words, the answers of the Soviet emigrés to the last question may very well have been strongly situation-oriented and not a consequence of a total immersion in a particular type of ethical system.

It would be possible to put this conjecture to a test by including another question in the questionnaire: "Do you think that Pavlik Morozov was a good person?"

At the time the question was asked, Pavlik Morozov was an authentic Soviet saint. This twelve-year-old lad is identified in stories about him as a son of a kulak, that is, a well-to-do peasant opposing Soviet collectivization policies in the 1930s. Pavlik's act of heroism was informing on his father who, it seems, concealed grain rather than deliver it at prices fixed by the authorities. The father was shot for this crime. Later the father's friends killed Pavlik as an act of revenge. Pavlik Morozov's story appears in school readers as an example of martyrdom in the cause of socialism.[3]

According to Lefebvre's theory, admiration of Pavlik Morozov's action strongly reflects adherence to the second ethical system: informing on one's father, thus sending him to his death, is evil; but since this action is demanded by loyalty to "Soviet Power" (the usual designation of the authorities), the "compromise" between good and evil is condoned. The reverence with which young Morozov's deed and his martyrdom are depicted seems to be a dramatic confirmation of Lefebvre's contention that the second ethical system dominates moral judgments in the Soviet Union.

Let us now imagine that Pavlik Morozov acted in the opposite way, that is, lied to the authorities who questioned him about the hidden grain and thus saved his father. Should this action not also be regarded as using evil means (lying) for good ends (saving father)? So in this case, too, as in the case of the doctor lying to his patient, either resolution of the moral dilemma can be interpreted as being dictated by the second ethical system, which effectively drains the concept of theoretical content. Moreover, Pavlik's preference for saving his father to being loyal to "Soviet Power," even though, as we have seen, it is consistent with the second ethical system, will surely not be consistent with official Soviet morality.

Actually, the question about Pavlik Morozov's deed *was* put to Soviet emigrés in another study. However, they were not asked to evaluate this deed directly. Instead, the respondents were asked how an "average Soviet citizen" would evaluate Pavlik's betrayal of his father (Lefebvre 1982, pp. 53–54). The reply was as expected: the Soviet emigrés guessed that the average Soviet citizen would approve of Pavlik's action. This may very well be the case. However, had the immigrants been asked to evaluate Pavlik from their own point of view (which was not done), it is practically certain that their evaluation would have been strongly negative. Lefebvre would presumably interpret this deviation from the second ethical system by taking into consideration the fact that the emigrés had rejected this ethical system, as evidenced by the fact that they left the Soviet Union. But then the question arises why in other contexts they still exhibited attitudes that are presumably typical of adherents to the second ethical system.[4]

The same objection can be leveled against Lefebvre's interpretation of styles of conducting international negotiations. Ronald Reagan's stark distinction between the "empire of evil" and "the land of freedom" can be interpreted as a refusal to compromise with an adversary, while his enthusiastic exacerbation of the arms race can be interpreted as using evil means to achieve what he sees as good ends. From this point of view, Reagan's attitudes can be seen to be in accord with the second ethical system.

Similarly, Lefebvre's interpretation of Soviet behavior can be turned upside down. The Soviet leaders are most adamant when they insist that socialist and capitalist *ideologies* are incompatible. They will hear nothing about an "ideological detente." On the contrary, it is on the ideological level (or "front," as Soviet leaders are fond of saying) that the struggle must go on, until the socialist ideology is victorious.[5] But when ideologies are "personified," e.g., by regimes of socialist and capitalist countries, the Soviets insist on the possibility of peaceful coexistence (read compromise).

What matters is not the vindication or refutation of Lefebvre's characterization of ethical systems prevalent in the Soviet Union and in the West. Much more interesting is the conjectured connection between "the end justifies the means" ethos and a dedication to *struggle*, to perceiving the world as always divided between the blessed and the damned, between forces of light and forces of darkness. In fact, it is this compulsion that is primary. The "end justifies the means" mentality is simply a consequence. If the other side is seen as the epitome of evil, beyond redemption, then no price seems too high to pay for annihilating it.

We might mention in passing that, at least in the context of the Cold War, the view of the adversary as beyond redemption has been as characteristic of the attitude of the American ruling elite as of the Soviet. It is true, however, that the compulsion of seeing *every* controversy as a confrontation has been carried to far greater lengths in the Soviet Union than in the United States. The view to be presented here is that, just as the cult of property represents a perversion of the ideal of individual freedom, so the cult of struggle represents a perversion of the ideal of collective freedom.

Freedom Conferred by the Collective

In addition to the three versions of freedom in which the human individual was at the center of attention, Mortimer Adler singled out two other versions.

Political liberty. Here collectivity makes its first appearance. The individual is still prominent, because it is his right to participate in the political process (vote, run for office, etc.) that is identified with political liberty. However, since effective political action can be taken only by organized groups of individuals acting together, it is actually the freedom of groups to act in the political arena that constitutes political liberty. Nevertheless, the freedom of groups in this conception is derived from the ideal of the freedom of the individual to associate with like-minded individuals. It is a pooling of individual interests that constitutes the interest of a politically acting group.

Government in this conception exists to protect the "natural rights" of individuals. The American Declaration of Independence spells this idea out:

> ". . . all men are endowed by their Creator with certain unalienable rights . . . to *secure* these rights, governments are instituted among men." (Emphasis added.)

The notion of "natural right" is implied in the conception of freedom as Freedom of Self-Determination. However, according to the conception embodied in Political Freedom, this freedom must be "secured" (presumably against encroachments). The government is conceived as the servant of the collectivity and as a guardian of the citizens' freedom.

Collective freedom. Finally, the conception of Collective Freedom implies that the freedom of the individual acquires meaning *only* in the context of a collectivity of which the individual is a member. On this score, the exponents of Collective Freedom agree. However, notions abut what sort of collectivity assures the freedom of its members differ widely. The differences are apparent in a comparison between the following passages.

> The union of the subjective with the rational will is the moral whole, the State, which is that form of reality in which the individual has and enjoys his freedom but on the condition of recognizing, believing in, and willing that which is common to the whole, and this must not be understood as if the subjective will of the individual attained its gratification and enjoyment through the common will, as if this were the means provided for its benefit, as if the individual, in his relation to other individuals, thus limited the freedom, in order that this universal limitation—the mutual constraint of all— might secure a small piece of liberty for each. (Hegel 1837/1944, p. 38.)

> Only in a classless society has each individual the means of cultivating his gifts in all directions. . . . In the previous substitutes for the community, in the States, etc., personal freedom has existed only for the individuals who developed within the relationships of the ruling class, and only insofar as they

were individuals of this class. The illusory community, in which individuals have up till now combined, always took on own independent existence in relation to them, and was at the same time, since it was the combination of one class against another, not only a complete illusory community, but a new fetter as well. (Marx 1845/1947, pp. 74–75.)

Hegel explicitly rejects the idea that "governments are instituted among men to secure these rights," i.e., freedom of individuals. For him, the State is a "form of reality." To be sure, the individual enjoys freedom in this "reality" but only on condition that he wills what "the whole" wills, i.e., what the State wills. Hegel endows the State with a will of its own.

Marx, too, contends that the State acquires an independent existence. But in his view, the State is a "substitute" for the community. It assures freedom only for a class of individuals, those who belong to the "ruling class."

Opposite Views of the State:
Materialism and Idealism Again

Why did these two social philosophers, while agreeing on the primacy of the collective, come to such different conclusions about the role of the State? According to modern adherents of Marx's philosophy of history, this difference stems from opposite conceptions of the nature of "ultimate reality." Hegel is classified by Marxists as an "idealist," Marx as a "materialist" (cf. Chapter 6). These terms should not be confused with their common usage meanings in the context of priorities of needs or desires. In common parlance, a "materialist" is one who assigns high priorities to possessions of material goods or to the wherewithal of acquiring them (money); an "idealist" is one who has "ideals," i.e., is guided in his behavior by principles that reflect some sort of higher morality.

In Marxist philosophy, "idealism" and "materialism" refer not to different values but to different conceptions of reality. For the idealist, "ultimate reality" resides in ideas, whether they are inside people's heads, in the mind of a Supreme Being, or altogether disembodied. Hegel, a prime representative of this outlook, thought of history as a succession of realizations of what something he called the Absolute produced by its contemplations. The evolution of freedom, then, according to Hegel, was the evolution of the *idea* of freedom. Specifically, Hegel conceived of what he thought were the earliest civilizations (those of the ancient Middle East) as ascribing freedom to only *One*, that is, God, or, perhaps, the God-king. In the Hellenic civilization, the idea of freedom was supposed to have been extended to the *few*—the free citizens of a city state, and denied to many, the slaves. The extension of freedom to *all* was supposed to be accomplished by the idea of the State, by which Hegel doubtless meant the Prussian state, which he served and which he regarded as a "form of reality" endowed with a will. The individual, Hegel maintained, becomes free when he fuses his will to that of the State.

"Materialism" in Marxist philosophy is an outlook in which "ultimate reality" is embodied in matter. Natural laws, which govern all events in the universe, are laws of motion and of transformation of matter. When matter, following the laws of motion and transformation, becomes structured in certain ways, life emerges and with it eventually consciousness, thoughts, and ideas—all generated by what happens in their material substrate. The world exists quite independently of whether we perceive it. Moreover, since ideas are produced by the activity of human beings, they must be endowed with content, shaped by human experience. Consequently, there is no such thing as "freedom" in the abstract. If "freedom" means anything at all, it must mean freedom to do this or that. In particular, human freedom is enhanced by progressive emancipation from the constraints imposed by the environment. Hence man attains freedom by shaping his environment to suit his needs. This is done by productive labor which, according to Marx, is the unique characteristic feature of our species. It is, therefore, in the sphere of labor, i.e., of production, that the meaning of freedom is to be sought.

It is through this chain of reasoning that Marx ultimately came to his views about the role of the State in a society where people are differentiated by their roles in the production process, that is, in a class-structured society. If the paramount reality of history is the struggle between the upper (exploiting) and the lower (exploited) classes, the function of the State must be (according to Marx) to keep the lower classes in subjugation. The State with its coercive organs (the police, the army, the press, etc.) is the instrument of class rule. It follows that in a classless society there will be no need for the State. It will then "wither away." But the classless society can be achieved only by a "social revolution." In Marx's time, the French Revolution was still in living memory. Marx witnessed the revolutionary upheavals of 1848 and the Paris Commune, a short-lived "proletarian dictatorship" proclaimed after the defeat of France by Prussia in 1870. The uprisings were crushed, but in Marx's view, these defeats only sharpened the "class consciousness" of the proletariat. He believed that the "final" social revolution leading to the establishment of a "classless society" was inevitable.

It is not clear whether Marx was convinced that the social revolution would necessarily be violent. Nor did he have a clear idea of how, when, or where it would start and by whom it would be led except that, according to his theories, it would have to start in an "advanced" country, where the level of production was already high and the process of production sufficiently organized to be "taken over" by the organized proletariat.

In contrast, V.I. Lenin, the most ardent disciple of Marx, had very definite ideas about how the social revolution was to come about:

1. It would have to be led by a highly disciplined elite, well versed in "theory" and supported by the industrial working class, which was to seize political power and use the still-existing state apparatus to *keep* that power until the society was restructured, primarily by socializing all important means of production.
2. Nothing could be expected from an orderly political process, especially one keeping within the rules of parliamentary procedures. Parliamentary systems were used to camouflage the rule of the bourgeoisie (cf. Britain's) and true democracy could be realized only when the power of the present ruling class, the bourgeoisie, was broken.
3. A social revolution might well start in a "backward" country.

This last tenet of Lenin's faith was inspired by the "almost" successful revolution in Russia following Russia's defeat by Japan in 1905. Russia's defeat in World War I and the collapse of the Czarist government rekindled Lenin's hope that the social revolution foretold by Marx would occur in Russia. Returning to Russia from exile in April 1917, Lenin assumed the leadership of the radical wing of the Russian Social Democratic (Marxist) party, which seized power by an almost bloodless coup a few months later.

To Lenin, struggle was the meaning of life. His elder brother, whom he revered, had been hanged for allegedly participating in an assassination plot against Czar Alexander III. Lenin himself, however, rejected terrorism, not because of an aversion to violence but because he firmly believed that revolutionary leadership required mastery of "revolutionary science" rather than romantic fervor. To Lenin, Marx was first and foremost a scientist, who fully explained the "laws of motion" of society quite in the same way that Newton fully explained the laws of motion of heavenly bodies. And just as natural science became a powerful weapon in the conquest of nature, so Marxist social science would be a powerful weapon in the hands of the revolutionary proletariat in overthrowing the oppressing class and reorganizing society.

Lenin was an avid reader and a tireless intellectual worker. Devoid of personal vanity, he was nevertheless totally ruthless in dealing with opponents, being completely convinced that having "mastered" Marxist theory, he was in possession of "objective truth." Of course physical violence was in those days unthinkable in internal political struggles within revolutionary parties. Lenin browbeat his intellectual opponents by adroit use of acerbic polemics. In tracing the roots of the obsession with struggle that has marked the entire political history of the Soviet Union, it will serve us well to examine Lenin's polemical style.

Lenin's Philosophical Crusade

Lenin promoted to an unassailable dogma the view that idealism was the ideological weapon of the bourgeoisie and materialism the ideological weapon of the proletariat. It is on the ground of this ideological struggle that he attacked his colleagues, Marxists all, whom he took to task for sliding into "idealist positions." The bill of particulars was spelled out in a book entitled *Materialism and Empiriocriticism* (Lenin 1909/1964). Central in the charge of heresy was the interest that the "heretics" showed in the philosophical implications of the "new physics."

The first decade of the twentieth century saw the birth of the theory of relativity and of quantum theory, both destined to change radically our conceptions of space, time, and causality. A framework of cognition facilitating this revision, called "positivism," had been formulated by the prominent physicist E. Mach, who had a profound influence on Einstein. According to Mach's positivist outlook sense impressions are the primitive elements from which our perceptions and concepts are constructed. The role of a scientific theory is that of describing these sense impressions as "economically" as possible. This idea was a precursor of the so-called "operational definition," in the light of which the paradoxes of relativity and quantum mechanics are resolved.

In *Materialism and Empiriocriticism* Lenin directed a devastating attack on Mach and, since his colleagues Bogdanov, Lunacharsky, and others had expressed sympathetic interest in Mach's ideas, he castigated them too. The technique was that of imputing guilt by association. Lenin asserted that Mach's positivism was nothing but Bishop Berkeley's idealism in a new guise. From this identification, Lenin deduced that any attitude except total rejection of the ideas of Mach and all of its heretical spin-offs amounted to falling into a trap set by the bourgeoisie to subvert the revolutionary movement.

It is possible that Lenin used the materialism-idealism issue as leverage in an ordinary power struggle against political rivals. On the other hand, there is no reason to doubt that Lenin was entirely sincere in his fundamentalism. Quite possibly he actually believed that the formulations of the new philosophy of science (attempts to come to terms with the revolutionary metaphysical implications of relativity and quantum phenomena) were really part of a nefarious scheme on the part of the "bourgeoisie" to blunt the "philosophical weapon" of the working class, namely, dialectical materialism, which, Lenin was convinced, was incompatible with "positivism," "empiriocriticism," and all other camouflaged versions of idealism. This conjecture is supported by the following passage:

> Entirely in the spirit of Marx and in close collaboration with him, Engels in all his philosophical works briefly and clearly contrasts the materialist and idealist lines in regard to *all* questions, without . . . taking seriously the endless attempts to "transcend" the "one-sidedness" of materialism and idealism, to proclaim a *new* trans-some-kind of "positivism," "realism," or other professional charlatanism. . . . Either materialism consistent to the end, or the falsehood and confusion of philosophical idealism . . . (Lenin 1909/1964, p. 318.)

The either/or mentality so conspicuous in Lenin's polemical style marked the entire history of Bolshevism, first as a faction in the Social Democratic Party, then, after the faction had taken power and was renamed the Communist Party, as the only legal party in post-revolutionary Russia, finally as the strictly hierarchically organized, fully bureaucratized power elite. In the early struggles, the slogan that guided Bolshevik tactics was "Those who are not with us are against us." In the years of reconstruction after the civil war, the "struggle" went on on various "fronts": the "struggle" for production efficiency, the "struggle" against illiteracy, the "struggle" against religion, the "struggle" on the cultural front, etc.

There was even a "struggle on the musical front." I recall a conference on music in the 1920s at which a heated discussion erupted over the question whether a certain instrument was truly a "people's instrument" or a relic of feudalism. One speaker chided "proletarian" music theoreticians for their simplistic belief that the minor mode was an expression of bourgeois ideology, while the major mode reflected proletarian class consciousness, citing counterexamples to prove his point. I recall a criticism of a string quartet, in which the critic found symptoms of "Kautskyism." (Kautsky was a prominent German Marxist, against whom Lenin launched some of his most bitter diatribes.)

Thereby a metaphysics based on the idea of the primacy of struggle in the unfolding of history (of both the inanimate and the animate worlds) grown on the soil of politics, was transformed into a dogma.

The Paradigm of Struggle as Political Clout

In the wake of the policy of forced collectivization of agriculture in the Soviet Union, the first wave of terror engulfed the country. The "class struggle" was now directed against the "kulaks," identified primarily by their opposition to collectivization. (Understandably, as these were the relatively well-to-do peasants.) After the expropriation of the kulaks and their "liquidation as a class," the "class struggle" could be regarded as officially ended in the Soviet Union. At any rate, the constitution of 1936 declared that the social structure of the U.S.S.R. accommodated three classes "friendly toward each other," the workers, the collective farmers, and the intelligentsia (in this context white collar workers). Nevertheless, the idea of the class struggle was not easily abandoned. It continued to serve as political clout. Stalin declared that the closer Soviet society approached the final apotheosis (Communism) the *sharper* the class struggle would grow, since the bourgeoisie would become more and more desperate. Perhaps he meant the class struggle on the global scale. Whatever was meant to be the arena of the "final" class struggle, we see in this rhetoric a compulsion resembling an addiction. We shall have more to say about a similar addiction in the next chapter.

The Onslaught on Genetics

Perhaps the most bizarre antics characterizing the Soviet addiction to struggle was the Lysenko affair. As the authoritarian principle came to dominate ever broader areas of Soviet life, science did not escape its grip. Dialectical materialism was declared to be the only "correct" philosophy of science, reflecting the only "genuinely" scientific view of the world. Citations from the "classics" of Marxism-Leninism (expanded to Marxism-Leninism-Stalinism), of which a major portion came from *Materialism and Empiriocriticism*, became mandatory in all writings with any sort of philosophical bent and in most scientific writing as well, at least in the prefaces. Eternal vigilance guarding against heresy was demanded of everyone. An insurance of sorts, at least in the short run, against being purged as a heretic was to accuse someone else of heresy. Soviet intellectual life took on a resemblance to Hobbes' war of everyone against everyone. In a way, it resembled the world of business competition, except that the gains and losses were much more extreme. Some rose to pinnacles of power and prestige. Others, often the same ones, when the political winds shifted, were cast into pits of disgrace, ostracism, exile, or worse.

Trofim Lysenko climbed to the very top of the pyramid. His qualifications were ostensibly in biology. Actually, he was a plant breeder, a disciple of I.V. Michurin, who was a sort of Soviet counterpart of the American plant breeder Luther Burbank, the inventor of the grapefruit and many other useful or pleasant fruits of the soil. At one time Lysenko gained favor by developing a frost-resistant variety of wheat. It is now firmly established that such artificially bred varieties arise through selectively directed recombinations of genes. Lysenko, however, would hear nothing of genetics.

Genetics had enjoyed a healthy development in the Soviet Union. The names of Vavilov, Dubinin, and many other luminaries of the field were well known in the world of biology. Following the rediscovery in 1900 of Mendel's seminal work, genetics was a rapidly growing field of sophisticated research where important breakthroughs were made leading to dramatic advances in understanding mechanisms of heredity and the driving forces of biological evolution.

Lysenko declared war on genetics. Whether he was motivated by the monomaniacal fixations of a crank or by contempt for all theory of the sort that Thomas Edison often showed, or simply by the tempting opportunity of exercising power over others by browbeating them (he enjoyed Stalin's favor), we will probably never know. Of much greater importance than Lysenko's motives is the setting in which the browbeating took place. It had the appearance of a scientific conference (a session of the Lenin Academy of Agricultural Sciences, July 31–August 7, 1948) but in effect amounted to public heresy hearings, at which participants, invited to present their views in scientific papers, were forced to recant as three hundred years earlier the Holy Inquisition had forced Galileo to recant.

In the years immediately after the Soviets' victory over Germany, there were several intellectual lynchings of this sort, in which the faithful were given an opportunity to vent their wrath on would-be subverters of the true religion. Perhaps the function of these orgies was to provide an outlet for pent-up aggressive impulses. If so, they could be regarded as dramatic confirmations of the frustration-aggression theory.

The main accusation was invariably that of abandoning the true faith of materialism for the false faith of idealism. Here are some typical examples of the oratory recorded at the genetics (or rather the anti-genetics) conference:

> Weismanism, which made its appearance at the turn of the century, followed by Mendelism-Morganism, was primarily directed against the materialist foundations of Darwin's theory of evolution. . . . (Proceedings of the Lenin Academy of Agricultural Sciences 1949, p. 15.)

These were the opening shots in the "final struggle" against idealism in biology. The following example is of imagery suggesting a routed enemy making his last desperate stand:

> Our Morganists, retreating all along the line in face of the pressure of Michurinist fact, are trying to make a stand on a front which is least subject to the attack of the Michurinists. This front is cytology. . . . (p. 594.)
>
> Different beings resort to different means of defense: the lion defends himself with its claws and the bull with its horns, the hare relies upon the swiftness of its legs, the mouse hides in a hole, and the cuttlefish—it secretes a dark fluid and escapes from its enemy into the murk. Our anti-Darwinists are fond of imitating the tactics of the cuttlefish, with the only difference that the latter is of course glad if it can only get away from its enemy, but our Morganists hurl abuse at their opponents from their murky cloud. (p. 600.)

And here is a celebration of victory.

> Comrades, we may record with pleasure that our Soviet biologists, armed with the Michurin doctrine, have already demonstrated the fallaciousness of Morganism up to the hilt. Nobody will be led astray by the Morganists' false analogies between the invisible gene and the invisible atom. Far closer would be an analogy between the invisible gene and the invisible spirit. They want a discussion. But we shall not discuss with the Morganists! (Applause) We shall continue to expose them as adherents of an essentially false scientific trend, a pernicious and ideologically alien trend, brought to our country from foreign shores. (Applause)
>
> The future in biology belongs to Michurin, and only to Michurin. And with this, permit me to conclude. (Applause) (pp. 602–603.)

The climax of the "conference" was Lysenko's announcement in the final session:

> The question is asked in one of the notes handed to me. What is the attitude of the Central Committee of the Party to my report? I answer: The Central Committee of the Party examined my report and approved it. (Stormy applause. Ovation. All rise.) (p. 605.)

From Ideals to Cults

We can see a parallel between the transformation of the ideal of individual freedom into a cult of property and the transformation of the ideal of collective freedom into a cult of struggle. Whatever became clear in retrospect about the economic roots of individualism, there is no reason to doubt that the Founding Fathers of the United States actually believed that in establishing the American republic they were ushering in the Age of Freedom. It so happened that the most immediate and concrete opportunities that were opened up by the newly won freedom were those for getting rich. The Freedom of self-realization, coupled with favorable circumstances, overshadowed the freedom of nurturing values nobler than pursuit of gain. Besides, in a society where riches became a measure of worth, enrichment brought power, and it is the powerful that exert the strongest influence on the ideology that is to become dominant.

The ideal of collective freedom that energized the European revolutionary movements seemed to be realized in struggle. For it is organized struggle that welds collectives. The obverse side of fury against the enemy is loyalty to one's own. From its inception to the German invasion of 1941, the Soviet power elite, in spite of its gross incompetence in developing the nation's economy to provide at least a modicum of prosperity for the population, held on to power by pretending that the "class struggle" was still going on and that the fate of the country depended on its outcome. There was no real "struggle," of course. The "class enemy" had been either expropriated or forced to emigrate in the first years after the revolution. During the civil war of 1918–1921, some resistance was offered by the remnants of Czarist armies. After that there was no way of organizing any serious challenge to the regime. The fiction of the "class struggle" continued to be nurtured *in order* to prevent any such challenge.

Overnight the German invasion turned the fiction into stark reality. An enemy materialized. And what an enemy! Perfidious, ruthless, vicious, genocidal; everything one would wish in an enemy. The cult of struggle now stood in good stead. The people rallied. At the cost of enormous and heroic sacrifices, the enemy was beaten back. But there was no respite. The fiction of the struggle was kept alive, whipped up by the leaders, who thought, consciously, that in the atmosphere of perpetual struggle lay the security of the regime. Above all, the armed forces (which indisputably had saved the country from Nazi conquest) acquired an aura of sanctity. It is probably true that reverence for the armed forces as the defenders of the country would persist in the population of the Soviet Union even if loyalty to the regime became eroded by apathy and cynicism.

The following is an account of an emigré from the Soviet Union of how the memory of the "defense of the motherland" is kept alive.

During the few months preceding May 9 of this year [1985], deafening shooting and explosions were heard from our TV screens. We were preparing to celebrate the fortieth anniversary of the end of World War II.

Some years ago on a warm summer evening, I heard a sickening cry through my open window. 'Waaa . . . aar!' Before I realized that these were just children playing, I was bathed in cold sweat. . . .

Recently on the eve of the fortieth anniversary of victory, we were shown an altogether unusual programme: "Children in the War." . . . For two hours we glorified "the youngest participants in the war" . . . 15-year-olds, 12-year-olds, even 10-year-olds. . . . I was reminded of Nazi newsreels showing Hitler inspecting adolescents with which the Thousand-Year Reich was trying to stop breaches of the front.

Here is a weekly series, "I Serve the Soviet Union." Again deafening explosions, infantry shouting "Hurrah!" No, thank God, this is not war. It is only an imitation. Maneuvers "in conditions approximating battle" . . . The narrator is heard saying, "The heirs of victorious soldiers learn to be victorious." (Deutsch 1985.)

The cult of struggle in the Soviet Union, like the cult of property in the U.S., is an ideological analogue of a "hang-up" in a person. It is these hang-ups, rather than commitments to ideologies like "Free Enterprise" or "Socialism," that block the way to a rapprochement between the superpowers and the liquidation of the Cold War. We will return to this theme in Chapter 11.

Notes

1. Boolean algebra is a mathematical system in which 0 and 1 are the only elements. The operation of addition is defined by the rules $0 + 0 = 1 + 1 = 0$; $0 + 1 = 1 + 0 = 1$. The rules of multiplication are $0 \times 0 = 0 \times 1 = 1 \times 0 = 0; 1 \times 1 = 1$.
2. The result of the experiment would have been more enlightening if the Soviet respondents were recruited from residents of the Soviet Union. At the time the study was made, however, the use of Soviet subjects for this purpose would have been out of the question.
3. In the course of radical reevaluations associated with *perestroika*, Pavlik Morozov was officially repudiated in April 1988.
4. To what extent actions like Pavlik Morozov's would be approved by ordinary Soviet citizens before *perestroika* is an open question. It is interesting to note, however, that in the U.S. a controversy arose over similar though milder denunciations. Cases were reported of children informing the police that their parents were drug users. Both strong approval and strong disapproval of these actions were publicly expressed.
5. Although in Marx's formulation of the sociology of knowledge the term "ideology" is reserved for a distorted world view, the Soviets in the heat of polemic "on the ideological front" inadvertently imply that their completely enlightened Marxist-Leninist view of the world is also an "ideology."

9

Addiction to Power

Addiction is a term given to a medical problem manifested in extreme dependence on some substance inhaled, ingested, or injected into the bloodstream. Tobacco, alcohol, and several narcotics are common examples of addictive substances. If taken repeatedly, these substances produce changes in the chemical balance of the body causing great distress that can be relieved only by continuing intake. Characteristic of addiction is the increase of dosage required to relieve the distress. It is this progressively intensified dependence that produces the well-known social problems of addiction superimposed on the medical problem.

In a more general sense, any need that becomes progressively more insatiable may be called an addiction. In this way, addictive needs can be distinguished from nonaddictive ones.

The needs that human beings share with other animals are nonaddictive. This is not surprising, since a need that became addictive would in all likelihood have been selected against in the process of evolution. These nonaddictive needs include hunger, thirst, sleep, and sex. Typically, each of them, once satisfied, remains dormant for some time. Thus, a cycle is established in which the need undergoes periodic fluctuations. A gradual rise in intensity gives way to an abrupt fall following satiation which, in turn, is followed by a gradual rise, and so forth.

In addition to these periodic nonaddictive needs, human beings may also have addictive ones. (Other animals are not known to have addictive needs except when these are deliberately induced in them by human beings.)

Not all addictive needs are regarded as harmful in the sense of impairing health or causing severe social problems. Indeed, great artists and scientists can be regarded as being "addicts" of sorts. A creative artist may become more and more sensitized to certain aesthetic values. That is, his "taste" becomes progressively more refined. In a way, this change in sensitivity resembles an addiction if, as a result, the artist makes ever greater demands on himself. Difficulties in meeting these demands may be a source of considerable anguish. Nevertheless, an "addiction" of this sort seldom destroys the "addict," and the anguish may be actually a source of satisfaction. (The distinction between ecstasy and suffering is sometimes blurred.) The same can be said of the wholly dedicated scientist in pursuit of esoteric knowledge, ever elusive, since solutions of truly significant scientific problems often spawn more problems, sometimes of steadily increasing difficulty, while accumulation of esoteric knowledge only whets the appetite.

There is, however, one form of psychologically insatiable appetite that is almost always destructive. This is the lust for power. This lust is marked by the most essential feature of addiction. More power increases the need for more power. This is a result principally of the social results attendant on the acquisition of power.

Addictive Features of Power

There are two kinds of goods or commodities: conservative and nonconservative. A conservative commodity is one whose total available amount remains constant in the same way that the total amount of matter in a given region without sources or sinks remains constant. (The term "conservative" derives from "conservation of matter.") If some amount of a conservative commodity passes from A to B, A will have less of it and B correspondingly more. This is not necessarily true of nonconservative goods. A prime example is information. If A gives a piece of information to B, B is that much richer in information, but A has not thereby become poorer. He has not lost the information that he gave to B.

Goods can also be distinguished by their abundance. Some are so plentiful that even though they are in principle conservative, their allocation is not subject to the usual economic considerations. Air, being matter, is a conservative good, but we are not yet in a situation where air must be rationed or sold.

It stands to reason that competition is likely to be most intense for commodities that are both conservative and scarce. Power is a prime example of such a "commodity." It is impossible to increase A's power over

B without at the same time reducing B's power over A, at least in the same dimension. Nor can power be regarded as an abundant commodity, because by its nature power must be measured always relative to others' power. It makes no sense to speak of the "total" amount of power in a society (at least when we speak of power that some persons have over others). It makes sense to speak only of the relative shares of power possessed by individuals or groups. Competition for power is a prime example of a *zero-sum game* (cf. below).

The addictive aspect of power derives from the circumstance that the more of it acquired, the more intense the need for it becomes. This is because persons who rise to high positions of great power usually make enemies. Aware of this problem, Machiavelli, in his treatise on power (1532/1950), advises the prince who has just taken possession of a province and is unable to take up residence there to make sure that all those who may challenge his power are destroyed. This, however, is usually easier said than done. In eliminating enemies, the prince is likely to make more enemies. He will need more power to protect the power he already has. This cycle is quite analogous to that set up in the development of drug addiction. As larger doses of the drug are needed to satisfy the craving, the craving becomes stronger.

History abounds in examples of power addiction among potentates, and much literature exploits the theme of the destructive effects of this addiction. Here we are interested primarily in its social dynamics. What sort of social and political milieus are most conducive to emergence of intense power struggles as the most essential process of political life? And what are the consequences of these struggles?

It stands to reason that struggles for power will be most intense in societies where the perceived "rewards" of power are greatest. But what are these "rewards"? Obviously one thinks of them as opportunities provided to the possessors of power to compel others to do their bidding. But this is not all. In fact, the *instrumental* value of power loses importance as power accumulates, for then the *intrinsic* value of power becomes dominant. Just as very rich people value money primarily for its money-making potential, so power is valued because it is necessary to have power in order to gain more. This aspect of power was masterfully expressed in Orwell's novel *1984*.

The scene is a torture chamber. The victim is Winston Smith, who dares to defy the totalitarian state by harboring independent thoughts. The torturer is O'Brien, a high Party functionary, who enticed Smith into a trap by posing as a sympathizer.

"Power," O'Brien explains to Smith, "is not a means; it is the end. One does not establish a dictatorship in order to safeguard a revolution; one makes the revolution in order to establish the dictatorship. The object of persecution is persecution. The object of torture is torture. The object of power is power."

Power Over People

What gives people power over other people? Clausewitz says in the opening sentences of *On War*, "War is an act of violence by means of which we force the adversary to do our will." How is this done? Clausewitz says that the aim of war is accomplished when the adversary's army is destroyed, for then the adversary is "helpless" to resist our will. We know that this is frequently the case. A victor often "dictates the peace terms" to the vanquished. This presumably means that the government of the defeated country (if it still exists) issues edicts or decrees or makes laws as prescribed by the victor; or else the victor takes over the government and issues the orders. But then what happens? To mean anything, orders have to be obeyed. Why do people obey orders or laws? The commonsense answer is that people obey in order to avoid the penalties imposed for disobeying. Most people accept this answer. But it stands to reason that if *everyone* disobeyed, no authority, however powerful, could punish *everyone*. Why then does not everyone refuse to obey?

Of course, the crux of the matter is that it is not necessary to punish everyone for everyone to obey. Setting a few examples usually suffices. However, why a whole population can be intimidated by a "few examples" still remains to be explained.

Consider the following situation, admittedly an extreme one, but one which is known to have occurred on several occasions. A group of some hundreds of victims are being marched to execution accompanied by a few armed guards. What will happen at the end of the march is known to all. In any case, there is no doubt about it when, having arrived, they are told to dig a trench. If the hundreds of victims fell upon the guards, a few would surely be killed, but only a few, since the guards could not shoot more than a few before they were overpowered. Thus, most of the victims could escape. To be sure, their chance of survival would be small, but would still be greater than zero, which it remains if they do not resist. But the victims do not fall upon the guards. In order to succeed, the attack must be coordinated. And it is precisely this that they are not able to do. Not one can be sure that everyone will jump the guards. Everyone knows that if he is the only one or only one of a few that try it, he will surely be killed. Logically it makes sense to take the chance (since otherwise death is certain), but it takes an *act of will* to act "logically." Few can rule over many as long as too few of the many can mobilize a will to resist.

We know that at times such will is mobilized and people are able to resist tyranny. However, a necessary condition for such mobilization is the inculcation of a feeling in individuals that the will they are mobilizing is a *collective* will. Among animals, such collective will is sometimes ignited as when a large number of prey animals mob a predator.[1] Doubtless this ability to act collectively spontaneously is a product of natural selection, established over many thousands of generations. As we have seen, the instinct repertoire of human beings, if it exists at all, is not large. Evidently the social situation in which successive generations of human beings find themselves changes too rapidly for the evolution of genuine social instincts to take place.

Actions guided by a "collective will" can be incorporated into human behavior through learning, but such learning involves communication and organization. In our example, the victims could mob the guards if they had previously organized themselves and agreed upon a signal that would trigger the attack. Under these conditions, everyone (or most) might have accepted the risk of dying immediately (actually shortening life by just a few minutes) in order to increase everyone's chance of surviving from zero to some small but positive quantity. All this requires a certain state of mind. And this is precisely the state of mind that the victims have *not* acquired. In fact, whenever rule depends on terror, the main problem faced by the ruler is to keep the ruled in a state of mind that makes it seem impossible to resist the ruler's power.

In the past, when subjugation of lower social strata was frank and often brutal, the rulers exercised their power by monopolizing weapons. The words "cavalry," "cavalier," and "chivalry" are all etymologically related to "horse" (*cheval*), reminding us that in feudal Europe knights rode horses to battle while the peasants fought on foot. In Russian the word for "pawn" (in chess) is derived from "pedestrian"; in German, the word for "pawn" is *bauer* (peasant). In feudal Japan, the Samurai had a monopoly on swords, the weapon that became a fetish of that caste.

In modern times populations are kept in line by open and protracted terror only in totalitarian states and to some extent in states that have emerged from the colonial system, in many of which the monopoly of weapons passed from the erstwhile colonial authorities to national armies. The army officers, usually trained by the colonial authorities, did not hesitate to take advantage of the power bestowed by this monopoly.

Democratic regimes of industrially advanced countries rely on internalized habits of law-abiding behavior developed in societies where life is comparatively comfortable for majorities. Even totalitarian regimes, however, cannot rely on continued terror to preserve their power. To a large extent, stability is ensured by the same sort of "legitimacy" that is accorded regimes of liberal democracies. This legitimacy, however, is reinforced by modern methods of controlling large populations.

Fixation on Orthodoxy

In the Soviet Union political control was exercised until recently by a virtual monopoly of both education and communication, not only of the media (press, radio, television, educational institutions) but also of content. The goal of this control was undoubtedly that of guarding the orthodoxy of officially approved ideology. In fact, this goal was often explicitly stated. It is instructive to see how this fixation came about.

The Russian monarchy collapsed as a result of defeat in World War I. The collapse followed a pattern established in Europe. The empire of Napoleon III collapsed following the defeat of France by Prussia in 1871; the German, Austrian, and Turkish empires, like the Russian, fell after their defeats in World War I.

In March 1917, Czar Nicholas II of Russia was completely isolated. Everyone in Russia welcomed his abdication—nobility no less than common folk. In spite of the humiliating defeats and the hardships of the war, a burst of public optimism greeted the formation of a provisional government and the announcement that a constitutional assembly would be convened to decide on the form of government for Russia. For eight heady months, Russians reveled in "freedom." Meetings were held everywhere. In speeches, articles, and slogans, people expressed their hopes, their commitments, their convictions. Brass bands blared out the once-forbidden "Marseillaise." And, of course, innumerable political parties, groupings, factions, unions, societies, and every variety of grass roots organization sprouted.

But the war went on. Millions were at the front away from their families and from their normal occupations, which for the vast majority was tilling the soil. The war was a key issue on which the views were sharply divided. Perhaps "divided views" is not quite the right phrase. One thinks of "division" of views on an issue in terms of pros and cons, manifesting a certain symmetry of commitments, convictions, or values. This was not the case with the war issue in Russia in 1917. For the peasants the war was not a historical event or the outcome of a policy or a commitment of a nation, the way it might appear to people who read newspapers. For the illiterate Russian masses, the war was nothing but a disastrous disruption of their lives. Only habits of obedience to the "authorities" (who for centuries had imposed their rule by wielding whips) kept the peasants in the trenches. When the "authorities" suddenly collapsed, there was nothing to keep the masses obedient. Not infrequently, soldiers lynched their officers before going home. Often they took their weapons with them. (Memories of peasant revolts were still alive.) The peasants "voted with their feet," as Lenin wryly remarked, revealing his contempt for formal parliamentarian democracy, which, to his way of thinking, was the bourgeoisie's instrument of class rule.

The public debate on the war issue was confined to the intelligentsia. In Russia, this term comprised professionals, students, all the sectors of the public sufficiently literate to think in political terms and sufficiently interested in ideas to debate "issues." Since the intelligentsia was divided on the war issue, if anything more inclined toward the continuation of the war "to a victorious end" (a slogan of the time), it was possible to get the impression that the whole population was divided. This, however, could not be said of the masses—only of the "public," i.e., the articulate sector of the population. For the vast majority, there was only a heaven-sent opportunity to return to normal life. The Bolsheviks understood this. Their success in seizing power in the fall of 1917 can be attributed to their ability to grasp an unprecedented opportunity.

The front collapsed. The soldiers, many of them armed, went back to their villages and ousted the landlords. The workers seized factories. "Revolutionary committees," composed of determined armed men, assumed dictatorial power in urban centers. The slogan of the Bolsheviks during the political free-for-all had been "All power to the Soviets." These were councils, similar to those formed in the aborted revolution of 1905. At that time, the Soviets were Councils of Workers' and Peasants' Deputies. In 1917, they became Councils of Workers', Peasants', and Soldiers' Deputies. After the overthrow of the Provisional Government these councils came to be dominated by the Bolsheviks. Soon afterward, all rival parties and factions were expelled from them. Virtually the entire power of the state was concentrated in the Bolshevik Party, now renamed the Communist Party.

The undisputed leader of the Bolsheviks was V.I. Lenin. Our purpose in quoting at length from Lenin's writing in the philosophy of science (cf. Chapter 8) was to convey something of the man's fanaticism. Few authors have been so completely committed to the paradigm of struggle. In this Lenin resembled Clausewitz. Just as the latter regarded moderation in war as an absurdity, so Lenin directed his most bitter diatribes against those who attempted to reconcile Marxist philosophy with trends of thought stimulated by developments in physical science, of which Marx could not have had the slightest conception. To Lenin, these attempts appeared blasphemous.

> From this Marxist philosophy, which is cast from a single piece of steel,
> you cannot eliminate one basic premise, one essential part without departing
> from objective truth, without falling prey to bourgeois-reactionary falsehood.
> (Lenin 1909/1964, p. 306.)

He hurled what amounted to accusations of agnosticism at his colleagues
and warned them that their doubts were sown in their minds by their
enemies—the bourgeoisie—whose avowed goal was to corrupt the true
faith and thus deprive the proletariat of its ideological weapon. In singling
out one of those "agnostics" for ridicule, he commented thus on the latter's
plaintive cry: "Perhaps we have gone astray, but we are seeking."

> The trouble is that it is not *you* who are seeking, but *you who are sought.*
> You do not go with your Marxist (for you want to be Marxists) standpoint to
> every change in the bourgeois philosophical fashions; the fashions come to
> you, foisting on you their new falsifications, adapted to the idealist tastes.
> . . . (p. 323.)

Just as for Clausewitz only complete annihilation of the adversary and
obtaining of absolute power over him was a worthy outcome of a war, so
for Lenin only the complete demolition of an opponent's position on any
question whatsoever was a satisfactory outcome of a polemic. Of course
he did not seek the physical annihilation of all who did not agree with him
or who seemed to stray from the true path. The mass extermination of
dissidents was to come later, under Stalin. When the ideological struggle
became bloody, the polemic did not need to be applied in the tortuous
way Lenin applied it in his fights against heretics. Still, a foretaste of what
was to come is discernible in the following ominous passage of Lenin's:

> . . . not a single Marxist could be found in whose eyes such statements referring
> to specific heresies would *not* place Anatole Lunacharsky *exactly* in the same
> category as Peter Struve.[2] If this is not the case (and this is not *yet* the case),
> it is exclusively because we are fighting *while there is still ground* for a fight
> along comradely lines. (p. 325.)

The emphasis on *yet* tells the story. Lenin never tired of warning his
colleagues of the traps set for unsuspecting Marxists by bourgeois ideologues. "A single claw is enmeshed," he wrote, "and the bird is lost." If
the "seekers" continued in their apostasy, they would have to abandon
willy-nilly the "materialist" camp and join the camp of "idealist bourgeois
reaction." Later the same "inexorable logic" would send practically all of
Lenin's erstwhile comrades-in-arms to their deaths. The road to treason is
through some initially seemingly trivial errors. Since "you cannot remove
a single . . . part without . . . falling prey to bourgeois-reactionary false-

hood," it follows that those errors, like cracks in a dam, will inevitably grow into major breaches in one's ideological armor and finally to desertion to the enemy camp. There is no middle ground.

In the browbeating of his colleagues, Lenin gave clear indications of power addiction. However, it is difficult to imagine that he could have used Stalin's methods of eliminating opponents, imagined opponents, or rivals by resurrecting the methods of Ivan the Terrible. Lenin was immensely proud of his intellectual prowess. He sincerely believed that he knew "objective truth," that the doubters should and could be brought into the fold by persuasion. He probably thought that his chains of argument were as unassailable as proofs of mathematical theorems. His intellectual charisma was in fact enormous. He did convince his colleagues of the errors of their ways and welcomed them back to the ranks of the saved when they struck their colors. (For example, Lunacharsky, mentioned above, became Commissar of Culture in Lenin's government.) There was hardly a Bolshevik who at some time or other was not taken to task by Lenin for ideological lapses, but all of them played prominent parts in the established power elite until the advent of Stalin, who made short work of them. In all likelihood, Lenin would have been horrified, as Trotsky was, at Stalin's blood purges had he lived to see them.

Lenin was addicted to intellectual power. This was the power he wielded to bring his fellow revolutionaries into line. Stalin, who before the revolution was practically unknown in intellectual revolutionary circles, was addicted to ordinary brute power, the power of a despot, wielded through organized terror.

Stalin ruled the Soviet Union as a complete autocrat for a quarter of a century. To him—perhaps more than to any other tyrant—O'Brien's dictum, "The object of power is power," applies. Of course, the idea is not new. It pervades Machiavelli's treatise on the use of power, where the prince is advised to take advantage of every human weakness, to exploit gullibility, sycophancy, and vanity, all with the single aim—consolidation of power. What is to be done with power does not fall within the scope of the treatise (Machiavelli 1532/1950).

Stalin may or may not have read Machiavelli. But he did not have to read him, since the techniques of seizing and holding power come naturally to the power addict. Actually, the statement is a tautology, since power addiction is a consequence of virtuosity in the acquisition and retention of power. It is those to whom the tricks come naturally who become addicts.

Physical elimination of all potential rivals was, of course, the most distinguishing feature of Stalin's reign. But the purges extended far beyond the circle of potential rivals. Stalin believed in terror for terror's sake, not necessarily because he was a sadist (although he may have been) but because he was convinced that terror is an impressive credential of power. For power to be effective, people have got to believe that you have power, and terror is a sure way of demonstrating this.

The tyrant most admired by Stalin was Ivan the Terrible. In a conversation with Nikolai Cherkassov, who was to portray the czar in a film, Stalin revealed something about himself when he mentioned two traits that he regarded as flaws in Ivan's character. One was Ivan's periodic bouts with his conscience, when, following orgies of tortures and executions, he would retreat to a monastery and wallow in remorse. The other weakness was Ivan's failure to "finish the job," i.e., to destroy completely the Russian nobility (the boyars), who, in Stalin's opinion, stood in the way of "progress." "Progress," of course, was identified with making Russia a great power. The obvious allusion in Stalin's remarks was that his own character was unimpeded by Ivan's shortcomings. (Apparently, the elite of the Communist Party appeared to Stalin as the modern counterpart of the boyardom. At any rate, he set out to do the job on them that Ivan failed to do on the Russian nobility.)

As it happened, Stalin's initials were the same as Ivan's. The czar was called, as was traditional in old Russia, by his first name and patronymic, Ivan Vassilievich. Stalin's name and patronymic was Iosif Vissarionovich. It is said that he signed his secret orders of liquidation "I.V." and on occasions even used the full pseudonym, "Ivan Vassilievich."

While a direct line of causality from Lenin's intellectual autocracy to Stalin's despotism cannot be convincingly drawn, the fact remains that rejection of compromise, resort to overwhelming force, demand of iron discipline, and intolerance of dissent became the hallmarks of the Soviet regime. There is therefore some substance in Lefebvre's characterization of Soviet culture as being based on what he calls "The Second Ethical System" (cf. Chapter 8). However, we retain our reservations about the theoretical underpinnings of Lefebvre's hypothesis.

Disavowal of Rationality

Nazi totalitarianism arose almost simultaneously with the Soviet variety. While the parallels between the two are conspicuous, the differences are equally important. The sociological origins of the Nazi and the Communist movements were quite different. The difference is reflected in the ideologies, which, in spite of important common features, stem from strongly contrasting outlooks. The roots of Communism are distinctly intellectual. Marx, who is naturally regarded as the most articulate exponent of Communist thought, was a serious scholar, immersed in the world of sophisticated philosophical ideas of his time. He was as much at home with English and French social philosophers as with Germans. He was, of course, obsessed by a fixed idea (as many great thinkers have been), believing that he had discovered "laws of social development" as fundamental for understanding history, psychology, and social structure as knowledge of the laws of mechanics are essential for understanding the motions of bodies subjected to forces.

In using an abrasive and acerbic style of argumentation, Marx was not alone. It was common enough in his time. Lenin continued the tradition. It so happened that the imperatives of power "froze" the intellectual content of Communist ideology in sterile clichés, stopping all further development. From then on, if argumentation was used in "exposing" enemies of the regime, that is to say, in verbal struggles for power, it was reduced to ritual. It was meant to elicit signal reactions, not to convince anyone of anything except to show on whose side there was power. It was the powerful side's exclusive prerogative to attach labels to people to be destroyed. The labels doomed them.

Although the arguments were reduced to invocations and anathemas, they were *used*. In a way, tribute was paid to the intellectual origins of Communism by using, at least in public, verbiage that had the appearance of an intellectual argument. Communist thought stemmed from the "progressive" heritage of Western Europe. Many of its ideas originated in the French Enlightenment and were inspired by the rise of democratic institutions, by the triumphal march of natural science and its challenge of dogmatic religion, finally by the appearance of "genuinely scientific" social philosophy presaging the final emancipation of *humanity* (not just of a class or a nation) from bondage imposed by necessity. "Scientific socialism" prophesied the age of genuine freedom. This was the language of hope. For a long time, this hope helped relieve the misgivings that "people of good will" had about the deeply disturbing features of the Soviet regime.

National Socialism had no humanistic roots. From the start, its propaganda was soaked in hatred, primarily, of course, directed against the Jews but also against everything else that was cherished by the "people of good will": ideals of liberty, equality, and fraternity, peaceful resolution of conflicts, full use of reason in arriving at truths, tolerance—in short, all values and sentiments that have come to be called "civilized."

The Nazis despised both the idea of human brotherhood and the idea of individual autonomy. They extolled tribalism both in the sense of exclusiveness and in the sense of submerging individual freedom. They deliberately fostered cruelty in young males. They told the young "to think with their blood" and "to spit on freedom."

Disavowal of Law—the Triumph of Power

One of the most conspicuous features of Nazi totalitarianism was the deliberate disavowal of law as a guide in social life. Hannah Arendt (1958) points out that when the Nazis came to power, they did not annul the Weimar constitution. One would have thought that this would have been their first act. The Weimar Republic came to stand in the eyes of the Nazis for corruption of Germany by the Jews, Communists, and traitors. It contained the trappings of Western democracies, which the Nazis despised. There is no need to belabor the point, because "Weimar" was one of the most frequently used hate-words in the Nazi vocabulary. Yet they did not use the occasion of their political victory in 1933 to proclaim the end of the "shameful" Weimar era by rescinding its symbol, the Weimar constitution. Why?

According to Arendt, a principal objective of totalitarian rule is the denial of the very idea of "law." To abrogate the old constitution and to proclaim another in its stead, no matter how authoritarian, would still imply that the Nazis needed some sort of legitimization. And this is what despotic rule eschews. Despotic power must reside in the *person* of the ruler, who is supposed to embody the *will* of the nation (or race). It is this will, not something formulated in coherent language and written on paper, which demands obedience and loyalty.

Arendt goes on to point out that it is a mistake to regard the totalitarian state as a monolithic bureaucracy, where everyone knows who is below and who above, who can be bullied and before whom one must cringe. On the contrary, the lines of authority in a totalitarian state (except for the supreme and unlimited authority of the Leader) are often vaguely drawn. Uncertainty breeds insecurity, and insecurity—the sort of chronic apprehension that one *may* have done something wrong—is just what the totalitarian state deliberately induces in everybody. Terror may be dormant, but it is always there. In Germany, evidence of this stratagem was provided by the fact that when the Nazis came to power, they did not fire the old bureaucracy. For the most part, the officials remained at their posts. But *another* system of administration was introduced parallel to the bureaucracy, the party apparatus, creating a system of dual control, in which it was never entirely clear whom one had to obey when a crunch came.

Arendt ascribes this feature of totalitarian rule also to the Soviet regime. Power resides both in government and in the Party organs. The function of this dual control, according to Arendt, is the same as it was in Nazi Germany—to avoid *formal* legitimization of authority.

With regard to the constitution, it seems at first thought that the parallel breaks down. In 1936 Stalin actually "granted" a constitution to the Soviet people. It was supposed to reflect the "victory of socialism" in the Soviet Union. Presumably, the last spasms of the class struggle in the Soviet Union occurred in the early 1930s when the kulaks resisted collectivization of agriculture. "Liquidation of kulaks as a class" signaled the conclusion of the last class battle. With the disappearance of the "class enemy," the many regrettable, albeit allegedly necessary, repressive features of the "dictatorship of the proletariat" could be dispensed with. Accordingly, the constitution of 1936, proclaimed as the most democratic in the world, guaranteed all sorts of civil and human rights, including freedom of speech, press, and assembly, the right to a fair trial, inviolability of personal property, and many other provisions of a similar nature.

The constitution was solemnly and unanimously adopted on the very eve of the great bloody purge of 1937–1938, in which practically all the erstwhile leaders of the Communist Party were accused of treason, espionage, sabotage, and conspiracies to perpetrate terrorist acts. Among those liquidated were all who worked on the drafts of the constitution, except one.

One is tempted to conjecture that in "granting a constitution," Stalin pursued the same goal as did the Nazis when they did not bother to rescind the Weimar constitution, that is, to demonstrate that totalitarian rule is not subject to law, even to law established by the regime itself. There is a telling scene in Arthur Koestler's novel, *Darkness at Noon*. Rubashov, a high Party functionary, caught in the dragnet of Stalinist terror, is being interrogated. He wants to know why he has not been subjected to "direct physical pressure."

> "You mean physical torture," said Gletkin [the interrogator] in a matter-of-fact tone. "As you know, that is forbidden by our criminal code."
> "Besides," Gletkin continued, "there is a certain type of accused who confess under pressure, but recant at the public trial. You belong to the tenacious kind. The political utility of your confession at the trial will lie in its voluntary character."

Having pointed out that torture is prohibited in the Soviet Union, the interrogator in the next remark blandly explains to his victim why he was not tortured, as if to emphasize the meaninglessness of law.

Disavowal of Responsibility

Related to the disavowal of law is disavowal of responsibility, which in regimes based on law is associated with authority. A principle established in the Nuremberg trials was that disavowal of responsibility for atrocities ordered by superiors was not a valid defense. But of course fixing the responsibility for the atrocities on those who actually carried them out (whether they followed orders or not) did not absolve the superiors who ordered the atrocities. Note that the Nuremberg principle applies only to atrocities. Normally, where authority is linked with responsibility, the superior, but not those who carry out his orders, is responsible for the results. If the results are "good," the superior gets the credit, if "bad," he gets the blame. The totalitarian system, however, absolves the *superior* from responsibility by making it unnecessary for him to give explicit orders to his underlings. The superior can simply hint at what he wants done. The underling is supposed to be attuned to the will of the superior, so that he is expected to know without being told what he is supposed to do.

A dramatic (though possibly unwitting) demonstration of this principle appeared in a Soviet film about the battle of Stalingrad, shown shortly after the end of World War II. The hero is a general in the besieged city who knows that a great counteroffensive (which in fact led to a devastating defeat of the Germans) is being prepared. But the details of this counteroffensive are so secret that not even this general, whose division is to play an important part in the operations, can be informed of them. He is supposed to *guess* how to deploy his troops. He knows (and says so) that if he guesses wrong, he will be shot. But of course he guesses right. He is attuned to the will of the Supreme Leader. So much is clear from the message of the film. Arendt, however, would add that there is more to keeping the general ignorant than prevention of information leakage. The lack of specific orders absolves the supreme dictator from any responsibility if anything should go wrong.

The Illusion of Omnipotence

The strongest compulsion to which power addicts have fallen victim is that of proving to self and to others that their power knows no bounds. Orwell captured this compulsion in the following passage from *1984*:

> Smith: But how can you control matter? You don't even control the climate and the law of gravity.
> O'Brien: We control matter because we control the mind. Reality is inside the skull. There is nothing that we could not do. Invisibility, levitation, anything. I could float off this floor like a soap bubble if I wished to. I do not wish to, because the Party does not wish it. You must get rid of those nineteenth century ideas about the laws of nature. We make the laws of nature.

Smith: But you do not! You are not even masters of this planet. What about Eurasia and Eastasia the rival empires. . . . You have not conquered them yet.

O'Brien: Unimportant. . . . We can shut them out of existence. Oceania is the world.

Smith: But the world itself is only a speck of dust. And man is tiny—helpless! How long has he been in existence? For millions of years the earth was uninhabited.

O'Brien: Nonsense. The earth is as old as we are, no older. How could it be older? Nothing exists except through human consciousness.

Smith: But the rocks are full of the bones of extinct animals.

O'Brien: Have you ever seen those bones? Of course not. Nineteenth century biologists invented them. Before man there was nothing. After man, if he could come to an end, there would be nothing. Outside of man there is nothing.

Note the curious twist. Although Oceania is a transparent caricature of Stalinist Russia, O'Brien bases his arguments on the tenets of "idealism": nothing exists but the mind. Whoever controls the mind controls everything. Therein lies the secret of absolute power. And of course in practice the rulers of totalitarian states proceed in just this way, realizing consciously or not that their power resides in the control of the mass mind.

Dehumanization

The appetite for power stems from a desire to control one's environment. Inanimate things and animals are easier to control than human beings, partly because they are more predictable. It follows that control over human beings can be facilitated if people are made less than human. Military training is designed to do just that. Traditionally military training began with getting recruits to execute collective movements in unison in response to sharply barked commands: "Forward march!" "Company halt!" "About face!", etc. In the heyday of standing armies, when battle tactics were modeled after parade-ground maneuvers, this training may have had some value as preparation for fighting. It would seem, however, that when as a result of tactics developed in the French Revolutionary and Napoleonic Wars, the rigid battle maneuvers were abandoned, "close order drill" (as the training in moving in unison was called) should have been abandoned as a waste of time. The fact that it was and is retained reveals its fundamental function: to dehumanize the soldier, to instill in him the habit of instant, unconditional obedience.

Dehumanization is reflected in the words used to designate human beings reduced to instruments. In Russian military terminology, infantrymen used to be called "bayonets" (as in "a force of so many bayonets"), and cavalrymen "sabres." Nowadays, factory workers are called "employees," but traditionally they were called "hands."

The Nazis' brutal treatment of their victims also seemed to serve the purpose of dehumanization, but not with the view of utilizing the dehumanized in the same way (since many were marked for slaughter). Rather, the atrocities served as tests to see how far dehumanization could be carried. Hannah Arendt writes:

> The concentration and extermination camps of totalitarian regimes serve as the laboratories in which the fundamental belief of totalitarianism that everything is possible is being verified. . . .
>
> Total domination, which strives to organize the infinite plurality and differentiation of human beings as if all of humanity were just one individual is possible only if each and every person can be reduced to a never-changing identity of reactions, so that each of these bundles of reactions can be exchanged at random for any other. (Arendt 1958, pp. 437–438.)

Soviet totalitarian ideology never abandoned the rhetoric of European humanism. All the sacrifices demanded from the population, the repressions, the whole system of total control over all aspects of life, all the manifestations of despotism had to be either denied or rationalized as necessary, i.e., as forced upon the regime by the realities of the age. The vision of emancipated humanity living in peace and freedom in the future for the sake of which everything in the present had to be endured was kept intact.

In contrast, the rhetoric of the Nazis harmonized with their practice. Brutal power over people was practiced with sadistic zest. Extermination of human beings was planned and systematically carried out as the Nazis sought to perfect their methods of dehumanization. Their success is evidenced ironically in the attempts of some of the organizers of genocide to save their victims "needless suffering." Once dehumanization is complete, one can attend to the problem of "humane slaughter." The following excerpt is from a report of Untersturmbahnführer Dr. Becker (a physician?) dated May 16, 1942, on the gassing of Jews in vans in which they were transported:

> The gassing is not done properly. In order to complete the operation as quickly as possible, the gas is released all at once. In this way, the executed suffer death by asphyxiation instead of being put to sleep as intended. Following my instructions, in consequence of releasing the gas at the proper rate,

death sets in more quickly and the prisoners fall asleep peacefully. Distorted faces and excretions are no longer observed. (Rosenthal 1979, p. 31.)

Technolatry

The following are excerpts from an article that appeared in the Toronto *Globe and Mail*, December 24, 1985.

Despite thousands and thousands of dollars of research, SDI's "Star Wars" toy line was a complete bust. Advertised as "An exciting working-scale replica of the real Star Wars plan President Reagan wants for Christmas," the SDI toy was in fact a dud. Company spokesman Clarence Thunderbust, Jr. said, "We tossed the vision into children's heads, to see how it would dance sugar-plumwise. But the darn thing wouldn't work, the batteries died, all our scale drawings got sold to the Russians, and I cut my finger on it! . . ."

The problems with the SDI Star Wars toys were formidable: they required 3,492,205 size D batteries (not included), at $8,000 the toy was too expensive; and the catchy name, Peace Shield, was too sissy for today's kids.

The Star Wars toy worked by reflecting flashlights off mirrors in space (the ceiling). But the mirrors got dusty, broken or covered with fingerprints. The flashlight beams could be blocked by cigaret smoke, tin foil and even steam from the kettle. The add-on set of ABM missiles didn't work properly, either. The elastic-band-powered rockets went off too soon, or wouldn't hit the target or got confused by the radar image from the family cat.

The name of the company spokesman (Thunderbust) and the exact number of batteries required to run the toy (3,492,205) gave the piece away as a hoax. But until I noticed these cues, I took the article seriously. The grotesque hypertrophy of the war toy industry is in evidence everywhere, testifying to the particular mode of power addiction of Americans—technolatry, the worship of machines.

Mark Twain's Connecticut Yankee begins his fantastic narrative with these words: "I am an American. My father was a blacksmith. My uncle was a horse doctor. I can make anything. . . ."

Note that this champion of American know-how does not say, "I can *do* anything." This was to come later with Superman and his comic book variants. The Yankee says he can *make* anything, implying command of skills expressed in work, i.e., dominance over things, not over people. And it is this know-how that enables him—almost—to turn King Arthur's sixth-century world into a facsimile of nineteenth-century America. Almost, but not quite. He becomes "boss." But he does not bully people. He ignites a spark of freedom in them by giving them skills, and he believes that eventually these skills would emancipate the people from obscurantism, superstition, and dogma.

But he fails. In the end he has to fight the knights who symbolized the enslavement of the human spirit by fear and ignorance. And even though his small band of converts is armed with machine guns and succeeds destroying the flower of knighthood, they are overpowered and perish.

The denouement of *Connecticut Yankee* reflects on Mark Twain's profound pessimism about human nature. In many ways, this pessimism resembled Freud's. At the same time, Mark Twain, the artist, could depict with uncanny insight the ebullient optimism of still-young America, nurtured by unbounded faith in the omnipotence of technology. Here was the source of the power addiction of Americans.

Worship of despots, the mark of totalitarian regimes, is foreign to Americans. Their hero worship is largely confined to champions. Mostly in sports. To maintain their image as heroes, these must project a folksy modesty, must show themselves in other respects as "regular," i.e., average. Megalomania is not admired. Power worship expresses itself in technolatry. It is here that the danger that the American military establishment presents to the world is the greatest. Witness the following comments:

> On the battlefield of the future, enemy forces will be located and targeted almost instantaneously through the use of data banks, computer assisted intelligence evaluation, and automated fire control. With the first round kill probabilities approaching certainty, and with surveillance devices that can continuously track the enemy, the need for large forces to fix the opposition physically will be less important.
>
> Hundreds of years were required to achieve the mobility of the armored division. A little over two decades later we had the air-mobile division. With cooperative effort, no more than 10 years should separate us from the automated battlefield. (General W. Westmoreland, cited in Dickson 1971, p. 169.)

This projection into the future is surely a power dream but not a Machiavellian one. The dreaming general does not see himself as a potentate, who has outwitted and destroyed all his enemies in the manner of a Stalin or a Japanese shogun. He dreams not of personal power but of power conferred on the "good guys" by sophisticated technology. Power resides in technical virtuosity, not in virtuosity of intrigue or psychological perspicacity, as it had been pictured by Machiavelli.

The same mentality shines through Ronald Reagan's dream of omnipotence conferred by the new space technology. The film "Star Wars" was the obvious source of inspiration for the "Strategic Defense Initiative," as evidenced by the epithet "evil empire" applied to the Soviet Union. (The enemy was so named in the film.) Altogether, there is reason to believe that the American president of the 1980s spent many of his thinking hours in fantasy. One source of fantasy is the president's past as an actor in adventure films. We have seen how protracted contact with mass entertainment media sometimes induces confusion between what is depicted and reality. This may have happened to the president. He has been heard to relate incidents in a way that made it seem that he participated in them, whereas they were actually incidents depicted in films in which he acted. The other source of fantasy may be science fiction and the electronic version of comic books, video games. In any waiting room or other place where people with time on their hands congregate, one sees these video game machines. Youngsters and adults engage in combats with monstrous robots flitting across the screen, keeping score as they zap them with their laser guns. All this occurs against a background of a starry sky to show that war has been duly updated by being transported to outer space.

There is, of course, a connection between addiction to struggle and addiction to power. One proves oneself to be powerful (to oneself) by emerging victorious in struggle. It is, however, instructive to note the sharp difference in the mood in which violent struggle is presented in the Soviet Union and in the United States. In the Soviet Union, depicted combats are filled with pathos. Heroism, readiness to sacrifice one's life at every opportunity, and above all passionate, all-consuming patriotism mark every episode. Thus, combat is never free from tragic overtones. The exuberance of power is often played down. In America, in contrast, depicted combat sometimes resembles slapstick comedy. For instance, much of Saturday morning television is devoted to animated cartoons aimed at children. (Children are important targets of certain kinds of consumer advertising, e.g., breakfast foods, toys, etc. While having little or no disposable income themselves, children often promote the advertised products by persuading their parents into buying only those brands.) The content of the animated cartoons is pervaded with violence. The cartoon characters chase each other, flatten each other, throw each other off cliffs. But the victims recover instantaneously, and the chasing and the fun goes on and on. It is not likely that this make-believe frequently incites children to commit mayhem or murder as "serious" television violence sometimes does. But it is not unlikely that viewing "funny" violence may induce the idea that violence is fun.

Hegemony

Although the attitudes reflecting power addiction may be quite different in different cultural milieus, international power conflicts exhibit recurrent common features. D. Senghaas (1986) calls attention to the "hegemony cycle" in the international arena. Since navigation became global, different European states assumed successively a dominant position in the realm of world trade, access to resources, etc. Spain and Portugal held these positions, doubtless achieved through an earlier start in exploratory voyages. Then dominance passed to Holland, later to England as a result of her victories over France, her principal rival. Through the nineteenth century, England's hegemony was firmly established.

A new factor in the acquisition and retention of hegemony was introduced during the Industrial Revolution, namely, superior productive capacity and especially technological, organizational, and institutional innovation. Hegemony was usually backed by military power, e.g., the colonial system. However, as power conferred by superior economic potential became the basis of hegemony, the importance of military power decreased. After World War I, economic hegemony passed largely to the United States and at that time did not need to be maintained by far-flung conspicuous garrisons, as it had been in the colonial empires.

Senghaas describes cycles that have marked recent struggles for hegemony. The existing hegemonial power is challenged by a "younger" aspirant—more dynamic, bold, innovative. Eventually, often as a result of wars, hegemonial status passes to a challenger. In maturity, the hegemonial power enjoys a "golden age," when its prosperity and influence are at their peak. But eventually "aging" sets in. New challengers appear, more vigorous, with resources not yet fully mobilized, more innovative and imaginative. Another challenger takes over, and a new cycle begins.

The United States emerged as the most conspicuous victor of World War II, having suffered no exhaustion and no trauma remotely comparable to those of the other "victors." It assumed an unquestioned, dominant position in all aspects of world economy, a position that enabled it to prescribe the "rules of the game." Its cultural influence also became pervasive. Everywhere everyone seemed to aspire to the "American way of life."

The "golden age" did not last long. In consequence of the extremely rapid recovery of both Western Europe and Japan, the relative economic position of the United States declined. Senghaas presents the following telling figures. In 1950, the U.S. share in total world production was 34%, in industrial production 60%. By 1980, these shares fell respectively to 23% and 30%. Currency reserves during the same period fell from 50%

to 6%. In 1956, 42 of the world's largest concerns were American, in 1980, 23. These losses were mainly to America's allies. In addition, however, the hegemony of military power, which Americans believed they possessed through the monopoly of atomic weapons, was also challenged, namely, by the Soviet Union, which had been transformed from an ally to an "enemy."

The U.S.S.R. was not in a position to exercise hegemony in the economic sphere. The claim of successes of the world socialist system coupled with "insoluble contradictions in the capitalist camp" (cf. below) had no basis in reality. However, the Soviet Union did establish *political* hegemony in bordering countries, e.g., in Eastern Europe, Mongolia, and (in varying degrees) in some outlying countries, e.g., Cuba, Angola, Ethiopia, Vietnam, Afghanistan. Although the success of this expansion has been far from spectacular and has even been marked by some notable reverses, the United States from the beginning regarded it as a horrendous threat. This fear was not confined to the American power elite, but pervaded most of the population. What remained of American influence from the "golden age" of U.S. hegemony kept the same fear alive in Western Europe. Thus, the decades following World War II have been marked by what Senghaas calls a "hegemonial crisis."

The U.S. response to this crisis has been oscillating. Initially, bristling anger predominated, marked by threats of "massive retaliation" for infringements on the "free world" (i.e., on American hegemony). As the military might of the Soviet Union grew, and especially after the debacle of Vietnam (an attempt to stop "Communism," equated to Soviet expansion), a period of halfhearted attempts at accommodation, the so-called detente, followed. After disengagement in Southeast Asia, American military spending actually declined while social welfare spending increased significantly. During the Nixon, Ford, and especially Carter administrations, there was talk of new directions in world politics, a recognition of "emerging complexities," demanding a "constructive response." There is little evidence that these changes toward adjustment to global realities were stimulated by new insights. Rather, they were reactions to the ever more conspicuous decline of the U.S. as a world power, to the oil crisis, to the emergence of the Third World as a political force, in short to the trend toward "multipolarity" (instead of bipolarity) in world politics.

However, budgeting reorientation in favor of social welfare at the expense of the military establishment stimulated a reaction both in the defense community and in conservative business circles. What Goldwater could not achieve in 1964, Ronald Reagan and his backers were able to accomplish in 1980—an electoral victory of a reactionary coalition, intent on dismantling the "welfare state" and giving the military a blank check.

There was no longer any question of reestablishing a global economic hegemony. The American economy had lost its vitality, in no small measure because of the squandering of material and human resources to nurture the insatiable and nonproductive war machine. Thus, only one road remained open—to establish hegemony based on military power.

The theory of hegemonial conflict resembles the "realistic" approach to international relations in that a struggle for power is regarded as a principal force in global politics. The "realistic" theory of international relations de-emphasizes the role of ideology both in its descriptive and its normative aspects. So does the theory of hegemony. The irrelevance of ideology as a factor in local hegemonial conflict is also conspicuous. For instance, in Kampuchea, where a civil war has been going on since 1979, support for the coalition that includes the Khmer Rouge is given by both Thailand and China. This support is contrary to all expectations on ideological grounds, since Thailand is one of the most "anti-Communist" states in the region, and China has abandoned Communist orthodoxy, while the Khmer Rouge represents Communist fanaticism gone berserk. In comparison with the atrocities perpetrated by the Khmer Rouge on the population of Kampuchea when it was in power (1975–1979), the excesses of the Chinese "cultural revolution" (since disavowed by the Chinese regime) pale into insignificance. Thus, support for the Khmer Rouge by both China and Thailand (who are themselves ideological adversaries) can be explained only on one ground, namely, resistance to the establishment of hegemony by Vietnam on the Indo-Chinese peninsula. In addition, the Chinese see this hegemony as an extension of Soviet hegemony, which they have committed themselves to resist.

There is, however, an important difference between hegemonial conflict and the sort of power struggles envisaged by the "realist" school of international relations. Central to the realists' conception of a power struggle is the idea of a "balance of power." Political scientists of the "realist" persuasion, who, like H. Morgenthau (cf. below), reject the idea that war is an instrument of rational foreign policy, regard a "balance of power" as a desirable stable state of the international system. As Senghaas points out, however, attempts to establish or restore a balance of power have usually led to war. It was rather periods of hegemony that were relatively free of wars (Pax Romana, Pax Britannia). Moreover "balance of power," if it can be established at all, requires more than two contestants of comparable potential. For then, "counterweights" can be provided whenever balance is disturbed. Britain, espousing balance of power until World War I, played that role, now siding with Prussia against France, now with France against Germany. Thus, whatever equilibrium may have existed in the international system dominated by European states was a dynamic, not a static, equilibrium.

In a bipolar world, counterweights are not available. In fact, the "superpowers" are so named because the destructive potential of each exceeds by several orders of magnitude that of any combination of states that does not include its rival. A polarized struggle for hegemony excludes "balance of power," i.e., compromise, accommodation, division of "spheres of influence," indeed all the means of "settling" the power struggle short of giving up the creed that national security resides in the last analysis only in military power. According to the theory of hegemony, a bipolar power struggle, if pressed to its logical conclusion, must end in a Clausewitzian battle of annihilation like that between Rome and Carthage. It is for this reason that the present hegemonial crisis presents an unprecedented threat to humanity.

In a hegemonial crisis, encroachment by one side upon the hegemonial domain of the other is likely to be met with violence totally incommensurate with the importance of the encroachment. It is quite conceivable, for example, that substantial modifications of economic and political systems in states within the domain of Soviet hegemony would have presented no threat whatsoever to Soviet security. Nevertheless, the Soviet Union responded with violence to democratization attempts in Hungary in 1956 and in Czechoslovakia in 1968. It coerced Poland into crushing a democratization process in 1981. Similarly, the United States has engaged in a long series of covert and overtly violent operations whenever it has felt its hegemonial prerogatives threatened.

The increasing commitment of the United States to a militarily coercive global policy is particularly disturbing, because it has been accompanied by strident support in broad sectors of the population. The blatant glorification of violence is a forceful reminder of the public mood in Germany in the years preceding World War II. We have pointed out the possible background of the parallel, namely, deflation of the illusion of invincibility and the ready acceptance of simplistic explanations of the defeats: ("stab in the back," "loss of national will," and the like).

Comparisons of intensely disliked regimes to that of Nazi Germany have become meaningless by repetition. Indeed, such comparisons can be easily refuted by pointing to unique aspects of Nazi depravity. The methodical extermination of men, women, and children in human slaughterhouses elicits stronger repugnance in most people than the most brutal massacres perpetrated in fits of mob fury, by victorious armies, or in communal strife. It is, nevertheless, instructive to compare societies extolling violence, not with the view of assessing degrees of their depravity, but in order to examine parallel manifestations of power addiction. It seems that these manifestations transcend wide cultural and ideological differences.

Notes

1. Birds have been observed mobbing an owl that ventured abroad in the daytime. In an experiment birds were observed collectively attacking a stuffed cuckoo. Aside from interspecific wars, e.g., among ants, these are among the relatively rare instances of genuine interspecific aggression, as distinct from predation.
2. P.B. Struve, an erstwhile Marxist, shifted to the right on the political spectrum to found the "Cadet" party (the Party of Constitutional Democracy). In Lenin's eyes, Struve was a renegade. Putting Lunacharsky "in the same category as Peter Struve" was tantamount to calling him a traitor to the cause.

10

The Cult of Violence

So far we have pictured the paradigm of struggle in contexts where the goal of the struggle—at least in its concrete manifestations (as contrasted with metaphysical allegories)—remained clearly in focus. The goal was victory, and somehow victory brought with it a resolution of the conflict. The class struggle was pictured as culminating in the victory of the proletariat and with it the establishment of a just society without exploitation and without repression. Lenin, in attacking his colleagues who deviated from fundamentalist Marxism (as Lenin interpreted it) thought he was doing it for their own good. Victory meant forging the party of the proletariat into a disciplined fighting machine capable of overthrowing the bourgeois social order.

We now turn to the preoccupation and fascination with "struggle as an end in itself," as a way of life. Victory becomes incidental, much as winnings eventually become incidental to a gambling addict. We see here yet another instance of means transformed into ends.

The Professionals

The most conspicuous instances of dedication to struggle as a way of life are found where war became a major, at times the only, occupation of a group. Such a group can comprise a whole society. The North American Plains Indians were noted for their continual warmaking. We have men-

tioned Cossacks inhabiting the border regions of Muscovy; their chief occupation was fighting and raiding. In India, the Sikhs valued arms over
any other possessions, and were totally preoccupied with making war. Of
all the states of ancient Greece, Sparta was the most militarized. A young
Spartan's education was concentrated almost entirely on the acquisition of
martial skills and attitudes regarded as the marks of a good soldier. For
the Samurai of Japan, fighting was the most important occupation in life.

In all these instances, preoccupation with physical struggle, i.e., violence,
can be traced to a selective process. If a group occupied primarily with
war is open to volunteer recruits, its membership becomes self-selected.
Those who join are likely already to have inclinations to violence. The
Cossacks, urban gangs, the French Foreign Legion, and the Tonton Ma-
coute of Haiti can be cited as examples.

More common are situations where membership in the fighting profession is either hereditary or is conferred by authorities. In the Turkish
Empire, the Janissaries were a warrior caste, whose members were recruited by careful selection from Christian boys. The Japanese Samurai
were a privileged hereditary caste, completely separated from "common
people" whom they could kill at will.

Besides self-selection, characteristic of volunteer groups, and selection
by authorities in building a fighting force to keep them in power, a selective
process also goes on inside an individual who becomes a member of a
group trained in violence. In the last analysis, all learning is a selective
process. Consider the learning of a muscular skill, as in playing an instrument or skating. Initially, muscular movements involved in the activity are
made more or less at random. Some of these are more efficient than others
in producing desired effects. In the process of learning, the less efficient
movements are inhibited, the more efficient ones reinforced. All this happens without the learner being aware of how it happens. Our nervous
systems are constituted in a way that makes a selection process of this sort,
which is frequently unconscious, possible.

So much is known. A generalization to formation of attitudes is admittedly conjectural, but it is not unreasonable to assume that something like
a selection process takes place in the shaping of any strong commitment.
We do not hesitate to acknowledge the existence of independent minds.
Still, the degree of this independence is an open question. We know that
normally children are socialized, that is, are taught to adopt the mainstream
mode of cognition and attitudes of the culture in which they grow up. The
same can be said of special sectors of a culture, in particular, of occupations.
The individual normally identifies with others whom society designates as
a category. The modes of cognition and the values of that category are
internalized. We can suppose that initially the mode of thinking and feeling

was in flux. But as in the case of muscular skills, some modes or patterns are inhibited, others reinforced until the personality is molded to fit the mentality and the value system of the caste, sect, or professional group to which the individual belongs.

In this process, the transformation of means into ends is especially noteworthy. Thus, violence, which initially may have been a means (of survival or of imposing dominance or of seizing plunder) becomes a value in its own right by being constantly reinforced, while inhibitions of violence (which may be natural to human beings) are themselves inhibited by social disapproval.

If professional fighters occupy a high position in a stratified society so that membership in the profession is a matter of pride, additional positive attitudes toward violence are reinforced internally as well as by approval of peers. For example, in feudal Japan only noble families and the Samurai were permitted to have surnames. The Samurai's sword was more than a weapon. It was a symbol of status that set the warrior totally apart from common people.

When firearms were introduced into Japan, the Samurai did not adopt them. Swordsmanship had become a passion, a focus of the libido. A similar mentality seems to have gripped a large sector of the American population, except that the handgun rather than the sword has become the fetish. For example, attempts to restrict the possession of handguns have been energetically resisted by well-organized lobbies opposing gun control. Perusing the literature put out by these groups, one gets the impression that a pistol or a revolver is identified by the American male with his manhood and that being deprived of one is something like castration. In the 1980s, one southern town even passed an ordinance making it *mandatory* for each family to own a gun.

Status, pride, and glorification of violence frequently go together. Conceptions of gentlemanly behavior appropriate to an army officer in nineteenth-century Europe usually involved an obligation to defend one's "honor" (or the "honor" of a lady) by violence. Challenging to a duel in response to an "insult" was obligatory, as was the acceptance of a challenge. The penalty for shirking this obligation was ostracism. However, duels could be fought only with social equals, implying that deigning to fight with someone to the death, if necessary, was a gesture of respect.

In eighteenth- and nineteenth-century Europe the sword was part of an officer's apparel. In some countries even professors carried swords on official occasions. Since a professor was not expected to use the sword in the way it was intended to be used, we can only conclude that high social status was established by this symbol of violence. It is interesting to note that as late as World War II, Japanese fighter-plane pilots carried swords in the cockpit. It is also instructive to observe that in the nineteenth century several European monarchs, notably those of Russia, Germany, and Austria, adopted military uniforms as their formal apparel.

We see a conspicuous example of the way violence, first regarded as a means, comes to be perceived as an end in itself in those comments of Clausewitz on war when he allows his feelings to shine through. Clausewitz's conception of international politics was the Hobbesian world writ large with sovereign states playing the part of Hobbes' individuals "in the state of nature," i.e., waging a war of everyone against everyone. Hobbes's way out of the eternal struggle, as we have seen, was the surrender of individual liberty. The analogue in the case of the state would be the surrender of sovereignty. This solution was not available in Clausewitz's time (any more than it is available today). Consequently, political wisdom entailed effective ways, using the means at one's disposal (i.e., the army) to pursue political aims. These, in Clausewitz's time were easily definable in terms of expanding the domain and the influence of the state and resisting the expansion of other states. It would seem, then, that if war was to support the goals pursued by the State (read "the prince," for he was the embodiment of the State), war had to be fought "rationally." (Today we would say, in accord with cost-benefit analysis.)

In spite of his view of war as a rational instrument for attaining goals extrinsic to war, Clausewitz recognized a fundamental aspect of war that resides in its own dynamics rather than in application of "rationality." Namely, he regarded "moderation" in war as an absurdity. The key idea in Clausewitz's philosophy of war is that the one overriding objective of war is victory, and victory means annihilation of the military potential of the adversary, thus rendering him helpless to resist the will of the victor. Since both sides pursue the same objective both offensively (striving to annihilate the adversary) and defensively (resisting annihilation), it follows that neither side can stop short of expending its total effort. Only complete victory or complete defeat can stop this mobilization of effort. Clausewitz realized that wars were seldom fought in this way in his time, that is, before "total war" was invented (although Napoleon's style of warfare was a foretaste of what was to come). This failure of war to proceed to the conclusion dictated by its inner logic was attributed by Clausewitz to an effect analogous to friction. Just as in the absence of friction physical bodies would move in strict accordance with the idealized mathematical models of theoretical mechanics, so a war would develop in accordance with its "true nature," if it were not for human foibles, such as failure to grasp opportunities, lack of will, considerations extraneous to the true war aims, or war weariness.

Now it has been argued (e.g., by Vagts 1937) that Clausewitz was not prescribing how wars should be fought but only describing how war *would* be fought under idealized conditions. (In the same way, a physicist does not say how bodies *should* move but only describes how they *would* move in the absence of friction.) However, it is not always easy to distinguish between "would" and "should." There are passages in *On War* that are clear exhortations rather than analyses of the logic of war. How are we, for example, to understand the following passage?

> Let us not hear of Generals who conquer without bloodshed. If a bloody slaughter is a horrible sight, then that is a ground for paying more respect to War, but not for making the sword we wear blunter and blunter by degrees from feelings of humanity, until some one steps in with one that is sharp and lops off the arm from our body. (Clausewitz 1832/1966, Vol. 1, p. 288.)

Equally telling are the following excerpts from Clausewitz's letters to his fianceé:

> My country needs the war and—let us admit openly—the war only can bring me to the happy goal. In whichever way I might like to connect my own life with the rest, the world, my way always takes me across a great battlefield; without my entering upon it no permanent happiness will come to me. The day after tomorrow . . . there will be a great battle, for which the entire Army is longing. I myself look forward to this day with joy as I would to my own wedding day. (Schwartz 1878, pp. 219, 226.)

The Spectators

For the professional soldier violence is a way of life, and it is not surprising that many members of the military profession become addicted to it. That it is not necessary to lead a life of violence to become addicted to the vicarious experience of violence is evidenced by the huge popularity of bloody sports at various times in various places. The fondness of the Roman mobs for gory spectacles in the era of decadence of the Roman empire is well documented. In modern civilized societies gladiatorial combats and feeding people to beasts are taboo. These have given way to bullfights, cockfights, and boxing. There is, however, plenty of opportunity to see brutality and killing of people. Television, especially in America, continues to nurture the addiction to violence.

The average American youngster, by the time he/she has reached the age of fifteen, has witnessed about 15,000 killings on television. What are the effects of this exposure? It is often taken for granted that the persistent day-in-day-out watching of human beings killing human beings predisposes people to violence, in fact, in two ways: by social learning and by desensitizing one to others' suffering. A great deal of social learning takes place by imitation, especially in children. Instances of murder and torture perpetrated by children in ways directly imitating adult acts of violence shown on television have been reported. Examples:

> In San Francisco, three teenaged girls lured two younger girls down a lonely path and sexually molested them. In Chicago two boys attempted to extort $500 from a firm by means of a bomb threat. In Boston a youthful gang set a woman on fire with gasoline. In all three cases police officials concluded that the crimes had been directly inspired by shows the adolescents had recently watched on primetime television.
>
> Witnesses say a gunman armed with two rifles and dressed in Army fatigues yelled and laughed hysterically as he moved through a paintbrush factory on a fatal shooting spree. Five workers died. Three other persons, including the alleged assailant and a policeman were wounded. . . . Police, unable to arrive at a motive for the rampage, were exploring possible parallels to a recent "Hawaii Five-O" television segment involving a multiple slaying. . . . Many characteristics, including the assailant's garb, method of operation and a bag of candy found in his pocket, resembled the television program. . . . Receipts found for one rifle and ammunition were dated shortly after the broadcast. (Cited in Aronson 1984, p. 202.)

Habitual watching of killings and beatings may desensitize people to the suffering of others. During the Vietnam War, Americans watched battle scenes on TV while eating snacks and sipping beer. Some said that the sudden concretization of war shocked Americans into opposition to it. This is open to doubt. The mass media had previously blurred the distinction between pretense and reality. For instance, addicts of soap operas have been known to become so immersed in the lives of the characters that they behaved as if they believed them to be real, e.g., sent them Christmas and wedding gifts, advised them on how to cope with their problems, and so forth. It is possible that the telecasts of battles produced the reverse effect. *Reality* was perceived as pretense. After all, battle scenes in movies were known to be only pretense. And television screens do not look much different from movie screens.

If desensitization through habituation really takes place, then the value of "concretizing" the horrors of our age (e.g., by films such as *The Holocaust*) can be questioned. In fact, in spite of the best intentions, antiviolence propaganda of this sort could have a partially opposite effect. Habituation can lead to acceptance.

The commonsense conjectures about the effects of presenting violence and brutality to mass audiences have been challenged. At times the challenges are based on usually justified criticisms of conclusions drawn from statistical correlations. For instance, causality, especially causality in a particular direction, cannot be inferred without qualification from positive correlations of variables. Positive correlations established between the severity of television violence preferred by children and the extent to which they resort to aggressiveness in the solution of their problems (Robinson and Bachman 1972) cannot be regarded as conclusive evidence that watching television predisposes children to violence. It is possible that children who have a "natural" predilection to violence prefer severely violent programs.

One ought, however, to take into account the fact that an important source of skepticism regarding the brutalizing effects of television violence is the mass media business community. The sharpest criticisms of conclusions based on correlation between smoking and lung cancer come from persons linked to the tobacco industry. It is declared that those correlations may well be due to the fact that people predisposed to lung cancer have stronger craving for tobacco. Whatever the actual basis of the correlations, the fact remains that both the addiction to tobacco and the addiction to vicarious experience of violence are lucrative sources of profit.

The most credible explanation of why so many Americans like to watch violence on television to the extent of having made vicariously experienced violence a way of life is that they have become accustomed to it. Why, then, did they accept it when it was first presented, presumably before they had become accustomed to it? Violence on TV was a direct continuation of violence in films. Film violence was built around sagas about the combats between cowboys and Indians, sagas depicting (largely imaginary) exploits of the early settlers of the American West. There are other traditions in American folklore, the strongest being the glorification of success, either in courtship or in sports or in business. Violence is not normally associated with these exploits, except in some forms of sports. When, then, did violence become predominant? It may have been a case of accidental fixation by a positive feedback effect. If initially violent entertainment had an edge on other forms, this genre would be further reinforced, as the more familiar, which, in turn, caused it to be selected for because of the edge in popularity ratings (or box office figures)—a sort of snowball effect. All this is, of course, conjectural, but in our opinion as good an explanation as any.

Russia has not had a tradition of mass entertainment centered almost entirely on violence. As we pointed out in the preceding chapter, the violence in Soviet films and television is focused on just one theme: defense of the motherland. Unquestionably, this theme is kept in the foreground of public consciousness as a means of insuring steadfast loyalty to the regime. Whether this fixation has induced an addiction to vicariously experienced violence in the Soviet public is unknown, since the content of the programs does not necessarily reflect the preferences of the viewing public and field studies by impartial observers have not been carried out in that country.

The Terrorists

As one would expect, the label "terrorist," being a term of opprobrium, is usually affixed to individuals, groups, or actions with the view of arousing repugnance. All too frequently, attempts to come to agreements on a definition of terrorism get sidetracked into arguments about whether acts of violence of a given kind are or are not justifiable. Thus, a definition of terrorism that would include holding passengers of an airliner as hostages and, perhaps, killing them, may trigger a demand to include also the fire-bombing of cities or torturing political prisoners in order to turn attention to the abominable nature of these actions. This may or may not serve to clarify the essential aspects of a phenomenon we wish to analyze.

Most will probably agree that the assassination of a head of a state, a lynching, the murder of kidnapped persons in response to a government's failing to meet a politically relevant demand, the extermination of a village "to set an example," or the bombing of a crowded public place have essential features in common. One may decry all these manifestations of violence or one may seek justifications for them. If, however, one wishes to understand such events, one must first delineate as clearly as possible what one is going to talk about. It is worth remembering that the purpose of a definition is not to discover or to reveal the "essence" of something, much less to justify or to condemn it, but simply to circumscribe the scope of discourse.

In this discussion, we will include under "terrorism" acts of usually lethal violence that are characterized by the following features:

1. They are perpetrated (with one exception to be noted below) by persons not "licensed" to commit such acts. This excludes the police or members of the armed forces.
2. They are perpetrated against persons who are not usually armed.
3. Their intent is distinctly political.

The one exception is where violence committed by "accredited" agents, e.g., police, covert agents of espionage or subversion, or members of the armed forces, will be subsumed under "terrorism" if such actions are clearly calculated to intimidate a population suspected of aiding or sympathizing with revolutionary groups. Strictly speaking, these actions are not exceptions in the sense of our definition, since the "license to kill," normally accorded to policemen and soldiers, is not acknowledged to sanction killing unarmed and unresisting civilians. But in the interest of clarity, we specify such actions explicitly under "terrorism." The reason for doing this is that intimidation is one of the principal goals of terrorism. In the case of "unaccredited terrorism," it is the authorities who are supposed to be intimidated. In the case of accredited punitive actions against civilians, it is the population.

This distinction suggests two classifications of terrorism, namely, (a) terrorism against authorities and (b) terrorism against a population with the view of keeping it submissive. A well-known example of the latter type of terrorism was the far-flung activity of the Ku Klux Klan in the southern United States during the Reconstruction era. The murder squads of dictatorial regimes in impoverished countries, either deliberately organized by the regimes or "winked at," are the best known contemporary examples.

It is on this ground that frank genocide, such as the extermination of Jews, Gypsies, and the mentally ill by the Nazis, or of Tasmanians by the British, abominable as these atrocities are, will be excluded from the category of violent actions that we have subsumed under terrorism. The aim of genocidal actions is not *intimidation*, since the victims are not expected to comply or to submit. It is simply *extermination*.

The indiscriminate slaughter of civilians, as in modern total war, will also be excluded, even though the threat of such killing could be interpreted as intimidation of the victims' governments (to be discussed below as a principal aim of terrorism). In the minds of the authorities who sanctioned the mass bombings of cities in World War II, the purpose of these actions was the destruction of the enemy's war potential, which is not a goal pursued by terrorists.[1]

Two kinds of terrorism against authorities can be distinguished: "nationalist" and "ideological." Nationalist terrorists are usually members of ethnic minorities who regard themselves oppressed because of their ethnic origins. The Kurds in Iraq and Turkey, the Basques in Spain, and the Moluccans in Indonesia are examples of such groups. Palestinian terrorists can also be included in this category. Even though the activists of this ethnic group are largely outside of Israel and so do not constitute an "ethnic minority" within that country, their goal (a national homeland) is like that of nationalist terrorists everywhere else. In fact, the Israeli terrorist groups operating against the British before the establishment of Israel were also nationalist terrorists. Since these groups operated also against Arab civilians, they fall into both categories of our first classification: terror directed against authorities and terror directed against a population.

Ideological terrorism aims at instigating a "social revolution." It is this form of terrorism that is most relevant to the theme of this chapter. The most prominent of the early ideological terrorists were Russians, some of humble origin like Sergei Nechaev (1847–1882), others of the gentry like Michael Bakunin (1814–1876). They were all fired by what they felt as love for the oppressed, toiling masses, particularly the peasants, and by genuine unquenchable hatred for their oppressors. Their outlook was simple. The degradation of human beings by the tyrannical czarist regime was to them the epitome of evil, to be fought by killing its representatives. Successful assassinations would demonstrate to the masses that their oppressors were not all-powerful and would kindle the revolution. Their self-image was romantic, as can be seen in the following excerpts from *The Revolutionary Catechism*, essentially a handbook of terrorism, attributed by some to Nechaev, by others to Bakunin.[2]

> The revolutionary is a lost man; he has no interests of his own, no feelings, no habits, no belongings. . . . The revolutionary knows only one science, that of destruction . . . all the tender feelings of family life, of friendship, love, gratitude and even honor must be stilled in him by a single passion for the revolutionary cause . . . day and night he must have one single thought, one single purpose: merciless destruction. . . .

Along with this fixation on destruction, there was another—a boundless faith in the instinctive wisdom of The People, i.e., the "dark" (illiterate and therefore unspoiled) peasant folk, who in the romantic imagination of the terrorist anarchists appeared as the epitome of virtue. For this reason, the transformation of the czarist nightmare into an idyllic cooperative society seemed simple enough. The main task was to smash the oppressive State. Thereby The People would be emancipated and would do the rest. This idea is also spelled out in the *Catechism*:

> . . . we must draw close to the people: we must ally ourselves mainly with those elements of the people's life which ever since the foundation of the Muscovite State have never given up protesting, not just in words but in deeds, against anything directly or indirectly tied to the State; against the nobility, the bureaucracy, the priests, against the *kulaks*. We must ally ourselves with the doughty world of brigands who in Russia are the only true revolutionaries. . . .
>
> All our organization, all our conspiracy, all our purpose consists in this: to regroup this world of brigands into an invincible and omni-destructive force.

The reference to brigands stems, no doubt, from memories of the peasant revolts led by Stepan Razin in the seventeenth century and Emelian Pugachev in the eighteenth.[3]

Nechaev was probably mentally unbalanced. In his travels over Europe meeting with numerous circles of Russian revolutionaries in exile, he invented fantastic stories about himself, for instance, that he escaped from the notorious Peter-Paul prison. He enjoined revolutionaries to break "every tie with the civil order, with the educated world and all laws, conventions . . . and with ethics of this world"; and he followed his own advice. On one occasion he tried blackmail, on another he murdered a colleague who would not carry out his orders. As is sometimes true of completely self-assured egotists, Nechaev had tremendous charisma. When he was finally actually incarcerated in the Peter-Paul fortress for political prisoners, he "converted" 69 guards to the "cause" and almost succeeded in organizing a jail break. In those days, the czarist government dealt gingerly with famous political prisoners. It dealt much more severely with the guards. Nechaev died in the fortress at age thirty-nine, reportedly of scurvy.

The most important exponent of ideological terrorism in the nineteenth century was doubtless Michael Bakunin, son of a Russian country gentleman. As a student of philosophy in Germany, he was influenced by the Young Hegelians, as was true also of Karl Marx. Unlike Marx, however, Bakunin had no use for "scientific analysis." He rejected Communism categorically, for he would have nothing to do with the State, even in its role as an instrument of proletarian dictatorship preparing for its own "withering away," as forecast in the Communist creed. He worshipped "liberty," which he envisioned in Hobbesian fashion as the absence of restraints. His rhetoric is very similar to Nechaev's. "Let us put our trust," he wrote, "in the eternal spirit which destroys and annihilates only because it is the unsearchable and eternal creative source of all life. The urge to destroy is also the creative urge." Bakunin's influence was much wider and deeper than Nechaev's, probably because his personal integrity could not be impugned. Because of his enmity toward every activity that might involve discipline, he became an archenemy of Karl Marx.

While Marx with his emphasis on organization was most influential in Imperial Germany (where the then Marxist Social Democratic Party became the largest single political party), Bakunin's disciples multiplied in Italy and in Spain. How much his success in the south of Europe can be attributed to the "Mediterranean temperament" will not concern us. Probably the miserable conditions of the Italian workers and of the Spanish peasants and their deep mistrust of everything and everybody connected with the government contributed much to the spread of anarchist movements in those countries. Toward the middle of the nineteenth century, church lands in Spain were expropriated by the State and sold to private landowners. The ancient charitable privileges of the poor to eke out a livelihood on those lands were lost. The desperate peasants, turned paupers, reacted by burning churches (blaming the Church for betraying them) and, soon afterward, manors. They also raided Civil Guard posts, where they obtained arms. They became what today we call guerrillas. Needless to say, these outbursts led to ruthless and indiscriminate reprisals.

The Italian poor were as susceptible as the Spanish to anarchist and terrorist ideas. While technical progress increased both agricultural and industrial productivity by at least 300 per cent in the last decades of the nineteenth century, wages remained at the same level. Attempts to form labor unions were suppressed by terrorism from above. With rising prices, Italian workers became steadily poorer. They emigrated en masse to America, where many banded together in anarchist groupings.

The turn of the century witnessed three spectacular assassinations within three years. In 1898, an Italian anarchist killed Empress Elizabeth of Austria. An Italian anarchist cell in Paterson, New Jersey, condemned King Umberto of Italy to death; the sentence was carried out by an Italian emigrant, father of a baby son. He was sentenced to life imprisonment and committed suicide. In 1901, President William McKinley of the United States was shot and mortally wounded by an American-born anarchist of Polish extraction. Doubtless all of these killers regarded themselves as martyrs, sacrificing their lives for the Cause. The statement of McKinley's assassin may well speak for all of them: "I have done my duty. The President was the enemy of the workers. He went about saying that the whole nation is prospering. He was a liar. I believe we should not have leaders. It is right to kill them. I am an anarchist."

The prevalence of ideological terrorism in Italy, Spain, and Russia during the nineteenth century and its comparative rarity in Germany and England can be ascribed to the fact that the misery of the victims of the Industrial Revolution in the northern countries was to some extent alleviated by reforms and by gradual introduction of social services, especially in Germany, which at the height of its imperial power had the most advanced system of social welfare in Europe. All the more remarkable is the resurgence of ideological terrorism at a time when the economic reconstruction of Europe after World War II was completed.

Whatever can be said about inequalities in modern industrial societies, a sober examination of the lives of the workers in those societies makes the conclusion inescapable that their plight does not compare with that of their counterparts a century and a half ago. For one thing, labor unions, which once could lead only a precarious semi-underground existence, became established as institutions to be reckoned with economically and wooed politically. Ghetto poverty still festers, and in fact is increasing in U.S. and British cities. It is not in this milieu, however, that revolutionary agitation finds attentive response, as it did when the *working* poor (rather than the chronically unemployed) were the "wretched of the earth." In the last two decades, genuine ideologically inspired terrorist organizations appeared in West Germany, Italy, and Japan. Further, it seems that the typical recruits into these organizations have been young intellectuals from predominantly middle class families. These young people went about preparing and executing elaborate terrorist actions: kidnapping, murder, and bombings. How is this phenomenon to be explained?

We might venture an explanation from a psychological point of view. Somehow the "frustrations of modern life" drive young people from predominantly middle class backgrounds to violence. Since effective perpetration of violence requires coordination and cooperation, organizations dedicated to violence are formed. The fraction of violently inclined individuals in the population may be minuscule, but since it is these who are self-selected to join terrorist groups, the existing groups act as catalysts and grow. Moreover, a positive feedback of escalation sets in. When terrorists are caught and imprisoned, a new "cause" appears—that of freeing the imprisoned comrades. Hijackings and kidnappings are terrorist acts specifically geared to the task of forcing the release of those previously imprisoned. Since on the whole the numbers of imprisoned grow, so do the terrorist actions.

In our opinion, however, psychological predilections alone do not tell the whole story. We must see what there is about the ideational environment of our age that has provided an impetus for a resurgence of ideological terrorism in our time. As we inquire into this matter, we shall see further ominous implications of the conditions underlying the resurgence of terrorism generally.

Assuming that deep-seated destructive urges drive individuals to join terrorist groups, we can suppose that ideology consistent with terrorism provides a pseudo-ethical justification of violence. Thereby the destructive urges can be channeled and realized. Moreover, belonging to a group leading a precariously dangerous existence and tightly bound by total loyalty nurtures also the needs for affection and self-esteem.

Ulrike Meinhof, a leader of the once-dreaded RAF (Rote Armee Fraction) in West Germany, strikingly resembles the women who played leading parts in Russian revolutionary organizations a century earlier. Her childhood and youth were spent in an atmosphere of religiously inspired pacifism. She was the author of articles and producer of radio programs and films devoted to the plight of the *Gastarbeiter* (people from poor countries of southeastern Europe imported into Germany as temporary immigrant labor), the homeless, the institutionalized children, and the like. An excerpt from a speech by Ulrike reveals the transformation of these humane impulses into implacable hatred spiked with self-pity. (This and the following excerpts from writings produced by the Rote Armee Fraction are cited in Hobe 1979.)

> . . . that is what we are, that is where we come from: a brood spawned by the processes of destruction and annihilation of the metropolitan society, ruled by the war of everyone against everyone . . . by the law of anxiety and achievement compulsion, by gains of one at the expense of another, by the splitting of the society into men and women, young and old, healthy and sick, Germans and foreigners. . . . We come from the isolation of row houses of suburban concrete silos, from prisons and asylums, from brainwashings through the media through the ideology of helplessness, from depression, from disease, from insults and abasement of human beings, of all human beings exploited under imperialism.

The articulate eloquence of the passage reveals the background of the author: the same bourgeois milieu against which the scathing accusations are directed. Of course, the social origin of a social critic need not discredit the criticism, but the "theoretical" underpinnings of the intellectual terrorist does. Her group (the RAF) put out a large volume of material which was eventually gathered and published by the "establishment" press. The writings of the RAF have a verbal resemblance to Marxist theoretical writings, being permeated with the terminology of that outlook. In contrast to the writings of Marx, Lenin, and Mao, however, which are held up by the RAF ideologues as models of revolutionary theory, the verbiage of the writings has no discernible connection to the social reality which the authors purport to describe.

These theses can be summarized as follows:

1. The proletariat, the "revolutionary subject" of the Marxist theory of social change, has betrayed its mission, having been coopted by the ruling class.
2. The Leninist thesis that the revolutionary proletariat must be led by a highly disciplined, completely dedicated elite is correct.
3. The Communist parties, which were supposed to constitute these elites, have betrayed their mission.
4. The rising importance of the intellectual worker in the new "mode of production," the substrate of all social relations according to Marxist theory, has assigned the role of the revolutionary elite to the students— the future intellectual workers.
5. By highly publicized acts of terrorism (e.g., assassination of functionaries of the ruling class) the "masses" will be shocked out of their complacency, which is induced by "false consciousness."

"We must attack in order to waken the consciousness of the masses.
The bombs that we hurl against the apparatus of oppression we hurl
also into the consciousness of the masses."

6. The masses will then rise to revolt led by their avant-garde—the
students.

" . . . the fighting units will be supported by The People, will take cover
among The People, swimming in it like fish in water."

Confluence of three currents is evident in these theses. The verbiage, as
noted above, stems from Marxist writings: "class consciousness," "proletariat," "false consciousness," "mode of production," and the like. The
idea of the "urban guerrilla" swimming among The People, like fish in
water, is an adaptation from Mao Zedong's theory of social revolution,
which actually succeeded in China. The romance of terrorism is a heritage
of nineteenth century violent Anarchism. However, a new dimension has
been added to the individualist terror of Nechaev and Bakunin: the idea
of a worldwide terrorist *organization*. (The Anarchists rejected any idea
of organization out of hand. Recall the statement of McKinley's assassin,
"We should not have leaders.") In our age of instantaneous communication
and near-instantaneous transportation, the idea can become reality. It is,
however, nationalism (not pseudo-Marxist terrorism with its heavy ideological baggage) that portends to become the core of an international
terrorist network, because substantial logistic support for such a network
comes from states playing international power politics, not waging an imagined "class war."

Modern technology provides the terrorists with sophisticated weapons
and facilities for a global organization. In addition, this same technology
makes the target of terror exceedingly vulnerable. The airliner is a natural
target of international terror. Several hundred people can be *certainly* killed
with one blow. The event will be immediately publicized worldwide. The
"Establishment" all over the world will utter cries of indignation and anguish, a source of ecstatic satisfaction for the terrorists, unmistakable evidence of their power as a force to be reckoned with. The usual precautions
taken by authorities to protect their functionaries (bodyguards, and the
like) have become pitifully inadequate. Airport security necessitates armies
of personnel, and its visibility destroys the feelings of arrogant self-assur-
ance ascribed by the terrorists to the "enemy." The fears induced by each
terrorist act are not allayed by the sight of men with submachine guns at
ticket counters and departure lounges. Most important, acts of terrorism

provoke governments to retaliate, which lends to indiscriminate massacres the appearance of "war."

In this way, punitive actions by governments and especially outbursts of mass violence against ethnic minorities (whose cause nationalist terrorists purport to espouse) play into the hands of nationalist terrorists. Provoking such outbursts seems to have been a deliberate policy of the Moslem separatists when India gained independence. The objective of terrorist acts by the separatists appears to have been that of triggering communal violence against the Moslem population, which would make them receptive to the idea that only a state of their own would protect them from genocide. A similar tactic seems to be pursued today by the Sikh separatists in India. The anti-Sikh pogroms following terrorist acts by the Sikh nationalist extremists are welcomed by the latter, because they tend to convince the Sikhs that an independent Punjab is their only guarantee against extermination by the Hindus.

Terrorist organizations provide a niche for those for whom violence has become a way of life. They have made it unnecessary for these people to nurture their addiction by entering the service of the "establishments," which was once the usual procedure, e.g., enlisting in the French Foreign Legion, where one had to submit to harsh discipline and be under constant domination of arrogant officers. In terrorist groups, the fascination with the power to kill is coupled with genuine camaraderie and dedication to what appear to be lofty ideals.

The first overt military action against a state accused of instigating worldwide terrorism was undertaken by the United States against Libya, with the cooperation of the United Kingdom, which gave permission to the American attacking planes to take off from British bases. Although we have excluded overt military actions by one state against another from the category of terrorist actions, the attack by the United States on Libya nevertheless reflects two distinguishing features of terrorism: (a) the use of violence for the sole purpose of demonstrating one's power; (b) contempt for law and for peaceful resolution of conflicts.

The attack on Libya could not be rationally expected to check further acts of terrorism on the world scale. Even if Libya were utterly devastated, the innumerable obscure gangs would carry on. Therefore the raid could have only one purpose: to deny to oneself and to others that one is actually helpless to deal with terrorism. Of course, all terrorist acts are gestures of helplessness. One of their main purposes is to deny helplessness.

Since a justification of rule by law is the protection of the weak against the strong, contempt for law is inherent in all power politics. Such contempt, shown in violation of treaties, has been especially conspicuous in the behavior of the United States toward its southern neighbors. Article 15 of the Charter of the Organization of American States reads:

> No State or group of States has the right to intervene directly or indirectly, for any reason whatever in the internal or external affairs of any other State. The foregoing principle prohibits not only armed force but also any other form of interference or attempted threat against the personality of the State or against its political, economic, and cultural elements.

Since 1954, the United States has been instrumental in the overthrow of the governments of Guatemala, the Dominican Republic, and Chile; carried out an armed attack on Cuba; committed explicit acts of war against Nicaragua (e.g., mining its harbors); and refused to recognize the judgment of the International Court of Justice in the latter case. It is in the light of the firmly established image of a state contemptuous *of its own laws* (treaties to which the U.S. is party are incorporated into the law of the land) that the attack on Libya (in violation of Articles 33 and 37 of the United Nations Charter) may be seen *in its futility* as an act of terrorism.

Justice as Private Enterprise

Readiness to resort to violence has characterized all powerful states. What is particularly disturbing about the growing addiction to violence of the United States in the past forty years is that it may be a reflection of a profound psychological disturbance on a mass scale. The per capita murder rate of the U.S. is many times that of Canada in spite of the close cultural similarity between the two countries. The pervasive violence in mass media entertainment has been mentioned. The linkage of sadistic fantasies with ideological self-righteousness and taking the law into one's own hands is another symptom of terrorist predilections. A favorite genre of criminal fiction in the United States is the "private eye" novel. The hero, a private detective, unlike the Scotland Yard investigator, operates completely outside the law. Invariably a bachelor, a "lone wolf," he roams the urban jungle, singlehandedly bringing criminals to heel by beating them at their own game: setting traps and bloody fighting. Mike Hammer, the hero of Mickey Spillane's novels, is especially articulate in explaining himself.[4]

> Yeah, and I'm going to kill some more. . . . I hate the lice that run the streets without being scratched. I'm the guy with the spray gun and they hate me too, but even if I'm a private cop I can get away with it better than they

can. I can work the bastards up to the point where they make a try at me and I can shoot in self-defense and be cleared in a court of law.

It will be recalled that shortly before the April 1986 raid on Libya, U.S. warships entered Sidra Bay, which Libya had declared to be her territorial waters, provoking an attempted attack on the intruding vessels, which led to an air strike "in self-defense." The much larger raid in April was also declared as an act of "self-defense," following the death of a U.S. soldier in the bombing of a Berlin discotheque.

Even more revealing is Mike Hammer's braggadocio as a defender of democracy.

. . . those Reds just aren't the kind who can stand the big push. Like it or not, they're still a lousy bunch of peasants who killed to control but who can be knocked into line by the likes of us. They're shouting slobs who'll run like hell when class shows and they know this inside their feeble little heads.

And so on to the final victory.

The Dragon is tethered and all the world will know why and nations will backtrack and . . . tear up the knotheads in the Kremlin and maybe their satellite countries will wise up and blast loose and maybe we'll wise up and blast them, but however it goes . . . Communist philosophy will get the hell knocked out of it.

The Roots of Violence-Oriented Politics

It is not necessary to assume that Ronald Reagan got the inspiration for his global policy from this literature. Rather it is the literature that reflects the mood of a significant sector of the American public, as it must, since this literary merchandise is produced for a mass market. Given a sufficiently large sector of the voting public in this mood, politicians who cater to it can get elected. To stay in office, they adapt policies to the mood.

The problem remains of explaining the mood. Here we can only speculate. Psychology offers no compellingly convincing theory, only analogies. A disturbing analogy is that with Germany in the 1930s. Routine comparisons of pugnacious heads of state with Hitler amount to little more than affixing a derogatory label, which becomes shopworn through promiscuous use. A comparison of the American mood in the 1980s with the German in the 1930s should be seen not as a reference to Nazi Germany as a universally recognized standard of political evil but rather as a conjecture that *both* moods could be regarded as corroborations on the scale of an ideology (i.e., collective thought) of the frustration-aggression hypothesis. Germany's decisive victories of 1864, 1866, and 1870[5] were followed by an era of euphoria, a belief in the invincibility of German arms, and a sense of mission—the spread of German *kultur* among the backward peoples. It is against this background that the defeat of 1918 appears as a crushing frustration. The resurgence of German nationalism expressed in the veneration of Hitler, who told the Germans that they were the greatest, the bravest, the purest, and so forth, could have been expected on the basis of the frustration-aggression theory.

America's decisive and easy victories in the war against Spain in 1898, Germany in 1918, and the Axis powers in 1945, also created a mood of euphoria, a belief in "The American Century," based on the invincibility of America's might, a sense of mission in the spread of American-style democracy and the American way of life among the economically and politically backward peoples. But this dream of benevolent omnipotence was challenged by the rise of a rival superpower. The standoff in the Korean war and the defeat in Vietnam must have been experienced as crushing frustrations. Thus, the aggressiveness of the American regime in the 1980s also fits into the frustration-aggression theory.

Of course, as we pointed out in Chapter 3, the frustration-aggression theory alone is not a sufficiently general theory of aggression. It acquires much more explanatory power when it is coupled with a social learning theory and a theory of cognitive dissonance. In the present case, these connections can certainly be established, namely, on the scale of the entire population (rather than of individuals) providing a theoretical basis of the ideology based on violence as a way of life.

Notes

1. Here the distinction becomes blurred. It is generally recognized that neither Dresden nor Hiroshima were of military importance, so that their destruction could be said to have had just one purpose: to intimidate the population. On the other hand, in total war, the entire population of a country is a military resource; so that actions calculated to break its will to resist can be "defended" as military operations, which we have excluded from acts of terrorism. We must emphasize once again that no distinction on moral grounds is made here between military operations and terrorism. The distinction is based on the attendant ideologies in which the two kinds of violence are rooted.
2. The excerpts from the *Revolutionary Catechism* are all from the writings of

Bakunin cited in Hyams (1975). Hyams conjectures that the *Cathechism* was essentially the work of Nechaev and that Bakunin edited it.

3. Stepan (in folklore "Stenka") Razin (d. 1671), a folk hero celebrated in song, was a Cossack chieftain who became a river pirate on the Volga. His flotilla of galleys fought pitched battles, on one occasion annihilating a Persian fleet. Eventually captured, he was cruelly tortured and put to death. Emelyan Pugachev (d. 1775) was also a Cossack, who proclaimed himself Czar Peter III (thought dead) and led a revolt of destitute peasants. He was able to capture Kazan, whence he threatened Moscow. When his fortunes waned, he was betrayed and executed. Pushkin's story, "The Captain's Daughter," is based on the events during Pugachev's revolt.

4. The excerpts are from M. Spillane's novels, *My Gun is Quick* and *The Girl Hunters*.

5. Otto von Bismarck, Chancellor of Prussia, maintained that national interest is effectively pursued not by diplomatic maneuvers but by "blood and iron." In quick succession, Prussian armies crushed Denmark and forced her to give up the provinces of Schleswig and Holstein; then defeated Austria in a six-weeks' war, depriving her of her dominant position in the German-speaking realm. In 1870, Bismarck provoked a war against France. Prussia's decisive victory led to the integration of all German states except Austria into the German Empire.

11

Ideological Issues of the Cold War

There is a widespread belief that the source of the hostility between the United States and the Soviet Union is a clash of ideologies. On the American side the confrontation is said to be between "Communism" and "Democracy." On the Soviet side, the confrontation is said to be between "Capitalism" or "Imperialism" and "Socialism." The different terms reflect the prevalent attitudes in the respective populations, or at least the way these attitudes are depicted in the mass media. In the United States "Communism" is a bad word and "Democracy" a good one. In the Soviet Union "Socialism" is a good word, while "Capitalism" and "Imperialism" are bad ones. It behooves us to look closely at the content of this alleged ideological confrontation, its genesis, its effects, and what it portends for the near future.

"Rightist" and "Leftist" Ideologies

The basic distinction between "rightist" and "leftist" ideologies lies, according to R.J. Glossop (1983) in the distinction between priorities ascribed to two principles: (a) the principle of *merit*, a basic value of the rightist ideology, and (b) the principle of *equality*. Glossop defines "leftist" ideology as "everyone should have the same amount of goods because ultimately the amount of contribution one makes or how qualified one is depends on factors outside of one's control." He defines "rightist" ideology as one based on the conviction that some people deserve to get more than others because they "contribute more or are more qualified in some way."

Further, Glossop points out, one should make a distinction between an *economic* and a *political* ideology. A person could be a rightist with respect to economic ideology but a leftist with respect to political ideology and vice versa. One could, that is, hold to the principle of merit with regard to the distribution of goods but to the principle of equality with regard to the distribution of political power; or one could believe in equal distribution of goods (regardless of merit or qualifications) but hold to the principle of merit with regard to political power. Presumably, then, the democratic capitalist societies are rightist on the economic dimension and leftist on the political dimension; while the present socialist societies are leftist on the economic dimension and rightist on the political dimension.

Whatever these distinctions say about economic or political beliefs that people could have, even a cursory glance at present day "capitalist" and "socialist" socieities shows that none of them approximate the ideal states they espouse. Gross inequalities on both the economic and political dimensions characterize the structures of both types of societies. Since, however, we are here interested in ideologies, it behooves us to inquire to what extent the beliefs described by Glossop (which are widely thought to underlie the "clash of ideologies" and hence the hostility and distrust characterizing the relations of the superpowers) have actually been internalized by their respective elites and populations. If they are as strongly entrenched as we may be led to believe on the basis of the rhetoric that pervades the discussions of ideological issues, then we must conclude that ideology has returned in full force as an instigator of war after having been dormant for some centuries.

The Historical Role of Ideologies in Large-Scale Conflicts

Recall that whatever role ideology, in the shape of religious doctrines, may have played in the wars of the sixteenth and early seventeenth centuries, after the end of the Thirty Years War it was completely eclipsed as a factor in European warfare. The monarchs of the eighteenth century cannot be said to have differed in their worldviews, and the imposition of an "ideology" (or religion) on the vanquished played no part in the war aims of that time.

Nor can ideology be said to have played an important role in the wars fired by nationalism, despite the fact that the U.S. entered World War I under the slogan of "making the world safe for democracy." Whether or not that slogan had any basis in the actual commitments of American

political leaders, aside perhaps from Woodrow Wilson, the settlement that
followed did not reflect any ideological victory. On the contrary, the country where a radical shift of ideology can be said to have occurred (Russia)
withdrew from the war and played no part in the settlement. And the only
country where ideological rhetoric was used, the U.S., withdrew from the
"peace" that followed, refusing to participate in attempts to restructure
international politics with the view of preventing a repetition of the
bloodletting.

World War II was another matter. The rhetoric of ideology fueled the
energies of both camps. If any war in modern times can be said to have
been ideologically motivated, World War II is it: the avowed aims of both
sides had to do with the establishment of a world order. Note, however,
that in that war the two countries that are now said to be committed to
incompatible ideologies fought on the *same* side. Further, on the very eve
of the war, the two countries which, judging by the rhetoric of their ruling
elites, had been the bitterest ideological enemies imaginable, concluded a
non-aggression pact, arranged for the partition of a victim of Nazi aggression and amicably delineated their respective spheres of influence.

It seems, therefore, that the question of to what extent the ideologies
that are widely believed to be essential obstacles to a rapprochement between East and West have actually been internalized by the elites and/or
by the populations is not an easy one to answer. It may help to examine
the origins of the beliefs that are said to constitute these ideologies and
what role they now play in the internal and external policies of the two
countries.

Origins of Ideologies

Ideologies are usually formulated by persons who possess considerable
background and are articulate in expressing abstract ideas. Formulated
ideologies usually contain thoughts about the nature of man, interpretations
of historic events, and the like, or, as was the case before literate societies
became secularized, theological considerations. In this respect, the circumstances in the United States and in the Soviet Union were parallel but in
other respects they were widely different. They were parallel in the sense
that ideological foundations in both countries were provided by highly
erudite people, who, in turn, received their ideas from sophisticated philosophical sources.

In the United States, it was the Founding Fathers and their immediate
successors who laid the foundations of what is usually regarded as the
American creed. Thomas Jefferson, a highly educated man, well versed in

the writings stemming from the French Enlightenment, was the author of the Declaration of Independence. James Madison played a leading role in the framing of the American Constitution, and James Monroe in articulating a foreign policy reflecting America's distancing of itself from European politics and by implication from European ideologies.

The principal ideologue of the Russian Revolution, V.I. Lenin, was also a person of unquestioned erudition. Writing more than a century after the American Founding Fathers, Lenin was thoroughly acquainted with the background of the ideology they espoused—the works of the English utilitarians and of the leading figures of the French Enlightenment. He applied Marx's devastating critique of the ideology that grew out of the "bourgeois revolutions." The ideologies that underlie the rhetoric of American and Soviet politicians were originally formulated by highly sophisticated thinkers who, whether or not they can be credited with keen insights or blamed for falling victims to delusions, were surely original, independent, and sincere.

This is as far as the similarity goes. The subsequent history of American and Soviet ideological formulations is quite different. We have seen how the entrenchment of Stalinist despotism was accompanied by the decimation of practically all the prominent political leaders and of large sectors of the intelligentsia in the Soviet Union. Any originality of thought in the realm of social philosophy, not to mention critical commentary on the "classics" of Marxism, which in Stalin's days comprised the writings of Marx, Engels, Lenin, and Stalin, *and only those*, was entirely out of the question. Any attempt in the way of criticism of these "classics" was tantamount to risking one's life and certainly jeopardizing one's career. Even more, to *praise* the ideas of Lenin or Stalin in words that were not repetitions of standard clichés was risky. It was risky to give evidence of any spark of original thought in fields from which the ingredients of Soviet ideology had come. Inevitably, the ideas of Marx, Engels, and Lenin (all imbued with considerable intellectual content) became encrusted in cliché-ridden verbiage. Absolutely nothing was added to them, if we discount Stalin's exhortations to work hard and to be vigilant, as contributions to the "science of society in the period of building socialism."

For this reason, it is impossible to say that the ideology created by Marx, Engels, and Lenin has remained a living body of beliefs or convictions in the population of the Soviet Union. Courses on Marxism-Leninism or on dialectical materialism are still compulsory in all higher institutions of learning, and surely the youngsters in middle and elementary schools are thoroughly indoctrinated in the tenets of the official faith. But in the complete absence of any critical approach, it is unlikely that those tenets are internalized as anything but slogans and clichés, somewhat in the way catechism answers are memorized by Catholic or Lutheran youngsters. We cannot, therefore, say with assurance that the Soviet people "subscribe to the Communist ideology." The life of the great majority of them is taken up with mostly mundane matters, especially since the business of daily living in the U.S.S.R. is difficult and demands considerable ingenuity. The situation is probably not much different from that in many other countries, including the United States. While the day-to-day existence in America is for the most part not nearly as difficult as in the Soviet Union, the very opportunities it provides serve to steer attention of the great majority away from contemplation of ideological matters. Certain values are simply taken for granted, but most people do not get very excited about them; there is no ardor in their faith other than in their patriotism or nationalism.

The intellectual worlds of the two countries are quite different. Whatever is said by social critics about de facto restrictions on intellectual freedom in the United States, the fact remains that there is the widest latitude for the development of critical social thought. Whatever "sanctions" can be pointed to against nonconformist ideas are trivial compared to the sanctions that have been applied in the Soviet Union. Consequently, one can expect to see a development of social philosophies in the United States against the background of a rich historical experience—the early days of the republic; the scene of growing tensions over the slavery question, culminating in a civil war; the heady years of rapid industrial development coupled with the conquest of the West; entry into the arena of international politics; the Great Depression, which shook the foundations of the complacent ideology of individualism; finally the experience of power in World War II, and being "thrust into the role of a world power."

The history of the Soviet Union since its birth has been no less stormy, but until 1986 there was no trace of genuine critical analysis of that history. Until then the traumatic events of the 1930s were not even mentioned. The metaphor of the "iron curtain" could be more aptly applied to *internal* blackouts of an entire historical period than to the information barriers between the Soviet Union and the outside world.

How have the two ideologies fared in their roles as the intellectual underpinnings of the political and social systems of the United States and the Soviet Union, respectively? Let us first look at what has happened in the United States.

An Economic Model of Politics

As we saw in Chapter 7, the ideals of individual freedom in the United States were intimately linked with a pristine faith in free enterprise. Although shaken by the Great Depression, this faith returned with full force after the victory of 1945. The conviction that the victory should be credited to the socioeconomic system of the United States deserves as much or as little credit as the conviction expressed in the Soviet Union that the victory of the Soviet Union over Germany must be credited to the superiority of "socialism."

While faith in the "free enterprise system" survived in the United States, so did energetic criticism of it, as one would expect in an open society. In fact, the strongest case for the viability of capitalism has been made in America by the firm linking of the open society to the free enterprise system.

In this linkage, classical economics has been imbued with a *political* meaning. The ideological structure of American politics is presented as a counterpart to Adam Smith's "free market." Whether this picture does or does not correspond to American political reality, one can take it as representative of post-World War II American ideology, formulated in a climate of intellectual freedom and therefore immune to accusations of sycophancy.

As economic model of American politics is developed in *The Calculus of Consent* by James Buchanan and Gordon Tullock (1965). The original subtitle of the book was *An Economic Theory of Political Constitutions*; but the authors changed it to avoid the impression that their primary orientation toward politics is "economic" in the vulgar sense of economic determinism.

The Calculus of Consent satisfies all the criteria of an explicitly formulated ideology. It offers a "model of man" in the sense of pointing to the presumed mainsprings of human motivation. From this model, a model of society emerges.

There are two ways of viewing a model of anything: as a description of its "essence," i.e., of what it would be like if this "essence" were not subjected to disturbances and fluctuations; or as a description of what the thing modeled *ought* to be like, an ideal to live up to. In some social philosophies the boundary between the two conceptions of a "model" is not sharp. For instance, in *The Republic*, Plato describes society as it ought to be. But his theory of ideals suggests that this is the way society *would* be if it were not corrupted by change. Similarly, Clausewitz describes war as it would be if it were not for what he calls "friction," circumstances that prevent war from being what it "really is" in its essence. Clausewitz tries to stay on that level of idealized description. Nevertheless, he is so fascinated by his supposed discovery of the "essence" of war that he slips into normative language, maintaining that war *ought* to be bloody.

This boundary between the descriptive and the normative modes is vague also in *The Calculus of Consent*. Much of what the authors say about the political dynamics of a "society of free individuals" could be construed to apply to a model of that society in the descriptive sense: what it would be like if it could function according to the dynamics attributed to it. At the same time, the attitude of the authors toward such a society is distinctly one of approval. In their view, this is the way a "good society" ought to function.

First, let us look at the "units" of which the society described in *The Calculus of Consent* is composed. A "unit" of this sort is offered as a model of the human being. To the authors' credit, they recognize that their model and the ideology on which it is based "stand or fall" with the validity of their assumptions regarding this unit. They know that a cogent challenge of the ideology they espouse must be directed at their basic "model of man." They show this awareness by anticipating the challenge: "The most controversial aspect of our approach is the assumption that we shall make concerning the motivation of individual behavior." (Buchanan and Tullock, 1965, p. 17.)

This assumption is embodied in what P.H. Wicksteed (1933, Vol. 1, pp. 175–180) called "non-tuism." "Tu," of course, is the Latin word for "Thou" and can be construed as the polar opposite of "Ego." Hence "non-tuism" could be identified with "Egoism." However, the pejorative connotations of egoism are emphatically excluded from Buchanan and Tullock's account of human motivation. They call their approach *methodologically individualistic*. Individualism in this sense does not necessarily involve narrowly hedonistic or self-centered motivations of individuals. It does involve a metaphysical assumption that individuals are the units of social reality. It also involves, as the authors specifically state, a rejection of an "organic" model of society which attributes to "the whole" a mode of existence that not only transcends the sum of individual existences but is somehow "more real" than the individuals who compose it (cf. Hegel's conception of the State).

The authors are right in recognizing their assumption as controversial and contribute to the clarity of their exposition by making it explicit. Besides, a clearly formulated ideology in their work is meant to be a challenge to rival ideologies, for instance those derived from Marx's models of society. It is for this reason that we have singled out this work for discussing the ideological issues of the cold war.

A Biological Analogy

The assumption that individuals are the "real" units of society and the ultimate determinants of social choice can be challenged by transcending the individual-centered point of view via an analogy.

We know that organisms are composed of cells and that each cell can be regarded as a living unit, not self-sufficient, to be sure, but nevertheless endowed with essential mechanisms for preserving its identity. We also surmise that the earliest forms of life were single-celled plants and animals. Later organisms composed of many cells evolved. For a time, however, the borderline between a collection of essentially autonomous cells and fully integrated organisms was not sharp. Even today some forms of life, for example, sponges, exemplify a borderline case. A sponge can be filtered, whereby its cells are separated and assume independent existence. But if given a chance, they coalesce again into an apparently single organism.

In such cases there is no difficulty in recognizing two levels of "biological reality." The cells of the sponge are "real" and so is the whole sponge. One can argue that everything the sponge "does" can, in principle, be described in terms of what its individual cells "do." However, "in principle" here is a very important qualification. "In principle" everything a human being does could be described in terms of what each of its constituent cells "does." But we would not want to use this principle as a foundation of a behavioral theory. When it comes to studying or describing the actions and motivations of the human individual, we don't pay much attention to what the cells do, except when we study quite elementary forms of behavior like reflex responses or when we analyze the simplest forms of perception such as sensations. In our present state of knowledge it is a hopeless task to try to put these elementary perceptions and actions together to give a picture of an individual's full repertoire of behavior, let alone his attitudes or motivations.

The controversial aspect of the assumption embodied in "methodological individualism" can now be discerned in the light of the analogy. It is not absurd to suppose that human societies have emergent properties that cannot be described or explained as resultants of the properties or actions of the individuals that compose them. It is difficult for us to assign a level of reality to a society conceived organically because we are ourselves individuals and have access to our own consciousness that convinces us of our "reality" (cf. "I think, therefore I am" of Descartes). This is only part of our problem. We in the Western industrialized world are immersed in a semantic environment in which the primacy of the individual, his interests, motivations, autonomy, and inviolability are constantly reiterated. It is difficult to transcend this fixation. But if we are to *understand* (which, of course, does not necessarily mean accept) other ideologies, we must make the effort.

Let us return to the implications of "methodological individualism." As the authors emphatically point out, this basic assumption does not picture human beings as necessarily "selfish." A person may be motivated to act "altruistically," as when he suffers discomfort, privation, even death, in order to make others more comfortable or less deprived. Such actions do not refute the assumption of individualism because the assumption is satisfied as long as the individual does all these things in order to increase his own satisfaction. Actually, the assumption blurs the distinction between "selfishness" and "altruism" because in the light of it, an "altruist" acting in ways that give him satisfaction acts "selfishly."

Buchanan and Tullock seek to describe the workings of a society in terms of composite actions to the individuals that compose it. Hence individual interest becomes here a tautological concept. It is that which motivates the actions of the individual *whatever* he does or attempts to do. The nature of that interest is not given *a priori* (e.g., maximization of profit). It can be established only *a posteriori* in the light of the individual's behavior. Here the descriptive mode of Buchanan and Tullock's model is in evidence. The normative aspect comes into focus when it appears that a society composed of individuals acting in this manner is identified with a "good" society.

The resemblance of the Buchanan-Tullock model to Adam Smith's "free market" is conspicuous. In fact, the authors explicitly point out the connection between the economic relation and the political relation representing cooperation on the part of two or more individuals.

> The market and the State are both devices through which co-operation is organized and made possible. Men co-operate through exchange of goods and services in organized markets, and such co-operation implies mutual gain. The individual enters into an exchange relationship in which he furthers his own interest by providing some product or service that is of direct benefit to the individual on the other side of the transaction. At base, political or collective action under the individualistic view of the State is much the same. Two or more individuals find it mutually advantageous to join forces to accomplish certain common purposes." (Buchanan and Tullock 1965, p. 19.)

From this passage it appears that the fundamental relationship between the units of a society is an "exchange relationship." Men cooperate because some have something that others don't, who have something they can give in exchange. Thus, the exchange benefits both.

People also decide to act collectively for their common advantage. So they must *decide* collectively *what* collective action to take. Since opinions of people differ in this regard, they must establish *rules* for choosing among different collective actions. But opinions may also differ about what rules to adopt. Recourse to designing rules for resolving differences about what rules to adopt would lead to infinite regress. This can be avoided only if on some level there is unanimity. In the simplest case unanimity is reached on the first level above substantive decisions. People agree on rules for resolving differences about what collective action to take. "Majority rule" is a simple example of such a rule. There are, of course, others.

Once the rules of social choice have been agreed upon, they can be used to make collective decisions in each specific case. The set of such rules can be called a *constitution*.

The political model just described is a model of political democracy. The exchange principle enters the political process via formation of interest groups, i.e., collections of persons acting together in the political process. These, in turn, can make larger coalitions where reciprocal support for certain political actions is given, a process that politicians call logrolling.

The basic mode of Buchanan and Tullock's exposition is normative. A society based on the exchange principle is described as a "society of free individuals" with the usual connotations of "freedom." However, the model is also meant to be a description (a highly idealized one) of the American political system. It appears to have captured some important aspects of that system *at least as they appear to its partisans*.

The Communist Models of Societies, Present and Future

At this point, for the sake of a well-organized exposition, a parallel (idealized) model of Soviet society, which reflects Soviet ideology, would be presented. From the juxtaposition of the two models, theoretically, the ideological issues of the Cold War would be delineated. Unfortunately, such a scheme, for reasons stated above, could not until recently be realized. The imposition of absolute conformism in all public discussions of the Soviet Union dealing with the nature of Soviet society, the Soviet State, its institutions, and its ideals, made all such discussions sterile. It is impossible to say how much of what was said or written was actually believed. Discussions of Soviet society by persons not subject to the compulsory conformity are not of much help. These fall into three classes: partisan pro-Soviet, partisan anti-Soviet, and more or less objective studies. The first two reflect the ideologies of the authors, and it is hard to say to what extent they were shared by the Soviet people. The "objective" studies do not penetrate the inner world of the Soviet people. They may have been accurate descriptions of institutions, the political process, or everyday life, without touching on matters related to ideology.

The only recourse seems to be to go to the sources of Communist thought. The ideology depicted there is often *attributed* to present-day Communist leaders. This attribution may be totally mistaken. However, the fact that it is attributed to them is relevant to the theme of this chapter.

Fundamental in the original ideology of Communism is a rejection of the exchange model of society. Two other models serve in its stead, one of a pre-Communist society, one of a Communist society. Ideas about the transition from the one to the other are also an important and integral part of Communist ideology.

Two models of society that Communist ideology juxtaposes to the exchange model are the threat model and the love model. The terms are borrowed from the writings of Kenneth E. Boulding (1974), who has no reticence about using terms with connotations that to some would seem inappropriate in analyses of societies. Since we are reproducing his ideas here, we will also adopt his terminology.

A society is held together by the *threat* principle if it consists of at least two classes distinguished by a dominant and a dominated position. Most societies (according to Marx, all civilized societies) have been of this sort. The dominated class can be regarded as being forced to perform its function in society by threats. These threats can be crass and explicit (e.g., whip-wielding overseers of slaves) or camouflaged.

Now it is possible to view societies based on threats as "exchange societies." One can point out that a slave performs his task in exchange for being fed or not being beaten. But most would agree that this interpretation would be stretching the point. A society based on slave labor would hardly be regarded as a "society of free individuals," as a society based on the exchange principle is supposed to be.

For reasons discussed in Chapter 7, Marx regarded a capitalist society as one based on threat, not on exchange, as Buchanan and Tullock characterize it. Marx would say that the contractual arrangement entered into by an employer and a worker is not an example of an exchange relationship, because the worker, depending entirely on access to tools of production, has no choice but accept the employer's terms. We will not argue the point. We will only note that societies based on what Buchanan and Tullock would call an exchange relationship have been common in the history of civilized societies. The third type, a society based on the love relationship, has not been observed. According to Marxist theory, it is a society of the future.

Here is it appropriate to explain that in discussing the "love relationship"

Boulding does not use the word "love" with its usual strong connotation of affection. A love relationship in this de-sentimentalized sense is one where services are rendered not in order to avoid threatened reprisals for failure to do so, nor in the expectation of getting something in return, but because the recipient of the services is entitled to them by virtue of what he, she, or it *is*. "Love" in its everyday meaning fits situations of this kind. We say parents protect and nurture their children because they "love" them. If we are interested in the phenomenological aspects of love, then to test this proposition we must somehow take a reading of parents' inner feelings—a psychological problem. But if one uses the word "love" in the political-economic sense, as the term is used by Boulding, this is not necessary. To validate the statement, it is only necessary to establish that children are cared for, not because they threaten reprisals if they are not, nor because they pay for their care, but because they are children.

Here it is possible to get caught up in endless arguments about the "true" meanings of threat, exchange, and love. Some would insist that all relationships are "in the last analysis" reducible to threat or exchange relationships. They argue that parents care for their children because they are threatened by censure or even by criminal prosecution if they don't; or, that they care for their children because they expect to be cared for by them in old age, and the like. All these attempts to reduce a variety of situations to varieties of a single situation may be motivated by an understandable desire to create a "unified theory" or to "milk" a concept for all it is worth. Often, however, such attempts are counterproductive, particularly when distinctions are more important than analogies. We believe that the distinction between various bases of cooperation (or compliance) in social life, such as the three principles mentioned, are important enough to be kept in focus.

The essence of Communist ideology, as it is depicted in official pronouncements, is a distinction between the hitherto existing societies based on threat and a future society based on love. Communist idealogues tend to lump the threat and exchange principles of social organization together, to expose the alleged freedom associated with the exchange relationship as a camouflaged form of a threat relationship.

That the envisaged Communist society is to be based on love can be seen in the slogan that describes its "political economy" (or rather the absence thereof): "From each according to his ability, to each according to his needs." The slogan is, in fact, a denial of the exchange principle because it implies the abrogation of bookkeeping either of services rendered or of benefits received. Arrrangements of this sort are not confined to fantasy. They exist in reality, albeit only in the microcosm, as it were. (A nuclear family with small children may exemplify a "society" of this sort.) More rare, but not unknown, are communes, groups considerably larger than a nuclear family, but still having the distinctive features of a "love" relationship in the sense that individuals receive benefits simply because of *who* they are, not because of what they are expected to do or refrain from doing. Of course these expectations are implicit in the concept of membership, but the important distinction between this "love" relationship and the "threat" or "exchange" relationships is that no credit–debit accounting is kept. A member who fails to fulfill expectations is not penalized in proportion to the seriousness of his transgression. If the transgression is serious enough, he is expelled.

The idea of a commune based on love is, of course, much older than Communism. It appears fully developed with the advent of Buddhism and Christianity. We have evidence that many of the early Christians lived in communes. Further, the commune was institutionalized in monasteries, and sects living in communes have survived to our day.

What distinguishes Communist ideology from, say, the Christian is that the Communist ideologues claim to have provided a *scientific* analysis of societies based on the threat principle (exploitative or class societies) and to have provided a theory of history from which predictions can be derived of a transition from exploitative to non-exploitative (classless) societies.

Communist Materialism

Communist ideology is often called "materialistic" and, because of the connotations of this term in common usage, deprived of "spiritual" values. "Materialistic," as the term is used in the lexicon of Communist ideology, reflects something quite different: namely, a refusal to attribute processes or events to the will or purpose of a supernatural being and the belief in the existence of matter independent of its being perceived. While militant atheism still arouses emotional reactions in believers, the "independent existence of matter" has lost its salience as a divisive issue. In the nineteenth century, however, it was very much alive in bitter polemics between the "materialists" and the "idealists." Many staunch defenders of faith and piety were in the ranks of the latter. This partly explains the violence of Lenin's polemics.

That atheism does not necessarily entail rejection of "spiritual" values is evidenced in the early writings of Marx, which centered on the concept of "alienation," a feeling of malaise, at times of despair, engendered by estrangement from things and from others in the world outside oneself. The concept can be traced to antiquity, for example, to the writings of Plotinus (A.D. 204–270), who conceived of the undivided One unfolding in its various manifestations and in the process becoming differentiated, hence no longer an undivided One. Inherent in this image is the view that "matter" is on a lower level of existence than the One, its antithesis. Later Hegel was to take up this theme in its religious garb. The central idea was again the disintegration of "wholeness" into a diversity where the parts became "estranged" from each other. The romantics, reacting to the stresses produced by the early phases of the Industrial Revolution associated alienation with the division of labor. Here they anticipated Marx, as is evident from Schiller's remarks on the soul-destroying effects of specialization.

The process of embedding the concept of alienation firmly in materialism was completed by Marx, who interpreted alienation as the forced separation of the worker from the product of his labor (which the capitalist appropriated). This separation, as Marx understood it, was not simply depriving the worker of mere "ownership" of what he produced. Since Marx laid great stress on productive work as the distinguishing feature of the human being, the expression of his "essence," as it were, the separation of the worker from his product amounted to depriving the worker of a part of himself, hence to alienation in its deepest sense.

The "love" system envisaged in the Communist society entails, therefore, not only the end of exploitation of man by man (presumably accomplished by abolishing private property of means of production), but also the end of alienation, both of persons from the product of their work and of persons from each other.

So much for the ethical aspects of Communist ideology. Its claim to being "scientific" stems from Marx's mature work, in which the theme of alienation with its psychological implications is practically abandoned, giving place to detailed analysis of economic dynamics under capitalism. The main argument presaging the collapse of the capitalist system rests on the presumed contradiction between the "anarchic" nature of capitalist competition and the highly organized mode of production, both generated by capitalism. Marx purports to show that inevitably capitalist enterprises will merge into ever larger ones, culminating in giant monopolies. Concurrently, the population will be progressively "proletarianized" since the small producers and traders (which Marx identified with the middle class or the "petty bourgeoisie") will be unable to compete with the monopolies. Eventually the middle class will vanish. The ever-more sharply exploited proletariat will rebel against the intensified exploitation, will overthrow the capitalist social order, and will take over the economy (which will have been already organized and so is ready to be taken over). The profit motive will no longer drive production; the satisfaction of human needs will be restored as the motive.

Thus the inevitability of Communism turns out to be neither a Utopian prophecy akin to the prophecy of the Kingdom of Heaven, as in eschatological Christianity, nor a consequence of military conquest, as in its vulgarized versions depicted by anti-Communists, but a result of the inner dynamics of capitalism. By extension, Marx interpreted the entire history of civilized societies in terms of the dynamics generated by class struggles. It is this appearance of a logically rigorous, demystified account of history and quasi-rigorous de-sentimentalized analysis of the human condition that lends support, in the opinion of the Marxists, to the claim that Marx was to social science what Newton was to physical science.

Do the Ideologies Clash?

Even if we assume that ideology has played the role of an instigating factor in some wars (for which there is little evidence), to ascribe the *present* war readiness of the superpowers to a clash of ideologies, as those ideologies have just been described, is farfetched indeed. The difference can be ascribed to different emphases on the two aspects of the human condition: the autonomy of the human individual and the fundamentally social nature of the human animal. (Marx remarked that man was social long before he became man.) That both can be realized is evidenced by numerous "islands" of rationality and dedication to humane values, where autonomy does not necessarily reflect itself in "non-Tuism" (complete independence of utilities assigned by different people to different situations) and where merging one's aspirations and gratifications, at times one's very consciousness, with others does not necessarily destroy the uniqueness of the individual. In fact, in the most intimate of human relations, that between a man and a woman in conjugal union, the greatest gratification comes from the awareness of both the uniqueness of each and of the merging of the I and the Thou, as is directly experienced in a complete orgasm.

The clash is not between the specialized one-sided interpretations of freedom (which with some effort can be seen to complement each other in the two ideologies), but rather between the distortions of these interpretations. These distortions are not confined to misrepresentations of the opponent's ideology. They stem also from corruption of one's own creed. It is here that the accusations and mutual recriminations take root and reinforce each other.

The ideological issues are important to the extent that emphasis on them makes the horrendous aspects of each regime salient. Let us look at the worst aspects of the Soviet regime as they appeared to Americans, particularly to Americans who could be expected to be in basic sympathy with the proclaimed goals of the Soviet peace policy. There are three loosely defined significant sectors of the American public that fit into that category: pacifist church groups, so-called grass roots peace movements, and intellectuals. "Left wing" groups and labor are deliberately excluded from these categories. The former have always been politically insignificant and fragmented—the staunch Soviet sympathizers among them a dwindling fraction. As for "labor," which in the Communist picture of world politics is usually cast in the role of a potential ally of the Soviet Union, its political complexion, at least in the United States, has become increasingly conservative during the decades following World War II and, to the extent that it has an articulate attitude on world politics at all, it is rather hostile to the Soviet Union.

Assuming that the desire of the Soviet leadership to defuse the nuclear time bomb and to establish some sort of modus vivendi with the "capitalist world," particularly with the United States, is genuine, it would seem to be in their basic interest to cultivate allies on this issue among the groups mentioned. To be able to do so, they should be aware of the primary concerns of those groups, of what motivates them to action, of what inhibits them from acting in given ways—in short, of the principal levers of their motivations.

The Religious Issue

As is generally known and, of course, must be known to Soviet leaders (since Soviet scholars have amassed much information on all aspects of American life), there is no established religion in the United States. This absence of an established church is not simply a matter of omission. It is expressly prohibited in the American constitution. Whatever can be said of prejudices festering here and there against various religious groups, the equal status of all such groups is constantly, publicly reiterated. In the armed forces chaplains of three principal faiths are provided. At public ceremonies, care is taken to balance invitations to priests, pastors, and rabbis to officiate in the proceedings. Appeals for more participation in religious life are phrased to emphasize the "faith of your choice." Moreover, the churches and sects have multiplied to the extent that it is impossible to keep track of them.

Whatever be the sociological or political implications of this peculiar development of religion as "free enterprise," religious tolerance has been firmly embedded in popular consciousness. It is easier in America to win popular support for the "right to worship in accordance with one's conscience" than for any other human right. Political dissidents have been on occasion persecuted in the United States; heretics, since the adoption of the constitution, have never been.

Much has been made in American propaganda of the "persecution of religion" in the U.S.S.R., eliciting angry denials by the Soviet government. Nevertheless, allowing for the usual exaggerations of hostile propaganda, the fact remains that at various times religious minority groups have been persecuted in the Soviet Union.

The Issue of Democracy

What has been said about religious groups applies equally to other peace-oriented grass roots activities. Persecution of so-called "independent peace groups" in the Soviet Union surely dampened the fervor and so reduced the effectiveness of the peace movement in the West. Again, the root of this difficulty has been the well-nigh pathological suspicion by Soviet authorities of any organized activity that was not instigated and controlled from above. Spontaneous demonstrations of any kind, even in complete sympathy with the avowed policies of the government, were frequently condemned as "hooliganism." This adamant hostility toward all initiatives from below made the claims of the Soviet regime to the status of an embodiment of "genuine democracy" a mockery in the eyes of American grass roots organizations, in which democracy is synonymous, if not necessarily with dissent, at least with complete freedom from government interference.

It can be argued that the issue of peace ought to take precedence over all others. The persistence with which the issue of peace is pursued by American grass roots peace groups could remain unaffected by the image of Soviet society projected until recently by the Soviet regime. Opponents of detente in the United States got much political mileage from the depressing history of repressions that have marked the Soviet regime from its origin. The cruel treatment of the dispossessed "kulaks" (an epithet which, in the absence of any recourse available to the persecuted, could be affixed to anyone); the terror of 1937–1938, when local NKVD functionaries were said to have been given "quotas" of "enemies of the people" to be liquidated; the summary uprooting and deportation of ethnic groups during World War II on suspicion of possible disloyalty; the witch-hunt on "rootless cosmopolitans" in the late 1940s; finally the chilling affair of the "doctors' plot," said to have been preparatory to a nationwide pogrom and deportation of the entire Jewish population to remote regions, aborted only by the timely death of Stalin, all have left their scars.

These are said to have been excesses of the Stalin era, supposedly things of the past. There was a brief period of "de-Stalinization" when grim episodes were recounted and the lawlessness of the repressions was condemned. Soon, however, a curtain of enforced silence descended on the entire era. Searching analyses of deeper systemic causes of the social storms in the decades preceding and following World War II are at this time out of the question. The single phrase "personality cult" was supposed to provide a blanket explanation of the entire pathology and thereby choke off all further discussion.

It is this *enforced silence* that created a bad image of Soviet society in the minds of American peace activists. Most genuine devotees of peace understood that "linkage" of the peace issue with the human rights issue is self-defeating, that peace is worth struggling for regardless of the nature of the Soviet regime, past, present, or future. But *recruitment* of people into the peace movement from among the masses of ordinary Americans became extremely difficult because of that image. Soviet denials often heard from apologists for Soviet domestic policies, for example, statements to the effect that "there are no political prisoners in the Soviet Union," that the 1968 intervention in Czechoslovakia saved that country from "counterrevolution," etc. were deemed most insulting to the intelligence and most difficult to accommodate. It is, perhaps, fortunate that books like *Solzhenitsyn's Archipelago of Lies* (Iakovlev, 1974)[1] have had a negligible circulation in the United States. On the other hand, it is *unfortunate* that a book like *Siluety Vashingtona*, by the same author (1983), is available only in the original Russian. Propagandists of both sides are at their best when they report on the seamy or gruesome features of the other society. They are at their worst when they exalt their own.

The Issue of Intellectual Freedom

The third sector of American society whose goodwill could contribute significantly to political pressure for detente is comprised of the intellectuals, people who "feel at home" with ideas, get satisfaction from analyzing and manipulating them, and assign importance to this activity by attributing large scale historical changes to it.

In America, intellectuals are very largely concentrated in academe. The main reason for this is that in politics, business, and the entertainment "industry" intellectual activity does not bestow prestige. The same could be said of the professions, e.g., medicine, law, engineering, architecture, and so forth, where technical competence rather than ideational creativity is the main source of prestige. In academe, on the other hand, the American intellectual has found a comfortable social niche. He/she can pursue a career as an intellectual (i.e., acquire prestige at least among colleagues) and at the same time engage in remunerative activity in accord with the ethical prescript of mainstream American ideology.

Being immersed in a professional life where advancement depended on administrative decisions, the intellectual could either give priority in career advancement by adjusting his or her "ideational creativity," if necessary, to the mainstream ideology, or else espouse the cause of intellectual freedom (specifically academic freedom). It may have been for this reason that "intellectual" freedom became an especially salient issue in the United States.

The suppression of intellectual freedom has had a long history in America. It flared up especially vigorously during the McCarthy "witch-hunts" of 1947–1953. It was against the background of this harassment that the American intellectuals witnessed the horrendous anti-intellectual campaign in the Soviet Union, which occurred during those last years of Stalin's reign. Whatever goodwill toward the Soviet Union accumulated among the American intellectuals during the war was quickly dissipated.

We have seen an example of an "intellectual lynching" in the Lysenko affair (cf. Chapter 8). The word used in the Soviet press to describe such orgies was *razgrom*, having the same root as *pogrom* (*grom* means thunder). A pogrom, as is widely known, was an outburst of mob violence against the Jews. *Razgrom* means demolition, especially a crushing defeat of enemy troops. Like genetics, other disciplines were demolished, among them cybernetics, mathematical statistics, and certain branches of psychology. Not all demolitions were accompanied by public performances like the *razgrom* of genetics. Usually an authoritative article sufficed to instigate abolition of institutes and to ruin careers of scientists and scholars.

In the course of de-Stalinization, practically all the scientific disciplines proscribed during the intellectual purges were "rehabilitated." Cybernetics, in particular, received emphatic official blessing and developed in the context of its applications to automatic control systems and computer science. This rehabilitation was accompanied by fairly frank acknowledgment of the "mistake" associated with its suppression. By and large, however, the issue of intellectual freedom *as such* was not raised in these official rehabilitations; emphasis was on the importance of the rehabilitated discipline to the development of technology and of applied science in general.

Rehabilitation of disciplines does not really have a bearing on the issue of intellectual freedom any more than rehabilitation of repressed individuals has a bearing on the issue of human rights. These issues revolve not around specific instances but around principles. The suppression of intellectual freedom as a policy was until recently never admitted, much less denounced by Soviet authorities.

What repelled the American intellectual most about the suppression of intellectual freedom in the Soviet Union was its totality effected by a virtually complete monopoly by the government and the Party of all means of public information and communication. Not only was freedom to write and publish ideologically dissenting views reduced to practically zero, but also the right to *read* was severely curtailed, not so much by specific prohibitions (although forbidden literature has often been confiscated in searches) as by making such literature inaccessible. Large sections of libraries, called *spets-khranenie* (special storage) were closed to all except those who could demonstrate a need to have access to them, for example, those with authorization based on being engaged in a relevant research project. These sections included practically all works containing criticisms of the Soviet social, political, or economic system, as well as works of authors who, by falling out of grace, became "un-persons." Whenever an intellectual was repressed or emigrated, mention of his name was eradicated in all sources except those that escaped the attention of persons directed to undertake the purge. His or her face disappeared from group photographs. Entries about him or her disappeared from encyclopedias. For example, following the liquidation of Lavrenti Beria, chief of Stalin's secret police (the last Stalin-type liquidation in the Soviet Union), libraries both in the Soviet Union and abroad subscribing to the *Great Soviet Encyclopedia* received a page of the encyclopedia with instructions to substitute it for the page containing the entry "Beria." An expanded article about Bering, after whom the Bering Strait was named, conveniently filled the space which Beria's biography, career, and the then highly valued services to his country had filled. The procedure was blandly called "updating." It was practices of this kind that lent frightful realism to Orwell's anti-utopian nightmare, *1984*. Equally disheartening was the failure of Soviet authorities to realize that instructions of this sort to librarians in the West inevitably strengthened the conviction that intellectual repression in the Soviet Union was chronic and absolute.

If a "clash of ideologies" has indeed been an obstacle to the establishment of a lasting peace based on friendly relations between the United States and the Soviet Union, then it was not the divergence of the ideologies, as they are themselves conventionally depicted, but the virtual absence of opportunities for open and sincere debate about them that blocked the way of political rapprochement.[2]

U.S. Support of Soviet Hard-Liners

Let us now look at the obverse side of the genuine ideological issues of the Cold War. Assuming (for the sake of a symmetrical argument) that the U.S. government fears an attack by the Soviet Union, it would be prudent on its part to cultivate "allies" within the Soviet Union, that is, support forces (if such could be mobilized) that would oppose any aggressive intent that the leaders of the Soviet Union have with respect to the United States. In contrast to the potential allies in the cause of peace that the Soviet Union might encourage within the U.S. (grass roots peace activists, intellectuals, etc.), the United States cannot hope to find analogous groups within the Soviet Union.

There remains only the "dovish" wing of the power elite. There is ample evidence that such a wing exists, even though explicit divergence of opinion on major policy issues is rarely publicized. Presenting a front of absolute unanimity to both their own populations and to the outside world has been an inviolable principle guiding the *modus operandi* of the Soviet leadership. It is this "dovish" faction, whose view of the realities of the nuclear age is clearer, who are relatively emancipated from the paralyzing grip of encrusted dogma, that could be cultivated as "allies" in the cause of reversing the drift to catastrophe via the establishment of a lasting detente preparatory to a firm peace.

The main obstacle to strengthening the position of such potential allies is the chronic muscle-flexing Rambo posture of the American establishment. This belligerency is not confined to rhetoric. On repeated occasions it has taken the form of aggression throughout the world: subverting and overthrowing governments, some of which had been democratically elected, to replace them with "authoritarian" regimes pledged to "fight communism."

With the resurgence of the Radical Right during Ronald Reagan's administration, the instigation and support of putsches and counterrevolutions, which had been an integral component of American foreign policy since the end of World War II, was coupled with bombastic saber-rattling, as if calculated to goad the Soviet Union into a similar state of frenzy. Nor was this policy of provocation confined to rhetoric. The United States made it clear that it had no intention of doing anything that might impede the acceleration of the arms race. A case in point was the announcement of a commitment to the so-called Strategic Defense Initiative program, essentially extending the arms race into space. The visions projected to sell the program to Congress and to the public reflect the megalomania of power addiction. These visions can be traced back to the views of Lyndon Johnson who, when still a senator, realized that considerable political mileage could be extracted from advocacy of an extensive space program. The Romans, he recalled, ruled the known world by controlling the roads. The source of British power as a world empire was control of the seas. Control of air became the key to victory in World War II (as it appeared to the Western Allies). The next step seemed obvious.

The feasibility of the SDI ("Star Wars") program became the subject of a heated debate in the U.S. Scientists were overwhelmingly skeptical about the prospects of its success. Warnings that the program constituted a severe intensification of the arms race and probably precluded meaningful arms control agreements were also heard. However, the administration held all the trumps: promises of virtually unlimited funding for research, development, and production, a trough at which millions could feed. There was something for everyone: for the worker as well as for the corporation, for the technician as well as for the "pure" scientist, including the theoretician and, of course, for the strategist. Roman emperors held on to power through the largesse of bread and circuses. The war system has become its present-day counterpart.

We expressed doubts about the extent to which received Communist ideology (with its strong ethical component) is taken seriously by the present Soviet leadership. However, the other side of that ideology, namely, the eschatological interpretation of history, fits well into the strongly power-oriented view of the leadership. The Reagan administration has given the Soviet leaders weighty reasons for believing that the prophesied onslaught of capitalism (in its "final stage") on the stronghold of socialism is now being prepared and will occur (unless checked) in the very near future, perhaps in a matter of a few years.

Mikhail Gorbachev. the first "young" leader to come to power in the Soviet Union, has launched a peace offensive couched in concrete proposals for reversing the arms race, coupled with unilateral initiatives of the GRIT type (cf. below). The initial U.S. response has amounted generally to dismissals. The proposal for a comprehensive test ban was rejected on the grounds that it was "not in the national interest of the United States"—an answer analogous to a curt "because" in reply to any question beginning with "why."

The fear of the Soviet leadership that the United States is actually preparing to annihilate the Soviet Union must be very real, because it is confirmed not only by the still-believed tenet of Communist ideology to the effect that the capitalists may unleash a war against the Soviet Union at any time in order to eliminate the threat of Communism. Over and above this reinforcement, there is another that fits the image of the U.S. as an expanding empire, continuing the expansion begun long before there was a threat to capitalism. Evidence of this dynamic expansion can be found in utterances of American statesmen and politicians from the very first decades of the American republic. Already in 1789 Jeremiah Morse, a Congregational minister of Boston, wrote in a book on geography (anticipating geopolitics of a later day):

. . . it is well known that empire has been traveling from east to west. Probably her last and broadest peak will be America . . . the largest empire that ever existed. (Cited in Van Alstyne 1960, p. 69.)

President John Quincy Adams wrote more explicitly:

In looking forward to the probable course of events, it is scarcely possible to resist the conviction that the annexation of Cuba to our Federal Republic will be indispensable to the continuance—and integrity—of the Union itself. (Cited in Morison and Commager 1962, Vol. 2, p. 417.)

Commodore Perry expressed similar views on the future American role in the Pacific:

It is self-evident that the course of coming events will ere long make it necessary for the United States to extend its jurisdiction beyond the limits of the western continent, and I assume the responsibility of urging the expedience of establishing a foothold in this quarter of the globe as a measure of positive necessity for the establishment of our maritime rights in the east. (Morison and Commager 1950, p. 315.)

The ideological rationalization of these imperialist ambitions came to be known as Manifest Destiny, an outlook in which the United States saw itself as a bearer of a mission and its conquests as the manifestations of some cosmic purpose. The following sample of senatorial oratory immediately following the victory of the United States over Spain may serve as an illustration:

We will not repudiate our duty. . . . We will not abandon our opportunity in the Orient. We will not renounce our part in the mission of our race, trustee under God, of the civilization of the world. . . . We will move forward to our work . . . with gratitude . . . and thanksgiving to Almighty God that He has marked us as His chosen people, henceforth to lead in the regeneration of the world. . . .
Our largest trade henceforth must be with Asia. The Pacific is our ocean. The power that rules the Pacific . . . is the power that rules the world. And with the Philippines, that power is and will forever be the American Republic. (Cited in R.J. Bartlett 1956, pp. 385–388.)

These remarks are mentioned here to show how easy it is to make one's own country appear as a rapacious conqueror. It is equally easy for the leaders of a country to undermine their own credibility. S. Ulam presents grounds for doubting the sincerity of Soviet "peace offensives":

Soviet leaders' ideology was extremely helpful in allowing them to justify to themselves as well as to their followers those drastic shifts and improvisations which led their opponents, flustered and furious, to protest Russian "insincerity," attempts to "lull the free world to sleep," etc. To such accusations the answer was and is invariably that the "objective historical circumstances have changed" and indeed are always changing, and with them the appropriate policies. (Ulam 1968, p. 570.)

The most persistent image of the Soviet Union as the core of the projected Communist world state is based on Marxist-Leninist rhetoric, as it flowed from the pen of Josef Stalin. Actually, there is no way of knowing whether *Problems of Leninism* was written by Stalin himself or was pasted up from ritually repeated phrases under his direction. It does not matter. The book is a model of banality and obfuscation. Nevertheless it was treated by John Foster Dulles, Secretary of State in Eisenhower's administration, as seriously as it was by Stalin's sycophants. The following excerpt, in Dulles' opinion, commits the Soviet Union for all time to instigating a world revolution and setting up a monolithic Communist world dictatorship:

Up to a certain period the development of the productive forces and the changes in the realm of the relations of production proceed spontaneously, independently of the will of men. But that is so only up to a certain moment, until the new and developing productive forces have reached the proper state of maturity. After the new productive forces have matured, the existing relations of production and their upholders—the ruling classes—become that "insuperable" obstacle which can only be removed by the conscious action of the new classes, by the forcible acts of these classes, by revolution. . . .

"We are living," says Lenin, "not merely in a state, but in *a system of states*, and the existence of the Soviet Republic side by side with imperialist states for a long time is unthinkable. One or the other must triumph in the end. And before that end supervenes, a series of frightful collisions between the Soviet Republic and the bourgeoisie will be inevitable. That means that if the ruling class, the proletariat, wants to hold sway, it must prove its capacity to do so by military organization also." (Cited in Dulles 1957, p. 10.)

Needless to say, it is just as easy to select other excerpts both from American and Soviet sources that solemnly insist that the keystone of the one or the other foreign policy is peaceful coexistence and renunciation of force (except in self-defense, of course) in international relations.

Rhetoric is not a good indicator of policy, much less of ideology, if by ideology we mean an internalized worldview. Recall that in its earlier meaning (e.g., in Marx's social philosophy), ideology referred to an *un-*

consciously held worldview. We have used the term in a broader sense; but we have kept the connotation of a *commitment* to a set of beliefs or attitudes. Political rhetoric need not reflect such commitments. However, this rhetoric can be frequently of use in ascribing intentions to others, on the basis of which one's own policies can be justified. So it is in the case of the ideological war of words that has marked the Cold War.

Internalized Ideologies or Hang-Ups?

When discussing the issues of the Cold War we must distinguish between different aspects of ideology and the different roles they play in the confrontation. To begin with, an ideology can be understood as an internalized world view of the whole population, usually coupled with an ethos. In this sense an ideology can be utilized in mobilizing populations to exert intense efforts, to risk their lives, to kill others, and so forth. Americans seem to have an internalized view of this sort, reinforced by a characteristic mode of living. It is an individualistic view with great stress laid on self-reliance and "freedom" in the sense of Circumstantial Freedom of Self-Realization, i.e., freedom from interference, especially by authorities, with one's way of making a living, pursuit of a career, place of domicile, etc. Although many of these freedoms are in effect limited by disparities of social status and income, considerable leeway remains, probably greater than outside the United States. There are the freedoms realized by the mobility provided by the automobile, absence of systematic police surveillance, greatly loosened family relations, absence of an established Church (to which one automatically belongs at birth), to name a few, not available even today in several European countries. The concept of community, while not entirely absent in the U.S., is perhaps weaker here than elsewhere, again because of extreme geographical and considerable social mobility.

This internalized ideology is in harmony with the mainstream of the "American way of life" and provides the basis of political support for politicians who extol it. (Those outside the mainstream—the unemployables, the slum dwellers, the chronically poor—are not sufficiently enlightened to provide an organized political counterforce.) Whether in the era of conventional warfare this political support would have been sufficient to mobilize the population for an all-out war effort (as in World War II) is an open question. In the nuclear era, such mobilization is no longer necessary. A tremendous expenditure of effort and resources is diverted to *preparations* for war, but these do not involve casualties, and the squandering of resources is not generally resented. Rather, the waste appears as robust economic health as well as "protection of the American way of life." In sum, the political support required to keep the country on a war footing is freely given.

In the Soviet Union, in contrast to the United States, the waste of labor, scientific talent, and resources diverted to the preparations for war is felt keenly, and there are no delusions about the "economic benefits" of a war economy. The waste is rationalized in the form of a routinely iterated litany of ideological orthodoxy. It is not likely that this orthodoxy is presently internalized by the general population or, for that matter, that it ever was. Thus, an ideology woven into the very fabric of everyday life (the way the mainstream American ideology is) did not play a part as a support for Soviet policies. This has made no difference, however, because the Soviet ruling elite did not require public support. It required only acquiescence, which was insured by the monopoly of the means of information and communication.

The aspect of Communist ideology that makes credible the constant danger of attack on the "first socialist state" by the most powerful "capitalist state" is an important source of the compulsions under which Soviet policies, in particular the compulsive "catching up" policy, were formulated and pursued. It is these ideologically based "hang-ups" that the American stance of implacable hostility toward the Soviet Union helps to preserve. It is difficult to imagine how more effective political support can be given to the most adamant Cold Warriors in the Soviet Union than by pronouncements such as this one, by a top U.S. arms control adviser to the Reagan administration:

> The United States should plan to defeat the Soviet Union and to do so at a cost that would not prohibit U.S. recovery. Washington should identify war aims that, in the last resort, would contemplate the destruction of Soviet political authority and the emergence of a post-war world order compatible with Western values. (Gray and Payne 1960.)

A pronouncement of this sort surely matches the apocalyptic prophecy of Stalin. It strengthens the siege mentality, the principaal hang-up of Soviet leadership, not only in its manifestation in the arms race but also in the compulsion to retain a stranglehold on all aspects of Soviet life, that is, to maintain a garrison state.

In the United States, too, it is hang-ups rather than the internalized ideology of individualism that maintain the frozen posture vis-à-vis the Soviet Union. As we have seen, one of the most powrful hang-ups in the makeup of Americans is technolatry—the deeply rooted conviction that application of technical know-how is the key to every "victory," whether over nature or over enemies. It is this hang-up, grafted on the faith in

America's mission in spreading the blessings of "freedom," that underlies the aggressiveness of America's foreign policy and helps keep the Cold War going.

Notes

1. The brochure is an ill-tempered and clumsy diatribe against the writer Alexander Solzhenitsyn and the physicist Andrei Sakharov, both Nobel laureates. Solzhenitsyn was expelled from the Soviet Union, Sakharov was banished to "internal exile" in a provincial city. He was freed and rehabilitated in 1986. "Archipelago" in the title of Iakovlev's brochure is an allusion to Solzhenitsyn's *The Gulag Archipelago* (1975), an expose of the Soviet system of concentration camps.
2. Under the leadership of Mikhail Gorbachev, release of considerable numbers of Soviet dissidents from prisons was reported. A policy of "glasnost" (openness) has been announced, with indications that criticism of the state by citizens will be tolerated. A "Soviet Spring" would go a long way toward removing the obstacles in the way of forging a firm peace alliance between intellectuals of East and West.

12

The End of Ideology

The following item appeared in the *Japan Times*, May 26, 1984:

> Twelve warships from Britain, France, the United States, and Japan will join in a two-day ceremony starting today to honor a Japanese admiral who annihilated an imperial Russian fleet in 1905. Organizers say the Soviet Union has not been invited to send a representative to the ceremony. . . .
>
> The ceremonies scheduled for today and Sunday mark the fiftieth anniversary of the death of Fleet Admiral Heihachiro Togo.

Togo died on May 30, 1934. The ceremonies commemorating the fiftieth anniversary of his death may have been scheduled on May 26–27, because these dates fell on a weekend. Or, perhaps, because May 27, 1905, was the date of the Battle of Tsushima, which made Togo Japan's national hero.

Nohoru Yogi, director-general of the Japan Socialist Party's International Department, was quoted in the same issue of *Japan Times* saying, "It's an example of unnecessary heightened tensions. Why should we remember events of a time when both Japan and Russia were fighting expansionist wars under imperialist regimes?"

One would think that in the Soviet press, where imperialism is persistently condemned, a similar attitude would be expressed. But the comments on the event in *Pravda*, the organ of the Communist Party of the Soviet

Union reflect something quite different. In an article entitled, "A Spiritualist Seance in Kagoshima," we read:

> Of what was the spirit of Admiral Togo, summoned from non-being, supposed to remind the Japanese public? On the night of February 9, 1904, the Japanese navy, commanded by this admiral, treacherously attacked the Russian squadron stationed in Port Arthur.[1] Two battleships and a cruiser were disabled. Simultaneously, the cruiser *Varyag* and the gunboat *Korean* were attacked [in another port]. They took on the enemy in an unfair fight and were sunk by their own crews.

Pravda continues its comments on the Russo-Japanese war:

> At the time, England played a foul inciting role, intent on using others to undermine Russia's influence in the Far East. Under pressure from London, Turkey refused passage to the Russian Black Sea Fleet.

From these remarks it appears that in 1984 Soviet leaders regarded the Russia of Czar Nicholas II as a hapless victim of England, Turkey, and Japan, which were intent on frustrating Russia's national interests. No mention is made of the role that Russia's imperialist expansionism may have played in the struggle for power in the Far East. It is instructive to see what V.I. Lenin, the founder of the Soviet state, thought about the events of 1904–1905.

> Progressive, advanced Asia has dealt an irreversible blow to backward and reactionary Europe. . . . It was not the Russian people but Russian autocracy that started the colonial war. . . . It was not the Russian people but autocracy that was ingloriously defeated. The Russian people gained from that defeat. (Lenin 1905a/1925.)

About the defeat of the Russian fleet in the Straits of Tsushima, Lenin wrote:

> The great armada, huge and clumsy, senseless, helpless, monstrous like the Russian Empire, set out squandering tremendous amounts of money and coal, evoking contemptuous comments in Europe, especially after its brilliant victory over British fishing boats in flagrant violation of all custom of neutrality. . . . (Lenin 1905b/1925.)

In *Pravda's* account, the British fishing boats become "British ships following in the Russian fleet's wake, informing the Japanese of its strength and position."

Lenin :

> Like a mob of savages, the Russian armada fell upon the Japanese fleet, superbly armed, equipped with the latest means of defense. . . . The Russian fleet is completely destroyed. . . . The autocracy plunged the people into a senseless, shameful war. . . . It now faces a well deserved demise. (Lenin 1905b/1925.)

In 1984, the Battle of Tsushima was recalled in a different spirit. The Soviet periodical *Novoe Vremia* praised the gallantry of Captain Iegoriev, commander of the cruiser *Aurora*, who urged his sailors: "Let us face our last hour with dignity! Let us not be deprived of our honor!" The armored cruiser *Suvorov* went on firing with its last gun and went down with the "flag of St. Andrew proudly waving."[2] Many other acts of heroism are recounted in *Novoe Vremia*. The mention of the *Aurora* is especially noteworthy. This was the same cruiser which, according to handed-down tradition, fired the shot signaling the attack on the Winter Palace in Petrograd on November 7, 1917, the start of the Bolshevik Revolution, and is now preserved as a national monument. No mention of the famous shot is made in the article.[3] Indeed, it would be out of place, since the Russian sailors fighting the Japanese are pictured as most loyal and fervent patriots of imperialist Russia, which Lenin so severely castigated in his contemporary account of the events.

These excerpts demonstrate the transformation of Communist ideology, originally based on internationalism and class solidarity, into conventional nationalism. Another point made by the juxtaposition of Lenin's and *Pravdas'* comments is that the idea of publishing such a juxtaposition in the Soviet Union would have been unthinkable in 1984. While specific errors committed by the State or the Party in the past were sometimes mentioned (invariably to show that they had been corrected), no inconsistency in the expression of basic policies or of the sanctified ideology could be admitted, nor any evidence of it publicly discussed.

An exponent of the so-called realist school of international relations would find nothing surprising in the transformation of Soviet rhetoric from revolutionary internationalism to state power-oriented nationalism. The basic idea of the "realist" school of thought in political science is that power is to politics what wealth is to economics.

The Theoretical Framework of Political Realism

A foremost exponent of the realist school of political science in the United States, Hans Morgenthau, has spelled out clearly the basic tenets of this approach.

First, it is assumed that politics, like all forms of human activity or like all social phenomena, is governed by "laws," meaning in this context not laws ordained by legislatures but natural laws, analogous to those that govern physical and biological phenomena. Moreover, these laws are supposed to be rooted in "human nature," which is a given and has remained unchanged "at least since the classical philosophies of China, India, and Greece endeavored to discover these laws" (Morgenthau 1962, p. 4).

Second, political realism identifies "interest" as the driving force in the behavior of states and defines interest in terms of "power." This reiterates the perceived analogy between the contents of economics and that of politics; as wealth is to economics, so is power to politics.

The adoption of power and power relations as the focus of interest in political science confers *autonomy* on that discipline by setting politics "as an autonomous sphere of action," distinguished from other spheres, such as economics, ethics, aesthetics, or religion. The implication is that it is possible to develop a theory of political action independent of the economic setting in which it takes place or independent of the ethical standards of the society in which it occurs.

Perhaps we would be doing Morgenthau an injustice if we interpreted this view to mean that economic conditions in a state or the ethical standards of its leaders exert no influence on the political goals pursued or on the means used to attain them. What Morgenthau more likely means is that pursuit of power serves as a common factor in all political action. What *form* power takes and what *means* are used to pursue it may well change with circumstances generated outside the political sphere. But whatever be the form of action or the means employed, the way to understanding politics is through understanding how power is pursued and used.

So far, no moral judgment is made about political action so defined. The theory is offered as an *efficient* theory. It is maintained that a better and deeper understanding of political behavior can be attained if explanations of this behavior are sought in the existing or envisaged power relations rather than, say, in the philosophic or political sympathies of statesmen. One should not be misled by the way statesmen present the rationales of their political actions, which may well be in terms of philosophical, ethical, (or generally ideological) considerations. The underlying motivating force, according to the political scientist of the realist persuasion remains couched in considerations of power and of power relations.

Morgenthau goes further, however. He regards a foreign policy based on the tenets of political realism as a "rational" foreign policy and regards a rational policy as a good policy, since it minimizes risks and maximizes benefits "and hence, complies both with the moral concept of prudence and the practical requirements of success" (p. 8).

Third, political realism takes due cognizance of the fact that the meaning and content of interest, defined as power, changes with the times and with circumstances. It is, therefore, empirically oriented. Moreover, it is pragmatic as well as realistic. The way of transforming the world for the better, seen through the prism of political realism, is via manipulating the forces operating at the time in accordance with the (presumed) laws governing those forces rather than by adhering to abstract ideals without taking realities of concrete situations into account.

Here Morgenthau expresses skepticism concerning the historical role of ideologies as forces that transform the political world or as forces that can be harnessed to effect desirable transformations.

Fourth, while recognizing the moral significance of political actions, political realism recognizes the "tension" between moral and political imperatives. Morgenthau denies the universal applicability of moral precepts in the political sphere. The supreme virtue in politics, in the realist's view, is prudence—a pragmatic principle which dictates weighing the consequences of alternative political actions and deliberately choosing the one that, as far as the political actor can see, is likely to lead to the most advantageous consequence.

In our discussion of rationality below (cf. Chapter 14), we will offer just such a definition of rational action. However, as we shall see, we shall have to come to grips with formidable conceptual difficulties as we analyze the consequences of this definition.

Fifth, political realism categorically rejects all claims by nations of being instruments of Providence, executors of God's will, Chosen People, and the like. All forms of crusade are anathema to the political realist. Ideology is not only denied the role of "midwife of history," but is also excluded as a basis for justification of political actions. On the other hand, seeing our own aspirations and those of others as based on interests (instead of being driven by missionary zeal) enables us to recognize the legitimacy of the aspirations of others. Perceiving others to be like us (in the sense of being motivated by similar interests) contributes, in Morgenthau's opinion, to international understanding and forestalls adventurism and fanaticism in the international arena.

As we examine historical events in the sphere of international relations, we can interpret many of them from the point of view of political realism, i.e., in terms of the interests of the parties involved, and from some other standpoint, say, of moral principle or international law. The strength of the political realist interpretation, according to Morgenthau, is that it explains more. That is, when the two explanations imply different additional facts or hypothetical events, usually the realist explanation accounts for the additional facts better or predicts a more reasonable hypothetical event than other explanations.

A case in point is the violation of Belgian neutrality by Germany at the start of World War I. This act brought Britain into the war on the side of France. The violation was a breach of a treaty, and Britain, as a guarantor of Belgian neutrality, could be said to have entered the war to fulfill her obligations under the treaty. At the same time, it had been Britain's policy for centuries not to allow a hostile power to dominate the Low Countries. So Britain's entry into the war could also be explained on the basis of interest. To decide between the two explanations, we could speculate on what was likely to have happened, if not Germany (at the time a potentially hostile power) but France (at the time a friendly power) had violated Belgium's neutrality. The consensus of opinion at the time was that Britain would not have entered the war on the side of Germany against France (Morgenthau 1973, p. 13).

Considerably more telling is the history of relations between the United States and China. Following the victory of the Chinese Communists over the Nationalist forces, the Soviet Union and China made common cause in the Cold War against the United States. In fact, the Korean War was seen by many American policymakers as a prelude to a war with China. The United States resisted stubbornly all attempts to admit China to the United Nations and to give her a seat on the Security Council, to which she was entitled by the U.N. Charter. The United States continued to insist that the government in Taiwan was the legitimate government of China. The U.S.S.R., of course, supported mainland China's claims.

In the meantime, however, the relations between the U.S.S.R. and China deteriorated to the point that it was widely believed that a war between the two Communist giants was imminent. Eventually, the attitude of the U.S. toward China was reversed. China was admitted to the United Nations and to the Security Council. The representative of the "Republic of China," as the government in Taiwan called itself, was expelled. For a while it even seemed that China's foreign policy leaned toward the U.S. For instance, the Chinese viewed positively the presence of the U.S. warships in East Asian waters, although the original task of that force was to protect Taiwan against China. Evidently China came to regard that force as a counterweight to the Soviet presence in the Far East. China was engaged in a number of sporadic border wars with Vietnam, which is allied with the Soviet Union. While Sino-Soviet relations are somewhat more relaxed today than they were ten years ago, one could evaluate the relations between "Communist" China and "Imperialist" United States as considerably more cordial than between "Communist" China and "Communist" Soviet Union. Clearer evidence for the greater relevance of power politics compared to ideological affinities would be hard to find.

Thus, there is considerable evidence in support of Morgenthau's contention that a theory of international relations based on interest, defined as power, provides more consistent explanations of the behavior of states than theories based on predispositions of statesmen, in particular on ideological affinities or antipathies. However, Morgenthau's contention to the effect that foreign policies based on realist principles (i.e., calculations of power relations) are generally more rational and therefore better policies is more problematic.

Morgenthau's judgment appears to be suggested by some traumas and fiascos of recent history as well as by the threats posed by the ideological interpretation of the continued confrontation between the superpowers. Surely, World War II was unleashed by an "ideology," namely, the conviction inculcated into the population of Germany by the Nazi propaganda machine that they, as members of a superior race, had the right to conquer and enslave other people. It is well to remember the futility and destructiveness of the so-called religious wars of the sixteenth and seventeenth centuries.

Morgenthau takes a somewhat different tack when he enumerates failures of policy based on miscalculations of power relations. He rightly points out that "power" is meaningful only as a relative, not as an absolute, concept. One can speak of the power of a nation only in relation to that of other nations. Since these relations change, estimates of power based on criteria characterizing only the nation in question can be seriously misleading. Thus, France at the close of World War I was regarded as the greatest military power in the world. The quality of the French armed forces (of their equipment, staff work, etc.) was no lower in 1940 than in 1919. So France continued to be regarded as "the strongest" power. In fact, the calm on the French-German front during the first months of World War II was seen as evidence that Germany did not dare attack "the world's finest army." France's crushing defeat in the spring of 1940 demonstrated that the French army, although its "quality" as such had not deteriorated, was no match for the Germany army.

Persistent misjudgments of relative military power by England and France led to their failure to form an alliance with the Soviet Union in 1939. (The Soviet Union was still regarded as "weak" on the basis of stereotypes of "Russian backwardness," hence not a valuable ally.) Failure to threaten Germany with a two-front war may also have helped to precipitate World War II. The obverse side of this underestimate of Soviet military power is the present conviction in Western military circles that Soviet land forces cannot possibly be contained by conventional weapons. This conventional wisdom provides the rationale for "nuclear deterrence," which is based on the constant threat of nuclear war.

If one accepts Morgenthau's views that more accurate estimates of the relative power of nations could have led to more "rational" and hence better foreign policies, in particular to avoidance of wars, then one can share his disdain for "ideology" as a guide to international relations on normative as well as on rational grounds. We will say, in passing, that the kind of "ideologies" Morgenthau had in mind are precisely the sort that have led to international disasters in the past and threaten global disaster today. If so, one can welcome, as Morgenthau undoubtedly would, the "end of ideology" as a factor in international relations. This conclusion is less than convincing, as we shall see, if "ideology" is viewed from another perspective.

"End of Ideology" in America?

Commenting on the riots that took place in Watts (a suburb of Los Angeles) in 1965, S.I. Hayakawa, a widely read writer on general semantics, wrote:

> Power in America is always limited and shared power, exerted by alliances and coalitions of political parties, business groups, churches, unions, minority blocs, and the like. New Left leaders adroitly escape power (and therefore responsibility) by refusing to enter into alliances or coalitions, which they term "making deals" and "selling out." Standing on their moral and ideological purity, they prefer the blazing rhetoric of moral denunciation to the give-and-take and the hemming-and-hawing of practical negotiation—for jobs, for better schools, for housing, for political support.
>
> From the New Left, therefore, Negroes can expect nothing: not money, nor power, nor jobs, nor better schools, nor housing, nor political leverage.
>
> The only hope for minorities, including the Negroes of Watts, lies in the broad center of both major parties—in those whose minds are neither in an imaginary past nor a visionary future, but in the realities of the present—in those who in the pragmatic, commonsense tradition of American life, will continue to hammer out the agreements and accommodations that we all must make to live together in peace and progress. (Hayakawa and Goodfield 1966.)

The reference to the "New Left" concerns the upsurge of political activity in the 1960s, which was sharply critical of government policies. This activity had strong ideological overtones. It contained a substantial admixture of rhetoric severely critical of American society and of the values dominant in it. This is not to say that the movement was not centered on specific issues. There were, in fact, two such issues. The civil rights campaign was clearly aimed at dismantling the pattern of racial discrimination. The other focus of protest was the Vietnam War. So it could not have been diffuseness of goals or a utopian orientation that set the New Left apart from "practical" political movements. More likely it was its tactics that made it politically impotent in Hayakawa's estimation. Instead of seeking out and manipulating the accessible levers of political power, the New Left spent its energies organizing mass meetings, protest marches, and "teach-ins," calling for establishment of social justice, as well as meaningful desegregation and an end to U.S. intervention in Vietnam. In this way, the movement presumably alienated not only those who held the reins of power but also the bulk of the population that constituted the mainstream of American life.

The "New Left" called itself that to call attention to its divergence from the "Old Left," the Socialist and Communist movements which practically dissipated after World War II. The American Socialist Party reached the pinnacle of its voter appeal in the presidential election of 1912, when its candidate, E.V. Debs, polled over a million votes. The old Socialist Party appealed directly to workers. Most of its support came from labor unions, which in those days led a precarious existence under perpetual threat of intimidation and harassment. The "class struggle" took concrete forms frequently erupting in violence, especially during strikes. A substantial measure of support for the Socialist Party came also from some minorities, still identified as immigrants and largely of the blue collar working force. Of these, the large Jewish contingent, primarily in the garment industries of New York, formed an important sector. These refugees from czarist persecutions brought with them the ideational baggage of the Russian revolutionary movement, a sort of simplified Marxism. The image of "workers exploited by bosses" was in those days not far removed from the reality of New York sweatshops.

The condition of the working man in the coal mines, the steel mills, the stockyards was similar: dank, unsanitary surroundings, long hours, low pay, bullying foremen, slum dwellings, lack of social services of any kind. To the extent that the worker was able to turn his attention from his personal plight to the common condition of those like him, he was attracted to the promise of socialism.

The Socialist Party opposed America's entry into World War I. Eugene Debs was jailed. While in prison, he again ran for president and received 920,000 votes. After the war, the Socialist Party, never a major political force, declined into insignificance. The reason was partly intimidation. In 1919 and 1920 Socialist Party and union headquarters were raided either by police or by gangs of self-appointed defenders of "Americanism," so-called vigilantes. Another blow to the Socialist Party was the split resulting from the formation of the Communist Party, which, following the "line" set by the Third International, directed their most vituperative campaign against the Socialists, who were accused of having betrayed the working class, among other things. Finally, a contributory factor in the decline of the Socialist movement was the "prosperity" of the 1920s. Immigration was severely restricted. Many of the earlier immigrants, no longer "green-horns," took advantage of opportunities presented by the comparative social mobility in America to rise into the middle class. Having internalized the individualist ideology of the mainstream, the erstwhile worker lost interest in the class struggle and in a radical restructuring of society.

During the Great Depression of the 1930s, the "Old Left," based on the labor movement and on loyalties generated by the class struggle, attained greater visibility and strength than ever before in American history. Union membership rose from three to fifteen million and comprised almost a third of the labor force. Organization was facilitated by a number of legislative measures guaranteeing the right to collective bargaining and inhibiting to a certain extent intimidation of workers by employers. However, no labor party appeared in the political arena. The Communists played an important role in union organization and rose to positions of power in some unions. But there was never the slightest chance that the Communists could achieve any significant successes in electoral politics.

The forces of the Left supported the Democratic Party, whose formidable political strength during the Roosevelt era was vested in a de facto coalition of labor, Blacks, ethnic minorities, and liberal intellectuals. The South (where the Blacks were still largely disfranchised) had voted traditionally Democratic since the end of the post-Civil War Reconstruction, although the political complexion of the white South was far from liberal, let alone radical.

The very success of the labor movement and of the liberal sector of the American public in putting through measures related to legitimizing union-ization and providing basic social services gave the *coup de grace* to what remained of the Socialist movement in the United States.

As Daniel Bell put it, American egalitarianism (which facilitated social mobility) was a "surrogate of socialism" to the American masses (Bell 1960). In the years when recent immigrants constituted a large portion of the American working class, revolutionary energies were diluted by assim-ilationist ambitions: Americanization was usually identified with moving into the middle class. In the 1930s the goal of the labor movement was not the restructuring of American society, but rather being accepted *into* so-ciety as a sector "in good standing," to be mentioned along with "business groups," "church groups" (products of egalitarian ideology in religion), and all the other "interest groups" whenever issues of public interest were on the political agenda. In fact, in collective bargaining negotiations, labor leaders and managers sitting across the table from each other grew indis-tinguishable, either by their appearance or by the style of their arguments.

At the time Bell's *The End of Ideology* appeared (1960), it seemed indeed that "ideology was dead" in the United States. The attack on the Left soon after the end of World War II spiked the feeble attempts of the Communist Party to assume an active political role. Communists had had considerable influence in American intellectual circles in the 1930s. Sympathy for the Soviet Union as a bulwark against fascism played a considerable part in that influence. The nonaggression pact between the Soviet Union and Nazi Germany was a severe blow to the pro-Soviet intelligentsia. Strong pro-Soviet sympathies were rekindled during the war, only to be extinguished in the wake of resumed persecution of intellectuals in the Soviet Union. Scientists, writers—all those with whom intellectuals of the West could find a common language and shared values—were vilified, exiled, or killed. The *razgrom* of genetics described in Chapter 8 typifies the anti-intellectual campaign of Stalin's last years. The sudden outburst of officially sanctioned anti-Semitism completed the alienation of American intellectuals from Communism. The Communist Party itself practically committed suicide by abandoning all pretense of a "united front" of progressives and resuming the narrow sectarian line of the 1920s. Whatever influence Communists retained in the labor unions was eliminated by the purges in the immediate postwar years. The unions were intent on not losing their hard-won legitimacy by harboring "subversives."

The expected postwar depression did not materialize. Hunger for consumer goods in short supply during the war and accumulated money not spent during the years of "scarcity" ushered in a postwar prosperity reminiscent of the 1920s amid similar political quiescence. It is in this setting that Bell developed the theme of his book.

This was on the very eve of the next resurgence of the "Left"—the "New Left," which was distinctly ideological in its orientation. The constituency of this movement was not primarily in labor. It comprised, in the first instance, young people, predominantly students and, in addition, church groups and similar "grass roots" constituencies, spontaneously sprouting "community organizations." The civil rights movement, essentially a massive assault on segregationist practices, was sparked by the Supreme Court decision of 1954, which declared racially segregated schools unconstitutional. The slowness with which integration of schools was implemented and the resistance to it (at times verging on violence) gave impetus to the movement. The first "battles" in the war against racial segregation were the Montgomery, Alabama, bus boycott of 1958 and the Selma, Alabama, protest march of 1960, which was attacked by the police.

The other wing of the mass protest movement of the 1960s was the resistance to the Vietnam War. The participants were to a large extent students and sympathetic faculty members of universities. Events called "teach-ins," reminiscent of the "sit-ins" of striking workers in the 1930s, were impressive demonstrations of how seriously "ideology" was taken in the United States in the 1960s. In that decade, the "Left" found a new cause—resistance against the drift toward war, which became especially apparent as the arms race between the U.S. and the U.S.S.R. took off in earnest.

The teach-in was conceived as an alternative to a strike. The first focus of opposition to U.S. intervention in Vietnam was in universities—understandably so because the draft threatened the students. There was no way of "selling" that war to them. The rhetoric of the postwar American administrations defending U.S. interventions as defense against Communist "takeovers" was too crude to appeal to most of the educated. (No doubt the reluctance to go overseas to fight in jungles ten thousand miles away helped to diminish the influence of the rhetoric.) In late winter 1965, the U.S. Air Force started systematic bombardment of North Vietnam, thus initiating American forces to overt combat operations. Massive transport of ground troops soon followed, leading to full-scale involvement of the U.S. in a war overseas.

On March 16, 1965, Alice Herz, an elderly lady, set herself on fire in Detroit, Michigan, as an act of protest against this war. Many were profoundly shocked. Groups had already formed on campuses to plan some fitting protest actions to publicize repugnance against the new openly violent phase of U.S. counterinsurgency policy. A faculty-student strike was proposed at the University of Michigan. However, the initial support for this action was weak. To go ahead with it would result in a publicized failure that would discourage further efforts. Next, it was proposed that faculty members use their classroom time to inform the students about the background of the war. This plan was also dropped, as only a few faculty members were sufficiently informed, and so only a few students would be reached. Besides, using classroom time for "propaganda," replacing instruction for which the faculty members were paid, might invite disciplinary action, and it was an open question how much of an impact such an action would make on public opinion.

Finally, the idea of the "teach-in" surfaced. Instead of striking, thus curtailing teaching (in violation of contracts) or diverting the content of teaching (which might also be interpreted as failure to discharge responsibility), concerned faculty members announced that they would devote a full *night* to teaching about the issues involved in U.S. intervention in Southeast Asia. This action could be publicized as the "opposite" of a strike, as deliberately increasing the teaching load beyond the contractual obligation.

The university administration went along with this plan. Facilities (lecture halls, classrooms) were made available to the organizers of the first teach-in, which took place on the night of March 24–25, 1965. Over three thousand students attended the several lectures, seminars, and open discussion sessions that took place between 8 P.M. and 8 A.M.

Supporters of the war marshaled a counterdemonstration. About 100 students picketed the building in which the teach-in was held, carrying signs that read "Better Dead than Red," "Drop the bomb!" and so on. There was a bomb threat in one of the halls, which had to be evacuated while it was searched. All these events added zest and excitement to the proceedings and accentuated a feeling of solidarity among the participants.

The next day, the State Department sent a team to the University of Michigan to explain U.S. policy. The "counter-teach-in" was attended by about 300 students. (Possibly many were sleeping off the vigil of the previous night.) That night, a teach-in took place at the University of Toronto. Within weeks, teach-ins were held at scores of American campuses. The culminating affair was the National Teach-in held in Washington, D.C., on May 15, 1965. It was attended by 5,000 persons and broadcast by a telephone hookup to about 40 campuses (Menashe and Radosh 1967).

The anti-Vietnam War movement and the civil rights movement were genuine *ideological* challenges to U.S. foreign policy and to racial attitudes prevailing in the United States. They could not be identified with "interests" of the sort that converted American domestic politics into an analogue of the marketplace, as Buchanan and Tullock pictured it in *The Calculus of Consent*. The demand of an end to racial segregation and the disfranchisement of Blacks could not be converted into an issue of give-and-take politics any more than the demand for the end of the Vietnam War, *because* these issues were ideological. Martin Luther King and other civil rights activists, Benjamin Spock and other antiwar activists, tried to reach the conscience of Americans, rather than appeal to their "interests."

Among the most prominent opponents of the Vietnam War and a key participant in the National Teach-in was Hans Morgenthau, author of *Politics Among Nations*, discussed in the beginning of this chapter. He condemned the war from the point of view of political realism, arguing that "defense of South Vietnam" (as the intervention was rationalized by the Johnson administration) could not by any stretch of the imagination be regarded as in the "national interest" of the United States, since Southeast Asia was entirely outside of its (presumably) legitimate sphere of interest. From the same standpoint, however, Morgenthau was not in a position to condemn U.S. intervention in the Dominican Republic, where a democratically elected government was overthrown by U.S. Marines. The Dominican Republic did fall within the (presumably) legitimate sphere of influence of the United States. Domination of Vietnam could not realistically be expected to be maintained indefinitely; domination of the Caribbean could. Nor would Morgenthau be in a position to condemn the Soviet invasion of Afghanistan, nor its military intervention in Czechoslovakia, nor the pressure on Poland resulting in the crushing of the democratic upheaval in that country in 1980–1981.

Political Realism and Pragmatism as Ideologies

Once the "national interest" of a state is identified, the consistency of Morgenthau's views on intervention is unquestioned. Challenging those views on moral grounds is pointless, since the stance of political realism explicitly subordinates moral considerations to those of interests defined as power. This sharp division is, in turn, consistent with the view that each sphere of human activity is autonomous. Economics is based on one set of values, ethics on another, and so forth. The values of politics are specific to that sphere and values properly considered in other spheres ought not impinge on political considerations.

Morgenthau, however, implicitly invokes values extrinsic to the political sphere (as he defines it) when he points to the disastrous consequences of basing foreign policy on ideological doctrines. He unequivocally condemns crusades, holy wars, conquests rationalized as civilizing missions, and the like, presumably not only on the grounds that they fail to "minimize risks and maximize benefits" strictly in terms of a power calculus, but also on the grounds that war is bad for humanity. We infer as much from his statement to the effect that "the autonomy of the political sphere against its subversion by other modes of thought does not imply disregard for the existence and importance of those other modes of thought."

"Political realism," he goes on, "is based on a pluralistic conception of human nature. . . . A man who was nothing but 'political man' would be a beast. . . . A man who was nothing but a 'moral man' would be a fool. . . . A man who was nothing but a 'religious man' would be a saint. . . ." (Morgenthau 1973, p. 14.)

If international relations are determined by policies designed by human beings—presumably composites of "political," "moral," and other classifications—then the question of how the political sphere can be guarded against "subversion by other modes of thought" without these human beings turning into beasts is left unanswered.

There is a basic difficulty with both Morgenthau's picture of "de-ideologized" theory of international relations and Bell's picture of "post-ideological" America. Both are based on underlying ideologies, but not recognized as such. In fact, recalling once again the meaning that Marx assigned to "ideology," we see that, in that context, being unaware of one's own ideology is essential to having one.

Bell presents a vivid panorama of postwar American society, scanning the world of business, the world of politics, the world of work, the world of crime. A principal theme of the book is the decline and final disappearance of the "socialist vision" in America and the sociological reasons for its dissipation. Part III of the book is called "The Exhaustion of Utopia." The familiar world of pragmatic politics has taken its place.

In Chapter 6, we offered several ways of classifying ideologies. One was on the basis on their orientation toward the past, the present, or the future. Pragmatism is an ideology in which the present, rather than the past or the future, commands the center of attention.

The pragmatic orientation is the problem-solving orientation. When the existing state of affairs does not correspond to a desired state of affairs, the problem-solving attitude turns attention to the concrete nature of the discrepancy. To formulate a problem means to spell out in concrete terms— that is, in terms that can be related to concrete observations—just what it is about the existing state of affairs that distinguishes it from the desired state. One then scans one's memory or experience or store of knowledge to see whether means are available to remove undesirable features or to add desirable ones to what is *given*. If these deletions or additions can be accompanied by manipulating matter, one resorts to technological solutions. If changes are required in relations among people, solutions can be sought in the realm of politics. At all times, however, results of manipulation are monitored. One takes account of where one *is* and at each step decides where one wants to be next, given the constraints of the situation and the means at one's disposal. The past is examined only to see which means have worked and which have not in (presumably) similar situations. The horizon of the future is limited by how much can be expected to be accomplished starting from where one *is*.

The dynamics of pragmatic politics are well described by Buchanan and Tullock (1965). Acceptance of those processes as realizations of democracy and as contributions to the preservation of social peace constitutes acceptance of the pragmatic ideology in the sphere of politics.

This acceptance (and a recommendation to others to accept it) is clearly evident in S.I. Hayakawa's comments cited above: "The only hope . . . lies . . . in those whose minds are neither in an imaginary past nor a visionary future, but in the realities of the present. . . ." The same attitude is implicit in Bell's description of the American scene, especially in his reference to the illusions of nineteenth-century European revolutionary utopianism. He cites Charles Fourier (French socialist thinker, 1772–1837), who promised that under socialism people would be at least ten feet tall,

Karl Kautsky (German Social Democrat, 1854–1938), "the embodiment of didactism," who proclaimed that the average citizen of the socialist society would be a superman, and Antonio Labriola (Italian Marxist philosopher, 1843–1904), who told his followers that their socialist-bred children would each be Galileos and Giordano Brunos. To these visions, Bell juxtaposes the gospel of Samuel Gompers, founder of the American Federation of Labor: "The working people are in too great need of immediate improvements in their condition to allow them to forego them in their endeavor to devote their entire energies to an end, however beautiful to contemplate. . . . The way out of the wage system is through higher wages."

Bell's acceptance of the present-oriented ideology has a broader philosophical base. He concludes his book by calling attention to what he regards as the lesson of the intellectual history of the past hundred years embodied in Thomas Jefferson's wisdom "aimed at removing the dead hand of the past, but which can serve as a warning against the heavy hand of the future as well: 'The present belongs to the living.' "

The same lesson seems to be embodied in the reproach addressed by Alexander Herzen (Russian humanitarian and revolutionist, 1812–1870) to an earlier revolutionist:

> Do you truly wish to condemn all human beings alive today to the sad role of caryatids . . . supporting a floor for others someday to dance on? . . . This alone should serve as a warning to people; an end that is infinitely removed is not an end, but, if you like, a trap; an end must be nearer—it ought to be, at the very least, the laborer's wage or pleasure in work done. Each age, each generation, each life has its own fullness. . . . (Cited in Bell 1960, p. 375.)

The ideology underlying political realism is also present-oriented, as is implied by the term "realism" itself—an orientation in which things "as they are" remain at the focus of attention. This orientation also induces an implicit *acceptance* of "things as they are." Morgenthau envisages a possible future when the national state is no longer the primary form of political organization (in the sense of being a repository of power). He also recognizes that the interest of a national state is a product of its history and would therefore disappear in the course of history. Indeed national states themselves come on and off the stage of history. Nevertheless, Morgenthau insists, whatever transformation can be brought about in the contemporary world can be brought about only by manipulating perennial forces that have shaped the past and will shape the future, that is to say, *presently* operating forces, in particular in the international arena, the power relations among states.

In classifying ideologies, we also distinguished between those primarily oriented toward constancy and those primarily oriented toward change. The terms "static" and "dynamic" refer to corresponding theories of physical systems, personalities, societies, etc. In the present context, the term "static" ought, perhaps, to be avoided because of its connotation of quiescence or stagnation. "Equilibrium" comes closer to the meaning of constancy, as it applies to systems that preserve constancy as a *consequence* of dynamic interactions. For example, there is a vast amount of activity inside a gas confined in a volume, if one regards the molecules of the gas as "acting units": they move wildly about, colliding with others, changing course, and so forth. Nevertheless, the gas can be said to be in a *dynamic equilibrium*. Buyers and sellers may be engaged in vigorous activity (the stock exchange may resemble a madhouse). But assuming the operation of the classical "laws" of supply and demand, exchange rates fluctuate around equilibrium values.

A central concept in the realist conception of international relations is *balance of power*, which is regarded as a stabilizing factor. A realistic foreign policy is guided by calculations of power relations. If a balance of power or a near-balance exists, so the theory goes, and if statesmen are realists, their pursuit of interests will be circumscribed by the existing power relations. If a balance truly exists and if political leaders of national states are committed to preserving it, then whatever deviations in the power of one state or a coalition of states will occur relative to others will be "corrected" by corresponding shifts of policy.

The American system of government, too, can be said to be based on a balance of power, a system of "checks and balances," as it is usually called. The Founding Fathers saw to it that power was not concentrated in the Executive. The independence of the Judiciary from either of the other two branches of government is generally conceded to have served as the basis of civil liberties and human rights to which America owes its (for the most part justified) reputation as a haven of individual freedom.

The same system of checks and balances is supposed by the proponents of a "de-ideologized" exchange system to operate in American workaday democratic politics as various interests groups maneuver for political advantages, form and dissolve coalitions, determining a sort of resultant of a large number of force vectors that constitutes policy.

We have repeatedly called attention to the distinction between a descriptive and a normative theory. The former purports to do no more than offer a cogent description of the way things are; the latter, on the other hand, says something of the way things ought to be. Bell's theory of de-ideologized politics and Morgenthau's theory of political realism can be understood both as descriptive and as normative theories. As descriptive theories they are convincing, being supported by a great wealth of evidence.

As normative theories, clearly they are value-laden rather than value-free; sometimes, especially in the case of Morgenthau, explicitly so. That author sees international politics based on national interest and on the power calculus as the most promising way to peace, and he is unquestionably in favor of peace. Bell, too, although not as explicitly, points to the "end of ideology" with satisfaction as a maturation of domestic politics, promising a lasting social peace. Hayakawa and Goodfield (1966) state this hope explicitly: ". . . agreements and accommodations that we all must make to live together in peace and progress."

Theories related to the physical world (explaining how it works) are necessarily value-free. The physical world does not care how we feel about it, and human cognition is mature to the extent that human beings recognize this fact of life. A large number of social scientists believe that the social sciences should also be value-free, since they regard the recognition of the independence of questions regarding "what is" and those regarding "what ought to be" as a foremost principle of scientific cognition. Note that this judgment is itself a value judgment, since it states what the scientific mode of thought ought to be like. But is the distinction between value-free and value-laden knowledge as sharp as this judgment assumes it to be? Consider the difference between the *effects* that statements about the world have on the world. They have no effect on the physical world: whatever we write, say, or think about physical reality has no impact on that reality, which remains what it is regardless of the way we perceive it or talk about our perceptions. The situation with social reality is different. What we write, say, or even think about social reality is *ipso facto* part of that reality. Thus, if we change our perceptions or judgments, at least a part of social reality also changes.

The realist mode of thinking about politics creates a certain image of political reality, in particular of international relations. This image is internalized by many persons who play or will someday play an active role in this reality, as statesmen, public servants, negotiators, authors of books about political reality, and the like. Internalized, the image perpetuates itself. If it is *believed* to correspond to reality, the persons who will be recruited into political life will be predominantly those who agree with that belief. Unlike the physical world, the world of culture, of social relations, of international relations, exists inside the heads of people. To a very large extent (though by no means in all respects) it is what it is believed to be. It is for this reason that ideologies are important components of social reality.

However, ideologies become obsolete. Bell has shown, convincingly, in our opinion, that the nineteenth century revolutionary ideology centered on the class struggle and on a vision of humanity emancipated in a socialist world became obsolete in consequence of the radical changes in the structure of Western industrialized societies. The ideology of the class struggle and the vision of a socialist world were important inputs into the processes that produced these changes. But the fact remains that *that* ideology has become exhausted. This does not mean by any means that ideology has simply disappeared from politics in industrialized democracies. All we can say is that another ideology has replaced the revolutionary ideology that was spawned in the wake of the Industrial Revolution. The change in the mode of production, which Marx correctly believed to be a prime mover of social change, was responsible for the dramatic change in the structure of Western societies, *not*, however, in the direction predicted by Marx (proletarianization of the masses) but rather in the opposite direction; the absorption of the bulk of the populations of industrialized countries into the middle class, in which revolutionary ideology withered.

Even more clearly obsolete is the ideology underlying political realism in the sphere of international relations. The circumstance that makes this obsolescence clear is the advent of weapons of total destruction that have rendered meaningless the use of violence in pursuit of national interests. One excludes reality from one's field of perception when one views these weapons as just another "technological advance" necessitating rethinking of military strategy in order to be able to regard these weapons as additions to "national power." In a few hours, activation of the global nuclear arsenal can destroy completely the infrastructure of civilization, and within a few months quite probably all human life. This is not an assertion subject to various interpretations, one whose validity depends on values we assign to conditions and events. It does not derive from our ideas about social reality. It derives from our knowledge about *physical* reality and from our knowledge of what it takes to sustain life. Knowledge of these matters is as reliable as human knowledge can possibly be. It cannot be rationally refuted. It can, however, be simply ignored by excluding from consciousness the events to which it refers. A fixation on the ideology underlying "political realism" effects this exclusion.

Let us examine the content of that ideology as it applies to the theory of international relations. States are assumed to be actors, i.e., entities having "interests," designing strategies to pursue them, implementing these strategies, and so forth. These "interests" are embodied in images of political reality in the minds of persons who, by virtue of the authority vested in them, make the decisions that constitute policies. That these decisions can be implemented is a consequence of "legitimacy" conferred on the authority of the decision makers. That is to say, a sufficient proportion of the population has so internalized habits or imperatives of obedience to authority that the actions ordered will be executed. The vast organization of human activities called the State owes its continued existence to this internalization of imperatives and habits of obeying legitimate authorities.

That states so defined still exist is beyond dispute. Note, however, that the *system of states* that produced the political reality on which realist political theories focus no longer exists. That system comprised essentially the states of Europe and the relations in which they stood vis-à-vis each other from about the middle of the seventeenth century to the outbreak of World War I. It is with regard to that system that the theory of international relations embodied in political realism, in particular the theory of the balance of power, applies most convincingly. In fact, a multinational system (comprising more than two states) is practically necessary as a setting for the operation of a balance of power, whereby disruptions of equilibrium are corrected by readjustments. In a bipolar system, without "third parties" free to direct their weight to restore the balance, such adjustments are difficult to imagine, for they would necessitate voluntary *reduction* of power by the side that "got ahead."

This is surely the case in the present arms race between the United States and the Soviet Union. A political realist who believes that a balance of power is the best guarantee of peace would hardly look with favor on this arms race. The theory of national interest defined as power has nothing to say about how such an arms race might be stopped, let alone reversed. The root of the difficulty is that the theory does not indicate how "national interest" is to be determined. One must assume that it is to be defined by the political leaders of the national states comprising the international system. For all practical purposes, the power of the present international system (as power is presently defined by political leaders) is concentrated in the Big Two. And it is precisely here that national interest is defined by each side as possession of destructive power at least as large as, preferably larger than, that possessed by the other. The fact that this conception of national interest has reduced the concept to an absurdity cannot be derived from the theory.

Curiously, while Morgenthau does not seem to realize that "political realism" is just another ideology, he does realize that "balance of power" is one, that it serves as a concept in terms of which aggressive actions of states can be rationalized. He specifically mentions the outbreak of the Seven Years War in 1756, which was rationalized by both warring sides, England and France, in terms of preserving the "balance of power" in Europe. Likewise in 1813, when the Allied Powers submitted conditions of peace to Napoleon, they justified them as a restoration of the "balance of power." Napoleon justified his rejection of these conditions *on the same grounds*.

At this point in time, the "balance of power" fetish serves as the perpetual justification for each escalation of the nuclear arms race. Indeed, the ever-elusive "balance of power" is the driving force toward war behind every arms race in a bipolar system in which the leaders are mesmerized by the "realism" of the struggle for power.

To be sure, there are states outside the bipolar system, and they do engage in wars. It is said that since the end of World War II, there have been a total of twelve days when some war has not been going on somewhere on this planet. Those states sprouting in the debris of the colonial system bear little resemblance to the states of eighteenth- and nineteenth-century Europe which were bound by a network of diplomacy (not to speak of kinship ties among the monarchs and a common ideology), where the catalogue of "interests" was compiled and where the ideas comprising the realist theory of international relations arose. Iran and Iraq are presently at each other's throats not in consequence of "continuation of politics by other means" but in consequence of suicidal stupidity. The same can be said about the numerous wars that will probably for years wrack the fringes of the industrialized world. The most reasonable explanation of these outbursts is that those states have been supplied with weapons by the industrialized states who profit by the trade, enabling the rulers of Third World states, for the most part winners in often murderous scrambles for power, to go on a rampage. Diplomatic skills, the supposed key to keeping power politics within tolerable bounds, cannot have been acquired by Qaddafi or Khomeini, for example.

It is not these wars, however horrendous they are, that threaten humanity. It is the superpowers who literally hold the power of life and death over all of us. It is their relationship that holds the key to whether our species can survive or must become extinct because it became maladjusted to the environment which it itself "secreted": the environment of obsolete ideologies. But discarding obsolete ideologies does not mean an end of ideology. What Einstein meant by a "substantially new manner of thinking" is a substantially new ideology, one that is conducive to survival rather than to extinction. Einstein would probably have agreed that preoccupation with the struggle for power would have no place in it.

Notes

1. Port Arthur, which unlike the Russian port Vladivostok, is icefree, was wrested by Japan from China in 1894, then from Japan by Russia. It fell to the Japanese on January 1, 1905, after a siege of several months.

2. The article in *Novoe Vremia* was cited in the German periodical *Der Spiegel*, No. 30, 1984, pp. 92–93.
3. However, the identity of the cruiser is established in another article (*Pravda*, April 30, 1984) on the history of the ship, where her participation in the Battle of Tsushima is recounted along with eulogies to the heroic behavior of its crew.

THE STRATEGIC APPROACH

13

The Strategic Mode of Thought

So far our discussion of conflict has centered on its determining or contributing factors: genetic, psychological, or ideological. These factors can be said to "act upon" participants in a conflict, for example, by making them predisposed toward engaging in conflict, by shaping their attitudes toward others, or toward conflict as such, or by channeling conflict into specific modes, such as violence, polemics, or sublimation.

In this and the following chapters concerned with the strategic dimension, we will look at conflict from the point of view of a participant as a *subject*, not as an object influenced by circumstances over which he has little or no control. As a subject the participant in a conflict is, to begin with, clearly aware of the conflict situation he is in, of the presence of one or more adversaries and, most important, of the goals to be achieved in consequence of emerging victorious. In other words, we will be concerned with the thought processes of a participant who sees the conflict as a *problem*.

Awareness of a problem arises from an awareness of a discrepancy between an existing and a desired state of affairs, hence an ability to imagine a still nonexistent but presumably attainable state of affairs. An attempted solution for a problem consists of searching for ways and means of getting from "here" to "there." This way of dealing with the situation is usually regarded as rational. A rational or problem-solving attitude is often juxtaposed to an emotion-dominated one, manifested in reactions which may provide internal gratification but which are often inappropriate or futile from the problem-solving point of view. In approaching conflict from the point of view of a participant acting as a problem solver, we shall be concerned with the "rational" conduct of conflict.

People concerned with strategy in the context of military science, for example, tend to identify the strategic mode of thought with rationality in conflict situations. It will be our task to examine this conception of strategic thinking more closely. To do this, we shall have to offer some definitions. We will accept a definition of strategy proposed by a military writer: "A strategy is a plan of action designed in order to achieve some end; a purpose together with a system of measures for its accomplishment" (Wylie 1967, p. 9). "Rationality," being a more general concept, is more difficult to define to everyone's satisfaction. Some aspects of rationality, however, are widely recognized. We tend to regard a person as "rational" if, in choosing among available courses of action, he takes into account the consequences of his choice. Another mark of rationality is maintaining contact with reality, that is, relating one's beliefs to some actual experiences, one's own or others'. Still another, in the context of problem solving, is a realistic appraisal of the efficacy of the means used in the pursuit of a given goal. Finally, rationality involves an ability to think "logically," that is, to avoid unwarranted generalizations and errors in going from premises to conclusions. Unwarranted generalizations are the most common lapses of rationality from which no one is immune. However, one aspect of rationality might be being aware of this universal limitation.

None of these criteria can be unambiguously established. Different people have different conceptions of "reality." Perfectly rigorous deductive logic cannot be applied outside of mathematics. No generalization is perfectly reliable. In applying the criterion of taking into account consequences of actions, it is not clear how long-term consequences are to be weighed against immediate ones. Thus, we can at most form impressions of the *degree* of rationality that we can reasonably ascribe to a given approach to a problem. In our evaluation of strategic thinking, as it is reflected in writings on military strategy, we will point out the constraints on the exercise of rationality characteristic of this mode of thought.

Strategy as a Philosophy of War

The usage of the term "strategy" is not confined to military contexts. We hear of strategic management, of strategies on the football field, strategies in conducting an election campaign, and numerous others. It is true, however, that the term suggests military language. Etymologically, "strategy" is related to "generalship." Indeed, in most cases, reference to strategy is made in conflict situations, as in competitive business, competitive sports, and competitive politics, as well as in war.

In the literature on military science, "strategy" is also used in another way, namely, to describe a particular conception of war, its "essence" (to use an antiquated concept) or, more concretely, its purpose, its function in human societies and, at times still more concretely, the roles assigned to the various branches of the armed forces, including views about their relative importance. In short, a "strategy" is often identified with a particular "philosophy" of war.

By way of example, Carl von Clausewitz, often acclaimed as an outstanding philosopher of war, maintained that the overriding, in fact, the single objective of war is the destruction of the adversary's armed forces. He spelled out both the means to be used and the end to be gained by war. The means are decisive battles; the end is the destruction of the adversary's will to resist and consequently the imposition of the victor's "will" on the vanquished.

Emphatically reiterating this conception of war (which Clausewitz repeatedly did in his magnum opus *On War* [Clausewitz 1832/1966]) may seem to some as belaboring the obvious. That this is not so can be seen by examining the almost diametrically opposite view of war of Mao Zedong. Mao was concerned with a war dominated by guerrilla operations. Large-scale confrontations with the enemy were avoided, not sought. There was no prospect of annihilating the enemy's armed forces in engagements. Rather, those forces were expected to disintegrate in consequence of loss of support by the population converted to the revolutionary cause.

To cite another example contradicting Clausewitz's theory of war, Japan's "will to resist" was broken in 1945 in spite of the fact that the bulk of her land forces was still intact. It seems Clausewitz's philosophy of war, like Mao's, was shaped by his own war experience: in Clausewitz's case in the Napoleonic Wars, in which the great land battles played a decisive role; in Mao's case in the revolutionary war in China.

J.C. Wylie brings out important differences between *sequential* and *cumulative* strategies. In the former, success consists in sequential expansions of controlled territory. For example, the struggle between Germany and the Soviet Union during World War II was marked at first by a large expansion of territory controlled by the Germans, later by the loss of that territory to the Soviets, who pushed on into the heart of Germany itself, thus achieving victory.

In contrast, battles on the seas and especially in the air do not result in expansion or contraction of well marked territories controlled by the adversaries. Rather, encounters result in differential losses of military potential (ships, aircraft). It is assumed that the cumulative effect of these losses eventually becomes decisive.

The different ways of waging war on land, sea, and in the air induce different commitments by respective specialists in the different armed forces. Understandably, each emphasizes the decisive role of his own branch. Partisans of the different branches become prominent figures in military science literature by eloquent and, for the most part, strongly biased espousal of different philosophies of war. To Clausewitz, war was synonymous with land battles. Champions of the navy, like the American strategist A.T. Mahan (1917), were inspired by the dominance of the British Empire based entirely on the control of the seas. Enthusiasts of air power, by the nature of that power, identify control with destructive potential. The most vociferous of these wrote in the first decades of the twentieth century, when aviation appeared as the "wave of the future." No doubt, the ability of the airplane simply to ignore the traditional defenses (trenches, pillboxes, and all the other descendants of classical fortifications) seemed awesome. Giulio Douhet, an ardent partisan of air warfare wrote:

> . . . Two new weapons, the air arm and poison gas . . . will completely upset all forms of war so far known. . . . Air power makes it possible not only to make bombing raids over any sector of the enemy's territory but also to ravage his whole country by chemical and bacteriological warfare. . . . Three kinds of bombs are needed. The explosives will demolish the target, the incendiaries will set fire to it, and the poison gas bombs prevent the fire fighters from extinguishing the fires.
>
> In order to assure an adequate national defense, it is necessary—and sufficient—to be in a position . . . to conquer the command of the air . . .
>
> Any diversion from this primary purpose is an error. (Douhet 1921/1972, pp. 6–7, 20, 28.)

Constraints

The Situational Constraint

Wylie correctly points out that each of these four philosophies of war, the continental (Clausewitz), the maritime (Mahan), the aerial (Douhet), and the guerrilla (Mao), is situation-bound. It "works" only in a proper environment. Napoleon's land victories did not pave the way to the conquest of Britain, because the British commanded the sea. In fact, Napoleon had floundered already in Russia, because he did not reckon with the fact that the Russians would refuse to abide by the rules of "civilized warfare," i.e., capitulate when Moscow was occupied. Mao and Castro's guerrillas were victorious, but Che Guevara's were not. Even less likely is a successful revolution led by guerrillas in countries where, instead of a peasantry, desperate in its misery and easily imbued with revolutionary fervor, the population consists predominantly of a highly urbanized middle class with a strong stake in existing institutions. The revolution on which Italian and German terrorist groups pinned their hopes must remain a romantic dream. In spite of the destruction wreaked by Anglo-American forces on German industry and civilian population, German war production actually kept increasing to the very end of World War II. German civilians did not demand peace after 36 hours of bombing, as Douhet thought they would.[1] Germany was brought to her knees only when almost her entire territory was occupied.

Constraints of Past Experience

Rationality is frequently identified with the ability to learn from experience. Inevitably, however, what is learned from experience involves *selection* of apparently causal relations. Such selection can often be misleading, especially if it entails unjustified generalizations.

One of the most persistent controversies in the philosophy of war is that revolving around the relative merits of "offensive" and "defensive" operations. Clearly, the advantages and limitations of each are determined by specific situations. Superiority over the enemy appears to provide an opportunity for destroying or crippling him by a bold attack. Faced with a superior enemy, a military commander might regard defense as the more prudent course.

Aside from recognizing the obvious relevance of specific situations, however, military theoreticians have espoused different views on the *overall* importance of offensive and defensive strategies in the conduct of a war. It stands to reason that their views must have been substantially influenced by their own special expertise. In addition, however, recent historical experience has played a major role in the formulations of military doctrine.

Throughout the nineteenth century, French strategists were outstanding partisans of the offensive. Quite likely the memory of Napoleon's successes which, in their estimation, bestowed glory on French arms, was a determining factor in their outlook. In fact, Clausewitz, an outspoken exponent of the offensive, was more assiduously read and ardently admired in France than in Germany. The importance Clausewitz attached to the morale of the troops fitted especially well into the prevailing mood of the French military. Something called "élan" was supposed to be a decisive factor in battles, and the outcomes of battles were assumed to be the obvious decisive factor in the outcome of a war.

We find clear expression of this idea in the writings of Ardant du Picq, who appears to have been inspired by Marshall M. de Saxe and Count J.A.H. de Guibert (cf. below). Du Picq dismissed the notion that victory in battle is decided by a sort of physical shock, like an impact of a heavier body on a lighter one. The decisive factor, he insisted, is psychological.

> In battle, two moral forces, even more than two material forces are in conflict. The stronger conquers. The victor has often lost . . . more than the vanquished. . . . With equal or even inferior power of destruction, he will win who is determined to advance, who . . . has the moral ascendancy. . . . The moral impulse lies in the perception by the enemy of the resolution that animates you. Maneuvers . . . are threats. He who appears most threatening wins. (Cited in Possony and Mantoux 1941, p. 210.)

French military thinking at the start of World War I was dominated by these ideas. Ferdinand Foch, an enthusiastic disciple of Clausewitz, wrote: "The will to conquer: such is victory's first condition and therefore every soldier's first duty; but it also amounts to a supreme resolve which the commander must, if need be, impart to the soldier's soul." (Foch 1918, p. 287.)

Clearly, these sentiments extol the offensive. One does not exercise "the will to conquer" sitting behind fortifications. World War I, however, turned out to be a sitting war on the Western front. Barbed wire and the machine gun should have soon convinced both sides of the futility of attacking strongly fortified positions. But the lesson was learned only at the cost of millions of lives. Jean de Pierrefeu recalls Foch's behavior during a battle:

> . . . bursting like a tornado into every headquarters, his face contorted, . . . gesticulating in jerky spurts . . . to a general who in anguish tells him, "My troops are yielding overwhelmed by numbers; if I do not get reinforcements, I cannot answer for anything," he replies with a sweeping angry gesture: "Attack!" "But . . . ," says the general. "Attack!" The general tries to insist . . . "Attack, attack, attack!" bellows Foch and dashes out to charge like an electric battery . . . other faltering spirits. (Pierrefeu 1923, p. 308.)

The French did not win World War I in the sense of achieving victories. The Germans lost it by exhaustion, by hunger, by being bled white in futile attempts at offensive, as in the eight-month-long battle of Verdun, in which successive waves of attacking infantry were blasted by artillery shells, mowed down by machine gun fire, poisoned by gas.

Thus was born the "legend of Verdun," the conviction that modern fortifications can withstand any assault. After World War I, the French military doctrine became anchored in defense. Already after the disastrous offensive of 1917, Prime Minister P. Painlevé, speaking to the Chamber of Deputies, said, "There will be no more offensives."

The "legend of Verdun" was cast in concrete in the form of the Maginot

Line, against which all future onslaughts of the Germans were supposed to shatter. When these onslaughts were unleashed in the spring of 1940, France was defeated in a few weeks.

It seems that lessons were indeed learned by military theoreticians from successive wars, but often the wrong lessons. In fairness, however, it must be recognized that farsightedness was not uncommon among the strategists. The future of aviation and of mobile armor was forecast by imaginative military thinkers. These were frequently set up (in retrospect) as examples of progressive and creative thought. It should be kept in mind, however, that predictions which justify themselves remain in the memory far more frequently than those which do not.

Ideological Constraints

The strategist is, by definition, concerned with the art and science of war. It is conceivable that his interest does not extend beyond that of a scholar, in which case his theory of war will be a purely descriptive one; he will attempt to draw more or less general conclusions from his analyses of historical instances and trends. For the most part, however, strategists who theorize about war are themselves deeply committed to particular doctrines. Accordingly, their theories are normative, not merely descriptive. They extol certain forms of warfare and deprecate others.

The strategist's ideas may be in line with currently dominant ideas or opposed to them. Whether in the latter case he is free to espouse his views (which entail criticism of prevalent ones) depends on his political environment. In some societies sharp critique of existing policies or doctrines may preclude professional advancement but is not fraught with more serious dangers. In other societies to criticize the established doctrine may mean to risk one's life. Whether conformist or critic, whether in the latter case he can be frank or must hide behind a smoke screen, a strategist can be assumed to accept the basic tenets of the ideology that governs the thinking of the power elite of his society. If he is a critic, his criticism (explicit or implicit) is directed at the means, not at the goals of the elite, for in most cases he is himself a member of that elite and therefore is subjected to the ideological constraints imposed either on it or by it.

The Soviet Strategists

One would expect that ideological constraints on strategic thinking would be especially severe in the Soviet Union because of the intense indoctrination that pervades all Soviet educational institutions, especially the military. And indeed examination of Soviet strategic literature gives this impression. One excerpt is given to illustrate:

> The appearance of a new methodology in the study of military phenomena was related to the birth of the dialectic method, which uncovered great opportunities to elucidate the rules governing changes in the nature of war and the methods of its conduct.
> The founders of this scientific method, K. Marx and F. Engels, showed that industrial development, railroad construction, and the appearance of new types of weapons and equipment caused changes in army organization and in the development and expansion of theoretical military concepts, and, consequently, the necessity for a more complete study of war. (Sokolovskii 1963, p. 87.)

The passage seems to imply that Marx and Engels were primarily responsible for the realization that railroads and the like were important new factors in the conduct of wars. As we have pointed out, however, it is difficult to assess the extent to which the officially sanctioned ideology, Marxism-Leninism, is actually internalized by the Soviet power elite, particularly by the military. Ritualized affirmation of faith pervades every politically or philosophically sensitive public discussion in the Soviet Union. In what follows we will try to trace ideological influences on Soviet military thought as they are manifested in the history of the Soviet military establishment.

Before the establishment of Stalin's autocracy, there was an intense ideologically inspired controversy about the function and organization of the military establishment of the Soviet Union. A large proportion of the officers who had served in the czarist army formed the backbone of the anti-Communist forces, against which the Bolsheviks fought a three-year-long civil war. But many of these officers, taking seriously the apolitical conception of the military profession, remained loyal to the new regime. The issue of the controversy revolved around those officers. Political leaders who were pragmatically oriented valued competence above ideological purity; the ideologues insisted on a complete break with the past and on building a revolutionary army on entirely new principles. A compromise of sorts led to a system of political commissars attached to the commands of army units. One of their functions was to keep the commanders under surveillance. This system of dual control (orders of commanding officers had to be countersigned by the commissars) was for the most part deeply resented by the military professionals. Throughout the history of the Red Army, the commissars were at times removed, at times reinstated.

In the early years of the Soviet regime, the role of the Red Army in the international arena was also an ideological issue. It will be recalled that the struggle between Stalin and Trotsky ostensibly revolved around the question of whether Soviet foreign and military policy was to be based on the expectation of an imminent world revolution or whether the Soviet Union was to "dig in," i.e., effectively withdraw from the world scene and devote all of its energy to "building socialism in one country." The latter course was taken in the wake of Stalin's political victory. It enabled an all-out effort of rapid industrialization and the building of a formidable war machine.

The effects of this fortress mentality were twofold. On the one hand, isolationism precluded military adventures and provided a credible rationale for a belief that the Soviet Union was genuinely dedicated to peaceful coexistence. Against the background of this belief, the militarization of Soviet society appeared as a response to the ever-present threat of war that the "imperialists" could unleash at any time in order to destroy what they supposedly perceived as a horrendous threat—the "first socialist state." The siege mentality has remained long after World War II, as can be seen from the following passage:

> The success of the world socialist system, which has become a decisive factor in the development of human society, the . . . insoluble contradictions in the capitalist camp, and the desire of peoples for peace clearly show the imperialists that their intentions to dominate the world cannot be realized. All this causes the imperialists, and primarily the American imperialists, to make greater efforts to ward off their inevitable destruction and, by means of war, to change the course of world events now so unfavorable to them. This is the reason that contemporary imperialism poses a threat to peace and the security of nations. (Sokolovskii 1963, p. 82.)

The other effect of Soviet isolationism between the two world wars, coupled with Stalin's increasingly pathological suspicions, was an internal climate of xenophobia and witch-hunting culminating in the bloody purges of 1937. The senior officer corps of the armed forces was decimated in those purges. Among the victims was M. N. Tuchachevsky, considered by some to have been among the most able of Soviet commanders and a hero of the Revolution. It is said that the initial crushing defeats suffered by the Soviet armies at the start of the German invasion were direct consequences of the bloodletting and the attendant demoralization in the armed forces.

In the historical sections, *Soviet Military Strategy* includes an account of the civil war of 1918–1921, but nothing about the operations in the war against Finland (1939–1940), in which the Red Army suffered serious reverses. The operations of the "Great Patriotic War" (1941–1945) are depicted as successful solutions of "problems," the net result of which has been to raise Soviet military science and military art to new heights. Projections of operations into the future mention nuclear weapons, and the "radically changed nature of war in the nuclear age" is given its due. At the time the book was written, the idea that the next major war may have no "victor" in any reasonable sense of this word was evidently still proscribed. The idea that war has become irreversibly meaningless as "defense" is nowhere in evidence.

This does not apply, however, to the Soviet analysis of *American* nuclear strategies, the futility of which (in helping to attain the presumed war aims of "American imperialism") is pointed out as convincingly as it is by American critics, who are liberally cited (cf. Trofimenko 1968). In fact, in this connection, Lenin is credited with prophetic powers for his remark in 1918 to the effect that "modern technology makes war more and more destructive; but a time will come when war will become so destructive that it will become altogether impossible" (cited in Trofimenko 1968, p. 9). Characteristically, however, insights of this sort seem to make not the slightest difference to the Soviet military establishment (any more than to the American). The order of the day remains to learn how to use the new technology effectively, to achieve military "parity" at any cost, to raise the "art of war" to new heights of perfection as a bulwark of "defense."

The American Strategists

The writings of American strategists are free of ritualized genuflections. Hence their true ideological content is much more transparent, and the sincerity of the authors is more credible.

Two principal themes emerge. One is a boundless faith in technology; the other the conviction that through proper exercise of power, it is possible to "win the hearts and minds" of practically everybody, inducing aspirations to the "American way of life." Recent events have cast doubt on both of these articles of faith, but the faith persists, particularly in the form of technolatry, which has tended to overshadow the missionary zeal.

The aborted attack on Cuba in April 1961 provides ample evidence of the role of self-deception in the mainstream ideology of the American power elite. The events were penetratingly analyzed by L.S. Etheredge (1985). He lists several delusions that led to the Bay of Pigs fiasco.

The actual ground fighting in the Bay of Pigs invasion was to be done by Cuban expatriates who arrived in Florida by the tens of thousands. It stands to reason that these people were motivated to emigrate for a wide variety of reasons. Some were accustomed to the sort of life that flourished under the Batista regime, a life of predation essentially, sharp money-making schemes, rackets—in short, the sort of life that could not possibly continue under an austere Communist regime but for which America offered a welcome haven. There were others who were simply attracted by the opportunity of improving their standard of living, e.g., professionals and businesspeople. They took advantage of the initial liberal emigration policy of Cuba and the liberal immigration policy of the U.S. to make the move. There were also doubtless still others who regarded themselves as Cuban patriots. Many of them may have been followers of Castro, but were disillusioned by what they regarded as an oppressive dictatorship established soon after the victorious revolution.

American missionary zeal induced in John Kennedy and his advisers a grossly exaggerated estimate of the proportion of men in the invading force motivated by genuine democratic fervor, on which the morale of the invaders crucially depended.

The obverse side of the same coin was a gross underestimation of the Cubans' loyalty to the new regime. Kennedy and his advisers believed that the troop landings would trigger a widespread rebellion. Nothing of the sort happened. It has been reported that Castro had over 200,000 persons arrested on the day after the start of the invasion. But this operation could hardly have been carried out (if it was carried out at all) without massive support for the Castro regime at least in the face of foreign invasion.

A more subtle manifestation of missionary zeal was in the attempt to keep American involvement secret at all costs. It was largely for this reason that Kennedy refused to commit the Air Force in support of the invasion when it seemed (at least to the invaders) that success depended crucially on air support. In fact, the whole scheme had to be scrapped after success failed to materialize immediately, in order to maintain the fiction that the attack was entirely an undertaking of Cuban patriots. At that time, the American administration did not want to make the U.S. appear as an "aggressor," a role not entirely in accord with the image of a democracy devoted to peace and to a law-abiding international order.

In Chapter 9, we cited an eloquent expression of technology worship in a speech by General William Westmoreland, in which he prophesied the "automated battlefield" within a decade. The speech was given more than ten years ago. The "automated battlefield" is still a utopian dream. But much more important is the fact that since General Westmoreland gave that speech, the United States armed forces, wielding the most advanced military technology ever used in warfare, had to withdraw from Southeast Asia, where they could not subdue a people fighting a guerrilla war. To be sure, the "stab in the back" excuse was invoked (referring to the antiwar protests at home), and the failure of the American public to give whole-hearted support to the war may well have been an important factor in the defeat. But this is just the point: the conviction that superior technology can win wars in all circumstances turns out on occasions, for whatever reason, to be an illusion. One can only conclude that continued faith in omnipotence of technology is an ideological compulsion.

Strategic Doctrines in the Nuclear Age

Examining the constraints on "rational" military science, we find that they become progressively more severe on the higher, more abstract levels. On the lowest (most concrete) level, military science is concerned with the effective use of weapons. Such skills can be objectively evaluated. On the next level, we find tactics and logistics. The former deal with effective conduct of combat. These methods can also be evaluated in specific situations, for example, the relative effectiveness of open or closed battle formations, concentration or dispersion of pressure, coordination of different weapons in attack and defense. Logistics has to do essentially with supplying combat operations with materiel and personnel. In particular, logistics involves estimates of the possible scope of operations, the carrying capacity of roads, availability of storage facilities, and the like. Reliable knowledge about all these factors can be obtained. Contact with reality is still intact. Once we pass from these concrete, clearly identifiable operational problems to "general principles," the "theories" become progressively more obscure and all too frequently dissolve into either banalities or into jargon devoid of identifiable content. It is here, especially on the highest level of strategy—global politics—that ideological bias contributes to the break with reality.

Loss of contact with reality is especially evident in "doctrines," which are supposed to serve as guides in constructing strategies involving the use of nuclear weapons. Here loss of contact with reality is inevitable, since whatever relevant experience may have guided the formulation of "classical" doctrines, *no* such experiences are available as guides to nuclear strategies. Moreover, since nuclear wars can hardly be expected to occur repeatedly, whatever experience is gained in the first (and very likely the last) nuclear war would be of questionable value to survivors, if any. Keeping this irrelevance of experience to the design of nuclear doctrines in mind, let us examine some that have been publicized in American strategic literature.

Massive Retaliatory Power

For four years from 1945 to 1949, the U.S. had the monopoly on the atomic
bomb, which meant, thinking in purely military terms, that it could launch
an atomic attack against the Soviet Union without fear of a retaliatory
atomic attack. That it did not do so is sometimes attributed to the superior
morality of Americans, although this point cannot be driven home except
by showing that if the Soviet Union enjoyed such monopoly, it *would* have
launched an atomic attack on the U.S. Speculations of this sort contribute
nothing to understanding the mentality of the military establishments of
the superpowers or the hegemony of the military view of world affairs in
either country. The fact is that the world was spared another outburst of
genocide during the time when it was thought that genocide could be carried
out with relative impunity.

There was no dearth of threats, however. As late as 1954, when the U.S.
monopoly of atomic weapons was a thing of the past, John Foster Dulles,
then U.S. Secretary of State, gave full vent to self-righteousness when he
warned the Soviet Union that "Communist aggression" would not remain
unchastised. And since nuclear superiority was the only basis for thinking
that the U.S. could get away with chastising the Soviet Union for any
instance of what the U.S. perceived as "Communist aggression," we must
assume that the allusion was to a nuclear attack.

In a speech before the Council of Foreign Affairs on January 12, 1954,
Dulles said:

> Local defense will always be important. But there is no local defense which
> alone will contain the mighty land power of the Communist world. Local
> defenses must be reinforced by the further deterrent of massive retaliatory
> power. . . . Otherwise, for example, a potential aggressor glutted with man-
> power, might be tempted to attack in confidence that resistance will be con-
> fined to manpower.
>
> The way to deter aggression is for the free community to be willing and
> able to respond vigorously at places and with means of its own choosing.

A few days later, Dulles amplified his remarks:

> The question of circumstances under which you retaliate, where you retal-
> iate, how quickly you retaliate, is a matter which has to be dealt with in the
> light of facts of each particular case. One thing I want to make clear beyond
> the possibility of doubt is that I don't believe you should tell the enemy in
> advance just where, how, and when you plan to retaliate. The whole essence
> of the program is that the action should be an action of our choosing and he

is not to know in advance what it is, and that uncertainty on his part is a key to the success of the policy.

Taken literally, the policy enunciated by Dulles could be interpreted to mean that the United States might drop atomic bombs on Moscow if guerrillas made headway in some Latin American country, since events of this sort were at the time (and still are at this writing) routinely labeled as "Communist aggression." While retaliations of this sort might have been regarded as overreactions, intervention with atomic weapons in the Indochina war on the side of the French *was* seriously considered. However, the massive retaliation policy lost whatever attractiveness it may have had as an adjunct to the policy of containment when the Soviet Union acquired a nuclear capability to be taken seriously. For the possibility of being subjected to "counterretaliation" did not escape the strategists. Gradually, talk of "massive retaliation at times and places of American choosing" subsided.

"Mutual Assured Destruction"

The nuclear arsenals grew. Along with them, means of delivery were developed that obviated the use of aircraft. A bomber requires several hours to fly from the United States to the Soviet Union or vice versa. An intercontinental ballistic missile can make the trip in less than an hour. It can be intercepted only by another missile and interception is incomparably more problematic than the interception of a plane by a plane or by a ground-to-air missile.

Eventually both sides acquired capacity for inflicting unacceptable damage on each other. Estimates of the amount of damage that could be inflicted varied, but one could reasonably assume that each side became capable of completely obliterating the "society" of the other. It is difficult to imagine what a sudden death of a complex society would be like. The analogy with death is suggested by irreversibility. In order to appreciate the analogy, one must conceive "society" as a living system, which it, in fact, resembles in many ways. No individual in modern society is self-sufficient any more than one cell of a multicellular animal is self-sufficient. At every step and turn, the survival of a human individual depends on assistance from others. He does not forage for food; he obtains it from stores at accessible locations, whither the food has been brought from more or less distant sources by means of rapid transportation. These, in turn, could not function without access to stores of fuel, repair shops, and the like. In most cases, the individual's needs are met in exchange for money, with money serving as the medium of exchange, because everyone believes that it can be exchanged for whatever is needed. When a person is hurt or ill, there is usually help available, so that most trauma or illnesses are temporary. People are shielded against the elements by clothing and dwellings. If these were made unavailable, most people would soon die of exposure. Although people live in very close quarters in cities, sanitary facilities prevent outbreaks of lethal epidemics. Breakdown of such facilities (which would certainly result from nuclear attacks) would immediately lead to massive deaths. Attacks on individuals with the aim of appropriating whatever food, clothing, or living space they have are rare in civilized societies, first because most people are supplied at least with bare necessities, and second, because most people have been "socialized," i.e., inhibited from committing violence; finally because society provides some protection for the weak against the strong. A disruption of normal functions in a society, functions of which we are seldom aware because we take them for granted, would remove all inhibitions. The most violent would enjoy a short-term advantage until they, in turn, fell victim to each other's violence.

A society "dies" when all the sources of support and integrating mechanisms disintegrate. The capability of each side in the present superpower confrontation to "kill" the society of the other means that such total destruction can be wreaked in just this manner. It means that people would be dying suddenly by hundreds of thousands in close quarters, and that it would be impossible to remove the corpses. It would mean that the short-term survivors would be crazed by thirst, hunger, and agony.

It is important to divest oneself of the idea that destruction of this sort would be similar to that resulting from the bombardment of European or Japanese cities in World War II. Horrible as were the ordeals of Hiroshima or Dresden, there was still an "outside," where the survivors could escape, places to which children could be evacuated, intact parts of the country from which help could be expected.

The destruction of cities in World War II was analogous to wounds inflicted on an organism. Evidently, these wounds were far from fatal. But we know that wounds inflicted on an organism *can* be fatal and that death is irreversible. So far, history has seen only slow deaths of societies. Moreover, it was not always certain whether a society actually died or was transformed into another. This ambiguity stems from the slowness of the process. There is every reason to believe that a nuclear holocaust would result in *sudden* deaths of societies, something history has never witnessed and therefore about the consequences of which we can have no idea.[2]

Mutual Assured Destruction (MAD) was the name given to the strategic posture which supposedly deterred each superpower from attacking the other because the other had the capacity to kill the society of the attacker.

This posture had several attractive features. It represented a sort of balance of power which is held in high esteem by some scholars in the field of international relations. If one assumes that the temptation to attack is greatest when one feels that one is more powerful than the intended victim, balance of power seems a way of reducing this temptation. Of course, one way of preventing a nuclear attack would be by doing away with nuclear weapons. Such proposals, however, were until recently never considered seriously by either side of the present confrontation. The usual reason for dismissing nuclear disarmament has been, on the American side, presumed impossibility of preventing cheating without far-reaching inspection procedures, and on the Soviet side, refusal to submit to such procedures. In effect, both sides did their best to spike all hopes for nuclear disarmament.[3]

An attractive feature of the "balance of terror" represented by MAD was that it did not depend on verification procedures. The achievement of a finely tuned balance did not seem to matter as long as it was obvious to both sides that each could completely destroy the other. The logic of the situation implied that once mutual destruction was guaranteed, there was no need to escalate the arms race because there was no point in achieving a capability of destroying the other side several times over. In this way, the highly desirable goal of stabilization seemed attainable.

Mutual assured destruction depended on a *second* strike capability of both powers, since a first strike would presumably be inhibited by fear of retaliation. In this way it seemed that rendering the first strike suicidal would in fact eliminate the likelihood of the second strike altogether. It seemed that a sufficiently horrendous threat of annihilation was an insurance against annihilation.

Now the second strike had to be targeted not on the military installations of the adversary, but on his population centers, for two reasons. First, whereas complete destruction of the adversary's military installations could not be assured without greatly increasing the accuracy of the delivery systems, complete destruction (in the sense of "killing" the adversary's society) could be actually carried out if the strike were directed against population centers. Second, assuming that the first strike would consist of missiles fired from silos, there would be no point in hitting the silos after they had ejaculated.

In order to enhance the deterrent effectiveness of MAD, the population centers would have to be helpless against the incoming retaliatory strike. In effect, therefore, if both superpowers "agreed" upon a MAD stance, they would thereby pledge their populations as hostages, in this way reassuring the adversary that they could not undertake an attack without inviting the annihilation of their own population. This reassurance was explicitly incorporated into what was probably the only significant arms control agreement between the two superpowers. The agreement specified that no antiballistic missiles would be developed by either side at more than one site. According to the logic of MAD, antiballistic missiles (ABM) would have a destabilizing effect, since an attempt to protect one's own population against a *retaliatory* attack could be interpreted as a preparation to initiate a first strike.

It appeared to those who believed in a "rational" solution to the problem posed by nuclear weapons that the MAD posture would provide such a solution. It became clear, however, that nuclear deterrence was neutralized by the very horrendousness of the threat it posed. If MAD were sufficient to deter a nuclear attack, it might for that reason not be sufficient to deter "lesser" aggressions, because punishing such aggressions by a nuclear retaliation would invite a nuclear counterretaliation. Thus, the would-be "aggressor" would count on impunity, being protected by the very balance of terror that was supposed to deter him. The Communists could be expected to "nibble away at the Free World," as the saying went, referring to the many "brushfire wars," revolutionary upheavals, and the like in the impoverished world, all of which Americans routinely labeled as instances of "Communist aggression."

Aside from the inadequacy of the MAD posture, at least from the American point of view, the stabilizing potential of MAD turned out to be illusory. The arms race continued, attesting to the inherent instability of the deterrence system.

"Flexible Response"

As has been said, nuclear deterrence turned out to have low credibility. A threat that cannot be carried out (because the threatened party could reciprocate the chastisement) is eventually ignored. The "flexible response" doctrine was supposed to reestablish credibility of threats by "making the punishment fit the crime." Local "aggressions" were to be met by local responses. This would mean that the U.S. would have to take its self-appointed role as world policeman literally. Bases would have to be acquired all over the world, strategically located to enable the U.S. to dispatch forces appropriate to the task assigned to them in quelling "aggression" wherever it occurred.

The special appeal of the flexible response policy was that it emphasized the retention of control over the situation. Not a spasm but an application of pressure of appropriate controlled intensity should be the response to encroachment on the world order that the U.S. was determined to preserve. The working out of the details of contingent plans required a great deal of work, but this was, of course, welcomed by the defense community, since it called for just the sort of expertise that it possessed. In particular, the notion of a "limited war" gained ground.

Henry Kissinger, in his book *Nuclear Weapons and Foreign Policy* (1957), argued that (limited) nuclear war "need not be as destructive as it appears when we think of it in terms of traditional warfare." In traditional warfare, so his argument goes, great store was put on disruption of the production, communication, and transportation facilities of the enemy. This necessitated attacks on heavily populated areas. In a nuclear war, industrial potential will play a smaller role. Thus, with cities no longer serving as key elements in the enemy's fighting potential, there will be less need to attack them, with consequent great loss of life.

Further, in World War II, control of the air was of prime importance, and since enemy aircraft could be most effectively destroyed on the ground, it was necessary to attack airports, many of which were located near cities. In a nuclear war control of the air is not an issue if nuclear bombs are delivered by missiles. In sum:

> In these circumstances, it is possible to conceive of a pattern of limited nuclear war with its own appropriate tactics and with limitations as to targets, areas, and the size of weapons used. Such a mode of conflict cannot be improvised in the confusion of battle, however. The limitation of war is established not only by our intentions but also by the manner in which the other side interprets them. It, therefore, becomes the task of our diplomacy to convey to our opponent what we understand by limited nuclear war, or at least what limitations we are willing to observe. . . . If the Soviet leadership is clear about our intentions, . . . a framework of war limitation may be established by the operation of self-interest—by the fear of all-out nuclear war and by the fact that new tactics make many of the targets of traditional warfare less profitable. (Kissinger 1957, p. 185.)

Flexible response and its corollary, limited war, are an extension of deterrence. It is assumed that each side fighting a "limited war" will be deterred from escalating it by fear of counter-escalation by the enemy. In fact, what Kissinger is proposing is collaboration with the enemy in keeping the war within "acceptable" limits. From the professional's point of view, this conception of warfare is superior to the mutual assured destruction stance. It is difficult to avoid seeing the absurdity of MAD: it implies that the one and only purpose of weapons of total destruction is to prevent their use. One can hardly blame military leaders and strategists for being repelled by this inglorious culmination of the "art of war," trapped between uselessness and self-destruction. Limited war provided a way out. It presented a plethora of problems to be solved, new tactics to be worked out, and a rationale for retaining war as an option in the conduct of foreign policy while not ignoring humanitarian concerns.

Above all, the professional is concerned with dispelling the conception of nuclear war as "the end of everything." In the United States especially, where a great deal of literature on strategy and related subjects was directed at the general public, appeals to adopting a coolheaded attitude, "learning to live with the bomb," "thinking about the unthinkable," etc., are a recurrent theme.

H. Kahn's book, *On Escalation* (1965), is especially revealing in this respect. The core of the book is an "escalation ladder" with 44 rungs, representing a range of severity of conflict between the two nuclear powers. The lowest rungs represent "subcrisis maneuvers" (political, economic, and diplomatic gestures). Then come "traditional" crises (show of force, significant mobilization); "intense crises" comprising large conventional war; "barely" nuclear war; "bizarre" crises (e.g., declaration of limited nuclear war), and so forth. When we consider that nuclear strikes occur already on rung 15 and that there are 29 more rungs to go until the epitome is reached in the "spasm"—all-out nuclear war—we can appreciate how complex and sophisticated the game of escalation can be.

It seems that *On Escalation* was meant to make two points. First, that the popular conception of nuclear war as "the end of everything" was an oversimplification, a crippling fear reaction, blocking a coolheaded analysis, which, in Kahn's estimation, was indispensable for dealing with the "problem" posed by nuclear weapons. Second, to represent escalation (and, incidentally, de-escalation) as an option in dealing with the adversary, Kahn apparently intended to create the impression that the situation could be "controlled" and that the business of the strategist is to learn how to control it to advantage—for example, by sliding up and down the escalation ladder as the situation may require. In the light of sophisticated strategic analysis, the nuclear age could be presented as a fountain of opportunities instead of a paralyzing threat. An excerpt from the book given below lends credence to this interpretation.

Kahn did a great deal of lecturing on matters pertaining to nuclear strategy to audiences consisting, as he writes, of "college students, businessmen, members of the League of Women Voters, etc." To illustrate the point about exercising control, he would ask them what they thought would (or should) happen if a single hydrogen bomb were dropped on New York. At first, the answer would be that the President should order a crushing retaliatory blow on the Soviet Union. A few years later, however, presumably after exposure to lectures on flexible response, the audiences became much more sophisticated, as Kahn notes with satisfaction. A lively discussion would ensue. Searching questions would be asked.

Someone would suggest that the President get in touch with his opposite number in the Kremlin and inquire why there was only one bomb.

Kahn would stimulate further discussion by explaining that the one bomb on New York was indeed a deliberate act by the Soviet Union and that the Soviets could destroy the U.S. totally even by a second strike. Then

> . . . almost all would agree that there should be retaliation but that it should be limited. Most suggest that Moscow should be destroyed, but many object to this on the grounds that this city is much more important to the Soviet Union than New York is to the United States. These usually agree that the destruction of some smaller city, such as Leningrad or Kiev, would be an appropriate counterescalation. . . .

"In the past five years," Kahn concludes, "almost everyone in the U.S. who has any interest in these problems or is even modestly well informed has, as a result of both serious and fictionalized discussions, learned that there are possibilities for control in such bizarre situations." (Kahn 1965, pp. 185–186.)

Prevailing Strategy

There was a time when wars had goals that were extraneous to themselves. In other words, wars were *about* something: territory, slaves, resources, political control, trade monopolies, dynastic interests. The outcome of a war was in line with what the victor aspired to. The victor took over a territory, brought slaves home as a labor force, put his relative on an empty throne. Here and there strategists still depict the coming war between the superpowers as a war for political hegemony or resistance against it. This, however, is done mostly by force of habit, as it were. A coolheaded appraisal of the consequences of a nuclear war reduces all the standard war aims to absurdity. Indeed, once mentioned, the "issue" over which World War III will presumably be fought is soon forgotten. The discussion centers entirely on *how* the war should be fought, not on *why*.

Actually, the issues over which wars are fought, even if these are real, not imaginary, are of no real concern to the military professional. (This is the essence of the "political detachment" of the defense community.) It is as pointless to ask why the adversary is an adversary as to ask why the chess player across the board is an adversary. The adversary, as far as the defense community is concerned, is *given*. He has to be given; otherwise the military profession has no *raison d'être*. The irremovable adversary provides the military profession with a standard answer to all questions concerning why wars must be fought: because the adversary is there.

In a way, the tacit abandonment of the "limited war" doctrine can be credited to its realistic evaluation by the defense community as wishful thinking. The inevitability of a war going to its logical conclusion—total annihilation of the adversary—once represented by Clausewitz as an "ideal," has now been recognized as inherent in the dynamics of the nuclear age. However, "annihilation of the adversary" has acquired a new meaning: it now comprises the destruction of everything and everyone, not just of the adversary's army.

One would think that in the light of this new reality, the defense community would reexamine its role in society, for instance, ponder the question what can possibly be meant by "defense." At this writing, however, no such self-examination is in evidence. On the contrary, with the installation of Ronald Reagan as President of the United States, the American defense community acquired unprecedented self-confidence and exuberance. Magnificent vistas opened before it. The idea of "victory" as the goal of war was revived in the ascendance of the so-called "prevailing strategy," centered on the design of a plan of war in which the United States would emerge as victor over the "Evil Empire," as President Reagan, borrowing the term from the movie *Star Wars*, characterized the Soviet Union.

Can a General Theory of Strategy Be Constructed?

J.C. Wylie notes that a general theory of strategy would have to extend beyond military science to include all sorts of conflict situations. It would have to "provide a common and basic frame of reference for the special talents of the soldier, the sailor, the airman, the politician, the economist, and the philosopher in their common efforts toward a common aim" (Wylie 1967, p. 99).

Do all these professionals have a common aim? The soldier, the sailor, and the airman apparently do: one of their common aims as professionals is to understand war more thoroughly in order to conduct it more effectively. So a general theory of strategy should, presumably, provide a common frame of reference for this common aim. How about the politician and the economist? Wylie includes them, because he is impressed by B.H. Liddell Hart's "indirect approach" as a contribution to military strategy. Liddell Hart (1967) sees the "unbalancing" of the adversary as the aim of war, namely, disorganizing the *system* on which the adversary's power depends. This system embodies not only the territory, not only weaponry, manpower, and production capacity, but also certain realizable *rules* that bind and integrate all the activities of a society. To effect a disorganization of such a system, military action must be combined with a large repertoire of other actions directed against the adversary's economy, the morale of his population and the like. It is for this reason that a general theory of war should provide a common frame of reference for the economist and the politician as well as for the military men. Indeed, E.M. Earle (1941/ 1960, p. 504) emphasizes this point when he calls attention to Hitler's *nonmilitary* preparation for war—imbuing the Germans with a fanatical creed, sowing discord among erstwhile or potential allies against Germany, and so forth.

Wylie points out that the economist and the politician are engaged in activities analogous to war, even when they are not directly involved in a war effort—namely, they are engaged in techniques of exercising *control*, and control can be exercised, according to Wylie, only by wielding power. No matter that the content of power is different in different contexts. All power is acquired in consequence of success in a struggle for power, that is, in conflict. Therefore, by a "general theory of strategy" one must understand a general theory of conflict, specifically a general theory of rationally conducted conflict. It is probably for this reason that Wylie included also the philosopher among the professionals for whom a general theory of conflict should provide a "common frame of reference." Perhaps he had in mind the philosopher's concern with the nature of "rationality" itself. Whether he did or not, we shall be concerned with this question. The next two chapters will be devoted to it.

The Theory of Games as a General Theory of Conflict

An attempt to construct a completely general theory of rationally conducted conflict was, in fact, made. The result was the theory of games. There is an unavoidable trade-off between the generality of a theory and its relevance to specific situations. The wider the range of validity of a theory, the less content it has. In the extreme case, if the validity of a theory is universal, the theory becomes unfalsifiable and so loses all content. In the case of a theory of war, a completely general one might assert that "the stronger side always wins." Since by any sensible definition of "stronger," the winning side must be regarded as the stronger side, the assertion is a tautology. It only indicates how the word "stronger" is to be used and says nothing about what it takes to win a war. On the other hand, if "stronger" is given a meaning independent of *ex post facto* observations of outcomes of conflicts, any statement to the effect that the stronger side always wins can turn out to be wrong. Numerically inferior forces have been known to defeat superior ones. Better-equipped armies have been known to be defeated by poorly equipped ones, and so forth. In sum, a completely general theory must be devoid of content, while the incompletely general ones must be situation bound.

Nevertheless, there is a type of theory which, being general, must be "devoid of content" but which is nevertheless not trivial for that reason. Such is a mathematical theory. Mathematical theories are completely deductive. They are concerned exclusively with implications of propositions. They are not concerned with the "truth" of propositions in the sense of their correspondence to observable facts. For this reason, they are said to be devoid of (empirical) content. But they nevertheless disclose important *logical* relationships which cannot be appreciated without the application of the deductive techniques developed in the theory.

The theory of games is a mathematical theory of conflict. As such it is concerned neither with any specific content of a conflict situation, nor with the genesis of conflict, nor with its effects, nor with its psychological components. It is concerned only with the logical structure of conflict situations.

To a certain extent, game theory can be regarded as a normative theory of conflict, that is, a theory of the way a conflict *would* be conducted if the participants were completely "rational." As we shall see, however, this conception of game theory can be only partly justified. If a normative theory is understood as one that indicates how a conflict *ought* to be conducted, that is, one that singles out optimal strategies, then game theory can be normative only in certain circumscribed contexts. Nevertheless, the idea that game theory *is* a theory of "rationally conducted conflict" persists. There is a sociological reason for this which we will discuss below (cf. Chapter 16). Our task will be to delineate the validity of this idea.

The principal value of game theory as a general theory of conflict is not pragmatic. Expertise in game theory will not help anyone become a competent strategist, let alone achieve expertise in some specific game of strategy like chess or poker. Rather, the value of game theory is revealed in the process of rigorous analysis of the logical structure of certain idealized types of conflict. In the light of this analysis, the shortcomings of "strategic thinking" in many types of conflict situations become apparent. Here game theory becomes a powerful tool of *critique* of the strategic mode of thought.

The most important insight gained from game-theoretic analysis of conflict is that the meaning of rationality is many-tiered. Game theory can be regarded as a branch of a general theory of decision, specifically the branch that deals with situations involving conflicts of interest. As we consider the simplest decision situations (not yet involving a conflict of interest) and progress stepwise to more complicated ones, we shall see that the new problems posed at each extension necessitate the introduction of new concepts. In consequence, the notion of rationality becomes progressively more complicated. The meaning that suffices on a more primitive level of decision making no longer suffices at a higher level. In this way, the hierarchical structure of rationality is disclosed.

At one point in the examination of more complex decision situations an adversary appears on the scene. Since we are dealing with a theory of "rational" decision, "rationality" must be ascribed also to the adversary. Here the strict game-theoretic conception of strategy enters the analysis. In the context of game theory, a strategy is not merely a "plan of action . . . in order to achieve some goal . . . together with a system of measures to achieve its accomplishment." It must be a plan of action that includes anticipation of all possible contingencies, including the measures that can be taken by the adversary as he attempts to frustrate the goal to be achieved.

This attribution of "rationality" to an adversary is part of the definition of "rationality" in the context of game theory. Clearly it must serve as a basis of any theory of "rationally" conducted conflict. How generally is this principle observed in the design of military strategy? That it is not entirely ignored is evidenced by the wide use of "gaming" as training for future military operations. By splitting their forces into opposing teams (the "Reds" and the "Blues"), commanders exercise their strategic prowess by planning operations with due regard for the stratagems available to the "enemy." With the development of sophisticated computer technology, much more extensive and complex military operations can be simulated, whereby apparently "optimal" strategies can in principle be designed for a great variety of situations.

As we examine the conception of military strategy on levels higher than those of field operations, we find that considerations involving the reactions of potential adversaries become vague, and are sometimes altogether absent. A case in point is E.M. Earle's attribution of strategic brilliance to Hitler, who designed a grand scheme of conquest in which both military and political operations were supposedly ingeniously meshed. Hitler spelled out the scheme in *Mein Kampf* (Hitler 1925/1943). The ultimate goal was the expansion of Germany's power to the east to provide "living space" for the future, greatly increased German population. This could be accomplished, Hitler thought, only if Germany could avoid a two-front war. (Apparently, the memory of the defeat in World War I was fresh.) Accordingly, before undertaking conquest of eastern Europe, Germany had to crush France in the sense of eliminating her as a European power. To accomplish this, according to Hitler, Germany had to seek an alliance with Britain and Italy. And so on.

Admittedly, this scenario constituted a plan. But there was nothing in this plan that provided for alternatives in the event that success was not achieved in the intermediate phases—for instance, in the event that Britain refused to ally herself with Germany, or in the event that France was not defeated, or in the event that conquest of Russia with the view of enslaving the Russians proved impossible.

To cite another example, the so-called "Strategic Defense Initiative" undertaken by the United States also qualifies as a plan of action designed to achieve a goal, namely, protection against a nuclear attack. The means to implement this plan are supposed to be realized in consequence of new knowledge obtained from a vast research undertaking projected over several years and involving a mobilization of a whole army of scientific and technical personnel. Computer-aided exercises involving the "Reds" (attacking) and the "Blues" (defending) were included in the research projects, designed to generate problems to be solved in the development of the new weapons systems. Thus, in this context also, the principle of ascribing rationality to the opponent seems to have been applied. But the horizon defining the range of projection in these exercises has remained conspicuously limited. By definition, the unforeseeable cannot be foreseen. But even what can be foreseen in these exercises is constrained by the frame of reference in which strategic thought operates.

A case in point is the dynamics of an arms race. It stands to reason that when in a military context an adversary has been identified, one has identified oneself as the adversary's adversary. Given approximately equal levels of scientific knowledge, technical competence, and resources devoted to "defense," it is clear that advances in military technology, whether quantitative or qualitative, by one side will be sooner or later matched by the other. The result can, therefore, in no way be regarded as an increase in security for either side. Yet every such *projected* advance is heralded as a contribution to "national security." As in the case of the persistence of the idea that game theory is essentially a theory of rationally conducted conflict, the reasons for the persistence of the idea that increasing sophistication of military technology contributes to national security are sociological. These will be discussed in Chapter 16.

Strategic planning is often identified with problem solving, and in many ways it involves just that. The efficacy of problem solving, however, depends in great measure, often crucially, on the investigated problem "staying put" as it is being solved. All too frequently, it does not "stay put," in which case the futility of typical "technical fixes" becomes apparent. The most conspicuous manifestations of such failures have been in side effects of the measures undertaken to solve the problem originally posed. Massive use of insecticides, once thought to be a boon to agriculture, often had ecological effects that aggravated the problem instead of solving it. Many of the so-called wonder drugs had to be abandoned because of horrendous side effects. The degradation of the environment in consequence of burgeoning industrialization has put the entire enterprise of "conquering nature" into question.

Neglect of side effects (although common) is not necessarily inherent in strategic planning. But the strategic mode of thought is *conducive* to leaving certain kinds of side effects out of consideration. For central to this mode of thought is the actor conceived as a *subject*, from whose (fixed) point of view the efficacy of various courses of action is evaluated. The subject acts on his environment (which often includes others like himself), thereby changing the environment (considered as an *object*) presumably in ways to suit his needs. In designing the means for attaining his goals, the actor may become aware of prospective changes not originally envisaged. These he may take into account in assessing the efficacy of his means. What he is not likely to take into account are the changes that may be produced in *himself* in consequence of his impact on the environment, in particular, changes in the image of himself that will define his future relations with others. Having defeated his enemies, he thereby becomes an enemy of their friends. If the actor is a coalition rather than an individual (e.g., a junta, a revolutionary organization, or an alliance), the success of a strategically sophisticated and ruthless exercise of power may inspire cliques or individuals *within* that organization to employ the same methods to seize power themselves. Witness the fate of so many leaders of successful revolutions at the hands of their colleagues. Witness the transformation of successful revolutionary organizations into despotic power elites. An important insight induced by game-theoretic analysis reveals the self-defeating nature of "non-tuism," that is, viewing every problem from the point of view of an "ego," the *actor* (whether an individual or a coalition), fixed once and for all. It is an insight that sheds doubt on the concept of rationality inherent in the strategic mode of thought.

Another important result of game-theoretic analysis is that the value of a strategy may depend crucially on how many others in a conflict or a competitive situation are using it. This insight turned out to be an important input to theoretical biology. The initial conception of an organism's adaptation to its environment did not take into account the competitive aspect of adaptation. For example, if a certain mechanism for utilizing moisture present in the soil becomes, in the process of evolution, optimally adaptive, it is optimally adapative for all organisms in that environment *provided* moisture is plentiful. If, however, moisture is scarce so that competition for it is a factor, then a "strategy" may be optimal only if a small fraction of organisms use it. It may cease to be optimal if a large proportion use it. Since successful adaptation is manifested in reproductive advantage, the relative number of organisms using the initially optimal strategy will increase, and this increase may result in the strategy becoming maladaptive. Its "success" becomes the cause of its "failure" (cf. Riechert and Hammerstein 1983). Operation of the same principle is observed in business competition. A successful competitive strategy tends to be imitated and thereby may cease to be successful.

In Chapter 2, we mentioned patterns of cooperative behavior, e.g., restraint in combat, that have evolved in some animals as adaptations, thus providing counterexamples to the conception of the struggle for existence always awarding victory to the strong and fierce. Such a counterexample was produced in a recent experiment simulating an evolving population.

The initial phase of the experiment was a contest in which participants were invited to submit computer program that were essentially strategies for playing many iterations of a certain game. Every program submitted was then paired with every other as well as with itself. The scores resulting from these paired "combats" were then cumulated, and the program that got the highest score was declared the winner of the contest. A program called TIT-FOR-TAT won the contest. A second contest was announced together with the description of all the programs submitted in the first contest and the scores obtained by them. TIT-FOR-TAT was again submitted (by the same contestant) and again got the highest score. The really instructive result of those contests was not that TIT-FOR-TAT was "strong" but, on the contrary, that it was "weak" in the sense that when matched with any other program it never got the higher score. It either tied or got a lower score. The question how, then, did TIT-FOR-TAT manage to win both contests is easily answered. The "strong" programs, i.e., those designed to beat others in paired encounters, "succeeded" and thereby lowered their scores. The designer of TIT-FOR-TAT acted on the principle "let's you and him fight." The idea was poignantly expressed in a recent cartoon showing assorted insects joyfully dancing against a background of mushroom clouds. Limitations of the efficacy of power shed light on the limitation of strategic thought.

The next phase of the experiment was a simulation of evolution. The evolving population now consisted of computer programs similar to those submitted to the contests. Here, too, they were matched with each other. The scores were translated into reproductive advantage or disadvantage. That is, a number of copies of each program was either added to or withdrawn from the population following each encounter depending on the scores obtained by the programs matched in these encounters. In this way, the relative numbers of the various programs in the population changed. The "evolution" was allowed to run. Eventually, TIT-FOR-TAT "took over" in the sense of being the only program represented in the population (Axelrod 1984).

Previous simulations of this sort (cf. Maynard Smith and Price 1973) suggested the idea of an "evolutionarily stable strategy" (ESS). A strategy in this sense represents a genetic profile of a deme. An ESS is one which, if adopted by a population, cannot be "invaded" by a mutant or an immigrant in the sense of being pervaded by the deme represented by the "invader." An evolutionarily stable strategy represents a *collective* rather than an individual adaptation. We do not usually speak of "rationality" in nonhuman contexts. In human contexts, however, such collective adaptation could well be ascribed to *collective rationality*.

Recent history is replete with strategies that were initially successful but eventually failed *because* they were competitively successful. Napoleon's initial successes could be attributed to his use of massive armies of recruits instead of the meticulously trained standing armies used by his enemies. But when the practice of *levée en masse* spread, the advantage was lost. When the United States was the sole possessor of the atomic bomb, it could contemplate intimidating the Soviet Union, but when the Soviet Union acquired the weapon, intimidation became problematic. It would be foolhardy to deny that strategists are unaware of this fact of life. That arms races nevertheless go on can be attributed to compulsions to "stay ahead" at all costs, or to "catch up" at all costs. These "problems" are immediate and, in the minds of the decision makers of the competing states, painfully pressing. Pressure is a well known "dissolver" of rationality.

As a rule, in human affairs, immediate and pressing problems obscure the long-range view. In particular, in the long run, the problem originally posed may change so radically in the process of being attacked that the solution becomes meaingless or self-defeating. In the case of arms races, however, it is not necessary to suppose that the long-range effects are not apparent. In fact, we are now actually witnessing these long-range effects— the cumulative effects of the arms race. And we can easily project them into the immediate future. Increased national security is not one of them.

Still, horrendous as these effects seem to many, those actively participating in the arms race, i.e., designing strategies for continuing it, may not deplore these effects at all. Perusing the literature on the history of military science or "the art of war," one cannot but feel that the authors regard the process as "progress." There is no question that military thought has undergone "progressive" evolution. Indeed, military science and technology, being by-products of general science and general technology, exhibit, as do their sources, a unidirectional progressive development. The evolution of strategic thinking has kept pace. It exhibits a corresponding growth in creativity and imagination. Writers on strategy speak of the

"Renaissance" of military thought following centuries of "stagnation." They eulogize the "genius" of Napoleon, Clausewitz, and Moltke. They celebrate the broad sweep of geopolitical thought such as Mahan's (1917). They see the promise of a new "flowering" of strategic thought instigated by the age of nuclear weapons, by the information-processing revolution, by "high tech." They welcome each new "generation" of the devices either directly dedicated to destruction or to aiding it. Recall the euphoric tone of General Westmoreland's speech (cf. chapter 9).

Whether one welcomes or deplores the advances in military doctrine, the art of war, and strategic thought depends on commitments to one or another set of values. But to what extent strategic thought can be regarded as a manifestation of rationality can be seen in the light of rigorous analysis of its logic in the context of generalized conflict. It is to this matter that we will now turn our attention.

Notes

1. In March 1930, a few days after his death, an article entitled "The War of 19—" by Douhet appeared in *Revista Aeronautica*. In it Douhet describes a hypothetical war in Europe that he expected to break out in a few years, which would consist entirely of bombardments from the air and would last a few days. The article was appended to the 1972 edition of *Command of the Air*.
2. The reported total destruction of Carthage by the Romans or of Khorasan by Genghis Khan might be cited as examples of "sudden death" of societies. However, the structure of the global system was much looser in those days: the rest of the world could go on living as if Carthage or Khorasan never existed. It is, on the other hand, unthinkable that the sudden death of the United States or the Soviet Union or Western Europe or, as is not unlikely, of all three could go unnoticed or be taken in stride by the rest of the world. For such an event there is no remotely analogous precedent.
3. Since this was written, the Soviet Union has given strong reason to believe that its leadership wants to be genuinely committed to significant disarmament and to peaceful coexistence.

14

Limits of Individual Rationality

The voice of protest against the drift toward catastrophe frequently reflects anguish. At times, peace activists have used scare tactics to prod people to action. Again and again the immediate results and the probable aftermath of nuclear attacks have been depicted in all their obscene detail. The emphasis on the depravity of a war of total destruction may have produced a significant shift in the conception of war. For many, war is no longer identified with a natural disaster, but rather with a deliberate, horrendous crime.

The stance of the strategist throughout the decades of peace activisim, now mounting, now ebbing, has been that of coolheadedness and tough-mindedness. Morality, the strategists often point out, may have its place in a more perfect world, but not in the present world of international relations. The situation calls for realistic appraisal, solid expertise, above all a hardheaded reliance on reason rather than on emotions. Understandably, the layman shrinks from "thinking about the unthinkable." So it is up to the professional to live and act in the murky world of modern science-oriented defense.

In assessing the role of this stance in our time, it behooves us to examine the claim of "rationality" on the part of those whose expertise in technical matters having to do with the use of up-to-date implements and the paraphernalia of war is indisputable.

Decisions Under Certainty

Perhaps the simplest and, for this reason, the most widely accepted criterion of rationality is the extent to which a person, having a choice of several alternatives, chooses by taking into account the consequences of his choice.

Actually, this definition of a "rational person" does not signify much. It does not specify what it means to "take into account." Even if we think we understand this phrase intuitively, we are left in the dark about the extent of the "time horizon" within which the consequences are to be "taken into account." Most important, no mention is made of the circumstance that often the consequences depend not only on the actions of the actor himself but also on the state of the environment in which the acts are performed. In particular, the environment may contain other actors, who, too, may be "rational" and whose actions have significant influence on the outcomes of the actor's decision.

All these matters are often not at all easy to clarify in real life situations. For this reason, if we wish to undertake a systematic analysis of decision problems that a "rational actor" faces, we must begin with simplified models of decision situations. In these models, the verisimilitude of situations in all their complexity is sacrificed in order to gain clarity and tractability.

The simplest imaginable decision situation is one where the actor has at his disposal a small number of alternative courses of action (choices) and knows with certainty what consequence will result from each of these available actions. Here no more is required from a "rational actor" than that he "knows his own mind." That is, he must be able to rank the consequences from the most preferred to the least preferred.

Of course, in assuming that there is a one-to-one correspondence between actions and consequences and that the consequence of each action is known to the actor, we have assumed a great deal. The problems associated with determining these consequences are often formidable, and a great deal of expertise may be required to solve them. It is often this expertise that the professional has in mind when he dismisses the layman's misgivings and anxieties as stemming from ignorance or from misplaced sentiment. Actually, however, technical expertise of this sort has little to do with the problem of rationality, as this problem arises in a theory of decision. Indeed, the *decision* problem in situations where consequences of actions can be determined with certainty, difficult as it may be to determine them, is trivial; the decision prescribed to the "rational actor" is simply that of choosing a course of action that leads to the most preferred consequence.

Decisions Under Risk

Non-trivial decision problems reveal themselves only when the consequences of actions are *not* uniquely determined by the actions; that is,
when each of the available actions may lead to one of several possible
consequences, and it is not known with certainty which it will be.

The usual conception of a solution to a problem involving decisions under
risk involves two new concepts, which need not be invoked in decision
situations where the outcomes of decisions are certain. These new concepts
are *utility* and *probability*. The utility of an outcome is a measure of how
much it is worth to the actor. When an actor ranks the possible outcomes
of his actions from best to worst, he assigns utilities to them in that order
of magnitude. Thus, utility is always person-bound.

The actor could represent the utilities by numbers, for example, by
assigning the largest number to the best-preferred outcome, the second
largest to the next-most-preferred, and so on, down to the smallest number
assigned to the least preferred. An important question in the theory of
decision is how much latitude the actor has in assigning these numbers.
To fix ideas, suppose there are three outcomes, A, B, and C, preferred in
that order. To express these preferences, 3 could be assigned to A, 2 to
B, and 1 to C. But if nothing further is said about the preferences, 100,
3, and -12 would do just as well, because these three numbers stand in
the same order relation to each other as 3, 2, and 1.

The scale that assigns only an order of magnitude is called an *ordinal
scale*. An ordinal scale suffices for solving some kinds of decision problems
but not all. In our discussion of decision under risk, we shall need a scale
"stronger" than the ordinal scale. One scale is stronger than another if
there is less latitude in assigning positions on that scale. An example of a
scale stronger than an ordinal scale is an *interval* scale, best illustrated by
conventional temperature scales such as the Celsius or the Fahrenheit. Let
us see why these scales are stronger than the ordinal scale.

A conventional temperature scale is characterized by the choice of a
point of origin on it and the size of a unit. For example, the point of origin
of a Celsius scale (0°C) is the temperature of melting ice. Its unit is so
chosen that 100 of these units (degrees) brings the temperature up to that
of boiling water. On the Fahrenheit scale, 0°F is the temperature of a
mixture of salt and ice, while 100°F was what Fahrenheit mistakenly thought
was the normal temperature of the human body. What distinguishes an
interval scale is that once the zero point and the unit have been chosen,
there is no more latitude in choosing the numbers to be assigned to the
remaining magnitudes. Another way of saying this is that given four magnitudes, x, y, z, and w, the ratio of the differences $(x-y)/(z-w)$ must remain
invariant however the zero point and the unit are chosen.

The other concept that we shall need in the theory of decision under risk is that of probability. Most people have an intuitive understanding of probability as the degree of likelihood of an event. We say the probability that it snows in Toronto on some day in January is rather large, but that the probability that it snows on some day in May (though this sometimes happens) is rather small. By convention the largest number assigned to a probability is 1, which is the "probability" of an event that is certain to occur. The smallest number assigned to a probability is 0, which is the "probability" of an impossible event. All the intermediate numbers are probabilities of uncertain events, such as how a tossed coin will fall or whether it will rain next Sunday.

Probabilities of events are related to observations via observed relative frequencies of events. Thus, if we toss a coin very many times, we shall very probably observe that the fraction of times it will fall heads is quite near one-half. If we toss a pair of well constructed dice, we shall observe that an "eight" will come up very nearly $5/36$ of the times, and so on.

Some philosophers thought that they could derive results like these by reasoning alone. For instance, there are 36 possible ways a pair of dice can fall. Of these, 5 ways make an "eight," namely, (4, 4), (3, 5), (5, 3), (6, 2), (2, 6). Thus, the relative frequency of an "eight" ought to be $5/36$. However, this reasoning contains a tacit assumption, namely, that each of the 36 ways a pair of dice can fall is "equally likely." But whether it "really" is equally likely or not can be established only by observation. Thus, the probability of an event can be established in the last analysis only by observation. Moreover, it takes many observations to establish the probability of an event (by noting the relative frequency of its occurrence in the repeated observations). An important implication of this principle is that there is no such thing as an "objective" probability of a single event. "Objectively," i.e., through observations, the probability of an event can be established only in the context of repeated events, so that the event in question can exhibit a relative frequency. Let us keep this in mind when we discuss some comments on "probabilities" of events that by their nature cannot occur more than once or at most very few times.

We are now ready to formulate a decision problem under risk and to indicate its "rational" solution. The word "rational" was put in quotation marks to indicate that we are speaking here not of rationality as a property of decision makers that has a completely general universally accepted meaning, but rather of "rationality" that is defined in a very special way.

Assume that an actor has a choice among m alternatives, labeled 1, 2, . . . m. Assume, further, that the outcome of his choice will be determined not only by the alternative he chooses but also by the state of the environment, usually called "the state of nature." Examples of "states of nature" are rainy weather, fair weather, stock market rising, stock market

	S_1	S_2	.	.	.	.	S_j	.	.	.	.	.	S_n
A_1	u_{11}	u_{12}	.	.	.	.	u_{ij}	.	.	.	.	.	u_{in}
A_2	u_{21}	u_{22}	.	.	.	.	.	.	.	.	.	.	u_{2n}
.		.	.	.	.	.	.	.	.	.	.	.	.
.		.	.	.	.	.	.	.	.	.	.	.	.
.		.	.	.	.	.	.	.	.	.	.	.	.
A_i	u_{il}		.	.	.		u_{ij}	.	.	.			u_{in}
.		.	.	.	.	.	.	.	.	.	.	.	.
.		.	.	.	.	.	.	.	.	.	.	.	.
A_m	u_{ml}	.	.	.	.	.	.	.	.	.	.	.	u_{mn}

Decision under risk in matrix representation

Figure 14.1. The rows, A_1, A_2, ... A_m, represent the available courses of action; the columns, S_1, S_2, ... S_n, the relevant states of nature.

falling, summit meeting that resulted in a disarmament agreement, summit meeting ending in an impasse, etc. In our formulation, we will be considering only those "states of nature" that are relevant to the problem at hand.

Suppose there are n such states, labeled 1, 2, ... n. Then the whole situation can be pictured in the form of an m x n *matrix*, that is, a rectangular array of m rows and n columns. Each of the m rows represents an alternative available to the actor. Each of the n columns represents a possible state of nature. A *cell* of the matrix is, thus, an intersection of a row and a column. It represents an outcome which results if the actor chooses a particular row and the state of nature happens to be the one represented by a particular column. We will designate the cell, that is, the intersection of the i-th row and the j-th column by (ij).

The utility (u_{ij}) of each outcome (to the actor) is entered into the corresponding cell. A matrix depicting a decision problem under risk is shown in Figure 14–1.

The problem now is to choose among the available alternatives (i.e., to choose a row of the matrix) in a way that can be defended as "rational." A basic concept that provides a solution to this problem is that of *expected utility*, defined as the weighted average of the utilities associated with each row of the matrix, where the weights in this average are the probabilities assigned to the different possible states of nature. Thus, if these probabilities are given by p_1, p_2, ... p_n, and if the utilities associated with alternative i are u_{i1}, u_{i2}, ... u_{in}, then the expected utility of alternative i will be given by $p_1 u_{i1} + p_2 u_{i2} + \ldots p_n u_{in}$. The "rational choice" is then defined as the alternative whose expected utility is largest.

The justification for this solution of the decision problem under risk is usually expressed in terms of long-run expectations. If an actor is confronted with the same sort of problem many times in succession and each time chooses the alternative that maximizes expected utility, then his total actual gain of utility per decision will be with great probability very near the expected gain, i.e., maximized in the context of the problem. This principle is applied to many business situations, where utility is usually identified with quantities of money and where situations of the same type present themselves recurrently. Insurance and gambling enterprises are the best known examples. Investment portfolios are also sometimes constructed on this principle. We must now see to what extent the principle of maximizing expected utility is justifiable as a principle of rational decision under risk in situations where our two assumptions may not be valid. These two assumptions are (a) that utilities are identified with amounts of money and (b) that the situation calling for a decision under risk recurs many times.

Let us first keep the first assumption and drop the second. To fix ideas, consider the choice between two slot machines and for simplicity suppose that each machine either pays out the jackpot or pays nothing. Suppose also that the probability that each machine pays out the jackpot on any try is known. If the sizes of the jackpots are equal, common sense dictates that the rational choice is the machine that pays out with the larger probability. If the probabilities are equal, it stands to reason that one should choose the machine that delivers the larger jackpot. What if neither the probabilities nor the sizes of the jackpots are equal? The principle of maximizing expected utility prescribes the machine associated with the larger *product* of the amount delivered and the probability of delivering it.

This last conclusion will not be as readily accepted as the first two. Consider a choice between a machine that pays out a very large jackpot with a very small probability and one that pays a small jackpot with a medium probability. Some people may prefer a larger probability of winning even if the winnings are smaller. Others will prefer the "long shot" with the larger prize. It is not at all certain that all will agree that it is the products of probabilities and gains that decide the issue.

Such disagreements can be ascribed to the fact that the utility of an amount of money is, for most people, not proportional to the amount of money. As a matter of fact, if this were not the case, then we would have to conclude that the insurance company that sells insurance and people who buy insurance cannot both be "rational," since if the expected value of the insurance (the product of the amount paid out and the probability of getting it) is positive for one, it must be negative for the other. The fact that most will readily ascribe rationality to both the seller and the buyer of insurance can be accounted for by assuming that for the insured there is a "diminishing returns effect": even though the utility of money increases with the amount, it does so at a decreasing rate. It is commonplace to observe that a dollar is worth more to a poor person than to a rich person. Similarly, the loss of a large amount of money even with small probability has a greater "disutility" than paying the amount of the premium. For this reason, it is rational to pay the insurance premium. The same reasoning does not apply to the insurance company, because it deals with very many policies, so that the expected amount of benefits paid out is very nearly equal to the actual amount that will be paid out, which is more than compensated by the premiums received. To put it in another way, for the insured, the probability of a disaster is probability of a *single* event; for the insurance company, the probability of paying a benefit can be translated into the actual average amount paid out per case.

When the events to which utilities are assigned are not readily quantified, in the way, for example, amounts of money gained or lost are, the problem of assigning utilities to such events can become extremely difficult, especially if the outcomes are defined in terms of intangibles. In weighing outcomes of decisions against each other, a person may have to assess the utility (or disutility) to him of making a good or bad impression, retaining or losing a friend or romantic relationship, enhancing or forfeiting self-respect, getting wet as a consequence of having failed to take an umbrella or lugging an umbrella in fine weather, and the like. In all these cases, we assume some risks are incurred, namely, that a "wrong" decision will be made, and these have to be weighed against the advantage to be gained in consequence of having made a "right" decision. In each case, the risks are associated with the fact that the "state of nature," now or in the future, is not known with certainty.

The principle of maximizing expected utility sounds fine as a principle of rational decision. However, we must constantly keep in mind that the principle can be applied *only* if the following two conditions are satisfied: (a) utility on a scale at least as strong as the *interval scale* must be assigned to each possible outcome; and (b) probabilities must be assigned to all relevant states of nature. These probabilities need not be "objective," i.e., determined by observed relative frequencies. They may be no more than degrees of belief of the actor that one or another state of nature obtains (or will obtain). The rationality of a decision is always defined relative to the *decision maker's* estimates of probabilities and relative to the utilities that the outcomes have *for him.* To what extent these assignments are themselves to be regarded as rational is an entirely separate problem, which leads to inquiries having nothing to do with the situation at hand.

A Momentous Risky Decision

In October 1962, President Kennedy of the United States had to make a decision, the outcome of which might have been a global nuclear war. The Soviets had installed missile sites in Cuba, from which the United States could be attacked with nuclear weapons. President Kennedy and practically all his subordinates and advisers regarded this situation as intolerable. Yet, to their way of thinking, there seemed no way of getting the Soviets to remove these installations by negotiation. Or perhaps they thought that pursuing the normal course of diplomacy in a situation of this kind would irreversibly impair the prestige of the United States or else cause a political furor leading to a loss of power by the political party which Kennedy represented. Whatever were the blocks to attempts at peaceful settlement, the consensus of opinion at the top was that the U.S. should assume a threatening, uncompromising posture, that is, *force* the removal of the missiles rather than invite negotiations.

Clearly, the choice involved a grave risk. Now "taking a calculated risk" is usually regarded as a frequently necessary step in effective decision making. Practically every decision involves some risk that it will turn out to have been wrong. So risks are unavoidable. Let us, however, see what could possibly be meant by a "calculated risk." What is there to calculate? If a rational decision is one that maximizes expected utility, then, of course, calculations are in order. If probabilities have been assigned to possible states of nature and utilities (on an interval scale or better) to the possible outcomes, then one knows exactly what and how to calculate. The expected utilities of each of the available alternatives are to be calculated by multiplying the utility of each outcome associated with each of the alternatives by the probability of the state of nature that produces the outcome, then adding all these products. One can then compare the sums so obtained and choose the alternative for which the sum is largest.

Could this procedure have been applied in the Cuban missile crisis? To give this approach the benefit of the doubt, let us assume that the simplest possible model of this decision problem is an adequate representation. Let Kennedy choose between two alternatives: threaten force or ask for negotiation. Suppose further that the Soviets have a choice between yielding and standing firm. (In the case of proposed negotiations, yielding means accepting the proposal, standing firm rejecting it.) The resulting decision matrix is represented in Figure 14–2.

The utilities u_{ij} can now be interpreted.

u_{11}: utility to U.S. if offer of negotiation is accepted by U.S.S.R.
u_{12}: utility to U.S. of being humiliated if offer to negotiate is refused

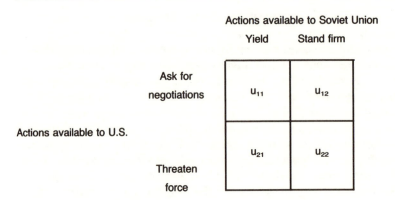

Figure 14.2. Actions available to Soviet Union and U.S.

u_{21}: utility to U.S. if U.S.S.R. is humiliated by yielding to threat
u_{22}: utility to U.S. of head-on confrontation, possibly nuclear war

Now if probabilities could be assigned to the choices of the Soviet Union and utilities (at least on an interval scale) could be assigned by the U.S. to each of the four possible outcomes, the problem could be reduced to calculations. In this context, taking a "calculated risk" would have a concrete meaning. Without specifications of utilities and probabilities, the phrase means precisely nothing. It serves as window dressing to make it appear that decisions are made "rationally."

It is said that at the meetings of the National Security Council and the Joint Chiefs of Staff Kennedy asked each participant in turn what he thought the probability was that a war would break out if the U.S. sent an ultimatum to the Soviet Union or else, if bypassing an ultimatum, the U.S. would simply launch a surprise attack against Cuba. A "surgical strike," they called it, alluding to the accuracy of the attacking weapons, which could presumably "take out" the missiles without doing too much "collateral damage."

The strategists and generals gathered at that momentous meeting obliged. Some estimated the probability of war as 0.30, some as 0.40, some as 0.60. Obviously, there is no way of estimating these probabilities on the basis of observed frequencies, which alone could provide some objective basis for the estimates. By its nature, a nuclear war cannot occur with a "frequency." It probably cannot occur more than once. Therefore the estimates given by the strategists and generals were entirely subjective. It is doubtful that even those subjective estimates were based on any serious thinking through. Most likely, they were given simply because some answer had to be given to the president's thoughtless question. The most that could be said about those estimates is that if they were small, they reflected a hope that a war would not break out; if large, the fear that it would (always assuming that the participants in that session regarded the outbreak of a war between the U.S. and the U.S.S.R. as an undesirable event).

Since there is no way of removing the subjective element from estimates of probabilities of unique events, we must suppose that these estimates are strongly influenced by what decision is desired. We can suppose that the members of Kennedy's staff who strongly desired military action against Cuba would have estimated the probability of war to be small (if they thought Kennedy did not want war). Those who had misgivings would give larger estimates.

Let us now look at the other component of expected utility, which has been proposed as a reasonable index for arriving at a rational decision in risky situations, namely, the assignment of utilities to the outcomes. The subjective nature of these assignments is even more conspicuous than in the case of estimated probabilities. There is no such thing as an "objective" utility. Utility, if it can be defined at all, must always be defined with reference to a specific actor (who need not be an individual). A person might be hard put if asked to assign a "utility" to an event like a nuclear war. Nevertheless, here, too, attempts have been made to lend an aura of "no-nonsense" objectivity to the "problem." Herman Kahn, for example, estimated this utility in terms of the number of "acceptable casualties." There is hardly any need to point out that "utility estimates" of this sort are only reflections of certain thinking habits acquired in the course of certain highly specific activities. They are rather a caricature of objectivity.

Aside from all these difficulties, there is another reason why the "calculated risk" paradigm does not apply to situations in which presumably "rational adversaries" confront each other. In "assessing the risk" of a nuclear war during the Cuban missile crisis, the probabilities assigned to that event were actually probabilities assigned to the event that the Soviet Union would be adamant or compliant in response to the ultimatum (or to a "surgical strike") by the U.S. In effect, therefore, the attitude of the Soviet Union was regarded as a "state of nature" quite in the same way that the weather is regarded as a state of nature. There is, however, a fundamental difference between a state of nature (like the weather) and the choice between alternatives made by an actor. Granted that whether it will rain or not can be formally regarded as a "choice" made by nature, the fact remains that in making that "choice" nature does not serve her (or anyone else's) interests. Nature is neither malevolent nor benevolent. She will not make it rain just because Ms. A left her umbrella at home; nor will she make fine weather for that reason. An adversary is an alto-

	C_1	C_2	C_3	C_4
R_1	2	3	−11	−4
R_2	−1	5	0	−2
R_3	6	−7	3	−5

Game 14–1

gether different kind of actor. An adversary has interests of his own. He will guide his choices by what he thinks *his* adversary is going to do. A method of inquiry that takes such "sizing up" of the adversary into account, *including* his thinking about the strategic aspects of the conflict situation has been developed in the *theory of games*, to which we now turn our attention.

Two-Person Antagonistic Games

A basic distinction is made in the theory of games between conflicts with just two participants (*two-person games*) and those with more than two (*n-person games*). Two-person games are further divided into *constant-sum* and *non-contant-sum* games. Constant-sum games are also sometimes called *games of complete opposition* or *antagonistic games*. The term "constant-sum" derives from the circumstance that in such games what one player gains in utility, the other necessarily loses. Hence the sum of the gains, which may be positive, negative, or zero, is constant in every outcome of the game. Without loss of generality, this constant can be taken to be zero. Thus, constant-sum games are also often called *zero-sum* games.

Like decision problems under risk, two-person games can also be represented by matrices. Here the rows of the matrix represent the choices available to one of the players, whom we will henceforth call Row, and the columns those available to the other player, who will be called Column.

A *play* of the game consists of simultaneous, i.e., independent choices —of a row by Row and of a column by Column. The chosen row and column intersect in one of the cells of the matrix. When the matrix represents a general two-person game, there are two entries in each cell, one representing the *payoff* (the utility of the outcome) to Row, the other to Column. If the game is zero-sum, there is no need to enter both payoffs. By convention, only the payoffs to Row are entered. The payoffs to Column will then be numerically equal with the opposite sign. An example of a zero-sum game so represented is shown as Game 14–1.

To illustrate a play of the game, suppose Row chooses R_2 and Column chooses C_4. The entry in the cell at the intersection of this row and this column dicates that Row has lost 2 units and, consequently, Column has won 2 units.

We turn to the question that may have occurred to the reader, namely, how general is this representation of a game. Game theory was originally developed in the context of analyzing so-called *games of strategy*, of which chess, go, bridge, and poker are examples. In these games, each player makes many choices in the course of a play of the game. In chess, for example, these sequential choices are called *moves*. In our model, on the other hand, each player makes just one choice. It is shown in game theory, however, that in principle it suffices for each player to make a single choice in order for the entire course of the game to be determined. This single choice is a choice of a *strategy*. This term is borrowed from military parlance but has a special technical meaning in the theory of games. A strategy is an indication by the player of what he intends to do in every possible situation in which he can find himself in the course of the game. Once such a choice is indicated by each player, the play of the game can be constructed following the "instructions" implicit in the choices of strategies.

Let us look at Game 14–1 from Row's point of view. If Row knew how Column will choose, he would have no difficulty deciding on his choice of strategy. If Column should choose C_1, Row's best choice is obviously R_3; if Column should choose C_2, then R_2 is Row's best choice, and so on. But of course Row does not know how Column will choose. However, even in his state of ignorance, Row can make a "prudent" choice. He can examine the matrix to see what would be the *worst* possible outcome from his point of view in case he chose each of the rows. Thus, if he should choose R_1, then -11 would be the worst possible payoff; if R_2, the worst payoff would be -2, and so on. A strategy could be regarded as "prudent" if it *guarantees* some minimum payoff to the player who chooses it. Observe that the three worst payoffs to Row resulting from his choice of each of the three rows are -11, -2, and -7. Of these three minima, -2 is the maximum. Accordingly, it is called the *maximin*. This maximin guarantees a payoff of at least -2 (i.e., a loss not greater than 2) to Row, for should Column choose a column other than C_4, Row would get more than -2.

Suppose now Row decides, as yet provisionally, to choose R_2, so as to get a guaranteed payoff of at least -2. To see whether this choice is optimal, he should ask himself what Column would do, if he knew how he (Row) would choose. For if the choice is indeed optimal, Column, attributing rationality to Row, will have figured out that Row will choose R_2. How then should Column choose? This is the question that Row must ask himself. He must put himself in Column's shoes, as it were. The answer

	C₁	C₂	C₃	C₄
R₁	-2	3	1	-2
R₂	-2	5	0	-2
R₃	-8	-11	3	-5

Game 14–2

is clear. If Column thought that Row would choose R_2, Column would choose C_4. Now Row asks himself what *he* would do if he knew that Column would choose C_4. The answer is again clear. R_2 would still be Row's best choice.

We see that C_4 is Column's best reply to Row's R_2 and R_2 is Row's best reply to Column's C_4. The outcome represents a sort of "balance of power." It guarantees each player the best possible payoff under the constraint that the co-player, who in this case is a real adversary, since his interests are diametrically opposed, is rational and is also trying to get the most he can under the constraints of the situation.

The principle of choosing the alternative that guarantees the "best of the worst" is called the *maximin principle*. It seems to be a reasonable guide to choosing among alternatives in situations that can be adequately modeled as two-person zero-sum games, as in our example. As we have seen, if both players are guided by this principle, a sort of "balance of power" results. The choice of each is best against the choice of the other. However, this turned out to be the case only because Game 14–1 was one of a special type. Namely, the game possesses a *saddle point*. A saddle point is an entry in a matrix of a two-person zero-sum game which is at the same time minimal in its row and maximal in its column (with regard to Row's payoffs). This is the property that makes the saddle point an *equilibrium*, that is, an outcome from which neither player is motivated to shift if the other does not. In Game 14–1, the outcome R_2C_4 is an equilibrium, for if Column stays with his strategy C_4, Row, by shifting to another strategy, can only impair his payoff. Similarly, Column can only impair his payoff by shifting, if Row stays with strategy R_2. It has been shown that if a two-person constant-sum game has more than one equilibrium, the payoffs in all of them must be equal. Moreover, any two strategies of the respective players that contain equilibria among their outcomes always intersect in an equilibrium. It follows that a simple prescription can be given to both players in a two-person constant-sum game: choose a strategy that contains an equilibrium. Game 14–2 illustrates this result.

Note that in Game 14.2, outcomes R_1C_1, R_2C_1, R_1C_4, and R_2C_4 are all equilibria. Thus, R_1 and R_2 both contain equilibria, and so do columns C_1 and C_4. If Row is advised to choose a strategy that contains an equilibrium, he can choose either row R_1 or row R_2. Similarly, Column can choose either C_1 or C_4. If both choose either of the two equilibrium-containing strategies, the outcome will be an equilibrium.

Mixed Strategies

The situation becomes more complex if a game has no equilibrium. An example is shown in Game 14–3.

Observe that none of the four outcomes is an equilibrium. Row is motivated to shift from R_2C_1 and from R_1C_2; Column is motivated to shift from R_1C_1 and from R_2C_2. Let us see what happens if either player decides to choose his maximin strategy. Since the worst payoff for Row associated with R_1 is -1 and that associated with R_2 is 1, R_2 is Row's maximin strategy. Similarly C_1 is Column's maximin strategy. Outcome R_2C_1 results.

Now if the outcome is "rational" and both players are rational, then on the assumption that Column will choose "rationally" (i.e., C_1), Row should choose R_1, since that is the best response to C_1. But since Column is just as rational as Row, he will have followed Row's reasoning, and on the assumption that Row will choose R_1 will choose C_2, the best response to R_1, which again suggests that Row should choose R_2, not R_1. The reasoning goes around in circles, and there seems to be no way of prescribing an unambiguously optimal strategy to either player.

A major achievement of game theory has been the discovery of a way out of this impasse. The way out is provided by the concept of *mixed strategy*. A mixed strategy is essentially a probability distribution on the player's available strategies, which we will now call *pure* strategies. To fix ideas, suppose Row has at his disposal (pure) strategies R_1, R_2, . . . R_m and a random device by means of which he can choose any of these strategies with any desired probability. A roulette wheel can be thought of as an example of such a device. To choose a particular mixed strategy, Row divides the circumference of the wheel into arcs of lengths proportional to the probabilities with which he will choose among his available pure strategies. He then spins the wheel and chooses the strategy corresponding to the arc on which the ball falls.

The use of mixed strategies is well known in games of strategy. Consider poker. It may seem judicious to adjust the size of one's bet to the strength of one's hand, for example to fold if one holds a bust, to bet the limit if one holds a straight flush. An experienced poker player, however, is not likely to play this way. On occasions he will raise steeply when he holds

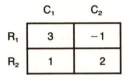

Game 14–3

a weak hand and only slightly when he holds a strong hand. The purpose is to keep the other players guessing. If he always determined the size of his bet by the strength of his hand, he would thereby reveal the strength of his hand. Then the other players would be likely to fold when he bet high and to raise when he bet low. The idea of bluffing is to induce the other players to think that you have a strong hand and perhaps to scare them into folding. The idea of sandbagging is to keep the other players in the game when you have a good chance of winning the pot.

The achievement of game theory was twofold in this context. First, it was shown that if the concept of strategy is extended to include mixed strategies, then it is always possible to prescribe an optimal strategy (pure or mixed) to each player in the sense that such a strategy guarantees the player a minimum *expected payoff* regardless of how the other chooses. Second, the way was paved for the development of algorithms for calculating these optimal strategies. The method is illustrated by "solving" Game 14–3, where by a solution of such a game we will mean a prescription of a strategy (pure or mixed) to each player.

Suppose Row chooses R_1 with probability 0.20 and consequently R_2 with probability 0.80. Then if Column chooses C_1, Row's expected payoff will be $(3)(.20) + (1)(.80) = 1.40$. If, on the other hand, Column chooses C_2, Row's expected payoff will be $(-1)(.20) + (2)(.80) = 1.40$. We see, therefore, that Row is *guaranteed* an expected payoff of 1.40 regardless of how Column chooses. Similarly, it can be shown that if Column chooses C_1 with probability 0.6 and C_2 with probability 0.4, then Column will obtain an expected payoff of -1.40 regardless of how Row chooses. Since neither player can gain over the guaranteed expected payoff by shifting away from the prescribed mixed strategy, while the other stays with his, it follows that these strategies are optimal in the sense that they guarantee a minimum payoff to each player and in the sense that a shift away from such a strategy (using a different mixture) can be exploited by the other player. For example, suppose Row, instead of using the mixture (0.2, 0.8), uses the mixture (0.4, 0.6). Then Column, by choosing C_2 can get -0.8, which is more than his guaranteed payoff -1.4. Consequently, Row will get less.

Calculation of optimal mixed strategies in so-called 2×2 games, where each of two players has two strategies available, is quite simple. It gets considerably more complex in larger games. Algorithms for solving games of arbitrary complexity have been developed as a by-product of solving linear programming problems.

Beyond the Two-Person Zero-Sum Game

So far, the only games we have examined involved two players with diametrically opposed interests. These comprise only a very narrow class of conflict situations. In what follows, we will examine more general types, involving more than two players or else two players with interests that are not entirely opposed. First, however, let us review the principles on which solutions of two-person constant-sum games were based.

We have described the maximin principle, according to which a player chooses a strategy that guarantees him "the best of all worst possible outcomes." It is clearly a pessimistic principle, being based on the assumption that whatever strategy one chooses, the adversary will choose a strategy that will result in the worst possible outcome (for self) associated with one's own chosen strategy. In the context of a game in which the interests of the players are diametrically opposed, this seems to be a prudent principle, since one can suppose that the adversary, being rational, will choose a strategy to maximize his own payoff and consequently to minimize self's payoff. If the maximin strategies of the two players intersect in an equilibrium, the maximin strategy, as we have seen, justifies itself. It awards to each player the best payoff he can expect under the contraints of the situation.

If the maximin strategies do not intersect in an equilibrium, optimal strategies turn out to be mixed. Intersections of these optimal mixed strategies are also equilibria in the sense that neither player can improve his payoff if he shifts away from such an intersection, while the adversary does not. We see, therefore, that the equilibrium principle can also be regarded as a principle of rational decision, at least in the context of two-person constant-sum games.

Finally, we can regard the so-called *sure-thing principle* as a principle of rational decision. This principle is illustrated in Game 14–4.

As before, the matrix represents a two-person zero-sum game. The entries are payoffs to Row. The payoffs to Column are the negatives of these. In this game, Row's strategy R_2 is said to *dominate* the other in the sense that it yields Row a larger payoff than the other *regardless* of how Column chooses. It is, therefore, difficult to avoid the conclusion that R_2 is Row's optimal strategy. Clearly, games in which one or the other player has a

	C_1	C_2
R_1	1	-10
R_2	10	-1

Game 14–4

dominating strategy are quite special. In general, whether one or another strategy yields a larger payoff to the actor who chooses it depends on the strategy chosen by the other player.

Strategic analysis of two-person zero-sum games is especially simple, because these three principles of rational decision—the maximin principle, the equilibrium principle, and the sure-thing principle—are closely related. If a player has a dominating strategy in such a game and uses the sure-thing principle to choose it, he has automatically satisfied the other two principles, as can be readily verified. If the game has no dominating strategy but possesses a saddle point, then the application of either the maximin principle or the equilibrium principle results in the same choice. If a two-person game has no saddle point, the maximin strategy is no longer optimal. However, optimal (mixed) strategies still intersect in an equilibrium. It follows that the equilibrium principle governs the rational decision in all types of two-person zero-sum matrix games. These games have the property that if both players choose a strategy that contains an equilibrium among its possible outcomes, the outcome will always be an equilibrium. Hence, in prescribing a rational choice, it suffices to instruct the player to choose a strategy that contains an equilibrium. In games that are not constant-sum, this is no longer the case, as will now be shown.

In non-constant-sum games, the sum of the payoffs may be different in different cells of the payoff matrix. Thus, the interests of the players may be no longer directly opposed. Such games have also been called *mixed-motive* games to indicate that the interests of the players may be partially opposed and partially coincident. As an example, consider once again the drastically simplified version of the Cuban missile crisis. Recall that the choices of the U.S. and U.S.S.R. were defined as between "yielding" and "standing firm." Each side preferred the outcome resulting from "standing firm" while the other side "yielded." In this respect, therefore, the interests of the two were opposed. However, it is reasonable to assume that *both* sides preferred the outcome resulting from a compromise (both yielding) to the outcome resulting from both standing firm (war). The situation is represented as Game 14–5.

We note that neither player has a dominating strategy. If the other yields,

U.S.S.R.

	Y_2	S_2
Y_1	1, 1	-10, 10
S_2	10, -10	-100, -100

U.S. (label to left of Y_1/S_2 rows)

Game 14–5

then standing firm awards the larger payoff. But if the other stands firm, then yielding is the preferable strategy. Hence the sure-thing principle cannot be applied.

Examining Game 14–5 for equilibria, we find two, namely at outcomes Y_1S_2 and S_1Y_2. Of these, S_1Y_2 is preferred by the U.S., Y_1S_2 by the U.S.S.R. Since these equilibria are in different rows and different columns, it follows that either strategy of each player contains an equilibrium. If our prescription to each player is (as in the case of the zero-sum game) "Choose a strategy that contains an equilibrium," it is possible that each player will choose the strategy that contains his preferred equilibrium. This means that the U.S. will choose S_1 (stand firm) and the U.S.S.R. will choose S_2 (stand firm.) The outcome will be S_1S_2, which is not an equilibrium and is disastrous for both. Thus, the application of the equilibrium principle is beset with difficulties.

There remains the maximin principle. This principle dictates Y to both players. The outcome Y_1Y_2 (compromise) results. It seems, therefore, that the maximin principle in this case yields an acceptable solution. Note, however, that the outcome Y_1Y_2 is not an equilibrium. Each player, by shifting away from this outcome, while the other stays with his strategy, can gain. The trouble is that if *both* switch their strategies, both lose heavily. In sum, we see that in the context of Game 14–5, each of the three principles of rational decision in conflict situations presents difficulties. The sure-thing principle cannot be applied in this game, because neither player has a dominating strategy. Application of the equilibrium principle may result in an outcome that is not only not an equilibrium but also the worst possible outcome for both players. Application of the maximin principle apparently leads to a reasonable outcome, but this outcome is not an equilibrium. Thus, both players may be tempted to shift away from it; but if both do, both will be worse off.

We shall see that Game 14–5 has a third equilibrium (in mixed strategies), but it, too, presents problems. At this time, let us examine another nonconstant-sum game, in which all three principles point to the same

	C_2	D_2
C_1	1,1	$-10, 10$
D_1	$10, -10$	$-1, -1$

Game 14–6

choice of strategy by each player, but the resulting outcome is not satisfactory.

Consider Game 14–6. We note that each player has a dominating strategy. Row does better by choosing D_1 regardless of how Column chooses. Should Column choose C_2, Row gets $+10$ by choosing D_1 but only $+1$ by choosing C_1. Should Column choose D_2, Row gets -1 by choosing D_1 but -10 by choosing C_1. The same reasoning applies to Column's choices. Hence the sure-thing principle dictates D to both players.

The maximin principle also dictates D, since by choosing D each player avoids the outcome that is worst for him (in which he would get -10).

Finally, outcome D_1D_2 is the only equilibrium in the game. Neither player can shift from that outcome, while the other does not, without impairing his payoff.

It would seem, then, that outcome D_1D_2, being dictated by all three principles of rational decision so far considered, would be an eminently rational outcome. Note, however, that both players are worse off in that outcome (getting -1 each) than they would have been in outcome C_1C_2 (where both get $+1$). The question naturally arises whether there may be other principles of rational decision in conflict situations that lead to outcomes that are intuitively acceptable, as most people would agree outcome C_1C_2 is. It appears at first sight that if an agreement could be effected between the two players, the acceptable outcome Y_1Y_2 in Game 14–5 and C_1C_2 in Game 14–6 could be realized. An "agreement," however, implies the existence of some way of enforcing it. Enforcing an agreement, in turn, implies that sanctions can be applied for violations. By definition a sanction has negative utility for the actor subjected to it. Recall that the payoffs entered in a game matrix are utilities. Therefore, if choices of some strategies are punished, corresponding negative utilities must be added to the utilities of the outcomes associated with those strategies. In the case of the above games, the punished strategies would be S in Game 14–5 and D in Game 14–6. But if these sanctions were sufficiently large to make the choice of S (or D), i.e., violations of agreements, unattractive, this would mean that the structure of the game would have been changed. We would escape from the paradoxes associated with these games only by substituting other games for them, which would amount to evading the problem instead of coming to grips with it.

A *conceptual* way out of the difficulty is provided by the recognition that the concept of "rationality" is ambiguous, if the context in which it is applied is not specified. It seems necessary to distinguish between *individual* and *collective* rationality. The principle of individual rationality is invoked in the answer to the question, "How shall *I* choose in this situation so as to do the best I can under the circumstances?" The answer to this question in the context of Game 14–6 is unambiguous: "Choose D." The principle of collective rationality is invoked in the answer to the question, "How shall *we* choose in this situation so as to do the best we can under the circumstances?" The answer to this question in the context of the same game is equally unambiguous: "Choose C."

In formal decision theory, the concept of collective rationality is closely related to that of *Pareto optimality*. An outcome of decisions made by a set of actors is called *Pareto-optimal* if there is no other outcome that could have resulted in that situation, which *all* of the actors would have preferred. Thus, in Game 14–5, Y_1Y_2 and in Game 14–6 C_1C_2 are both Pareto-optimal. Note, however, that each of these games has three Pareto-optimal outcomes. All the outcomes except S_1S_2 in Game 14–5 and all except D_1D_2 in Game 14–6 are Pareto-optimal, since in each case there is no other outcome that *both* players would prefer. The principle of collective rationality dictates a Pareto-optimal outcome. However, in case there are several such outcomes, it is not clear without further analysis how the outcome is to be selected among them.

We will examine this problem and its proposed solutions in the next chapter. For the moment, let us return to the problem of choosing a strategy when there is no opportunity for making an enforceable collectively rational decision.

If there is no way of enforcing an agreement to choose Y_1Y_2 in Game 14–5 or C_1C_2 in Game 14–6, we are left with the equilibrium principle as apparently the only principle of rational decision. The attractive feature of this principle is that an equilibrium outcome is, by definition, "self-enforcing," since neither player can gain by switching his strategy while the other does not. Outcome D_1D_2 in Game 14–6 has this property. As we have seen, this outcome is not Pareto-optimal, hence unsatisfactory from the point of view of collective rationality. However, those who argue that solutions of matrix games must be selected from among their equilibria point out that being content with a non-Pareto-optimal outcome is the price one must pay for not having made provisions for enforcing agreements. This argument addresses itself to an ethical issue raised in connection with games like Game 14–6, which we will now examine.

Game 14–6 is well known in game-theoretic literature. It was discovered in 1950 by M.M. Flood and M. Drescher in connection with some experiments in decision making. Shortly thereafter it was given a name—Prisoner's Dilemma—by A.W. Tucker and has stimulated a great deal of interest among psychologists, political scientists, sociologists, and philosophers. The anecdote invented by Tucker to illustrate a setting in which such a decision problem might arise explains the name.

Two men are arrested on suspicion of burglary. Articles stolen have been found in their possession, hence there is sufficient evidence to convict them of possession of stolen goods, which carries a penalty of one year in jail. There is not sufficient evidence, however, to convict the men of burglary unless one or both confess to that crime. To induce confessions, the prosecutor resorts to the following stratagem. The men are kept in separate cells and have no opportunity to communicate, and the situation in which each finds himself is explained to him.

The penalty for possession of stolen goods is, as has been said, one year in jail, and this is what each of them will get if neither confesses to burglary. The maximum penalty for burglary is five years in jail. However, if both confess, this will constitute extenuating circumstances, and the sentence will be reduced to three years. If only one confesses to burglary, he will not be prosecuted at all (for having turned state's evidence). The other, who did not confess, will nevertheless be convicted on the strength of his erstwhile colleague's evidence and given the maximum sentence of five years. Each man now faces a decision problem: to confess or not to confess?

Examination of all possible outcomes indicates clearly that it is in each prisoner's individual interest to confess. For should the other confess, confession results in only a three-year sentence, while not confessing will result in a five-year sentence. Should the other not confess, refusing to confess will result in a one-year sentence, while confessing will bring immediate freedom. The strategic structure of the game turns out to be identical with that of Game 14–6. Individual rationality dictates confessing. But if both confess, both will get three years in prison, while if both hold out, both will go to prison for only one year (being convicted of the lesser crime).

Now the ethical implications of the problem are apparent. A familiar unwritten law of the underworld is that one does not snitch on one's partners in crime. Often violation brings severe penalties, especially in organized crime circles. Aside from these penalties, however, the taboo against cooperating with the police has been strongly internalized by many who make their livelihood outside socially approved activities. One finds similar taboos among inmates of institutions like boarding schools or prisons where, alongside of enmities among the inmates, strong feelings of solidarity are developed when dealing with the common enemy—the authorities. These feelings of solidarity are based on mutual trust, and it is for this reason that betrayal is regarded as a heinous offense. The notion of "trust," however, does not enter strategic analysis. To see the implications of this conceptual constriction, let us analyze a game consisting of several iterations of Prisoner's Dilemma.

Prisoner's Dilemma Iterated Many Times

To fix ideas, suppose Prisoner's Dilemma is played 100 times, the number of plays being known to both players. One might think that a tacit agreement would develop in the course of the iterations, to effect successive cooperative outcomes C_1C_2. Indeed, once this pattern is established, both players might be expected to be "deterred" from defecting to D by the threat of retaliation, which would lead to the inferior outcome D_1D_2. However, pursuing the analysis to the end, we see that such a tacit agreement cannot be established by a pair of individually rational players. For if both know that the 100th play is the last, both must conclude that the outcome of that play is a foregone conclusion, namely, D_1D_2, since "deterrence" cannot be effective if the play stops then. But if the outcome of the 100th play is a foregone conclusion, then the 99th play effectively becomes the "last play," and the same reasoning applies to it. And so on. Situations of this sort have been called *social traps*.

In experiments with iterated Prisoner's Dilemma, "locking in" on C_1C_2 is frequently observed if the sequence of plays is long enough, even if the number of iterations to be played is known to both players. But we must attribute this result to the fact that the players have not followed strategic reasoning to its final conclusion. Had they done so, that is, had they been competent strategists, they would have come to the conclusion that cooperation in this context is impossible and would have chosen the uncooperative strategy D all 100 times. Or all 1,000 times, if the game were to last that long. Or all 1,000,000 times. If it seems bizarre to associate this conclusion with "rationality" and if there is no escape from it, that is, if it is a rigorously logical consequence of applying principles of individual rationality, then it seems necessary either to abandon the principle of individual rationality that leads to this conclusion or to declare individual rationality to be inadequate in dealing with conflict situations in which the conflicting parties have some common interest. We opt for the latter alternative. Paradoxes are often resolved by refinement of concepts by making distinctions where none had been made before. So it is in the present case. A clear distinction between individual and collective rationality provides an escape from the paradoxes generated by the analysis of Prisoner's Dilemma.

The Game of Chicken

Let us turn to Game 14–5. This game has also been widely discussed in connection with strategic analysis. It has been nicknamed "Chicken" after a game which has a similar structure once played by spirited youngsters. Two parties get into cars some mile or so apart and race toward each other straddling the middle of the road. To avoid collision, one or both must swerve. The idea is to demonstrate "nerve," that is, to make it appear that one will not swerve. If the driver of the other car wants to live, he will swerve and thereby demonstrate loss of nerve, earning the contemptuous epithet of "chicken" (coward).

In the arena of international relations, the game is called "brinkmanship," after the expression of John Foster Dulles, American Secretary of State in Eisenhower's administration. Dulles declared that on occasions he brought his country to the brink of war. In this way he could prove to America's adversary that America had the will to emerge victorious in confrontations.

The stance is obviously flawed. Since the game is symmetric, in the sense that both players are in the same situation, advice given to one ought to be good for the other. But if both players take this stance, the outcome will be disastrous for both. For the same reason of symmetry, neither of the two equilibria of Chicken can be regarded as a solution to the game. One of these equilibria favors Row, the other favors Column. Since the situations of both players are identical, neither equilibrium can be preferred to the other.

Besides the two asymmetric equilibria at outcomes S_1Y_2 and Y_1S_2, Game 14–5 has a third equilibrium, an intersection of mixed strategies. This one is symmetric. It is calculated in the following way. Each player determines for himself a mixed strategy that will make the other player indifferent between his two strategies. In Game 14–5, this mixed strategy turns out to be (10/11, 1/11); that is, strategy Y is to be chosen with probability 10/11, strategy S with the complementary probability 1/11. If Row uses this mixed strategy, then Column's strategy Y_2 yields an expected payoff of 0. Strategy S_2 yields the same expected payoff. Consequently, Column is indifferent between the two strategies. Similar reasoning applies to Row if Column uses the same mixed strategy. Now if neither player is motivated to shift away from this intersection (being indifferent between the alternatives and therefore between all mixtures of the alternatives), we can call the intersection an equilibrium. Since it is symmetric, it rates as a possible solution to the game. Note, however, that this equilibrium is severely unstable. To see this, consider what happens if a small fluctuation occurs in, say, Row's mixture, so that he chooses Y_1 with a slightly larger probability than 10/11. If Column detects this perturbation, he can afford to use S_2 more frequently, because in this game the more cautious one player is, the more reckless the other can afford to be. But if Column becomes more reckless, Row must become still more cautious. A positive feedback sets in, which will drive the "system" either toward Y_1S_2 or to S_1Y_2 depending on the direction of the initial perturbation. We shall encounter a similar instability in a model of an arms race to be discussed in Chapter 18.

In sum, equilibria leave a great deal to be desired as solutions to non-constant-sum games. As we have seen, intersections of strategies containing equilibria are not necessarily equilibria. If a game has more than one equilibrium, the problem arises of how to choose among them. This problem was energetically attacked by J.C. Harsanyi (1977), who singled out a unique solution to every matrix game including generalizations of such games to more than two players. However, Harsanyi was obliged to take recourse to the concept of "tacit bargaining," supposedly engaged in by players who are rational and who regard other players as equally rational. Harsanyi has even introduced the possibility of communication between the players. Usually, opportunity to communicate is associated with so-called *cooperative* games, in which bargaining can be explicit. Harsanyi, however, reserved the designation "cooperative" to games where not only explicit communications can pass betweeen the players but also enforceable agreements can be made. In Harsanyi's treatment, communication may be permitted also in a non-cooperative game; it is only the possibility of making enforceable agreements that make a game "cooperative." Because equilibria are self-enforcing, Harsanyi regarded them as the only candidates for solutions to non-cooperative games. He then went on to establish criteria by means of which an essentially unique equilibrium could be singled out from all the equilibria of a game as *the* solution.

However, if it takes "tacit bargaining," i.e., a sort of tacit understanding, to establish *the* solution to a non-cooperative game, it is difficult to see why such "tacit understanding" cannot effect a solution that is more advantageous to both players than a non-Pareto-optimal equilibrium solution. A tacit understanding to achieve an outcome better for both than the equilibrium outcome in Prisoner's Dilemma would lead to the outcome C_1C_2 in Game 14–6 and to outcome Y_1Y_2 in Game 14–5. Admittedly, the cooperative outcome would be more difficult to achieve in Prisoner's Dilemma than in Chicken, since it has nothing (but Pareto-optimality) "going for it." It is not an equilibrium. It violates the maximin principle. It violates the sure-thing principle. Outcome Y_1Y_2 in Game 14–6 is not so encumbered. Since neither player has a dominating strategy in this game, the sure-thing principle does not apply. To be sure, Y_1Y_2 is not an equilibrium. But it does satisfy the maximin principle. Moreover, it is preferred by both players to the symmetric mixed strategy equilibrium, since it yields a payoff of 1 to each player, while the mixed strategy equilibrium yields an expected payoff of only 0.

As we have seen, Harsanyi's argument in favor of equilibria as solutions to non-cooperative games is that they are self-enforcing. That is to say, their rationale does not depend on the players' mutual trust, except for a belief in each other's individual rationality, which, in turn, is defined in a way that excludes the notion of trust.

The exclusion of trust from the concept of rationality also leads to the absurd solution of iterated Prisoner's Dilemma whenever the number of iterations is known to both players. For if each decided to trust the other, not to "stab him in the back" on the last play, "deterrence" would be sufficient to keep the players producing the cooperative C_1C_2 outcome. In fact, mutual trust coupled with "trustworthiness" (resisting the temptation to defect) could ensure a cooperative outcome even in a single play of Prisoner's Dilemma, if it were not for the powerful pressure of the sure-thing principle to play D. Note that the sure-thing principle is not involved in iterated play, because the unconditionally uncooperative strategy (D throughout the iteration) is no longer a *dominating* strategy in the iterated game. It remains, however, the only *equilibrium* strategy. It follows that at least in that context, it is the "orthodox" preference for equilibria that excludes the mutually advantageous solution based on trust.

Escape from Social Traps

Suppose the two actors playing Prisoner's Dilemma are given the opportunity to discuss the situation in which they find themselves and to enter agreements if they so desire. It is not difficult for them to realize that an agreement to choose C_1 and C_2 respectively is to their common advantage. But now another problem arises. Assuming that no external sanctions can be applied for breaking the agreement, each player can ask himself whether it is to his advantage to keep the agreement or to break it. The reasoning involved in an attempt to answer this question goes on in exactly the same way as the reasoning that had led to the choice of D in the absence of the agreement. For if the co-player keeps the agreement, breaking it is surely advantageous, because it results in the largest of the four payoffs. If the co-player breaks the agreement, keeping it brings the largest loss. Therefore it is imperative to break the agreement.

Resisting the temptation to break the agreement in order to get a larger payoff reflects "trustworthiness." Assuming that the co-player is trustworthy reflects "trust." Both players must be both trustworthy and trusting if the agreement is to be kept in the absence of external sanctions. It is easy to see that trustworthiness itself is not sufficient. For even if one resists the temptation of violating the agreement in pursuit of gain but mistrusts the co-player, i.e., suspects that he will not keep the agreement, then in the context of Prisoner's Dilemma, one must violate the agreement "in self-defense," as it were.

This reasoning can be pursued on still higher levels. For example, one can be both trustworthy and trusting. Being trusting means that one does not suspect the co-player of being untrustworthy. But one can suspect the co-player of not being *trusting*. If one does, one must assume that the co-player will violate the agreement ("in self-defense"); so again one is led to the conclusion that one has no choice but to violate the agreement. There is no way out of this vicious cycle except *refusing to entertain such thoughts*.

Can such a refusal be regarded as a mark of rationality? Surely not, if the paradigm of individual rationality, i.e., the principle of "non-tuism" (cf. Wicklesteed 1933), is to be preserved at all costs. But a refusal to enter the vicious cycle ("Can I trust him? Can I assume that he trusts me? Can I assume that he assumes that I trust him? . . .") is surely consistent with collective rationality. It rests on the assumption that the Other is a mirror image of Self. In consequence of this assumption, the thought that an advantage can be gained by double-crossing the Other is rejected, because it leads to the conclusion that the Other entertains the same thought. A "double double-cross" entails a loss for both. The objection that the mirror image model is inconsistent with the independence of consciousnesses of different individuals is not relevant, because the "independence of consciousnesses" is itself an assumption. It is, in fact, equivalent to the assumption that individual rationality is the only "real" rationality. This stance reflects an inability or unwillingness to extend the concept of rationality to contexts beyond the two-person zero-sum game.

This unwillingness or inability is all the more strange because trust and trustworthiness pervade all areas of social activity which would be paralyzed otherwise. Without giving the matter a second thought, we entrust our lives every day to perfect strangers each time we cross the street in a marked crosswalk where pedestrians supposedly have the right of way, every time we board a plane, every time we eat a meal in a restaurant, or take a drug prescribed to us. It is *because* we take the trustworthiness of people for granted that we fail to appreciate how crucial trust is for the functioning of normal social life. The exclusion of trust and trustworthiness from classical decision theory rests on a mistaken notion that they cannot be incorporated without invoking principles of "morality" which, in the interest of logical rigor, ought to be excluded from the concept of rationality. That this is not so can be demonstrated by the following game:

An unspecified number of players (everyone can play) are invited to submit whole positive numbers, 1, 2, . . . 10, . . . 1,000, . . . as large as they wish. The person submitting the largest number will be awarded a prize in the amount of one million dollars divided by the number submitted. If more than one person submit the largest number, the prize will be divided equally between them.[1]

Note that it is collectively rational for everyone to submit "1." Then the million dollars will be divided equally among the participants. Note further that an individually rational strategy does not exist in this game. To see this, imagine the game played by three participants. Each could reason as follows:

"Suppose each of us submits '1.' Then each will get $333,333.33. This is not bad, but if the others submit '1' and I submit '2,' I get $500,000.00, which is better. I must, however, realize that each of the others thinks the same way. If each of us submits '2,' each gets $500,000/3 = $166,666.67. But if I alone submit '3,' I get $333,333.33, which is twice as good."

And so on. Thus, no equilibrium, hence no individually rational solution exists in this game. In order to realize the collectively rational outcome, each getting $333,333.33, each *must trust the others* and must assume that *each of the others trusts him*. "Morality" does not enter this conclusion. Here trust and trustworthiness are in everyone's self-interest.

The relevance of social traps to the confrontation between the superpowers is obvious. Identifying national security with military superiority or with the equally elusive notion of "parity" is tantamount to being impervious to any ideas based on collective rationality. Indeed, the most frequent reason given for rejecting proposals based on collective security invokes the dangers involved in "trusting" the other side. The dismissal of "trust" as an attitude reflecting "naiveté" or "misguided idealism" is said to be dictated by "sober rationality" or "hardheaded realism." The fact remains, however, that three persons playing the "Largest Number" game stand to gain $333,333.33 each if they trust each other and remain trustworthy, while three persons trying to "beat each other" or "catch up with each other" in a race to infinity stand to get nothing.

Notes

1. A similar game, invented by Douglas Hofstadter (Hofstadter 1985, pp. 751ff) was actually played by readers of *Scientific American*. Participants were invited to submit entries to a "lottery," in which the prize was $1,000,000.00 divided by the number of entries submitted. A participant could submit any number of entries. The collectively rational strategy in that game was for each of the participants to give him/herself a very small chance (depending on the estimated number of participants) to submit an entry. In this way the probability that just one entry would be submitted would be maximized. The winner of the lottery could then at his/her discretion share the million dollars with the others. As expected, the publishers' million dollars was quite safe, since several of the participants submitted fantastically large numbers of entries, which reduced the prize to practically zero.

15

Cooperative Games and Strategic Bargaining

In a two-person zero-sum game, cooperation serves no purpose. Whatever one player gains, the other must lose. Consequently, if one player prefers one outcome to another, the other must have the opposite preference. Thus, there is no outcome that both prefer to another, which would be the only possible basis for cooperation.

In a mixed-motive two-person game, there is a partial coincidence of interests. Hence cooperation can be advantageous to both players. The players can cooperate by coordinating their choices of strategies. Such coordination entails *binding agreements* to choose strategies that jointly result in some particular outcome. For example, in Prisoner's Dilemma (Game 14–6), the players can agree to choose C_1 and C_2 respectively so as to achieve the outcome C_1C_2, which both prefer to the equilibrium outcome D_1D_2. If the rules of the game provide for binding agreements of this sort, the game is called *cooperative*.

It is clearly in the interest of both players to coordinate their strategies in such a way as to achieve a Pareto-optimal outcome. In general, however, a cooperative game will have more than one Pareto-optimal outcome. With regard to these, the interests of the players generally diverge. Thus, a play of a cooperative game can be regarded as consisting of two phases. In the first phase, the players, recognizing their communality of interest, coordinate their strategies so as to achieve any of the Pareto-optimal outcomes. In the second phase, they contend for the outcome among these, since here their interests diverge. They bargain. When a bargain is struck, the

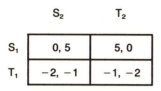

Game 15–1

players choose their strategies so as to achieve the outcome, or, more generally, a *mixture* of outcomes (as explained below) on which they have agreed. This result will constitute the solution to the game.

Bargaining involves (explicitly or implicitly) threats and promises. Promises are benefits offered by one player to the other in return for agreeing to cooperate in order to achieve some proposed outcome. Threats are indications of disadvantages that will accrue to the other players if he does not agree to some proposed outcome. The carrying out of a threat entails the choice of a strategy that will lead to an outcome disadvantageous to the other player. Threats and promises will be illustrated in the context of Game 15–1, which follows.

First let us see what the outcome of this game is likely to be if it is played by two rational players as a non-cooperative game, i.e., without opportunity to bargain. Note that both players have dominating strategies (cf. Chapter 14), namely, S_1 and S_2, respectively. If they apply the sure-thing principle, the outcome will be S_1S_2, which favors Column.

Without possibility of communication, there is nothing Row can do to improve his payoff. His choice is between S_1 and T_1. If he chooses S_1, his payoff will be 0, since it is in Column's interest to choose S_2. If Row chooses T_1, Column's best choice is still S_2, so that T_1S_2 will be the outcome. Thus, Column will be "punished" but so will Row. Aside from a possible satisfaction of punishing Column (which is not taken into account in the representation of the game), Row can do nothing to get more than 0.

But now suppose communication is possible. Row can now *threaten* to choose T_1. A threat is effective if it is coupled with a promise. In the context of Game 15–1, Row's communication to Column might take the following form:

"I will choose S_1 if you agree, after getting 5 in the outcome S_1S_2, to give me one-half of your take." (This is a promise.) "Otherwise, I will play T_1, in which case you cannot get more than -1." (This is a threat.)

Column can reply something of this sort:

"If you play S_1, I will give you 1." (Promise.) "If you play T_1, you will get -2, because I will certainly play S_2." (Threat.)

The bargaining can go on whereby each, in turn, may reduce his demand or yield a bit to the other's. If they converge on an outcome that they agree upon, the bargain is struck.

In the context of a game theoretic model, bargaining is pictured not quite in this way for a technical reason. Recall that the payoffs in a two-person game are expressed in units of utility. Because of the way the determination of an actor's utilities was defined in Von Neumann and Morgenstern's treatise (1947), the zero point and the unit of utility of each player was left arbitrary, i.e., could be chosen independently. In consequence, addition of the utilities of different actors does not make sense in this context: it is something like adding apples and oranges.

For this reason, Row cannot ask Column to give him a part of his payoff in return for choosing S_1. There is no way this part can be subtracted from Column's payoff and added to Row's. But there is something Row can ask of Column. If the game is played many times, he can demand that Column play T_2 a certain portion of the times. For example, if Column plays S_2 and T_2 with equal frequencies, while Row plays S_1, Column will be in effect giving Row one-half of his take. So the bargaining can be about the fraction of times Column is to play T_2, while Row continues to play S_1. A particular distribution of frequencies among a set of outcomes is what is meant by a mixture. Alternatively, if the game can be played only once, Column could use a random device to choose between S_2 and T_2. The bargaining will then be about how this device is to be calibrated to determine the probabilities with which Column will choose S_2 or T_2.

Intuitively we can see that Column has a stronger bargaining leverage than Row because, if there were no opportunity for negotiation, S_1S_2 (which favors Column) would be the only rational outcome. But how can this bargaining advantage be expressed in the bargain to be struck? And what can we mean by "rationality" in this context apart from avoiding the non-Pareto-optimal outcomes T_1S_2 and T_1T_2?

A common procedure in formal decision theory is to specify certain properties of a solution to a decision problem which we "feel" would reflect rationality and then to draw the consequences of demanding that the solution have these properties. John Nash (1953) listed four such properties of a solution to a two-person cooperative game. They are:

1. *Symmetry*. Whatever be the solution, it should be invariant with respect to the interchange of the players. This means that if the players change roles (Row taking the part of Column and vice versa), the solution ought to remain the same. That is to say, the solution should specify how the *roles* of the players are rewarded and should not depend on *who* the players are. Symmetry can also be interpreted as an equity criterion. It reminds somewhat of the principle of "equality before the

law," according to which a civil suit, for example, is decided entirely on the merits of the case and not influenced by the identities of the litigants.

2. *Linearity*. The solution should be independent of positive linear transformations of the payoffs. Recall that the solution of a two-person cooperative game was defined not in terms of the numerical payoffs but in terms of probabilities or relative frequencies with which the Pareto-optimal outcomes are chosen. A positive linear transformation on the payoffs is effected if all the payoffs of a player are multiplied by some positive constant (which means that the unit of utility is changed), or if a constant is added to all the payoffs of a player (which means that the zero point of utility is shifted), or both. Linearity means that if the utilities of either or both players are changed in either of these ways or both, the solution (as defined above) remains the same.

3. *Pareto-optimality*. The solution of the game should be one of the Pareto-optimal outcomes or some mixture of them. This property of the solution reflects the collective rationality of the players.

4. *Independence from irrelevant alternatives*. If the game is reduced by removing some outcomes in a way that does not affect the optimal threats that the players may make in their bargaining, and if the solution of the original game is not thereby removed from the possible outcomes, then the solution of the game should not be affected.

It turns out that every two-person cooperative game defined by a payoff matrix has a solution that satisfies all four of Nash's criteria. Moreover, the solution is essentially unique. It reflects the relative bargaining powers of the players (as these are defined by the structure of the game, not by the players' bargaining abilities). By way of example, the solution of Game 15–1 is a mixture of the two Pareto-optimal outcomes S_1S_2 and S_1T_2 which prescribes the choice of S_1S_2 60% of the time (or with probability .6) and S_1T_2 40% of the time, thus awarding 2 units to Row and 3 to Column. Should the payoffs be changed by a positive linear transformation, the mixture defining the solution would remain the same, although the numerical payoffs would, of course, change. To see this, suppose Row's payoffs have all been multiplied by 100. Now the game matrix looks like Game 15–2:

The same mixture of S_1S_2 and S_1T_2 would now award 200 to Row and still 3 to Column. One would think that Row would now be better off than Column. But this conclusion is not warranted, for he only seems to be getting more. It is as if in the original game both players were paid off in dollars and in the transformed game Row would be paid off in pennies, while Column would still be paid off in dollars. In the context of this model,

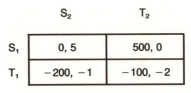

Game 15–2

the numerical payoffs cannot be compared. It is only the frequencies with which the Pareto-optimal outcomes are chosen that can be compared. Column's stronger bargaining position is reflected in the fact that the solution prescribes that he "get his way" (namely, that outcome S_1S_2 is realized) 60% of the time (or with probability .6), while Row "gets his way" (his preferred outcome S_1T_2) only 40% of the time (or with probability .4).

The "strategic" aspect of strategic bargaining has to do with the choice of threats. In Game 15–1 it is easy to see that the choice of T_1 is the only threat Row has at his disposal against Column. Similarly, Column needs only to threaten S_2 whatever Row does. Thus, the "threat point" of the game (with respect to which the solution is calculated), namely outcome T_1S_2, is determined. In the marketplace, where the bargaining is over the sales price of an item, the threat point is "no sale," i.e., the buyer threatens not to buy if the seller does not accept his offer, and the seller threatens not to sell unless the offer is increased. If a bargain is struck, both the seller and the buyer gain utilities that are larger than their utilities for "no sale." That is to say, the bargain is Pareto-optimal, while "no sale" is not.

Note that in the theory of the cooperative game, the problem shifts from choosing optimal strategies in playing the game to choosing optimal *bargaining* strategies, e.g., choosing demands, threats, and promises. As in the theory of the non-cooperative game, a solution is found, one that reflects not only the relative "strengths" of the players but also their common interest (which always exists in a cooperative game). Moreover, this solution need not be an equilibrium of the game. For example, the solution of Game 15–1 is not an equilibrium, since Column can improve his payoff by shifting to his pure strategy S_2 (while Row stays with S_1). Similarly, the solutions of Chicken and of Prisoner's Dilemma played cooperatively are Y_1Y_2 (cf. Game 14–5) and C_1C_2 (cf. Game 14–6) respectively, which, as we have seen, are not equilibria.

Of course this "emancipation" from non-Pareto-optimal equilibrium solutions is affected by the introduction of the possibility of making binding agreements, on which the entire theory of cooperative games depends. It can be said, therefore, that in passing to cooperative games, game theory has assumed the format of a theory of *conflict resolution* instead of (or in addition to) being a theory of rationally conducted conflict, as it was originally conceived. The emphasis on conflict resolution is even more evident in the theory of cooperative n-person games (where n>2), to which we now turn our attention.

N-Person Cooperative Games

The players in a two-person cooperative game coordinating their strategies so as to realize their common interest (a Pareto-optimal outcome) can be said to have formed a *coalition*. If the number of players of a cooperative game exceeds two, there are several ways in which the players can form coalitions. For example, in the case of three players there are five ways: (a) players 1 and 2 in coalition, the third by himself; (b) players 1 and 3 in coalition, the second by himself; (c) players 2 and 3 in coalition, the first by himself; (d) each player by himself; (e) all three players in coalition. As the number of players increases, the number of ways coalitions can form increases very rapidly.

In the theory of the n-person cooperative game, the principal problems revolve around the effects of the *possibilities* of forming different coalitions on the solution of the game. As before, the solution is conceived as the apportionment of payoffs among the players. In the "classical" theory (i.e., as originally formulated), the payoffs are assumed to be given on a sufficiently strong scale so that comparison of utilities of different players and transfers of utilities from one player to another are possible. For all practical purposes, utility is now conceived to be a transferable conservative commodity (like money). That is, player 1 can now give player 2 a number of "utiles," whereby player 1 becomes that much poorer and player 2 that much richer. These "side payments," as they are called, play an important part in bargaining related to coalition formation, for example, in invitations to join coalitions or threats to leave a coalition to join another.

The Characteristic Function

Suppose that a certain group among the n players of an n-person game has formed a coalition. Call the entire set of players N and the group that has just formed a coalition S. Call the set of the remaining players N–S. The players in S can coordinate their choices of strategy in any way they wish. It is clearly in their common interest to coordinate their strategy choices so as to get the largest *joint* payoff under the constraints of the situation. (Recall that it is now meaningful to speak òf the sum of payoffs accruing to different players.) The constraints are embodied in the circumstance that the players in N–S can also form a coalition in a way that assures *them* the largest joint payoff under the same sort of constraints. Now if the interests of the players in S and those in N–S are diametrically opposed in the sense that the more one coalition can get for itself, the less the other can get, the n-person game is called constant-sum (or zero-sum). In this case, each coalition can expect that the other coalition will coordinate its strategies in such a way as to keep the joint payoff accruing to S to a minimum. However, the payoff to a coalition can be pushed down only so far, that is, to the amount that the coalition is guaranteed. This minimum amount guaranteed to coalition S by the structure of the game is called the *value* of the game to S. In fact, every possible coalition S (where S now ranges over all the possible subsets of N) commands a certain minimum guaranteed payoff, the value of the game to it. This value is designated v(S). We say v(S) is *given* when we know what value is associated with every one of the possible coalitions among the N players. The mathematician says v(S) is a *function* of S.

In the theory of the cooperative n-person game, attention is focused on this function, called the *characteristic function* of the game. In fact, the characteristic function can be said to *define* an n-person cooperative game studied from the point of view of the effects of opportunities to form coalitions on the final allocation of payoffs among the players. A game so defined is said to be in *characteristic function form*.

In the original formulation of n-person game theory, it was always assumed that the characteristic function is *superadditive*. This means that whatever any two coalitions could achieve separately in the sense of the magnitude of the sum of their payoffs, they could achieve together by merging into a single coalition and, in general, more. This seems to be a reasonable assumption since whatever strategies the two coalitions could choose when they are playing independently, they can also choose when playing as a single coalition. In addition, there are joint strategies they can undertake when they have the opportunity to coordinate their choices, which they cannot undertake when they have no such opportunity. Note, however, that in this conception, the *costs* of forming a coalition are not considered. Such costs may be associated with the creation of communication facilities (for coordinating strategies). Or, in political contexts, some coalitions may be precluded for ideological reasons. The exclusion of such coalitions can be formally expressed by making the costs of forming them prohibitively high. In what follows, we will assume that all coalitions can be formed without cost and that, therefore, the characteristic function is superadditive.

A superadditive characteristic function implies that it is always *collectively* rational for players to merge into coalitions. In particular, it is always collectively rational to form the *grand coalition*, i.e., the coalition consisting of the entire set of players N, since the joint payoff v(N) guaranteed to N is at least as large as what the members of N can get in sum if they partition themselves into smaller coalitions. In this case, the question which coalition will form is bypassed. It is simply assumed that the players, being collectively rational, will form the grand coalition. The only question remaining is how this joint payoff v(N) is to be apportioned among the members of N. One would think that the final apportionment would be a result of a bargaining process. Bargaining in this context means making and considering bids to join some coalition, where the incentives are offers of certain portions of the joint payoff that the coalition can guarantee itself. All this bargaining is supposed to go on before the grand coalition forms. Its outcome then determines the apportionment of v(N) among the players and constitutes the solution of the game. We will illustrate the process by the simplest possible n-person cooperative game.[1] We will call it "Divide the Dollar."

How "Stable" Can a Solution of an N-Person Cooperative Game Be?

The three players are A, B, and C. They are promised a dollar if they can agree on how to divide it among them. The rules of the game specify that an agreement is reached when a majority of the players have agreed how to divide the dollar. Further, a time limit is set on the reaching of an agreement. If no agreement is reached when the time limit expires, the offer of a dollar is withdrawn, and no one gets anything.

We can imagine that A and B, who happen to be near each other when the bargaining begins, come to an agreement to divide the dollar equally between them. Since they are a majority, this decision can be final. Thereby C is left out, and he is powerless to force the other two to give him a positive share of the dollar. However, C can resort to a stratagem. He approaches B with the following proposition. "In coalition with A, you, B, will get 50¢. I will make you a better offer. Leave A and join in a coalition with me. I promise you 60¢. The deal is obviously to the advantage of both of us. You will get 60¢ instead of 50¢. I will get 40¢ instead of 0¢."

We will suppose that the time limit has not yet expired, so that the bargaining can go on until the announcement of the final agreement is made. The original apportionment of the dollar was (50, 50, 0), where the numbers in parentheses are the payoffs to A, B, and C respectively. After

B has (tentatively) accepted C's offer, the apportionment is (0, 60, 40). Now A is the loser. He offers B 70¢ if B will leave C and come back to him. Again, both A and B stand to gain from this bargain. B will get 70¢ instead of 60¢, while A will get 30¢ instead of 0¢. However, B's good fortune is short-lived, since he is now vulnerable to being deprived of all his share by A and C. Indeed, A and C have excellent reason for joining in a coalition and thus appropriating the whole dollar instead of just 30¢ between them. Suppose, then, this happens, and the two agree to split the dollar equally. If now B approaches A, offering to restore the original agreement and is rebuffed, he can offer A a greater share, say 60¢. Should A accept this offer?

A little reflection shows that no matter what arrangements the three agree upon, there will always be two of them, who can both do better and can enforce the new arrangement (in which both do better) because they are a majority.

Thus a problem practically forces itself on the attention of the game theorist—to propose some properties that a solution to an n-person game in characteristic function form should possess in order that it be in some sense "stable." The question what could be meant by "stability" in this context is in itself a problem. If the formation of the grand coalition is collectively rational, one would wish the members to be "satisfied" with the solution in the sense that no subset S of the players would be motivated to break away from the grand coalition to form one of their own. This they would be motivated to do if $v(S)$, the amount that they could jointly get as a coalition exceeded the sum of the payoffs that the solution awards them. It turns out, however, that if the n-person game is constant-sum, no such "stable" allocations exist. Our "Divide the Dollar" game was an example of one such game. Thus, questions can be raised about the necessary and/or sufficient conditions for such a "stable" allocation to exist. Another way to proceed with the development of n-person game theory is to define "solutions" in some other way so as to guarantee the existence of such solutions for all or for a sufficiently broad class of games in characteristic function form.

The ramifications of this theory are of interest primarily to the mathematician and are beyond the scope of this book. Of central interest to the student of *conflict* is the fact that in the theory of the n-person game in characteristic function form, the principal theme of game theory as it was originally formulated, namely, the rational conduct of conflict, was dropped by the wayside, as it were. Instead *conflict resolution* became the central theme as manifested in the problem of allocating the joint gain of a cooperative enterprise in a way which in some sense can be defended as "fair" or "stable."

We will illustrate this approach to conflict resolution by another simple three-person game which captures the essentials of the approach.

The scenario involves a lion, a tiger, and a fox who go on a hunt together and succeed in killing a deer. The problem arises of how to divide the prize. Having heard of parliamentary procedures, the three agree to abide by the decision of the majority; but they realize that they do not have equal status, and so the 100 votes to be allocated among them must reflect the differences.

Lion declares that as King of the Beasts he should have 51 votes. But the others, realizing that controlling 51 votes would enable the Lion to award the entire deer to himself, refuse to go along. After some discussion, they concede that Lion, as King of the Beasts, can claim 50 votes, which will give him veto power (since an absolute majority is required for a decision) but not dictatorial power. Tiger thereupon claims 49 votes, and the Fox must be content with a single vote.

If their votes represented voting shares in a corporation and if the deer were a dividend, then the portions of the deer awarded to each would be proportional to the numbers of votes. However, in this "political" situation in which the majority takes all, the rules are different. We can readily see that, as in the Divide the Dollar game, no apportionment can be "stable." Here Lion must be a member of any majority-commanding coalition, but he needs another member to form a majority. To induce another to join, he must offer him a portion of the prize. But whatever he offers one, the other can break up the coalition by offering to take less. If Tiger and Fox form a coalition, they can jointly demand some portion of the deer, since Lion cannot by himself enhance a decision. But how much can they demand? And how vulnerable is their coalition to the offers that Lion can make to the one or the other in return for leaving his partner and joining him? We see intuitively that Lion is in the strongest position. But how do we express the relative strengths of all three positions to obtain a basis for allocating corresponding portions of the prize?

To show that the problem has no unique answer we will describe three different solutions, each of which can be regarded as "reasonable."

The Power Indices

The basic idea underlying the calculation of power indices is that the power of a member of a decision-making body is reflected in how valuable a coalition member he is. We will now assume that the set of players of an n-person cooperative game form a decision-making body. Their task is to decide how their joint payoff, $v(N)$, is to be allocated. It seems reasonable to determine each member's share by assessing his "value" to a coalition that he joins. If the characteristic function of the game is superadditive, each additional player joining a coalition already formed can be said to "bring something into it" if the resulting larger coalition commands a larger value (as is indicated by the characteristic function). On this basis, we can assess the power index of a player by averaging his contributions to all the possible coalitions that he can join. It can be shown that the indices calculated in this way add up to $v(N)$, hence can represent the corresponding portion of $v(N)$ that can be claimed by the player. The power index calculated in this way is called the *Shapley value* of the game. In the special case where coalitions are distinguished only as being "winning coalitions" (with value 1) or "losing" coalitions (with value 0) it is called the Shapley-Shubik index (Shapley and Shubik 1954).

In calculating this power index, we assume that the grand coalition forms by accretion. Some player starts by forming a "coalition of one" and by inviting another player to join him. Then the resulting coalition of two invite a third player and so on. With three players the grand coalition can form in six different ways corresponding to the six different orderings (permutations) of the three players: LTF, TFL, FLT, FTL, TLF, and LFT, where the players have been represented by their initials.

Consider the order LTF. Lion as a "coalition of one" can claim nothing, not being a majority. With Tiger he becomes a majority. Therefore it is Tiger who changed a losing coalition into a winning one. In this situation, Tiger can claim the prize. Examining all six orders, we see that Lion changes a losing coalition into a winning one four times out of six. Tiger and Fox do this once each (in LTF and LFT respectively). Therefore "Lion's share" is $\frac{2}{3}$, while Tiger and Fox get $\frac{1}{6}$ each. The allocation reflects Lion's stronger position and also the fact that the difference between Tiger's 49 votes and Fox's 1 vote makes no difference here. What matters is that Tiger and Fox's situations are exactly the same. Both need Lion to form a winning coalition. The Lion needs either but not both.

There are other ways of assessing the relative power of the players. The so-called *normalized Banzhaf index* is calculated in the following way. For each player, consider the winning coalitions of which he is an *essential* member, i.e., those which he can change from winning coalitions to losing coalitions by leaving them. Lion is an essential member of three winning coalitions, namely the grand coalition, the Lion-Tiger coalition and the Lion-Fox coalition. Tiger and Fox are essential members in one coalition each, both with Lion. Therefore according to this criterion, Lion's share is $\frac{3}{5}$, while Tiger and Fox get $\frac{1}{5}$ each (Banzhaf 1965).

Finally consider only the *minimal* winning coalitions, i.e., those in which every member is essential. Lion is a member of just two such coalitions,

Lion-Tiger and Lion-Fox. Tiger and Fox are members of one each, both with Lion. Therefore, according to this criterion, the allocation is ($\frac{1}{2}$, $\frac{1}{4}$, $\frac{1}{4}$) to Lion, Tiger, and Fox respectively. This allocation reflects the Packel-Deegan power index (Packel and Deegan 1982).

In presenting three different ways of calculating power indices, that essentially being the relative strengths of the players' bargaining positions as a basis for allocating a joint gain, we sought to demonstrate an important feature of collective decision making, namely the importance of a *prior agreement* on the principles that are to serve as guidelines for the decisions. We have seen that three different principles have led to three different allocations. There is no way of justifying any of the principles on objective grounds. Each reflects some aspect of "fairness," i.e., taking into account the players' bargaining positions in determining the allocation. Whenever a prior agreement exists on the principles to be applied, a basis for conflict resolution exists. These prior agreements correspond to *laws* in societies governed by law. Agreements on a higher level, that is, on principles to be used as guidelines for enacting laws, are called *constitutions*.

The Strategist's Conception of the Non-Constant-Sum Game

It is worth noting that the relevance of non-constant-sum games to the study of conflict was first pointed out by T.C. Schelling (1958), a political scientist who subsequently wrote extensively on strategic bargaining (Schelling 1960).

As we have seen, a two-person non-constant-sum game model of conflict provides an opportunity for communication between the players. If, as is generally assumed in this context, the players can make binding agreements, they can achieve Pareto-optimal outcomes (even though these may not be equilibria) to their mutual advantage. The conflict aspect of such a game is centered on the choice among these Pareto-optimal outcomes, some of which are preferred by one player, some by the other.

The theory of the cooperative game provides methods for resolving this conflict by applying certain principles on which the players may be able to agree in advance, for instance, the four principles advanced by Nash.[2] Thus, although the theory takes into account possible *situational* disparities between the players' bargaining positions, it also includes considerations based on "fairness" or "equity."

As an example, consider Game 15–1. In the absence of communication, S_1S_2, the intersection of dominating strategies, is the only rational outcome. The underdog (Row) has no way of putting pressure on the top dog (Column) to induce him to share some of his gains in iterated play. If communication is possible, however, Row can threaten to "strike" (i.e., play T_1). Nash's principles determine just how much Column should share with Row to neutralize the pressure.

However, the introduction of communication can also *detract* from a reasonable solution to a non-constant-sum game. Consider the game of Chicken. In the absence of communication, the prominence and apparent prudence of the maximin strategy suggests a compromise (Y_1Y_2 in Game 14–6). If communication is possible, however, a posture of reckless "resolve" on the part of one player ("I will play S no matter what you do, and you better believe it!") may result in an asymmetric outcome of a symmetric game or else, if both players adopt this posture, in disaster.

In this way, opportunities to communicate serve to transport the conflict *to another level*, the level of bargaining, threats, counterthreats, and so forth. We have seen how the theory of the cooperative game provides for resolution of conflicts on that level. The strategist, however, is typically interested less in equitable methods of conflict resolution than in effective strategies of *winning*. Thus, the emphasis in the literature on strategic bargaining is predominantly on ways of "outbargaining" the adversary, that is, still on the antagonistic aspects of conflicts, even of mixed-motive conflicts.

This orientation is clearly reflected in T.C. Schelling's book, *The Strategy of Conflict* (1960). In assessing the contribution of strategic bargaining to the theory of deterrence, Schelling writes:

> We have learned that a threat has to be credible to be efficacious, and that its credibility may depend on the costs and risks associated with the fulfillment for the party making the threat. We have developed the idea of making a threat credible by getting ourselves committed to its fulfillment, through the stretching of a trip wire across the enemy's path of advance, or by making fulfillment a matter of national honor and prestige. . . . We have considered the possibility that a retaliatory threat may be more credible if the means of carrying it out and the responsibility for retaliation are placed into the hands of those whose resolution is stronger. . . . (Schelling 1960, p. 6.)

Schelling summarizes the task of strategic bargaining in international relations as the "rational non-use of force." The attractiveness of this conception is understandable from the point of view of the contemporary military professional. Practically overnight the concept of war as the "continuation of politics by other means" became vulnerable. It became practically impossible to justify the use of weapons of total destruction to achieve "political goals." The inversion of Clausewitz's dictum, "Politics is the continuation of war by other means" can save the *institution* of war from danger of extinction by suggesting that strategic skill could be developed to the fullest extent in conflicts involving "non-use" of force. In fact, successful blackmail amounts to non-use of force to get one's way.

The difficulty in using blackmail as a stratagem of international conflict in the nuclear age is that carrying out the threats embodied in the blackmail is fraught with danger if the opponent possesses destructive potential comparable to one's own. Thus, the threat in the form of "Do (or don't do) this or else you will be attacked by nuclear weapons" does not sound convincing if a nuclear attack can be retaliated in kind. The threatened party may well defy the threatening party in the belief (perhaps justified) that the former would not dare to carry out the threat for fear of retaliation. This is why placing "the responsibility for retaliation . . . into the hands of those whose resolution is stronger" has a special fascination to the designer of bargaining strategies. More generally, the threat can be made even more credible if the threatening party *has no choice* but to carry out the threat if the carrying out is delegated to an agency completely outside the threatening party's control.

The so-called Doomsday Machine embodies the idea of deliberately relinquishing control. A Doomsday Machine is a stockpile of nuclear weapons sufficiently large to destroy the planet. It is technically possible to construct such a machine, because this stockpile need not be delivered to the enemy's territory, so there is no limitation on its size. It can be kept on the owner's territory. The machine is programmed to activate the stockpile if, say, a nuclear explosion takes place on the territory of the owner. The existence of the Doomsday Machine must, of course, be made known to the enemy. The enemy now cannot assume that the attacked party will not dare retaliate for fear of counterretaliation, because the decision to retaliate or not to retaliate is no longer his. The machine will surely retaliate. Moreover, the owner of the Doomsday Machine cannot be blackmailed to dismantle or defuse it, because it has been programmed to be activated if any such attempt is made.

The Game of Chicken

A similar idea is involved in the advice given by Herman Kahn to those who play Chicken.

> The skillful player may get into the car quite drunk, throwing whisky bottles out the window to make it clear to everybody just how drunk he is. He wears very dark glasses so that it is obvious that he cannot see much, if anything.

As soon as the car reaches high speed, he takes the steering wheel and throws it out the window. If his opponent is watching, he has won.

One can see the force of this reasoning. But what if the opponent is not watching? Kahn has foreseen this contingency also:

If his opponent is not watching, he [the "skillful player"] has a problem; likewise if both players try this strategy. (Kahn 1965, p. 11.)

It is not clear whether the last remark was supposed to be a sarcastic comment on the proposed "winning strategy" or a way of indicating that the author disavows responsibility for the disastrous consequences of his advice. We will find, as we examine other instances of reasoning common in the strategic community, that the important distinction between game theory and "classical" decision theory (involving just one actor), namely, that in game-like conflicts, the value of any strategy depends crucially on how many players are using it, tends to be ignored. For example, in Game 14–5, strategy S is worth 10 if only one player uses it but it is worth −100 if both players use it. The principle applies whether the game is played cooperatively or non-cooperatively. As illustrated by Kahn, Chicken is played (implicitly) as a "semi-cooperative" game, where although binding agreements are not to be expected, nevertheless communication takes place, and is taken into account in designing strategies.

Now "what to communicate" to the co-player comes to the forefront as a strategic problem. Kahn says the "skillful player" will send a message which says in effect that he can no longer swerve (because he has thrown his steering wheel away). If the other player is "rational," he will swerve. Here, however, is the rub. If sending such a communication is a mark of skill, i.e., is a good strategy, it must be good for both (because the game is symmetric). But if both use it, both have a "problem."

Randomized Threats

The discussion of so-called randomized threats conveys the full flavor of the strategic approach to mixed-motive games. An important distinction is drawn between randomized threats and randomized promises. Randomization can be used as a substitute for divisibility. If only large indivisible prizes can be promised, then promising such a prize "probabilistically" can, under proper circumstances, be regarded as giving a fraction of the prize. We have seen how this concept figures in the Nash solution to a cooperative two-person game played once. A "success" in this case is

	S_2	T_2
S_1	1, 0	0, 1
T_1	0, 0	−y, −x

Game 15–3

costly. That is, if the random event directs keeping the promise, the giver of the prize suffers a large loss.

The situation involving randomized threats is different. The threat can be said to have failed if it is ignored, i.e., if the other commits the transgression which is to be punished. Frequently, however, the punishment meted out to the other is also costly to self. Retaliation against a nuclear attack by a nuclear attack comes to mind. Except for the satisfaction provided by revenge, retaliation is worthless (assuming that one's own society has already been destroyed). Yet retaliation must be resorted to if a commitment to punishment (the content of the threat) has been made. Why? I have not heard a satisfactory answer to this question, but it is regarded as beyond dispute that a lethal attack will be "avenged" by an equally lethal attack. Thus, the greatest losses may be associated with a threat that has failed (i.e., one that has been ignored). Randomization of threats is supposed to dilute this loss. From the point of view of purely formal calculation, a threat of total destruction carried out "with probability p" is supposed to be equivalent to a p-th fraction of the destruction.

Schelling illustrates a randomized threat, shown below as Game 15–3 (Schelling 1960, p. 178).

Here x and y are positive numbers. Contrary to the game-theoretic convention by which Row and Column are supposed to choose their strategies simultaneously, here Column is supposed to choose his strategy first, then Row. Before Column chooses, however, Row is entitled to make a threat. It is easy to see that Row prefers $S_1 S_2$ to $S_1 T_2$, while Column has the opposite preference. In the absence of a threat by Row, Column would play T_2. Row, however, can threaten to play T_1. Now if Column plays T_2, $T_1 T_2$ results, which entails a loss for both players. So making a threat entails a risk for Row.

Now Row can attentuate this risk by threatening to choose T_1, not with certainty, but with a certain probability. Row now faces the question of how large should this probability be to make the threat worthwhile. Row could assume that Column would try to maximize his expected utility, namely, the average between 1 (the payoff in $S_1 T_2$) and −x (the payoff in $T_1 T_2$), weighted respectively by $(1 − \pi)$ and π. This expectation is, therefore, $1 - \pi - \pi x$, which is negative if $\pi(1 + x) > 1$. Column can be expected, therefore, to be deterred from choosing T_2 if $\pi > 1/(1 + x)$.

It is not *a priori* certain, however, that Column will be deterred. If the threat succeeds, i.e., if Column is deterred from choosing T_2, Row gets 1. If not, that is, if Column chooses T_2 in spite of the threat, Row gets $-y$. Suppose the threat succeeds or fails (with π larger than the minimum established by the above formula) with probabilities $1 - p$ and p respectively. Since Row chooses S_1 and T_1 with probabilities $1 - \pi$ and π respectively, his expected gain (should the threat fail) will be $-\pi y$. If Row assigns probability p to the event that the threat fails, his expected gain will be $1 - p - p\pi y$. This will be larger than 0 if $\pi < (1 - p)/py$. Combining the upper and lower limits on π, we get the inequality.

$$(1 - p)/py > \pi > 1/(1 + x).$$

If the inequalities are incompatible, i.e., if $1/(1 + x) > (1 - p)/py$, then it is not worthwhile making the threat at all. If, however, the inequalities are compatible and if $(1 - p)/py < 1$, that is, if $p/(1 - p) > 1/y$, then a randomized threat is preferable to a certain threat.

We have pointed out that in the context of the two-person constant-sum game, it is natural to conduct the analysis from the point of view of one of the actors. Paradoxes generated by the divergence of individual and collective rationality do not enter the picture. We have also seen how in the context of the mixed-motive game, paradoxes appear if analysis is conducted as before from the point of view of one of the players, or even from the point of view of both players but from that of each player separately. However, the problems acquire another "dimension," namely, communication. If a mixed-motive game is played cooperatively, communication can be used to insure Pareto-optimal outcomes and later to bring the players to an agreement about the final outcome, which will reflect both their common interests and their relative bargaining positions.

Finally, we have seen that in the strategic approach to the mixed-motive game, bargaining becomes the center of interest and acquires a markedly antagonistic flavor. Bluntly put, the main goal in bargaining now becomes that of gaining the largest possible advantage over the adversary. Even though the analysis is conducted in the context of a mixed-motive game, it is pursued entirely in the spirit of the constant-sum game.

And this is not all. The fixed probabilities assigned to "success" and to "failure" of a threat converts Game 15–3 into something between a genuine two-person game and a game against nature. It is not quite a game against nature because whether Column plays T_2 with certainty or a mixture of S_2 and T_2 depends on whether Row makes a threat or not. But if Row does make a threat, Column's behavior is not the behavior of a player in a genuine two-person game. His choice of S_2 or T_2 is like alternative states of nature to which fixed probabilities have been assigned. It may be of interest to examine this model as such. But it amounts to "depersonalizing" Column, making him, to a certain extent, less than a genuine player.

"Shortcuts" of this sort are common in models illustrating strategic analysis. They probably stem from confining the focus of attention to a single actor, the decision maker, who is presumably advised on how to act in the pursuit of his interests. Traditionally, the rest of the world in these analyses has been depicted simply as "the environment." In game-against-nature models, this environment was assumed to be stochastic. That is, fixed probabilities were assigned to its various states. Game theory was a large step forward. The environment now contained actors as rational as "our" actor. It became necessary to imagine oneself in *their* shoes, not in order to empathize with them but in order to assess how the "environment" is going to act in pursuit of *its* interests. And this is as far as the analysis can go if the determination of optimal strategies in the pursuit of self-interest is to remain in the focus of attention.

Games Nations Play

R. Jervis (1970) elaborated greatly on the theme of strategic negotiation. His book, *The Logic of Images in International Relations*, represents an intertwining of the semantic and pragmatic aspects of language in international relations. Essentially, the game nations play is a game of communications. The content of communications consists of *signals* and *indices*. Signals are "statements or actions, the meanings of which are established by tacit or explicit understanding among the actors." Indices are "statements or actions that carry some inherent evidence that the image projected is correct because they are believed to be inextricably linked to the actor's capabilities or intentions." In other words, signals convey *intended* meanings. They may be intended to inform or to deceive. Indices convey *unintended* meanings. They reveal something about the source. Signals and indices have counterparts in communication between individuals. The content of a communication is conveyed by signals, that is, the accepted meanings of words. The state of mind of the speaker, his feelings, attitudes, and thoughts of the moment, not intended to be conveyed, are communicated by indices, for example, the tone of voice, gestures, demeanor, and the like.

Evaluation of messages is complicated by the circumstances that indices can be manipulated and so can be used to deceive. The task of evaluation entails deciphering *both* the signals and the indices, estimating the veracity of the former and the genuineness of the latter.[3] A perusal of the chapter headings of *The Logic of Images* reveals the important role that the author assigns to the problem associated with deception and discovery of deceptions: "Manipulation of Indices," "Restraints on Lying," "Incentives for Lying," "The Utility of Ambiguity," "Coupling and De-Coupling of Indices," "Challenges Avoided or Created by Claims about One's Own Motives," and so forth.

The whole spectrum of activity described reinforces the conviction that the "actors" in the international arena are playing an immense game of strategy, enormously complicated by changing rules, changing interpretations of the rules, shifting coalitions, and fluctuating stakes. There are two ways of viewing this description. One is to take it at face value as a description: here are the stratagems that states use in jockeying for positions of advantage, in bullying or flattering, conning, blackmailing each other. If the description is accurate (and there is little reason to doubt its accuracy), it is a contribution to our understanding of the "psychology" of states, as it is reflected in the behavior of their representatives in the international arena. Another way of viewing this work is to see it as a manual for learning successful techniques of strategic negotiation. It may be that diplomats of one country learn the techniques sooner than those of another. Then the former may have an advantage over the latter at the bargaining table. Any advantage, however, is bound to be short-lived. If the techniques are indeed effective, professional bargainers are sure to learn them and rather quickly at that. This will cancel any initial advantage of the "leading" state and possibly reverse it. The situation is the same as with military skills. New skills confer an advantage. The side which has failed to acquire them suffers defeat. But defeat is an excellent teacher. When Peter the Great of Russia won his bloody victory over the Swedes at Poltava, he invited the defeated generals taken prisoner to dinner and raised a toast "to our teachers." And, of course, the situation with respect to technological innovations is the same. Maurice Saxe, like Guibert (cf. below), one of the "advanced" military thinkers spawned by the French Enlightenment, anticipated the overthrow of eighteenth-century dogmas. He understood that eventually the advantage conferred by technological innovation would be canceled. However, before this happens, he argued, the state that introduced them first would reap benefits on the battlefields. And at any rate, the advantage would be likely to last for a long time. "So reluctant are all nations," he wrote, "to give up old customs." (Cited in Vagts 1937, p. 83.) Besides, Saxe pointed out, if the enemy were to adopt new ways, skills, or weapons, this would serve only to demonstrate their excellence. It is well to realize, however, that the lag between the adoption of new technologies or skills by states and their potential enemies keeps getting shorter. When it comes to matters related to competition in the international arena, nations not only learn but also *learn to learn*, that is, get better at learning. This applies to techniques of strategic bargaining as well.

The same situation exists in all areas of keen competition, be it strategic bargaining, games of strategy, sports, or any form of virtuosity. Competition drives the participants to master their art. Hardly anyone holds permanent advantage over the others. There is an overall "progressive" result, however. The state of the art improves. Chess becomes more sophisticated with each generation. Athletic records are broken. Virtuosity of performance in many different fields soars to new heights. All this "progress" makes life richer, nurtures enthusiasms, inspires efforts, refines sensitivity, creates aims in life external to preoccupation with self. There is reason to believe that this "externalization" of libidinal strivings is conducive to mental health.

These positive by-products of competition are realized, provided two conditions are satisfied. First, the competitors must have a common loyalty to something beyond their egos, hence be able to share enthusiasms that unite them. They must be not only competitors. They must also be afficionados. Admiration for victorious rivals dilutes the bitterness of defeat. Second, the "progress" resulting from competition must contribute positively to the human condition. The world must become a better place because of it.

Now the first of these conditions was frequently satisfied in the history of warfare. Both Clausewitz and Jomini were ardent admirers of Napoleon, in spite of the fact that the former was in the service of his enemies throughout the Napoleonic wars, while the latter was on Napoleon's staff. Also the devotion of many military professionals to their profession is genuine. One needs only to read their works to be convinced. The second condition, however, cannot be satisfied in the military sphere because of the very nature of the "art of war." Whatever the positive functions of military prowess may have been in the days when the armed forces of a country could be regarded as its defenders, the *overall* contribution of military "progress" has been to make killing and destruction more pervasive. This is the inevitable result of every "improvement" of every piece of equipment, offensive or defensive.

"Progress" in strategic negotiation, i.e., "the continuation of war by other means" should also be considered from this point of view. It may seem at first thought that emphasis on strategic bargaining (skill in strategic "non-use of force," as Schelling puts it) amounts to deflection of skills from violent to clever ways of getting one's way, a proper adjustment to the nuclear age. There is, however, an obverse side to this "progress," namely, its contribution to the intellectualization of war. We will address ourselves to that theme in the next chapter.

Notes

1. More accurately, the game to be described is the simplest possible *essential* three-person cooperative game, that is, one in which joining in a coalition is advantageous at least to some players.
2. It is at this point that game theory turns away from problems of applying strategic skills in getting a maximum advantage in a conflict situation. In singling out ways of arriving at solutions based on equity principles formulated in advance, game theory becomes essentially a theory of conflict resolution.
3. If one stays within the paradigm of strategic conflict, then adroitness in controlling the indices attendant on one's communications becomes an adjunct of strategic skill. Pushkin alludes to this skill when he describes Eugene Onegin as a young profligate: "His eyes, now tender, quick and clear/Or shining with a *summoned* tear." But of course as skills are acquired in using apparently involuntary indices to deceive, skills are also acquired by potential opponents in not letting oneself be deceived.

16

The Intellectualization of War

Addiction to power and addiction to violence reinforce each other when resorting to violence succeeds. The success induces the sense of power. Traditionally, American mass entertainment has induced in audiences an identification with heroes who succeed in vanquishing opponents often by resorting to violence. Children, for whom vicarious experiences are especially vivid, are particularly susceptible to identifying violence with power and power with success, and such success with virtue. The emphasis on violence and threats of violence in America's posture in the international arena of the 1980s has surely been a contributing factor to the unprecedented boom in the sale of war toys in the U.S.

Douglas Thomson, president of the Toy Manufacturers of America, has been quoted as saying that the phrase "war toys" is not recognized in the industry. Guns are called "guns," and the figurines depicting violent heroes are called "action figures." Sales of "action figures" grew from $622 million in 1984 to $840 million in 1985, an increase of 35 percent in one year alone.

Adults don't play with "Thundercats," "Blasterhawks," and other such bellicose-sounding war toys, except perhaps surreptitiously. Instead they play games where exercise of strategic skill induces a sense of power. These games are very old and their popularity probably remains constant through the ages and does not necessarily reflect growing preoccupation with vicarious experience of power as does the dramatic increase in the popularity of war toys. However, the *content* of games of strategy may be indicative of prevailing preoccupations. For a long time, Monopoly was a leader in

325

strategic board games "with content." Accumulation of power was depicted
in terms of building a business empire, "taking over" enterprises, forcing
competitors into bankruptcy, and the like. As the Cold War grew in intensity and prominence, world conquest games, such as Risk, became
popular. The principle was the same as in Monopoly, but the entities "taken
over" were now countries instead of businesses, and the currency of power
was military might instead of money. The advent of computers opened up
entirely new vistas. The following enthusiastic description of a parlor game
called "Balance of Power," designed to be played against a human adversary or against a Macintosh computer, speaks for itself.

> Subtitled "Geopolitics in the Nuclear Age," the game is an exploration of
> superpower diplomacy played on a world map. You choose to be either the
> U.S. or the U.S.S.R. (In a one-player game, the computer takes the other
> side. You can also play against a friend.) In brief, you decide whether to
> support or undermine the governments of each of 60 countries: you can send
> economic or military aid to either government or rebel forces, conduct covert
> operations to destabilize unfriendly regimes, apply diplomatic pressure, sign
> treaties, station troops. The object is to increase your sphere of influence and
> international prestige—at your opponent's expense—while avoiding nuclear
> war, in which both sides lose. The dynamics of the game consist of challenging
> your opponent's moves; at every step the other side takes, you can send a
> diplomatic protest which can expand into a full-scale crisis. Your opponent
> has the same opportunity. It's a grand global game of "chicken" played for
> the highest stakes.
>   It's an intriguing adult simulation, provocative as well as entertaining. A
> carefully thought-out game could take days, and as an educational tool, I
> could see Balance of Power a month-long project in a high school social science
> class.
>   But what strikes me most forcefully about the game is how beautifully it
> uses the Macintosh's resources. You can display vast amounts of political,
> social, economic, and military data about the world ranked in several ways,
> on cross-hatched maps. Every "event" triggers changes in status reports, maps,
> and newspaper displays. And the algorithms for analyzing the progress of the
> world situation over the course of a game's eight-year span are very com-
> plex. . . .
>   If I gave out little stars or little disks for computer programs, this one would
> get the highest ranking. This is what computers should do. (Shapiro 1986.)

It is naive to think that people in the Pentagon or in the Kremlin play
games of this sort to get ideas about global strategies. And it is wrong to
think that game theory has anything to teach about playing this game (any
more than it has anything to teach about playing chess, contrary to the
prevalent image of game theory). What we have here is a dominance of

game mentality, an ideology that pictures life as a set of overlapping games which everyone plays and tries or ought to try to "win." Monopoly transported people into the harsh but just (in the sense of rewarding the competent) world of business—a man's world, a world of no-nonsense bottom-line reality. Now it is Balance of Power, transporting people into the somewhat frightening but exhilarating, justly stern and starkly "rational" world of geopolitics—the new reality.

Karen Novak, manager of communications of Mindscape, the software company that produces Balance of Power, has been quoted saying that it is a *peace* game. The claim is made on the basis of the fact that, formally speaking, Balance of Power is a non-zero-sum game (cf. Chapter 15): if, as a result of strategic maneuvering of the players (representing respectively the U.S. and the U.S.S.R.), a nuclear war erupts, both lose. Thus, a "common interest" has been built into the game. The essential feature of the game, however, remains competition for "prestige points" acquired by no-holds-barred power ploys. We read in the manual of the game ". . . if a government of another nation seems unalterably opposed to you, you should (with great regret) seek to eliminate it."

It is possible that Balance of Power was meant to enlighten the public about the pitfalls of power-politics-as-usual in the nuclear age. It is, however, an open question whether it does so or whether it serves to bolster the view of the public that the Cold War is the basic world-political reality of our age and that the sole objective of a foreign policy is the acquisition of power and prestige at the expense of an adversary. It is also possible that the game *exploits* the addiction to power of the general public, nurtured by the blatantly aggressive policies of the present American administration. The threat of mutual destruction may serve to add zest to the game.

The most glaring deficiency of rationality in thinking about war is found in the way the game-theoretic mode of reasoning has fostered the intellectualization of war in the strategic community. Because of seemingly irremovable misconceptions, we must reiterate at the risk of redundancy that the game-theoretic mode of reasoning is not identical with applications of game theory. Affixing the epithet "game theorists" to strategists is demonstrably unjustified and makes the critics of strategic thinking vulnerable to accusations of ignorance. It is nevertheless true that the appearance of game theory on the intellectual horizon aroused most lively interest in strategic circles. Actual applications of the theory are still only a very small part of strategic thought. The keen interest stems from the implication deduced from game theory that mathematically rigorous thinking focused on the search for optimal strategies in conflict situations is *possible*. And this idea surfaced at a time when it seemed that nuclear weapons had drained military science of all intellectual content and made it obsolete.

Here we have a plausible explanation of the emphasis placed by writers of the strategic community on intricacies of strategic problems in the nuclear age. Schelling went so far as to point out that game theory has opened up a new area of military science: the development of theories concerned with the rational *non-use* of force (in addition to the traditional theories dealing with the rational use of force). This extension may, perhaps, be regarded as a response of the strategic community to the prospect that the use of military force in the nuclear age would, after all, make military science, as well as everything else, irrelevant. Intellectualization of war has given military science a new lease on life.

"A Long and Heaithy Future"

Colin Gray, who regards himself as a member of the "strategic community," gives evidence of keen insight into this latest phase in the evolution of war as an institution and, incidentally, into the reason why the intellectualization of war blossomed most luxuriously in the U.S. It was he who called attention to the openness of American society as a key factor in broadening the conception of the military professional.

> . . . only in the United States is it possible for individuals with relative ease to have "mixed careers" involving occasional periods of official service, university teaching (or affiliation at least), "think tank" research, private consulting, and possibly employment in the defense industry. (Gray 1982, p. 2.)

It is this sort of cross-fertilization encounters—opportunities to mingle different kinds of experiences, to adjust rapidly to one or another style of life as one's circumstances demand—that produces a rich soil for creative work and strong motivation to work with enthusiasm and devotion.

In the United States, the free and easy exchange of ideas and personnel between civilian and military professional environments has given rise to what Gray calls the "Golden Age" of strategic thinking. He writes as a prophet of the Age of Science might have written during the Renaissance:

> It is safe to predict that strategic studies will enjoy a long and healthy future. Those scholars who believe that, in all save rococo variations, nearly the last important word has been written on issues of interest to strategists, may confidently be proclaimed to be in error. (Gray 1982, p. 7.)

One recalls the wistful comment of R.A. Millikan toward the end of the nineteenth century that physics had come to the end of its creative period and that nothing remained for physicists to do but push the precision of measured physical constants to the next decimal point. This gloomy prognosis was made a few years before the discovery of radioactivity, the formulation of relativity theory, and of quantum theory.

Gray goes on to list the "catalysts of inquiry" that drive strategic studies of today forward and open up new vistas. These are policy need, technological innovation, dissatisfaction, idle curiosity, and personal career motivation.

> *Policy needs* stem from bureaucratic competition. A policy maker in some agency may feel that he understands the problems related to the particular role his agency plays in defense, but he knows that other policy makers in other agencies may have different ideas in which they usually have proprietary interest. The rivalries of the various branches of the armed forces are well known. The navy is concerned with its particular strategic and tactical problems, the army with its, the air force with its. They must compete for funds, attention, prestige, and career opportunities for their personnel. Each needs solid technical or scientific arguments to bolster its position. They turn to the strategists for the wherewithal of such support. This demand keeps the strategists busy in their think tanks and universities.
>
> *Technological innovation* is an obvious source of demand for the skills of the strategist. Each advance in weaponry requires appropriate adaptation of strategic thinking. Moreover, the time is past when the military bureaucracies resisted strategic innovations suggested from outside their ranks. The lesson about the decisive role of technology in war has been well learned. The so-called technological imperative manifests itself in a chain reaction. The scientists discover something. The engineers say they can build it. The military say they've got to have it. So it comes into being. Now the question arises what is to be done with it. It is the strategist's job to think up uses. In this way, technological innovation becomes a catalyst of strategic thought.
>
> *Idle curiosity* stimulates strategic thought by "the intrinsic fascination of the subject matter." A scholar so moved may discover that his research is policy-relevant even though it is not policy-oriented. (Gray 1982, p. 9.)

Here we may have serendipity at work, the principle that often underlies important scientific discoveries. Faraday played with wires wound on empty thread spools and discovered electrical inductance. Thus was the principle of the dynamo discovered and the age of electricity ushered in.

Even aside from the lure of developing future applications, idle curiosity in its pure form often plays a vital role in keeping the strategic community alive and well.

R. Isaacs gives an eloquent account of his preoccupation with developing the theory of differential games. To be sure, dogged pursuit of success and of vindication of his ideas appear to have been foremost in his mind. But what he really feels passionate about is the thrill of discovery, the joy of knowing. Kepler must have felt this way when his three laws of planetary motion fell neatly into place. Kekulé must have felt this way when the carbon ring appeared to him in a dream in the form of a snake biting its tail. Let Dr. Isaacs speak for himself:

> Progress of pursuit games was steady, when a colleague, Arnold Menger, brought me two air-war games, which later appeared in my book as the two versions of the war of attrition and attack. The first he had solved but the second baffled him. I was able to see that the cause was a universal surfeit. New vistas opened: there was scope for my techniques beyond pursuit and evasion contests. I coined the name, "differential games" . . . .

Isaacs goes on to describe his trials and tribulations in attempting to arouse interest for the theory in military circles. He made little progress. Finally, he decided to write a book on the subject.

> During the galley proof stage, there was a national meeting on control theory. . . . The experience was unique and bizarre. The speakers were largely grappling with one-player versions of differential games such as I had solved years before. I had the eerie feeling of a bird who could fly with two wings watching fledglings attempt it with one. The eminent Pontriagin had come from Russia to present the featured address. Its title? Differential games! How had this phrase, then published only in my Rand reports, reached the Soviet Union? His topic? A pursuit game, virtually the isotropic rocket, which he treated splendidly and plainly had just made a beginning.
> Since then the subject bloomed. There have been national meetings exclusively on it and now an international one. It has even attained sufficient orthodoxy for the bestowal of research grants. Even the ears of the armed services, once so tenaciously sealed, are open a bit, for I have seen sponsored papers on the military use of differential games.[1] (Isaacs 1974.)

The most telling part of this narrative is Isaac's account of Pontriagin's appearance at the meeting. It does not matter in the least that Pontriagin is in the service of the "enemy." He is first and foremost a respected colleague, a master of the field, to the mastery of which Isaacs himself aspires. Isaacs is happy that one of the great mathematicians of the generation was attracted to the same problems that were a challenge to him. It matters not that Pontriagin has evidently scooped him. Generosity and solidarity of common concerns overshadow rivalry. Finally, what is most remarkable is Isaacs' fleeting bewilderment about how Pontriagin heard about the phrase Isaacs coined ("differential games"). Could a thought about espionage within the hallowed halls of the Rand Corporation have crossed his mind? If it did, this thought may also have been overwhelmed by a warm feeling of collegiality.

Dissatisfaction is a natural catalyst of strategic thought wherever opportunities for definitive tests of ideas are lacking. That opportunities for testing nuclear strategies are lacking should be obvious. The proving ground for testing strategic or tactical ideas in the pre-nuclear age was the battlefield. Sound ideas presumably led to victories, unsound ones to defeats. There is no way of testing nuclear strategies short of nuclear battles. Failing that, freewheeling doctrines meet each other head-on in lively debates, which presumably sharpen the intellect and inspire new ideas. Opportunities for criticizing nuclear doctrines are provided in think tanks and in professional literature. Searching questions can be asked about every one of them, which the proponents of the doctrines are honor-bound to answer. This takes considerable ingenuity and provides plenty of leverage for stimulating debates. Again, the unique openness of American society and the loose criteria used in evaluating professional credentials contribute to the liveliness of the discussions.

The role of career opportunities in maintaining the strategic community does not need to be spelled out.

A picture of the strategic community in America emerges. In its composition, it hardly differs from many other American "communities," as groups with common professional interests have come to be called: business, academic, the several professional communities. Compared to other societies, American society is markedly homogenized. There are some sharp distinctions between the white collar, the blue collar, and the destitute populations; however, within the white collar sector there is less differentiation than elsewhere, less "class distinction" and, by and large, no wide differences in outlook on politics, on the human condition, on matters of philosophical concern. Perhaps somewhat apart is the intellectual sector of the middle class, encompassing mostly people with higher education, among whom groups with genuine interest in ideas can be found. The "strategic community" belongs to this sector and, except for the peculiar content of the ideas at the center of their concerns, the members of that community are like all other intellectuals in America. Dr. Colin S. Gray can be taken as a representative of that community.

Strategic Studies and Public Policy

Most of the content of his book (Gray 1982) is devoted to the debates about war strategies and "postures" that the United States should adopt to meet the "problems" generated by the existence of nuclear weapons.

These "problems" revolve mainly around three principal themes: deterrence, arms control, and limited war.

The theme of deterrence emerged via the introduction of the policy of "Massive Retaliation" (cf. pp. 49–56). As expected, the policy raised a host of questions, all of which proved to be valuable grist for the intellectual mill. The richness of the subject matter can be appreciated by just perusing the list of these questions: (pp. 56–57):

> In the context of stable mutual deterrence, what is the value of strategic forces? [Consider the intellectual effort required to operationalize "value."]
>
> Is a strategy of large-scale nuclear retaliation incompatible with Western values? '[Questions of ethics must be given their due. The accusation of amorality should be countered with something.]
>
> Is the United States prone to seek a technological peace when really it is only a political peace which can provide lasting security?" [Due attention is paid to opponents of "technological fixes."]
>
> Since the decision to initiate nuclear use must be pregnant with fears of retaliation, what style of foreign policy will encourage foreign observers to believe that nuclear action will be taken under some circumstances?" [The recurring problem of credibility of threats.]
>
> Can one speak of a permissive or a restrictive public mood in relation to nuclear strategy?

Here it is worthwhile to examine Gray's views on American public opinion. So far, he has kept pretty scrupulously out of the picture, living up to the promise given in the introduction: "Although I have strong opinions on particular contemporary policy questions, such advocacy as there may be in this book is strictly secondary to the book's major purpose—to record and interpret the evolution of the field of strategic studies in its relation to public policy" (Gray 1982, p. 1). On the question of public mood in the United States, Gray ventures to present his own opinion. In his view, the American public is not sensitive to the intricacies of defense strategies. Americans may give credence to the charge that wars are "unwinnable", or they may be angered when wars are not won, which, Gray says, is not the same thing, possibly alluding to the dissatisfaction with the way the Vietnam war was conducted. However, Gray argues, the "finer points of credibility are not good campaign material." He cites evidence for this: Adlai Stevenson suffered a decisive defeat in the election of 1952. The public trusted a five-star general.

"How can the 'great question' between a healthy economy and adequate defense be resolved?"

None of these questions, Gray points out, has been settled. The debate is still very much alive. From the way Gray answers the numerous "charges" against the doctrine of massive retaliation (14 in all), one gets the impression that a summary rejection of the doctrine was not justified. According to Gray, "massive retaliation" did *not* mean that the U.S. would respond with a nuclear attack on Moscow to every transgression attributed to "international communism." There was plenty of room for "measured response" in the doctrine. Later this was spelled out explicitly in Schelling's refinement, namely, the introduction of the element of uncertainty into the prospect of retaliation. Credibility is not enhanced if one draws a line on the map and says, "If you or your proxies encroach on this line, we will destroy Soviet society." Far more effective is the warning, "If you do this or that, we will be compelled to react in a military manner so that the *chances* of our finding ourselves in a central war [the technical term for nuclear attacks on homelands] will increase beyond your (and our) ability to calculate" (Gray 1982, p. 60, emphasis added).

There have actually been concrete proposals of realizing "the threat that leaves something to chance." Suppose for simplicity that the nuclear arsenal can be activated by pushing a button (the popular conception of how a nuclear war will start). Instead of one button, have twenty, each of which activates the nuclear arsenal with a certain probability. This probability increases from, say, .05 through increments of .05 to 1.00. Deterrence (with something left to chance) can now be realized in the form of Russian Roulette. The mildest threat is to push the button that activates a nuclear attack with probability of "only" .05. If this doesn't work, one can go on to the .10 button and so on.

Perhaps this is a caricature but, if so, only because it is obviously simpleminded. The threat ". . . we will be compelled to react in a military manner so that the chances of our finding ourselves in a central war will increase .. ." sounds more sophisticated than the threat modeled by Russian Roulette. But it is as impossible to evaluate the merits of the one as of the other. For that matter, it is as impossible to evaluate the merits of the various strategies and postures as it is to evaluate the merits of the arguments of the scholastics about the burning theological questions of their time.

A case in point is the debate on the question, "How should a central nuclear war be waged?" (Recall that "central war" is the name given to a war consisting of "nuclear exchanges" against each other's homelands.) It is on this question that Herman Kahn's big volume *On Thermonuclear War* (1960) made strategic history. Until then, it was generally supposed that, given symmetric retaliatory capacity ("stable strategic balance"), a central nuclear war was not something to seriously think about. Sensible and cautious men do not embark on collective suicide. But strategic thinking does not stagnate. Attention inevitably turned to "What if?" *On Ther-*

monuclear War, Gray writes, was Kahn's achievement: ". . . to thrust the reality (or strategic fiction possibly) of nuclear war under the noses of those who write about preventing it . . . Kahn's message was that nuclear catastrophes may come in different sizes."

The relevant citations from *On Thermonuclear War* are about "three types of deterrence."

> Type I deterrence refers to the deterrence of an attack by the fear of retaliatory blow by a damaged SAC[2] or a preemptive by a SAC which has gotten tactical warning. Type II deterrence refers to the deterrence of provocative actions by fear of a premeditated first-strike by the nation being provoked. Type III deterrence refers to the deterrence of provocative actions by a counteraction which is expected to be so effective that the net effect of the "aggressor's" action is to cause him to lose in position." (Kahn 1960, p. 282.)

Refinement of concepts is a central theme of all of Kahn's writings on war. His often-repeated message is a recommendation not to shrink from "thinking about the unthinkable," which, in fact, is the title of one of his books (Kahn 1962).

The advice is sound enough, but if taken, it can affect the thinker in two different ways. Thinking about the unthinkable can sharpen the awareness of what the hypergrowth of the war system has brought about and so could stimulate people to take organized action aimed at dismantling the system. Or else "thinking about the unthinkable" could have an opposite effect. It could serve to "intellectualize" war and so to produce an "adjustment" to it. In fact, teaching the public to "learn to live with the bomb" is a major proselytizing effort of the strategic community.

Differentiation and refinement of concepts is the principal mark of intellectualization. The technique could be used therapeutically. It is possible, for example, that a pathological fear of, say, snakes could be greatly attenuated if the person with the phobia could be induced to differentiate between different species of snakes. Quite possibly it is the undifferentiated concept "snake" induced by a sudden act of recognition, that triggers the fear. Learning to differentiate "breaks up" the concept and inhibits the triggering action. This is essentially what Kahn is trying to do with his differentiation of various concepts associated in the public mind with the specter of nuclear war.

Along with the three types of deterrence, Kahn distinguishes also between several different kinds of world wars. He calls them World War III, World War IV, V, . . . VIII (Kahn 1960). Perhaps his intent was to shock the reader by giving the impression that after World War III there will be more to come. Actually, the roman numerals refer not to successive wars but to the types of world war that could be fought in the 1960s, 1970s, 1980s, and so on (*On Thermonuclear War* was published in 1960), taking into account the projected developments of technology. Again, however, the intent is clear—to defuse the fear reaction by inducing the reader to "refine and differentiate" and thereby accustom himself to thinking "calmly" about war. Kahn's "escalation ladder" (cf. Kahn 1965) with its 44 rungs is the most conspicuous example of this technique.

In sum, the objective apparently pursued by strategists, as they explain the intricacies of strategic thinking to the public, is to wean people away from "emotional" reactions to what the strategists are doing, namely, considering "rationally" the prospect of war and of the problems of waging it in the nuclear age. In assessing this stance, we must see what can possibly be meant by "rationality" in the context of preparing for and waging war.

Can War Be a "Rational" Enterprise?

By "war" I will mean not only what is commonly understood by war—e.g., battles, bombardment—but also all activities undertaken in connection with the organization of war. Some of these are already subsumed under "war" as the word occurs in common usage, for instance, transport and deployment of troops and weapons. I will, however, extend the definition to cover all activities related to the preparation for war even when a state of war in the accepted sense does not exist. Thus, the design of war plans, the manufacture of war material, research directed to designing and improving weapons, training of military personnel, even the development of strategic theories will be subsumed under "war," even though these activities do not in themselves directly embody organized killing and destruction.

In other words, in this discussion, I will speak of war not as a recurring *event* (the common conception) but as an *institution* within a society, an area of activity and preoccupation which has a continuous, rather than sporadic, existence.

"Rationality" in this discussion will have several meanings which are related but not identical. First, "rationality" can be understood as a property of a person as in the statement "John is rational" or else as a property of an action as in "John acted rationally." By the latter statement, we will mean that John had a clear idea of some goal and used means which he believed would help him to achieve that goal. By "John is rational" we will mean that John usually takes into account not only the immediate gratifications resulting from his actions but also longer-term consequences, depending on how far ahead the consequences of actions have been foreseen and deemed relevant to the attainment of the envisaged goal.

"Rationality" can also refer to the degree of "realism" embodied in a person's behavior. This is the most controversial aspect of the definition. We may, as a matter of course, regard someone as "irrational" if his actions are severely constrained by some idiosyncratic superstition. But if this superstition is deeply embedded in a system of beliefs dominant in the person's environment, such a criterion may not be appropriate. For example, at one time, tomatoes were thought to be poisonous. One could hardly call someone "irrational" if he refused to eat tomatoes in those days.

Finally, "rationality" can be related to logic. In this sense, derivation of mathematical truths is a prime example of rational activity because these derivations are examples of complete logical rigor. In common parlance, however, "logic" seldom refers to the sort of rigor that characterizes mathematical reasoning. A person's arguments are often presumed to be "logical" if the way in which they are presented is *reminiscent of* stating assumptions and deriving inferences. Often arguments of this sort do not withstand careful scrutiny. Inferences drawn do not necessarily follow from the assumptions. Extrapolations of limited experiences are mistaken for reasonable inductive inferences, converses of statements assumed to be true are also unjustifiably assumed to be true (e.g., all cats are mammals, therefore all mammals are cats), and so forth. Few people are familiar with these technicalities. But many are impressed with logical-sounding arguments and mistake resorting to such arguments for a mark of rationality.

Especially prevalent is the notion that "rationality" is the opposite of "sentiment." This notion reflects confusion between the tone of discourse and its content. A related notion also identifies "rationality" (by which is actually meant a certain detachment or a certain vocabulary) with maturity, self-discipline, and intelligence; and "sentiment" (again identified with a certain tone or a certain vocabulary) with immaturity, naiveté, or self-indulgence.

A review of a book (Rapoport 1964) by a member of the strategic community (Brennan 1965) will serve as an example of this juxtaposition of reason and sentiment. The theme of that book was a different juxtaposition, namely, of strategic thinking about war and of the sort of thinking that is induced by a refusal to dissociate the meaning of war in our day from its concrete results, namely, the physical and biological events associated with it.

> *Strategy and Conscience* is an anguished book, written by a man who points to some problems that more of us should spend more time thinking about.

But its chief claim to distinction, unfortunately, rests more on the intensity of its anguish than on the accuracy of its reporting or in the perceptiveness of its analysis. . . .

The first serious complaint I have with this book is that the author has not specified, and probably has not even clearly determined in his own mind just where he is shooting from, and this seems to interfere with his understanding of some important issues under examination. The great majority of us accept the idea that national military force may sometimes be used with justice in defense of important national goals or human values. Thoughtful people who adhere to this view are often confronted with line-drawing problems of degree. For example: Under what circumstances is it ethically reasonable to use how much military force? Under what circumstances is it reasonable to threaten what kinds of hostages? How many people can be risked as a consequence of some particular deterrent system?

We hear the principal theme: Anguish paralyzes reason. The essence of reason is analysis. Analysis means differentiation, gradation. Another mark of rationality is objectivity. Nothing is more objective than numbers, because everyone can agree on the meaning of a number. It is in this spirit that Herman Kahn proceeded to seek an answer to the last question posed by Brennan.

If 180 million dead [the population of the U.S. at the time] is too high a price to pay for punishing the Soviets for their aggression, what price would we be willing to pay? (Kahn 1960, p. 29.)

He found the answer he wanted readily enough:

I have discussed the question with many Americans and after about fifteen minutes of discussion, their estimates of an acceptable price generally fell between 10 and 60 million, clustering toward the upper number.

Let us return to Brennan's review. He goes on:

A few—pacifists—reject this kind of thinking altogether and hold that the best overall defense of human values resides in the complete rejection of military force, even when the rejection is by some countries only and not by all. For this view, the dominant problem is a missionary one, to convince the rest of us that we are working in the wrong general framework and that the gains of strict pacifism are worth the obvious risks. . . .

Now I do not find [the author] making overt missionary arguments that we should renounce all forms of military violence. . . . The major part of his argument is couched in a mode that suggests that he accepts the standard

framework, though I think he does not in fact. The book seems imbued with
a kind of surreptitious pacifism.

Recall Lenin's polemic against his colleagues (cf. Chapters 8, 9) who
questioned the meaning of "materialism" in the light of the revolutionary
discoveries in physics at the turn of the century. He accused them, in effect,
of "surreptitious idealism." *Tertium non datur.* One is either a materialist
and thus on the side of the revolutionary working class, or one is an idealist
and therefore an ally of the bourgeoisie. And this is what Brennan seems
to be saying with regard to attitudes about the use of military violence.
Either admit frankly that you are a pacifist and start preaching unilateral
disarmament, or else play the game like the rest of us: distinguish and
differentiate; draw lines; above all do not succumb to "anguish" or similar
sentiments, which stifle "rational thought."

It could be argued, however, that excluding affect is not always a sign
of rationality. Quite the contrary. Some psychoses are marked by just
that—absence of affect. One should not confuse the coldbloodedness of
the modern warrior with, say, the coolheadedness of the surgeon, who
must not flinch from cutting human flesh. Here exclusion of feelings (of
empathy, for example) is essential on purely *physiological* grounds. If the
surgeon got upset by the sight of blood, if his hand were to shake, he might
kill the patient. What, on the other hand, would be the consequence of
shifting attention away from megatons, thrust factors, kill-ratios, windows
of vulnerability—to evoking a mental image of actual events occurring in
a "nuclear exchange"?

Sixty million turns out, according to Kahn, to be an "acceptable price"
to pay for "standing up to the Russians." But "sixty million" conveys as
little about the reality of the events that would snuff out these sixty million
as "six million" conveys about the events that transpired in Auschwitz,
Treblinka, and Maidanek.

There are bounds beyond which it is senseless to draw lines of distinction.
Sacrificing thirty million lives to protect the prestige or the dignity of a
state is not "better" than sacrificing sixty million. By the same token, had
the Nazis slaughtered three million instead of six million, their crime would
not have been only "half" as horrendous.

Emotion is not an antithesis of rationality. Granted that in certain situations emotion is a hindrance to effective functioning, generalization is
not warranted. Some outstanding scientists have felt exuberance on making
momentous discoveries. This elation did not prevent them from drawing
carefully reasoned conclusions from them. Some have felt keen anguish
while struggling with a problem. This did not prevent them from using the
full might of their intelligence in grappling with it. True, all traces of

emotion are usually eliminated from the final product, as demanded by the decorum of scientific discourse. In the present situation this cannot be done because contemplating the end of the human race with apparent equanimity, far from being a sign of "rationality," amounts to a distortion of reality. Continuing to discuss "strategies" of fighting a nuclear war entails entering a world completely insulated from all normal human concerns. When strategists speak about events involving the incineration of hundreds of millions of men, women, and children, exclusion of affect serves a different purpose, namely, that of turning attention away from the enormity of the crimes being planned. Here rationality in the accepted sense of the word is compromised, because reality is implicitly denied.

Let us now examine samples of polemic purged of emotional content. Colin Gray conducts his polemic by setting up objections to different "options" that the strategic community has proposed as bases of a nuclear strategy for the United States. For instance, in discussing Mutual Assured Vulnerability (a euphemism for "Mutual Assured Destruction"?), Gray cites the following objection:

"Nuclear war would be a catastrophe unparalleled in world history."

Gray's comment:

> Nuclear war may or may not prove to be a catastrophe unparalleled in world history, but it is unlikely to be the functional equivalent of the cataclysmic bibilical flood, notwithstanding the recent claim advanced by some scientists to the effect that nuclear war would probably trigger climatic changes that could be fatal to life on earth. The new apocalyptic vision is of "nuclear winter." In the thirteen and fourteenth centuries, the Mongols and the bubonic plague[3] were viewed in much the same eschatological terms in which many people today view nuclear war. These "visitations from God" were terrible, but mankind remained in business." (Gray 1984, pp. 61–62.)

The "logic" of this argument rests on the following analogy. In the fourteenth century, people believed that the Black Death was a visitation from God and that humanity would be wiped out. But they were wrong; only about one-fourth of the population of Europe died. European history went on to blossom into a Renaissance. Therefore we need not take the warnings about the probable demise of humanity as a consequence of nuclear war too seriously, prospects of a nuclear winter notwithstanding.

Another example is the *post hoc–propter hoc* argument to the effect that nuclear weapons have kept the peace in Europe for forty years.

We have already pointed out that any model of a decision under risk must involve a utility associated with every action paired with every state of nature. Brennan in his review of *Strategy and Conscience* mentions the "obvious risks" engendered by pacifism without mentioning risks engendered by willingness to undertake military actions. As this is written, the United States government has still not formulated a reply to Mikhail Gorbachev's proposal to embark on a program of nuclear disarmament with the aim of completely eliminating nuclear weapons over a period of 15–20 years. Doubtless, assessment of "risk" will play a crucial role in the fate of this proposal. From the way American strategists assess risks, it seems certain that only one side of the risk will be considered, namely, the risk of regarding the Soviet Union as trustworthy when in fact it is not. But to formulate this as a problem to be solved "rationally," it is imperative to consider also the complementary risk, namely, the risk of regarding the Soviet Union as untrustworthy when it in fact is trustworthy (in this instance). Further, only if the utilities as well as the probabilities of both types of error are assigned numerical values, can this problem be solved "rationally" in the full sense of the word.

The last remark should not be construed as a demand that in every situation of risk a mathematical model must be constructed. At times, it would be fatuous to do so. At any rate, there is hardly any basis for assessing numerical values of utilities and probabilities in this situation. Both must remain entirely subjective. The only point made is that in situations of this sort claims of "objectivity" and "rationality" (as opposed to "emotionality" or "sentimentality") are vacuous. The selection of risks to be made salient, assessment of their magnitudes, and implicit assignment of values to outcomes feared or hoped for are all governed by subjective factors imbued with strong, albeit unrecognized, emotional content.

Technolatry, "Objectivity," and Cost-Benefit Tally

Perhaps the most conspicuous source of impressions that strategic thinking is rooted in rationality is the infusion of science into the preparation for war. The entry of science was provided via ever-more-sophisticated technology drawing upon ever-more-abstract theory. It has been said, not without justification, that World War I was a chemists' war (explosives, poison gas), World War II a physicists' war (radar, atomic bomb), and that World War III will be a mathematicians' war (guided missiles, completely automated weapons systems). As the more abstruse areas of science are drawn upon, the level of expertise required to utilize the resulting high technology rises steeply until the problems involved become completely incomprehensible to the layman. The vast complex of activity, great portions of it consisting of exchange of information coded in an esoteric language of indices and acronyms, defines a separate world *apparently* ruled by pure rationality.

Others have noticed the deceptive nature of the "rationality" generated by strategic thinking. Charles W. Tait (1965) wrote:

> The attraction lies not only in the directness and simplicity of actual military force. The air of technical efficiency and *objectivity* [emphasis added] which surrounds decisions made by computers; the impressive apparatus of intelligence agencies with their networks of agents and almost instantaneous transmission of top-secret, evaluated intelligence to policy makers; the jet transports, aircraft carriers, helicopters, radio communications from the Pentagon to forward command posts—all these give an illusion of purposeful action. Is it any wonder that they impress men who worship technical gadgetry and pride themselves on their ability to make speedy executive decisions?

Recall the glowing description of the new world conquest game played with the aid of an on-line computer: "You can display vast amounts of political, social, economic, and military data about the world ranked in several ways as cross-hatched maps. Every 'event' triggers changes in status reports. . . ." It may very well be that the "world system" at any given moment responds to complex interactions of political, social, economic, and military variables. In fact, the systemic view of the world (the topic we will discuss in the next chapter) assumes just such a reality. It is not the representation of global reality in this game that detracts rather than contributes to enlightenment; it is the assumption that political wisdom and virtuosity are encapsulated in the ability to assess the essentials of this complex reality, find the levers by which it can be manipulated, and use this knowledge in order to amass power at the opponent's expense, that is, in order to win the "global game of 'chicken' for the highest stakes," as the enthusiastic endorser of the game correctly describes it.

Here we have the extension of technolatry to the cognitive sphere: the prestige once lent to the struggle for power by sophisticated hardware is now lent by sophisticated software.

Erosion of reality awareness that results from the intellectualization of war is most striking in the decoupling of strategic considerations from the events that the implementation of strategies must generate. This decoupling is characteristic not only of the thinking of outspoken enthusiasts of the arms race and of the technocratic opportunities offered by nuclear war but also of the "moderates"—strategists concerned with the "destabilizing" effects of some weapons systems. Consider the following argument directed against the deployment of Multiple Independently Targeted Reentry Vehicles (MIRVs). Each of these "vehicles" carries ten warheads that can be dispatched independently to ten different targets. Assume that these missiles are to be used in a "counterforce" strategy, i.e., in an attack aimed at the adversary's missile sites. Assume further that given the present accuracy of long-range and middle-range ballistic missiles, it takes on the average two warheads to "take out" one site. It follows that by using missiles with single warheads the attacker spends two missiles for every site he destroys; so that if these contain single warhead missiles, he depletes his own stock of missiles faster than he destroys the adversary's. On the other hand, using MIRVs he spends one missile to destroy the adversary's five (assuming the same kill ratio). It follows that using single warhead missiles in a "counterforce" (read "first") strike is not "cost-effective", while using MIRVs is. For this reason possession of MIRVs should predispose the possessor toward launching a first strike. Moreover, if both sides have MIRVs, each is aware that the other is strongly tempted to launch a first strike and consequently is practically compelled to launch a preemptive strike "in self-defense." This is what is meant by the "destabilizing" effect of MIRVs.

There is nothing wrong with this argument as far as it goes. It sounds like a laudable attempt to inhibit the development of a "destabilizing" weapon, which would be bound to make "control" of the arms race more difficult if not altogether impossible. Consider, however, the assumption underlying this argument: "cost effectiveness" is tacitly assumed to be the most important consideration in a decision to launch or not to launch a nuclear attack. It is, of course, quite possible that such considerations *are* foremost in the minds of the strategists planning a nuclear war. But if so, this may well be a consequence of the fact that cost-effectiveness considerations are *believed* to be the most important considerations. The boundary between a *belief* in and the *acceptance* of a mode of thinking is often blurred. When one believes that a way of thinking is "normal," one learns to think in that way. But to think in this way is possible only if "cost effectiveness" considerations are formalized in some sort of arithmetic and hermetically sealed off from a realization of what a nuclear war entails on the level of *actual events*, not merely on the level of bookkeeping.

In this way, reality is shut out of consciousness, which is exactly what the intellectualization of war is supposed to accomplish. Except in the realm of pure mathematics, shutting out awareness of concrete reality is incompatible with rationality. Therefore the intellectualization of war, "thinking about the unthinkable," instead of facilitating a rational approach to the problem of war precludes it. "Thinking about the unthinkable" becomes possible precisely because the "unthinkable" is emptied of content. Only its verbal shell remains, expurgated of concrete horrifying referents, adapted to playing thrilling games, whether in living rooms or in the world arena.

Notes

1. An example of a differential game is a so-called game of pursuit and evasion. An antiballistic missile (ABM) can be programmed with a "pursuit strategy" calculated to intercept an attacking intercontinental ballistic missile (ICBM), which is programmed with an "evasion strategy" designed to help it elude the ABM. It is in the "interest" of the ABM to intercept the ICBM as far from the target as possible and in the "interest" of the ICBM to get as near to the target as possible. Hence the game is zero-sum. The calculation of optimal strategies for both the ABM and the ICBM involves formidable mathematical problems.
2. Before intercontinental ballistic missiles became the principal "delivery systems," nuclear attacks were planned in the U.S. by the Strategic Air Command (SAC), employing long distance bomber planes.
3. The Black Death (probably the bubonic plague) ravaged Europe in the middle of the fourteenth century. In some countries, two-thirds to three-fourths of the population died, in England even a greater proportion. It is estimated that in all of Europe about 25 million persons, or one-fourth of the total population, were killed by the disease.

PART

THE SYSTEMIC APPROACH

17

The Systemic View of the World

When some portion of reality is called a "system," it is perceived as a unified whole, something that stands out and is recognized as "itself." The clearest example of such a system is a living organism. The most characteristic feature of an organism is that it retains its identity even though its material constituents may be replaced within a short time.

The property of being a "system" in the sense of comprising a recognizable "whole" is not confined to organisms. Organizations, too, have this property. All the members of an organization (a firm, a battalion, a club) may be replaced, some quitting or dying, others born or recruited; yet the organization retains its identity.

Non-living systems also have this property. The water in a river empties completely into the sea and is replaced by other water. But the Nile is still the Nile, and the St. Lawrence is still the St. Lawrence. "You can't step into the same river twice," said Heraclitus, but the fact that he used the phrase "the same river" establishes its identity in spite of constant flux. A system is recognized as a whole, not as a conglomeration of parts. This is what is meant by "wholeness" as a property of systems.

Interrelatedness has to do with the way the internal structure of a system is organized. In fact, it is this internal organization, the *structure* of a system, that enables it to retain its identity. Inside the organism we find a vast complex of interconnected parts and interrelated processes. As the outside world impinges on the organism, signals are sent throughout its interior activating different reactions in a way that makes the organism respond "properly" to the impinging stimuli. By "proper" responses we mean those that are likely to help the organism preserve its identity, e.g., to stay alive.

Some systems other than organisms also possess such repertoires of self-preserving reactions. It is to this internal organization of systems that the term "interrelatedness" applies.

We humans, like all other organisms, owe our continued existence on this planet to the particular way we have adjusted to our environment in the course of our evolution. Unlike other animals, we did not accomplish this adjustment by modifications of our body parts. The carnivores have claws and teeth suited to their hunting and flesh-eating habits. We are also flesh eaters and at one time lived mostly by hunting, but we have no claws to speak of, and our teeth are not the teeth of carnivores. We can run and swim after a fashion but not as well as the animals that depend on running or swimming for survival. We have some body hair but not enough to keep us warm in cold weather. Our bodies are generalized, not specialized, except for two parts: hands and brains. Our hands are specialized for refined manipulation of things; our brains for thinking in abstract categories.

Our highly specialized brain not only endows us with a prodigious capacity for learning from experience but also enables us to learn from experiences of others (through communication by symbolic language) and from experiences accumulated over generations (culture).

In particular, the ability to think in terms of abstractions enables us to formulate in language relations between "causes" and "effects," i.e., to anticipate events as consequences of other events and to transmit these anticipations to others. It is this ability that has over centuries developed into *science*.

As accumulated knowledge grew, it became impossible for individuals to acquire it all. But a division of labor made it possible for the sum total of knowledge to grow. Individual scientists acquired and developed only narrow sectors of knowledge, now called *disciplines*. Each had its own sphere of interest, its own methods of investigation, inevitably its own terminology, and often its own criteria of reliability of the knowledge embodied in it. Thus, "fractionalization" of science came about, in consequence of which scientists in various specialized fields of knowledge could no longer communicate with each other, each being immersed in narrow, often esoteric fields of activity.

The systemic view of the world represents attempts to reintegrate various, often widely separated areas of knowledge so as to allow a coherent picture to emerge. Philosophers have always striven to present a unified view of the world. Indeed, this is why some classical philosophers are associated with systems—ways of viewing the world in terms of certain categories that are supposed to fit different aspects of reality into a coherent picture. However, these philosophical systems usually turned out to be products of freewheeling associations of ideas triggered by concatenations of words. Connections between these speculations and reality were frequently severed. This rupture became apparent at about the time science "found itself." This occurred in Europe during the Renaissance, when people's attention turned away from the "spiritual" world of religion toward the material world accessible to the senses. Science took off on its own, as it were, abandoning speculations unrelated to concrete experience in favor of the *experimental method*, which became the foundation of scientific investigations.

An experiment is essentially a way of arranging events so that an answer can be obtained to the question "What will happen under such and such (specified) conditions?" This is the "If . . . then . . ." paradigm of scientific cognition, the matrix in which causal relations between events are established.

Establishing Causal Connections

Causal connections between events have always been assumed. In fact, guiding one's actions by such presumed connections marks what is usually regarded as the very essence of intelligence. Before the advent of science, however, causal connections tended to be established haphazardly through chance associations of events, by unwarranted generalizations of experience, by associating connotations of words with events suggesting similar connotations. We call such unverified, generally fortuitous beliefs in causal connections superstitions. Whatever else science has done for the human condition, one thing is indisputable. Science has systematically waged war against superstition, not by substituting one set of beliefs for another but by demanding evidence for every presumed causal connection and challenging all beliefs not based on such evidence.

The experiment establishes evidence for a causal connection by the exercise of *control*. For this reason, experiments conducted with the view of adding to scientific knowledge are called *controlled experiments*. Control means eliminating factors that *also* could have caused the effects observed. If causal relations are established quantitatively, i.e., in a way that associates the magnitude of the presumed cause with that of the presumed effect, control serves to eliminate disturbing influences on the supposed relationship between the quantities. For example, courses of chemical reactions usually depend on both the pressure and the temperature of the environment. Therefore, in order to eliminate differential effects of pressure and temperature on the course of a chemical reaction, these must be controlled, i.e., kept constant. If it is desired to describe the influence of pressure and/or temperature on the course of the chemical reaction, then other factors, e.g., the concentration of the substances in the reaction, must be kept constant.

The same precautions must be observed in the study of social phenomena if we purport to establish relations between variables. For example, if we wish to know wheher there is a differential in the wage levels between social groups differing on one variable, e.g., sex, age, ethnic background, etc., we must be careful to keep other features of compared groups constant to exclude the possibility that the differential may be due to them rather than to the factor we are interested in.

The degree of control that can be imposed in field observations or in laboratory experiments varies widely. Perfect control is an ideal that can be approached in varying degrees but hardly ever attained. Relevant to this discussion is the fact that this ideal has had a powerful influence on the methodology of empirical science. For the most part, empirical science represents an *analytic* approach to knowledge. In order to get to know something about a portion of reality, the empirically oriented scientist first of all tries to *isolate* that portion from everything but the influences he is interested in or from his own interventions, whose effects he wants to study. He hopes to study each aspect of this portion of reality separately, then put all his findings together and let the complete picture emerge in this way. It is as if, in order to form an idea of what some solid object looks like, we studied different plane cross sections of it, hoping to put these together in our mind's eye to form an image of the three-dimensional object. Those who have studied descriptive geometry know how difficult it is at times to form such a picture.

The Mathematical Paradigm

The development of mathematics as a tool of scientific cognition opened up avenues for putting parts of a picture together. This possibility is expressed in the mathematically oriented definition of a system, which captures both the idea of "wholeness" and that of "interrelatedness" of internal parts (Hall and Fagan 1956).

A system, according to this definition, is described as a succession of *states*. A state of a system, in turn, is defined as a set of *values of specified variables*. A variable is often a number but may be any other attribute that can vary over a certain range. For instance, the position of a selector valve (which is one of several positions) can also be regarded as a variable.

A good example of a system defined in this way is the solar system. At any given time, each planet in our solar system has a position that can be defined by three numbers (its three coordinates in space). It also possesses a certain velocity, which can be specified by three numbers (its components in three mutually perpendicular directions). The totality of all these numbers associated with each of the planets constitutes the state of the system at a given moment of time.

Now these variables are all interrelated in the sense that the gravitational force is manifested in their mutual attractions and in the attraction exerted by the sun. These forces produce changes in the velocities of the planets, that is, both in their speeds and in their directions of motion, and therefore also in their positions. These changes, in turn, produce changes in the forces of attraction. In this way, the state of the system (the aggregate of all the values of the variables) keeps changing. A *trajectory* of such a system is a record of the values of all the variables as they change in a given stretch of time. The system can be said to be completely understood if its trajectory can be derived from the way the variables are known to interact. The solar system is completely understood in this sense, which accounts for the impressive accuracy with which positions of the planets relative to the sun can be predicted far into the future.

The content of the so-called exact sciences, the more or less mathematicized portions of the physical sciences, can be described in terms of models of systems understood in this way. The understanding rests on the fact that the variables singled out for describing the states of the systems are indeed the determinants of their behavior or at least of the aspects of their behavior that are of interest to the scientist who has described them. Furthermore, the laws of interaction among these variables are well known; at least, they are presumed to be well known *because* the calculated trajectories agree with the observed behavior of the systems.

The same applies to complex man-made artifacts such as machines, systems of controlled chemical reactions, weapons systems, and the like. To the extent that the operation of these artifacts is governed by known physical laws and to the extent that their structures (having been constructed by people) are known, their behavior can be predicted within certain margins of error. The realization of the predictions is *prima facie* evidence that the systems are understood.

There have been persistent attempts to extend this definition of systems and of methods of studying them to portions of reality beyond the inanimate world, for example, to portions of the living world exemplified by ecological habitats, certain social aggregates, certain interconnected physiological processes, and the like.

The degree of success of these attempts ranges from considerable to spotty. To understand the main difficulty of extending mathematical modeling to phenomena beyond the sphere of the physical sciences, it helps to examine the principal reason for the success of this method when applied to physical phenomena. This success has depended on two circumstances. First, the essential variables that describe a physical system have been singled out. These are spatial coordinates, the time coordinate, masses of bodies, and combinations of these by "legitimate" mathematical operations. For instance, addition is legitimate with respect to masses. The mass of a body composed of two bodies is simply the sum of their masses. A stretch of time formed by linking two such stretches in a succession is measured by summing its components. Multiplication and division are also legitimate operations when applied to physical quantities. Thus, compound variables, such as velocity, acceleration, density (mass per unit volume), force (mass times acceleration), etc., can be formed. Some of these compound variables turned out to be basic in the construction of physical theories—for example, energy, momentum, and power.

The branch of physics first to be mathematicized was mechanics. Later, phenomena involving heat and electricity were incorporated into mathematical physics. At all times the variables entering the mathematical models of physical systems were defined *operationally* and with precision. Operational definitions indicate what should be *done* (what operations undertaken) in order to observe or measure the thing defined. Operationalization served as a guarantee of semantic clarity. Precision legitimized mathematical operations.

The other equally important circumstance that insured the success of a mathematicized system theory was that the nature of interactions between the components of such systems was known. For example, gravitational force served as a basis for interactions between heavenly bodies, permitting the construction of a mathematical model of the solar system. Interactions involving transfer of heat, chemical reactions, and electrostatic and electrodynamic phenomena were all likewise known. Mathematical models of systems involving all such phenomena could be constructed. These systems represented a true synthesis of the analytic and the integrative approaches. Describing a system in terms of variables and their detailed interactions represented analysis. The emergence of gross properties of a physical system, for example, its energy, its entropy, or its stability, could be regarded as a successful integration.

These two conditions are seldom met outside the world of physical systems. The success of the physical sciences, as exemplified by consistent confirmation of mathematical models of physical phenomena inspired the so-called "reductionist" view, according to which *all* phenomena are ultimately reducible to interactions of material particles or fields of force or whatever other fundamental building blocks of physical reality may have been discovered. One may be comfortable with this view or not. But in any case, a philosophical view is not a substitute for a fruitful methodology. It is all very well to insist that every instance of human behavior is reducible to muscle contractions, hormone secretions, or nerve impulses. The conviction that this is so does not show a way of actually describing human behavior in these terms.

In sum, although a mathematical model of a system captures "wholeness" and "interrelatedness," the utility of such a model in providing a theoretical basis for empirical science is limited because of the formidable complexity of actually existing systems, especially those involving living organisms. On the other hand, attempts to study "interrelatedness" by breaking up interactions into simple cause-effect links (as in controlled experiments) may be misleading because they turn attention away from the complexities of causality. Actual causes of events are seldom simply sums of component causes.

Attempts to design ways of studying complex phenomena that could bypass the difficulties of following the path charted by the analytic approach are reflected in so-called *general system theory*. Strictly speaking, general system theory is not a theory in the sense of a logically coherent scheme providing explanations of some class of phenomena. Rather, it consists of several formulations of the systemic view of the world that take this view a few steps beyond the generalities in terms of which it was originally stated. The justification of subsuming these often-quite-diverse formulations under a "general system theory" is the theme that unites them all. They all represent examination of analogies.

Analogies

Analogy as a basis of an explanation is sometimes depreciated. Calling an explanation a "mere analogy" is tantamount to dismissing it as superficial. Yet all explanations are in the last analysis analogies. To explain something means to show that something which at first did not fit into a pattern actually does fit. We see a man running. "Why is he running?" we want to know. The question reflects our impression that the man's behavior does not fit into a familiar pattern: people do not ordinarily run in the street. When we are told that the man wants to catch a bus, his behavior does fit into a pattern: people trying to catch a bus do frequently run.

The principles underlying both this homely explanation and those underlying the most sophisticated explanations of science are essentially the same. Legend has it that Newton discovered the law of universal gravitation by pondering on the question of why an apple fell from the tree. Not so.

Newton came to the law of universal gravitation by wondering why the moon did *not* fall to the earth, that is, why the moon did not conform to the familiar pattern of falling objects. Analysis of the moon's motion showed that it *was* actually "falling" toward the earth. This becomes clear when one realizes that "falling" means not "moving toward" but "accelerating toward," that acceleration means rate of change of velocity, and that velocity involves direction as well as speed of motion. In this way, the motion of the moon can be seen to fit into the general pattern of falling bodies. All falling bodies move in orbits. The reason why the most familiar ones hit the earth is because their orbits intersect the surface of the earth. The moon's does not.

Misleading or superficial analogies are those suggested by incidental similarities or, as frequently happens, by connotations of words, or anthropomorphic notions. Superstitions stem from such analogies. Thunder sounds like growling; so it must be sounds made by an angry god. The lion is fierce and therefore brave; the rabbit does not fight and is therefore timid. Hence eating the heart of a lion will make one brave, while eating the heart of a rabbit will make one a coward. Scientific explanations, no less than superstitions, are based on analogies. The reason they are more reliable than superstitions is that the analogies on which they are based reflect *structural* (as distinct from connotational) similarities between phenomena.

Analogies Based on Identical Mathematical Structures

The most rigorously established analogies are those based on identical structures of reliable mathematical models of different phenomena. For example, the mathematical model of a harmonic oscillator moving through a resisting medium and that of an electrical system consisting of an inductance, a resistance, and a capacitance are structurally identical in the sense that both are represented by differential equations having exactly the same form. Only the parameters of the two equations have different physical meanings. The parameter that represents mass in the mechanical system corresponds to the parameter that represents inductance in the electrical one. The parameter that represents friction in the mechanical system represents resistance in the electrical one. The parameter that represents the rigidity of the spring in the oscillator corresponds to the reciprocal of the parameter that represents the capacitance of the circuit. Since both models are rather accurate representations of the two systems, whatever we can say about the behavior of the harmonic oscillator we can say about the behavior of the electrical circuit. We need only translate the terms used in one theory into the corresponding terms of the other.

Another instructive example of structural analogy is a frequently recurring distribution in time of a certain class of events. The "pips" in a Geiger counter and airplane crashes are events of this kind. Their distributions in time are rather accurately represented by the so-called Poisson distribution, which, in turn, reflects *absence* of a causal relation between successive events. This distribution was first discovered in a study of deaths caused by kicks of horses in the Prussian cavalry. To conclude from this finding (apparently linking radioactive decay with the behavior of horses) that horses are radioactive would be to succumb to the lure of a superficial analogy, the sort that superstitions are based on. Not the physical content but the mathematical structure of the models constitutes the analogy. In the case of the Poisson distribution this structure reflects the perfect "randomness" of the events examined. It follows that any departure of a sequence of events from a Poisson distribution in time *must* reflect some "non-randomness," residing either in the events themselves or in some outside influence. This suggests a search for such interpretations or influence. Therein lies the productivity of the approach based on examining mathematical analogies.

As in the case of mathematical models constructed with the view of deriving trajectories of systems, the use of mathematical models in establishing strict structural identities of systems with different contents is limited by the range of systems that can be accurately described by mathematical models. The use of analogies as building blocks of scientific theories, however, is not confined to identities of mathematical structures. Some less rigorous but nonetheless fruitful uses of analogy underlie the so-called *organismic* general system theory.

Organismic General System Theory

We will illustrate the organismic approach by a formulation by R.W. Gerard (1958). The model is represented by a matrix, whose rows are different levels of systems regarded as analogues of living organisms and whose columns are certain aspects (to be described below) possessed by all such systems.

The living cell can be taken to represent a living system on the lowest level. It constitutes a system by virtue of maintaining its identity in spite of the fact that its material content may be replaced during metabolism. This identity and integrity is maintained by certain homeostatic mechanisms that keep certain variables (e.g., concentrations or gradients within the cell) within certain limits. The gradients are maintained by virtue of the fact that the cell is an "open" system receiving matter and energy inputs from its environment and exuding matter and energy to the outside. From the analytic point of view, the cell is a vastly complicated system. From the organismic point of view, however, it serves as a unit in the structure of larger systems of which it is part.

On the next level are systems composed of cells, for example, organs or tissues. These, too, are organized entities, functioning in accordance with physical and chemical interactions within them and between them and their environment. These are, in turn, components of individual *organisms*, which appear on the next level of organization of living systems.

Continuing to still higher levels, we can take either the biological or the social path. The biological path leads to the usual biological taxa—species, genera, etc., on to ecological systems composed of large numbers of interacting species, all the way to the biota, the total living world on this planet. Or one can follow the social path to the small group (in humans, families, friendship circles), large organized groups, e.g., organizations, institutions, still larger organized aggregates of organizations and institutions, e.g., states, nations, to systems comprising states as units—the international system.

All these biological and social aggregates satisfy the system criteria in the sense that they maintain their identities. The mechanisms by which this is done vary widely, but in certain ways exhibit analogies. The ecological system may serve as an example. The components of such a system are the populations that compose it. The sizes of these populations can be taken as the quantified variables. The populations interact in many ways, for example, in predator-prey, parasite-host, or symbiotic relations. Within the ecosystem there are discernible food chains bearing a striking resemblance to metabolic cycles within the individual organism. The "identity" of the system is maintained in the form of a *steady state*. Even though individuals of each species die and additional individuals are born into the system, a certain balance is maintained as long as the ecosystem "lives." It may undergo slow secular changes through coevolution of its components. In the short run, however, random fluctuations in its composition tend to be "corrected."

Consider, for example, a predator-prey subsystem of such an ecosystem. If the population of predators increases, the population of the prey on which it feeds decreases by depletion, and this decrease eventually results in a decrease of the predator population because of the diminished food supply. Then the prey population can increase. Such cyclic adjutments are typical of stable systems. They are effected by so-called *negative feedback loops*, well known in technological systems. We shall have more to say on this theme in the next chapter.

Regulatory mechanisms must also be involved in maintaining the identity of social organizations. Institutions have regulations governing the composition of their memberships and so preserving certain of their characteristics. Countries have immigration laws. Distribution of wealth and income in societies depends on the operation of certain institutional mechanisms, which can themselves be regarded as constituting a system. The variables thought to be descriptive of that system's dynamics—production volumes, prices, wages, trade volumes, investment rates, tax rates—comprise the subject matter of a discipline completely devoted to the study of that system—economics.

Some of the analogies between the systems on the various levels can be established by appropriate mathematical models, such as parallel models of economic and ecological systems (Rapoport and Turner, 1977; Rapoport, 1986). For the most part, however, living systems are too complex to yield to rigorous mathematical modeling. Analogies between them are established through insight rather than through detailed analysis. Some of these analogies are quite obvious. An organism, e.g., an animal, engages in many immediately recognizable activities: it runs, sleeps, eats, copulates. Very different kinds of events on the microscopic level may be involved in each of these activities. The events that add up to "eating" in a cow or to "feeding" in a mosquito may have very little in common. Yet, we have no difficulty in identifying the two kinds of events as instances of the "same" kind of event, and we do this completely intuitively, without benefit of analysis.

Similarly, we recognize analogies between systems on different levels. A household, as well as its individual members, takes in food and exudes waste. The telephone system of a city bears a conspicuous resemblance to the nervous system of an animal. J.G. Miller's large volume *Living Systems* (1978) represents an attempt to establish a set of identity-preserving mechanisms (19 of them) supposedly common to all living systems.

The degree of confidence that analogies of this sort deserve varies. The crudely anthropomorphic ones (suggested by connotations of words as much as by supposed structural similarities) can be dismissed. For example, medieval models of a society identified the king with the head of an individual, the army with the arms, the peasantry with the back, and the Church with the heart. Between this naive analogizing and fruitful insights, there is a wide gradation of controversial intermediate conceptions. It is one of the positive contributions of the organismic systems approach that it has stimulated a critical scrutiny of theories suggested by such analogies.

The columns of Gerard's matrix designate three principal aspects of a living system: its structure, its behavior, and its evolution, or, as Gerard was fond of saying, its Being, its Acting, and its Becoming.

The *structure* of a system refers to a static aspect: the interrelations between its parts without reference to changes in time. For example, the structure of an individual organism is described by its anatomy. The structure of an organization (e.g., a business firm or a government bureau) is described by its table of organization, showing lines of authority, responsibility, or communications.

The *behavior* of a system refers to short-run dynamic aspects: its responses to inputs from the environment. For example on the level of the individual organism, a stimulus impinging on some sense organ may produce a response appropriate for warding off a danger or satisfying a short-term need. A nation may respond to what it perceives as a threat by mobilizing its military potential. Digestive organs respond to infusion of food by secreting substances that process it for being assimilated into the bloodstream. Behavioral changes are transient and usually reversible. On the whole, they serve to maintain some steady state. This is true especially on the level of organs, many of which perform homeostatic functions; that is, they keep levels of certain physiological variables (temperature, concentrations of substances in the blood, and the like) within tolerated limits.

The evolution of a system refers to long-run dynamics: changes over protracted time spans. These are, as a rule, irreversible. The evolution of an individual organism is usually called development. The zygote develops into an embryo, the embryo or fetus into a young, then into an adult individual. After maturation comes reproduction, senescence, and death. Families, institutions, and nations also go through a development. Large living systems viewed over historical periods of time are said to undergo evolution. The evolution of a society or nation is called its *history*.

Gerard's scheme is shown in Figure 17–1.

Interrelatedness of Disciplines Concerned with Living Systems

Gerard, who was interested in the organization of knowledge and of the acquisition of knowledge, pointed out how the cells of his matrix correspond to established disciplines of knowledge. For example, the structure of a cell is studied in cytology, that of a society in sociology. Psychologists study the behavior of individuals, political scientists of nations. An embryologist is interested in the development of a fetus, a developmental psychologist of a child, a historian of a society. In this way connections can be seen between the rows of Gerard's matrix. Connections between the columns can also be established. Structure has a distinct influence on function (behavior) and function on evolution, which, in turn, determines changes in structure. For example, on the level of the individual, the structure of its nervous system determines its short-term responses to the

	Structure	Behavior	Evolution
Nation		Political Science	History
Society	Sociology		
Organization		Management Science	
Group		Social Psychology	
Individual	Anatomy	Psychology	Embryology Developmental psychology
Organ		Physiology	
Cell	Cytology		

Figure 17.1. Biological and social science disciplines from the perspective of an organismic system theory.

environment. If the individual is capable of learning, these responses will guide its development, which, in turn, may produce irreversible changes in the nervous system.

Cognitive Implications of the Systemic View

Interrelatedness, *wholeness*, and *analogy* are the three basic concepts on which both the mathematical and the organismic general system theory rest. Awareness of these aspects of reality characterizes the systemic view of the world. It has had a profound effect on modern thought and attitudes. For example, awareness of interrelatedness of practically everything brought some of the dramatic dangers inherent in promiscuous use of technology to the forefront of attention. The climatic changes that turned large areas of the southwestern United States into a dustbowl were traced to attempts to increase arable acreage through deforestation. Initial enthusiasm for insecticides was dampened when their long-term adverse ef-

Table 17–1 (After Norton and Holling 1979)
Development of acaricide resistance in the Australian cattle tick

	Chemical Year introduced	Year in which resistance was widespread
Arsenic	1895	1936
DDT	1946	1955
BHC	1950	1952
Diazinon	1956	1963
Dioxathion	1958	1963
Carbiphenothion	1961	1963
Ethion	1962	1966
Carbaryl	1963	1963
Chlorpyrifos	1967	1970
Bromophosethyl	1967	1970

fects became apparent. Not only did the insecticides introduce toxic substances into the human food chain but they often defeated their own purpose. The decimation of the insect population drastically reduced also the bird population, which eventually resulted in increased rather than decreased populations of insect pests, on which the birds fed.

Aside from producing unintended and unwanted changes in the ecological balance, insecticides soon lost their effectiveness in consequence of adaptive mutations of the target populations. Table 17–1 tells the story.

The derisive term "technological fix" refers not so much to any resort to technology in solving problems as to acting thoughtlessly on the assumption that every effect has a "cause" and that to remove an unwanted effect, one need only find its cause and remove it. "For want of a nail," goes the old adage, "a horseshoe was lost; for want of a horseshoe, a horse was lost . . ." and so on to the loss of a rider, a message, a battle, and a kingdom. This homily illustrates thinking in terms of simple linear chains of causal events: E_1 "causes" E_2, which "causes" E_3, and so on.

Very few events have single causes and very few have single effects. Usually an event is the result of many antecedent events, no single one of which would have been sufficient to produce it. Likewise every event usually has many often unforeseen consequences. Instead of a chain of events $E_1 \Rightarrow E_2 \Rightarrow E_3$ we usually have diverging and converging lines of causality, as shown in Figure 17–2.

We are convinced, on common sense grounds, that causes always precede effects, so that the causal sequence always goes in one direction. This is so if each event occupies only a single moment (a "point" in time). But all events have durations. They are processes rather than happenings. So

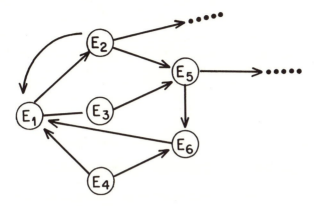

Figure 17.2. A network of causal relations.

there may well be a *mutual* causal relation between events. Event A may be a contributory cause of event B and vice versa. Awareness of this interchangeability of causes and effects should forestall many futile controversies as to what causes what. Are people trapped in poverty because they are "lazy" (i.e., lack motivation to work hard), or is their apathy the result of their poverty? The most reasonable answer is that each condition is a contributory cause of the other. Is the arms race difficult to stop because the superpowers distrust each other or do they distrust each other because each feels threatened by the increasing destructive potential of the other? Both, probably, and there are more contributory factors to each of the "cause-effect" feedback loops.

Failure to anticipate side effects has led to tragedies in applications of new medical technology. These have been dramatic and conspicuous enough to stimulate a radical change of perspective on the potentials of "wonder drugs." Much more extensive research is now done on possible harmful side effects before a new drug is released for general use. Researchers in the fields of pest and crop control are increasingly adopting the systemic view of their problems. It is now realized that many factors are to be taken into account in environmental management. These include, on the one hand, natural phenomena, such as the weather and ecological dynamics and, on the other, interventions.

Awareness of "side effects" is sadly lacking in the scenarios concocted in the defense community. When a nuclear war is depicted as a sequence of "cities exchanges" (cf. Rung #39 on H. Kahn's "escalation ladder," Kahn 1965), a score is kept on the number of cities lost by each side. It may be bizarre to speak of the events concomitant to these "exchanges" as "side effects" (cf. "collateral damage"—a term in the jargon of the defense community). For most people involved, they would be the "main effects." But even granting secondary status to the events that are sure to accompany "city trading" (Kahn's phrase), it seems difficult to believe that the principle of interrelatedness of phenomena (a cardinal principle of the systemic view) can be so hermetically excluded by people who speak knowingly and authoritatively of the vast networks of interdependence that comprise sophisticated weapons systems.

Inertial Properties of Large Systems

Traditionally, historical events have been viewed as results of actions of individuals who were in positions to command large numbers of people. A potentate, moved by ambition or by a grievance, would declare a war. Armies would clash; people would kill each other. One side would emerge victorious, the other defeated. And these events somehow influenced the further course of history. In his novel *War and Peace*, Leo Tolstoy explicitly challenged the view that individuals, however powerful, can affect the course of history. He denied that potentates could start or stop wars by their commands.

A part of Tolstoy's argument is unassailable. The potentate's commands would have no effect if the people he commanded were not already "programmed" (as we would say today) to obey his commands. The potentate's decision, therefore, to launch a war is not a *sufficient* cause of the war. But is it a *necessary* cause? Would that particular war have occurred even if no one gave the command to start it? Obviously, this question cannot be answered, because history cannot be rerun to see what would have happened under different conditions. From the perspective of the systemic view, however, some credence can be given to Tolstoy's theory.

Writing about the invasion of Russia by the French in 1812, Tolstoy compares it to previous invasions, for example, by the Mongols in the thirteenth century. The Mongol aggressive migrations were led by chiefs such as Genghis Khan and Tamerlane. It seems reasonable to suppose that there were powerful *systemic* causes of the invasions. Ecological changes in the grasslands of Central Asia may have produced strong population pressures, in consequence of which populations *moved in masses*. And since their coming would not be welcomed by the inhabitants of the lands they passed through, their movement took on the shape of pillage and massacre. Any organized action by large masses of people requires leadership, which consequently emerges. Tolstoy surmised that something of the sort happened in France. He thought Napoleon was only a figurehead who no more "caused" the invasion by the French of Russia than the figurehead on the prow of a ship causes the ship to move.

Tolstoy's systemic view of history cannot be dismissed out of hand. Recall the unfolding of events in the last days of July 1914. Neither the German nor the Russian mobilization could be stopped, no matter how powerful the Czar and the Kaiser appeared to be. The war machine, a system par excellence, once started, could not be stopped, at least not in time. It possessed an enormous "inertia."

Something of the sort may be happening in our time. Thinking in the traditional "voluntaristic" mode, we may believe that the American President or the Soviet General Secretary can, by issuing proper orders, stop or reverse the arms race. But is this so? If these orders came out of the blue, say as results of a sudden "conversion" or insight, would they be likely to be obeyed? Are the people who would have to pass these orders on "programmed" to obey *any* orders of the President or the General Secretary? Or will they obey only *some* kinds of orders, those that harmonize with the state of the system at the time?

Adam Smith's great insight into the operation of the "invisible hand" amounted to a discovery that large systems have properties quite unlike the properties of their constituent parts. Recall that in Smith's model of the free market, every producer, consumer, buyer, or seller acted apparently in the pursuit of his own interests without considering the interests of anyone else. Yet the whole activity resulted (Smith supposed) in benefits to everyone. If the free market system worked as Smith thought it worked, then the problem of social justice would be solved quite independently of whether the individuals comprising the society were "just" or not.

This picture also has an obverse side, noted later by the critics of the capitalist system. The gross economic inequities of the system were seen to be not the results of the capitalists' "greed," "callousness," or any other sentiment. The property of the *system* was said to be such that the rich in it would become ever richer and the poor ever poorer. The fact that in the Western world this ever-sharper polarization between the rich and the poor did not materialize may be evidence of the inadequacy of the theory as it was originally formulated. But this should not detract from the significance of the insight inspired by the systemic view, namely, that large systems acquire a dynamic and an inertia of their own, insensitive to actions of either malevolent or benevolent individuals. The prognosis derived from Marxist economics may still be realized on the larger global scale. In the decades since the emergence of states from the colonial system, the rich states (i.e., the industrialized countries) have been getting richer and the poor states (the so-called "developing" countries) have been getting poorer. It is quite apparent that no amount of philanthropy can provide a

quick fix to the situation. It is inherent in the dynamics of the present
global economic system.

Finally, we see the enormous inertial forces that seem to make the global
war system unresponsive to attempts to put it under constraints. One looks
in vain for an explanation of this resistance in the psychological makeup
of the individuals who seem to be the actors. Occasionally one finds ar-
rogance, callousness, and megalomania in the highest echelons of leadership. But one cannot help wondering whether Tolstroy was not right
after all. The system is governed by formidable forces over which no individual, no matter how powerful he seems, can exercise control. What is
happening is that individuals most attuned to the dynamics of the global
war machine are selected into the highest positions of leadership, where
they can act "naturally" and give the impression that they are influencing
the course of history.

Legitimizing the Biological Metaphor

Turning to the organismic models of systems, we see that they have conferred a certain legitimacy on views that are routinely called "anthropomorphic." In the writings of international relations specialists it is
customary to find statements about states endowed with human characteristics. "Germany was determined to . . ."; "Britain could not allow . . ."; "It was Russia's age-old dream to . . ." Objections to this way
of speaking rest on the argument that countries are not sentient beings and
therefore cannot have ambitions, desires, or dreams. At most, if such
assertions mean anything, it has been argued, they are just a way of saying
that the *rulers* of the countries manifested intentions, determinations, or
sentiments. The impressions we get about the thoughts of human individuals other than ourselves are all based on inferences that we make when
we observe their behavior. We *attribute* inner life to others, because they
are "like us."

A conspicuous example of a fruitful analogy suggested by organismic
system theory is between the nervous system of an organism and the communication system of an institution. This analogy is developed in great
detail and with profound insight by K.W. Deutsch (1963) in his *Nerves of
Government*. Analogies between a society and an organism go back to the
Middle Ages. At times, as stated previously, the monarch was identified
with the head (we still speak of heads of states), the army with arms, the
peasantry with the back, the church with the heart, etc. Analogies of this
sort have little or no theoretical leverage: once the comparisons have been
suggested, there is nothing to be inferred. In contrast, Deutsch's compar-

ison of the communication network of a government with the nervous system of an organism does suggest further exploration. In particular, the mathematical theory of information can be applied both to describing some aspects of the working of a nervous system and to some aspects of the working (or limitations) of a communication network connecting the various decision centers of an institution, e.g., of a government. Certain pathologies induced by deficiencies in neural function seem to have their counterparts in crises and failures affecting the working of a government.

Every metaphor contains an analogy. So does every scientific generalization. The reason scientific generalizations are taken more seriously than other types of analogies is because the analogies that underlie scientific generalizations are usually subjected to rigorous tests. Other analogies—for example, poetic metaphors—are not subject to such tests; nor do they need to be tested. Poetic metaphors *call attention* to something that may have escaped us and give us pleasure in new awareness. This pleasure is the essence of the appreciation of poetry. What poetic analogies and analogies generated by organismic system theory have in common is that both come into being by acts of *recognition*. In contrast, the analogies contained in isomorphic mathematical models are arrived at by *analysis*. Here we see the basic difference between the analytically oriented and the organismically oriented systemic view. They complement each other.

18

Arms Races

Negative Feedback

Negative feedback loops are regulating mechanisms that keep the state variables of a system within certain limits. The thermostat is a simple example of such a mechanism. When the temperature in a room falls below a certain preset point, the level of mercury in a thermometer falls below a certain critical value. This activates a switch turning a furnace on. The operation of the furnace makes the room warmer; as the temperature rises, the mercury level rises. When it passes a certain preset point, the furnace is turned off, and the room cools. In this way, the temperature of the room, a "state" of the system, is kept between the two critical values.

The same sort of mechanism keeps a person comfortable under an electric blanket. Here the person can become a component of the system. When one gets cold, one turns a knob increasing the current through the blanket. This makes the blanket warmer. When one gets too hot, one turns the knob in the opposite direction to reduce the current and cool the blanket.

Positive Feedback

Imagine a man and his wife sleeping under electric blankets, each with its own control. Each spouse regulates the temperature to suit his/her taste.

But now suppose some practical joker switched the controls, so that the knob on the man's side controls the current in the woman's blanket and vice versa. Suppose now the man feels too cool. He turns the knob thinking that this will make his blanket warmer. Instead he makes his wife's blanket warmer. Now she feels too warm and turns her knob to make her blanket cooler. Instead, she makes her husband's blanket cooler. Instead of getting warmer, the man is colder than before. So he turns the knob in the same direction (thinking this will make him warmer). He makes his wife still warmer! She turns her knob and makes her husband still colder. This process will continue until either a fuse is blown or one of the spouses realizes what is happening.

The arrangement we have just described contains a *positive feedback* loop. Here a disturbance from a steady state releases a process which *increases* the disturbance instead of reducing it. We can see that negative feedback loops characterize stable systems which can preserve states close to equilibria. Positive feedback loops characterize unstable systems, which cannot maintain themselves in a steady state.

A Simple Mathematical Model of an Arms Race

British meteorologist Lewis F. Richardson pioneered the field of study now called "peace research." In one of his early works (Richardson 1960a) he proposed a mathematical model of a system that shared some characteristics with an arms race. The system has both positive and negative feedback loops.

Imagine two countries, X and Y, each apprehensive about the intentions of the other. Each seeks "security" by building up an arsenal. We will call x the destructive potential of X's arsenal and correspondingly y the destructive potential of Y's arsenal.

Now X is motivated to increase its arsenal by the existence of Y's destructive potential and vice versa. For simplicity, suppose that the *rate of increase* of the arsenal of each is proportional to the level of the other's arsenal at that moment. The rate of change of x is denoted by dx/dt, that is, the ratio of dx, which is a small change in x, to dt, representing a small interval of time. The ratio can be positive (representing increase) or negative (representing decrease). To say that this rate is proportional to the level (y) of Y's arsenal, write dx/dt = ay, where a is a constant of proportionality. Actually, however, what motivates X to change the level of its arsenal (according to Richardson's model) is not the absolute level of Y's arsenal, but rather the "gap" between the level of Y's arsenal and that of its own. This gap could be represented by the difference of the levels. More generally, it could be represented by a *weighted* difference, where the weights would correspond to the relative importance X assigns to the level of Y's arsenal and to that of its own. Thus, we can write $dx/dt = ay - mx$, where m is another constant. (Here a is the weight X assigns to the threat represented by y, and m the weight it assigns to the "security" represented by x (its own arsenal level). The situation of Y is similar. It is represented by an analogous equation: $dy/dt = bx - ny$. Here b is the "threat" constant corresponding to X's a, and n the "security" constant corresponding to X's m. To complete Richardson's model of an arms race, we add constant terms to the rates of change to represent contributions to these rates of change of the arsenals independent of their levels. For instance, these additional constants, g and h, could represent standing "grievances" that the countries have against each other. Or else they could represent reservoirs of "goodwill." The system is now represented by a pair of *differential equations*:[1]

$$dx/dt = ay - mx + g$$
$$dy/dt = bx - ny + h.$$

A *state* of this system is now represented by the values of the pair of variables x and y. (They are variables, because they change with time.) There is, however, among these values, one pair of values that represents an *equilibrium* of the system when x and y remain constant. Clearly, dx/dt and dy/dt, the rates of change, are then equal to zero. If, therefore, we set the right sides of the above equations equal to zero and solve the resulting *algebraic* equations for x and y, we shall determine the values of the arsenal levels (if such exist) at which the arms race has "stabilized" itself. Such a pair of values does indeed exist if the straight lines represented by the two algebraic equations intersect, i.e., are not parallel. Since the lines are parallel only for special values of a, b, m, and n, we will assume that this is not the case. However, whether the arms race stabilizes at the intersection of the two lines representing the equilibrium of the system depends on another condition, to be described below.

We will find the intersection of the two lines graphically. That is, we will plot the two lines in a two-dimensional space, where the horizontal coordinate represents the values of x and the vertical the values of y. We note that the slopes of both lines are positive since the signs of the x and the y terms are opposite. Figure 18–1 shows the plots when the slope of the line $ay - mx + g = 0$ is larger than that of $bx - ny + h = 0$.

The rates of change of x and y are zero at the intersection of the two lines. Let us now see what happens when x and y assume values that are not at the intersection. One such point is shown as (x_0, y_0) in Figure

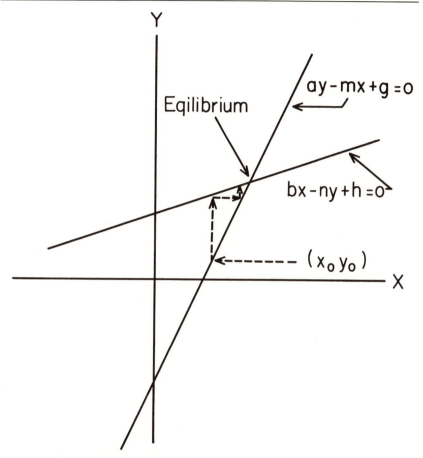

Figure 18.1. Richardson's arms race model. The stable case: the system tends toward equilibrium from any initial state.

18–1. The rates of change of x and y are always such that the system "tries" to reach one or the other straight line. In our case, the horizontal movement of the state of the system is "controlled" by X, the vertical component by Y. We can break up the movement into a sequence of small horizontal and vertical shifts. These are shown in Figure 18–1 by the broken dotted lines. We see that eventually the state of the system will approach the intersection of the two lines. It can be shown that this will be the case wherever we choose our initial state, i.e., the point (x_0, y_0). In this sense, the intersection of the two lines in Figure 18–1 represents a *stable equilibrium*. All deviations of the system from this equilibrium tend to be "corrected." Therefore, the arms race represented by this model will stabilize

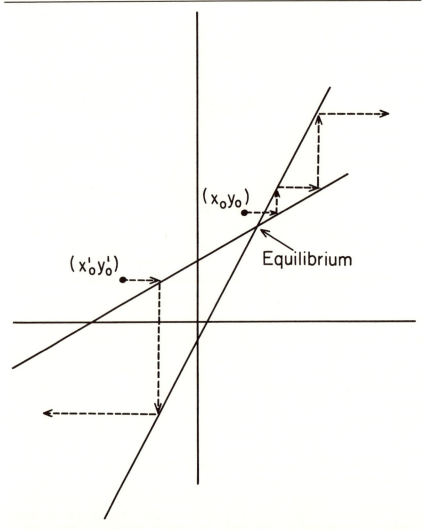

Figure 18.2. Richardson's arms race model. The unstable state: the slightest disturbance at equilibrium drives the system away from equilibrium toward either a runaway arms race or disarmament, depending on the initial state.

itself at a certain pair of values of x and y, the levels of the two arsenals.

Let us now examine the case where the slope of the line $bx - ny + h = 0$ is larger than that of $ay - mx + g = 0$. This situation is shown in Figure 18–2.

If we now represent the motion of the point (x, y) from some initial position not on the intersection of the two lines by successive horizontal and vertical displacements, we find that the point moves *away* from the intersection, making the numerical values of x and y ever larger, driving them either toward positive or toward negative infinity. This is the *unstable* case. Theoretically, the armament levels could remain constant at the equilibrium since their rates of change would both be zero at that state. However, the slightest deviation in one direction or the other would be magnified, and the state of the system would "take off" either toward positive or toward negative infinity. The direction in which it would "take off" would be determined by where it started from. This is shown in Figure 18–2. Starting at the point (x_0, y_0), the trajectory goes toward positive infinity; starting at (x_0', y_0'), toward negative infinity.

We must now interpret these purely mathematical inferences in terms of the content of the model. We have allowed for the possibility that the variables x and y assume either positive or negative values. In the context of the original meanings assigned to these variables (destructive potentials of arsenals), negative values seem to make no sense. If, however, more abstract meanings are assigned to the variables, an interpretation of negative values becomes possible. Let x and y stand for "degrees of hostility" of the rival countries toward each other. This interpretation has some bearing on the original meaning since the destructive potential of an arsenal intended to be used in the event of war with the rival country could be interpreted as a measure of hostility (or, perhaps of fear, which is related to hostility). If, then, positive values of x and y reflect degrees of hostility, negative values can be assumed to reflect the opposite attitude, namely, degrees of "goodwill." Richardson interpreted positive values of x and y as the respective excesses of the armament budgets over trade volumes between the two countries. Consequently, negative values would stand for excesses of trade volumes over armament budgets. In Boulding's conception (cf. Boulding 1974) arsenal levels reflect intensities of a threat relationship, trade volumes the intensities of an exchange relationship. Since threats are related to conflict, while exchanges promote cooperation, we see that Richardson's model incorporates a quantification of Boulding's notions.

We have seen that the constants g and h in the differential equations above represent "chronic hostility," if positive, and reservoirs of "goodwill," if negative. If both x and y were equal to zero (no arsenals, no trade), g and h would represent the rates of buildup of armaments (if positive) or of trade (if negative) when both X and Y are disarmed.

Next, we examine the conditions under which a system represented by Richardson's model will be stable or unstable. From Figures 18–1 and 18–2, it appears that the system will be stable if the slope of the line ay − mx + g = 0 is larger than that of line bx − ay + h = 0. Now the slope of the former line is given by m/a, of the latter by b/n. The condition m/a>b/n is equivalent to mn>ab. We conclude that the system will be stable in that case. If, on the other hand, mn<ab, the system will be unstable.

The interpretation of these conditions in terms of the meanings assigned to the parameters a, b, m, and n is straightforward. Recall that a and b are the "threat" parameters. They represent the sensitivity of X and Y respectively to the level of the adversary's arsenal. On the other hand, m and n are the "security" parameters. They represent respectively the importance that X and Y assign to the already-existing levels of their own arsenals. Thus we see that the condition of stability expressed mathematically by the inequality mn>ab can be interpreted to mean that the system is stable if the countries' confidence in their levels of arsenals already attained is sufficiently greater than their sensitivity to the levels of the adversaries' arsenals. This interpretation seems to make intuitive sense.

Richardson believed that the success of mathematical methods used in constructing theories of physical phenomena could be replicated in the social sciences. Being a meteorologist, he appreciated the difficulties of weather prediction. But in view of the reliability of physical laws, it appeared clear that these difficulties stemmed not from gaps in our understanding of physical phenomena but only from their complexity in specific situations. Richardson believed that these difficulties could be overcome as the mathematical models of social phenomena became more sophisticated and the mathematical methods of solving complex systems of equations became more powerful. For this reason, it seemed reasonable to him to begin with some very simple models of social phenomena (the above model of an arms race being an example) and gradually "build them up." The development of the approach would have to be coupled with putting successive models to empirical tests. Comparison of mathematically derived and observed trajectories of the systems represented by the models would suggest the direction of development. Such comparisons could be carried out only if the variables comprising the model represented observable quantities. It was for this reason that Richardson represented "degrees of hostility and of goodwill" by armament budgets and trade volumes respectively.

Richardson's model attracted some attention because it "fit" the arms race that preceded World War I. The adversaries were the Allies on one side and the Central Powers on the other. Richardson took the combined armament budgets of Russia and France to represent the "hostility" of the Allies and those of Germany and Austria-Hungary as an index of theirs. Further, he set the "threat parameters" of the two sides (a and b) equal

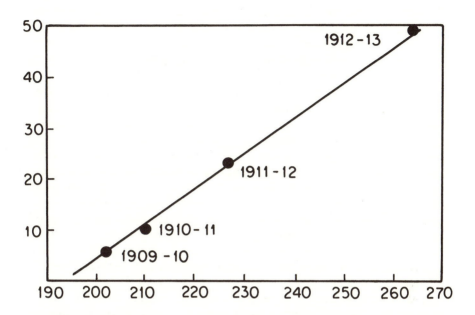

Figure 18.3. The arms race of 1909–1913. Horizontal coordinates: military expenditures of Allies and Central Powers in millions of pounds sterling. Vertical coordinates: yearly increases in combined military expenditures. According to Richardson's model, the four points should fall on a straight line.

to each other, likewise the "security parameters" (m and n). This simplification led to the single prediction of the model, namely, that successive *increases* in the combined budgets, when plotted against the combined budgets should fall on a straight line. Four successive yearly increases, 1909–1910, 1910–1911, 1911–1912, and 1912–1913 were plotted against the combined budgets in 1909, 1910, 1911, and 1912. The four points indeed fell on a straight line corroborating the prediction of the model. The plot is shown in Figure 18–3.

Critique

A sober evaluation of this "success" shows it to be anything but impressive. Actual "predictions" concerned only two of the four points of the plot, because two points were used to determine the straight line on which the points were supposed to fall. That the remaining two points did fall on this straight line does constitute a corroboration of the model, although clearly a rather weak one, because coincidence could not be confidently ruled out.

Another weakness of the model is revealed in its ad hoc feature. The start of the arms race could have been taken a year or two earlier. In assessing the military budgets of the opposing blocs, Britain might have been included on the allied side and Turkey on the side of the Central Powers. Would the agreement between the model and the data have been as good if the model were extended in this way? If not, was Richardson not guilty of selecting his data bases in a way most favorable to the model?

Richardson's approach can be viewed with justifiable skepticism, but only if the main purpose of constructing the model is assumed to have been that of predicting time courses of arms races. Regardless of how Richardson himself viewed his approach, its value lies not in its predictive power but rather in the conceptual framework it suggests for a systematic study of arms races and related phenomena. Within this framework important questions can be asked. For instance:

1. Can anything be said about the likelihood that an arms race can be stabilized at some equilibrium state?
2. Is mutual stimulation a necessary feature of an arms race?
3. How does one go about singling out the most relevant quantifiable variables in an arms race?

In fitting his model to data, Richardson had to estimate the "threat" and the "security" parameters. Recall that a necessary and sufficient condition for the stability of the system is that the product of the security parameters be larger than the product of the threat parameters. The estimated values of the parameters did not satisfy the condition of stability. Consequently, if the model was an adequate representation of the arms race, the situation must have been unstable.

It is difficult to imagine how an arms race could attain a stable equilibrium. Stability would mean that any deviation would be corrected. Suppose one of the adversaries "accidentally" increases his armament level above the equilibrium level. If the equilibrium were stable, this would mean that his tendency to *reduce* his armaments (in order to restore the equilibrium) would have to be stronger than the tendency of his adversary to "catch up." Conventional conceptions of national security being what they are, such a situation seems to be most unlikely.

Let us assume that instability is an inherent characteristic of arms races, i.e., that arms races are fueled predominantly by positive feedbacks. If Richardson's model is adequate, this instability has an obverse side, not usually taken into account. Namely, should a deviation from an (unstable) equilibrium occur in the direction of *reduced* armaments, a positive feedback process would also set in. Disarmament would proceed at an accelerated pace! That such a process has not been observed may mean that Richardson's simplistic model is not adequate (which is quite likely). Nonetheless, the *possibility* of a "disarmament race" is suggested by the model.

Such a possibility actually occurred to Richardson. Having noted that his model implied that the system was unstable, he argued that, had the "initial condition" prior to World War I been different, the process may have gone in the opposite direction toward disarmament, increased cooperation, possibly a united Europe.

There is no way of rerunning history. But the idea that the very instability of arms races makes a "disarmament race" possible need not be discarded. In human affairs, frequently what becomes thinkable becomes realizable. The fact that this principle applies typically to disasters should not turn our attention from the possibility of effecting a recovery from our present predicament.

Further Implications of Richardson's Model

In Richardson's model, mutual stimulation plays a crucial role. It is the threat parameters that drive the arms race. The security parameters, which represent the influence of one's *own* armament levels, *inhibit* the escalation. It is, however, possible to formulate a model of an arms race, where the level of one's own armaments stimulates further increases. Wagner *et al.* (1975) compared the trajectories derived from such a self-stimulating model with those derived from a Richardsonian mutual stimulation model. They found that the former fit the Arab-Israeli arms race of 1950–1970 better than the latter. The question immediately arises whether a self-stimulation model can be reasonably interpreted. It can in terms of the so-called "technological imperative." As we have seen, advances in one sector of technology depend on those in other sectors and, in turn, stimulate advances in still others. For example, development of intercontinental ballistic missiles has depended on advances in computer technology. Conversely, breakthroughs in computer technology suggested designs of self-guiding missiles that would not have been imagined otherwise. Thus, war technology has a built-in stimulant. Its growth could, in principle, proceed at an accelerated pace independently of threats in the form of advances in an adversary's war technology. Of course, both kinds of stimulation may be operating simultaneously.

It must be stressed that comparison of models in this context should not be regarded as a way of refining the theory. The actual context precludes any such refinement, simply because the processes represented by the

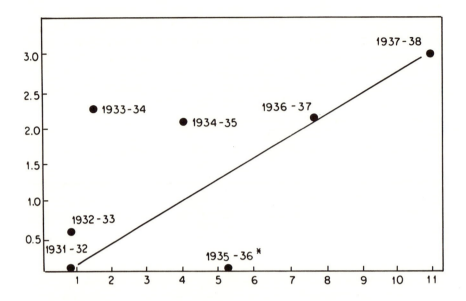

Figure 18.4. The Soviet-German arms race of 1932–1938. Horizontal coordinates: combined military expenditures in billions of old U.S. gold dollars. Vertical coordinates: yearly increases in combined military expenditures. The combined expenditures showed a *decrease* (in gold dollars) from 1935 to 1936; so the point should fall slightly below the axis (cf. Richardson, 1960b, p. 115).

models are far too complex to permit delicate quantitative "tuning" of the theory, which advanced mathematical methods have made possible in the exact sciences. The principal value of the models is heuristic. They suggest questions. Attempts to answer the questions often lead to other questions. In this way, one's own view of the phenomena under scrutiny becomes more sophisticated. One understands more in spite of the low predictive powers of the theory developed.

It is instructive to follow Richardson's attempts to find proper quantitative indices, in terms of which arms races could be systematically described. The problem arose after the abandonment of the gold standard by most countries in the 1930s. In the absence of a common monetary unit, comparison of military budgets of different countries became meaningless. At first, Richardson tried to translate the armament expenditures into equivalent gold units. The resulting plot of the Soviet-German arms race of 1912–1938 turned out to be wildly erratic (cf. Figure 18–4).

After much trial and error, Richardson finally arrived at a unit based

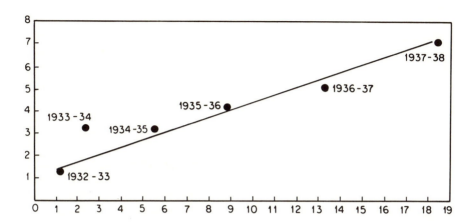

Figure 18.5. The Soviet-German arms race of 1932–1938. Horizontal coordinates: combined defense budgets expressed in million person-years. Vertical coordinates: yearly increases in the same units. The resulting fit to Richardson's model is much better than when the budgets are expressed in gold dollars (cf. Richardson, 1960b, p. 137).

on work time. In terms of these units, the Soviet-German arms race fit Richardson's model, though not nearly as well as the arms race of 1909–1913. The plot is shown in Figure 18–5.

Again we are led to view Richardson's approach with considerable ambivalence. On the one hand, the value of the model seems to have been enhanced: it seems to "point" to the proper index to be used as a measure of war expenditures, namely, work time. In fact, in bringing out this idea (which "restores" the validity of the model in a changed economic environment), it seems to corroborate the labor theory of value, on which Marxist economics is based. On the other hand, a skeptic might point out that if one searched long enough and wide enough for an index in terms of which the model could be corroborated, one would eventually be bound to find one; but this sort of corroboration would not be very convincing. It is always possible to find a pattern to fit one's preconceived notions. But then everyone's preconceived notions can be corroborated in this manner. Superstitions are based on just such "corroborations."

The "Qualitative" Arms Race

The difficulties of quantifying arms races were first thought to be related to the problem of finding the "right" index. Richardson first tried a gold monetary unit, then tried other indices, finally settling on work time. Nuclear weapons and especially delivery systems that coevolved with them made the indices related to all forms of expenditures all but irrelevant. In terms of their destructive power, nuclear weapons are actually cheaper than conventional weapons. ("More bang for a buck; more rubble for a ruble.") The resulting ambiguities have provided opportunities to apologists of the present Soviet-American arms race to deny its existence altogether by pointing to actual reductions in arms budgets that were observed in particular periods of time. In the same way, the Soviet-German arms race of the 1930s could have been denied by pointing to the drastic reduction of Soviet expenditures in terms of *gold* units in the middle of the decade.

A. Wohlstetter went to great lengths to challenge the interpretation of the arms race by some of its opponents. He cites instances when American strategic analysts actually underestimated rather than overestimated Soviet capabilities, thus refuting the charge that the American military establishment consistently exaggerates the Soviet threat in order to fuel the arms race. Wohlstetter dismisses critics of the arms race by pointing out the difficulties of pinning down the relevant indices:

> When we talk of "arms" are we referring to the total budget spent on strategic forces? The number of strategic vehicles or launchers? The number of weapons? The total explosive energy that could be released by all the strategic weapons? The aggregate destructive area of these weapons? Or are we concerned with qualitative change—that is alterations in unit performance characteristics—the speed of an aircraft or missile, its accuracy, the blast resistance of its silo, the concealability of the launch point, the scale and sharpness of optical photos or other sensing devices, the controllability of a weapon and its resistance to accidental or unauthorized use? When we talk of a "race" what do we imply about the rate at which the race is run, about the ostensible goal of the contest, about how the race is generated, about the nature of the interaction among strategic adversaries? (Wohlstetter 1974.)

All of these questions emphasize the futility of describing the arms race by some neat model and of drawing unambivalent conclusions from the description, such as one might wish to draw in order to call attention to the inherent dangers of arms races. By pointing out the complexities of the process, Wohlstetter implicitly disqualifies persons not versed in the intricacies of strategic considerations to pass judgment on the overall mean-

Table 18–1

Factors of increase in the different dimensions of the "quality of weapons" and of the "quality of life" from 1945 to 1985. (Source: Sivard 1985.)

Quality of Life		Quality of Weapons	
Longevity	1.3	Fire Power	24
Literacy	2	Speed of delivery	42
Income	2	Lethality	200
Education	4	Area of destruction	250
Suffrage	5	Range	262

ing of the arms race and on the dangers associated with it. For example, he points out (correctly) that just how an arms race is bound to "explode" in a war is not spelled out in any of the models, thereby throwing doubt on the "alarmist" aspects of arms race theories.[2]

A characteristic feature of the systemic approach is that it often deliberately ignores details in order to see the "big picture." As an example, consider the changes in weapons during the forty years from 1945 to 1985. It takes several dimensions to quantify these changes. For these reasons, they may be regarded as "qualitative" rather than "quantitative" (i.e., one-dimensional). An elusive concept like the "quality of life" can also be quantified on several dimensions. To decide whether an arms race actually took place in the forty years following World War II, we might compare the changes in the "quality of weapons" with changes in the "quality of life" during the period. The comparison is shown in Table 18–1.

In view of these "gross" effects unencumbered by at times bewildering details, it seems safe to answer the question that serves as the title of Wohlstetter's article ("Is There a Strategic Arms Race?") in the affirmative. At most Wohlstetter's critique refutes the oversimplified image of the arms race as a mindless compulsion-driven rush, an addiction to massive piling up of bombs. He calls attention to the intricacies of strategic assessments, to the growing realization that "quality" not quantity is decisive for killing ability, to the necessities generated by multi-pronged technological advances, in other words to the *rationales* of the arms race. None of these arguments, however, can disguise the gross overall burgeoning growth of destructive potential. As for "how the race is generated," the chronology speaks for itself.

Table 18–2 shows the sequence of innovations since 1945, as they were introduced by the United States and by the Soviet Union.

For the most part, it seems, the United States has played the leading role in the arms race in the sense of introducing technical innovations. The

Table 18–2
The "qualitative" arms race (after Craig and Jungerman 1986)

Date of innovation by U.S.	Weapons system	Date of innovation by U.S.S.R.	Initiator of innovation
1945	Atomic bomb	1949	U.S.
1948	Intercontinental bomber	1955	U.S.
1954	Deliverable hydrogen bomb	1955	U.S.
1958	Satellite in orbit[3]	1957	U.S.S.R.
1960	Submarine based ballistic missile	1968	U.S.
1970	Antiballistic missile	1968	U.S.S.R.
1972	MIRV	1975	U.S.
1982	Long-range cruise missiles	198?	U.S.

Soviet Union appears to have played the role of the follower, constantly trying to catch up. These roles are amply reflected in the rhetoric of the spokesmen for the governments. The emphasis in American rhetoric is on world leadership, on American moral superiority, on identification of moral superiority with strength (the "good guys" always win in American fantasies). Bellicose rhetoric reached its peak in the U.S. with the advent of the Reagan administration. Direct evidence of public support for the sharp change of style can be seen in the assessment of military expenditures. Figure 18–6 shows plots of proportions of American respondents in an opinion poll who felt that "too little" and "too much" was spent on "defense." In 1969, at the height of the Vietnam war, the majority (55%) thought military expenditures were excessive and only a small minority (10%) thought they were insufficient. In 1980, the proportions were reversed: 60% thought the expenditures were too small and only 10% thought they were too large. After Reagan's inauguration in 1981, the trends were again reversed (although the "too little" plot was still above the "too much" plot). The reversal was undoubtedly due to the drastic increase in military spending.

Turning to Soviet rhetoric, we note that it emphasizes "defense" in its literal, not euphemistic sense. The driving force of Soviet addiction to military might is *not* a vision of world domination, regardless of the persistent attribution of this vision to them in Western rhetoric, regardless of the expansionist policies of czarist Russia, and even regardless of the creation of the postwar satellite empire and support of so-called wars of national liberation. The mentality of defense, nurtured by a chronic fear of encirclement, of being a *specific* target of attack, is evident to anyone

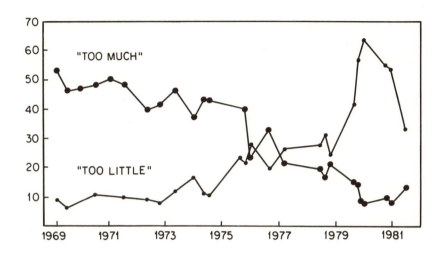

Figure 18.6. After Russett, 1983. Percentages of respondents in U.S. judging current military expenditures to be "too much" and "too little."

who cares to wade through the monumental output of Soviet rhetoric on this theme.

In sum, if the affects associated with the U.S.–U.S.S.R. arms race are compared, the mood prevalent in the U.S. is akin to euphoria—an intoxication with power conferred on the world's greatest, most virtuous, most free—by superior technology and unlimited resources to develop it beyond every imaginable horizon. The mood prevalent in the Soviet Union is grim. It is dominated by fear—fear of being "left behind," of being beaten because of one's "backwardness." This mood was already apparent in the feverish, chaotic forced industrialization of the 1930s. It was clearly reflected in Stalin's slogan, "The backward are beaten" (*"Otstalykh b'yut"*). As Stalin vividly pointed out, the Russians were beaten by the Tartars, the Teutonic knights, the French, and the Germans—beaten because of their "backwardness" (in Stalin's view). The lesson seemed obvious: Never again! The fear that if the Soviet Union "falls behind," it will be crushed, is real. Indices of military might are clear and objective. They can be constantly monitored. Keeping up provides concrete reassurance. Hence the key to "security" was always seen to be technology. Everything was subordinated to its growth. The formidable growth of industrial potential in the 1930s at the cost of immense sacrifices of human welfare was funneled mainly into military technology.

In spite of the very different psychological and ideological bases of Amer-

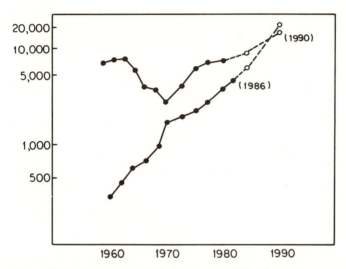

Figure 18.7. After Craig and Jungermann, 1986. The nuclear arms race. Vertical coordinates: numbers of nuclear warheads (logarithmic scale). Lower curve: the Soviet arsenal. Upper curve: the U.S. arsenal. The curves were projected from 1984 to 1986 and 1990.

ican and Soviet technolatry, the gross visible effects of these orientations are strikingly similar. The proverbial Martian, who sees only these gross effects and is unable by virtue of his wholly alien psychology to recognize or understand human motivations, would simply record the time courses of the conspicuous variables to get an overview of the process, which he would interpret in terms of *his* preconceptions.

This is what the system-oriented investigator does. Let us look at some of those records, which give us an immediate impression of what is happening on the grand scale.

Figure 18–7 shows the growth of the U.S. and U.S.S.R. strategic nuclear arsenals from 1960 to 1985, extrapolated to 1990.

Note that the vertical coordinates of the plots are given on a logarithmic scale. This means that a time course that looks like a straight line on such a graph is in reality exponential. Note also that between about 1962 and 1970, the arsenal level of the U.S. was actually *decreasing*. These data lend credence to the claim sometimes made by the protagonists of the U.S. position that an attempt was actually made by the U.S. to reverse the arms race. At the same time, however, the rate of growth of the Soviet arsenal was at its maximum (shown by the steepness of the curve in those years).

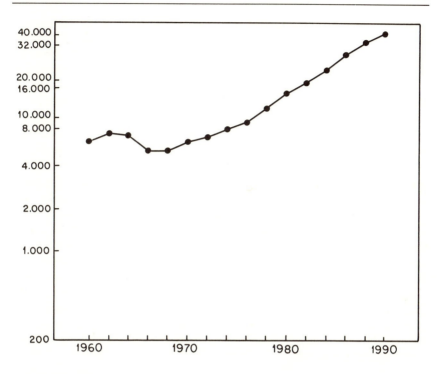

Figure 18.8. The nuclear arms race. Vertical coordinates: total numbers of U.S. and S.U. warheads projected to 1990. After about 1970, the curve is reasonably well fitted by a straight line on the logarithmic scale, corroborating Richardson's model.

This can be and has been used as evidence that the Soviet Union did not respond to the American attempt to reverse the arms race and that consequently the U.S. "had no choice" but to resume the race.

Suppose, however, our Martian looks at the process with an even lower resolving power. That is, he records not the trajectories of the two arsenals separately but lumps them together in a single trajectory. (This is what Richardson did when he tested his model of the 1909–1913 arms race.) The trajectory of the combined U.S.–U.S.S.R. arsenal is shown in Figure 18–8. It is an almost perfect straight line on the semi-logarithmic scale and therefore represents an *exponential* growth. Richardson would regard this trajectory as a vindication of his theory.

These results suggest that the farther we get from the arms races, the more similar they appear. This would not be surprising, since looking at the processes with lower resolving power removes details from the field of vision, and it is in these details that the differences are found. Obviously, getting farther away entails loss of information. At the same time, however, this very loss of information may reveal the "essentials" of the process, suggesting that it is driven by the dynamics of the large system in which it is embedded and is insensitive to particular circumstances, predilections of people in power, least of all to rationalizations in terms of which it is justified or criticisms leveled against it. One is forced at least to consider with an open mind an analogy between a system comprising the defense establishments of *both* the U.S. and the U.S.S.R. and a neurotic driven by compulsions of which he is unaware. We know that such compulsions exist because they can be induced experimentally, for example by post-hypnotic suggestion. A subject will act out these induced compulsions after he comes out of the hypnotic trance even though the actions appear to be absurd. When asked to explain them, he will offer equally absurd explanations. The Soviet-American system appears to behave under similar compulsions. Explanations of the behavior of the two superpowers are offered readily and with conviction. But whatever these rationalizations bring out, the overall effect remains the same. The arms race goes on. At times, it seems as if the stage has been set for the two sides to see their common interest. But something always happens to abort the process of de-escalation. An example of such a nearly successful attempt can be seen in the following episode.

When Disarmament Was Almost Within Reach

In January 1952, the United Nations Assembly set up a Disarmament Commission "to prepare proposals to be embodied in a Draft Treaty . . . for the regulation, limitation and balanced reduction of all armed forces and armaments, for the elimination of all major weapons adaptable to mass destruction, and for effective international control of atomic energy to ensure the prohibition of atomic weapons and the use of atomic energy for peaceful purposes only." (Resolution of January 11, 1952.)

Andrei Vyshinsky, the Soviet delegate, said that the proposal made him "laugh all night." Possibly the world reaction to the proposal made Stalin change Vyshinsky's mind. The decision to set up the Commission was carried unanimously.

The Western proposals to the Commission were embodied in six principles. These read in essence as follows.

1. The goal of disarmament is not to regulate but to prevent war.
2. All states must cooperate to achieve this goal.

3. Armed forces of all states must be reduced to limits required only to maintain internal security and to fulfill obligations under the United Nations Charter.
4. All instruments adaptable to mass destruction must be eliminated.
5. An effective system of international control to insure compliance must be instituted.
6. An effective system of continuing disclosure and verification of all armed forces and armaments must be provided for by international agreements.

In March 1953, Stalin died, and for a while hopes were raised that with the demise of his personal dictatorship the Soviet leadership might become more flexible. At that time, the American administration was not yet in the grip of a commitment to an unrestricted arms race, as it was to become later. In 1954, a United Nations Subcommittee on Disarmament consisting of the United States, Britain, France, and the U.S.S.R. met in London to try to achieve some progress toward abolition of nuclear weapons. The Western governments still adhered to the Six Principles. The memorandum laid before the Subcommittee by Britain and France was endorsed by all members except the Soviet Union. Once again, however, the Kremlin changed its mind. Vyshinsky in the last speech before his sudden death declared that the Soviet Union would go along.

The next meeting of the Subcommittee was in February 1955. This time concrete proposals were made by the Western delegates. These reflected the chronic apprehension that elimination of nuclear weapons would leave the Soviet Union with a formidable advantage because of its massive superiority in conventional forces. Accordingly, the Western proposal linked the prohibition of atomic weapons with a progressive reduction of conventional forces. In particular, the new production of all weapons of mass destruction would cease when conventional forces have been reduced by one-half. When these were reduced to one-quarter of their original size, elimination of existing nuclear weapons would begin together with the elimination of the last quarter of conventional forces.

This was on April 19, 1955. The Soviet replied on May 10. They accepted, in effect, the entire package submitted by the West. They also accepted the ultimate objectives of the Six Principles.

On May 12, the American delegate, speaking "as a representative of the United States" said:

> We have been gratified to find that the concepts which we have put forward over a considerable length of time, and which we have repeated many times during the past two months, have been accepted in a large measure by the Soviet Union.

The British delegate was equally gratified. He said he was glad that the Western "policy of patience" had

> . . . now achieved the welcome dividend, and that the proposals of the West have been now largely, and in some cases, entirely, adopted by the Soviet Union and made into its own proposals. (Quoted in Noel-Baker 1958.)

That same month in 1955, the occupation of Austria by the four powers ended and its independence and neutrality recognized. It seemed as if a major breakthrough toward peace was finally achieved.

Systemic Inertia

As this is written, 33 years after the near-breakthrough to peace, the world military stockpile has increased by a factor of at least fifty. What happened? It is easy to suggest answers based on strategic considerations. The Soviets always regarded their conventional forces as a counterweight to American nuclear superiority. Second thoughts about the concrete proposals made by the West (reductions of conventional forces) may have set in and forced a reversal of the Soviets' initial agreement to go along.

Ad hoc explanations of this sort seem less satisfactory against the background of *repeated* failures to halt the massive growth of the global arsenal at times just when it seemed that it could be stopped. A. Myrdal devotes a chapter in her book, *The Game of Disarmament* (1976) to a "History of Lost Opportunities," a dreary account of failures and frustrations, at times apparently of deliberate sabotage of any incipient movement toward the goal that everyone professed to share.[4]

Realization of the futility of war as an instrument of policy became widespread immediately after World War I. Even before that war, attempts had been made to "tame" war by banning "unusually cruel" weapons such as poison gas, dum-dum bullets, and the like. Conventions were signed governing the treatment of prisoners, protection of civilian populations, respect for neutrality, and so on. *All* of these agreements were broken. The treaty guaranteeing the neutrality of Belgium was declared by the Germans to be nothing but a "scrap of paper." Poison gas was introduced on the Western Front less than a year after the outbreak of World War I. In World War II, civilian populations became a principal target of military aviation. Soviet prisoners of war were starved to death by the Germans. The conclusion is inescapable that some sort of *systemic* forces blocked the implementation of all good intentions.

The cause of disarmament suffered the same fate. The covenant of the

League of Nations demanded the reduction of armaments to the lowest level consistent with "national security." A few years later, a Preparatory Disarmament Commission was established whose task was practically identical to that of the Disarmament Commission established by the United Nations in 1952 (cf. above). Both commissions were established just seven years after the ends of World War I and World War II, respectively. Negotiations went on interminably. Apparently, different parties had different ideas about what was consistent with their own (and with others') "national security." Still, an arms control plan prepared by Americans, the so-called Plan of 1932, providing for drastic curtailment of land, sea, and air forces *almost* succeeded. One is strongly tempted to believe that it would eventually have succeeded if it were not for the advent of Hitler in 1933. Interest in arms control dissipated quickly thereafter.

All of these failures when success seemed imminent may have been due to coincidences. Another possible though often discredited interpretation invokes various conspiracy theories. These are not to be altogether discounted, since cases when powerful munition industry interests attempted deliberate sabotage of arms control agreements have been reported. Explanations in terms of massive systemic forces seem to us to carry more weight. We will present two arguments in support of this interpretation, one based on concepts advanced by "organismic" system theory, the other based on statistical considerations.

How a Suicide Appears from the Outside and from the Inside

Imagine a person about to shoot himself. If we know something about his life and the situation he is presently in, we may feel we "understand" what he is about to do. Also the motions he is going through seem purposeful to us. We "understand" why he takes the revolver out of the drawer, checks the chamber, lifts the muzzle to his temple, and presses the trigger. All of these actions are parts of a purposeful act.

Now this person is a living system composed of very many subsystems, all interacting in complex ways with each other. They all participate in the actions that lead to the death of the "supersystem," of which they are constituents. The muscles act in a coordinated manner. Sensory inputs are properly processed. Nerve cells are activated and activate other cells and muscles. Impulses are transmitted as they are supposed to be over nerve fibers. All these activities function *normally*. Only their sum total is a disaster for the total system.

Organismic system theory recognizes the existence of living systems that are themselves composed of living systems. For example, our suicide appears as a composite of cells, organs, and tissues. The systemic aspects of the supersystem (its behavior or its evolution) cannot be understood entirely in terms of the analogous aspects of its components. The supersystem has *emergent* aspects of its own. Thus, the suicide's "purposeful" actions leading to his death are not deducible from the "normal" activities of his organs. It is only in that particular situation that these "normal" activities add up to his death. We can understand the given situation only in terms of the emergent events—the man's mental processes, his emotions—accessible to us, who are beings like him, but inaccessible to the cells that comprise him, systems that seem to go about their normal business.

How Humankind May Look from the Outside

Everything said so far does not seem particularly outlandish and will be accepted by many as a reasonable description of how a suicide looks "from the inside" and "from the outside."

Suppose now an extraterrestrial being (our "proverbial Martian" again) is observing humankind, which he perceives as an organism. To this being, people and their institutions appear as the cells and organs of a human being appear to us. The being sees more than the constituent parts. It sees analogues of mental processes and emotions of the living system, quite inaccessible to us, just as the mental processes and emotions of a human being are inaccessible to the cells and organs that comprise him. We will not assume that these "mental processes" of the organism have any resemblance to those that we directly experience (because they are totally inaccessible to us), but we can imagine that they exist. These "mental processes" may suggest to the extraterrestrial being that humankind is preparing to commit suicide. The elaborate preparations for death are convincing. If this is indeed the case, then the events that seem to us fortuitous snags, blocking the attempts to stop the arms race, are perceived by suicidal humanity as hindrances in the way of intended action. They are "removed" as they appear.

The above scenario is offered as a stimulant to thought rather than as an explanation. In particular, it is worthwhile pondering the question of what drives any apparent compulsion. We know that such compulsions do govern the behavior of individual human beings. We recognize some of them as pathological, and we realize that some of these are unconscious. Psychoanalytic theories, in particular, postulate such unconscious compulsions, by which they purport to explain instances of behavior which, taken at face value, appear bizarre or counterproductive but which, against the background of unconscious compulsions, are revealed as purposeful. While these theories leave much to be desired as scientific theories, they are not absurd. There is no reason why the implications of a theory of pathological compulsion cannot be examined on the level of humanity as a whole. We do not find the notion fantastic that whole societies can succumb to outbursts of destructive fury. Why should humankind be regarded as immune to this form of pathology?

A Statistical Model of "Mass Compulsion"

Some apparent manifestations of "mass compulsion" can be explained without recourse to fantasizing. Forms of human behavior which on the level of the individual appear to be entirely voluntaristic appear on the level of masses of individuals to be compulsive. An instance was observed in the United States shortly after practically every household became equipped with a television set. In those early years of television, commercials appeared only when programs changed, usually every half-hour on the half-hour. It was noted that at those times, the pressure in the water mains of cities dropped sharply for some minutes and was restored as quickly. It is certainly true that human individuls have the "free will" to go or not to go to the bathroom. The *mass* of such individuals, however, went to the bathroom on command, "by the numbers," as they say in the army.

Much of mass behavior is governed by statistical regularity. Numbers of vehicles on roads at various times are predictable within narrow margins of error, and so are the numbers of traffic fatalities. In fact, the latter can within limits be affected by imposing or relaxing restrictions. For instance, when low speed limits were imposed on American highways during World War II, the numbers of fatalities dropped significantly. As these limits were raised, the fatalities increased. It would seem that tens of thousands of lives could be saved yearly by restricting the speed of automobile travel. The reason this does not happen is because measures of this sort are not politically feasible, and this is also a matter of statistical effects. To become politically feasible, some proposed measure must be acceptable to sufficient numbers of people. These numbers are determined by *systemic* properties of a society. One can, therefore, say with justification that American society values human life (in the context of being jeopardized by automobile traffic) just so much and no more. This "personification" of American society is justified in this instance. It acts *as if* it had a will.

In a similar way, it can be argued that humanity as a whole or at least the portion that currently supports governments engaging in the global arms race "does not want" arms control or disarmament. Again it must be stressed, we are not speaking of what *individuals* "want" or "do not want." It may well be the case that a large majority of individuals "do not want" the continuation, much less the escalation of the arms race. But we are speaking of the resultant of a vast number of interlocking relationships. It is these relationships that *add up* to the support of a process which may be driving the human race to suicide. Here the analogy with the cells of a suicide becomes somewhat more credible.

Of course not all of the "cells" of the organism "humanity" participate in the process. But there are enough of them to insure the "statistical inertia." It seems that only the rulers of the superpowers could put a stop to the arms race by issuing directives. Such directives would have to be implemented and the implementation would have to consist of a large number of actions, most of which would be against the current: contracts canceled, standing directions rescinded, projects discontinued, and the like. It is commonplace to relate resistance to arms control or to disarmament to "interests," by which appetite for profits is usually meant. The "merchants of death" have been repeatedly blamed for arms races and for the wars which they prepared. It is true, for example, that large industrialists supported Hitler in his march to power, and it is reasonable to suppose that a revival of the armament industry was to them an alluring prospect. The American military-industrial complex surely plays a part in maintaining the arms race fever. Greed for profit in the usual sense cannot, however, be a motivating force in the Soviet Union. In spite of the much greater power of the Soviet ruling apparatus, it is almost certain that the resistance of the military establishment could play a significant role in blocking moves toward curbing the growth of the global war machine.

There is more to compulsion than greed for profits. People have other, no less powerful commitments. Some of the strongest in our age are commitments to one's profession, the source of quasi-libidinal gratifications and of ego strength. The same force operates in all societies. We submit that the idea that a "suicidal tendency" in driving the continuing arms race is not as fantastic as it may seem at first glance. It is not very different from other alarming processes, such as the drive to overpopulation and the accelerating degradation of the environment. These, too, may seem to our extraterrestrial being to be suicidal tendencies. Yet on the level of the individual they are nothing of the sort. Everyone goes about his business. The total result is manifested in inexorable trajectories of the global system: the Malthusian population curve, the increasing concentration of pollutants in the atmosphere, in the waters, and in the soil—in particular, the increased concentration of carbon dioxide, which through the greenhouse effect threatens to produce disastrous climatic changes. Adam Smith's invisible hand, which in the free market is supposed to aggregate all apparently selfish actions into a collective optimum, here produces an opposite effect. Everybody is just trying to get along, doing the accustomed things, supporting a family, pursuing a career, doing one's duty for one's country. What all these innocuous activities can add up to is the end of all of us.

Keeping the Arms Race Going

In 1985, the Soviet-American arms race was on the threshold of a new phase. The Americans were planning to extend the theater of war into outer space. The "Strategic Defense Initiative" was being sold to the public as a formidable defensive shield, presumably to protect the United States from nuclear attack and so "make nuclear weapons obsolete." The fatuousness of this selling job is not lost on anyone who is even minimally informed about the nature of the problems involved. But this makes not the slightest difference; the project has been launched. What is most important, politicians, entire governments have been committed, moneys have been dispensed, scientists and technicians recruited. All these activities contribute to the massiveness of the inertia of the process. The more invested in it, the more difficult it will be to stop it.

As if to provide additional evidence for the theory that all efforts to reverse the trend to disaster must fail, the infusion of the new stimulant into the arms race came at a time when a change of leadership in the Soviet Union kindled new hope of a revived detente. M. Gorbachev began a "peace offensive" immediately upon assuming office. His most dramatic moves were successive extensions of a unilateral moratorium on testing nuclear weapons. It is generally recognized that a comprehensive test ban would essentially stop the qualitative arms race, because new weapons cannot be developed without being tested. All the invitations by the Soviet Union to the United States to join in the moratorium were summarily rejected. The Soviets promptly defused the objections by offering to yield to any demands, but this made no difference. The Soviets accepted verification procedures which the U.S. demanded, apparently in the hope that they would be rejected because they had been previously rejected. Then the Americans retreated to a next line of defense. Testing was necessary, they declared, in order to assure the "reliability" of their nuclear weapons. If this assurance is important, it must also be important to the Soviets. It is clear, moreover, that "reliability" of nuclear weapons is a factor in plans for a first strike. "Reliability" of *retaliatory* weapons is not nearly as important, because the mere *existence* of these weapons is supposed to constitute deterrence. If, as has been estimated, the overkill factor of deterrence is 30 or 40, an adversary has only to fear that three percent of the bombs thrown at him will explode.

The United States is no longer concerned with the cogency of its arguments against a comprehensive test ban. Much more to the point is the statement issued by a White House spokesman to the effect that "A nuclear test ban is not in the security interest of the United States, our friends and allies." This answer is like the reason given to a child who persists in asking why he "can't": "Because I said so."

If one were deliberately to design a mechanism that would effectively frustrate any attempt to break out of the vicious cycle generated by the global arms race, one could not do it more effectively. Whenever one side seems to show some sign of coming to its senses, the other becomes adamant. Meanwhile the global arsenal keeps growing quantitatively *and* qualitatively.

Notes

1. Differential equations relate values of variable quantities to the rates of change of these values, in physical problems usually to their rates of change with respect to time. A *solution* of a differential equation or of a system of such equations specifies *how* the variables change with time, that is, the trajectory of the system represented by the equation(s).
2. Although Wohlstetter apparently dismisses the concept of the "arms race" as irrelevant to the present superpower rivalry, he unwittingly suggests specific research problems which were, in fact, taken up by some peace researchers a decade later (cf. Chapter 24 below), which shed further light on the process.
3. The successful launching of a satellite paved the way for the intercontinental ballistic missile. Thus, the lead in this weaponry is usually attributed to the Soviet Union.
4. In another instance, a near-success failed in a way that makes it difficult to dismiss the suspicion that it was wrecked by design. Toward the end of 1959, President Eisenhower announced that the U.S. (following a year of moratorium) would not resume atmospheric testing of nuclear bombs without advance notice. This announcement may have been a veiled invitation to the Soviet Union to extend its own moratorium. Chairman Khrushchev "apparently in response, announced that the Soviets would not resume testing unless the West did so first." Thereupon France started testing in the Sahara, which the Soviets interpreted as a violation of the implicit extension of the moratorium. In the summer of 1960, the flight of an American spy plane over Siberia was a pretext for aborting the summit meeting between Khrushchev and Eisenhower. The ban on atmospheric testing was not effected until 1963 (cf. York 1970, p. 30).

19

Indices, Parameters, and Trends

Quantification, Parameters, and Universal Constants

What we now call the "exact sciences" rest soundly on quantification and measurement. Modern physics was born when Galileo made measurements of the speed of falling bodies and the oscillation frequencies of pendulums. Modern chemistry began when chemical reactions were described in quantitative terms. It is not surprising that methods of quantification and measurement eventually spread to the behavioral and social sciences and that in the minds of many this development was interpreted as a sign of maturation of those sciences.

There is a fundamental difference between the role quantification has played in the physical sciences and the role it is currently playing (and is likely to continue to play) in the social sciences. The quantities singled out for attention in the physical sciences pervade their entire scope. The reason these quantitites appear in all theoretical discussions, always playing the same role, is that they are firmly believed to be reflections of fundamental physical reality embodied in well-nigh immutable laws. These are the conservation laws: conservation of mass and conservation of energy. They assert what remains constant in spite of change. It is these constancies that provide a solid base for all physical theories. In fact, all physical theory is based on assertions that, in spite of change, certain quantities remain constant. The changing quantities are represented by *variables*. The quantities that remain constant in a given context are represented by *parameters*.

In different contexts, the parameters themselves may become variables, but then other "more fundamental" parameters play the role of *constants*.

It is the existence of these constants that supports scientists' faith in the orderliness of the universe, without which there would be no motivation to pursue truth by the objective methods of science.

Indices

The question as to what extent the social sciences can follow in the footsteps of the physical sciences revolves around the question of whether constants analogous to the physical constants can be found in the realm of human affairs. For any rigorous theory is essentially a set of assertions about what remains constant in spite of change.

It is easy enough to construct quantitative descriptions of social phenomena. Measurement in the social sciences is, for the most part, counting. In economics, for example, the basic quantities of interest (prices, trade volumes, supply, demand, employment, gross national product, etc.) are established by counting. The sophisticated instrumentation of measurement that characterizes modern experimental physical science plays no part in the social sciences. In sociology one counts people in various categories. In political science, to the extent that it has become quantified, one counts votes or frequencies of events thought to be of importance.

These quantities, predominantly determined by counting, are called *indices*. There is no problem in constructing an index. The problem is that of estimating how important a part the index can play in a theory. In particular, can a process be described quantitatively by an equation, where the variables are indices, and the constants are parameters? If so, can the dependence of the parameters on the situation in which they occur be determined, and can the situation itself be expressed by an equation in which these parameters now play the role of variables, while other "more fundamental" parameters turn out to be constants characteristic now of a *class* of situations? In other words, can the method of theory construction which has laid the foundation of the physical science edifice be applied to the social sciences?

Let us see what this would involve in a mathematical theory of arms races. Recall that in Richardson's model time and armament budgets are the variables, while the parameters are the constants of the model, representing the intensity of mutual stimulation (the threat parameters), the degree of self-inhibition (the security parameters), and terms representing grievances or goodwill. We have seen that this model fits the data of the 1909–1913 arms race very well. If we found that the same model fit other arms races, possibly with different parameters, our confidence in the model would increase. If we discovered how the *parameters* depend on the circumstances of the arms race; better still, if we discovered a *trend* (a drift of the parameters in time), we would be well on the way to constructing a theory of arms races.

The difficulty in constructing such a theory is that historical changes in modern times are extremely rapid. Phenomena that we would like to conceive as repetitions of the "same" or at least of the "same kind" of phenomenon may be so fundamentally different from each other that no such assumption is justified. Still, we might learn something from comparisons. We have, in fact, compared the arms race of 1909–1913 with that of 1933–1938. As we have seen, in putting his arms race model to a test, Richardson drastically simplified it by equating the stimulation and the inhibition parameters of the Allies and the Central Powers respectively. This enabled him to plot increases in the combined arms budgets against the combined arms budgets. The parameter of interest now is the slope of the straight line that fitted the plotted points. In the 1909–1913 arms race, this slope turned out to be about 0.8. Treating the German-Soviet arms race the same way, we also got a fair fit to the straight line representing the theoretical relation between the combined arms budgets (expressed in work time) and yearly increases. Here the slope turned out to be about 0.3. This might mean that the net stimulation parameter of the second race was substantially smaller than that of the first. This finding could be interpreted in various ways provided it reflected something real, that is, provided the models were reasonable approximations to the dynamics of the arms races. This is, of course, a very big "if." The latitude available to the investigator in this instance is extremely great. "Nature" does not prescribe to him the choice of indices or parameters because the processes he studies are not subject to the well-nigh immutable laws that govern physical phenomena. For this reason theories constructed on the basis of models of this sort can never be accepted with much confidence. Given the wide latitude in choosing the relevant variables, some combination of them may well give good fits. But the greater the number of possible choices of the "building blocks" of the models, the greater is the probability that the fit occurred by chance. This probability can be reduced only if the model can be put to successively more severe tests. If there were a sufficiently large "population" of arms races and if they were conducted under approximately similar conditions, this approach could be promising. This, however, is not the case. Not only are arms races only occasional historical events, but, being separated in time, they may be governed by quite different sorts of dynamics.

As we have seen, the indices used to describe the two arms races were different. In the first, the indices were armament budgets (or differences between armament budgets and inter-bloc trade volumes). In the model of the second arms race, the indices were hours of work spent on war production. The reason for choosing a different index was that the previous one (based on gold dollars) did not "work." The trajectories turned out to be erratic. The reason was not difficult to see. The Great Depression that set in in the early 1930s and the abandonment of the gold standard deprived the figures based on the gold dollar of their meaningfulness. Richardson had to look around for another index, and he thought he found one in work time. The reason it seemed suitable was because, when this index was used to describe the arms race, the trajectory was "smoothed out" and moreover, the model that had worked so beautifully in the context of the first arms race turned out to give a pretty good fit in the second. In other words, the choice of the index was based on *ad hoc* considerations. Of several possible indices, this one turned out to "work."

It is important to note that consistent resorting to *ad hoc* selections of indices would in the long run be self-defeating, since if one searched long enough, one would be bound to find *some* index that would make *some* sort of sense. But this "success" could well be fortuitous. If one searches persistently for a pattern, one is bound to find a pattern in practically anything. All pseudo-sciences are based on this sort of "selective confirmation."

With this caveat in mind, let us look at index construction unrelated to theory building. An index can serve in its simplest capacity as a component of an objective description. Why, then, should one index be selected rather than another? The selection is made with the view of establishing some relation between two or more indices. This is the most primitive level of "theory construction," just one step removed from pure description. Because it constitutes a great deal of quantified social science, we will examine it in some detail. In particular, examining relations between indices has played a major role in investigations that have come to be called "peace research."

Correlation

It is consistent with the systemic view to compare large-scale conflicts such as wars with cataclysmic natural phenomena, such as floods, epidemics, and earthquakes. There is, however, one property of large-scale social events that justifies the hope that to a certain extent a hard science dealing with social events can be developed. By a "hard" science, we mean one of maximum objectivity, firmly rooted in quantitative data subject to verification by independent observers. The feature that justifies this hope is the *magnitude* of large-scale social events.

The discovery that gross masses of matter are actually vast conglomerates of minute particles, e.g., atoms or molecules, has revealed that the apparent simplicity of large-scale physical events is in actuality a sum total of vast numbers of much more complex events. Consider a cloud driven by the wind. The cloud appears to us as an "object," and its motion seems simple and regular, at least for a while. The whole mass seems to be moving in a given direction at a given speed. If, however, we were to look inside the cloud under sufficiently large resolving power to distinguish the molecules, we would find chaos. To be sure, the motion of each molecule is almost certainly determined by the laws of mechanics, but in their totality these motions seem to be entirely "random." Somehow this randomness sums to something definite, namely, the motion of the whole cloud in a given direction with a given speed.

In large-scale events involving human behavior, the same sort of statistical regularity is often observed. We may be convinced that each individual is free to go out on the street or not to go out at any time. In fact, in a large city, some people are on the street at all times. Nevertheless, the fact remains that the streets are crowded with pedestrians and traffic at 5:00 P.M. on weekdays and nearly empty at 5:00 A.M. Even though we cannot predict whether a particular person will be on the street or at home, we can predict with sometimes impressive accuracy how many will be on the street at various hours of the day. The same applies to such phenomena as accidents, marriages, divorces, enrollments in schools, and incidence of disease. All these events display *statistical regularities*. Although unpredictable in individual cases, many of them are fairly well predictable "in the large."

Over sufficiently protracted periods of time, however, the indices that reflect statistical regularities may show *trends*. And it is these trends that are of interest to the social scientist. The economist is interested in trends exhibited by the variables with which he is concerned, such as production and trade volumes, employment, currency exchange rates, and inflation rates. The sociologist may be interested in trends observed in crime statistics, and in the incidence of violence.

All these indices and trends may be of interest in their own right. However, interest in them may go beyond the purely descriptive level. In constructing a theory, one may want to assess the way these indices are interrelated. If such interrelations are in evidence, they may suggest cause-effect relations, which can serve as building blocks of a theory.

Now the degree of association between two or more indices can be assessed by calculating *correlations* between quantified variables. For instance, a sociologist may want to know whether there is a relationship between the number of years of schooling a person has received and his/her income. One way of finding out is by comparing the average incomes of people who have received different amounts of schooling. These averages will very probably be different. However, one may want to know more, namely, how important the amount of schooling is in influencing a person's income. Calculation of correlations between income and schooling answers this question.[1]

To fix ideas, suppose we examine the amount of schooling and the income of a number of individuals, a "sample" from the general population. We plot the income of each individual against his years of schooling. A relationship between these two variables would be established most definitely if the plot turned out to be a straight line with either a positive or negative slope. In the former case, we could say for that sample, "the more schooling the more income," and we could say it with certainty. Similarly, if all the points fell on a straight line with a negative slope, we could say with certainty, "the more schooling the less income." If all the points fell on a horizontal or vertical line, we could say that there is no apparent relation between schooling and income. In the former case, persons with different amounts of schooling would all turn out to have the same income. In the latter case, persons with different incomes would all turn out to have had the same amount of schooling.

In practice, plots of this sort hardly ever turn out to be straight lines. Typically, the points are scattered. But it is possible to assess the *degree* to which they approximately fall on a straight line. The greater the approximation, the stronger confidence we have that a linear relationship between the two variables exists. This degree of relationship is called a *correlation*. A perfect positive correlation attains the value $+1$, a perfect negative one -1. Values of correlation near zero indicate that no relationship between the two variables can be presumed to exist.

Suppose we have established a strong positive correlation between number of years of schooling and income. Can we say that more years of schooling "causes" a larger income? We cannot, because the influence may go the other way. It may be that persons with high income come from high-income families, and children from high-income families receive on the average more schooling than children from low-income families. In other words, correlation does not indicate the direction of causality, nor even that a causal relation exists, since both the amount of schooling and income may have been the effects of some other "cause." Nevertheless, correlation studies are sometimes useful in the development of a theory because they give indications of *possible* causal relationships.

Correlates of War

Many investigations subsumed under "peace research" have concentrated on the study of what are called "correlates of war." They were clearly motivated by a hope that some of the more prominent correlations might suggest where to look for the "causes of war."

The point of departure in a correlation study is a hypothesis in the form "the more of this, the more of that" or else "the more of this, the less of that." The strongest confirmation of such a hypothesis would be a finding that the correlation coefficient associated with the relationship between the two quantities in question is either $+1$ or -1.

The first task in a correlation study is to quantify the variables of interest. The "amount of war" has been quantified in different ways. Richardson's original measure was derived from the number of battle deaths. He regarded wars as cases of encounters that he called "deadly quarrels," i.e., encounters leading to violent deaths of some of the participants. Following the usage in astronomy, where brightness of stars determines their magnitude, and in seismology, where the severity of an earthquake is measured on the Richter scale, Richardson used a logarithmic measure to define the "magnitude" of a deadly quarrel, namely, the logarithm to base 10 of the number of deaths resulting from the encounter. Thus, a murder was assigned magnitude 0 (since the logarithm of 1 is 0). A small riot with ten fatalities would be assigned magnitude 1, since the logarithm to base 10 of 10 is 1. The magnitude assigned to a large riot with, say, 100 fatalities would be 2, to a small war with 1,000 battle deaths 3, and so on. The two world wars appear on this scale with magnitudes 7 and 8. A war of magnitude between 9 and 10 would wipe out the human race.

Singer and Small (1968) used five different measures for the "amount of war" and seven different measures for the degree of "alliance aggregation," an index whose relationship to the "amount of war" they set out to investigate. In these measures the "major powers" involved in wars or alliances are counted separately. Measures of alliance aggregation include proportions of the states comprising the international system that are members of an alliance at a given time. "Defensive alliances" (so designated in the treaties) are counted separately. In addition, two measures of "bipolarity" are included as measures of alliance aggregation. The calculation of these measures involves the average degree of freedom of states to join any alliance. In a completely polarized system (when all states are committed to one or another alliance), this degree of freedom reduces to zero.

The historical period examined was 1815 to 1945, i.e., from the end of the Napoleonic Wars to the end of World War II. Of the 35 correlations, only four turned out to be statistically significant at the .01 level of significance, all being positive correlations of "amount of war" with the percent of all states in any alliance. Needless to say, this result was disappointing.

When, however, the period examined was broken up into two periods, one from 1815 to 1899, the other from 1900 to 1945, a very different picture emerged. In the earlier period, 10 different correlations between the various measures of the "amount of war"[2] and different measures of "alliance aggregation"[3] turned out to be significant—all negative; while in the later period 11 such correlations were observed—all positive.

A conclusion suggested by these correlations is that in the nineteenth century, the readiness of states to enter alliances acted as an inhibitor of war, while in the twentieth century, it acted as an instigator. As has been pointed out, conclusions about causal relations and especially about the direction of causality based on observed correlations can be misleading. At best, correlations can alert us to what *may* be causal relations. If so, then the opposite effects of alliance aggregation in the nineteenth and twentieth centuries deserve further examination.

In favor of the argument that alliance aggregation is an inhibitor of war is the notion of "collective security." Presumably, strong defensive alliances deter wars of aggression. On the other hand, in favor of the argument that alliance aggregation is conducive to war or at least aggravates the severity of wars is the circumstance that allies are drawn into war by virtue of obligations assumed on entering the alliance. In a highly polarized international system (nearly total aggregation into alliances), opportunities for preserving a dynamic balance of power are lost. In a "loose" system, a non-aligned state can throw its weight toward the weaker side. According to this hypothesis, the number of opportunities for making new alliances should be inversely related to the incidence or severity of wars. Or, equivalently, if we define "degree of polarization" as a measure that varies inversely with the number of new alliance opportunities, then the incidence or severity of war should be positively correlated with the degree of polarization.

Can we see changes in the nature of the international system that would explain the greater weight of the inhibiting factor of alliance aggregation in the nineteenth century and the greater weight of the instigating factor in the twentieth? If we can, then the substantive meaning of the change of sign of the correlations as the system passed from the nineteenth to the twentieth century is brought out. If we cannot see such changes, we are motivated to look for them. In this way, the approach acquires some theoretical leverage.

Correlates of War-Proneness of States

The correlations examined by Singer and Small could be interpreted as a reflection of the war-proneness of the entire international system as a function of the degree of alliance aggregation. In what follows, we will examine correlations that could be interpreted as a reflection of the war-proneness of individual states as a function of so-called *status inconsistency*. We have already encountered a related concept in J. Galtung's theory of large-scale conflicts.

The notion of status applied to actors in the international arena is of early origin. Pope Julius II ranked the Christian princes of Europe in the order of their importance. The highest ranking monarch was, of course, the Emperor (of the Holy Roman Empire). Next came Rex Romanorum, Rex Hispaniae, Rex Franciae, and so on through the kings. The dukes followed: Dux Burgundiae, Dux Bavariae, Dux Saxoniae, etc.

In our time, no such authoritative ranking is available. Nevertheless, states are routinely ranked, even though our standards of importance may be quite different from those applied by Pope Julius. We tend to assign status to states on the basis of their achievements. In our time, these achievements are measured predominantly by economic indices, such as gross national product, at times by certain indices of modernization, for example centralization and capability. Centralization has to do with the facility with which a nation can be organized for some collective action. Often this means war, since war is the most prominent truly collective action in which states engage. In the nineteenth century, centralization was usuallly estimated in terms of transportation facilities. For example, Germany's war potential was strongly dependent on its railroad network, which had been constructed specifically with that end in view. Another index of centralization derives from communication facilities. Formerly, the telegraph and telephone systems and the efficiency of mail flow may have been suitable measures. In our time, the radio and television networks are so dense in practically all "developed" countries that this measure has lost its discriminating significance. Finally, degree of urbanization has been an important index of centralization. It has still retained its discriminating potential to a considerable extent.

Capability is reflected in production capacities and in population.

Aside from this *achieved* status, nations are aware of an *ascribed* status, that is, of the degree to which their importance is recognized by "the international community." This status is more vague and hence more difficult to measure. A motivation for designing an index for measuring ascribed status derives from a theory that relates the discrepancy between achieved and ascribed status to the war-proneness of states. Specifically, it is suggested that if the ascribed status of a state lags significantly behind its achieved status, a tension is created in its ruling elite, somewhat analogous, one supposes, to the "inferiority complex," to which aggressive tendencies in individuals are frequently ascribed.

One way of measuring ascribed status is by the level of diplomatic recognition rendered to the country, e.g., by the number and rank of its diplomats received abroad (Singer and Small 1966). Another measure may be the number of international conferences held in the country. The relevance of these indices changes. At one time, conferences tended to be held in countries regarded as "important" in other respects. Today, many international conferences are held in countries not otherwise regarded as "important." Switzerland, for instance, has probably hosted more international conferences than many other countries, and Austria has become a favorite center. The main reason for the popularity of these countries is surely their formal neutrality, which is quite unrelated to prestige derived from the usual indices of importance.

Another possible measure of ascribed status is the number of international organizations to which a country belongs. This index, too, has lost its discriminating power. Formerly, a country's "importance" was a factor in its acceptance into an international organization. Today open membership is the rule.

In constructing his model relating war-proneness to the disparity between achieved and ascribed status, I. Midlarsky (1975) used diplomatic representation as an index of the latter. However, he relates ascribed status not to the achieved status itself but rather to the rate of change of the achieved status. He assumes that the tension, which manifests itself in war-proneness, results from a feeling that one's *rate of progress* has not been given adequate recognition. Accordingly, he takes the difference between levels of achieved status at the beginning and end of a period, specifically, between 1860 and 1940, compares this change with the rate of change of diplomatic recognition during the period, then assesses the discrepancy between the two measures, which he then relates to war-proneness. For some countries, he gets a large positive inconsistency resulting from an excess of the difference of achieved status over the difference of ascribed status. For other countries, he gets a negative inconsistency, resulting from a deficiency of the difference of achieved status over the difference of ascribed status. He then classifies countries according to whether they are characterized by positive or negative inconsistency. Table 19–1 shows this classification, calculated according to two indices of achieved status.

Table 19–1 (After Midlarsky 1975)
Countries with large positive inconsistency and large negative inconsistency between status and achievement in relation to centralization and potential as measures of achievement.

Countries with large positive inconsistency	Countries with large negative inconsistency
With respect to centralization	
Britain	Czechoslovakia
Germany	Finland
Japan	Luxembourg
Russia (U.S.S.R.)	Poland
United States	
With respect to potential	
Brazil	Czechoslovakia
Japan	Finland
Germany	Luxembourg
Russia (U.S.S.R.)	Poland
United States	

Correlates of War-Proneness: Militarization of Economy

On common sense grounds alone, one would suspect that states that devote large fractions of their resources to military expenditures would be more war-prone than those that do not. This conjecture, however, contradicts the oft-repeated homily, "If you want peace, prepare for war." Results obtained by A. Newcombe et al. (1974) indicate that preparations for war as reflected in deflection of resources to that end tend to increase rather than decrease the likelihood of war.

Newcombe's null hypothesis is that military expenditures of states are linearly related to their gross national product. Thus, if the military expenditures of states plotted against their gross national products all fell on a straight line with a positive slope, the null hypothesis would be confirmed. It turns out, however, that the points so obtained do not fall on a straight line. When a straight line of "best fit" is drawn through the scatter plot, some points remain above it, some below, thus identifying the "overspending" and the "underspending" nations. This constitutes a prediction of which nations are war-prone and which are not.

In a variant of this model, a hyperbola asymptotic to the straight line

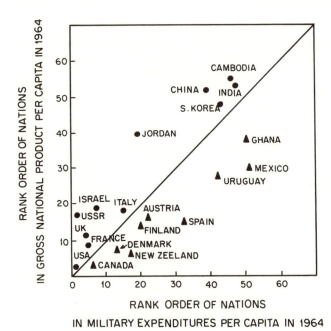

Figure 19.1. Nations below the diagonal appear as military "underspenders;" those above as military "overspenders." For a more complete plot, see Newcombe et al, 1974, p. 49.

so determined was used as the boundary separating the overspenders from the underspenders. The principle is the same. Alternative models of this sort are used in the process of searching for indices of the greatest predictive power.

Plots were made for the years 1964, 1965, and 1966 in order to test the robustness of the model. The results (using a straight-line boundary) are shown in Figure 19-1.

We observe that both high-income and low-income countries are among both the overspenders and the underspenders. The NATO countries (except Denmark and Canada) are overspenders. The Soviet Union is an overspender. Some of the Warsaw Pact countries (not shown in the Figure) are overspenders, some underspenders. Of the low-income countries, conspicuous overspenders are Egypt, China, Cambodia, and India. Almost all the Latin American countries are underspenders.

From these data an index called the Tension Ratio (TR) is calculated. The model predicts that countries whose TR exceeds a certain critical value are more likely to go to war than others. In the five-year period after 1964, the countries with TR greater than critical value were 21 times more likely to go to war than those with TR smaller than the critical value.

Dynamic Indicators

Dynamic indicators of system behavior are those that exhibit time courses. Study of such indices sometimes reveals interesting effects, especially during international crises. In this way, they are analogues to the indices associated with arms races except that they are manifested during shorter spans of time and can be much more convincingly described by continuous variables. Armament budgets are not really describable by continuous variables, since they are given as a rule for successive years. Since an arms race generally lasts only a few years, the budgets are given as discrete values, not as continuously changing quantities. The indices related to the progress of crises can be measured practically daily. Examples are indices derived from *content analysis* of materials published in the mass media during a crisis.

Content analysis treats massive verbal outputs (called corpuses) as generators of symptoms of underlying attitudes, perceptions, or intentions of actors who produced the corpuses. The method can be applied to compare corpuses produced by individuals or large systems such as states. Corpuses produced by states may be the contents of diplomatic communications or else selected contents of newspaper items published during the period of interest.

To serve as indices, the statements serving as messages have to be coded. For example, let us consider a content analysis of the time course of a crisis with respect to some symptoms. These symptoms may be degree of perceived hostility or degree of expressed hostility, intensity of threats as expressed or perceived, and the like. The utterances thought to be relevant to these symptoms are classified, perhaps according to the intensity of the affect reflected or according to the severity of actions threatened. These classifications reflect the theoretical orientation of the political scientist undertaking the analysis. This orientation usually has a psychological bent. The "psychology" of a state in a crisis is assumed to be a composite of the psychologies of its key decision makers. These, in turn, are defined as those who, by virtue of their positions in the power structure of the state "can make and implement decisions binding on the population of the state" (Zinnes 1968). The context of these decisions is the events related to an outbreak of a war.

Practitioners of content analysis in political contexts make hypotheses about interactions between the utterances that constitute the corpuses they examine. They assume that these interactions (evaluated statistically) reflect underlying interactions between psychological states. For example, on the basis of a statement the perceptions of the source (the author of the statement) can be inferred. On the basis of other statements the quality and/or the intensity of affects can be inferred. A hypothesis may be advanced that the perceptions of the actor (here, a state) affect the expressions of affects of that actor or his statement of intentions. In some cases, data inferred from verbal outputs can be compared with actual actions undertaken. In such a case, content analysis becomes linked with analysis of behavior. Examples of hypotheses advanced by D.A. Zinnes (1968) are (a) Perception of hostility by an actor directed against self is positively correlated with expression of hostility against the source; or (b) Expression of hostility on the part of actor X toward actor Y stimulates expression of hostility on the part of Y toward X. Clearly, these hypotheses are analogues to Richardson's mutual stimulation hypotheses on the level of a war of words.

These hypotheses can be put to a test as soon as the raw data, i.e., the statements as they appear in documents or in the press, have been coded and classified and the various types counted.

Zinnes (1968) applied the method of content analysis to the description of the crisis that preceded World War I and to testing hypotheses concerning the interaction of statements of various parties to the crisis. Her sources were documents representing internal and international communications between the principal actors: Russia, France, England, and Serbia on the one side of the confrontation, Germany and Austria-Hungary on the other.

The statements culled from the raw data were coded according to perceptions of hostility, perceptions of power, perceptions of friendship, and the like, and corresponding to expressions of different affects or intentions. The statements were also coded according to the sources and the targets at which the expressions of hostility were directed.

The data were processed with the view of testing hypotheses (a) and (b) above. The tabulation was done in three different ways, which Zinnes calls:

Model   I: no memory; the events of each day are tabulated with no reference to those on previous days.

Model II: limited memory; a weighted sum of the events of each day and those of three previous days are tabulated.

Model III: perfect memory; everything that happened from the beginning of the crisis is remembered without attenuation.

Table 19–2 (after Zinnes 1968)
Correlations (r) between perceptions of hostility and expressions of hostility. Hypothesis I: self-stimulation. Hypothesis II: mutual stimulation Model I: no memory.

Frequency	r	Hypothesis I significance	r	Hypothesis II Significance
All statements	.55	.01	.56	.01
Threat statements	.25	not sig.	.32	.01
Action statements	.29	.05	.30	.05

Intensity	r	Hypothesis I significance	r	Hypothesis II significance
All statements	− .02	not sig.	− .14	not sig.
Threat statements	− .20	not sig.	− .35	.01
Action statements	.11	not sig.	.07	not sig.

The use of several alternative ways of tabulating data will be discussed in the critique below.

Two pictures emerge. One is an overview of the crisis as it develops. Combining all statements of the corpus examined, i.e., treating them as the output of a single system, the investigator can see the crisis "at a glance," as it were, from its beginnings (the assassination of the Austrian Crown Prince on June 27, 1914) to the outbreak of World War I. Such an overview is shown in Figures 19–2 and 19–3. The other picture shows the extent to which the hypotheses concerning the interactions as reflected in correlations between the statements are corroborated. These results are shown in Tables 19–2 and 19–3.

In Figures 19–2 and 19–3 we see the sudden outburst of intensity in both perceptions and expressions of hostility toward the end of July. We also see a peculiar effect, this being that the *frequency* of statements perceived as hostile *drops* on July 31, the day Germany declared war on Russia. Perhaps this drop can be accounted for by noting that when war has been actually declared, the statements of the adversary are likely to be *labeled* as hostile less frequently, since it is taken for granted that the adversary, now unambiguously seen as such, is hostile. However, from July 31 to August 4, the frequency of statements perceived as hostile again rises. This may be due to Germany's reaction to England's threats to enter the war on the side of the Allies, which she did on August 4. Referring to Figure 19–3, we see that the frequency of *expressions* of hostility

Table 19–3 (after Zinnes 1968)
**Correlations (r) between perceptions of hostility and expressions of hostility.
Hypothesis I: self-stimulation. Hypothesis II: mutual stimulation. Model II:
imperfect memory.**

Frequency	r	Hypothesis I significance	r	Hypothesis II significance
All statements	.59	.01	.63	.01
Threat statements	.60	.01	.63	.01
Action statements	.26	.05	.28	.01

Intensity	r	Hypothesis I significance	r	Hypothesis II significance
All statements	.41	.01	.36	.01
Threat statements	.31	.01	.15	not sig.
Action statements	.51	.01	.54	.01

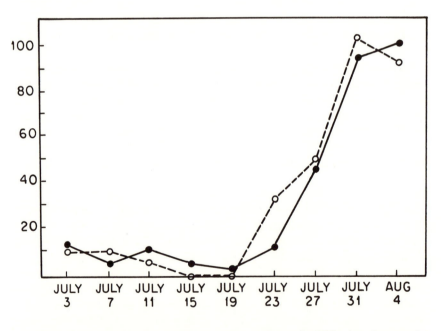

Figure 19.2. After Zinnes, 1968. Perception of threat (solid line) and expression of threat (broken line) during the crisis of 1914 by all states involved in the crisis. Vertical coordinates: units of intensity operationalized by methods of content analysis.

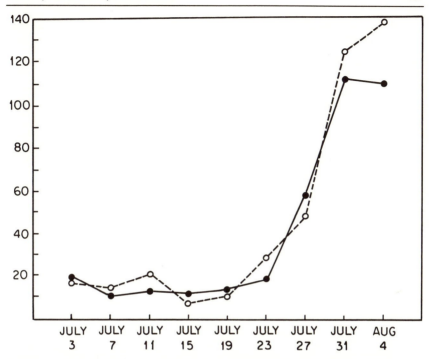

Figure 19.3. After Zinnes, 1968. Perception of hostility (solid line) and expression of hostility (broken line) during the crisis of 1914 by all states involved in the crisis. Vertical coordinates: units of intensity operationalized by methods of content analysis.

does not abate. They become steadily more frequent from the middle of July on.

These interpretations of the gross systemic effects of the crisis as reflected in the verbal outputs are, of course, conjectures. These conjectures, however, can be put to a test by examining the course of the crisis under "greater resolving power," namely for each of the participants separately. The interested reader is referred to Zinnes' paper.

Turning to Tables 19–2 and 19–3, we see that the confirmation of Hypotheses I and II is considerably stronger when the data are tabulated in accordance with Model II (imperfect memory) than in accordance with Model I (no memory.) Moreover, in the case of no memory we see an actual *negative* correlation between the perception of threat from the adversary and the expression of threat toward the adversary. Again several conjectures can be made concerning the meaning of this correlation and tested by further examination of the data suggested by the conjectures.

Besides the hypotheses related respectively to self-stimulation and mutual stimulation between perceptions and expressions, Zinnes offers two further hypotheses.

Hypothesis III: xEy ⇒ yPx states that expressions of hostility on the part
    of X toward Y are likely to be so perceived by Y.
Hypothesis IV: xEy ⇔ yEx states that expressions of hostility by X toward
    Y are likely to stimulate expressions of hostility by Y toward
    X. This hypothesis comes closest to the Richardsonian
    model (cf. Chapter 18) because it relates to interactions
    between actions of the same modality.

Note that the other three hypotheses are, in a way, refinements of Richardson's model, since they relate to interactions of actions of different modalities (perceptions and expressions). The results of testing Hypotheses III and IV also suggest a variety of conjectures, which can be tested by further examination of the data.

Critique

The most serious criticism leveled at the methods illustrated above is that they amount to "fishing expeditions." As we have seen, there is no "natural" way of selecting indices either static or dynamic that reflect the "essential" nature of a system or the "essential" features driving a system's dynamics. We have seen how in the case of Richardson's model, armament budgets that gave a good fit for the model in the case of the 1909–1913 arms race had to be discarded when the gold standard was abandoned. Eventually another index was found to be adequate, namely, work time. There is no guarantee, however, that work time will continue to be a relevant measure of the effort expended in preparation for future wars. If different indices have to be used in different situations, there is no assurance that the search for a "proper" index stops as soon as a satisfactory fit between data and model is established. It is common knowledge that any search stops after we have looked in the last place, since the last place turns out to be the "right place." This may be true for lost objects. In the case of a search for a "proper" index, however, fortuitous coincidences cannot be excluded, and the method loses its theoretical leverage.

A similar charge can be leveled against Singer and Small's search for the correlates of war. Recall that among their 35 correlations only four turned out to be "significant" according to standard methods of establishing significance of a correlation. Rather than dismiss the hypothesis that a correlation between alliance aggregation and war exists as supposed, Singer and Small desegregated the data to look at the wars of the nineteenth and twentieth centuries separately. They found that the virtual absence of significant correlations in the pooled data was due to negative correlations in the nineteenth century and the positive correlations in the twentieth canceling each other. Here the search for significant correlations ended because some were found. The question arises: Suppose none were found even after the data were desegregated; would the search have gone on until *some* significant correlations were found? If so, fortuitous coincidences cannot be excluded.

Let us now take a close look at the argument that in the nineteenth century "collective security" was an effective inhibitor of war, but in the twentieth century attempts to establish collective security by large alliances produced an opposite effect. This sounds plausible until one realizes that by far the largest "amount of war" in the twentieth century (until 1945) was produced undoubtedly by the two world wars, and these were characterized by the largest alliances ever formed. For instance, toward the end of World War I, Latin American countries declared war on Germany. Clearly, these declarations were purely ceremonial. Similarly, in World War II, there was a scramble to get on the bandwagon of the anti-Axis coalition when the outcome of that war seemed assured.

An even more severe cricitism can be leveled at Midlarsky's hypothesis regarding the relation between status inconsistency and war-proneness. It seems at first sight that Midlarsky's hypothesis is strongly corroborated. On the left side of Table 19–1 we find states that have engaged in severe wars during the period examined (Brazil being the only exception). On the right side we see states much less involved in wars, at any rate, states which could not reasonably be called "aggressive," having been victims of aggression rather than instigators or willing participants in war. On second thought, however, this confirmation of the discrepancy hypothesis turns out to be illusory. The countries on the left side of the table already enjoyed extensive diplomatic recognition at the beginning of the period examined. Consequently, there was little room for more recognition, and the difference between ascribed status in 1860 and 1940 turned out to be small. This accounts for the large positive discrepancy between the rate of change of achieved and ascribed status. Three of the countries on the right side of the table did not exist as independent states in 1860. Consequently, the increase (from none) in their ascribed status from 1860 to 1940 was large, and this accounts for the negative discrepancy. As for Luxembourg, although it existed as an independent state in 1860, the rate of change of its "achievement" between 1860 and 1940 was small: Luxembourg did not go through a dramatic industrialization or urbanization during that period.

Therefore its status inconsistency index, like those of the "young" states, turned out to be negative. Thus, Midlarsky's results in this instance must be regarded as due to an artifact.

Zinnes, like Singer and Small, casts her net wide. She advances four hypotheses and uses three different ways of tabulating data. One would surmise that *something* is bound to come out that would justify some conjectures. Yet Zinnes' results cannot be easily ascribed to fortuitous coincidences. They make too much sense. The very fact that certain correlations are *not* manifested when memory is shut out of interactions and are observed when it is included suggests that the results reflect some sort of reality.

In our opinion, content analysis is the most promising of the approaches inspired by the analytic systemic view of international relations. The importance of momentous decisions by leaders in situations of crisis cannot be altogether discounted, as, for example, Tolstoy discounts it in his philosophy of war. When it comes to massive verbal outputs, however, involving veritable floods of utterances made by many people reacting to that same deluge, the primacy of systemic forces seems much more convincing. That World War I did break out in the crisis of 1914 but that World War III did not break out in consequence of the Berlin crisis or of the Cuban missile crisis may have been a matter of chance. But the ebb and flow of threats and reactions to threats or of conciliatory gestures, as these are reflected in masssive corpuses, are not readily ascribable to decisions and directives. They may be true reflections of the state of a large system going through phases, tending toward an equilibrium or, driven by positive feedback, exploding. The wealth of data alone available for content analysis makes this method worthwhile to pursue.

A direct relation between militarization of the economy of a nation and the likelihood of its going to war seems to have been well established in the study of Newcombe *et al.* and in several related studies. But of course the interesting question of the direction of causality (assuming the relation is a causal one) is not answered by the data. Militarization may well contribute to war-proneness, but the reverse is also possible: war-proneness may contribute to the readiness to militarize the economy. As in many similar situations, the question of the direction of causality should not be posed in the expectation of an either-or answer. Causality may well go both ways. War-proneness, however generated, usually stimulates war planning, which in turn necessitates militarization. However, militarization may be an important contributory factor in focusing the energies and attention of rulers on war, its eventuality, and the like. The existence of a large and expensive military machine is in itself a source of temptation to use it.

It should be pointed out, however, that the direction of causality is not an issue in Newcombe's model. The aim of the model was to construct an index for "predicting wars." The index was tested (successfully) in *"post-dicting"* wars and for this reason can be regarded as a potential predictor. The practical utility of a predictor, however, depends on knowing the direction of causality, in the sense of knowing what to manipulate in order to produce the desired effect. In the present case, there is not much hope that either the military budgets or the war-proneness of states can be reduced by manipulation. For this reason, the direction of causality is not an issue. In another way, however, the findings are important: they cut the ground from under the cliché, "If you want peace, prepare for war."

The cognitive implications of peace research centered on the investigation of correlations are much more important than the pragmatic implications. The results of these investigations cannot be expected to give us a "handle" to affect the course of large-scale events, e.g., to prevent wars, resolve crises, and so forth. The "fishing expedition" investigations are of value in helping dispel all kinds of unfounded notions that make up the conventional wisdom about the "causes of wars." The studies put these notions under the glaring and merciless light of "blind" analysis, unencumbered by preconceived notions. For the most part, they return the verdict unproven.

Notes

1. A correlation can be regarded as a measure of confidence we can have in predicting the value of one variable when we are given the value of another associated with it. For example, if the correlation between the variables is $+1$ or -1, then once two pairs of values of these variables have been established, we can, given any other value of one predict with certainty the value of the other. If the correlation is numerically smaller than 1, we can make such predictions only with certain probabilities. Note that the strength of correlation does not refer to the strength of the effect one variable has on another. At any rate, this "strength" is not an "objective" relation, since its numerical value (the slope of the regression line) depends on the units in which the variables are measured.

2. Among Singer and Small's measures used for the "amount of war" were frequency of wars, their duration (e.g., nation-months), and severity (battle deaths).

3. The degree of alliance aggregation was measured by percent of states in any alliance, percent of states in defensive pacts, certain measures of "bipolarity," and so forth.

20

The War System

In his book, *A History of Militarism*, A. Vagts (1937) represents "the military way" as rationality in the conduct of war and subordination of the needs of the military profession to those of the state that it is supposed to serve. He pictures "militarism" as a set of attitudes developed in members of the military profession when the military establishment becomes self-serving. A conspicuous military caste, according to Vagts, is a pronounced symptom of militarism. Frequently, exaggerated feelings of self-importance develop in members of this caste, reinforced by distinguished dress, a code of honor, and at times, contempt for civilians. It may even happen that concern with war (which in Vagts' view is the proper primary concern of the military man) is eclipsed by other concerns having to do with the prestige of the military caste and its influence on affairs of state. Militarism may induce prejudices which prevent the military establishment from serving its country most effectively. Advances in military technology may necessitate shifts of emphasis from one branch of the armed services to another or may require eliminating some branch that has become obsolete (e.g., cavalry). But the militarist who often has a vested interest in old ways (since learning new ways requires effort) may resist "progress," putting the interests of his caste above the (supposed) interest of his country. The ethos of "the military way" as distinguished from that of "militarism," according to Vagts, requires that the effectiveness of the military establishment be kept as a supreme value at all times. By "effectiveness" he meant maximum potential for achieving victory in war at minimum cost in life and treasure.

Underlying Vagts' distinction between "the military way" and "militarism" is an assumption that Vagts apparently regards as self-evident, namely, that the military profession has a vital function in a society. It performs that function in war. Militarism, on the other hand, appears as a perversion of that function, engendered by the atrophy of allegiance to society and pursuit of goals benefiting only the profession.

The Art of War

It is impossible to give a definition of art that would permit us to distinguish unambiguously between activities or products which deserve to be called "art" and those which do not. Nor do we have a standardized account of the "method of art" analogous to what is presented in many textbooks as "the scientific method." To designate something as "art" means to appreciate it in some way and to attribute the appreciated excellence to some "creative" expression of an artist. All these criteria are entirely subjective, which is what separates them sharply from criteria applied in evaluating a work of science. Nevertheless, subjective criteria can serve as a basis of inter-subjective consensus. There is a great deal of consensus in characterizing the symphonies of Beethoven or the sculptures of Michelangelo as "art." On the basis of such inter-subjectively consonant criteria it is legitimate to speak of the "art of war." Some military historians succeed in conveying this appreciation of the creative aspects of military thought, which to a reader outside the profession appears quite similar to the appreciation of the creative aspects of art.

Liddell Hart's book, *The Ghost of Napoleon* (1933), is an example of such appreciation. It is based on a set of lectures given in 1932–1933 at Trinity College, Cambridge, under the title "The Movement of Military Thought from the Eighteenth to the Twentieth Century and its Influence on European History."

The first chapter is entitled "Generation—the Military Renaissance of the Eighteenth Century."

Liddell Hart uses the word "Renaissance" to mean the revival of interest in classical antiquity, in particular, the influence of Greek and Roman military masters on the military professionals of the eighteenth century.

It turned out, however, that the "military thought" of the eighteenth century, far from being liberated by creative energy released in the Renaissance, remained imprisoned in dogma. The core of the battle formation was massed infantry, a carry-over of the Greek phalanx. This was effective when shock (direct impact) weapons were predominant, but not with the advent of weapons that could kill at a distance. As a target for firearms, the massed infantry became in effect a limbless trunk. Liddell Hart refers to this period of military history as "the sterile state."

He goes on to tell how the precursors of Napoleon developed the idea of enhancing the mobility of the army by dispersion. As is often the case with creative innovations, the prophets of the wave of the future fought against encrusted thinking habits. They fought with conviction and passion, as can be seen in some excerpts from Jacques Guibert's major work on war (1770). His purpose, he wrote, was to assemble as the foundations of a science, "the results of every happy thought of all ages before us, with whatever could be added by present experience."

To Guibert the modernization of military strategy and tactics was dictated not only by military needs of the time. It was for him a matter of honor and integrity. He anticipated patriotism, which was not to become a full force in the European war system until the French Revolution. Liddell Hart points out that Guibert virtually put country before king, as is evident in the preface to his book.[1]

> May the day soon come that will give the sacred name of country its full significance and force, in making it the cry of the nation and the watchword of all who compose the State. May the ruler and his subjects, the great and the humble feel themselves honored by the title of "citizen."

In the role of a political moralist he wrote:

> What picture does modern Europe offer to the philosopher who contemplates it? Tyrannical, ignorant, or feeble administration, the virtues of nations smothered by their vices, private interests prevailing over the public good . . . oppression of subjects reduced to a system . . . If the philosopher, weary of so much rottenness, can find any objects more consoling to look at, it is on some of the small states and some moral and political truths which, filtering gradually through the false, will develop little by little, until at last perhaps they will reach the rulers, occupy the thrones, and make posterity happy.

It is interesting to observe that the young man,[2] writing in the Age of Enlightenment, longs to liberate "military science" (more properly the "art of war") from the dead hand of the past. The style, if not the content, of his arguments is similar to that of Thomas Paine who, writing not much later, tried to arouse thinking people against the yoke of religious dogma in the name of "common sense." Liddell Hart, writing a few years after World War I, gives an account of how the road was finally cleared for Napoleon's brilliant innovations in the art of war. His comments differ little from an enthusiastic music lover's work on the history of music. In the same spirit, such a historian might write of the precursors of Bach, Beethoven, or Wagner who paved the way for the magnificent contributions of the masters. Genuine commitment to a cause is often tinged with a sense of tragedy. In the writings of serious authors on war, this sense is often evident in their emphasis on "unlearned lessons" or else on lessons learned "too well" that had frozen into a dogma that eventually led to disaster.

Writers on the "art of war" generally agree that World War I was a disaster. They see no redeeming features in the slaughters that resulted from infantry rushing at fortified positions and being mowed down by machine guns or in the obscenity of poison gas attacks. Some of this repugnance can be ascribed to stirrings of ordinary human feelings. Liddell Hart, for instance, decries the ossified Clausewitzian dogma of numerical superiority being the key to victory that was manifested in the butchery on the Western Front in World War I.

> Even in the twentieth century, the generals would train their masses for the bayonet fight which Guibert in the eighteenth century had pointed out as a fantasy of theorists. In reality, it meant that they were training their masses to be massacred by machine guns. Not merely stalemate but massed suicide— more truly homicide—was the penalty of Clausewitz's theory of mass. (Liddell Hart 1933, p. 129.)

Liddell Hart compared war to a disease and appears to have seen something else in war than a science or an art. He calls for "scientific research into war's nature, conduct and effects." One looks in vain, however, for a further development of this theme. Instead, Liddell Hart suggests that the most important lesson to be drawn from two thousand years of war is the necessity of adapting methods of conducting war to the technical innovations that make the old methods obsolete.

> The failure to adapt theory to reality has been matched by the failure to adapt armament to technical progress—to adopt new weapons that invention made available at the time when they promised a decisive advantage. . . .
>
> Even when the Army had been provided with the Minie rifle, its value was forfeited in the Crimean War because we continued to rely on the bayonet. . . .
>
> The germ of the tank was seen during the Crimean War . . . But it was only a civilian, James Cowen, who saw the tactical possibilities of such a machine. (pp. 173–174.)

The examples go on and on. There is an obverse, "positive" side of this picture. William McElwee (1974) is full of admiration for Helmuth Moltke, who is credited with creating the formidable Prussian military machine. Moltke did better than adapt to technological progress; he *anticipated* its significance for war. He is credited with developing the dense railway system of Germany, entirely geared to serving his military machine. But again Kenneth E. Boulding's dictum, "Nothing fails like success," was vindicated. The very efficiency of the German railway system, which made it possible for a troop train to cross the Rhine every ten minutes on the way to the Western Front in 1914, made it impossible to halt the mobilization once it was on the way. Had the Germans halted mobilization in those early August days and accepted one of the many frantic offers to talk before shooting. World War I might have been avoided.

On the whole, however, regrets of this sort (that some wars were unnecessary or were bloodier than was necessary) are rare in the literature on "the art of war." Acclamation and critique center on ways of preparing for and conducting wars. Some periods in the history of war are described as "progressive," marked by imaginative innovation and seized opportunities (McElwee mentions "The Great Age of Moltke"), others as "stagnant." The most important "moral" in these books is addressed to the professional military men, who are enjoined to learn from the past, adapt to changing conditions in order that the science and art of war can continue to be part of the great creative achievements of humanity.

"Rational" and "Humane" Conduct of War

The "military way," as Vagts sees it, regards war as a means to an end and is committed to waging war as "rationally" as possible. The two criteria are identical, because compatibility of means and ends is a principal aspect of rationality.

Vagts, like Liddell Hart, criticized severely the conduct of World War I, sparing neither the French, the Germans, the British, nor the Russians. He was appalled by the bloodletting at Verdun. He castigated the Russians for their failure to supply their soldiers with enough rifles, for sending the men into battle unarmed to wait for their comrades to become casualties, so that they could take their rifles. He castigated the British military leaders for ignoring Lloyd George's plea for more machine guns per battalion and for failing to make full use of the tactical value of the tank. The effect of that weapon would have been greatly enhanced, Vagts explains, if it appeared on the battlefield suddenly and in large numbers. Instead, it was introduced haltingly, "experimentally," as it were. Instead of effecting a decisive breakthrough, the tanks merely warned the Germans, who learned how to deal with them and soon produced tanks of their own before the weapon could become decisive. Vagts accuses the Germans of the same mistake in failing to utilize fully the element of surprise when they introduced poison gas. Again the attempt was only halfhearted, which permitted the British to develop effective countermeasures and to produce poison gas of their own by the time the full force of that weapon could be exploited.

All this criticism appears to be directed at lapses of "rationality"—failures to exploit appropriate means to achieve the goal pursued. In the context of war, this is obviously victory. Liddell Hart criticizes military leaders for failing to learn the lesson, which they should have learned from two thousand years of experience with war: namely, to take advantage of available technology or to develop a technology suggested by advances in scientific knowledge. Another theme in the criticism of "militarism" from the point of view of the "military way" is failure to avoid "excessive" or "unnecessary" loss of life as, for example, in the eight-month-long Battle of Verdun.

Let us see what the outcome would have been had the military leaders been more "rational." More rationality would have meant introducing more destructive weapons by *both* sides, since what is rational for one would be rational for the other. This sort of rationality would conflict with humaneness, a virtue identified with the "military way" (as contrasted with "militarism") and the exalting of violence as the embodiment of martial virtues (cf. Clausewitz's remarks cited in Chapter 10).

In historical perspective, we can see the source of the contradiction. World War I, which in retrospect appears even to many military professionals as either a collective act of folly, a disaster, or a crime, cannot be associated with rationality. To say that World War I could have been conducted "more rationally" is a contradiction in terms.

A History of Militarism was published in 1937, practically on the eve of World War II. Mussolini had already conquered Ethiopia and waxed eloquent about the coming restoration of the Roman Empire. Hitler was rapidly building a gigantic war machine. Japan was engaged in the conquest of China, and her plans for further conquest in the Pacific were all too evident. It appeared as if the democracies had no choice but to prepare for armed defense against the coming onslaught by the highly militarized, openly aggressive states. In contrast to World War I, World War II, which everyone expected, seemed to have a well-defined, noble goal: defense against open and ruthless aggression *already going on*. The objective of this defense seemed clear: a decisive defeat of the aggressors leading to the dissolution of their violent regimes.

In the 1930s, "militarism," the dominance of politics by military establishments interested only in waging war and subordinating all policies to it, loomed as a threat to freedom-loving and peace-loving people. Since military defense seemed the only possible way of avoiding being conquered and enslaved, an ethically justifiable role had to be assigned to the military establishments of the democracies. The definition of the "military way" became essentially the definition of that role.

In 1937 Vagts could see America as a society immune to militarism. Never having had a nobility, America never had a military caste. Throughout the period of its dynamic expansion, it was not the soldier but the businessman who enjoyed the greatest prestige. In the heyday of American freewheeling capitalism, to become a millionaire was a much more common ambition among American youngsters than to become acclaimed as a war hero. The army helped in the expansion by killing off native Americans, but killing expeditions by the army were regarded somewhat in the same way as clearing forests. They didn't contribute directly to the nation's glory the way nineteenth-century national wars did in Europe. No Peter the Great, Frederick the Great, Napoleon, or Moltke is celebrated in American history.

Vagts probably foresaw, as many did, that World War II was imminent and that Americans would have to take part in it. But it is most likely that he foresaw American participation as an exemplary manifestation of "the military way," not of "militarism."

The American Way of War

In fact, this is what actually happened. The vast officers' corps of the American armed forces contained a large proportion of civilians recruited from the general population for their management rather than their martial skills. This was appropriate because a large part of America's war effort did not involve any battle experience. Great emphasis was placed on mobilization of production, services of supply, logistics, training, entertainment of troops—all regarded as components of a vital infrastructure for the war effort. Of all the major belligerents of World War II, the United States had the smallest proportion of professional military personnel in the armed forces. Some branches of the service never did participate in combat. For example, the Air Transport Command was a global airline, engaged in transporting personnel and materials to and from the far-flung theaters of war. Many of the commanding officers of this branch of the service were airline executives.

The comfort of the soldier was a major concern. Along with the war machines and ammunition, huge stores of consumer goods went overseas. The PX (Post Exchange) was a familiar installation in practically every permanent, even semipermanent, base. In these supermarkets, the GIs could buy candy, shaving cream, sweaters, cameras, and much else. Sanitary facilities, movies, and canned radio programs followed the American soldier all over the world. All these conveniences were regarded as necessary for the morale of the troops—probably justifiable in view of the fact that reverence for consumer goods appears to be ingrained in American conceptions of virtue, democracy, and loyalty to the United States. In their homesickness, American soldiers overseas fondly referred to the United States as the Big PX.

One could say that the U.S. waged World War II in a distinctly "non-militaristic" way. A large majority of the men inducted into the armed forces regarded themselves as civilians in uniform temporarily torn from their homes and normal occupations, expecting to return after victory (which no one doubted) to resume normal lives. In certain respects, however, Vagts could have seen this style of waging war as compatible with what he approvingly called "the military way." His conception of that style coincided with the image that most Americans had about the war—"a job to be done," rather than a drama of heroism, glory, or self-sacrifice. Americans waged war in a way to bolster the conviction that it was neither heroic nor romantic, but a necessary evil.

The Americans fought World War I "to make the world safe for democracy," and World War II became the "war to end war." Such sloganeering gave the wars a strong ideological component. But it was this very component that nurtured a non-militaristic attitude. The gulf between officers and enlisted men was narrower than in traditional military establishments. The enlisted man was provided with as many comforts as could be arranged. Technology and mass production, rather than élan in battle and readiness to sacrifice one's life at every opportunity, were regarded as the keys to victory. War aims were phrased as liberation of subjugated people rather than in terms of conquest and asserting the glory of arms.

The United States emerged from World War II practically unscathed. It suffered fewer casualties than any of the other major belligerents. There were no battles on its soil. The population was spared not only destruction but even serious shortages. What shortages there were, e.g., of automobiles, prevented a postwar depression by fueling a buying spree to satisfy the built-in appetite. Except for the fallen and their bereaved families, World War II was for most Americans an exhilarating experience.

The military were cordially thanked. Yet the social prestige of the man in uniform did not rise appreciably. None of the trappings of what Vagts calls militarism—gaudy uniforms, caste honor, dominance in political life—were in evidence in postwar America.

Only one feature of militarism can be ascribed to the American defense establishment that emerged from the war—the transformation of military power from the wherewithal to pursue the "national interest" to an end in itself.

This came about in spite of the inconspicuousness of the uniformed military in American life. The very fact that World War II was "fought" (i.e., managed) to a large extent by civilians, made it possible for the war establishment to continue to attract large contingents of civilians. In view of this massive influx, it seems necessary to revise the conception of the military professional. Clearly, the essential feature of the military occupation is not a uniform or a formal rank in the military hierarchy, but rather an immersion in an activity devoted primarily to war. As the war business was extended to solving complicated problems of planning and organization, and involving an immense array of specialists of all sorts, it became natural to subsume all the categories of specialists under military professionals. The difference between the man in uniform and the man in a business suit, both serving in the war business, has become blurred.

The crucial feature of the military profession, as we will use this term, is preoccupation with war and with all matters centered on war. The activities of the military professional may comprise development, procurement, and evaluation of weapons; scientific research related to the development of weapons; teaching subjects related to military science; covert activity related to waging secret wars; and, significantly, the design of strategies and the formulation of doctrines justifying them.

The Defense Community

There now exists in the United States a self-styled "defense community," comprised of the uniformed military personnel and a large civilian component including liaison personnel between the military and industry, a large scientific sector mobilized in the service of research feeding into development of weapons, a sector engaged in profitable arms trade, and an intelligence contingent engaged not only in worldwide espionage but also in subversion of unfriendly governments, and at times terrorist activity. Within this defense community is the most important "strategic community" composed of civilian strategists (cf. Chapter 16).

An important mark of the military professional is political detachment. This is an aspect of the military "professional ethic." It has been romanticized by Tennyson ("Theirs not to reason why; theirs but to do and die"). In a more prosaic vein, Clausewitz, a veritable apostle of military virtue, insisted that the military should be at all times subordinated to civilian authority. The army, Clausewitz taught, has just one raison d'étre—to serve the state.

In monarchical Europe, to serve the state meant to serve the monarch. The army was, therefore, an instrument of realizing the monarch's ambitions. For the military to be politically detached meant no more than refraining from developing its own ambitions apart from those of the monarch. Since, however, the monarch's ambitions were largely manifested in appetites for more territory or more influence in European affairs, they harmonized with those of the conscientious military. Notably in nineteenth-century Prussia, then in the German Empire, the military could afford to be politically detached.

When "national interest" can no longer be openly identified with an appetite for conquest, political detachment of the military becomes problematic, especially when fighting wars no longer can be done regularly and as a matter of course. During the nineteenth century, balkanized Latin America was a theater of many national wars, all futile and debilitating. Eventually such national wars ceased to be regarded as normal, and the role of the military in those countries became ambiguous. The military establishments then became fiercely political—"militaristic," as Vagts would characterize them.

Since World War II, the principal rationale for the continued existence of military establishments has been "defense." All the departments of war have become departments of defense. This rationale has become a national obsession in the United States and has sufficed to support, practically unimpeded, the growth of a huge war machine. In this milieu, the defense community could continue to be "apolitical" in the sense that *extra*-military justifications for its continued existence and growth became unnecessary. The defense community could remain entirely self-contained. Aside from lobbying for ever more support, it could divorce itself from politics. That is to say, "war aims" ceased to have any interest for it. The defense community could concentrate entirely on how to fight wars, completely ignoring the questions as to why they should be fought, the traditional stance of a non-political military establishment.

Note the work of the Institute of Land Combat, created in 1967. It was assigned the task of forecasting possible future wars and the role (if any) of the United States in them. The projections are for five-year periods. In the first five years of its existence the Institute identified nearly 400 possible wars in the period ending in 1990, of which more than a third might plausibly involve the United States. Each possible war was examined against the background of the terrain, climate, tactics, enemy, and so forth. About 600 new weapons or other pieces of equipment were mentioned, and ways of handling them discussed. This program gave the participants and possibly the administration the feeling that the U.S. was preparing itself for any possible contingency (quite in accordance with "the military way").

P. Dickson in his book *Think Tanks* (1971) lists some possible wars that have been examined in some detail. For instance:

Yugoslavia, U.S., and Italy pitted against the Soviet Union, Romania, Bulgaria, and Hungary.

U.S., Norway, West Germany, and Denmark versus U.S.S.R., East Germany, Poland, and Finland.

U.S., Libya, Tunisia, Italy, and West Germany versus United Arab Republic, U.S.S.R., and Algeria.

In retrospect it seems bizarre to think that preparations were made to fight a war in which Libya was expected to be an ally of the United States. But these projections were not meant to be prognoses. They were exercises, inspired by the stance of a mature military establishment, which is to be ready for every contingency, no matter how remote. (The European general staffs in their heyday were doing this all the time.) If a contingency should arise, one can imagine that a worked-out plan, prepared for just that situation, would be pulled out of the top-secret files and the communication channels would start sparking with coded messages sent over the whole planet, activating the giant war machine to do just what the contingency would require.

It is doubtful that an experienced military leader could take this scenario seriously. Nevertheless, from the point of view of the defense community, this exercise makes sense. It keeps military personnel and their civilian colleagues busy. It brushes aside the disturbing idea that all of a sudden the accumulated wisdom of the "science of war" has become completely and irrevocably obsolete. The profession must look to its own survival. It must keep its concepts and values viable and meaningful.[3]

We see in this activity another manifestation of a transformation of the conception of war as a means to an end to a preoccupation with war as an end in itself. Vagts would have called this transformation a degeneration of the "military way" into "militarism." It appears to us that in view of the fact that war has become obsolete as an instrument of rational policy, the persistence of war *as an institution* must be regarded as the persistence of militarism. There is no way of restoring the virtues of "the military way," because there is no way of rationalizing war as a way of pursuing ends *extrinsic* to war. Therefore the distinction between "the military way" and "militarism" has become meaningless.

To see how, in spite of its obsolescence, war has remained a chronic condition of human life, it will be helpful to examine the "war system." Let us look at war, not as a recurring event like an epidemic or some natural cataclysm, but as an institution, a "subsystem" embedded in human societies.

War as an Institution

War is certainly as old as civilization, if by civilization we mean a way of life associated with more or less permanent, settled human communities marked by a division of labor and a clearly differentiated social structure.

Almost the only thing that can be said of all wars is that they involve sustained large-scale organized violence and more or less skilled use of weapons. The latter feature is usually associated with the existence of a specialized occupation—that of the soldier. This occupation has been a mark of civilization. In precivilized human groups, often every able-bodied man participated in a war as a fighter.

Except for this common feature—organized, large-scale violence—wars have differed radically throughout history in their origins, etiology, and effects. Conceptions of war, too, have undergone changes. There were times when war was conceived simply as a means of livelihood, like hunting or fishing. At other times and places, war has been regarded as a heroic enterprise, a pious act, a punishment meted out by a deity, a way of extending political or economic control, a normal phase in relations among states, an abnormal phase of international relations, a natural disaster, a symptom of social pathology, a manifestation of an "aggressive instinct," and a crime.

Here we want to call attention to a particular feature of the practice and the conception of war, namely, an alternation of "phases"—a succession of "democratization" and "technocratization" of war.

Everyman's War and the Specialist's War

Tribal warfare was, for the most part, "democratic" in the sense that the people engaged in war faced each other as personal enemies. Everyone was involved. Objectives of warfare were often matters of survival. The conquest of Canaan by the Israelites, as related in the Old Testament, reveals the "total" character of that sort of war of conquest (cf. Chapter 2). Extermination was frequently the lot of the vanquished.

With the advent of empires, professional warriors carried out the military operations. The outcome of a war usually still affected entire populations. The defeated were subjugated, often reduced to servile status and burdened with tribute.

An extreme example of a directly opposite situation can be seen in the warfare of eighteenth-century Europe, the period of so-called "cabinet wars." These were fought predominantly by standing armies, bodies of highly trained men pressed into service for many years. These soldiers were only a small fraction of the population, or were mercenaries from other countries. The wars were fought for limited objectives, such as the conquest of a province or the legitimization or de-legitimization of a candidate for a throne. The outcomes of wars rarely had serious effects on the non-combatants. The general population often did not know that their countries were at war, much less the objectives for which the wars were fought.

Because the professional armies were expensive instruments, the risks taken in cabinet wars were tempered by prudence. Capitulation was no disgrace. Nor did patriotism (a later invention) play an important part as an instigator of war or as a morale factor. Military specialists frequently left the service of one prince to enter the service of another, much as corporation lawyers now move from one firm to another without incurring the onus of disloyalty.

The French Revolution introduced a radical change in the nature of European warfare. A new "actor" appeared in the arena of political events—masses of people moved by passion, enthusiasm, rage directed against age-old compulsions to render deference to and obey the traditionally privileged. A public execution of a king was not unprecedented, but that of Louis XVI created a much greater stir in Europe than did the execution of Charles I of England a century and a half before.

Military intervention by monarchies followed promptly. Meticulously trained Prussian and Austrian professionals met with humiliating defeats by the recruits of the French Republic. A new ideological dimension was added to war: the armed citizen believed that he had something to fight *for*.

Perhaps the upsurge of "morale" as a decisive factor in battles was not confined to the revolutionary armies. The Russian general Suvorov was also able to inspire his soldiers to fight furiously without regard for personal safety as a matter of pride rather than because of brainwashing by persistent drill. (It is said that Suvorov accomplished this transformation by exercising personal charisma.)

Another extremely important feature that made the citizen army a formidable fighting instrument was the expendability of the conscripted citizen-soldier. His training was much shorter than that of the professional. He did not have to be spared in battle. The battle could now be conceived as an extermination contest. That Napoleon well understood this new conception is evidenced in his massive use of artillery. This arm now achieved parity with the infantry and the cavalry in the "orchestration " of battles.

From the point of view of the *sociology* of warfare, the most important new feature of war that came in the wake of the French Revolution was patriotism. War became "democratized" again. Not only did the citizen become a direct participant in nineteenth-century war as a conscript. He became involved also as a civilian. The spread of literacy and the rise of the public press, the first of the mass media, contributed mightily to the ascendance of nationalism as a dominant public mood. The history of nineteenth-century Europe can be regarded as a history of struggles to weld populations into nations, to make them loyal to their mother tongue and cultural traditions, hence to a language rather than to a dynasty.

It is this "democratized" phase that is most prominent in the present generation's conception of war. Although the generation that has direct memories of World War II has passed middle age, and the generation with direct memories of World War I is almost gone, the two world wars stand out as "typical" wars of the "civilized" world. Their most distinguishing feature is their massiveness. The armies involved in them dwarfed all the armies of bygone eras. The war technologies developed during those wars deployed more energy of destruction than all the past wars together. The participation of the civilian populations both as auxiliary forces (producing weapons and supporting technologies) and as casualties had no historical precedent. The two world wars, especially World War II, represented total mobilization of societies aiming at each other's destruction.

The destructiveness of the two world wars gave rise to the conception of war as an anomaly or a disaster resembling an earthquake, a flood, or a severe epidemic. The latter analogy seemed especially apt in view of the important role that popular enthusiasm was thought to play in the instigation of war. This enthusiasm was variously attributed to deep-seated or "instinctive" hostilities toward people of other nationalities or to deliberate stimulation of such hostility through propaganda. But whatever was assumed to be the genesis of hostility, few doubted that hostility, whether natural or induced, was a principal factor in the etiology of wars.

This conception of war as the ultimate expression of personal hostility and aggressiveness is now becoming obsolete. To see this, consider the transformation of the "warrior" throughout the history of warfare. We see the warrior portrayed in ancient lore as strong, brave, and fierce. The warrior of old had to be strong, because he had to wield heavy weapons. He had to be brave, because he had to suppress in himself the instinct of self-preservation. He had to be fierce in order not to shrink from killing his own kind. With the advent of weapons that kill at a distance, these characteristics lost their importance. The killing power of a gun is not necessarily correlated with its weight, as is the killing power of a sword or a spear. As battles became encounters between ever-more-organized units rather than between individuals in single combat, bravery became less important. As the victim was removed from sight and earshot, fierceness was no longer a prerequisite for uninhibited killing.

Like any other profession, the military profession takes pride in "progress," in this case progress in the science and art of warmaking. Extrapolating present trends into the future, some military professionals write with undisguised enthusiasm about imminent developments in the technology of destruction. Recall the dream of the "automated battlefield," where the location of enemy forces is discovered by sophisticated sensors and electronic data processing, where fire is directed by computer programs, where unmanned devices crawl, run, or fly to destory the adversary's devices. While the dehumanization of war in the sense of severing human beings from weapons is still a science fiction fantasy, the dehumanization of war in the sense of making emotions associated with war irrelevant remains the principal result of sophisticated technology. It is no longer necessary to hate anyone in order to kill everyone.

The drastic changes in the nature of war throughout its history account for the very different conceptions of war and of its role in human affairs. We take the opportunity to reiterate the view that just because many events or processes are subsumed under the same label, they do not necessarily represent variants of the "same" phenomenon in the sense of stemming from a common origin or being subject to the same "laws." So it is with war. Clausewitz, following a time-honored philosophical tradition, set for himself the task of revealing the "essence" of war. His achievement was to reveal what war in Europe *became* in consequence of replacing the animated tin soldier of the cabinet wars with the motivated citizen-soldier of the Revolutionary and Napoleonic wars. It seemed to Clausewitz that in undergoing this transformation war revealed its "true essence." But war was to undergo even more radical transformations. No single concept can encompass all of them. The designation of all these very different manifestations of organized violence by a single word may be misleading, but we have no choice other than to continue established usage. The most we can do is warn against the misconceptions that it can entail.

And yet there is some justification in seeing unity in all these widely disparate manifestations of organized violence. In tracing the history of war, we are tracing the history of a system, specifically of an institution. Many institutions have undergone radical changes and yet have retained an identity of sorts. This conception of war as an institution is at variance with some now widely prevalent conceptions, for instance those that identify war with a *breakdown* of the international system or as an instance of large-scale social pathology. There is no way of deciding which of these conceptions of war represents its "true nature." They are different *aspects* of war. Each conception may be legitimate and may contribute to the understanding of the phenomenon.

War as a System Adapted to Its Environment

Regarding the war establishment as an institution in the organismic sense raises questions about its role as a subsystem in a state or in a society. We mentioned a school of thought represented in sociology and in anthropology called functionalism, according to which each lasting institution has a role in holding together the society in which it is embedded. In support of this view are certain consequences derived from the natural selection theory of evolution. This theory explains the existence of structures and processes characterizing biological organisms by pointing out that they exist by virtue of conferring reproduction advantages on their possessors. If societies or cultures evolve, we could assume that a selection process is operating on their differentiated characteristics conferring advantage on those characteristics that are conducive to the continued existence of the society or culture in question.

This analogy is beset with serious difficulties. The process of natural selection applies with full force in the biological setting where there are vast numbers of organisms differing in minute details and reproducing themselves at different rates. Natural selection acts over many generations of an evolving species. Nothing of the sort is observed in the world of "societies" or "cultures." It can be said of a species that if it is at least holding its own in the struggle for existence, it is (by definition) adapted to its environment. This cannot be said of a species on the verge of extinction. A species clearly on the way to extinction, as evidenced by a dwindling population is, by definition, *not* adapted to its environment. Unlike species composed of many individuals, we do not examine a "population" of societies or cultures. We examine single instances. Therefore, there is no objective way of assessing whether a particular society or culture is or is not on the way to extinction. For this reason the assertion sometimes encountered in functionalist sociological or anthropological literature, that lasting institutions play a positive role in holding a society together or in ensuring the continuity of a culture, is not always tenable.

Quite aside from the role that an institution plays with regard to the system in which it is embedded, it *itself* may well be adapted to *its* environment, and natural selection may play a part in conferring adaptive mechanisms on it. Let us see whether something of this sort can be said of war as an institution.

If we view the institution of war as an organism living within another organism (a society), then we can regard the various transformations of war as adaptations to the transformations undergone by its "host." The system and the subsystem coevolved. We need not, of course, assume any conscious "effort" on the part of the war system to adapt to the society in which it is embedded. All we need to recognize is the fact of its continued robust existence, which is *prima facie* evidence of its adaptability. Indeed, the transformation of war from an instrument used by monarchs to feed their ambitions into a manifestation of "national will" or "national vigor" coincided with the decline of absolute monarchies and the awakening of democratic ideas. When the great disillusionment with romanticized nationalist heroics threatened the existence of warmaking as an established, venerated institution, the military establishment found another safer niche: defense. The touted function of the war machine became that of ensuring the preservation of the ideals and values of its host society. The defense stance became especially impregnable in the Soviet Union. It was easily accepted by a population that had suffered through a long history of devastating invasions.

In the United States, "defense" is also a word to conjure with. There the war system has found another powerful support, namely, in the pervasive superstition that war, or at least a permanent war economy, is conducive to prosperity. Like all superstitions, this one is directly traceable to an unwarranted generalization.

On common sense grounds, it is difficult to see how the idea can persist that war or preparations for war are "good for the economy." Modern war is immensely destructive. Preparations for war are certainly unproductive. They create neither consumer goods nor capital goods (machines to produce consumer goods or other capital goods). If by a "good economy" one means an economy that provides the population with usable things and services, the war economy cannot possibly be as good as a peace economy in which things are produced for use by the population.

This common sense argument has two drawbacks. First, what is "usable" cannot be precisely defined without invoking certain values. Works of art can be regarded as "usable" or "unusable" depending on the extent to which art is appreciated. If art is regarded as something needed for a "good life," then an economy in which artists are supported cannot be charged with being wasteful. By the same token, it can be argued that huge arsenals contribute to the people's feeling of security, making the argument that tanks and bombs can be neither eaten nor worn nor used to produce eatable or wearable things inconclusive.

Second, although one of the properties of a "good economy" is a large productive capacity, it is well known that in capitalistic economies productive capacity is not sufficient. During the 1930s, the entire capitalist world suffered from severe depression. The productive capacity was there. The raw materials were available. A large labor force was available, and people were happy to work for a pittance if only they would be allowed to work. Yet the machines and the people stood idle. Certain stimuli were needed in order to activate the system. People with money had to be motivated to invest their money. People who had closed down their factories had to be motivated to open them, and this they would do only if there were prospects of selling the things produced at a profit. But there was not enough money in the pockets of potential buyers of these goods, and so the economy was paralyzed by several interlocking vicious circles.

In the United States, attempts to break out of these vicious cycles were made during Franklin D. Roosevelt's administration. These were attempts to "prime the pump" by government spending. This remedy was strongly resisted in big business circles, because "government interference" went against the prevailing laissez faire ideology. A large political coalition of low-income workers, ethnic minorities, Blacks, and so forth, supported Roosevelt's program. As it turned out, however, the volume of government spending was not sufficient to overcome the Depression. It was overcome only when America went to war.

The difference between stimulating productive and stimulating non-productive activity (such as production for war) is that the former eventually becomes satiated but the latter does not. Suppose, for example, cars are not produced because people wanting cars haven't the money to buy them. By stimulating the economy by government spending, some money is poured into people's pockets. Some start buying cars. The assembly lines start running again, people are hired, have even more money, etc. Eventually, however, the buying slows down, because people have enough cars. Of course, the economy can be stimulated still more; people can be induced to believe that unless they buy a new car every year, they can't be happy. Nevertheless, there are limits to how much the economy can be boosted by such stimulation.

Military spending need not have any limits. In the first place, there is no problem of the market becoming satiated. Weapons rapidly become obsolete—then to be scrapped and replaced by improved models, which are also sure to become obsolete. Moreover, there is always an adversary, who must be prevented from getting ahead, which means that there is never enough.

In this way, the idea took hold that military spending was the most effective way of stimulating the economy. Since the memory of the Great Depression made the stimulation of the economy by government spending acceptable in America, the idea persisted. It should be noted, however, that alongside that idea another has become an indispensable prop of open-ended military spending, namely, that these expenditures do *not* represent pure waste. They are presumed to buy "security." The more destructive power is amassed, the more secure people are supposed to feel. The two shibboleths, defense and security, have become firmly linked in the mass mind in spite of the fact that the weapons of total destruction cannot possibly "defend" anything or anybody and in spite of the fact that the feeling of "security" seems to decrease as the destructive power of the war machine increases. This idea, like the idea that war is "good for the economy," is also based on an unwarranted generalization.

Let us first examine the unwarranted generalization inherent in the belief that war or preparation for war is "good for the economy." Support for this idea followed from the sudden dissipation of the Great Depression as America started to prepare for war and then entered World War II. The volume of government spending exceeded by several orders of magnitude the amounts spent on public works projects, social welfare, and all other measures developed during the New Deal. Nor was the stimulation confined to orders to factories. A huge idle labor force was put to work, a large fraction of it inducted into the armed forces. Plant capacities were expanded. Even though most of the things produced were not consumer goods, people, who now had money, could buy up the surplus consumer goods, clearing the market, even creating a scarcity. This scarcity persisted during the war and was the principal reason why the expected postwar depression did not materialize. People with money accumulated for lack of things to buy were starved for goods that they had come to regard as necessities, such as cars and refrigerators. Buying stimulated production of new "necessities," such as television.

The unwarranted generalization in this scenario is that this state of affairs can continue indefinitely. War stimulated the American economy in the 1940s only because of very special circumstances—the existence of a large idle productive capacity and a large idle labor force. The two had been kept apart by a specific prejudice inherent in capitalist ideology, namely, that the incentive of profit is an indispensable component of production. It is this *ideological* factor that paralyzed the economy in the 1930s. An initial "overproduction" made it difficult to sell at a profit in a buyer's market. Production was curtailed, unemployment rose, buying power was reduced, goods remained unsold—a vicious circle wound down the economy. The incentive for war production by private firms is also profit, but there is no problem with selling what has been produced. The impulse to the American economy provided by war production at the end of the 1930s came from outside the system, as it were. The government stepped in as a giant buyer, buying at cost-plus. The idle labor force was brought together with the idle productive capacity, and this happened suddenly and dramatically. These were very special circumstances that produced the impression that war is "good for the economy."

However, an effective infusion of a stimulant is one thing and continuing infusion of the same stimulant quite another. By all reasonable measures of economic health, the American economy under the perpetual stimulation of military spending is declining. Superstitions, however, are exceptionally resistant to facts, especially when they are based on wishful thinking.

The unwarranted generalization underlying the second superstition, that the level of security is directly related to the level of the destructive force piled up, exemplifies the common fallacy of assuming a monotone relationship where none exists. In countries where undernourishment is chronic, there is a belief that obesity is a mark of health. Even in America, a belief persisted well into the 1920s that gaining weight was a sign of good health, while losing weight was a sign of poor health. Signs on public scales read "Your weight indicates your health. Are you gaining or losing?" Nothing has remained of this superstition, but it is difficult to find a person, at least in America, regardless of the level of income, who is not convinced that more income is always better than less income.

Like the obsession with body fat (still persisting in some cultures), the obsession with money (persistent in all societies with money economies) has all the earmarks of an addiction (cf. Chapter 10). The same is true of the persistent belief that power, as measured by the destructive potential of one's arsenal, provides "security." It is primarily for this reason that pumping money into the war machine does not appear to the majority of citizens of militarized states as waste. The gross national product of an economy includes military expenditures. The fact that what these expenditures buy represents neither wealth nor security remains obscured.

The adaptation of the war system to its host society was assured by the persistence of the above-mentioned superstitions. The internalized beliefs that a perpetual war economy is the basis of prosperity and that the war machine is the basis of security make the population not only tolerant toward this essentially parasitic growth but even proud of it.

The adaptation of the war machine to the society as a whole, however, does not tell the whole story. Its adaptation to the business sector of the society has been even more complete. Consider the values inherent in business activity in a free enterprise economy. As we have seen, there is a strong linkage between the idea of free enterprise and the idea of freedom in the ideology of laissez faire. But there are certain costs associated with economic freedom. It is all very well to admire the system in which the worthy win and to welcome the invigorating effects of competition. The system appears most attractive to the winners, considerably less so to the losers. To be a winner, one must acquire certain skills and exert considerable effort. One must take pains to familiarize oneself with the environment. One must use considerable ingenuity in seeking out profitable niches and in minimizing the costs of operation. The satisfaction that comes in the wake of a successful performance is rewarding, but the disappointment that comes in the wake of an unsuccessful performance is painful. For all too many, the system would appear even more attractive if everyone who played were a winner. The permament war economy has made this possible.

S. Melman (1974) shows through a case study how the military economy works. An American firm, undertaking to submit bids to the Department of Defense for some new products, assigned the job of preparing price estimates to a young engineer. Ordinarily, this procedure would involve consulting accounting records of one's own firm, reports containing information about costs of materials that would have to be used in the new products, work time estimates, and the like. Taking these estimates into account, the cost of a new product could be estimated. Then a profit margin would be added. There would be a trade-off in determining this profit margin. On the one hand, the firm would be aware that other competing firms would probably be making similar bids. This circumstance would create a pressure to make the profit margin small. On the other hand, the profit margin could not be reduced below a certain minimum which would make the contract worthwhile.

In estimating costs, the person entrusted with this task might consider the relevant costs in the past. He might use his expertise to design ways of bringing these costs down, in this way either making more room for a margin of profit without impairing the competitive position of the firm or keeping the same margin of profit and thereby improving the chances of getting the contract.

This is the way private enterprise works. Whatever virtues can be ascribed to the capitalist system are inherent in competition. It is competition that generates pressures to keep costs down, to reduce them if possible, to keep profit margins at reasonable levels, and to improve the quality of the products—which often means to improve at least the physical aspects of human life.

However, this is not the way the military economy works. The young engineer in Melman's case study who was assigned the task of preparing price estimates of new products proceeded to do so without consulting the records of the accounting department relevant to the estimates of the costs. *He was not permitted* to consult those records. How, then, one might ask, did he prepare the price estimates? By basing them on prices, *not* costs, of former products of his own firm and on prices of similar products of other firms. Occasionally, he could obtain some information from competing firms informally.

Melman concludes this story as follows: "This sort of job requirement proved to be unnerving to the engineer . . . because his training had instilled in him values about efficiency which he was unable to fulfill under the condition imposed on him. After a few years he left this job in disgust." (Melman 1974, pp. 27–28.)

The story illustrates the difference between *normative* costing and *historical* costing. Normative costing determines what the cost of an item *should* be if it is based on diagnosing and evaluating the costs of what goes into producing it. Historical costing is based on past prices used in price bidding. It is inevitable that historically determined costs escalate. If inflation is in process, it is natural to "allow" for it in estimating prices to be charged for the product, which will be read in the future, not today. The assumption that inflation will continue *makes* it continue—a realization of the self-fulfilling assumption principle.

There is a good reason for ignoring the actual costs in estimating prices of products bought by the military and for not trying to reduce them. A crucial difference between a civilian economy in a capitalist system and a military economy, which, Melman points out, constitutes *state capitalism*, is that the pressure to *minimize* costs operating in the former is replaced by a pressure to *maximize* costs in the latter. The one and only customer of military products is the government. There is no reason why the government of a militarized state should care what it pays for products. Why should it? *It* does not compete with another government that can show that it can pay less and so save the taxpayers' money. The government can always be counted on to pay whatever it is asked to pay. On the other hand, the more an item costs to produce, the more profit can be made by selling it if the margin of profit is a constant percentage of the cost. Besides:

> For the military-industry enterprise, higher costs mean more activity, more facilities, more employees, more cash flow . . . For the military-industry top managers in the Pentagon, cost increases in the sub-firms denote more activity under their control and are the basis for enlarged budget requests to the Congress. There is no built-in limitation on the cost-maximization process. The limits are external: the political acceptability of Pentagon budgets to the Congress and to the population as a whole. (Melman 1974, p. 34.)

Acceptability is insured by the robustness of the superstition that links military potential to "security," coupled with the superstition that whatever costs more must be better.

Is there, then, no competition at all under state capitalism, one might ask? Yes, there is. But the competitive standing of a firm is not determined by its efficiency, as efficiency is usually understood in the context of capitalism.

The military-industry firms compete with each other, but in their race for fresh contract and capital grants from the Pentagon managers, they do not vie for who can achieve a lower product price and cost but rather who can compete best in terms of a display of "competence." Competence, in the jargon of the military-industry world, means the readiness and ability of the particular firm to satisfy the Pentagon's requirements in the judgment of its top management. It means its ability to collaborate with Pentagon-level administrators to turn out the sort of product that the Pentagon wants with regard to details of product designing, testing, producing and servicing. It includes, for example, the capability for coping with very large numbers of design changes once a product has been specified. It includes the expectation that the firm has the stuff and the accompanying know-how for dealing with military managers and with the military user organizations on a continuing basis. It means knowing how to talk to the military, how to write the instructional and maintenance manuals needed for training people in the operation and maintenance of complex equipment. (Melman 1974, p. 35.)

Business firms that adapt themselves to these requirements prosper and multiply. Between them and the military establishment a symbiotic relationship develops. Together they form the so-called military-industrial complex. Other institutions adapt themselves to *this* environment: research institutes, institutions of higher learning. All of them together serve the needs of the war machine.

The Declining Economy

By all usual standards except the gross national product, the economy of the United States is in a state of decline. The gross national product index does not count because it includes the military sector. So unless one insists that the military sector is producing something of economic value, this component of the economy (which is vaguely referred to in most American economics textbooks as the "public sector") must be left out. When it is left out, a dismal picture emerges. To appreciate this picture, we must turn away from indices and observe actual events affecting people's lives.

In August 1969, as American astronauts made history by landing on the moon, the technology that serves the ordinary business of living was conspicuously breaking down. In New York City, the telephone service was falling apart. The commuter railroad service was falling apart. Electric power-generating plants of Consolidated Edison were suffering breakdown after breakdown. Even these concrete symptoms do not convey the actual picture. But the following opening paragraphs of an article by Martin Tolchin in *The New York Times* of January 15, 1973 does.

Packs of wild dogs pick through the rubble and roam the streets, sometimes attacking residents. As protection, many mailmen, health workers and deliverers carry dog repellent.

A drug pusher is murdered by a youth gang acting on a contract from a rival pusher. A youngster is nearly stomped to death outside a school in an argument over a Coca-Cola bottle. Merchants close their stores at sunset even though many are armed and some conduct business inside their stores behind bullet-proof glass.

This is the South Bronx today—violent, drugged, burned out, graffiti-splattered and abandoned. Forty percent of the 400,000 residents are on welfare, and thirty percent of the employables are unemployed.

Now let us look at the indices. In 1971, for the first time since 1893, the value of exports from the U.S. fell short of the value of imports. The balance of trade became negative. In the decade after 1960, imports of three classes of technological goods (non-electrical machinery, electrical apparatus, and transport equipment) increased by 600%. On September 16, 1985, the U.S. Department of Commerce announced that the United States had become a debtor nation. This led Gore Vidal to remark that on that date the American Empire died at the age of 71. The reference was to the transformation of the U.S. from a debtor nation to a creditor nation in 1914, thereby inheriting Britain's economic hegemony. (Presumably the mantle of economic hegemony has now passed to Japan, a nation which at this time is still virtually disarmed.)

A detailed analysis of the complex interlocking causes and effects that have added up to the decline of the American economy are beyond the scope of this book. It suffices to point out a commonsense conclusion. If resources, capital, and talent are diverted to economically unproductive activities, the economy *must* decline, and the consequences of the decline must affect the society adversely.

That this decline and these consequences are ignored or perhaps not even perceived by persons in power is a direct consequence of the fact that these persons identify with the sector of the economy that is robust and prospers—the military and its entourage.

We have a situation not unlike that of an organism infested with a parasite. The parasite, adapted to its host environment, thrives. It thrives because the vital resources of the host are diverted to *it*, and it does not need to give the host anything in return. Eventually, the parasite may kill the host and so destroy its own environment and perish. But the parasite does not know this.

Other Adaptations

Adaptation based on peculiarities of the variety of capitalism that has evolved in the United States could not have taken place in the Soviet Union. There the military attained its privileged position by assuming a distinctly credible defense function: invasions of Russia by rapacious enemies actually occurred throughout its history and within living memory, culminating in a truly murderous assault on the population. The fact that the prospects of another invasion of this sort are practically nil and that all the time-honored means of "defense" have become meaningless in the nuclear age makes no difference. Attitudes based on historical experience have remained geared to that experience. And yet, regardless of the credibility of its defense function, the Soviet military establishment must be seen, objectively speaking, as a parasite on the Soviet economy. The deeply ingrained attitude of reverence toward it in the population is its particular mechanism of adaptation.

In countries of the Third World, military establishments have assured their parasitic existence by direct use of force. At propitious times they would take over the government and run the country as it suited them, simply by virtue of possessing physical power. These establishments have adapted themselves to underdeveloped economies and underdeveloped political institutions.

In reviewing the analogies that suggest the organismic metaphor, it appears that a comparison of the war system to a malignant growth is somewhat more apt than the comparison to a parasite. A parasite invades the organism from the outside. Although it adapts itself to the organism's metabolism, it is foreign to the organism. The host is sometimes able to mobilize resources to destroy the parasite or drive it out. For example, the white corpuscles in the blood have precisely this function in ridding the body of invading pathogenic organisms. The effectiveness of these defenses depends on the defenders' ability to recognize the invaders as "alien."

In contrast, a malignant growth is composed of the organism's own cells. For this reason, malignant growths are usually deadly: the body treats the malignant cells as "its own." Similarly, a military establishment mimics a functionally necessary subsystem of a living system. It is aided in this mimicry by historical memory. There was a time when military establishments did perform functions necessary for the survival of the society which they served. These functions have atrophied. But military establishments, particularly those of the superpowers, succeeded in readapting themselves to new conditions, so that they are still regarded as functionally necessary. Therein lies their viability, and therein lies the mortal danger to the hosts.

Notes

1. The following excerpts from Guibert's work are cited in Liddell Hart 1933.
2. Guibert was 27 when his major work was published.
3. In countries where populations think of war as an evil (albeit at times a necessary one), the "glories" of war are played down. War is invariably depicted as "defense." Where a physical invasion of a country is difficult to imagine realistically, e.g., in America, "defense" refers to "values" or "our way of life." When it becomes difficult to imagine how weapons of total destruction can defend "values" (or anything else), "deterrence" is advanced as the most pervasive rationalization of the war machine. Indeed, "deterrence" is sold as protection against the war machine: it is supposed to prevent the machine from being activated.

PART

IN QUEST OF PEACE

21

Pacifism

Pacifism is usually understood as an unconditional rejection of war. A pacifist refuses to distinguish between a "just" and an "unjust" war or between an "offensive" and a "defensive" war. The pacifist's rejection of war is rooted in an internal aversion to violence. An extreme manifestation of this aversion is a refusal to justify even personal self-defense. In the Sermon on the Mount, Jesus advises against "resisting evil." In the biblical account of his life, Jesus meekly submits to his tormentors (although he presumably had the power to destroy them) and even refuses to defend himself against false accusations. The Christian martyrs are said to have followed his example.

Attitudes toward violence and toward war in particular range from this complete and unconditional rejection to enthusiastic acceptance and glorification. In Chapter 2 we cited military professionals who depicted war-making as an activity necessary for the preservation of the vigor of a nation and the moral fiber of its citizens. Attitudes of this sort can easily be attributed to these authors' dedication to their profession. Romantic celebration of war has, however, by no means been confined to its practitioners. It can be found anywhere among those who associate human virtue with "heroism" and who assign higher priority to causes or ideals than to personal safety. Heroism can be defined as transcendence of self and dissolution of the ego in an identification with something larger.

This transcendence can be manifested in glorification both of the "brotherhood of man" and of war by the same person. Witness the sentiments expressed by Friedrich Schiller, Germany's foremost romantic poet (1759–1805). He authored both "Hymn to Joy," the text set to music in Beethoven's Ninth Symphony, and "The Bride of Messina." The former contains the line:

All men shall be brothers.

In the latter we read:

Man is stunted by peaceful days,
In idle repose his courage decays.
Law is the weakling's game.
But in war man's strength is seen
War ennobles all that is mean,
Even the coward belies his name.

In examining negative attitudes toward war, we can distinguish between those based on religious or ethical grounds and those based on an analysis of the role wars have played in human affairs. Rejection based on religious or ethical grounds is predominantly personal and rooted in a philosophy of life. Rejection based on analysis is a social or political outlook. Attitudes related to rejection of violence lead to conclusions about how an individual should behave. The critical attitude of social pacifism toward war leads to conceptions of how a society or, on a larger scale, the world order should be organized. In a systematic discussion of pacifism and of views related to it, we must examine these outlooks with respect to two criteria: how the rejection of violence, in particular of war, is *qualified* by the conditions under which it emerges and according to the cognitive foundations of the attitudes involved, whether they are grounded in religious or philosophical convictions, in a personal predisposition, or in a normative theory of society.

Personal Pacifism

Uncompromising insistence on interpreting the teachings of Christ as an unconditional rejection of violence has been evident throughout the ages. Outstanding among "personal" pacifists was Leo Tolstoy, who took the injunction, "And I say unto you, resist not evil" literally and absolutely.

The clearest example of this attitude is found in Tolstoy's story, "The Godson." A poor peasant, unable to find anyone to be godfather to his son, goes wandering in search of one. A stranger whom he meets on the road accepts his invitation but disappears after the baptism, never to be heard of again. When the lad grows up, he goes wandering in search of his godfather. A stranger, to whom he tells of his quest reveals himself as the godfather. He bids him go to his house and await his return.

The house turns out to be a castle. The godson had been told that he is free to go everywhere except into one room. Naturally, curiosity makes him go in. The room turns out to be a control center, from where all events in the world are influenced. (The godfather is actually God.) Watching people's lives unfold, the godson interferes on numerous occasions, always on the side of the good; but, as it turns out, always with disastrous results, which the godfather reveals to him upon his return. (The godson thinks he spent only a few minutes in the control room, but actually years have gone by.)

In one of his interventions, he killed a robber who was about to murder his mother. For this he is punished by having to take upon himself all of the robber's sins, for which the robber would have had to bear the penalty, had he not been killed and thereby absolved.

In another story, a humorous one, written in the style of a folk tale, Ivan the Fool, who in Russian folklore represents the power of innocence, triumphs over all forms of evil through invincible simplemindedness, immune to temptation and hence invulnerable to being taken advantage of. The secret of Ivan's power is his inability to *see* evil.

By a fantastic concatenation of circumstances, Ivan becomes king of a country. But he remains true to his character and habits. Tired of idleness, he goes out into the fields to plow. When people point out to him that he is a king, his rejoinder is, "A king's got to eat, too." His answer to a man who accuses another of having stolen his money is, "Well, he must have had need of it." Soon all the clever people in that country realize that Ivan is a fool and leave. Only fools remain to lead a hardworking, pacific life.

The devil, intent on corrupting Ivan, disguises himself as a general and enters Ivan's service. He urges Ivan to let him organize an army. Ivan, as always, consents. A proclamation is issued commanding every male of military age to enlist under the penalty of death for refusing. The fools are puzzled. They come to Ivan to ask him how he alone can put all of them to death. This question Ivan cannot answer. "If I were clever," he says, "maybe I could explain this to you. But, as you know, I am a fool." "So we won't enlist," say the fools. "So don't," says Ivan.

Frustrated, the devil enters the service of a neighboring king and persuades him to invade Ivan's kingdom. The inhabitants, of course, don't resist. The devil orders the soldiers to burn the villages and to kill the cattle. The fools still don't resist. They plead with the soldiers: "If you need our things, dear souls, why don't you just take them? Why destroy them?" The soldiers become demoralized, and the army falls apart.

In banking on the moral power of nonresistance, Tolstoy assumed the existence in every human being of a conscience, which is silenced only if victims of aggression resist, for resistance provides the rationale for violence. If Tolstoy's hypothesis is not accepted, that is, if it is assumed that whole categories of persons can be completely "freed" from conscience, the concept of nonresistance to evil as a way of "fighting" evil collapses. Recent history suggests that the hypothesis of a universal conscience in human beings that inhibits against doing harm to innocent others is not tenable.

Emphasis on the power of conscience is the most essential aspect of personal pacifism. Analogues of Christian pacifism are found also in Buddhism, Bahaiism, and other pacifist religions. They all emphasize the necessity for expelling violence from one's *own* psyche as a precondition for reducing the amount of violence in the world. This theme, along with the rejection of activism, is also developed in "The Godson." In his wanderings, the godson meets people in predicaments created by their failure to use suitable means to attain desirable goals. A woman tries unsuccessfully to wash wooden boards using a dirty cloth. Some shepherds try to build a fire by piling logs on a fire that is still too small. (The message: First cleanse yourself, then try to get others to cleanse their souls; build a fire inside yourself before trying to ignite it in others.)

Was Tolstoy, the champion of Christian meekness, a meek person? Did he follow his own prescripts of first eradicating anger in his own soul before preaching gentleness to others? There is ample evidence that he did not. There was one context in which Tolstoy was an ardent advocate of resistance, and in his advocacy he revealed a fiery anger and annihilating scorn that matched the vituperative style of any revolutionary. Tolstoy preached unyielding resistance to orders to commit violence. The following comment is on the army regulation which enjoins the soldier to obey all the orders of his commander except those that tend toward the injury of the czar:

> If the soldier before obeying the orders of his commander must first decide whether it is not against the czar, how then can he fail to consider before obeying his commander's orders whether it is not against his supreme King, God? And no action is more opposed to the will of God than that of killing men. And therefore you cannot obey men if they order you to kill. If you obey, and kill, you do so only for the sake of your own advantage—to escape punishment. So that in killing by order of your commander you are a murderer as much as the thief who kills a rich man to rob him. He is tempted by money, and you by the desire not to be punished, or to receive a reward. . . . Christ taught men that they are all sons of God, and therefore a Christian cannot surrender his conscience into the power of another man, no matter by what title he may be called, King, Czar, Emperor, and that therefore one should not obey them. . . .

And therefore if you indeed desire to act according to God's will, you have only to do one thing—to throw off the shameful and ungodly calling of a soldier, and be ready to bear any sufferings which may be inflicted upon you for so doing. (Tolstoy 1901/1968, pp. 34–35.)

Although in these passages (which abound in Tolstoy's pacifist writings) Tolstoy departs from the Christian ideal of the utter meekness called for in his doctrine of "nonresistance to evil," he remains true to the conviction that the only true pacifism is rooted in the *individual's* personal rejection of violence. Tolstoy rejected all forms of organized action, in particular the sort of organized action that constitutes politics. The reason was probably Tolstoy's disdain of "civilization." He believed that only the simple peasant could embody real virtue and he deeply distrusted all social "movements," however eloquently they espoused ideals resembling those of Christianity.

In his late life, Tolstoy became a world celebrity as a great writer and as a pacifist. He received innumerable letters asking his opinions on various schemes of preventing wars, establishing peace, and generally improving the human condition. The following excerpts from his reply to a letter he received from the organizers of a "peace conference" reveal his skepticism, bordering on contempt, for all such schemes.

The Conference, it is said, will aim, if not at disarmament, then at checking the increase of armaments. It is supposed that at this Conference the representatives of governments will agree to cease increasing their forces. If so, the question involuntarily presents itself: How will the governments of those countries act which at the time of the meeting happen to be weaker than their neighbors? Such governments will hardly agree to remain in that condition—weaker than their neighbors. Or, if they have such firm belief in the validity of the stipulations made by the Conference as to agree to remain weaker, why should they not be weaker still? Why spend money on an army at all? (Tolstoy 1968, pp. 113–114.)

In its extreme form, personal pacifism may reflect an ethos of resignation, i.e., rejection of all attempts to influence the course of events. The only actions approved by such a position are those directed at self-perfection and rendering direct assistance to persons in pain or in need. Closely associated with this attitude is an emphatic rejection of the "the end justifies the means" rationalization of action. Ends are held to be irrelevant; actions are to be evaluated only on the basis of themselves without reference to the goals they are supposed to serve. Again, we turn to Tolstoy's parables for an eloquent illustration of this ethic:

Two brothers are devoted to each other and to helping others. One day, they find a treasure. One of the brothers refuses to have anything to do with it, but offers no explanation. The other reasons that although much evil can be done with gold, also much good can be done with it. He takes the treasure, leaves his brother, and devotes himself to large-scale philanthropy: charities, hospitals, and so forth. When the gold is spent, he seeks to rejoin his brother, only to find his path barred by an angel with a flaming sword, who explains to him that he is not worthy of his brother. Only by love and labor can one help others. Buying such help is worthless as an act of love or charity.

Tolstoy's parables vividly illustrate a variety of pacifism rooted in an individualistically anarchistic ideology—a distrust of all forms of organized social action. Thus Tolstoy explicitly castigated socialism, liberalism, feminism, and all the progressive Western "isms." We find the same rejection of "progress" in the writings of Henry David Thoreau (1817–1862), as is evident in his sarcastic comments on visions of technological utopias.

In discounting social organizations as tools of effective action for a common good, Thoreau expressed a profound contempt for politics.

> What is called politics is comparatively something so superficial and inhuman, that practically I have never fairly recognized that it concerns me at all. The newspapers, I perceive, devote some of their columns specially to politics or governments without charge, and this, one would say, is all that saves it; but as I love literature and to some extent truth also, I never read those columns at any rate. I do not wish to blunt my sense of right so much. I have not got to answer for having read a single President's Message. A strange age of the world, this, when empires, kingdoms, and republics come a-begging to a private man's door, and utter their complaints at his elbow! I cannot take up a newspaper but I find that some wretched government or other, hard pushed on its last legs, is interceding with me, the reader, to vote for it. . . . (Thoreau 1863/1937, p. 824.)

For all his skepticism, however, about organized action, Thoreau unwittingly contributed to a central idea later incorporated in modern political pacifism, namely, the idea of civil disobedience.

The impulse appears to have been the war that the United States waged against Mexico (1846–1848). This war was strongly supported by the pro-slavery forces and opposed by the anti-slavery forces. The slavery issue was central, because the South expected that newly acquired territories would eventually become slaveholding states. The industrializing North was emphatically opposed to this extension. As frequently happens, moral convictions were in harmony with economic interests.

Thoreau's condemnation of the war was rooted in both his profound hatred of slavery and in his pacifism. His civil disobedience consisted of refusing to pay a tax. He was put in jail, but was freed the next day when someone paid the tax for him. He was not grateful for this well-intentioned favor.

Thoreau's conception of civil disobedience was entirely consistent with his individualistic philosophy. There was no question of organizing a "tax strike," such as was (unsuccessfully) attempted during the Vietnam War. For Thoreau, civil disobedience was no more than an action (or a refusal to act) that is forced on a person who remains true to the dictates of his conscience. In this way, Thoreau's level of moral development would correspond to Kohlberg's highest (sixth) stage.

Specifically, Thoreau takes to task those who campaign for changing the law but obey it as long as it is still on the books.

> Unjust laws exist: shall we be content to obey them, or shall we endeavor to amend them, and obey them until we have succeeded, or shall we transgress them at once? Men generally under such a government as this, think that they ought to wait until they have persuaded the majority to alter them. They think that, if they should resist, the remedy would be worse than the evil. But it is the fault of the government that the remedy *is* worse than the evil. *It* makes it worse. . . . Why does it not encourage its citizens to be on the alert to point out its faults . . . ? . . . If the injustice . . . is of such a nature that it requires you to be the agent of injustice . . . then, I say, break the law. (Thoreau 1849/1937, p. 796.)

This essay of Thoreau's originally published under the title "Resistance to Civil Government," became Gandhi's textbook in his campaign of passive resistance against British government in India. In Gandhi's campaign for the independence of India, we have a transition from personal to political pacifism. Gandhi derived his revolutionary energy from deep religious convictions. He was strongly influenced by Tolstoy, particularly by Tolstoy's emphasis on the autonomy of the individual's conscience. In his essay, "The Kingdom of God Is Within You" (1899), Tolstoy emphasized the role of fear as the principal guarantee of obedience to the State, implying that in overcoming this fear, the individual frees himself from the compulsion to obey. Recall how in his "Tale of Ivan the Fool," Tolstoy makes it seem absurd that an individual, a king, can force a whole population to obey him against their will. Specifically, about the subjugation of India by the British, Tolstoy wrote:

> What does it mean that thirty thousand men . . . have subdued two hundred million . . . ? Do not the figures make it clear that it is not the English who have enslaved the Indians, but the Indians who have enslaved themselves? (Tolstoy 1937.)

Tolstoy's meaning is clear. A people can be enslaved only if it consents to be enslaved. Tolstoy's ideology, based on a faith in the complete autonomy of the individual. limited his vision to the internal life of the individual. Like Thoreau, Tolstoy believed that collective consciousness is the sum of individual consciousness; so that only if each individual develops within himself the strength to resist encroachment on his autonomy can a people remain free. He did not see that a collective of weak individuals can become strong if each individual's initially inadequate will is reinforced by that of others.

A prominent American pacifist was A.J. Muste (1885–1967). Like Tolstoy's, Muste's pacifism was rooted in Christianity. Unlike Tolstoy, however, Muste was an ardent activist. As an act of protest, he climbed over the fence of a missile base. He was arrested for refusing to take cover during a civil defense drill. He demonstrated against nuclear testing on the White House lawn and in Moscow's Red Square. Walter G. Muelder, Dean of the Boston University School of Theology, said of Muste that he made the peace movement:

> . . . an aggressive and dynamic force for social change and has compelled Christian thought to accept full responsibility for the qualitative texture of social life. He did not, like many pacifists, find it possible to stand pat on traditional peace attitudes and static political answers, but has infused the peace movement with a faith that all the institutions of society can be transformed in principle to nonviolent ones. This means that he remains a radical on all social fronts and is not a single-cause pacifist. (Cited in Hentoff 1967, pp. xiii–xiv.)

Until 1936 Muste accepted fully the Marxist-Leninist position both in politics and metaphysics. He rejected this ideology completely when he became convinced that the ideal of Communism was totally corrupted by addiction to power. Referring to the events of the great purges in the Soviet Union in the 1930s, he wrote:

> "If one looks squarely at these and many other such facts, touching all organizations in the labor movement, then I think one is driven to the conclusion that the root of the difficulty is moral and spiritual, not primarily political or economic or organizational. Inextricably mingled with and in the end corrupting, thwarting, largely defeating all that is fine, idealistic, courageous, self-sacrificing in the proletarian movement is the philosophy of power, the will to power, the desire to humiliate and dominate over or destroy the opponent, the acceptance of the methods of violence and deceit, the theory that "the end justifies the means." There is a succumbing to the spirit which

so largely dominates the existing social and political order and an acceptance of the methods of capitalism at its worst. (Muste 1967, pp. 198–199.)

Muste's "return to pacifism," as he put it, was total. In this respect, and in insisting that true pacifism must be rooted in the soul of the individual, Muste resembled Tolstoy. The following passage reveals the personal nature of his pacifism.

> Pacifism—life—is built upon a central truth and the experience of that truth, its apprehension not by the mind alone but by the entire being in an act of faith and surrender. That truth is: God is love, love is God. . . .
>
> Such an affirmation one must accept and make, first in one's own soul. If it is not there, it exists only in formulas and abstractions. The individual must therefore be won and saved. (p. 201.)

Religious Pacifism

It is interesting to observe that scenarios of a warless world were produced in antiquity by the Hebrews, who at the time they were conquering Canaan were among the most warlike (as well as cruel) people in the Middle East. The Lord of Hosts, leading the children of Israel forth into battle, demanded extermination of the conquered population (cf. Chapter 2). The Hebrews' turn to pacifism is understandable in view of the fact that they themselves became victims of militarily superior conquerors. It is interesting to note that visions of future perpetual peace were associated with disarmament: "And they shall beat their swords into ploughshares and their spears into pruning hooks. Nation shall not lift up sword against nation, neither shall they learn war any more." (Isaiah 2:4.) Even predation is sometimes excluded from that future: ". . . And the lion shall eat hay like the ox." (Isaiah 11:7.) Unlike the Lord of Hosts, the Messiah was depicted as the Prince of Peace.

The early Christians, originally a Judaic sect, divested themselves of the idea of the elect people and extended the vision of a peaceful world to all of humanity. For a time, the Church entertained the idea of a world empire bound together by a universal religion.

On the personal level, Christian pacifism was at times manifested in refusal to do military service. However, already in the third century, Origen, foremost among the early Christian theologians, apparently felt it was necessary to rationalize this refusal by a claim that it by no means reflected disloyalty to the state or to the monarch. He wrote:

To these enemies of our faith who require us to bear arms for the commonwealth, and to slay men, we can reply: "Do not those who are priests at certain shrines and those who attend on certain gods, as you account them, keep their hands free from blood, that they may with hands unstained and free from human blood offer the appointed sacrifices to your gods; and even when war is upon you, you never enlist the priests in the army? If that, then, is a laudable custom, how much more so, that while others are engaged in battle, these too should engage as the priests and ministers of God, keeping their hands pure, and wrestling in prayers to God on behalf of those who are fighting in a righteous cause, and for the king who reigns righteously, that whatever is opposed to those who act righteously may be destroyed? And we do take our part in public affairs, when along with righteous prayers we join self-denying exercises and meditations which teach us to despise pleasures, and not to be led away by them. And none fight better for the king than we do. We do not intend to fight under him, although he require it. But we fight on his behalf, forming a special army—an army of piety—by offering our prayers to God. (Cited in M.C. Smith 1903, pp. 14–15.)

Here we can discern the idea of the "just war" taking root, which was to be fully developed a century and a half later by St. Augustine and was to dominate the mainstream of Christian thought about war for centuries to come. Genuine pacifism found sanctuary only in more or less isolated sects like the Quakers and the Mennonites.

The chief source of inspiration for Christian pacifism is without doubt the New Testament, particularly the Sermon on the Mount. However, there have been other contributing factors. The operation of these other factors can be seen in the history of some sects. The Reformation introduced centrifugal forces into Christianity. It was not long before sects split off from the major Protestant churches. Frequently those sects were subjected to persecution, which led to alienation from the state. In at least one case we can suppose that it was this alienation that established the uncompromising pacifist position of the Anabaptists, from which the Mennonite pacifist sect descended.

An incident in the early history of the sect points to its by-no-means pacifist origin. The first leaders of the Anabaptists were scorned by Luther, denied access to churches, and driven from the cities of Northern Europe. They became involved in the Peasants' War in South Germany, which broke out a few years after Luther's break with the Roman Church. Led by Thomas Muenzer, one of the Anabaptists' "prophets," the war became a revolt against all constituted authority and an attempt to establish an ideal Christian commonwealth. In fact, the Anabaptists succeeded with the help of some allies in establishing a theocracy in Muenster in Westphalia, which lasted from 1532 to 1535. The town was besieged and taken, and the leaders of the insurrection cruelly tortured and executed. The persecutions that followed dispersed the Anabaptists over several countries, which accounts for the several names of the sect's descendants and for their attitudes toward the state.

The Anabaptists firmly believed in rendering obedience to the state, which they regarded as an institution ordained by God as an instrument for maintaining order in human communities. They recognized the right of the state to wield the sword in fulfilling this task. There was one area, however, that the Anabaptists regarded to be outside the state's jurisdiction. They denied the magistrate's right to exercise authority over spiritual matters. They insisted that it is the Christian's duty to refuse obedience and suffer the consequences rather than act against his conscience. They also drew the logical consequence of this conviction, namely, that it is impermissible for a Christian to hold government office.

The Anabaptists' firm espousal of the separation of church and state, which at that time was regarded by both Catholics and Protestants as a heresy, was another pretext for their persecution. A self-stimulating process of alienation may have set in, which led to the rejection of the most prominent and universal activity of the state, namely, waging war. It is noteworthy, however, that not only were the Anabaptists anything but pacifists at the time of the Muenster affair, but also that pacifism gradually disappeared from their ideology in Western Europe toward the end of the nineteenth century, remaining only in some Swiss communities and in France, (Brock 1968, p. 7). In Russia, however, where the Mennonites (descendants of the Anabaptists) found refuge in the eighteenth century as farmer settlers, pacifism and other features of Mennonite culture survived until after the Russian Revolution. In fact, it was the apprehension that the czarist government would withdraw the exemption from military service that had been extended to the settlers that led many Mennonites to emigrate to America.

Several pacifist sects live in isolated communities with minimal contacts to the outside world. Members of such communities usually possess high degrees of competence in farming or other productive occupations. Coupled with a predilection for simple, sober living and hard work, their isolation has enabled these people to attain comfortable prosperity. Quite possibly these communities represent the same sort of adaptation that monasticism attained in the Dark Ages. The monasteries served as refuges from the pervasive violence that raged in Europe during the centuries after the breakup of the Roman Empire.

In sharp contrast to the Mennonites, the Quakers do not shun public offices and do not isolate themselves from the society at large. Their conception of pacifism stems less from the formal commandment embodied in the Sermon of the Mount than from personal conviction that war is wrong. This conviction is of course couched in religious terms, but the emphasis remains on its internal source. The Quakers speak of an "Inner Light," a strongly individualistic and introspective interpretation of salvation. Tolstoy's essay, "The Kingdom of God Is Within You" (1899) reflects the same introspection. The Quakers have eschewed all forms of hierarchical organization. Perhaps for this reason, they have practiced their religion in the "outside world," applying its principles to mundane matters. In this respect their Christianity differs from Tolstoy's, who rejected all forms of organized social action, and from other Christian pacifist sects which did have a social organization but which withdrew from public life.

The Quakers' conception of Christianity was clearly manifested in the so-called Holy Experiment, William Penn's determined attempt to incorporate nonviolence in a government. By a peculiar chain of circumstances, Penn was given a charter to establish a British colony in North America, which he named Pennsylvania after his father, Admiral (*sic*) William Penn. Penn realized that an absolute renunciation of force by a government was impossible. Pennsylvania had prisons and even the death penalty. Still, by the standards of the seventeenth century, the government of the colony was remarkably humane. Penn's chief achievement was to demonstrate that Europeans could live in peace with "savages."

Because of the influx of immigrants, the Quakers soon became a minority in Pennsylvania. They nevertheless governed the colony from 1682 to 1756. Their pacifism became an issue on several occasions when England went to war, for example, in 1689–1697 ("King William's War") and in 1739, upon the outbreak of the war with Spain. Quaker rule survived these crises. Pressures, however, built up within the Quaker community. Among the dissidents was a group led by one George Keith. It is noteworthy that the original issue of the schism was a theological quibble. Keith emphasized the importance of the authority of the Bible as against the Quaker doctrine of the "Inner Light." An incident involving bringing a river pirate to justice brought the dispute to a head. Keith maintained that the exercise of governmental authority by use of force was inconsistent with Christian nonviolence. "A pair of stocks, whipping post, and gallows are carnal weapons, as really as sword and gun, and so is a constable's staff, when used, as it hath been by some to beat and knock down the bodies of some obstinate persons." (Cited in Brock 1968, p. 91). Indeed, Keith and his followers could not see why it was permissible to use force against domestic wrongdoers but not against the Indians.

Eventually, the Quakers' greater emphasis on the "Inner Light" rather than on the authority of the Bible led to an actual challenge of the Scriptures, a grave matter in those days. One John Jackson, in a pamphlet entitled "Reflects on Peace and War," rejected the belief that God ordered the Hebrews to slaughter the populations of conquered lands. The accepted explanation of the contradiction between the sanctioning of those atrocities and the commandment to love one's enemies was that in his inscrutable purpose, God actually commanded the Hebrews to perpetrate genocide but that he revealed his "true nature" in the New Testament. Jackson simply denied this by stating that the Jewish chroniclers were mistaken, that no such dispensation was ever given. "Those authors," he wrote, "whoever they were, were fallible men like ourselves, liable to mistaken views of the divine character and will." (Cited in Brock 1968, p. 370.)

The most distinctive feature of Quakerism is a sense of mission to act as catalysts in conciliation of enemies. The doctrine of the Inner Light sustains their belief in the power of the human conscience which can be awakened in anyone. The Quakers' reliance on conciliation was manifested in the Pennsylvania period when resorting to courts of law was permitted only if efforts to settle disputes by arbitration failed. In recent years Quakers' conciliation efforts have extended to the political sphere. Brief accounts of some of their activities in this area will be given in Chapter 23.

The difference between the Anabaptists' and the Quakers' pacifism lies in the difference between doctrinaire and personal sources of convictions. There is no reason to doubt the sincerity of the fundamentalist pacifist sects condemning war. Yet, because the source of their conviction is projected to an external agency (the command of a deity), they find it easy to rationalize violence in its most depraved forms. Proselytizing members of Jehovah's Witnesses (a pacifist sect) have been heard explaining that the Canaanites deserved to be slaughtered because they practiced human sacrifices. On several occasions, mass murderers explained that they were given explicit orders by God to kill. On one occasion, the author was told by a Moslem scholar that Islam is the most pacific of religions, because "Islam" means "peace" in Arabic.

In contrast, the source of Quaker pacifism, being projected inward, is independent of doctrine. It is predicated on a conviction of personal freedom. In Adler's classification of types of freedom, it would come under the Freedom of Self-Perfection. The same inner source of pacifist convictions can be ascribed to the ideology of early peace movements, still rooted in religious beliefs but no longer bound by sectarian doctrines. The American Peace Society, founded in 1828, is an example. The Society's position is stated in the first issue of its periodical, *Harbinger of Peace*.

> We do not as a society agitate the question, whether *defensive* war can be carried on on Christian principles. We receive into our communion all who seek abolition of war, whether they hold to the lawfulness of defensive war,

or condemn all war in every shape, whether they allow a latitude of construction to the injunctions of our Saviour, or take the exact and strict letter of them. We endeavor to avoid all "doubtful disputation," and to walk peaceably with all who will walk with us, whether they go further, or not so far, as the majority of the society. (Cited in Brock 1968, p. 484.)

Explicit reference to the ultimate freedom of the individual is contained in a pamphlet published by a group affiliated with the American Peace Society. Addressed to a juvenile readership, it contains the following dialogue between two brothers:

Frank: . . . But I thought they could compel you to train, whether you wanted or not.
William: That would be a difficult matter. How would they go to work to compel me to buy a gun and cartridge box tomorrow morning, and go to the common, instead of going to my store as usual?
Frank: I thought they could prosecute you if you did not go.
William: Very well. Then according to your own account, I can choose which I please, either to train or be prosecuted. I prefer the latter.
Frank: But they will put you in prison.
William: Very well. Still I have the choice of training or going to prison, just which I like best. This is not compulsion. (Cited in Brock 1968, p. 514.)

The insight that *ultimately* the individual is free to obey the dictates of his conscience, rather than the commands of others, coupled with the insight that the individual's will to obey his conscience can be mightily reinforced by a similar determination on the part of others, led to the emergence of political pacifism.

In our own day, religious pacifism has acquired a political complexion in the sense that some religious bodies have gone beyond condemning war in the abstract by publicly declaring their opposition to specific government policies—those which appear to increase the danger of war or to make war unspeakably horrible. In Japan, the first victim of an atomic bombing, Buddhism has "gone public" in this sense through proselytizing activities of Soka Gakkai, its secular arm, said to have 10 million members over the world. The teachings of Buddha are deeply rooted in pacifism—for the most part, however, the pacifism of resignation.There is no trace of resignation in the activitier of Soka Gakkai, which has established networks of pacifist activism among the youth, women, students, and other groups, already bound by some form of solidarity and finding an additional bond in peace activism.

Much attention was attracted by the recent declaration of the American Catholic bishops:

> Any act of war aimed indiscriminately at the destruction of entire cities or of extensive areas along with their population is a crime against God and man himself. It merits unhesitating condemnation. . . . (National Conference of Catholic Bishops 1983, p. 33.)
>
> The whole world must summon the moral courage and technical means to say "no" to nuclear conflict, "no" to weapons of mass destruction, "no" to an arms race which robs the poor and the vulnerable, and "no" to the mortal danger of a nuclear age which places before humankind indefensible choices of constant terror or surrender. (pp. 101–102.)

The statement is particularly significant because it amounts to a rejection of the concept of the "just war," which from the days of St. Augustine has been a tenet of the Catholic creed. No less significant is the circumstance that this explicitly stated fundamental modification of the Catholic position on war was a consequence of "changed material conditions," as a materialist would say. It was nuclear weaponry, new means of destruction, analogous to a new means of production emphasized in the Marxist theory of ideology, that has rendered the concept of a "defensive war" fought with nuclear weapons meaningless. And it was a readiness to relate theologically supported principles to what a nonreligious person would call the "real world" that has apparently led the American bishops to express unconditional condemnation of nuclear war. As such, the declaration appears to be an expression of "relative pacifism," that is, of condemnation of a particular type of weaponry rather than condemnation of war as an institution. As we shall see, however, in this instance, "selective" or "relative" pacifism is a substantial step toward total pacifism.

Political Pacifism

The political pacifist espouses nonviolence on essentially rational grounds. Following G. Sharp (1973) let us review various methods of conflict resolution that have been used throughout history.

Removal of causes. There is considerable merit in the argument that the way to liquidate or attentuate a conflict is to remove its causes. It follows that it makes sense to try to discover the causes of a conflict. But knowledge of the causes does not confer an ability to remove them. Witness the difficulty in removing the most obvious "cause" of war—armaments.

Increased understanding of the opponent. It is true that many conflicts are aggravated by failure of the opponents to understand each other's motives. Often, however, a greater understanding of the motives has aggravated a conflict instead of alleviating it.

Compromise. "Splitting the difference" often works as a way of resolving a conflict, but is often impossible to apply if the conflict is about ideology or sovereignty or something equally indivisible.

Negotiation, conciliation, arbitration. Successful conflict resolution by these processes typically involves compromising, which entails the limitations mentioned above.

Democratic institutions. Methods based on strict observance of legal procedures and respect for the rights of individuals cannot be applied except where democratic institutions already exist—a very serious limitation in today's world.

World government. This idea remains in the realm of utopian thinking. As is sometimes pointed out, a world government might lead to the same sort of dominance by the strong over the weak that characterizes the politically divided world of today.

Violent revolution. Typical outcomes of such revolutions are replacements of one power elite by another with no solutions for the problems arising from abuse of power and from power struggles.

War. As a method of "conflict resolution," war has proved itself a complete failure. In fact, war is fundamentally incompatible with the idea of conflict resolution.

Apathy and impotence. These attitudes characterize the philosophy of resignation that is sometimes reflected in personal pacifism. Submission is, of course, a most direct way of preventing conflict. But identifying avoidance of conflict with conflict resolution seems to amount to evading a problem instead of coming to grips with it.

One can pose the question as to why it is at all necessary or desirable to resolve conflicts. Some maintain that conflict is what gives meaning to life, and we have seen how perpetual conflict is sometimes adopted as a way of life. We have also seen how conflict, continuing until one side is victorious, is nature's way of assuring vigor in all life. However, conflict does not appear this way to those who abhor violence either on emotional or pragmatic grounds. These people see its often horrendous effects on the human condition. The most powerful rationale for conflict resolution is avoidance of violence. Prevention or attenuation of internal violence is the most conspicuous feature of a society commonly regarded as "civilized."

There are two contexts, however, in which avoidance of violence is most generally regarded as impossible. Both have to do with removal of injustices. One form of injustice is perpetrated when a country is invaded and its inhabitants dominated or exploited by the invaders. Another form of injustice is seen in the exploitation of a population by the country's own power elite, which apparently cannot be induced to change its ways by nonviolent means. Violence in defense of a country against invaders goes under the name of a "just war." Violence aimed at depriving a tyrannical elite of its power goes under the name of a revolution. The establishment of social justice by violent revolution is frequently aborted, however. Any war in our age has become so destructive that one cannot in good faith speak of a "defensive" war as defending anything.

The proponents of nonviolent resistance point out that the idea of a defensive war and that of a violent revolution both are based on an implicit identification of power with the potential to resort to violence. For example, it is generally assumed that the power of a tyrannical government is based on the ability of that government to kill, imprison, or otherwise inflict injury on any numbers of the population it controls. Likewise, it is assumed that an invading enemy establishes his control over a country by his unchallenged power to commit violence. However, the potential to do violence is not sufficient in order to control a population. Effecting control requires first that the population *accept* the idea that the potential to do violence is sufficient. This argument is clearly identical to that of Tolstoy, that enslavement can take place only with the consent of the enslaved. However, Tolstoy failed to see that a collective can acquire power when the individual merges his consciousness with that of the collective.

Recall the story of the march of several hundred persons to the site of their execution. They are led by a half-dozen soldiers armed with rifles. Concerted action by the victims could overpower the soldiers. Several would get killed in the process, but the rest could escape and perhaps have some chance of surviving. The reason this does not happen is because none of the victims believes it can happen. So no one takes action. The power of the soldiers over the victims is based not only on the loaded rifles but also on the belief of the victims that resistance is futile.

People believe that their rulers have power over them, and for this reason the rulers have power over them. A little reflection, however, shows that no power elite can force an entire population to do anything if they refuse to do it. Even an individual cannot be forced to do anything against his will. At most an individual can be restrained from doing something by physical constraints. But preventing someone from doing something and forcing someone to do something are two different things. Doing nothing requires no act of will. Doing something always requires an act of will, because voluntary actions must be coordinated. For example, it is impossible to force a person to sign his name. He can be *apparently* forced to do so by threatening him with reprisal if he does not. These threats are successful only if the person prefers avoiding the reprisals to signing his name, not otherwise. If *everyone* preferred suffering punishment to signing his name, it would be impossible to force anyone to sign his name.

Concerted action confers power on the weak to resist the strong. This principle is well known and has vindicated itself as effective in innumerable circumstances. Strikes are the best-known examples. A strike is a prime instance of nonviolent resistance to perceived injustice. Violence has been frequently perpetrated on strikers, and strikers have often resorted to violence against strikebreakers. However, the latter violence is not essential to the success of the strike, and the former violence has often been ineffective in breaking a strike. On the whole, the strike can be regarded as a moderately effective weapon against injustices at the workplace: low wages, long hours, poor working conditions, and so forth.

Nonviolent Struggle

The question we wish to investigate is to what extent nonviolent resistance is effective as a political tool available to people for use against their own tyrannical governments and as a substitute for military weapons as a means of resisting an invader. The potential effectiveness of political pacifism is dependent on the effectiveness of this tool.

Political pacifism differs from personal pacifism in two important respects. First, the practice of political pacifism does not depend on the participants' aversion to violence on emotional, religious, or ethical grounds. Many, perhaps even a large majority of persons mobilized into nonviolent resistance movements, are motivated by such aversion. But it is in principle possible to espouse nonviolent political action and to take an active part in it without the internal commitment that characterizes the personal or religious pacifist. Nonviolent resistance can be regarded as a technique of struggle. Conduct of such a struggle requires organization, discipline, at times strategic and tactical competence. Nonviolent struggle in many ways resembles military action except, of course, that resorting to violence is eschewed. This very eschewal can be regarded as a specific technique of the struggle. In some instances the goal of nonviolent struggle has been not conflict resolution in the sense of compromise or conciliation but victory. The key idea of nonviolent action is that fighting the enemy with weapons of *his* choice is futile, when the enemy's power far outweighs one's own.

The same principle governs techniques of self-defense such as jujitsu, where the adversary's strength is used *against* him. It is also related to the principle of "indirect strategy" in ordinary warfare. Liddell Hart, a noted authority on military strategy, wrote:

> To move along the line of natural expectation consolidates the opponent's balance and thus increases his resistance power. . . . (Liddell Hart 1967, p. 25.)

Similarly, in confrontations between people victimized by a tyrannical government and the repressive forces of government, acts of violence on the part of the former are just what the enemy expects. Soldiers have been trained to expect violence from an enemy, and they have been told that the resisting population was an enemy. When the enemy behaves in the way he is expected to behave, the soldier feels comfortable because he knows what to do. As on the battlefield, violence is met with greater violence in an attempt to insure victory.

The other argument for nonviolent methods of struggle has to do with the adverse effects of violence on the *victors*, especially in the aftermath of violent revolutions.

A. J. Muste abandoned Marxist-Leninist ideology as a result of complete disillusionment with the Soviet regime during the great purges of the 1930s. The czarist regime, he pointed out, was overthrown in March 1917 in a practically bloodless revolution. Bread shortages in the capital sparked massive street demonstrations. Soldiers ordered to fire on the marchers refused; the authority of the government fell apart; the Czar was forced to abdicate. A provisional government was formed, and the country was immersed in a heady climate of political freedom.

The Bolsheviks, who overthrew the provisional government by force, were put in the position of having to defend their action. Regardless of the merits of that defense, it had an inadvertent side effect, namely, an *ideological* commitment to violence in politics. Once this commitment was made, violence against all rival political parties could be rationalized. (The standard rationale was the necessity of violence for defense for proletarian dictatorship.) Finally, violence was turned inward upon the party's own members, culminating not only in mass expulsions from the party but also in executions. It is estimated that between 70 and 80 percent of the members of Lenin's Central Committee faced firing squads during the Stalinist terror of 1936–1938.

Gandhi's Struggle

Foremost among the leaders of nonviolent political action was Mahatma Gandhi, who was able to combine religious commitment to nonviolence with powerful personal charisma to lead a mass movement. Gandhi began his career as a revolutionary in South Africa, where he made common cause with the victims of structural violence. Later, in the struggle against the British occupation of India, his charisma and his formidable political astuteness came to full fruition.

One of the early nonviolent resistance actions led by Gandhi was directed not at the British but against upper caste Indians. The issue was the inhuman treatment of the so-called "Untouchables," the lowest stratum of the Indian caste system. The scene was Vykom in Travancore, one of the states ruled by an Indian maharaja. (These absolute rulers were left in power by the British in the interest of greater efficiency in dominating the subcontinent.)

The particular issue chosen as the focus of the action was the use by the Untouchables of a road which led directly to their (strictly segregated) quarters but which went past a Brahman temple. The Untouchables were forbidden to walk on that road, because presumably they would defile the temple as they passed it. Not all the high-caste Hindus were bigots in matters of caste. Some, dedicated to social reform, took up the cause of espousing the human rights of the Untouchables. Some of these joined a group of Untouchables to walk demonstratively past the temple. (Some 35 years later, when the civil rights movement was launched in the United States, whites joined blacks in deliberately breaking segregation laws.) The orthodox Hindus attacked the procession. The police intervened and arrested several of the demonstrators, who received severe sentences.

The most fundamental principle of nonviolent resistance is perseverance. This is where the difference between individual and massive dedication to nonviolence becomes apparent. If an individual persists in his nonviolent resistance, he can be destroyed. Unless his death induces others to follow his example, its effect dissipates. In contrast, massive resistance cannot be crushed in this way. As some resisters fall, others take their places, determined to resist nonviolently to the last resister. Success is not guaranteed, but neither is success guaranteed to the determined army unit fighting to the last man.

In the Vykom affair, the strategy worked. More volunteers joined the protesters. A cordon of police was placed across the road to keep the demonstrators out. The demonstrators stood before it, pleading with the police to let them pass.

It should be noted that this particular action had the "conversion" of the enemy as one of its goals. The underlying assumption is that the enemy has a conscience and that it can be reached. The injunction to "love one's enemy" is taken seriously in this practice. But "loving one's enemy" and the goal of "converting" him is not an essential feature of nonviolent resistance.

The demonstration lasted for months. The monsoons came. The demonstrators stood until the water reached their shoulders. (The police took to boats.) Finally, the cordon was removed. But the demonstrators did not move. They were still not satisfied. They were determined to just stand where they stood until the orthodox Brahmans said, "We cannot any longer resist the prayers that have been made to us, and we are ready to receive the Untouchables." This action was an important input into the strengthening movement in the cause of caste reform (Sharp 1973, p. 82).

The most publicized action against the British started with the Great Salt March in 1930. Indians were fobidden to make salt and therefore had to buy it. This was a crude form of direct exploitation backed by police power. Whether this reaching for pennies in the pockets of the destitute was an important source of misery was not the issue. The Salt March was organized as a conspicuous act of defiance. People went to the seashore and made salt out of sea water. The gesture was well chosen. It was noteworthy. Above all, it called attention to the avarice of the colonial rulers who took advantage of the indispensability of salt to squeeze money out of poor people.

The action was a distinct success in the sense of serving as a signal for a massive nonviolent revolt. Each action stimulated others—mass meetings, huge street demonstrations, speeches in defiance of anti-sedition laws, and especially boycotts. Certain products were concrete material symbols of British rule, in particular, cloth. One of the most common forms of economic exploitation of colonies was the appropriation of their raw materials at cheap prices, shipping them to the industrial centers of the colonial power for processing, then shipping the products back to the colony to be sold at high prices. Development of manufacturing industries in the colonized country was thereby discouraged. Gandhi's success as a leader of a nonviolent revolution was due in large measure to his ability to single out actions in which practically everyone could participate and which in their totality undermined the authority of the colonial power. Moreover he could think of actions other than demonstrations. The effectiveness of demonstrations is limited by the fact that it is difficult to maintain a high level of effort. It is not easy to mobilize people for a demonstration as massive as the preceding one. In contrast, simple activities that can be performed every day amount to a *sustained* effort, an important necessary ingredient of a nonviolent revolution. Economic boycott is an example of such an action: all it requires from each individual is refraining from buying a specific product or service. In doing so, each can feel that he is actually "fighting the enemy," "injuring him where it hurts most," since economic exploitation is the principal basis of colonialism, and at the same time scrupulously observing the commandment of nonviolence. In order to add an active component to the essentially passive boycott, Gandhi recommcnded self-employment in home manufacture; he himself set an example by spinning yarn.

The American Civil Rights Movement

Gandhi's objective—ending British rule in India—resulted in no less than the breakup of the British Empire (of which India was by far the most important dependency). It is not surprising, therefore, that it took a world war for this goal to be achieved. The objective of the American civil rights struggle was much more modest—the dismantling of legal racial segregation patterns. Nevertheless, it took about the same length of time for this goal to be achieved and, in a way, it can be said that a world war was a factor in assuring the ultimate success of the struggle.

The American armed forces were still segregated in World War II, but Blacks no longer served in exclusively servile roles as they had in previous wars. They also took part in combat. This experience could not but shake the foundations of the habit of unquestioning submission that had been instilled in Blacks by bullying and terror.

An important event marking the beginning of the breakdown of officially sanctioned racial segregation was the 1954 decision of the U.S. Supreme Court declaring segregated schools unconstitutional. This decision invalidated a previous decision finding the doctrine of "separate and equal" educational facilities as in accord with the Fourteenth Amendment to the Constitution, which guarantees equal rights of citizens. The 1954 antisegregation decision was supported by arguments to the effect that separate educational facilities, regardless of their physical condition, were *ipso facto* unequal. Denying black children the right to attend the same schools as white children already deprived them of "equality."

It took years until the order of the Supreme Court to dismantle segregation in schools was implemented, but the effect on the Blacks was immediate. An incident in Montgomery, Alabama, sparked nationwide acts of nonviolent resistance reminiscent of the events in India during the 1930s. Like all other public facilities, the city buses in Montgomery were segregated. The seats in the front were reserved for whites, those in the back for Blacks. The sign marking the segregation was movable. During the hours when there were few whites on the bus, the sign was sometimes moved forward to make more seats available for Blacks. However, during the rush hours, as more passengers boarded than could be seated, Blacks were supposed to give up their seats to whites.

On December 1, 1955, four Blacks were asked to vacate their seats. Three complied, but one, a Mrs. Rosa Parks, refused and was arrested.

On December 5, a one-day boycott of the buses was organized and proved 100% effective. The boycott continued. As expected, repressions followed. When the Blacks organized car pools to take each other to work, the drivers were harassed. A city ordinance was passed outlawing car pools. Another prohibited the use of taxis at reduced rates. (Segregation extended to taxis, and the Blacks had their own.) Threats were made, averaging thirty per day, against the leaders of the boycott. Among the leaders was the young preacher Martin Luther King, Jr., who became the "American Gandhi."

Nothing succeeded in breaking the new spirit of the Blacks. The Ku Klux Klan, a white terrorist organization that had been intimidating Blacks for ninety years, staged a march through the Black district in Montgomery. The usual reaction of the Blacks to such marches had been to cower behind locked doors and drawn window shades. This time they stood in open doorways and watched. Some waved.

Suddenly fear was cast off. Fear is the principal weapon of structural violence. It is effective if the victim "cooperates" by succumbing to feelings of terror, which paralyze resistance. Once fear is dissipated, formidable energy can be released. This energy can be channeled into violence against the oppressor, the usual pattern in violent revolutions. Occasionally, however, it can be channeled into nonviolent resistance with impressive results.

The Montgomery bus boycott lasted a year, until the United States Supreme Court ordered desegregation of the buses. Terrorist acts against Blacks followed, but they repelled many whites. The local newspaper, several white ministers, and the businessmen's association supported desegregation or, at any rate, urged compliance with the law. In the wake of this clear victory a nationwide civil rights movement was launched, almost entirely based on nonviolent actions.

By no reasonable standard can the Blacks of the United States be said to have achieved full social or economic equality. Yet the main instruments of structural violence—apartheid and terrorist intimidation—have for all practical purposes been made ineffective. Whatever problems spawned by entrenched social inequalities remain, the American Blacks' struggle for civil rights and, above all, for human dignity must, like the struggle led by Gandhi, be regarded as a pronounced success. Both the principal leaders of those struggles, Mahatma Gandhi and Martin Luther King, Jr., died as martyrs.

Types of Nonviolent Action against Oppression

In *Exploring Nonviolent Alternatives*, G. Sharp (1971) cites 85 cases of nonviolent action in the last four hundred years. They are classified according to their targets, in almost all cases perpetrators of structural violence. A sample of instances will illustrate the range of the issues.

Actions against oppression of minorities. Civil resistance of Tamils in Ceylon (Sri Lanka), 1956–1957. Civil resistance struggles by the Indian minority in South Africa, the so-called "coloureds," in 1906–1914. This was the first action in which Gandhi was involved.

Actions against exploitation and other economic grievances. "Boycott" of Captain Charles Boycott by Irish peasants in 1880. Boycott, a rent collector for an earl who charged exorbitant rates, shared with Lynch of the United States and Quisling of Norway the dubious honor of having contributed his name to the vocabulary as a common noun. Among the prominent strikes were the British general strike of 1926 and the strike of the Delano grape workers in California in 1965–1970. The latter aroused sufficient sympathy for the striking agricultural workers to instigate a boycott. Supermarkets in Toronto, Canada, did not go so far as to bar California grapes, but they did put up signs on the grape bins which read, "If you support the striking grape pickers, do not buy these grapes." A cynic might point out that in this way the stores kept the goodwill of the strike supporters without antagonizing the nonsupporters by refusing to carry the grapes. On the whole, however, this stratagem helped the strikers by publicizing the boycott.

Actions on religious issues. Examples comprise early Christian reactions to Roman persecutions, the Roman Catholics' struggle against the Prussian government over mixed marriages in 1836–1840, and the South Vietnam Buddhist campaign against the Ngo Diem regime in 1963.

Actions against particular injustices and administrative excesses. Before armed struggle erupted in the American colonies against British rule, resistance included boycotts, political noncooperation, and tax refusal. Persians resorted to an anti-tobacco tax boycott in 1891. There were general strikes for broader suffrage in Belgium in 1893, 1902, and 1913. In Russia peasants resisted passively against forcible grain collections in 1918–1921. The bus boycott in Montgomery, Alabama, inspired similar boycotts in Johannesburg, Pretoria, Port Elizabeth, and Bloemfonstein in South Africa in 1957.

Actions against long-established undemocratic rule. Examples include major aspects of the resistance against Spanish rule in the Netherlands, especially 1565–1576; Hungarian passive resistance against Austria, 1850–1867; Korean national protest against Japanese rule, 1919–1922; and South African Pan-Africanists' defiance of pass laws in 1960.

Actions against new attempts to impress undemocratic rule. Passive resistance was practiced against the French and Belgian occupations of the Ruhr in 1923. The Danes resisted nonviolently against the German occupation in 1940–1945. There was a general strike in Copenhagen in 1944.

Sharp classifies these actions also according to where they occurred: 49 in the West, 23 in the East. Almost 40 percent occurred in "democracies," 60 percent in "dictatorships."

A large majority of these actions would come under the rubric of non-violent resistance to structural violence, that is, by "underdogs" against oppression by "top dogs."

Nonviolent resistance directed against an enemy who would ordinarily be regarded as a military adversary deserves special attention, for it is in this area that some insights or experience could be obtained with regard to the serious problem posed by the widely accepted imperative of self-defense.

The cornerstone of pacifist ideology is the conviction that violence begets violence. If, therefore, violence perpetrated by humans against humans is an evil to be eradicated, the use of violence with the aim of eradicating violence is self-defeating. Acceptance of the Christian injunction to love one's enemies is a logical consequence of this view. It seems, however, that very few people can in all sincerity "love their enemies." Even those who, following the example of Jesus as depicted in the New Testament, offered no resistance to persecutors or tormentors did not necessarily internalize this attitude. They may have disciplined themselves to behave as Jesus urged them, but how they felt about it is anyone's guess.

In our day, this manifestation of the purest form of pacifism is extremely rare. Actions of nonviolent resistance do not rate as examples, since they are acts of resistance (not of nonresistance). Self-immolation (suicide by fire as an act of protest) can be regarded as a manifestation of violence rather than of nonviolence, deflected upon oneself with the aim of dramatizing the injustice resisted.

In view of the failure of nonresistance to take root, we can surmise that its practice is beyond the capacity of most human beings. Nonviolent resistance makes no demands on the way the participant feels toward his enemies. It demands only discipline of action. It was probably for this reason that nonviolent resistance has had a visible history and is presently attracting considerable attention. Significantly, only eight of the 85 cases of nonviolent action cited by Sharp could be unambiguously classified as "pacifist" in the religious sense of the term—that is, coupled with affects of empathy for the oppressor and by deliberate attempts to "convert" him by awakening his conscience.

The strength of the strategies of nonviolence that do not satisfy the criteria of "pure" pacifism is that they do not violate what may be a psychological imperative, the need of self-defense. They involve only the use of unconventional methods of self-defense which can be justified on pragmatic as well as on moral grounds. In our age, in which pragmatism is a widespread ideology, this approach seems especially fitting.

Civilian Defense

Civilian defense (not to be confused with "civil defense") comprises techniques of resisting military aggression by non-military means. It can be regarded as a method of waging war, pursuing a goal not unlike that defined by Clausewitz as the fundamental goal of a military campaign, namely, the destruction of the adversary's armed forces. It differs from conventional war in that it excludes violent means. The destruction of the adversary's armed forces does not involve killing or physically incapacitating enemy soldiers. The aim of civilian defense is to render the enemy's military forces useless either by undermining the enemy soldiers' will to fight or by depriving the enemy of the fruits of his supposed victory.

Civilian defense entails withdrawing all forms of cooperation with the enemy who has occupied the country. Civilian defense cannot prevent the occupation of the country defended, but it can destroy the advantage of occupation to the invader. Once instances of successful civilian defense have been noted, this form of defense can also act as a deterrent to aggression.

Underlying the rationale of civilian defense is the assumption that a consequence of a military defeat is the occupation of the defeated country by the enemy who expects to derive certain benefits from the occupation. These may consist of annexing the country or part of it, exploiting the country economically, imposing a regime on the occupied country that would fall under the influence of the victor's regime, utilizing the strategic position of the country for military bases to be used in future conquests, and so forth.

Realization of every one of these objectives requires cooperation on the part of the population of the occupied country. In fact, reaping the fruits of a military victory, that is, incapacitating the adversary's armed forces, also requires the cooperation of the defeated. In this case, cooperation is especially easy to obtain, since dependence on armed forces to defend the country implies accepting the rules of the game. Recall Clausewitz's definition of war as an act of violence aimed at compelling our adversary to submit to our will. Clausewitz goes on to point out what appears to him an obvious corollary: the way to compel the adversary to submit is to destroy his armed forces. This corollary is justified if the will to resist resides entirely in armed forces, so that without these armed forces the adversary *feels* helpless and has no choice but to submit to the will of the victor.

The legend of Samson is instructive in this regard. According to the legend, Samson's hair was the "seat" of his prodigious strength. His Philistine wife Delilah betrayed him by giving him a haircut. Taken literally, the story is a fairy tale. Underlying it, however, is a sound psychological principle. If Samson firmly *believed* that his strength resided entirely in his hair, then it is not surprising that his will to resist dissipated when he was shorn. The principle applies to the role of armed forces. If one accepts the rule of the game in which states vie for power over each other, then one is bound to capitulate once the source of that power has been destroyed. If the population is accustomed to obeying the rulers, their capitulation compels them to obey the new rulers if, as a result of defeat, the sovereignty of their state is destroyed.

Civilian defense is based on a conviction that a population can be induced to refuse to obey. Sharp points out that this method of defense is not offered as a "solution" to the problem raised by the hypertrophy of violence in human affairs. Full application of civilian defense, as Sharp describes the method, has never been tried. Only sporadic, partial attempts can be cited. Therefore we do not know how effective this form of defense can be under what circumstances. But this is just the point Sharp emphasizes. In view of the tremendous investment in research and training related to war, it seems reasonable to invest some effort to try to get more knowledge about this alternative to war which, on *a priori* grounds, offers some hope of escape from our present predicament.

Questions regarding civilian defense fall into two categories. One relates to what civilian defense could accomplish. The other relates to the prospects of having this method of defense accepted and implemented in place of conventional military defense.

Arguments in favor of civilian defense attain full force if one can assume that a given population can be *totally* mobilized for nonviolent resistance. The setting in which civilian defense is supposed to operate is a country that offered no armed resistance to an occupying force. Occupation of a country has some objective. If we discount for the moment destruction of the population as an objective, the realization of the goal of occupation requires the participation of the population in what the invader is trying to do. If the invader wants to utilize the population as cheap (or slave) labor, the people must work for masters appointed by the invader. If the invader wants to impose a puppet regime on the occupied country, the people must obey the decrees of that regime, and its bureaucracy must be recruited from the native population. And so on.

The will to resist in the absence of an armed force amounts to the will to refuse to obey. The refusal must be absolute. It must yield to no threats and no promises. Of course such refusal will lead to reprisals, including killing. But resistance offered by armed forces also leads to loss of life. Governments have no compunction in demanding from their citizens readiness to "die for their country." A government committed to civilian defense needs to ask for no more. The determination to "fight to the last man," not infrequently observed in conventional warfare and regarded as a supreme military virtue, applies with equal force in the context of civilian defense in the form of "refusing to obey to the last person" and should also be regarded in that context as a supreme civic virtue.

Refusal to obey—total, uncompromising, and steadfast—is the key to successful civilian defense. In the face of it, the invader cannot attain the objective of an occupation except possibly that of slaughtering the entire population, which since the Holocaust seems to be a farfetched objective. The invader can find no quislings and therefore cannot establish a native puppet government. His decrees are ignored. The institutions he attempts to establish with the view of incorporating the occupied country into his cultural, economic, or political system cannot perform their functions. The police of the occupied country do not cooperate in tracking down the leaders of the resistance, their radio transmitters, their press. The occupying personnel are subjected to total boycott. No one exchanges a single word with them. When they enter a restaurant or a shop, they are ignored. Their morale cannot fail to be shaken by this treatment especially if they had been told, as, for example, the Soviet forces occupying Czechoslovakia in 1968 were told, that they were "protecting" the country.

Without more actual experience there is no way of knowing whether the psychological strains to which the occupying forces would be subjected might not bring about dramatic political changes. Or, given some face-saving formula, these tactics might actually lead to withdrawal of the occupying force, which would be the main objective of this defensive operation. The possibility of such a victory should not be excluded from consideration at least at some times, in some places, and in some circumstances. We must try to find out more about the potentialities of this strategy and of these tactics.

We turn to the question of the feasibility of civilian defense as a substitute for military defense. It stands to reason that the best chances for implementing such a transformation are in small, democratic countries with a homogeneous population relatively free of internal strife, especially in countries with no significant investment in military establishments. At the present time, except for Andorra (a minicountry), only Costa Rica has demonstratively abolished its armed forces. That country, therefore, is a good candidate for joining a society of countries dedicated to civilian defense. Sweden, being small, democratic, neutral, and homogeneous, would also be a good candidate except for its large and sophisticated war machine. Switzerland's military is not a realistic instrument of conventional military defense under present conditions, but the Swiss are apparently emotionally devoted to it, perhaps as a symbol of national unity (offsetting linguistic and cultural heterogeneity). Austria, on the other hand, would be a good country for experimenting with a civilian defense program.

The sort of training that a civilian defense program would require must start in the schools and be imbued with the same sort of imperatives that characterize the training and indoctrination of populations in highly militarized countries, e.g., Sparta, Prussia, and the Soviet Union. However, the training could not amount to "brainwashing" of the sort that often pervades military training. There is no need to insulate the population trained in civilian defense from the realities of our nuclear age, as soldiers must be insulated if they are to be induced to believe that war still makes sense. On the contrary, training in civilian defense can be coupled with a solid education in the real (rather than imagined) political and ideological issues of our time.

The strongest argument in favor of the feasibility of organizing a country for civilian defense is that this task bypasses the psychological difficulties posed by purely pacifist indoctrination. It seems extremely difficult, perhaps impossible, to induce most people to "love their enemies." *Some* people can, perhaps, embrace this attitude. A small minority, however, cannot make a significant change in the psychological and ethical nature of a society. It is just such a change that Einstein had in mind when he declared a fundamental change in our "way of thinking" to be necessary for avoiding the final disaster.

There is no need to instill "love" of the enemy in civilian defense training. But neither is it necessary to instill hatred, as is usually done in conventional military training. Hatred is probably damaging. The damage often manifests itself in veterans of protracted and brutal wars. The most appropriate attitude toward the enemy in civilian defense training is contempt, perhaps tinged with pity. At any rate it would be an attitude of justified superiority, as a matter of fact, not only in terms of moral values but even, in a way, in terms of "military" sophistication. The basic tenet of civilian defense is that in a struggle against an enemy stronger numerically and technically, it is sound strategy to refuse to meet him on his terms, to resort to "weapons" that he does not possess and tactics with which he is not familiar. In this respect, the principles governing civilian defense resemble those recommended by Liddell Hart in conventional warfare—avoiding doing what the enemy expects, confusing him by doing what he does *not* expect, presenting him with problems that he cannot solve because of the nature of his capabilities and commitments.

It should be easier to mobilize a population to the cause of civilian defense than to the cause of "gentle" pacifism, because in mobilizing for civilian defense the usual charges leveled against pacifism can be refuted. The civilian defense "soldier" is not a "coward" or "sissy." On the contrary, he or she must possess superior courage and fortitude. The civilian defense "soldier" does not shirk his or her duty to his or her country. On the contrary, participation in civilian defense demands ultimate dedication to one's country, readiness for self-sacrifice and, above all, the strictest sort of discipline. Civilian defense is in a very fundamental sense democratic, because it enlists everyone—men, women, and children. The unity of purpose—the achievement of a completely clear goal, namely, ridding the country of the invader, provides the opportunity of practicing the ultimate form of participatory democracy—cementing a common will.

Civilian defense requires expertise at least as sophisticated as military expertise. Preparations require extensive and intensive investigations for the development of effective strategies and methods. Talent presently recruited into military research by providing inducements having to do with opportunities for "creative" work can be expected to be recruited as easily to research on civilian defense, indeed more easily if we assume that some scientists and technicians have misgivings about using their expertise for killing and destruction. Most of this research would be in areas related to human behavior, many as yet insufficiently explored. But there would be room also for technology-related research, e.g., on clandestine communication networks, sabotage, and the like.

Sharp discusses the question to what extent civilian defense can be used to complement military defense and the related question to what extent the expertise of the military can be utilized in the service of civilian defense. These questions arise in connection with the problem of replacing military defense by civilian defense in countries with substantial military establishments. If there is stiff resistance from the military, it might be judicious, according to Sharp, to organize a civilian defense system alongside the military defense system. Since the organization would involve activities similar to those carried out by the military (training, organization of operating units, planning operations, etc.), it is conceivable that some of the military might lend their professional skills for these activities. It would be necessary, however, to keep the two organizations completely separated. There should be no overlapping personnel. Military personnel working for civilian defense should sever their connections to the military establishment. This is necessary to guard against cooptation. The subservience of the U.S. Arms Control and Disarmament Agency to the defense establishment has rendered the agency impotent and its mission meaningless. It must be constantly kept in mind that the ultimate goal of civilian defense is to supplant the military establishment completely. Any coexistence must be viewed as temporary, pending the phasing out of the warmaking agency.

Expansion and perfection of a civilian defense establishment would not lead to an analogue of an arms race. Any race of this sort would be a genuine rather than an illusory contribution to the national security of the countries involved. The reason is obvious: civilian defense by its very nature cannot possibly be interpreted as a threat. This is not the case of conventional defense which, no matter how defensive it seems to one side, can always be interpreted as a threat by the other. Civilian defense is a safe way of pursuing national security, if perceived threats to it are indeed confined to aggressive intentions of others.

Non-Provocative Defense

This form of military defense represents an attempt to justify military measures as genuine self-defense by removing from them all aspects of threat. The difficulty of establishing a weapon as "purely defensive" is that most apparently defensive weapons are important components of offensive weapons systems. The walls of a fortress cannot attack the soldiers trying to reduce the fortress, but they shield an armed force which can attack if the fortress is not reduced. To call the armor of a battleship a purely defensive piece of equipment is manifestly absurd. The same can be said of anti-ballistic missiles (ABM). As such they are clearly defensive weapons, being directed only at the attacking missiles of the adversary, not at his armed forces or his population. However, to the extent that anti-ballistic missiles confer some protection against *retaliatory* strikes, they can be seen as serving an offensive strategy, for example, a surprise attack on the adversary's military installations. The ABM Treaty between the U.S. and the U.S.S.R. concluded in 1973 was a result of both sides recognizing the destabilizing effect of "defensive" weapons. The controversy over the so-called Strategic Defense Initiative ("Star Wars"), proclaimed by the American military as a vast "defensive" system, has revolved around the same issue. Even the staunchest enthusiasts of this project do not seriously maintain that it can provide meaningful protection to the population against a nuclear attack. What is claimed is that the system designed to shoot down attacking ICBM's can protect one's own offensive weapons and make a totally devastating first strike against them unlikely. The system should deter the Soviet Union from attempting such a strike. But a "defensive" system that protects offensive weapons is analogous to the armor of a battleship. Calling such a system "defensive" is resorting to a semantic trick.

A weapon can be called purely defensive if it cannot serve to protect an offensive weapon or personnel that can be used for offensive operations and if the only way it can do damage to the adversary is by being activated by the adversary himself. A "stationary attrition defense" has been proposed as a system of this sort (Boserup 1985). The idea of "non-provocative defense" arose in connection with the "problem" of defending Europe against the Soviet Union. The expectation of a Soviet attack on Western Europe has been a principal rationale for the "nuclear deterrent." The argument goes that the Soviet Union's conventional forces are far superior to those of NATO. Further, it is assumed that given the opportunity, the Soviets would invade Western Europe in order to impose Soviet-type regimes on those countries. The question of whether such a move would make political sense is usually bypassed. From the purely military point of view, this question need not be raised, because from that point of view it is not the intentions or the preferences of the adversary but only his *capabilities* that should be the point of departure in designing a strategy. The fact that there has been no war in Europe since 1945 is frequently cited as evidence that "nuclear deterrence works," that is, provides stability by offsetting Soviet conventional superiority.

It remains clear, however, to those whose framework of thought extends beyond military thinking that what appears as security measures to one side may be interpreted as threats by the other. This insight led to the investigation of possibilities of designing a non-provocative defense of Western Europe. One such proposal for a "stationary attrition defense" involves an area of defense deployed in depth and dispersed over the entire region to be defended.

The system would consist of two components. The task of the first, the attrition force, deployed in a belt perhaps 20 kilometers deep, would be to delay, disrupt, and decimate an enemy advance. Behind this force mobile armored units would be stationed. These would be small, hence incapable of attacking beyond the borders of the country defended. They would engage the now-weakened attacking forces in battle. Alternatively, the region behind the border could be defended by stationary obstacles and land mines.

It is suggested that a defense of this sort would be non-provocative, because the forces constituting it could not be used in offensive operations in the enemy's territory. At the same time, the defense would not be simply a version of a Maginot Line which, once penetrated, leaves the country defenseless against invading forces. Weapons produced by modern technology, for example high precision missile launchers and armor-piercing projectiles, are supposed to inflict sufficiently serious losses on the invader to insure his defeat by the mobile armored forces stationed farther back, if the invader continues to advance. Moreover, concealment and camouflage, as well as familiarity with the areas defended, are supposed to contribute to the staying power of the defenders.

This sort of defense can by no means be subsumed under nonviolent resistance. It is at one extreme of a spectrum representing possible peace-keeping policies, the other extreme of which is total nonresistance. The method deserves some consideration as a contribution to peace-keeping, because it retains features of deterrence and at the same time eliminates the principal objection to presently existing deterrence policies, namely, their inherent threats which undermine the adversary's sense of security and in this way make him dangerous. At the same time, a system of non-provocative defense still makes use of military personnel and military technology and thus presents less of a threat to one's own military establishment. It is less likely to evoke energetic resistance than civilian defense with its pacifist overtones.

Boserup's arguments in favor of non-provocative defense are all based on accepting the need of deterrence by military means. The first argument is that conventional deterrence can be made ineffective by "self-deterrence." The present forces defending Western Europe cannot restrict themselves to strictly defensive operations. They must resort to counterattack. But the very circumstances that are supposed to deter the Soviets from attacking Western Europe may deter the defenders from counterattacking. This is the fear of escalation from conventional to nuclear warfare. Non-provocative defense would not be paralyzed by self-deterrence.

The second argument is based on the supposition that the Soviets would be motivated to attack only if they could expect such an attack to be decisive, quick, and likely to yield significant gains. Non-provocative defense, being a defense in depth, would make such a victory unlikely. The widely dispersed forces would have to be defeated one by one, each at considerable cost.

The third argument is the expected effect of a protracted war of attrition on the Soviet Union's allies in Eastern Europe (and, in fact, on Soviet citizens). Every Soviet "success" in this war would, presumably, raise the specter of a nuclear war, and "the instinct of national survival," if nothing else, would actually induce them to obstruct the war effort of the Warsaw Pact as best they could (Boserup 1985, p. 208).

We turn to the possible attitudes of the opponents of military establishments to the proposed scheme. Some proponents of civilian defense might lend some support to a non-provocative defense policy, because a conversion of a military establishment of a European country to a non-provocative defense strategy might conceivably change the nature of the establishment. For instance, it could contribute to its democratization, since the dispersion of the defense forces would necessitate the development of

highly self-reliant units of perhaps a dozen or so. The defense would resemble guerrilla warfare more than conventional war. If the goal of non-
provocative defense is effective deterrence, and if the deterrence actually
works, it may never come to actual warfare. The structural changes that
a non-provocative denfense strategy would necessitate in the military establishment might contribute to its eventual transformation into a purely
symbolic institution such as the Swiss military establishment has, for all
practical purposes, become.

"Selective Pacifism" and Abolitionism

If "pacifism" is reserved to designate unconditional rejection of violence
(as we defined this word in the beginning of this chapter), then "selective
pacifism," that is, opposition to a particular war or to the use of a particular
class of weapons, seems to be a contradiction in terms. However, selective
pacifism can at times be a precursor of abolitionism—unconditional opposition to the *institution* of war, an outlook that coincides with pacifism
in several respects.

Clearly, opposition to a particular war need not stem from any pacifist
convictions. A war may seem to some to have been undertaken at a wrong
time or against a wrong adversary or it may be seen to serve another
adversary. Opponents of one war may be enthusiastic supporters of another. For example, there was strong opposition to the war against Mexico
(1846–1848) in the northern United States. This war was strongly supported
by southern politicians, who hoped to acquire the conquered territories
with the view of extending the slave system into them. Those same northern
politicians who ranted against the immorality of the war against Mexico
as an unabashed war of conquest wholeheartedly supported the war against
the seceding southern states. Many voices were raised within the American
military establishment against the war in Vietnam on the grounds that the
Indochinese peninsula was not an advantageous site for a confrontation
with the Soviet Union.

Opponents of nuclear weapons are also found among military professionals. If military power continues to be seen as a means for securing
certain political, economic, or strategic advantages, then nuclear weapons,
because of their horrendous destructiveness, are useless for these purposes.
The same military professionals who advocate reduction or even abolition
of nuclear arsenals argue for increasing and "modernizing" conventional
armaments, which presumably *can* be used in wars waged for political,
economic, or strategic objectives.

Opposition to certain kinds of weapons on humanitarian grounds has led to various "conventions," prohibiting the use of dumdum bullets, poison gas, bacteriological weapons, and the like. It is difficult to see what relevance these prohibitions have to humanitarian concerns. At the time dumdum bullets and bayonets with sawtooth edges were prohibited, nuclear weapons had not yet been invented. At the present time sticking a jagged bayonet into a soldier is illegal in the eyes of international law, but killing millions by dropping a nuclear bomb is presumed legal.

If opposition to a particular war or opposition against a particular weapon were all there was to "selective pacifism," then clearly it would be pointless to include a discussion of this subject in a chapter on pacifism. Organized opposition to a particular war, however, or to a particular weapon may, on occasion, be a beginning of a process of enlightenment with important consequences for opponents and for their social environment.

There is no denying that the opposition to the Vietnam war was energized primarily by the fact that university students were threatened by the draft. Of course all young men in the United States were threatened, but the university students, having daily opportunities of making contact with each other and of identifying themselves as an interest group, were in a much better position to render *organized* opposition. In this they were aided by a non-negligible fraction of university faculties. The opposition took the form of so-called teach-ins, so named to remind of the sit-in strikes of the 1930s.

The success of the teach-in movement can be attributed to the fact that it engaged people who were both strongly emotionally involved in the issue and who, being in constant contact with each other, could rapidly organize themselves. The format of the teach-ins was the familiar format of classroom instruction: seminars, lectures, discussions, where the strong emotional commitment could be coupled with a thirst for knowledge.

The wide publicity given to the teach-ins contributed to the rapid development of the anti-war movement in the late 1960s and early 1970s, eventually involving the general population. Significantly, Martin Luther King, Jr., the charismatic leader of the civil rights movement, lent his support to the protests. Mass meetings, marches on Washington, and other forms of protest involving many thousands of people became highly visible events and for some time acquired considerable political significance.

After the withdrawal of United States troops from Vietnam, this peace movement, having achieved its purpose, disappeared. Peace activists can draw important lessons from the experience. The anti-Vietnam War movement had the potential of turning into an "abolitionist" movement, directed not at a specific war but at the *institution* of war. This potential stemmed from the fact that in the process of organizing the protests, at first in the teach-ins but eventually on the community level, information had to be gathered and disseminated. New slogans did not suffice. To counter the sure-fire slogans of the anti-Communist phobia endemic to the United States, it was necessary to expose the demagoguery, misinformation, and hypocrisy in the rationalizations of the war being fed to the population. These exposures were possible in the United States, which continued to be an open society, one of its great redeeming features. In spite of the initial efforts to suppress the information, the publication of the Pentagon Papers revealed the deceptions and manipulations used by the defense establishment and the administration in preparing and conducting the Vietnam War.

The protest movement against the Vietnam War had an important enlightenment component, *educating* the public not only on the subject of the way a specific war was ignited and fueled, but also on the nature and role of the military establishment in our age when war as an institution has lost its *raison d'être*.

The same potential exists at the present time for transforming the "selective pacifism" directed primarily against nuclear weapons into "abolitionism" (a movement analogous to the anti-slavery movement of the mid-nineteenth century), directed against war as an institution. As with the anti-Vietnam War movement, an abolitionist movement would be nourished by enlightenment.

Nuclear weapons are products of highly sophisticated science. The first warning against incorporating such weapons into arsenals for future wars was voiced by the world's foremost scientists—in fact, two men who had made vital contributions to the creation of these weapons—Albert Einstein and Leo Szilard. Another physicist, one of the most important figures in the history of nuclear weaponry, Robert J. Oppenheimer, had opposed the production of the hydrogen bomb. His opposition was based on both technical and moral considerations. He was wrong in insisting that the hydrogen bomb was technically infeasible, and this error had reverberations that strengthened the position of arms race enthusiasts. The moral issue, however, could not be dismissed easily by scientists who had not succeeded in isolating the moral from the technical issues. *The Bulletin of Atomic Scientists*, published since 1945, became their voice of conscience.

Scientists have been engaged with the moral and ethical problems of the nuclear age since its inception. This engagement was strongly reinforced by the fact that as "selective pacifists," that is, opponents only of nuclear weapons, scientists could play a leading and natural role in educating the public about nuclear weapons and their effects. Many books authored by peace activists contain a wealth of information originally disseminated by scientists (cf. Caldicott 1984, Malcolmson 1985). Scientific expertise has become firmly welded to peace activism.

Other professionals followed the lead of atomic scientists who, by pressing for the abolition of atomic weapons, linked concerns rooted in professional ethics to general human concerns. Some actions of these professionals made a considerable impact on public opinion. For instance, in 1983 the U.S. Department of Defense invited the medical community to prepare a plan for treating casualties resulting from a nuclear attack. The reply was a categorical refusal. The physicians pointed out that there is no way of doing anything significant in the way of "treating casualties" after a nuclear attack. The sheer number of casualties would exceed the number of *normally* available hospital beds by several orders of magnitude, and, of course, it would be absurd to expect that these facilities (and the presently available medical personnel) would remain available after an attack. In short, to pretend that the country could be "prepared" to cope medically with a nuclear attack would amount to perpetrating a cruel hoax on the population.

Canadian professional associations primarily engaged in educating the public about nuclear war include Science for Peace (initially an organization of natural scientists that eventually extended membership to social scientists), Physicians for the Prevention of Nuclear War, Psychologists for Social Responsibility, Lawyers for Social Responsibility, and several locally based groups.

In the process of educating the public about the nature of nuclear war, the educators themselves become educated about matters going beyond their professional concerns. This happens when they come in contact with the broad public and sometimes also with policymakers and others concerned with geopolitical, technical, and strategic problems related to the confrontation between the superpowers.

An encounter between Helen Caldicott, a physician who became a peace activist, and President Reagan in December 1982 conveys a great deal about the nature of that education (Caldicott 1984, pp. 15–21). Caldicott began the conversation by relating how she became concerned with the high level of radioactive fallout resulting from atmospheric testing of nuclear bombs. The fallout penetrated grass and in that manner polluted milk with strontium-90, which settled in children's bones. To this President Reagan replied that he did not want a nuclear war but that the way to prevent it is to be stronger than the Russians. He went on to describe the Russians as godless Communists, and so on. When Caldicott asked whether he had ever met a Russian, he said no, but "we hear from the emigrés."

Caldicott got the impression that Reagan was not interested in discussing medical and ecological consequences of a nuclear war. He seemed completely preoccupied with matters having to do with fighting the Russians. He was worried about the Russians' civil defense preparations and that

Americans were not matching them. When Caldicott asked him where he got his data on Russian civil defense, he seemed not to know. When Caldicott suggested that they might have come from T.K. Jones, Reagan did not know who T.K. Jones was. (He was at the time the Deputy Undersecretary of Defense for Research and Engineering, Strategic and Nuclear Forces, in the Pentagon—one of the officials in charge of civil defense policy.) When Caldicott mentioned a Russian TV program in which three American and three Soviet physicians described to an estimated audience of 100,000,000 to 200,000,000 Russians the medical consequences of nuclear war, Reagan replied that they all couldn't have watched the program, because they don't all have television sets.

It might seem that the most frightening aspect of that scene is that a person apparently so poorly informed and as intellectually limited as the President of the United States has virtually the power of life and death over hundreds of millions of men, women, and children, the vast majority of whom had nothing to do with the way this power was conferred on him and had nothing to say about how this power might be used. The actual situation is worse. Potentates come and go. Some are intelligent, others stupid. The vision of some is distorted by phobias or hatreds; others are cooler and more humane. The crux of the matter is that the personal characteristics of the leadership are only a secondary source of danger. The real source of danger is the *institution* of war. A basement filled with dynamite is the real source of danger to the apartment house above it. The people going through the basement with matches in their pockets are only a secondary source of danger. Some may be careless; others more careful. But the danger will not go away until the dynamite is removed.

Legally, the President of the United States has the power to dismantle his nuclear arsenal. In actual fact, he could not do it even if he wanted to. If he tried, he would probably be impeached or assassinated. The global arsenal was created by the defense communities of technically advanced countries. This arsenal is the pride and glory of the professionals who comprise those communities. Talent, dedication, and much hard work is invested in them. Their existence is declared to be indispensable for national security. One is never secure, so the argument goes, unless one is as strong as, preferably stronger than, a potential adversary. And there is always a potential adversary. These beliefs are as unassailable as the belief in God in a theocratic state. To nurture the arsenal, to create conditions for its unimpeded growth, to protect it from misguided politicians are imperatives. They constitute the ethos of the profession, just as saving lives or relieving pain constitutes the ethos of the medical profession, just as making as much money as possible under given constraints is the ethos of many business professionals, just as nurturing and protecting children is the ethos of parenthood. The imperatives may not be equally keenly felt by individual members of the defense communities, but as a *collective* they must obey them. The obedience is assured by a vast network of obligations and relationships.

Once one sees the situation in this way, "selective pacifism," which originally may have been directed against a specific war or a specific class of weapons, becomes *abolitionism*, a struggle by whatever means one can muster against war as an institution.

Recall the words of S. Amos:

" . . . practices and institutions, which at the time seem to be necessary conditions of social and political conditions of all people, and yet stand condemned as counter to principles of morality, justice, and political expedience, vanish . . . and become so far obsolete as to be with difficulty revived, even in imagination."

We cited this passage and others as reflections of a naive faith in progress. Particularly pathetic appeared Amos's arguments that wars will inevitably become more humane and " . . . as the knowledge of the Sciences and practice of the Art of Government progresses," will disappear altogether.

Amos was wrong in supposing that it is the moral worth of a practice or institutions that keeps them alive. It is rather being adapted to their social environment that keeps practices and institutions alive. Indeed, to say this is to assert a tautology, since "remaining alive" in a social as well as in a biological sense, is *prima facie* evidence of being adapted to an environment. If so, however, then the converse is equally valid. Loss of adaptation spells extinction.

The hope that the institution of war may become extinct is nurtured by the observation that institutions *do* become extinct. Chattel slavery is virtually extinct. Absolute monarchy is well on the way to extinction. Hereditary monarchy, while not extinct, flourishes precisely where it has adapted itself to its social environment which entailed, as in the case of the monarchical democracies of Europe, a surrender of political power by the monarchs.

The institution of war can become extinct in one of two ways. As a consequence of a war of total destruction, humanity may become extinct and with it all its institutions, including war. Or war may become extinct by being abolished, as slavery was abolished, as the Holy Inquisition was, in effect, abolished, as absolute monarchies were abolished in Europe.

Abolitionism is a variant of pacifism dedicated to the liquidation of the institutions of war via general and complete disarmament, via closing all military training centers, academies, research institutes, think tanks, and the like. In view of its program, abolitionism clearly reflects a revolutionary ideology. However, being a variant of pacifism, it rejects all forms of violence ordinarily associated with revolution. In this sense, abolitionism is consistent with all forms of political pacifism. It differs in its goals from most forms of political pacifism in that the latter are, for the most part, directed against institutions that perpetrate structural violence, while abolitionism is directed specifically against warmaking institutions.

There is no *a priori* way of singling out tactics most consistent with the abolitionist view. Evaluation of tactics involves the usual trade-off between principle and opportunity. At times it is necessary to take into account that certain measures apparently reducing the risk of war or attenuating its severity may serve to undermine the abolitionist program by making war or preparations for war more legitimate or acceptable. A prime example of such measures is so-called civil defense, strongly advocated by the most hawkish elements of the defense community. The main thrust of the arguments for civil defense refers to its apparently purely defensive nature; the measures are designed to protect civilian populations, not weapons systems. Related to this argument are humanitarian concerns. On the basis of calculations, which may be valid, certain kinds of civil defense measures can reduce the casualties resulting from a nuclear attack.

The first argument is specious. While civil defense is designed to protect the civilian population, it can be argued that the protection provided is against a *retaliatory* strike, since it makes little sense from the strategic point of view to launch an unprovoked first strike against the civilian population rather than at military installations. But the preparations to protect the population against a *retaliatory* second strike can be interpreted as preparations for launching a first strike. Therefore civil defense can be severely destabilizing.

Cogent as the above argument is, it has little bearing on the abolitionist's opposition to civil defense. The abolitionist's main objection in civil defense plans and measures is that they must necessarily involve the participation of civilians. Such participation tends to *legitimatize* preparations for war and therefore also the defense establishment as a functional institution. This is in direct opposition to the abolitionist's goals.

For similar reasons, the abolitionist will, in general, refuse to support or to welcome various conventions aimed at making war "more humane." It is not likely that any such conventions will be added to the existing ones, which already appear ludicrous in view of the rapid and ubiquitous proliferation of ever-more-ingenious ways of killing, unforeseen in the conventions. The most one can say about the utility of the old conventions is that they can sometimes be invoked to demonstrate their futility and to make vivid the atrocities perpetrated in war. Still, such accusations will be used sparingly by the abolitionist since they can be interpreted to mean that if the conventions were strictly adhered to, warmaking could be made "legitimate."

The abolitionist's position on arms control may be ambivalent. The arms control agreements involved in SALT I and SALT II may be said to have contributed to the legitimization of the arms race by defining "acceptable" advances in weaponry. At the same time, these agreements might under proper circumstances be steps in the direction of disarmament. There is no general rule to guide the abolitionist's attitudes to the various developments of the Cold War. Suffice it to say that the abolitionist will try to evaluate these developments according to whether they tend to make the global military establishment weaker or stronger.

Of special importance in this regard is the impact of the developments on the broad public. The abolitionist knows that the achievement of his goal (the de-legitimization and dismantling of the institution of war) can be achieved only in consequence of sufficient public enlightenment that can be translated into political actions. It is for this reason that immediate political feasibility of measures espoused by abolitionists need to be a foremost consideration. Repeated and persistent exposure of the complete loss of the *raison d'être* of the global war machine and of the purely parasitic or malignant role that military establishments are now playing in human societies is the one activity that must remain prominent in the abolitionist's public life without regard to the feasibility of the abolitionist's program. Every other activity relevant to the struggle for peace can be adapted to a particular social or political environment.

A dramatic transition from a selective pacifist to an abolitionist position is reflected in the recent declaration by the American Roman Catholic bishops regarding the immorality of nuclear war. Traditionally Roman Catholic doctrine, following the teachings of St. Augustine, distinguished between "just" and "unjust" wars. For the first time, a fundamental change was heralded by the statement of the American bishops to the effect that a nuclear war cannot be "just" under *any* circumstances.

This declaration may appear to be a reflection of selective pacifism, since it selects a particular class of weapons for condemnation. However, together with a reasonable assumption concerning the dynamics of modern war, the declaration becomes in effect abolitionist. This assumption is to the effect that the likelihood of any major war in our age becoming nuclear or, at any rate, omnicidal, is exceedingly high.

The doctrine of "limited war," in particular nuclear limited war, is a product of the academic contingent of the American defense community. The basic assumption of this doctrine is that restraint in a war between the superpowers would be in the interest of both sides (to avoid total mutual destruction) and therefore would be exercised.

Note that this argument rests on the assumption that the superpowers have a common interest. If so, and if the military establishments of the superpowers are supposed to serve the respective interests of their countries, then on the basis of this common interest, the military establishments must prefer the following situations in one of two orders: (a) no war is preferred to a limited war, which is preferred to an all-out war; or (b) a limited war is preferred to no war, which is preferred to an all-out war. If (a) is the order of preference on the basis of the superpowers' common interest, then the only rationale for the hypertrophied arsenals—deterrence—collapses, since the arsenals become altogether superfluous. If (b) is the order of preference, then the two are sure to engage in a "limited war," which means deterrence is sure to fail.

There remains the possibility that the superpowers have no common interest, that is, if it comes to war, their interests must be diametrically opposed. They would be playing a zero-sum game. This is the fundamental assumption from which Clausewitz begins his argument that a war developing "naturally", i.e., in accordance with its "true essence," must end in a complete victory for one side or the other, where victory is identified with the annihilation of the opponent's armed forces and consequently of his ability (or will) to resist. If that is the case, then limited war is an absurdity.

In the abolitionist's view, the military establishments of the superpowers do have a common interest. This common interest may even extend to the prevention of war. It does not, however, extend to taking any measures that might reduce the prestige, power, or affluence of the defense communities. This interest is opposed to the common interest of the rest of humankind for two reasons. First, it maintains the constant threat of annihilation over the whole of humankind. Second, it drains the resources of humankind just as a parasite or malignant growth drains the resources of its host. For this reason, the abolitionist sees humanity divided into two parts: the warriors and the victims.

The terms "warrior" and "victim" were introduced by Freeman Dyson in his book *Weapons and Hope* (1984). The stated objective of that book was to provide a basis for a dialogue between the two subpopulations of humankind with the view of making it possible for them to understand each other's concerns. Before we face the question of what the content of such a dialogue might be, let us elaborate somewhat on the idea of "slicing" humanity along the line that separates "warriors" from "victims" and how it fits into the abolitionist's ideology.

A good way to form an idea of what separates the "warriors" and the "victims" is to compare two passages, one in a language that fits the concerns of the warriors, the other in a language that fits the concerns of the victims. The following excerpts were taken from a discussion of various criteria which, in the opinion of the authors, should be taken into account in the design of a defense strategy. Specifically, the excerpts deal with criteria of deterrence. The authors define and evaluate a number of them.

a. *Number and weight of offensive weapons (for a given budget)*. Criteria of this general type are used in a surprisingly large number of cases by military correspondents, columists, and other "experts" who should know better. . . . Little thought is required to dismiss such crude counting devices. . . . A missile that can carry a small bomb and deliver it within 10 miles of its target presents nothing like the deterrent threat of a missile that can carry a large bomb and deliver it within two miles.

b. *The number and value of enemy targets that can be destroyed (for a given budget)*. This is a criterion that makes a little more sense. It takes into account not only the numbers of our offense bombers and missiles but also their operational effectiveness. . . . It is still, of course, an ambiguous criterion, and requires more precise definition. For example, what target system—population, industry, or military bases—should we use to keep score . . . ?

c. *The number and value of enemy targets that can be destroyed (for a given budget) after an enemy first strike*. This is much closer to what we want. It requires us, in allocating our given budget, to reduce the vulnerability of our force whenever money spent on reducing vulnerability . . . will increase our "strike-second" capability more than the same money spent on additional bombers or missiles and the personnel to operate them. (Hitch and McKean 1965, p. 126.)

The following excerpt is from a description of what the first atomic bomb used against an "enemy target" did to people.

People exposed to heat equal to that of the sun at the instant of explosion were vaporized and left only their shadows on the pavement behind them. Children were seen running along the streets with their skin falling off their bodies like veils. A woman lay in the gutter with her back totally burned, and as she died, her baby suckled at her breast. A man stood acutely shocked holding his eyeball in the palm of his hand. Bodies lay in all areas. Tongues were swollen and protruded from the mouths, eyes were eviscerated by the blast and hung on the cheeks. To quote a survivor: "In one small space amid a pile of bricks, a young woman's head faced towards me, and a look of innocent beauty still remained on her face." (Caldicott 1984, p. 57.)

The juxtaposition of these excerpts (both typical of the respective literatures produced by the warriors and the victims) should leave no doubt that there is no point of contact between the two worlds. Thus, the difficulties of setting up a "dialogue" between the people inhabiting these two worlds seem insuperable. We need to examine the way this gulf between the world of the warriors and the world of the victims shapes the abolitionist's views.

To begin with, let us note that this complete separation of perspectives is quite common. Let us examine an instance of it in a context devoid of the strong emotional content that inevitably characterizes the separation of the warriors from the victims. We can imagine the planet Earth as a tremendously rich panorama of sceneries: arid deserts and rain forests, green fields and boundless oceans, teeming cities and silent glaciers. We can think of our Earth as the home of billions of beings in many ways much like ourselves, at times strikingly different.

All of these images vanish from the field of vision of an astronomer looking at the Earth as a member of the solar system. In this context, the Earth can be thought of as a mass concentrated in a point. All that matters is the motion of earth relative to the sun and to the other planets, also pictured as point masses. To the astronomer who seeks to understand the solar system (where "to understand" means to predict the courses of the planets), this is *all* that matters.

Now this difference between the perspectives, in fact, this *incompatibility* of the perspectives is nothing to get excited about. We can, if we wish, shift at will from one perspective to the other. This is not so in the case of the perspectives of the warrior and the victim. Trying to combine the two would become for most people in either camp extremely painful in view of extreme cognitive dissonance (cf. Chapter 5). One or the other perspective must be shut out of consciousness. The warrior who thinks in terms of "operational effectiveness" of offensive weapons and of the vulnerability or value of the "target" must, in order to preserve his sanity, prevent the real physical and biological referents of the "target" from encroaching on his train of thought. Likewise, if we imagine the man holding his eyeball in his hand or running children shedding their skins, we cannot easily undertake a cost benefit analysis of "exchanging targets" or worry about the best way of "keeping score" in the business of destroying "population, industry, or military bases," as C.J. Hitch and R.N. McKean advise the designers of defense strategies to do.

For this reason, the "rationality" of the warriors' concerns has as little meaning for the victim as the agony of the latter has for the warrior. Each must "shake off" whatever thoughts from the world of the other intrude on him. The warriors do this all the time (if, indeed, they had not at the outset of their careers made themselves immune to these thoughts). The abolitionist who has adopted the victims' world as his own does likewise. In this respect, the abolitionist's outlook is identical to that of the absolute personal pacifist.

However, the abolitionist differs from the personal pacifist and from the religious pacifist in important respects. Unlike the personal pacifist, the abolitionist does not see the awakening of individual conscience of all or of most individuals as either a necessary or a sufficient condition for establishing permanent peace. He differs from the religious pacifists because his opposition to war is independent of sectarian religious beliefs. Unlike the Quakers' approach to peacemaking, the abolitionist's is not based primarily on conciliatory conflict resolution. Finally, the focus of his activities is not primarily nonviolent resistance against oppression.

It goes without saying that the abolitionist can have great respect for all of those other approaches to peace, and he can make common cause with their proponents. But the focus of the abolitionist's attack is on the *institution* of war, which means concretely an attack (usually political) on the institutions devoted to the preparation for and waging of war and to training people in the business of making war. In this sense, the abolitionist is a direct descendant of the anti-slavery abolitionist and of the eighteenth- and nineteenth-century republican, whose goal was the abolition of monarchy as an institution. He regards Freeman Dyson's dichotomy of humanity into warriors and victims as fundamental, one which should override all other dichotomies that define "us" and "them," e.g., along national, ethnic, racial, religious, or sexual divisions.

In this sense, the abolitionist resembles the Marxist, who also emphasizes a fundamental overriding dichotomy, namely, a dichotomy along class lines. Unlike the Marxist, however, the abolitionist regards the warrior-victim dichotomy as more fundamental (in our age) than any class dichotomy. Like the Marxist, he banks on a growing consciousness of the underdog, the victim, who will come to realize his true interest and will emancipate himself from the dominant ideology. Unlike the Marxist, however, the abolitionist does not subscribe to a fixed doctrine of the historical process and entertains no eschatological visions. His ideology is distinctly present-oriented and pragmatic. His tactics are compatible with gradualism. He has no illusions about an impending breakdown of the war system, except, of course, in consequence of a total war, which he works to prevent.

On pragmatic grounds the abolitionist may support arms control, partial disarmament, prohibition of particular weapons of mass destruction, and so forth. But this support will be predicated on a single criterion: does a measure serve to weaken or undermine the war system and its serving institutions, or does it, on the contrary, in the guise of "security" measures, tend to legitimize it? The clearest case of the latter type of measures are civil defense programs, ostensibly undertaken to save civilian lives, especially programs undertaken by states possessing nuclear weapons.

The political aspects of the abolitionist's work may manifest themselves in electoral politics, supporting outspoken opponents of arms races and of interventionist global policies, obtaining access to decision makers open to rethinking of security issues, or organizing massive opposition to specific policies or actions of governments that enhance the danger of war or amount to preparations for war.

Outside of politics proper, the abolitionist's principal efforts are in the field of public education in its broadest (not merely formal) sense. His role in this field entails dealing with special problems generated by his position.

What are the prospects of Isaiah's prophesy, "Nation shall not lift up sword against nation, neither shall they learn war any more" being realized and the institution of war becoming extinct before it extinguishes the human race? Recall once again S. Amos's conviction that "institutions, which . . . stand condemned as counter to principles of morality . . . vanish in an almost inconceivably short space of time and become so far obsolete as to be with difficulty revived even in imagination." The fundamental and unconditional immorality of war has been recognized for centuries and eloquently expressed in the sixteenth century by Erasmus of Rotterdam:

> If there be anything in the affairs of mortals which it becomes us deliberately to attack, which we ought indeed to shun by every possible means, to avert and to abolish, it is certainly war, than which there is nothing more wicked, more mischievous or more widely destructive in its effects, nothing harder to be rid of, or more horrible, in a word more unworthy of a man. . . . (Cited in M.C. Smith 1903, pp. 18–19.)

At the time Erasmus wrote this indictment of war, the worst excesses of war that ever ravaged Europe were still to come. On this evidence alone, S. Amos's naive optimism could be dismissed without comment. Yet by changing his prediction only slightly, one can make it sound much more reasonable: "Institutions, which become *maladapted* to their social environment must vanish."

We have seen that war has been able to survive as an institution because its methods and its supporting ideology were sufficiently flexible to adapt to social change. It seems, however, that with the advent of weapons *literally* of total destruction, the adaptive potential of war has been exhausted. This time it appears to be really a question of whether humankind is able to abolish war or whether war extinguishes humankind. The conviction that this is so is the source of the abolitionist's courage and determination.

22

Conceptions of a World Order

Attitudes toward war range from enthusiastic celebration of it (cf. Bernhardi 1914; Hitler 1925/1943) to unconditional rejection (Erasmus 1517/1946). Intermediate positions distinguish between "just" and "unjust," "defensive" and "offensive" wars, between struggles for freedom and defense of the status quo based on privilege, etc.

In this chapter we shall be concerned with predominantly negative attitudes toward violent conflict stemming from conceiving of it as a violation of an existing "international order" or else as a phenomenon that occurs because of a *lack* of a world order. Complementary to this conception of war is a conception of peace as a result of establishing or reestablishing an order usually involving states with a common interest in maintaining such an order but occasionally conceived on the global scale. Attempts to reach such order are reflected in various projects aimed at attenuating the debilitating or devastating effects of war and/or establishing a machinery for conflict resolution.

Early Attempts to Regulate War

"International law" had its origins in attempts to regulate war among states that had peaceful intercourse with each other in periods between wars. An early example of an institution concerned with such regulation was the Amphictyonic League in ancient Greece. Although the Greek city-states frequently went to war against each other, the Greeks felt themselves to be members of the same Hellenic culture, differentiating between themselves and the "barbarians." The Amphictyonic League had only a Hellenic basis. In that institution we also find attempts to arbitrate among the city-states.

The Romans had certain regulations governing the taking of booty. Significantly, the persons of ambassadors were held inviolate. Strongly committed to legality, the Romans scrupulously observed the rule of declaring war before embarking on it.

The Turkish conquests in the fifteenth century, climaxed by the capture of Constantinople and the dissolution of the Eastern Roman Empire in 1453, contributed to attempts to form a defensive alliance of Christian states. Any such alliance is an amalgam of peaceful and warlike intentions. Internal peace is sought in the interest of presenting a united front against a common enemy.

One of the earliest explicitly spelled-out projects of such an alliance is that credited to King George of Bohemia. It was worked out in 1462–1464, significantly, only a few years after the fall of Constantinople. The preamble of the proposed treaty begins with the following curious statement:

> In the name of our Lord Jesus Christ . . . Let this be known to one and all for all eternity. We learn from the writings of ancient historians that Christianity once flourished and was blessed with men and goods, spreading far and wide that it held in its womb one hundred and seventeen rich kingdoms; that it also brought forth so many people that for a long time it held a large part of pagandom including the Holy Sepulchre; in those days there was no nation in the world which would have dared to challenge Christian rule. But we all know how lacerated it is today, how broken, impoverished, and deprived of all its former brilliance and splendor it is. For not long ago Christendom passed through such a change that if any of the ancient kings, princes, or notables were to rise from the dead and visit the Christian countries, he would not recognize his own land. (Czechoslovak Academy of Sciences 1964.)

We have no way of knowing whether the authors of this document really had such a notion of a Golden Age of Christianity or whether this gloomy picture of the decline of Christendom was meant to activate the Christian princes to make common cause against the Turks. The articles of the treaty, however, give evidence of political ideas remarkably advanced for the time. In fact, the treaty anticipates some of the principal features of twentieth-century collective security institutions such as the League of Nations, the United Nations, and the International Court of Justice. The organization proposed is definitely not a world monarchy nor an ecclesiastical state.

Retention of sovereignty by the various realms is emphasized. Yet a permanent peace among these sovereign realms is envisaged.

Provisions for active peacemaking are made in Article 5 of the Treaty:

> In order to facilitate the suppression of dissidence and wars, the very thought of which pains those who have to experience them, and in order to strengthen peace also among others faithful to Christ who are not parties to the present covenant, we hereby provide an order that if discord or war should occur between other Christian princes and magnates who are not included in our fraternity, our below described assembly shall dispatch in our name and at our mutual expense envoys whose task will be to restore concert between the parties to dispute . . .

And in Article 9, we read:

> And in order to settle individual matters in proper order, we have decided, first of all, to establish a single general consistory which will sit in the name of all of us and our whole assembly at the place where the assembly is sitting at that time, and from it, as from a spring, rivulets of justice will flow to all sides. This court shall be established in accordance with what our below described assembly or its majority may conclude and decide. . . .

For all its celebration of lasting peace, the horizon of the peaceful world had not yet been extended beyond Christendom. It was not until the seventeenth century that the idea of a "universal" law without regard to religious differences became explicit. No doubt the excesses of the Thirty Years War, a violent clash between adherents of Catholicism and Protestantism, stimulated some thinking about war in a secular vein. A major work in which that idea was embodied was *De Jure Belli et Pacis* (Grotius 1625/1962). This work was published in Paris in the midst of the Thirty Year War.

De Jure Belli et Pacis is remarkable in that it advances the idea of the Law of Nature as a basis of ethical precepts and posits a connection between these and a "universal" law that transcends the laws established by states to promote their own interests. It is not the idea of a "universal law" itself that was Grotius's original contribution, since this idea is discerned in religious teachings. Rather, it is the explicit insistence that "universal law" *transcends* state laws. It is therefore a challenge to the unlimited power of the state. Especially significant is the fact that this idea emerged just as the idea of completely sovereign states unsubordinated to the authority of the Church was emerging in Europe.

While Grotius drew a distinction between laws of states based on self-interest and an ethical principle of *right*, he did not go so far as to question the rolc of war as an acceptable method for settling disputes between states. He did maintain that war "may only be begun to pursue the right" and that the manner of conducting a war rests on fixed laws, presumably derivatives of the "Law of Nature."

International Law in the Spirit of the Enlightenment

The notion of international law independent of "The Law of Nature" and based on ethical imperatives alone comes to fruition with E. Vattel. Vattel's concern is with the obligations of nations, with the powers of the state, and with the duties of nations to one another. He seeks to look into the causes of "quarrels" between nations and into ways in which they could be settled without war and without humiliating either side. Ideas of arbitration and conciliation make their appearance in his work. *The Law of Nations* (1758/1916) was published when the French Enlightenment was in full bloom. And it is in the ideas of the Enlightenment that the idea of perpetual peace based on secular rather than religious (eschatological) notions came to fruition.

We observe a parallel development of two conceptions of a world order. One emphasizes international law regulating intercourse among states, specifying "legitimate" reasons for waging war and regulating the conduct of war. The other conception can be characterized as a dream of eventually achieved perpetual peace.

Until quite recently Europeans regarded Europe as "the world." The idea that Asian civilizations were also of this world and would possibly have something to say about how a world order was to be established simply did not fit into this conception. As for the rest of humanity, e.g., the Africans or the Polynesians, these were mentioned only as the "lower races" or subsumed under a similar category. They were to be *dealt with*, not considered as real actors in global politics. In the European view "perpetual peace" meant peace among the European states. Often the purpose of this peace was explicitly or implicitly that of strengthening European civilization against external threats. In some cases, however, genuine pacifistic ideas were interlaced with geopolitical ones.

One of the earliest works manifesting the "dream of perpetual peace" in the political rather than the religious mode was the *Memoirs* of M. de Bethune, Duke of Sully, published in 1634. A curious story is told about that book by M.C. Smith (1903). The French Abbé St. Pierre was supposed to have found it buried in an old garden and, inspired by it, wrote his *Projet de Paix Perpetuelle* (1713–1717). In his *Memoirs* Sully refers to a "Grand Design," which he attributes to King Henry IV of France. Smith conjectures, however, that this plan could not have originated with the king but was attributed to him by Sully to attract attention and, perhaps, to insure a more favorable reception.

The "Grand Design" envisages a Christian republic consisting of a union of fifteen European Powers. The union was to be formed on the principle of equality of its members. A legislative body with every Power represented was to "deliberate on questions that might arise, to occupy themselves with discussing different interests, to settle quarrels amicably, to throw light upon and arrange all the civil, political and religious affairs of Europe, whether internal or foreign."

Abbé St. Pierre expanded this scheme and worked it out in considerable detail. As in the case of the federation proposed by King George of Bohemia (cf. below), the union was envisaged as an alliance against the Turks. Indeed, the military force of the federation was to be applied to drive the Turks out of Europe.

The Abbé's project was received with considerable skepticism. Some aspects of it reveal obvious political bias. For instance, one of the provisions was that "the kingdom of Spain shall not go out of the House of Bourbon." (The book was written during the War of the Spanish Succession.) The primacy of France in the federation, in spite of the "principle of equality," was hardly disguised. Voltaire dismissed the scheme in a sentence (Voltaire 1771/1935, p. 351). Leibnitz wrote, "I have seen something of M. de St. Pierre's plea for maintaining perpetual peace in Europe. It reminds me of an inscription outside of a church yard which ran 'Pax Perpetua.' For the dead, it is true, fight no more. But the living are of another mind, and the mightiest among them have little respect for tribunals" (Leibnitz 1768, Vol. 5, pp. 65–66).

Of special interest to us is the circumstance that much of the skepticism that greeted St. Pierre's proposals stemmed from the loss of confidence in the ability of sovereigns to establish a lasting peace among themselves. J.J. Rousseau (1761/1955), in particular, thought that sovereigns would never submit to any authority over them. The poet William Cowper, Rousseau's contemporary, voiced the idea that war was one of the pleasures of regal existence:

Great princes have great playthings. Some have play'd
At hewing mountains into men, and some
At building human wonders mountains high
. . . .
Some seek diversion in the tented field,
And make the sorrows of mankind their sport.
But war's a game, which were their subjects wise,

Kings should not play at. Nations would do well
T'extort their truncheons from the puny hands
Of heroes, whose infirm and baby minds
Are gratified with mischief and who spoil,
Because men suffer it, their toy the world.

Here the idea of a revolution against the institution of war nurtured by monarchs comes over the intellectual horizon.

The Rationalist Conception of a World Order

The dominant ideas of eighteenth-century Europe are sometimes subsumed under "rationalism." This was the century in which the intellectual content of exact science blossomed. The spirit of the time is best exemplified in Laplace's remark to Napoleon, who had read (or said he had read) Laplace's great work on celestial mechanics and asked the author where God fit into his scheme of the universe. "I had no need of that hypothesis, sire," Laplace is said to have replied.

This same Laplace championed the idea of physical determinism. If there were a being, he argued, capable of encompassing the instantaneous positions and velocities of all the particles in the universe at a given moment of time, then, given sufficient calculating ability, this being could predict the state of the universe, that is, of the system characterized by the positions and velocities of the particles in it as variables, for all time to come.

The universe seemed to have been revealed as ruled by laws of nature, not by the will or whims of a sentient being. Robespierre tried to enthrone Reason as the deity to be worshipped by rational men.

In a way, the philosophy of Immanuel Kant reflects a culmination of rationalism, particularly in two works: *Ideas of a Universal History from a Cosmopolitan Point of View* (1784) and *Perpetual Peace* (1795). The latter work is especially relevant to the theme of this chapter.

The principal ingredients of *Universal History* are (a) the social basis of human development and (b) the progress of reason following the cognitive principle of science. The first idea is embodied in Kant's conviction that only in humanity as a whole, not in each individual separately, can the natural capacities of the human species reach full unfolding. In this respect, Kant was an evolutionist, an optimist, believer in the progressive development of humanity, and a forerunner of collectivist ideals. Both the right-wing philosophers (e.g., Hegel) and the left-wing social philosophers (e.g., Marx) owe a solid intellectual debt to Kant on this account. The second idea is embodied in Kant's statement that reason

. . . does not itself work by instinct, but requires experiments, exercise, and instruction in order to advance gradually from one stage of insight to another. Hence each individual man would necessarily have to live an enormous length of time in order to learn by himself how to make a complete use of all his natural endowments. Otherwise if nature should have given him but a short lease of life, as is actually the case, reason would then require an almost interminable series of generations, the one handing down its enlightenment to the other, in order that her germs, as implanted in our species, may be at last unfolded to that stage of development which is completely comformable to her design. (Kant 1784/1891, pp. 6–7.)

Here we have an early, clear expression of man's social nature, note-worthy because it is at odds with Kant's acceptance of Hobbes's ultra-individualistic view of the "war of everyone against everyone" waged by man "in the state of nature." In fact, Kant believed that "savages" lived in this condition.

The attachment of savages to their lawless liberty, the fact that they would rather be at hopeiess variance with one another than submit themselves to a legal authority constituted by themselves, that they therefore prefer their senseless freedom to a reason-governed liberty, is regarded by us with pro-found contempt as barbarism and uncivilization and the brutal degradation of humanity. (Kant 1795/1903, p. 130.)

The principal thought in Kant's essay on perpetual peace is that the civilizing process, which turned the "senseless freedom" of the "savages" into "reason-governed liberty" must be extended to the relations among states. It should be noted that "must" in this context was used by Kant both in its normative (moral) and its predictive sense. The latter stems from Kant's optimistic philosophy based on belief in Providence-ordained progress.

Another focus is an explicit attack on monarchy as a breeder of war. Referring to what he calls a sardonic inscription, "Perpetual Peace" on a graveyard, Kant raises the question of whether it is aimed at mankind in general or at the rulers of states, "unwearying in their love of war." He goes on to state the conditions of perpetual peace among states in six Preliminary Articles. They contain:

(1) A prohibition of secret reservation of material for a future war.
(2) Inviolability of independence of states.
(3) Abolition of standing armies.
(4) Prohibition of contracting national debts to finance future wars.
(5) Prohibition of interfering in the internal affairs of another state.

(6) Prohibition of excesses in the conduct of war which "make mutual confidence impossible in a subsequent state of peace."

These are followed by three Definitive Articles. In the first Kant explicitly reveals his view that the monarchical system is the root of war: "The civil constitutions of each state shall be republican." The second Definitive Article describes the structure of the international system as a "federation of free states." The last mentions the rights of men as "citizens of the world."

The influence of the ideas that energized the French Revolution are unmistakable in this essay written in the midst of that revolution. Even more significant, however, is the fruition of the idea that wars are spawned not primarily by the aggressive nature of men and only secondarily by ambitions of monarchs. Rather, the roots of war are in the monarchical system itself and, of course, in its trappings of that era: the standing armies, subversion of independence of states by inheritance or purchase, mentioned in Preliminary Article 2. In this way, a conception of a peaceful world order came to be based on a conception of a just political system. A half-century later, the idea was born that even more fundamental than a just political system as a basis for a peaceful world is an equitable economic system.

By suggesting that the roots of international anarchy are to be sought in the nature of the monarchical system, Kant anticipated the conception of a world order which gave rise to the Communist Manifesto (Marx and Engels 1848/1955).

Communist Manifesto

In this pamphlet, revolutionary internationalism makes its debut. The slogan "Proletarians of all countries unite!" is a way of saying that the workers, the underdogs of a capitalist society, have no allegiance to their respective states but only to each other. This disavowal of loyalty is a categorical rejection of the creed central in all nationalist ideology but especially that in the writings of the German state-worshippers inspired by Hegel.

Blueprints for a global proletarian republic are not found in the writings of nineteenth-century Marxists, because they shunned utopian images. Claiming their social philosophy to be based on sound scientific principles, they did not venture to predict what the world would be like in regard to its political structure, for example, aside from some vague references to the "withering away" of the state when the capitalist system was overthrown. They did, however, devote considerable attention to the role of global capitalism in shaping the existing world system and in instigating wars. Starting with the dynamic aspect of capitalism, they showed that the need for expanding markets is inherent in that dynamic. In their search for trade outlets, they maintained, capitalist states in the process of acquiring colonial empires or spheres of influence collide with each other, leading to wars among them. V.I. Lenin (1916/1969) developed this theory in considerable detail and supported some of its tenets with statistical data. A corollary to this view became that a peaceful world would be a "socialist" world.

Expressions of the inevitability of a "final" struggle between the "capitalist" and the "socialist" worlds are found in the writings of many Soviet writers. After the death of Stalin, however, the "inevitability" of an armed struggle disappeared from Soviet public statements related to the officially sanctioned conception of a world order. Dedication to struggle remained complete, but it was now conceived as a struggle on the ideological level, a contest "for the hearts and minds" of people, as it were. Belief in the ultimate success of the socialist system in proving itself to be superior to capitalism in providing for human needs gave confidence in the "final victory" of socialism.

Coexistence and Soviet Conceptions of a World Order

Coexistence of the "two systems" is now central in the Soviet leaders' conception of a world order. In this connection, it is interesting to note the interpretation of the above-mentioned fifteenth-century proposal of King George of Bohemia by the authors of the publication presented to UNESCO in 1964 by the Czechoslovak Academy of Sciences. The date was the 500th anniversary of King George's proposal. Doubtless national pride played a part in the gesture, displaying evidence that progressive humane ideals already flourished in the fifteenth century in what is now socialist Czechoslovakia. The following statements in the commentaries on the proposal are noteworthy:

> The most prominent place is occupied by proposals whose purpose was to exclude war from human society. This purpose is openly and exclusively followed in the first eight articles, that is, the whole of the first third of the project; these articles contain very detailed and complete regulations designed to eliminate wars, to settle disputes between states peacefully, and to punish those who disturb peace. War against the Turks is not mentioned once. (p. 18.)
>
> Mankind of the fifteenth century was shown the prospects of a world without

wars in which even the apparently insurmountable antagonism between the Christians and Moslems appeared to be replaceable by a situation for which we can hardly find a more fitting, modern-day term than "peaceful coexistence." This is clearly indicated by the final part of Article 13, which expressly envisages the possibility of peace between Christendom and the Turks. (p. 20.)

However, in the very Article 13 of the project just alluded to, we read:

> . . . we . . . pledge and swear to our Lord Jesus Christ, to his most glorious mother, the Virgin Mary, and to the Holy Roman Catholic Church that we shall defend and protect the Christian religion and all the oppressed faithful against the vilest prince of the Turks . . . and we shall not cease to pursue the enemy, if our assembly deems it expedient, until he is driven out of Christian territory or until it is jointly resolved to conclude peace, which may be done only if the security of neighboring Christians is deemed ensured.

To see in the fifteenth century proposal of a Bohemian king a precursor of "peaceful coexistence in spite of apparently insurmountable antagonism" may be an intriguing idea. However, a more realistic appraisal of the project would classify it with numerous attempts to forge alliances against a common enemy. Naturally, cooperation can be effective only if the allies are at peace with each other. For this reason, efforts to forge an alliance are often accompanied by appeals for cementing peaceful relations and generally celebrating the blessings of peace.

Conceptions of a "world order" that gives rise to such alliances are actually conceptions of an order comprising "us," to which "they " are, as a rule, juxtaposed. At times, however, it *seems* as if "we" comprise everyone who counts. Then the alliance appears (to everyone who counts) to be a genuine attempt to establish a world order assuring peace for everyone.

Collective Security and the Preservation of the Status Quo

After the defeat of Napoleon in 1814, the European powers who had formed a coalition against him (when he was already losing) gathered in Vienna to establish a "world order." It appeared to include all Europe, even defeated France, whose "legitimate" monarch, Louis (Bourbon) XVIII, was restored to his throne. For a while the alliance held together, because the conception of the world (European) order on which it was based, namely, the restoration of the prestige of monarchies shattered by the French Revolution and by Napoleon's armies, as well as the continued preservation of the status quo, was shared by the victors. They all felt threatened by the continued ferment of revolutionary ideas that once radiated from revolutionary France. The anti-revolutionary function of the alliance was seen especially clearly by Prince Clemens Metternich, the spokesman for Austria, which emerged as the dominant power on the continent. Metternich regarded the suppression of every stirring of "liberalism" as the sacred duty of every European power dedicated to peace, decency, and prosperity. Indeed, for a few years after what was regarded as "a world restoration," actions were undertaken similar to what today is called "counterinsurgency."

In 1820 the Neapolitans revolted against the Bourbon king. Metternich called the revolt "the work of a subversive sect." "The first duty and the first interest of foreign powers," he declared, "is to smother it in its cradle." Success, he was sure, would be certain "owing to our firm purpose to guard the old institutions against the assault of innovators and sectarians." (Cited in May 1963, p. 21.) Austrian troops were dispatched, did the job, and reinstalled the Bourbon king, Ferdinand. A revolt in Spain in the same year was crushed by the French, who thereby regained their prestige as a member in good standing of the "law and order" coalition.

Decisions to crush "subversion" everywhere in Europe were by no means unanimous. Britain's attitude was ambivalent, her interests having turned elsewhere—overseas, where a world empire was being built. When the Greeks revolted against their Ottoman masters, in Metternich's eyes they were a menace to the established order; but Russia wanted to help them. Not only were the Greeks Orthodox Christians and therefore entitled to the protection of the Czar, but also Turkey was Russia's traditional enemy sitting astride the Dardanelles, thus keeping the Russian navy bottled up in the Black Sea.

By 1825, the Quintuple Alliance (Russia, Prussia, Austria, Britain, France) was dead. In 1849, Czar Nicholas I still felt called upon to send troops to help Austria crush the rebellious Hungarians. But for all practical purposes the "preservation of the world order" by military intervention against any attempts to modify existing, for the most part autocratic, regimes became a lost cause. "National interests" overshadowed ideological commitments. A more convincing vindication of the "realist" theory of international relations is difficult to imagine.

Collective Security and the League of Nations

Yet something remained of the idea of including "everyone" (who mattered) in a collective security pact. Note that the Quintuple Alliance was not directed against any European power. It was supposed to be an alliance against the disturbers of established political orders and thus a collective security pact. The idea was revived in the formation of the League of Nations. As in the aftermath of the Napoleonic wars, European rulers were again reminded of the invariably negative balance resulting from a general war. Moreover, the political consequences of World War I were more definitively irreversible than those of the Napoleonic wars. The three most powerful dynasties, the Romanovs of Russia, the Hohenzollerns of Germany, and the Hapsburgs of Austria were toppled. Strong pacifist moods created revolutionary situations in both Germany and France. The League of Nations was, at its inception, a genuine attempt to establish international machinery for keeping the peace. Like the short-lived Quintuple Alliance, it, too, was based on a collective security pact. The members pledged to keep peace among themselves, to settle disputes peaceably, collectively to punish disturbers of the peace. These pledges were practically verbatim repetitions of the pledges that King George unsuccessfully urged the Christian princes to take four-and-a-half centuries earlier. This time, however, there was no "vilest prince of the Turks." Nor was there any explicit commitment to counterrevoltuion. The half-hearted attempts of intervention in Russia in 1919–1922, although they involved fourteen foreign powers, were abandoned.

The League of Nations was more inclusive than the Accord of Europe of 1815. The notion of collective security was extended to guarantee to small nations the right to exist—the principle of "self-determination." Doubtless this principle had its origin in the belief that one of the principal "causes" of World War I was Austria-Hungary's stubborn suppression of nationalist aspirations nurtured by the peoples comprising that empire. The principle of self-determination, however, was not extended to what we now call the Third World. The colonial system was kept intact.

Although Germany, the erstwhile enemy of the founders of the League of Nations, and the Soviet Union, initially a pariah, were eventually admitted to the League of Nations, that body was too weak to overcome the monstrous appetite for conquest that developed in the predatory newcomers in the international arena: fascist Italy, Nazi Germany, and Imperial Japan. World War II sounded the death knell of the League of Nations.

The United Nations

The United Nations was an attempt to revive the League of Nations, again based on the concept of collective security, this time to be realized by a frank recognition of the power distribution that resulted from the outcome of World War II. The power to enforce peace was vested in the Security Council, all of whose decisions were based on the unanimity of the Big Five, the U.S., the U.S.S.R., the U.K., France, and China. The inclusion of the latter was initially a fiction, because that huge country was represented in the Security Council by a government in exile, calling itself "The Republic of China" while exercising control over an island.

The Cold War had already started, and chances of agreement between the Soviet Union and the United States on matters involving contests of power were practically nil. The extension of membership to the new states emerging from the ruins of the colonial system spawned a host of unforeseen problems. The future of the United Nations, still functioning but facing an uncertain role in the unfolding of world politics, is a subject beyond the scope of this book.

It is interesting to observe that some contemporary conceptions of a world order, even if they transcend "national interest" as a focal concept, are tradition-oriented in the sense that they cannot transcend the identification of "legitimacy" with incumbent power. In this connection, a historical work by Henry Kissinger (1973) is revealing. The book deals with the lifework of Metternich. The title of Kissinger's book, *A World Restored*, reflects the author's conception of a world order. Although the book deals with events that unfolded almost two centuries ago, its message is clearly about the present state of the world. The principal idea is a juxtaposition of "legitimacy" on which the stability of the international system is assumed to depend and the impact of a "revolutionary power" on that system.

> . . . It is the essence of revolutionary power that it preserves the courage of its convictions, that it is willing, indeed eager, to push its principles to their ultimate conclusion. Whatever else a revolutionary power may achieve therefore it tends to erode, if not the legitimacy of the international order, at least the restraint with which such an order operates. (Kissinger 1973, p. 3.)

On the other hand:

> Stability . . . has commonly resulted not from a quest for peace but from generally accepted legitimacy. "Legitimacy" as here used should not be confused with justice. It means no more than an international agreement about the nature of workable arrangements and about the permissible aims and methods of foreign policy. (p. 1.)

Much wisdom is reflected in this distinction between "stability" and "justice." Going a step further, one could argue that in the last analysis justice can be realized only in a state of stability. For, whatever ideas may have been or may be current about justice being derived from "natural law" or God's will, or whatever, the realization of justice is possible only in consequence of sufficiently broad *agreement* about what is just. Thus, the relation between stability and justice turns out to be closer than Kissinger's comment might suggest. The critical distinction between legitimacy and justice, however, remains. It resides in the different identities of the parties to the agreement. For Metternich, legitimacy resided in an agreement among the mighty. In consequence of the events in France toward the end of the eighteenth century, this legitimacy was challenged. The overriding goal of Metternich's life's work was to restore the legitimacy of the old order. He was not concerned with justice.

In his book, Kissinger explains this goal to the modern reader with unmistakable allusions to the present situation. (The identity of the "revolutionary power" is unmistakable.) A stable world is not necessarily a conflictless world, but it is a world in which restraint in conflict can be practiced, in which there is place for diplomacy.

> And because in a revolutionary situation, the contending systems are less concerned with the adjustment of differences than with the subversion of loyalties, diplomacy is replaced either by war or by an armament race. (p. 3.)

It appears, therefore, from Kissinger's point of view that Metternich, much maligned as a "reactionary," actually did more for peace than all the revolutionary visionaries before and after him. If peace was not established and the prospect for a peaceful world is still dim, this is because the "legitimacy" of incumbent power continues to be challenged in the name of "justice." This may very well be the case. The fact remains that recognition of the legitimacy of incumbent power as a foundation of peace or at least of diplomacy and restraint in conflict continues to be valued by the possessors of that power. It amounts to the perpetuation of the "way of thinking," which Einstein maintained is driving the world to irreversible catastrophe.

Proposed Roads Toward a New World Order

Common to all transnational conceptions of a world order which challenge incumbent power is an explicit rejection of "national interest" as the overriding value in the conduct of human affairs. The actual images of a "postnational interest" world and especially the views about how it can be brought about vary widely. They range from advocacy of legalistic reforms, e.g., modifications of so-called international law or of procedures governing the activities of the United Nations, to the establishment of a world government with power comparable to that of present national governments.

There are also wide differences of opinion concerning priorities. Shall the human psyche be first cured of aggressive tendencies before we can think of a global cooperative commonwealth? Does the establishment of trust between nations deserve a commitment of efforts before we can think realistically about disarmament? Is disarmament a prior condition before trust can be established? That any designed world system must be politically feasible if it is ever realized is generally recognized, but opinions on what may be feasible today or tomorrow vary widely.

Hanna Newcombe (1974) has summarized sixteen major approaches to world order that are currently being advanced. These give a good picture of the present "state of the art":

1. United Nations Charter Revision
2. People's Constitutional Convention
3. Partial or Regional Federations
4. A New or Parallel Organization Separate from the U.N.
5. Gradual Expansion of International Law
6. Mundialization of (conferring "world status" on) Cities and Government Declarations for World Government
7. The World Citizens' Movement
8. Development through U.N. Peacekeeping Forces
9. The Functional Approach: Expansion of International Aid and Cooperation
10. Internationalism in Other than Political Areas
11. Drafting World Constitutions
12. Working through Certain Specialized Groups: Parliamentarians, Educators, Scientists, International Lawyers
13. Initiatives by the Non-Aligned Nations or by Becoming Non-Aligned
14. Political Parties with World Government Platforms
15. A World Language such as Esperanto
16. World Holidays

These approaches can be classified in a number of ways, for example, as gradualist versus revolutionary, institution-oriented versus people-oriented, or pragmatic versus utopian. The campaign for revising the U.N. Charter is an institution-oriented, gradualist approach. Attempts to establish a body as an alternative to the U.N. constitute an institution-oriented radical approach. Approaches 2, 6, and 7 are distinctly people-oriented. Drafting world constitutions could be regarded as a utopian approach.

All of these categories reflect specific philosophies of peace action. There is a widespread belief that large-scale conflicts could be prevented or attenuated if people could be got to "understand" one another more. At times "lack of understanding" is taken literally in the sense of people being unable to understand a foreign language. The proponents of a "world language" like Esperanto act on the assumption that if everyone could talk to everyone else directly, the amount of hostility and animosity in the world would decrease and that this would contribute to decreasing the incidence or severity of wars.

"Nationalism" is persistently held to be a principal source of international strife. The World Citizens' Movement is directed against nationalism. This approach, like mundialization of cities and the institution of world holidays, is distinctly a people-oriented approach with strong utopian overtones.

Institutional approaches are based on the assumption that changes are accomplished by effective use of political leverage. Proponents of these approaches envisage an extrapolation of some discernible world-political trends, such as the increasing scope and "democratization" of collective security arrangements as evidenced by the progression from the Accord of Europe (1815) to the League of Nations (1920), and the United Nations (1945). The Accord of Europe was firmly committed to a reactionary goal—the restoration of *anciens regimes* and eradication of all the changes stimulated by the French Revolution. The League of Nations was much more inclusive, gave voice to the idea that war was an evil, and developed some institutions engaged in humanitarian activities. The United Nations became even more inclusive and, in fact, became a forum in which representatives of impoverished peoples criticized the policies of powerful and affluent states. In particular, persistent demands for disarmament, arms control, a new world economic order, and the like now constitute a principal theme of the ongoing discussions in that forum.

On the whole, the demands remain unfulfilled, and the reason is obvious. The Charter of the United Nations provides no machinery for enforcing the resolutions of the General Assembly. Resolutions of the Security Council (dealing mostly with breaches of peace) could be enforced but require unanimity of the nuclear powers. It seems, therefore, that strengthening the authority of the United Nations could enhance its role as a body dedicated to the welfare of humanity as a whole, eventually turning it into the beginning of a world government. It is instructive to follow the history of these efforts.

The most comprehensive work to date centering on the institutional approach to the problem of creating a peaceful world order if G. Clark and L. Sohn's *World Peace through World Law* (1958). The main theme of this work focuses on two alternative plans. One is a far-reaching revision of the United Nations Charter; the other, the creation of a new world organization. Included in the proposed revisions are proposals (couched in formal articles) of planned disarmament, a U.N. peace force, a judicial conciliation institution, a world development authority, and a Bill of Rights.

The U.N. Charter provided for its own automatic review by specifying that the General Assembly consider the possibility of calling a Charter Revision Conference. This question was to be put on the agenda ten years after the signing of the Charter. The World Association of World Federalists viewed this provision as an opportunity. The first task was to see to it that such a conference actually took place. "Considering the possibility" of calling a conference was by no means a guarantee that it would actually be called. The second task was to prepare proposals for changing the Charter to be put before the conference.

The second task was duly attended to. Large collections of proposals were produced and published. Anyone interested can examine rich sources. Examples are "A U.N. Charter for Man" (Griftalconi and Weik 1954); hearings on the review of the U.N. Charter in the U.S. Senate (U.S. Senate Committee on Foreign Relations 1954); publication of a seven-year study by 500 conferees in the U.S. and 17 other countries (Millard 1961), and many, many others. Most of the proposals deal with strengthening the peacekeeping functions of the U.N., e.g., a proposal for a permanent U.N. force composed of volunteers, *not* national contingents; plans for complete and general disarmament with international inspections, and many more. Proposals of procedural changes deal with weighted voting in the General Assembly, abolition of the veto in the Security Council, and so forth. Many of the proposed changes reflect even more the goal of gradually turning the United Nations into a world government, for instance, "expanded legislative powers of the General Assembly, compulsory jurisdiction of the World Court, a world development authority for greatly expanding economic aid, a guarantee against violation of human rights . . ." (Newcombe 1967, p. 10).

Obviously, none of the proposals could be implemented unless a conference on U.N. Charter Revision were actually called. In 1955, the General Assembly did put the Conference on its agenda, as directed by the Charter, and did vote to hold the Conference, but it failed to set a date. Instead, it appointed a Committee which was to report to every Assembly and state its recommendation on calling the Conference. It has reported to every Assembly since. In each instance, the recommendation has been that the time for considering revisions was not yet right.

Resistance to revision of the U.N. Charter reflects the virtual impossibility at this time of even suggesting a possibility of encroaching on the sovereignty of the most powerful national states. This resistance defines practically the only area in which these states are in full agreement.

A more promising, pragmatic, institution-oriented approach is through existing nonpolitical (or presumably nonpolitical) organizations.

This approach to a peaceful world order is predicated on the idea that more can be accomplished by promoting conditions of peace than by removing the causes of war. There is ample evidence that cooperative interdependence is one of the firmest bases for peaceful relations among individuals and groups. This is true also in the nonhuman world. Intraspecific aggression rarely occurs between members of the opposite sex, doubtless because cooperation between members of the opposite sex is essential for the procreation of the species.

The crucial role of cooperative interdependence in conflict resolution was impressively demonstrated in a field experiment by Muzaref Sherif (1961). Two groups of preteen boys were kept apart in two summer camps until strong feelings of identification were developed in both. They were given organization names ("The Eagles" and "The Cobras"), flags, and so forth. Then an "accidental" meeting was arranged on a hike. From then on, strong feelings of intergroup hostility were developed, aggravated by competitive sport events. Many attempts at conciliation were made, such as meetings between the leaders, contact between rank and file members, providing favorable information about one group to the other. None of these reduced the hostility. Boys who talked to members of the other group were regarded as "traitors." Information was distorted to preserve the image of "the enemy." Apparently, cognitive dissonance was a formidable impediment to a change of attitude.

Only one intervention produced a fundamental change. The water supply broke down (this was deliberately arranged by the experimenters), and the only way it could be repaired was by a joint effort of the two groups. Thereupon "the false images rapidly crumbled and each group was open to reconciliation. It was then that 'summit meetings' and 'people-to-people' contacts were found effective. In other words, functional cooperation precedes political moves" (Newcombe 1974, p. 47).

The same idea underlies the functional approach to a world government. Bases of international cooperation involving members of both blocs already exist in the activities of several United Nations agencies, such as WHO, FAO, UNESCO, UNICEF, and so forth. Aside from these, postal service functions on the world scale involving a cooperative effort of all states. Codes regulating international air travel amount to legislation by a "world government" (of course with a very limited jurisdiction). Science devoted to the pursuit of knowledge and to the betterment of the human condition is in a very real sense a global cooperative enterprise. Except when the political struggle for power subverts its values, sport, even as it promotes the competitive spirit, at the same time nurtures cooperation through loyalty to its higher ideal of "sportsmanship." Wars between the city-states of ancient Greece were suspended during the Olympics.

It is possible that through these activities some progress toward a world government is being made, if only because progress is more surely made by starting from where one is than by looking longingly at where one wants to be.

Some identify regional federations and alliances as instances of the same gradualist approach to a world government. There is some evidence to support this view. After centuries of chronic warfare, the countries of Western and Central Europe have established a basis for a firm peace among themselves. It is now hardly thinkable that the most bitter enemies of bygone eras, e.g., Denmark and Sweden, England and Holland, or even Germany and France will go to war against each other. Some think that eventually these regional federations will continue to become more inclusive until a world federation arises. An obvious obstacle to this process is the circumstance that alongside of peaceful regional federations (e.g., the Scandinavian) there are others founded on military alliances (NATO, the Warsaw Pact). Internal cohesion in these alliances goes hand in hand with hostility toward rival alliances. Integration of potential enemies is not likely.

Conditions of "Positive Peace"

The frequently emphasized distinction between "negative peace" (absence of war) and "positive peace" (a just world order) poses the question of the extent of consensus on what constitutes a "just world order." Ideological rhetoric is a serious obstacle to such a consensus. For even if agreement on what is a "just world order" could be derived from universally shared values, the imperatives of the ideological struggle would be a formidable hindrance to *formulating* such an agreement.

M.S. McDougal and H.D. Lasswell (1966) proposed an ongoing study to be undertaken with a view to making a continual reappraisal of the degrees to which diverse existing public orders serve or despoil the realization of basic human needs. Recognizing that ideological confrontations might defeat the purpose of the study, they proposed that it be conducted in the non-Soviet world. At the time the project was proposed it was difficult to imagine that Soviet scholars would be permitted to collaborate with their Western colleagues in an undertaking of this sort.

McDougal and Lasswell point out that a framework for the study would be easy to establish because "the major systems of public order are in many fundamental respects rhetorically unified. All systems proclaim the dignity of the individual and the ideal of a worldwide public order in which this ideal is authoritatively pursued and effectively approximated" (McDougal and Lasswell, p. 49). The task can thus be concentrated on ascertaining by means as objective as possible the degrees to which the *components* of a just (i.e., shared value-enhancing) public order are realized in various societies. Eight of these components are singled out.

1. *Power.* Is power in a society widely shared or narrowly concentrated?
2. *Wealth.* What is the relative weight of property interests (savings, investments) and human needs (levels of consumption, hours of work) in determining economic policies? Does the system tend to increase or decrease disparities in assets or income? Is there compulsory labor?
3. *Respect.* Is status determined by birth? How protected are the rights of privacy of conscience, freedom from torture, humiliation, degradation?
4. *Well-being.* How available is health care, decent housing, adequate nutrition to everyone regardless of social status?
5. *Skills.* To what extent is education available to those that want it? To what extent are opportunities to practice skills available?
6. *Enlightenment.* How free is access to information? How available are facilities for transmitting and disseminating both information and interpretation of information, opinions, convictions?
7. *Rectitude.* How free is worship and education based on certain special spiritual values?
8. *Affection.* What protection is given to institutions fostering congeniality, e.g., the family? How free are associations based on love, friendship, commitment to common values?

These criteria will be readily recognized as the components of a just public order as it is conceived by Western liberals. For this reason, it will probably be dismissed as parochial by ethical relativists. Nevertheless, a collaborative project of this sort seems eminently worthwhile. No accusation can be made that it would be an attempt to *impose* a Western liberal order on the world. It entails no more than an investigation which, moreover, can be free from *explicit* commitment to the values implicit in the singled-out criteria. The object of the investigation would be to ascertain the *extent* to which various public orders actually satisfy the criteria. The question of the extent to which the criteria *ought* to be satisfied is left open.

The value of an investigation of this sort would be that of bringing the connection between the character of a public order and the satisfaction of human needs to the center of attention. Controversies concerning what these values actually *are* would, no doubt, go on. The important thing is to counteract the *dissociation* between the idea of order and the idea of human needs, which has marked all hitherto dominant conceptions of a world order derived largely, at times exclusively, from considerations associated with power relations among states.

23

Conflict Resolution and Conciliation

Fights, Games, and Debates

A dog fight, a chess game, and a debate are examples of three modes of conflict. The modes differ essentially in the objectives pursued by the conflicting parties. Strictly speaking, we cannot speak of the "objectives" pursued by fighting dogs. But if we could imagine ourselves in their skins, we would say that each dog tries to harm the other or to drive him away, at any rate to establish its own superiority over the enemy as the braver, the stronger, or the fiercer dog. Such is the objective of a "fight." At times the objective becomes that of eliminating the enemy altogether, destroying him physically. A duel, a feud, and a battle are examples of fights.

In a game the objective is also "to win." But a game is quite different from a fight. One does not win a chess game by harming the opponent, making him flee, or killing him. The emotional concomitants of a game are quite unlike those of a fight. The players do not normally experience rage or physical fear. Neither bravery, nor physical strength, nor fierceness are of help in winning a game. Certain intellectual faculties are essential: an ability to analyze the opportunities and the dangers of the situation, above all to see the situation as it appears to the opponent, to form ideas about how he is likely to act in the situation in which he finds himself, and to utilize this knowledge in designing one's own plans of action.

In a game the "elimination" of the opponent occurs only symbolically. The objective is really to *outwit* the opponent, to prove to him, to oneself, or to others one's superior mental virtuosity. Hatred of the opponent as a person is not usually a concomitant of a game-like conflict. Chess "enemies" may be the best of friends.

Finally, a crucial feature of a game, distinguishing it from a fight, is the existence of explicit rules known to both (or all) participants. The objective of a game is not just to win but to win by adhering to the rules agreed upon by all. Cheating (surreptitious violation of the rules) is either strongly condemned (as in card games), or is virtually impossible (as in chess).

In a debate, the objective is neither to eliminate nor to outwit the opponent but to *convince* either the opponent or, as is more common, a third party, such as a judge or a jury (as in a debate between opposing attorneys in a court of law) or a constituency (as in debates conducted in legislative bodies or the United Nations). In the latter case, the attempt is not so much to convince the constituency of the rightness of one's case as to reassure one's political supporters (or superiors) that their interests are being looked after. At any rate, in a debate one tries to exert influence either with the view of reinforcing or changing someone's way of thinking or with the view of projecting an image of oneself. A debate always revolves around *issues*. In contrast, there are no issues either in a fight or in a game aside from the objective of "winning," which is, properly speaking, not an issue, because there is no point in discussing it.

Because there are no issues in a fight or in a game, these conflicts cannot be resolved. Eventually they end, of course, but these endings are not resolutions in the sense that issues are "settled." We understand an "issue" in a sense that excludes the question of who is going to win as in a fight or a game. We sometimes speak about settling a fight, but this occurs only if a fight is *about* something *aside from* who is stronger, braver, or fiercer. This means essentially that the fight can be, in principle, *transformed* into a conflict of another modality, perhaps into a debate or into a process in which the issues are more thoroughly analyzed or understood. A chess game may be broken off by the players agreeing to a draw. This merely means that they are able to foresee that the game is bound to be a draw if carried to its conclusion. It is pointless to subsume this outcome under "conflict resolution." Only conflicts in which substantive issues of some sort are an integral part can be "resolved." A constructive or normative theory of conflict resolution deals with ways of structuring a debate or related processes, such as negotiation, arbitration, and conciliation, which include elements of debate.[1]

Rules for Constructive Debate

Consider a debate in which the opposing sides direct their arguments not at a third party but at each other. The objective pursued by each opponent is to produce a shift in the other's perceptions or ways of thinking so as to bring them closer to one's own. In order to bring about such a shift, one must thoroughly understand the opponent's position. In a debate, the opponents, usually at the start, state their respective positions. Just hearing the position of the opponent stated by him does not guarantee that the position will be understood. There are reasons for this. It is natural, when engaging in a debate, to be intensely concerned with one's own problem, that of presenting one's position most effectively. One is not easily distracted from constant preoccupation with this problem. Next, one can be expected to be preoccupied with the problem of refuting the position of the opponent. Therefore, as the opponent presents his case, one will be especially on the alert to pick out the weakest points in his argument. In planning to refute or discredit them, one is likely to pay little or no attention to what the opponent is saying. Finally, one may think one already has a clear idea of what the view of the opponent entails. In that case, one may completely ignore what the opponent is saying as he explains his position. To insure that each participant has a thorough understanding of the other's position, the following rule of debate has been offered (Rapoport 1960). Before being permitted to state his own position or to argue his own case, each participant must state the position of his *opponent* in such a way that the opponent will agree that his position has indeed been stated correctly.

This rule is a variant of a procedure used by Carl Rogers in what he called client-centered or non-directive therapy (Rogers 1951). In Rogers's view, advice or directions given to a patient seeking psychotherapy or counseling about what to do or what not to do is seldom effective, because the heart of the problem in most such cases is that the patient feels that he is not understood or is ignored or not cared for. In non-directive therapy, the therapist refrains from giving directions. He paraphrases what the patient tells him and presents it back to the patient in different words. Verbatim repetitions would be likely to defeat the purpose of therapy, since they could be interpreted as mockery. Paraphrased "reflections" of the patient's concerns would be more likely to be interpreted as evidence of understanding, perhaps of empathy with the patient's predicament. In this way, a trusting relationship would be established between therapist and patient, presumably a prerequisite to effective therapy.

Presenting the opponent's case to the opponent's satisfaction in a debate at least convinces the opponent that he has been heard and understood, a prerequisite for any prospect of bringing the position of the adversary closer to one's own. Note that each should be strongly motivated to present the other's case to the other's satisfaction, because the rule specifies that neither participant can present his own case before he has successfully presented the other's.

The next rule requires that each participant produce a "scenario" of a hypothetical situation in which the opponent's case would be justified. He must indicate under what circumstances he would act or feel or perceive as the opponent. This rule serves a dual purpose. First, it can lead to reduction of hostility induced by the initial, apparently irreconcilable positions by making salient a hypothetical situation in which the conflict of interests, attitudes, or perceptions would disappear. It would reveal a common ground of values or assumptions underlying the opponents' positions. If there is no common ground at all, the debate cannot possibly be productive. Situations that preclude the existence of a common ground are by no means uncommon. Whether the opponents are in fact in a situation of this sort should not, however, be prejudged.

Usually it is not difficult to hypothesize situations in which the opponent's position could be accepted. For instance, there is practically no assertion (except a self-contradictory one) that cannot under certain circumstances be true. If some one says "Black is white," the rejoinder may be, "That is so when one is looking at a photographic negative." Ordinary language contains enough ambiguity for practically any assertion to be interpreted in opposite ways.

The rule requiring conditional justification of the opponent's position focuses the substance of the debate on more or less objective matters of fact. After the conditions under which the opponent's position would be justified are specified, the task remaining is that of demonstrating that these conditions do not, in fact, obtain.

Recall the argument about whether a house is on the right or the left side of the road.

A: The house is on the right side of the road.

B: No, it is on the left side.

A: Yes, if you are driving north.

A's last remark states the condition under which his opponent's position would be correct.

B: But I was assuming that you were driving south. If so, then the house is on the left side.

A: I see. So we agree after all.

The conflict has been resolved.

The example is trivial, but the format represented by it applies in many serious controversies. This approach is analogous to that of the diagnostician who begins by *excluding* certain easily diagnosable conditions. In the same way, making explicit the assumptions underlying the opponents' positions serves the purpose of excluding controversies based on misunderstandings.

Negotiations conducted by persons acting on their own or empowered to modify the policies of the organizations they represent are closely related to genuine debates. The above criterion excludes negotiations in which the participants are bound to certain positions by their superiors, as is the case in many negotiations carried on in the context of international relations. Negotiations go further than debates, because presumably they are supposed to lead not merely to a modification of views but also to actions. When a seller and a buyer negotiate the sales price of a house, a successful outcome involves not only changes in each participant's opinion of what the house is worth in terms of money, but also leads to a deal.

R. Fisher and W. Ury (1981) listed a number of principles which they recommend as guides in the conduct of negotiations. Several of these are closely related to the abovementioned principles of constructive debate.

Perhaps the most essential of these principles is that of avoiding negotiating *positions* instead of *interests*. To illustrate, we will reproduce one of Fisher and Ury's homely but illuminating examples. Two persons in the reading room of a library argue over whether the window should be open or closed. Open and closed window represents respectively the positions of each of the conflicting parties. As long as their attention is riveted on these positions, a satisfactory resolution of their conflict is unlikely. A compromise in the form of a partially open window is not promising. Besides, such a compromise can be effected only if the two agree on how wide the window is to be opened. This may involve protracted negotiations without a guarantee of success. The librarian, to whom both appeal, resolves the problem after she has elicited from both information about *why* they want the window open or closed. One wants fresh air, the other is afraid of drafts. The librarian opens a window in the adjoining room, which lets fresh air in without a draft.

Over twenty years ago, the Soviet Union and the United States almost reached agreement on a comprehensive nuclear test ban. An issue remaining to be resolved was the number of on-site inspections to be allowed by each state per year. The Soviet Union insisted on limiting the number to three; the United States insisted on ten. These were positions. In principle, it might have been possible to keep bargaining over the number of inspections, just as the seller and the buyer argue over price. However, bargaining over quantities frequently leads to an impasse when each side is convinced that by remaining adamant, i.e., announcing the "last offer," it can get a concession that it would otherwise not obtain. So it was with the frozen positions: no more than three inspections versus no fewer than ten. The *interests* of the two parties never came to light, although, of course, these interests were well known. The United States was apprehensive of the Soviets' "sincerity" and was most concerned about the opportunities that the severe limitation of on-site inspections would provide for cheating.

The Soviet Union, on the other hand, was most apprehensive of being spied on. To its way of thinking, a large number of permitted on-site inspections would allow the United States to gather information other than what the inspections were supposed to provide. The negotiations were aborted. The interests of the two parties, as distinguished from their positions, were not what the negotiations were about. Had these interests (fear of cheating on the part of one, fear of espionage on the part of the other) been put on the line, some solution might have been found that would have allayed both of these fears.

Not all negotiations involving questions of "national security" end in failure. After a protracted negotiations process, a peace treaty was finally signed between Egypt and Israel, the most bitter enemies since the establishment of the state of Israel and the displacement of the Palestinians. A major stumbling block had been the Sinai Peninsula. The peninsula had been occupied by Israel since the Six Day War of 1967. The territory meant much to Egypt, not only because there was oil there, but also symbolically. Egypt, like Israel, had become a sovereign state only recently, after centuries of domination by the Greeks, the Romans, the Turks, and the British. Israel was most concerned with security against attack. In fact, the Yom Kippur War of 1973 started with a surprise attack by Egypt against Israel. Had the two states stuck to their positions, i.e., continued to argue to which state the Sinai Peninsula should belong, they might have spent much time drawing and and redrawing boundaries and in the usual squabbles about what to include or exclude. In this instance, however, where the atmosphere created at Camp David facilitated frank discussion, the parties were able to put their interests instead of their positions on the line. As a result, a solution was worked out—not a "compromise" solution ("splitting the difference"), but one that took the interests of both states into account. The peninsula was returned to Egypt, and large areas in it were demilitarized. Egypt's concern with sovereignty was satisfied, but Egyptian tanks were not poised on the borders of Israel.

Note the resemblance of the principle of focusing on interests to the principle of stating the position of the other side as a principle of constructive debate. To forestall misunderstanding, the two different meanings of "position," as this term is used by Fisher and Ury, and by us, must be pointed out. Fisher and Ury use "position" in the sense of an officially stated goal described in terms of what the side in question expects to be the result of a negotiation. In our sense, "position" is meant to include interests. Thus, to state the "position" of the other in the context of a constructive debate means to bring his interests to light. Of course, this can be done to the other's satisfaction (one of the prerequisites of a constructive debate) only if the interests of the other are properly understood.

Therefore, our principle of stating each other's "positions" is entirely in accord with the Fisher-Ury principle of creative negotiation, centering on interests instead of on "positions."

Objective Criteria

Arguments about facts can be much more easily settled than arguments about values or about future events. An argument about who was the greater general, Napoleon or Hannibal, can go on forever. If the stature of a general can be defined in terms of objective criteria, say, number of battles won, or people killed, or whatever generals are good at doing, agreement can be reached.

In our model of a constructive debate, we suggested a procedure whereby the dialogue would be reduced as far as possible to issues about relevant states of affairs. This was one reason for recommending statements of conditions under which the position of the opponent would be justified. Then the task of refuting the opponent or of inducing him to modify his position reduces to that of showing that the conditions under which his position would be justified do not *in fact* obtain. To the extent that these conditions are spelled out in concrete terms based on objectively verifiable facts, *both* participants can engage in a common enterprise. There is then an "authority" to appeal to that both may be willing to recognize.

Fisher and Ury's example illustrating the principle of appealing to objective criteria involves determining a "just" compensation for damage to a car in an accident. Discussing the situation with a claim adjuster of an insurance company, the owner of the car may call attention to the original cost of the car less depreciation (as conventionally estimated), what the car might have been sold for, what it would cost to replace the car, what a court might award as compensation for the damage, and so forth. All these are relatively objective criteria. Answers to questions regarding them can be obtained by consulting sources that were not originally designed to favor either the particular claimant or the particular insurance company.

Questions of "fairness" are often decided by procedures agreed upon *in advance*, when neither side knows in which position it may find itself. Recall Nash's solution to a two-person cooperative game. One of the criteria that the solution is supposed to satisfy is that of symmetry. The solution is supposed to be the same if the roles of the players are interchanged. In commenting on this criterion, we related it to the principle of "equality before the law." An impartial judge decides a case on its "merits," according to what the law says about the rights of the "plaintiff" and those of the "defendant," regardless of who these parties might be. Recall that objectivity refers to aspects of situations that appear the same to *independent* observers. Resorting to such criteria serves to reduce the salience of personal predilections, emotional involvement, and the like, which often block the way to conflict resolution.

Separating the People from the Problem

Closely related to the use of objective criteria is separating the people involved in the conflict from the issues. Fisher and Ury point out that the question of whether it is more advantageous to be a "hard" or a "soft" bargainer is not properly put. The argument usually invoked in favor of "hard" bargaining is that such a stance is more likely to force the other side to make concessions. The argument invoked in favor of "soft" bargaining is that such a stance is more likely to encourage the other side to cooperate. Actually, the partisans of "hard" and "soft" bargaining address themselves to two separate aspects of a conflict under negotiation. One aspect is that of getting a settlement that serves one's interests. The other aspect is that of preserving the relationship with the other side, if the relationship is valued. It seems that "being nice" to the other side serves to preserve a good relationship, while "being tough" might impair it.

Fisher and Ury point out that preserving good relationships depends on showing genuine and sincere respect for the persons one negotiates with. Their recommendation is to be "soft on people, hard on problems." Being "hard on a problem" does not mean sticking tenaciously to one's declared position. Rather it means insisting on exploring all different avenues that may suggest solutions. This can be done *jointly* with the other side. Being "soft on people" means being willing to find out more about why they feel as they do about the issues negotiated. One way of encouraging people to be frank about their feelings is to reveal one's own.

The principle governing "separating the people from the problem" is closely related to the rule of constructive debate that demands from each participant a statement of the other's case. To state the other's case to the satisfaction of the other often depends not only on the other's views of the issues involved but also on the other's feelings about them. Unfortunately, there is a strong prejudice in the world of bargaining and negotiations against bringing personal feelings to the surface and especially against revealing them to opponents. The approved stance of a negotiator is one of hardheadedness and toughness. These qualities do not necessarily imply inflexibility on substantive issues. Separating people from problems can be accomplished by arranging for informal contacts specially devoted to exploration of feelings about the issues off the record, as it were. Preservation of a relationship may depend essentially on the way these contacts are utilized rather than on the minimizing of conflict of interest when such a conflict actually exists. The key to productive negotiation is steering it so as to have both sides face the same *problems*.

Emphasis on the Non-Zero-Sum Nature of the "Game"

Note how Fisher and Ury's approach to negotiation differs from Schelling's (cf. Chapter 15). Schelling was one of the first "strategists" to recognize the non-zero-sum nature of the international "game." Every non-zero-sum game has two aspects: one involving the coincidence of interests of the players, the other the incompatibility of their interests. Turning once again to Nash's solution to the cooperative game, we see that this solution exhibits the two aspects. First, the solution must lie on the "Pareto-optimal set" of outcomes. There must be no outcome that *both* players prefer to the solution. Second, the solution (one of the outcomes on the Pareto-optimal set) must satisfy certain criteria. Now, by definition of the Pareto-optimal set, the interests of the players *on this set* are diametrically opposed. What is better for one must be worse for the other. Thus, after having agreed that the solution must be on the Pareto-optimal set, the players can forget about the non-zero-sum nature of the game and concentrate on the aspect which *is* zero-sum. There is, however, one feature of the *cooperative* game that must be taken into consideration, namely the opportunity the players have of communicating and therefore of bargaining, an opportunity that is useless in a zero-sum game, since in such a game there is nothing to bargain about.

It is precisely this opportunity to communicate that Schelling singles out for attention in his treatment of the non-zero-sum game. In his treatment, the most important opportunities provided by communication are those of making threats. In the formal setting of the game, these threats amount to making the opponent aware of the possibility that the threatener will, in the absence of concessions, resort to a strategy that will result in a non-Pareto-optimal outcome to the detriment of both. The possibility of communication created by shifting attention to non-zero-sum models of conflict opened up a wide range of problems dealing with bargaining strategies. It seemed as if the "art of war" was extended to an area where it could continue to flourish while the risk of the final holocaust could be avoided. As Schelling himself put it, he saw the making of a theory of a "rational non-use of force."

It is interesting to observe that the notion of the non-zero-sum game has finally hit the war game market. The Balance of Power game discussed in

Chapter 16 is an example. The objectives remain the same as in any competitive game such as Monopoly, Risk, and the many other global war games that have appeared throughout the Cold War era. The new twist in Balance of Power is that under certain conditions, when the parameters of the global situation exceed certain thresholds, a nuclear war occurs. In this case, "both sides lose." It is this feature that has been invoked by the inventor of the game (probably sincerely) as evidence that Balance of Power is a "peace game" rather than a "war game." Aside from avoiding the danger zones, the objectives pursued in Balance of Power are still geopolitical. The whole emphasis is on these. Victory for one side necessarily spells defeat for the other. Avoiding "nuclear war" means no more than being careful in the pursuit of one's own objectives.

The theory of productive negotiations, in contrast, emphasizes the cooperative aspects of the "game." It recommends an active *search* of ways to reformulate the game so that its perhaps unspecified cooperative aspects are revealed. While in strategic bargaining it seems advantageous to conceal one's true interests or even to misrepresent them, in constructive negotiation the opposite is the case. The contradiction is not as sharp as it appears because in strategic bargaining, positions rather than interests are central. The strategic negotiator will be well advised to keep secret the limits of his willingness to yield in modifying his position. The point made by Fisher and Ury is that emphasis on positions turns the attention of the negotiator away from his *own* interests, let alone from the interests of the other side. Above all, strategic negotiations do not encourage the conflicting parties to pursue an active search for solutions that may exist but which were not apparent because of the narrow concentration on positions.

Fisher and Ury dismiss the question of whether it is more advantageous to be a "hard" or a "soft" negotiator. Both stances are bad. If being a "hard" negotiator is rational for one side, it must be rational for the other. The result is an impasse. On the other hand, a "soft" stance may be an invitation to the other side to press hard for advantage and to get it without giving anything in return. The trouble with both the "hard" and the "soft" stances is that both refer to positions. It is preoccupation with positions as the bases of negotiation strategies that most often subverts the negotiating process. In productive negotiation, there is a use both for a "hard" and a "soft" stance but not with respect to positions. It is essential to be "soft" on people but "hard" on principles. Being soft on people reassures them of one's goodwill and creates an atmosphere in which mutual understanding is likely to be achieved. Being hard on principles focuses attention on rationality, fairness, and above all on mutual gains to be reaped from an agreement rather than on advantages to be won by one's own side.

Graduated Reciprocation in Tension Reduction

Negotiators in the international arena often serve only as mouthpieces of their governments and the negotiation process only as a platform for rhetoric. The negotiators frequently are not authorized to effect any agreement. In such situations, the eminently reasonable and potentially effective prescriptions embodied in Fisher and Ury's approach cannot be put to work.

Charles E. Osgood (1963) proposed an approach to conflict resolution that bypasses negotiations. Implementation of this approach presupposes a measure of goodwill on the part of each side and a realization that even with goodwill it may not be possible to resolve a conflict, because stands have been frozen in negotiations and it has become impossible to abandon or even to modify them without suffering serious losses. The greatest fear is that yielding may give the impression that one has lost one's nerve and so invite more pressure. The situation resembles a tug-of-war. As long as the forces are balanced, there is no movement in either direction. Once a movement begins, the momentum generated by it, however small, adds to the force of the moving side, which increases this momentum further, and so on, until the other side becomes helpless to stop it. Another fear that inhibits yielding anything in negotiations, no matter how little, is the fear of losing authority over one's own constituency, to which assurances of firmness and of the "rightness" of the position defended have been repeatedly and emphatically given.

A way of avoiding these obstacles is to make unilateral *non-negotiated* concessions. What makes such concessions possible is the circumstance that objectively they make no difference in one's situation. As an example, consider for simplicity the size of one's nuclear arsenal as an issue. The most common rationale for nuclear weapons refers to their presumed deterrent effect. "They've kept peace in Europe for forty years" is frequently heard as an argument stopper. What is usually not faced by the proponents of the deterrence argument is the question of why it is necessary to maintain an overkill factor of 40 or 50 to "deter" the other side from attacking. Is it not sufficient to have the capacity for completely destroying the adversary as an organized society to make an attack unattractive? And if the capacity for destroying the adversary once is not sufficient, is not the capacity for destroying him twice (for good measure) sufficient deterrence? If not, how about three, four, ten times? In short, if initially one can destroy the adversary 50 times over, and if one regards this potential to be a sufficient deterrent, it is difficult to deny that an overkill factor of 49 is equally impressive. But if so, what possible danger is there in reducing one's nuclear arsenal by 2 percent, i.e., from an overkill of 50 to one of 49? Putting the question this way reveals the above-mentioned obstacles to effective negotiation. If the declared objectives of negotiations had been a bilateral reduction of nuclear arsenals, the reasons for the failure of such negotiations may have been the unwillingness (actually, perhaps, the inability) of either side to make concessions, however trivial, even if such concessions were necessary to agree on the details of the procedures by which such reductions would take place. Abandoning negotiations bypasses this obstacle.

Suppose now one side unilaterally and unconditionally reduces its nuclear arsenal by 2 percent. Nothing is demanded in return. The step is undertaken with the view of signaling to the other side that one really wants to do something constructive in the way of reducing the nuclear arsenals from the present absurd and dangerous levels. Since this step was not undertaken in response to a demand, there is no loss of face. Moreover, no danger is associated with this step, assuming that the side that makes it is not hopelessly obsessed with the notion that one's safety is directly related to the number of tons of powder in the keg one is sitting on. The basic idea of *Graduated Reciprocation in Tension Reduction* (GRIT) is that the other side has found itself in a similar situation. It realizes that some concessions could be made without any danger in any reasonable sense of the word but that it has been unable to make them for the reasons stated above. If so, it is likely that the other side will be motivated to make some concessions in return, say, to reduce its arsenal by 2 percent.

If the other side does not respond, the 2 percent reduction can be restored, and nothing has been lost by the initial gesture of goodwill. On the contrary, the unreciprocated gesture could be used as leverage in propaganda picturing one's own side as accommodating and the other side as rigid.

If the other side responds, this can be used as an occasion to continue movement in the same direction. The whole procedure would then amount to a "reversal of the arms race" or a "disarmament race," if you will, where the prestige of one's own side depended not on its power to destroy the world but on its demonstrated willingness to remove such a threat.

An attempt to implement GRIT was once actually made. In June 1963, President Kennedy made a conciliatory speech, possibly intended to improve at least the tone of the relations between the United States and the Soviet Union. It was followed by a unilateral moratorium on testing nuclear weapons in the atmosphere. Besides being a signal to the Soviets that the U.S. might be willing to take further steps toward arms control, the moratorium was good public relations. Protests against testing nuclear weapons in the atmosphere had gathered impressive momentum. Emphasis on radioactive pollution of grass and with it of milk called attention to what the arms race was doing to children. Hundreds of thousands of baby teeth were donated by American children to a research group, which found them to contain strontium-90. These teeth were then put on public display. The moratorium on atmospheric testing could well have been a concession to a clear and intense public demand.

The Soviet Union responded immediately by stopping the production of a bomber plane. The U.S. continued with still another move, to which the Soviets again responded with an even larger one. However, the process was aborted when voices were raised in the American defense establishment pointing out that the "excessive" responses of the Soviet Union were making for a "loss of control" over the process, which could be "dangerous" (Etzioni 1967). In other words, attention was called to the danger of a runaway *disarmament* race. At any rate, further steps were discontinued in the fall of 1963.

Failure of the process to "take off" raises questions about the effectiveness of GRIT, not with respect to the opportunities it provides for reversing the arms race (from the short glimpse of it, it would appear to be quite effective in this respect) but with regard to the likelihood of it being accepted by the military establishments, particularly that of the United States. As we have seen, the prospect of "losing control" over the disarmament process was perceived by that establishment as a threat.

It is not easy to interpret this apprehension. It seems that the American military establishment was severely disturbed by the magnitudes of the Soviet concessions. If the security of the U.S. is perceived by the defense establishment as depending on its superiority in destructive potential over that of the Soviet Union, then why should a *decrease* of Soviet destructive potential be something to be concerned about? One possible answer is that failure to match Soviet reductions would put the U.S. on the spot as an adamant opponent of relaxation of tensions. Responding to the reductions might create a momentum for disarmament, which the American military establishment could not tolerate even if in the process of disarmament an edge in favor of the U.S. were preserved throughout. The conclusion is inescapable that the arms race is valued, at least by the U.S. military establishment, for its own sake, quite independently of what it is supposed to contribute to "national security."

In August 1985, the Soviet Union announced a unilateral moratorium on all tests of nuclear weapons. A total test ban treaty had been proposed repeatedly by the Soviet Union and was strongly supported even by Canada, America's staunchest ally. Resistance on the part of the U.S. under various pretexts blocked all attempts to make progress on this issue. Possibly the unilateral moratorium of the Soviet Union was an attempt to revive the GRIT idea. The U.S. failed to respond. Underground tests of nuclear weapons continued. A terse explanation was given to the effect that discontinuing the tests was not in the national interest of the U.S. Twice the Soviet Union extended its unilateral moratorium beyond the originally set limits. The U.S. made no positive response. At this time it appears that attempts to initiate GRIT have been aborted twice, both times by the U.S., in spite of the fact that the first attempt was initiated by the U.S.

Reconciliation

As we have seen, arms control negotiations are often paralyzed by rigid positions taken by the negotiators. These positions reflect certain conceptions concerning the requirements of "national security," usually conceived in terms of the magnitude of destructive power. The issues of arms control or disarmament negotiations are concrete, and in this respect they satisfy one of the principles of productive negotiation. They violate another cardinal principle, namely, they focus on positions instead of interests. But at least they are not likely to be bogged down in a deluge of ideological verbiage.

Very different sorts of issues characterize conflicts about political control. Here numbers, hardware, and the technical jargon that has grown up in the discourse on arms control play little or no role. Ideologically inspired rhetoric takes center stage. Obviously compromises, e.g., "splitting the difference," as in controversies over quantities, do not readily suggest themselves. To the extent that ideological issues are taken seriously by the negotiators and by their superiors, emotional factors may play an important role.

Such were the issues in the confrontations in which the Quakers have played an inconspicuous but important role.

In assessing the Quakers' role as conciliators, it is important to understand the problem generated by the Quakers' world view. This world view comes as close to that embodied in the teachings of Jesus as any of our time. At the same time, the Quakers realize that no amount of moralizing or of direct advocacy of brotherly love can have the slightest effect on persons engaged in conflicts generated by ideologies, political rivalries, or geopolitics. The conceptual repertoire relevant to the area of personal relationships on the one hand and to struggles for power on the other simply do not intersect. The Quakers, who are concerned with getting results in their conciliation efforts, not merely with preserving ideological purity, had to learn to think in the language of both worlds. From the accounts in *Quaker Experiences in International Conciliation* (Yarrow

1978), it appears that they have learned to do so and that whatever success they have had must be ascribed to this ability.

The Quakers' approach to conciliation is based on four types of activity: listening and asking questions, message carrying, understanding and assessment, and making proposals. Each requires proficiency in the conceptual language of the conflicting parties, but at the same time a detachment from it, since the dominant values of the world of power struggle do not intersect with those of internalized Christianity.

Listening performs a function in conciliation analogous to that in a constructive debate. In the case of conciliation, however, the listening is done not by the participants in the conflict but by the conciliators. This is unavoidable, since initially the participants *cannot* attentively listen to each other, each being completely preoccupied with the rightness of his own cause. The conciliator who listens attentively and who gives evidence of having heard and of trying to understand by asking questions provides some reassurance to a party to the conflict that his cause can be regarded *seriously* by someone who does not necessarily share the conviction that right is entirely on his side. This realization is indispensable if a dialogue is ever to take place.

Since direct contacts between the conflicting parties are either impossible or, if they take place, counterproductive, carrying messages is another important activity in the conciliation process.

The next phase—understanding—presupposes the ability to think in the conceptual language of the conflicting parties. This is difficult because this language includes concepts on which it is impossible to construct a basis for conciliation. These concepts generate ideological incompatibilities sharpened by verbal fixation of polarized values, adamance, hostility, and self-righteousness, categories that the Quaker must simply exclude from his own perception of the conflict. His problem is to find the *legitimate* concerns of both sides. Legitimacy here is a relative concept. It refers to where the participants of the conflict presently stand, not where they might be if their conflict were resolved.

Three case studies reported by C.H. Mike Yarrow (1978) involved negotiations between the two Germanies, between India and Pakistan, and between the opposing sides in the Nigerian Civil War. Two of these cases will be discussed here.

The Case of the Germanies

Divided Germany has been a most sensitive site of confrontation between the Soviet Union and the Western allies. Germany was regarded by both sides as the key to the domination of Europe. Reunification was a major geopolitical aim of both contenders, each attempting to bring it about on its own terms. The Western allies demanded "free elections" throughout the country. There was no doubt either in the Soviet Union or in the West that the form of government based on such elections would be of the Western type and would establish Germany as a bulwark against the Sovietization of Europe. The Soviets, for their part, were convinced that a Germany oriented toward the capitalist West would eventually become a threat to the Soviet Union, a partner in a military coalition against it, particularly because of the revanchist tendencies which the Soviet believed were being nurtured in the part of Germany dominated by the Western allies.

In addition to the conflict over the fate of Germany, the Soviets and the Western allies contended over the fate of Berlin. The erstwhile capital of Germany was divided into zones of occupation. Geographically, Berlin was inside East Germany. Soon the zones occupied by the Western allies were consolidated into West Berlin, while the Soviets kept control over East Berlin. As the conflict over Germany sharpened, the Soviets hoped that eventually West Berlin, an "island of capitalism" in the heart of Soviet-occupied Germany, would be abandoned by the Western allies as untenable and Berlin would become the capital of a socialist Germany. For the Western allies, however, West Berlin became a symbol of "liberty" and preserving its status became a gesture of defiance. The struggle over Berlin was perhaps the clearest example of the ideological component of the East-West conflict.

The attempt of the Soviets to isolate West Berlin by a blockade (1948–1949), prohibiting access by ground transport, was frustrated by an "airlift," a huge exercise in logistics, which proved effective in supplying the city for months. The city remained divided. In 1961, the division was made permanent by the erection of a wall through the middle of the city, a gruesome monument to the Cold War. The founding of two formally sovereign states, the Federal Republic of Germany in the West and the German Democratic Republic in the East, also portended a permanent political division of Germany. West Germany joined NATO; East Germany was incorporated into the Warsaw Pact.

The Quaker conciliation was able to single out the concerns of the two sides that could be viewed as "relatively legitimate," in the sense described. The West Germans found it intolerable that a part of Germany remained under foreign domination, which to them appeared despotic. The East Germans were intent on building a "socialist society," which they knew they could not do if Germany were unified by "free elections." In fact, it is doubtful whether free elections would legitimize any of the East European governments established with active Soviet support.

How legitimate, from the Quakers' own point of view, were the two causes? In view of the Quakers' insistence on putting themselves into the shoes of each side, the question does not seem to be very relevant. It does, however, bear on "relative legitimacy." The Quakers, being Christians and pacifists, could not share the values represented by the West German power elite, especially their enthusiastic buildup of military potential. Being deeply committed to the autonomy of the individual, they could not identify with the East German power elite, whose idea of "building socialism" was linked with total submersion of individual autonomy, and restrictions on free expression, free association, and so forth. Nevertheless, they could *assume* a sympathetic attitude toward the avowed goals of East Germans (represented as building an egalitarian society) and, what presumably came more easily, those aspects of a "free pluralistic society" that were defended in the West. Adopting this frame of mind enabled the Quakers to gain the respect, at times even the trust of the conflicting parties, a prerequisite to carrying out their mission.

The word that best describes the Quakers in their role as conciliators is integrity. This quality is by no means easy to achieve and to preserve in the activities undertaken. There is a strong temptation, for example, to say to each side what it wishes to hear. This might be an easy way of gaining the confidence of each side, a crucial achievement for the success of the conciliation. But a ploy of this sort would impair integrity, and ultimately the confidence gained would give way to suspicion, as it became clear that what the conciliators said did not represent their true convictions. The most important impression to be conveyed is that understanding of a participant's view is independent of agreeing with it.

Only when enough confidence in the integrity of the conciliators has been built up can making proposals be undertaken. This is the most sensitive phase of the conciliation process. Success can easily be jeopardized if a proposal appears threatening to one side or the other, for the confidence built up in the earlier stages of the process is fragile, easily shattered by the slightest suspicion that one is being manipulated.

As is known, conciliation between the two Germanies did take place. The East Germans got what they wanted—recognition as a sovereign state, which they deemed essential to the security of their program of building socialism. The West Germans did not achieve their originally stated goal of unification of Germany on their own terms. However, they did eventually rid themselves of the compulsions that precluded normalization of relations between Germans and Germans and remained a constant threat to peace. They could concentrate on developing West Germany as a major partner of the affluent West.

Even though the Quakers carefully avoided projecting their ideas on how the conflict between the two Germanies could be most effectively defused and eventually settled, they had considerable confidence in those ideas. It is here that political acumen, detailed knowledge of the issues as they appeared to the conflicting parties, and their own ethical orientation found a nexus. The Quakers were convinced that a *separation* of the two Germanies was a prerequisite to conciliation and that conciliation was a prerequisite to any further process of building a firm peace. For this reason, the Quakers did not share the Western view that the Berlin Wall was an unmitigated evil. It did, of course, appear so to the West Germans and kept arousing passions that stymied the conciliation process. Horrendous as the wall appeared as a crass violation of human rights, it was a necessary step in the separation—like physically separating two men fighting with fists and in danger of resorting to lethal weapons at any time.

The Civil War in Nigeria

The conflict in Nigeria generated problems much more complex than those generated by divided Germany. Nigeria was one of the many African states that emerged in the wake of the breakdown of the colonial empires. These states were in no sense "nations" as we understand the term, that is, regions whose populations have some feelings of communality, be it based on a common language, customs, mores, or shared historical memory. Rather, the colonies were administrative regions, whose populations consisted of many diverse tribes, clans, and ethnic and religious groups, often traditionally hostile toward each other. As the authority of the colonial governments dissolved, these enmities often erupted in violence.

At the time the Nigerian Federation gained its independence from Britain in October 1960, the country was divided into three regions quite different in language, customs, mores, and economic-political structures. The North was the most populous region, predominantly Moslem and feudal. The West was religiously heterogeneous and more urbanized than the other regions. The East was peopled predominantly by the Ibos, mostly Christians who lived in more or less autonomous villages. It was the situation of the Ibos that led to the severe civil war.

Political struggles reflected the diverse interests of the various groups. Rivalry, spurred by attempts to seize a dominant position in running the country, was intense. Initially, it appeared as if Nigeria, in some ways the most "advanced" of the African colonies, might evolve into a modern democracy. But in the scramble for private advantage, land grabs, and corruption, a disillusion with what "democracy" appeared to be set in. The stage was set for an army coup of the sort that pretends to save the country from chaos.

A coup duly occurred in July 1966. It was led by a group of young reform-minded army officers, mostly Ibos, who assassinated the Prime Minister, a prominent leader of the North and the Prime Minister of the Western region. The mutiny was put down by the army leaders, and a "strong man" was installed, an Ibo, who, however, was not involved in the coup. He proceeded to rule by stern measures, abolishing regional autonomy, intent on creating a strong unitary state.

Intense opposition developed in the North erupted in violence against the Ibos, many of whom had settled in that region. These people held key posts in both the bureaucracy and the economy of the country. It seems they were regarded by the others somewhat as the Jews were regarded in some European countries or the Chinese in some countries in Southeast Asia—as a shrewd, clannish, and pushy minority. The Ibo "strong man" was ousted in a countercoup. The lieutenant colonel who replaced him sought to restore the federal structure, but anti-Ibo violence got out of hand. Army soldiers joined in with civilians. Thousands were killed in the North. Some million-and-a-half fled to the southeastern "home" territory of the Ibos. The military governor of that region became the leader of a secessionist movement, and a civil war broke out.

The conflict in Nigeria, unlike the ideological-political conflict between the two Germanies, was kindled by passions generated by ethnic or religious strife. A conciliator in a situation of this sort faces problems rooted much more deeply in people's feelings and emotions: chronic hatreds, fears, grudges, resentments of humiliations, contempt for those perceived as inferior, and so on. This is the sort of situation where the empathetic approach of the Quakers can be most effective, simply because in their view, a conflict between human beings is primarily just that—a conflict between human beings, hence one in which the conciliator must see the participants as human beings, not as spokesmen for interests or positions. His job is to enable the participants to see each other in the same way. It is in precisely such situations, where human passions play a vital role in the genesis and dynamics of the conflict, that the Quakers can utilize their particular expertise to full advantage. They act as listeners and as facilitators of communication, helping the participants see each other as human beings.

The Nigerian civil war was further complicated by the plight of the Ibos, whose region, which they proclaimed as the independent Republic of Biafra, was blockaded by government forces. A famine resulted. The Quakers naturally felt obligated to organize relief for the starving Biafrans. This put the Quakers in a dilemma. The military outcome of the civil war was never in doubt. Biafra could not hope to gain independence by a military victory. The secessionists, however, continued to resist desperately, believing that defeat would lead to genocide. The obvious goal of the blockade was to starve Biafra into submission. Humanitarian aid to Biafra could well serve to prolong the war by enabling the secessionists to hold out. The Quakers had no choice but to do both: exert the utmost efforts to promote a negotiated peace, thus preventing a military victory by government troops and everything that such a victory might entail in the way of repressions; and at the same time do their utmost to relieve starvation in Biafra.

The goal of negotiated peace was not attained. However, in spite of the fact that the war ended in the military victory of the central government, the treatment of the vanquished was more magnanimous than anyone had dared to expect. There were no massive repressions and no executions. Many Ibos could return to positions in civil service and to normal partic------ipation in the life of the country. Yarrow (1978) attributes this compara------tively gratifying outcome in good measure to the Quakers' conciliation efforts. In view of the great respect for the Quakers expressed by both sides, the credit is probably well deserved.

Limits of Conflict Resolution

In discussing the biological roots of aggression, we pointed out the dis------tinction between aggression and predation. Among nonhumans, predation is almost exclusively interspecific. Cannibalism is exceedingly rare. If it occurs at all, it occurs sporadically, not as a way of life.[2] It is for this reason that we dismissed the idea that the roots of human aggression are traceable to the transformation of our prehuman ancestor into a predator.

Cannibalism among humans is also exceedingly rare, confined to sym------bolic or ceremonial consumption of human flesh. Europeans' accounts of cannibalism among the "savages" as regular meat-eating have been dis------credited. On the other hand, practices that could be interpreted as intra------specific predation have been common among humans. Some human groups turned to pillage as a way of life. Pillaging raids have often been accom------panied by slaughter of the plundered population. The genocidal warfare of the ancient Hebrews could be regarded as predation. It was rationalized as obedience to divine command. Recall, however, that the same deity who was believed to have "delivered" animals into man's hands to be preyed upon was also believed to have "delivered" the inhabitants of Canaan to the children of Israel, who appropriated their lands.

Is intraspecific predation a form of conflict? In distinguishing between predation and aggression, we pointed out that the usual feelings associated with human aggression (hatred, rage) may be completely absent in predation. If we accept the biblical accounts of the wars of conquest in Canaan, we can assume that feelings of intense hostility were aroused in the conquerors against their victims. There are, however, instances of humans preying upon humans where such feelings are not in evidence. For instance, some people living on rocky seacoasts have been known to extinguish the lighthouse lights with the view of plundering the ships that got wrecked as a consequence. The survivors, if any, who might testify against the plunderers were killed. It seems that this predation was seen by the people who engaged in it as no different from trapping and killing animals for food or fur.

Can we speak of "conflict" in situations of this sort? If so, does "conflict resolution" have any meaning in these contexts? We think not. The relation between a predator and his prey could, perhaps, be interpreted as a "conflict of interest." It is in the interest of the predator to catch and eat the prey and in the interest of the prey to escape from the predator. But this "conflict" is surely an instance of a zero-sum game, and therefore the concept of conflict *resolution* cannot apply to it.

Exploitation resembles predation in the sense that the exploiter uses the exploited for his own benefit. Whatever benefit he confers on the exploited is an incidental by-product. Pigs and chickens are fed well and cared for, but are nonetheless exploited. Indeed, domestication of meat-producing animals is a form of predation invented by humans.

Exploitation of humans by humans is marked by dehumanization of the exploited, as evidenced in the language of military and industrial organizations. The strength of infantry units was traditionally expressed by numbers of "rifles" (in Russia, "bayonets"), of cavalry units by numbers of "sabers," the size of a labor force by the number of "hands." This sort of dehumanization is different from that practiced by the Nazis. The killers in Nazi mass executions were often whipped into a frenzied state of intense hatred. In contrast, the dehumanization of soldiers and workers has been devoid of hatred. The "rifles," "bayonets," "sabers," and "hands" simply did not exist as human beings for the generals and entrepreneurs. They were only resources, entries in bookkeeping systems. In just this way, the populations that have become hostages in the current balance of terror have been dehumanized. Their numbers, below or above certain thresholds, represent "acceptable" or "unacceptable" casualties in the same way that numbers of soldiers expected to be killed or maimed in forthcoming battles were regarded in operations planned by staff officers.

We illustrated the gulf between the "warriors" and the "victims" by juxtaposing passages, one depicting key words like "target" as used by the warriors, the other describing what happens at the "target," seen as a place full of people instead of an object that is either hit or missed, something that serves as a token of a particular "value" (like a poker chip) in keeping score.

The question before us is whether the relation between the warriors and the victims can be reasonably regarded as a "conflict" and, if so, whether the conflict is accessible to resolution. An approach to "conflict resolution" between the warriors and the victims described by Freeman Dyson (1984) was to be a "dialogue" between them.

Dyson's argument is, in fact, a plea to distinguish between what A. Vagts (1937) called "militarism" and what he called "the military way." The warrior devoted to "the military way," as Vagts describes him, sees war as strictly a means to an end. The end can be a genuinely noble one, e.g., defense of one's country against aggression, invasion, enslavement, etc. Further, the warrior devoted to "the military way" regards the instruments of war strictly as tools to do the necessary job, that is, to defeat the enemy. He evaluates these tools strictly with respect to their efficiency in facilitating victory. Here humane considerations can also carry some weight, since there is nothing in "the military way" that can be interpreted as a manifestation of cruelty.

In contrast, the warrior devoted to "militarism," as Vagts describes him, sees war, or rather the institution of war, as something that benefits the military profession. In fact, at times he even forgets about war and what it is supposed to be waged for. He is more concerned with the privileges and prestige of the warrior caste. Indeed, the "militarist" has frequently blocked advances in the art of war when they threatened to make his particular expertise irrelevant or obsolete.

Such juxtaposition between "the military way" and "militarism" as in the work of Vagts and many others clearly amounts to a plea to save the military profession from degradation, to permit it to discharge honestly and efficiently the function assigned to it. In *Weapons and Hope*, Dyson pleads eloquently and passionately for the abolition of nuclear weapons. The horrendous effects of these weapons (well publicized by now) are the centerpiece in the support of Dyson's argument. But there is also another aspect to it. Abolition of nuclear weapons could be a step toward restoring to the military profession its dignity and its legitimate function. That these are subverted by nuclear weapons is beyond dispute. The military "virtues" are incompatible with indiscriminate slaughter of helpless populations. Aside from their omnicidal potential, however, nuclear weapons have no military value. The rationale of war, as it is depicted in "the military way" is, in the first instance, that of defending a country, its inhabitants, and its autonomy, perhaps even enhancing its prestige and grandeur—the rationale of war was not always confined to defense. Clearly, none of these ends can be served by a nuclear war, which, as Dyson emphatically points out, cannot possibly be "controlled" or "limited." This uselessness, as seen from the perspective of the "military way," by no means devalues nuclear weapons in the eyes of the "militarist," who sees in their development and in the exuberant growth of their support systems a source of prestige and power. Ironically, the disdain for technological advances that marked the militarist of the past (because they threatened to make his expertise obsolete or his cockiness look foolish) does not characterize the present-day militarist. He sees in these advances additional opportunities for growth and for exercising ingenuity and creativity. He has adjusted to the spirit of our age.

In setting the stage for a "dialogue" between the warriors and the victims, Dyson clearly sees the proponent of "the military way," not the "militarist" in the role of the warrior. He himself is in an excellent position to sketch the dialogue, because he sees himself in both roles. As a clear-thinking and feeling human being, he sees vividly the plight of the victims; as a consultant on military technical problems, he is immersed in the world of the warriors. He completely understands and has the deepest sympathy for the cause championed by Helen Caldicott, and at the same time he feels a need to explain and perhaps to justify positions taken by "responsible" warriors. He well realizes the difficulties.

> It is difficult to translate Helen's [Caldicott's] message effectively into the language of the generals, it is even more difficult to translate the legitimate concerns of the generals into a language which pays some respect to ordinary human values and feelings. The deliberately impersonal style of the warriors' world gives outsiders the impression that the warriors are even more inhuman than they actually are. There is prejudice and antipathy on both sides. The military establishment looks on the peace movement as a collection of ignorant people meddling in a business they do not understand, while the peace movement looks on the military establishment as a collection of misguided people protected by bureaucratic formality from all contact with human realities. Both these preoccupations create barriers to understanding. Both preoccupations are to some extent true. (Dyson 1984, p. 7.)

Two tasks face him. One is to make the victims and the warriors see each other as human beings rather than embodiments of wickedness or foolishness. The other is to show how the concerns of the warriors and of the victims can be cast into the framework of a constructive debate. He succeeds in both tasks. In the chapter entitled "Generals," the generals emerge as flesh and blood, "even as you and I." A whole chapter, one of the most perceptive in the book, is devoted to Robert Oppenheimer, a tragic figure, a brilliant scientist and a sensitive human being in the service of the war establishment. In the chapter entitled "Pacifists," Gandhi and

Tolstoy, Jean Jaures and George Lansbury take center stage. No one but a bigot could see these modern incarnations of biblical prophets as naive dupes.

No less impressive is Dyson's achievement in arguing both sides of each issue: "Star Wars," the ABM problem, fallout shelters, and the various nuclear strategies. He follows conscientiously the principle of stating the position of each side as strongly as he can, including the positions in defense of nuclear weapons, which he totally rejects. In stating the opposing position, he takes pains to define conditions, no matter how farfetched they seem, under which the position would be justified, thus avoiding giving the impression that the proponent of the position is crazy or depraved. For example, while rejecting the Mutual Assured Destruction strategy (cf. Chapter 13) as immoral and unworkable, Dyson nevertheless writes:

> The theory says that we need only to maintain a force of offensive nuclear weapons satisfying three conditions: the force must be powerful enough to destroy Soviet urban society, inaccurate enough not to threaten Soviet strategic weapons, and invulnerable enough to survive a Soviet attack. If these conditions are satisfied, then we have achieved a stable equilibrium. The situation is stable in two senses. We have crisis stability, meaning that even if we and the Soviet Union become involved in an intense crisis, neither side has any incentive to attempt a disarming first strike. We have arms stability, meaning that the forces required to carry out the assured destruction strategy have a limited size and need not grow constantly larger. (Dyson 1984, p. 240.)

Only after presenting the strongest possible case for the MAD posture (including the oft-repeated argument that it has "kept peace in Europe") does Dyson go on to demolish the position by showing that the conditions of stability do not in fact obtain.

Dyson has demonstrated convincingly that a constructive debate on issues of concern to warriors and victims is possible. Whether his reference to the "legitimate" concerns of the generals can be made meaningful is another matter. The question forces itself upon us: What are their *legitimate* concerns?

In light of Dyson's discussion, it turns out that the warrior's concerns are legitimate if they reflect the integrity of his profession. Dyson's juxtaposition of the concerns of two German generals reveals the meaning he assigns to "legitimacy." One of these generals is Alfred Jodl; the other is Hermann Balck. Jodl was convicted of war crimes in the Nuremberg Trials and hanged; Balck was acquitted.

Jodl was Hitler's chief of staff. He worked for six years planning and organizing the campaigns in which millions died. He was held responsible for these deaths. Balck was a field commander fighting in the front lines with his soldiers. He was accused of no war crimes. Thirty-four years later, at the age of eighty-five, he granted an interview in which he recalled his war experiences. He saw them as ingenious solutions to difficult tactical problems: surprising the enemy by turning up where he was not expected, using mules for transport when they were more efficient than motorized vehicles, and so on. In short, he was an enthusiastic and eminently competent practitioner of his trade. He was not called upon to be Hitler's partner in crime as Jodl was. In comparing Jodl and Balck, Dyson writes:

> Balck fought well because he enjoyed fighting well, and because he had a talent for it. As a professional soldier he took his job seriously but not solemnly. . . . Jodl doggedly sat at his desk, translating Hitler's dreams of conquest into daily balance sheets of men and equipment. Balck gaily jumped out of one tight squeeze into another, taking good care of his soldiers and never losing his sense of humor. . . . Jodl went on fighting to the bitter end because he had made Hitler's will his highest law. Balck went on fighting because it never occurred to him to do anything else. . . . Both Jodl and Balck were good men working for a bad cause. . . . Both of them continued to exercise their skills . . . when the only result of their efforts was to prolong Europe's agony. Both of them appeared to be indifferent to the sufferings of the villagers whose homes their tanks were smashing and burning. And yet the judgment of Nuremberg made a distinction between them. . . . Jodl was hanged, Balck was set free, and the majority of interested bystanders agreed that justice was done. . . . Rightly or wrongly, the public still approves the old tradition of military professionalism, giving honor and respect to soldiers who fight bravely in a bad cause. (Dyson 1984, pp. 154–155.)

The last sentence reveals the crux of the matter. The "legitimacy" of the warrior's concerns derives from the legitimacy of military professionalism, hence of the *institution* of war. A dialogue between the warriors and the victims can still promote "mutual understanding" and "mutual respect," can "separate people from issues," as recommended by Fisher and Ury. But no matter how this dialogue can serve to dilute the bitterness between the people involved or temper the contempt of the ones for the others, once the legitimacy of the war system is undermined, it cannot resolve the conflict between the *roles* of the warrior and the victim.

The legitimacy of the war system continues to be rooted in the right of self-defense extended from the individual to the state. The extension stops there. Only on that level does the rationale of maintaining a military establishment, hence of according legitimacy to the military profession, make sense. Each separate war machine can be legitimized by the existence of other war machines. Once, however, this framework of thought is transcended, the legitimacy of the *global* war machine comes into question. The only answer that can be given as to why it exists is "in order to prevent its being activated," which is absurd.

The right of self-defense can still be maintained. But if one refuses to "slice" humanity along the lines representing the separation of states or of blocs and insists on slicing it along the line representing the separation of warriors from victims (as Dyson did in the opening chapter of his book), then the victims can claim the right of self-defense against the warriors. Thereupon, the sincerity of the warriors, their devotion to their profession, their competence, and their integrity in upholding traditional military virtues may reveal them as good people, deserving respect and understanding. But the right of "self-defense" in the sense of defending the institution of war cannot be recognized any more than the right of the slaveowners can be recognized if slavery is to be abolished, any more than the "right to life" can be extended to a malignant growth.

The impossibility of reconciling the warriors and the victims (roles, not people) illustrates the limits of conflict resolution. It stands to reason that a conflict can be resolved only if the conflicting parties can find a common ground, recognize common interests or common values. This is usually the case when conflicts are generated by passion, resentment of wrongs, old encrusted enmities, and the like. It is possible that "people-oriented" techniques of conflict resolution can one day be applied to the conflict in Northern Ireland. These techniques have been successfully applied in family therapy and in conflicts on the community level; in short, in situations where the participants knew that they would have to continue to live together. The situation of the two Germanies was of this sort. Although it was primarily political, not personal, there was little chance of it erupting into an escalating power struggle.

Conflict resolution loses its relevance in situations where a power struggle becomes an end in itself. The conflict between the superpowers at times appears to be of this sort, to the extent that the arms race becomes its principal manifestation. In this context, "issues" are forgotten or are reduced to slogans to insure support of the populations. The struggle for supremacy is a zero-sum game, in which there is nothing to "settle." Only an illusory vision of victory and a numbing fear of defeat drive it forward. Even less relevant are the usual "understanding promoting" techniques, such as people-to-people contacts and the like. The trouble is not with people. It is not hatred or misunderstanding that feeds the arms race and keeps humanity on the brink of catastrophe. Dyson himself realizes this when he writes:

Germany was an extreme case of military professionalism run wild, and the judgment at Nuremberg was an exceptional nemesis. But every country which gives an exalted status to its military leaders runs a risk of catching the German madness. There, but for the grace of God, go we. (Dyson 1984, p. 155.)

There is, however, one weakness in Dyson's thesis. He does not seem to realize that military professionalism is *bound* to "run wild" when war has been deprived of all rational goals. For then the very "virtue" of the military profession (doing the job without bothering about ideologies or megalomanic dreams of crazy rulers) removes the question "Why war?" from the field of legitimacy. Only the question "How shall we fight it?" remains legitimate. The technological imperative dictates the answer. In a world where technolatry has become the professional soldier's religion, the distinction between soldiering as a trade (Balck's soldiering) and soldiering as a cult (Jodl's soldiering) vanishes.

The conviction that militarism cannot be tamed, only eradicated together with the institution that has constantly nurtured it, manifests itself in abolitionism—the refusal to come to terms with the war system.

Notes

1. The theory of the cooperative game provides a bridge between the game modality and the debate modality by introducing bargaining, which can be regarded as a primitive form of debate.
2. A notable exception is cannibalism among spiders, where the female devours the male immediately after being inseminated.

24

Problems of Peace Research

In industrially advanced societies, "rationality" is generally identified with the problem-solving mode of thinking. Awareness of a "problem" arises in consequence of a perceived discrepancy between an existing and a desired state of affairs. To pose the problem is to display such a discrepancy, for instance, between disease and health or between a broken-down machine and a properly functioning one.

Today there is a tendency to extend the problem-solving mode of thinking to dealing with the threat posed by the dramatic increase of potential for violence, especially for massive, highly organized violence called "war." The analogy between the failure of a social system (the disruption of orderly, peaceful interactions between individuals, groups, or states) and disease (breakdown of normal biological functions) seems compelling. Accordingly, activities subsumed under "peace research" or "peace education" have proliferated, especially in institutions of higher learning in the Western World.

Persistence of violence, especially war, is identified as an undesirable state of affairs; peaceful relations among individuals, groups, or states as a desirable one; the discrepancy as a problem. Solutions to this problem are often envisaged as the establishment of institutions for prevention or resolution of conflicts. A thorough study of conflicts with the view of designing a theoretically fruitful taxonomy, etiology, epidemiology, etc., appears to be a promising beginning in the search for solutions to problems associated with violence.

This sort of extension of the problem-solving mode to encompass the phenomenon of violence, especially of war, is beset with formidable difficulties. To see them, let us see what has contributed to the success of the approach in the areas of technology and medicine.

A machine is a system created entirely by people according to a preconceived scheme. The structure of such a system is entirely known in all its relevant details. Furthermore, the conditions under which the parts of the system interact in the prescribed manner are also completely known, since these situations are governed entirely by known physical laws: of mechanics, thermodynamics, electrodynamics, chemistry, and so forth. Diagnosis of the cause of malfunction or failure can, in principle, be absolutely correct. The problem-solving mode, namely, "treatment completely determined by diagnosis," e.g., replacement of a defective part, can be and usually is effective.

The situation with disease is considerably more complex. Although we routinely reproduce our bodies, we do not design them. The full structure of our bodies, not to speak of the interactions between their parts, are only superficially known. Progress in medicine has been essentially the accumulation of ever-more-reliable knowledge of the structure and functioning of living organisms. As the true causes of malfunctioning reveal themselves, prevention and cure of diseases become possible. It should be clear that the effectiveness of problem-solving in the realm of health, for all the progress made, does not approach the effectiveness of problem-solving in the field of technology.

We can, however, take solace in the following observation. If further progress in medicine depends on further accumulation of knowledge of conditions governing health and disease, we can be fairly sure that what is being discovered will "stay discovered." The laws governing the interactions of biological functions, although immensely more complex than those governing the interactions of machine parts, are still laws of nature. They are not likely to change just because we get to know more about them. For this reason, the taxonomy of diseases can be expected to retain its usefulness. It reflects an objective reality of sorts. The incidence of diseases may change radically, but we can suppose that present-day tuberculosis or cholera are the same diseases as those that ravaged populations in past centuries. In increasing our store of knowledge about our bodies and their afflictions, we can assume we are getting closer to "truth," to "what is." Hence the discrepancy between what is (the existing state of affairs) and what ought to be (the desired state of affairs) still makes sense.

Let us see whether the same considerations apply to the problem of violence, in particular to war.

If we see violence as a malfunctioning of a system, we must specify the system. But unlike an automobile or a vending machine or a foundry, the "system" whose malfunctioning is presumably manifested in violence cannot be obviously identified. People, who normally do not kill, kill each other in battle. Is this a result of something that has "gone wrong?" If so, with what? With people? If so, in what way? The units into which the people have been organized? Hardly. In fact, these units are often said to be functioning properly when they facilitate (rather than inhibit) killing. Have the governments of countries waging war "gone wrong?" Or is war, perhaps, a malfunctioning of a system, whose interacting parts are governments of countries? If so, how are these parts supposed to interact "normally?" It was once taken for granted that war is "normal" in the relationships between states. This view is less pervasive today. Still, conceptions of "normal" interactions among individuals, groups, and especially states are not nearly as clear as conceptions of normal functioning of living systems, and certainly not nearly as clear as conceptions of how a machine ought to function.

For this reason we face great difficulties when we try to set up some sort of a taxonomy of violence, in particular of wars. The difficulties multiply when we try to establish an etiology of violence. The roots of these difficulties are easy to see. The "systems" we have to deal with in our attempts to study violence systematically are neither constructed according to blueprints like machines, nor sharply defined by nature like most living organisms. The way we classify violence-prone systems depends on what we single out for attention. Different people who have thought of this problem have singled out different things. In our present state of knowledge, there are no compelling reasons for preferring one way of thinking to another.

Investigations of Causes of Wars

How a classification of instances of violence can depend crucially on what the classifier is interested in can be seen in Lewis F. Richardson's treatment of wars as instances of "deadly quarrels" (cf. Chapter 18). The result of this classification was the discovery that the distribution of "deadly quarrels" by magnitude resembled a well-known statistical distribution. Richardson conjectured that this distribution characterized sizes of groups "organized for violence" (Richardson 1960a). The finding that the distribution of sizes of war alliances, in contrast to the distribution of sizes of casually formed groups, seemed also to be of the same kind (Horvath and Foster 1963) lent some credence to this seemingly farfetched conjecture. Analysis of the stochastic process underlying the distribution suggested that it was due to the particular dynamics of the formation and dissolution of groups (Rapoport 1983, p. 180.) Just how these findings can be used to generate hypotheses about the causes of wars (let alone suggest how wars could be attenuated or avoided) is anything but clear.

There are troubling questions about the value of peace research centered on a search for the causes of wars. Consider once again the essential condition that has contributed to the impressive successes of medical research devoted to the investigation of the causes of diseases with the view of finding means of attenuating or preventing them. When some specific agent is discovered and is shown to be of value in preventing or curing a disease, very shortly its use becomes widespread. Some serious diseases have been almost eradicated (smallpox, polio) or greatly attenuated (tuberculosis, diphtheria) in just this way. What made this possible is an elaborate infrastructure of institutions, empowered to put the discovered agents to work. Hospitals are on the alert for just such developments in medical research. Public health institutions use the information provided by medical research to take preventive measures checking epidemics, and so on. The whole medical profession serves as a transmitter of scientific knowledge discovered in laboratories to institutions that can and do utilize this knowledge. Nothing resembling this infrastructure exists to use whatever is discovered about the "causes of wars" in preventing or aborting them.

Peace researchers concerned with causes of wars have been in a certain respect breaking through an open door. To see this, consider the difference between necessary and sufficient causes. We say A is a *sufficient* cause of B if whenever A occurs, B is sure to occur. On the other hand, A is a *necessary* cause of B if B cannot occur unless A occurs. A given cause of some event can be either necessary without being sufficient, or sufficient without being necessary, or both necessary and sufficient, or neither necessary nor sufficient.

If we search for a cause of an event with the view of producing the event, we need to find a *sufficient* cause of it. Then, if we can bring this sufficient cause about, we are sure to produce the event. If we are interested in preventing an event, all we need to know is a *necessary* cause of it, one which we can prevent from occurring. If we prevent this necessary cause from occurring, we thereby prevent the event in question from occurring. It follows that if our goal is to bring wars about, we should try to find sufficient causes of wars. On the other hand, if our goal is to prevent wars, we should be most interested in necessary causes of wars. For if we can somehow prevent these causes from occurring, we shall be able to prevent wars.

In this respect, the analogy between peace research and medical research holds. The goal of medical research is surely to prevent (or cure) diseases, not to cause them. From the practical point of view, only necessary causes of diseases, therefore, need be known. The fact that the medical researcher may be interested in sufficient causes of diseases reflects his or her scientific curiosity, which may be a valuable asset in the process of advancing science, but this knowledge is not necessary if the goal pursued is only the prevention or attenuation of a specific disease.

With regard to war, we can say with confidence that although *sufficient* causes of war are not known and have, in fact, undergone radical changes throughout history, a *necessary* cause is known with certainty: weapons. Without weapons there could be no war, at any rate no war that could threaten all humanity. In a sense, therefore, the search for "causes of war" need not go on. If what we are after is a necessary cause, we already know what it is.

But knowing the *necessary* causes of wars helps us not a whit in preventing or attenuating wars. This is so for a very concrete reason: there is no known way to put that knowledge to use. We are therefore back to the problem of the infrastructure. We know that by ridding the world of weapons, we could rid it of wars (the kind that count). But there are no institutions empowered to do just that. On the contrary, powerful institutions exist whose business it is constantly to increase the world arsenal and to make weapons progressively more destructive.

If this diagnosis is accepted, the prime task of peace research is clearly indicated: to reveal what stands in the way of global disarmament. It is not enough to come up with facile answers like fundamental aggressiveness of human nature or hostility and distrust among nations or vested interests. The point is that attempts to bring about some measure of disarmament have been made since the years immediately following World War I. Somehow or other these attempts have always come to naught. It is possible to trace chains of events that have blocked the implementation of all previous disarmament plans. However, chains of events are only strands of *networks* of events. The events do not generally have single causes and single effects. Cyclic or reciprocal interactions are the rule rather than the exception. To understand what is going on in any environment where human behavior, institutions, or patterns of culture are involved, we must investigate "everything." Can peace research be systematized and organized in a way that suggests a reasonable program and in a way that can be expected to produce knowledge relevant to the problems posed? How can the incidence and severity of wars be attenuated? How can wars be prevented? How can the institution of war be abolished? The nagging question "By whom?" must always be faced.

Building an Infrastructure

Again we turn to the history of medicine, because in spite of the very different problems associated with the struggle against disease and the efforts to promote peace, this history can teach us something of the way knowledge becomes transformed into ways of solving problems.

It can be reasonably pointed out that discoveries apparently unrelated to the problems of health and disease have contributed more toward solving many of the problems than direct quests for solutions. To take an obvious example, some of the most rapid and far-reaching advances in medicine can be attributed directly to the invention of the microscope, an instrument in no way related to the practice of medicine at the time of its appearance.

What the microscope did was reveal to human beings a world of which they had been totally unaware. Many answers to questions about the causes of disease were found in the course of studying that world. However, answers occur only when questions are asked. The world of microorganisms would not have provided important answers about the etiology of diseases caused by pathogenic organisms had not an infrastructure already existed receptive to questions about the etiology of diseases. This infrastructure was the medical profession and its adjuncts: hospitals, systems of urban sanitation, and the like.

This infrastructure existed and was supported for reasons other than that of contributing effectively to the preservation of health. Before the advance of scientific medicine, the medical profession probably killed more people than it cured. Semmelweiss's one-man campaign for sterilizing instruments used in assisting childbirth was spurred by his anguish about women who died of childbed fever. An epidemic of this killer of women giving birth was spread by physicians attending them. Superstition was rampant in medicine. Bleeding was standard medical practice in eighteenth-century Europe. Aside from some crude surgical procedures, first aid, and some commonsense advice, the medical profession had practically nothing concrete to offer in the way of arming humans against the ravages of diseases.

And yet, without this medical profession and its adjuncts, the discoveries that ushered in scientific medicine would have amounted to nothing. The medical profession was part of an infrastructure, a sector of society *concerned* with health and disease. It is through this infrastructure that scientific knowledge about health and disease spread. With the discovery of the role of pathogenic microorganisms, crude and frequently lethal surgical procedures could turn into lifesaving interventions. Knowledge about the direct connection between drinking water and typhoid fever could be put to use because crude sanitation facilities already existed in cities.

The role of the infrastructure as the recipient of new knowledge and an agency for transforming it into new practices can be clearly seen in many different contexts. The application of knowledge produced by physical science to industrial technology became possible only when an infrastructure in the form of the factory system of production was already in existence. And this institutional infrastructure, in turn, depended on the existence of another infrastructure, namely, the urban way of life—people living close together and therefore amenable to being recruited into the factory system. The ultrasophisticated technology of recent decades ("high tech") could not be mobilized in the service of war if an infrastructure—the defense community—were not already in existence. Moreover, this infrastructure had to be already imbued with certain attitudes, such as open-mindedness and enthusiasm for technical innovations, attitudes that did not characterize the military establishments of former days.

Prospects of preventing wars or ultimately abolishing the institution of war depend on the existence of an infrastructure analogous to those based on public concern with problems of health, disease, and "defense." Some features of such an infrastructure are already discernible in the widespread "peace movements," peace research institutes, peace education programs, etc. It is these that can play the role of producing, receiving, disseminating, and utilizing knowledge relevant to the promotion of peace.

A vital distinction between such an infrastructure and those underlying applications of technology or medical knowledge must be recognized. The infrastructure of war is most receptive to knowledge that points to "technical fixes." This has not always been the case. Technology became the focus of "military science" only when the industrial revolution was already in full swing. But the two world wars brought technology to the forefront of attention. In fact, the dream of the "ultimate weapon" has now become reality. Ironically, this technological fix may spell the end of war as an institution (along with the end of everything else). But the profound respect of the modern warrior, bordering on awe, for sophisticated technology persists. It has overshadowed the respect rendered to the traditional military virtues and to strategic virtuosity.

The infrastructure of health care is also receptive to technological fixes, although in recent decades this receptivity has been somewhat tempered by the increasing prominence of the undesirable by-products of many procedures and drugs. Doubts have arisen about the effectiveness of medical practices that concentrate entirely on diseases rather than on patients. "Holistic" medicine, with its emphasis on the importance of a personal relationship between physician and patient, has been receiving more attention. Factors directly related to prolongation or curtailment of life have been revealed that have little or nothing to do with medical technology. It has been found, for example, that old people live longer if they have pets. An affectionate relationship contributes to the "will to live" and to positive psychosomatic effects.

The infrastructure of peace activism, peace research, and peace education is probably not receptive to technological fixes. A quick fix would be the elimination of weapons, but elimination of these obvious "causes" of war is precluded by the absence of appropriate institutions. Given the difficulty of taking their toys away from warmakers, the most promising path toward the elimination of war seems to be the elimination of the will to make war. This goal can be pursued only by strengthening the infrastructure of peace. Providing a haven for research workers, attracting them to the peace infrastructure might help create a potential counterforce to the infrastructure of war.

The defense community understands the importance of an infrastructure. Not all of military research is directed toward finding technological fixes. As an example, consider the research on the theory of games, generously supported by the American military establishment. Can findings in the theory of games be applied to solving military problems? Yes and no.

Recall our discussion of differential games where the application potential of this theory was examined. Other examples come to mind. In a "game" between a bomber and a submarine, the problem is that of finding optimal searching strategies for the former and optimal hiding strategies for the latter. Methods of finding such optimal strategies have been developed in the theory of games. For the most part, however, game theory produces merely textbook examples of tactical problems analogous to the "word problems" used in the teaching of elementary algebra: people digging wells and racing on bicycles. It is argued that the value of these problems is that of teaching students to think mathematically. Similarly, it could be argued that the textbook examples of tactical problems developed in the theory of games serve to make officers think rigorously about actual tactical problems.

The military establishment has had and continues to have a more important reason for supporting research in the theory of games. Facilities for doing research *attract* mathematicians. This builds up an infrastructure of scientific talent that can serve the defense community. Not only the theory of games but many other branches of mathematical science and of "pure science" generally can be used as bait. If a scientist has misgivings about doing war research, these can be allayed by supporting his or her research that has no apparent connections to weaponry. This support is not a mere stratagem aimed at getting research done that has no *apparent* connection to making war but that can nevertheless be expected eventually to contribute to it. There may *really* be no connection between the research supported by the military and results relevant to its needs. What happens, however, is that the scientist is recruited into the war infrastructure. He may never be engaged in actual war research, but he will be available for consultation on problems related to his specialty.

It is very difficult for a person possessing some special competence to resist requests for help and advice that can be given on the basis of this competence. Professional pride based on extensive practical, theoretical, and hypothetical knowledge is one of the strongest motivations in our civilization. Knowledge is a wonderful commodity. It can be generously given without diminishing the store in one's possession. It can be given in exchange for compensation, thus satisfying appetites, or it can be given freely, thus satisfying vanity or more noble inclinations, those of sharing what can be shared without loss.

Technological Fixes

The pejorative connotation of the phrase "technological fix" stems from its association with a preoccupation with some narrow aspect of a problem while broader, more important implications are left out of consideration. Since problems that can be solved most directly and effectively are generally technological ones, it is technological solutions that present themselves most readily. Urban transportation problems are a conspicuous example. Vast networks of roads designed for fast-moving automobiles have made it possible to go quickly from place to place. But the very convenience of the automobile turned cities, especially in America, into wastelands. The inner cores were made unfit for habitation. The cultural function of the city as a community was undermined. The air was polluted. Public transportation systems deteriorated, intensifying the need for automobiles, which aggravated the problems further.

Technological fixes as pseudo-solutions to problems are nowhere as conspicuous as in arms races. The responses to an adversary's technological advances in weaponry are advances in one's own weaponry. Even one's own advances force the proliferation of technological fixes, because they pose new technological problems. Fixation on these problems sidetracks from consciousness really important questions, such as *why* the adversaries should plan each other's destruction in the first place.

Fixation on technological problems reflects a more general predilection of people to see sources of difficulties outside themselves. When a problem arises, it is easiest to assume that something has gone wrong "out there" in the external world. This suggests that one could solve the problem if one knew what to manipulate in what way. Francis Bacon's famous dictum "Knowledge is power" reflects this activist orientation. The whole scientific enterprise has been propelled primarily by this conception of knowledge. There is, however, another conception of knowledge, not as a way to power but as a way to wisdom. This conception is reflected in the thinking of philosophers, religious leaders, humanists, and, to a certain extent, by social scientists, those who single out *"das Verstehen"* ("understanding"), rather than prediction and control, as the proper product of social science. Often knowledge as a way to wisdom is identified with self-knowledge.

The Search for Self-Knowledge

The search for self-knowledge as a source of wisdom has not been crowned with the brilliant successes that have marked the triumphal development of science as a source of knowledge about the external world. It is commonplace to say that the reason for this discrepancy is that the accumulation of systematized reliable knowledge about the external world has been made possible by the discovery of reliable natural laws, which have no analogues in the realm of human affairs. But this is only a part of the story. The other important factor in facilitating the exuberant growth of the natural sciences has been the willingness of potentates (later of societies) to support it because its results fed the appetite for power. From the very birth of modern science to almost the present, limitless increase of power over nature has been regarded by most peole as an undisputed desideratum. The same could not be said of the thirst for self-knowledge.

  Self-knowledge does not confer power in the accepted sense, that is, power over the external world, least of all power over others. Its potential is essentially therapeutic. This is well recognized in psychoanalysis. Leaving aside the question of how concretely effective the techniques of psychoanalysis have been as a method of psychotherapy, the identification of mental health with self-knowledge reflects an ancient insight. It has been suggested that Marx's analysis of society and his theory of history could be regarded as an attempt to facilitate the creation of a humane society by a class (the industrial proletariat) that had attained an insight into the source of its plight (class consciousness). Leaving aside the question of how effective the inculcation of this insight has been in the context of social processes that have marked the recent history of the industrialized world, the projection of the basic idea of insight through self-knowledge to the level of a social class has been a step in the right direction. It remains to take the next step. The fundamental goal of peace research ought likewise to be therapeutic, directed toward imparting self-knowledge on the level of humanity.

Changing Our Way of Thinking

Many people accept the idea expressed in the preamble to the United Nations Charter that "wars begin in the minds of men." The corollary that points to the necessity of changing our ways of thinking also elicits agreement. Nevertheless, most people's notions about what is wrong with the minds of men that makes them a fertile soil for wars or how our ways of thinking should be changed in order not to let the seeds of war sprout are rather limited. For the most part, the psychological roots of war are associated with ideas about aggressiveness as an integral part of "human nature," and "changing our ways of thinking" with modifying our natures—for example, making us more peaceful. This is the simplistic view of the psychological underpinnings of war. Much of the content of this book has been devoted to attempts to demonstrate that "aggressiveness" is at most just one facet of the human psyche that contributes to the ubiquitousness and severity of conflicts and is, perhaps, not even the most important one.

So if getting rid of aggressive impulses or becoming more peaceful is not what is meant by "changing our ways of thinking," what is? The answer to this question should be the content of peace education. Knowledge required to answer this question meaningfully should be the main product of peace research.

How do we go about "changing our ways of thinking"? To answer this question, we might look to the past. We can examine ways in which people's thinking has changed throughout history. One thing we can be sure of: Changing ways of thinking is quite different from changing one's shirt. In changing my shirt, I take off the one I am wearing and put on another. The other is already there to put on. I can't change my thinking in this way. It is not a matter of discarding one "way" of thinking and adopting another which is already there, like a clean shirt. People change their ways of thinking by thinking. If they think hard enough, their way of thinking will change of its own accord. Thinking produces changes in thinking.

People's ways of thinking about war and peace and matters related to them are bound to change if they think hard enough and systematically enough about war and peace, especially if their thinking leads them to some form of action. Peace research is, in the first place, a way of thinking intensely and in a systematic and disciplined manner. In this way, it is like any scientific research, if by "scientific" we mean adhering to certain standards of observations, conceptualization, inference, evaluation of data, and the like. Formulation and solution of *problems*, a practice that characterizes applied scientific research, is only a phase of scientific research. There may or may not be occasions for applications of this sort, depending on the social environment in which the research is done. The effect on our ways of thinking does not depend on such opportunities. It is generated by thinking scientifically in itself.

Thinking Stimulated by Mathematical Models

By way of example, consider the research of Richardson on arms races (cf. Chapter 18). A drastically simplified differential equation model fitted the data from a few years of the pre-World War I arms race. Attempts to fit the same model to other arms races met with indifferent success. But this very lack of success stimulated thinking about the sort of systemic parameters that may be of importance in affecting the trajectories of variables associated with arms races. Whether or not such parameters are found, these exercises stimulate thinking about arms races as systemic phenomena, processes driven by their own built-in dynamics. And this way of thinking already differs radically from the way of thinking that pictures an arms race as a sequence of events, each reflecting an attempt to enhance "national security." This change in the way of thinking is engendered by "immersion" into a certain type of research activity.

The differential equation models of arms races are not good models in the sense in which "good models" of phenomena are usually understood in the natural sciences. And even if they were "good" in the sense of generating accurate trajectories, one is at a loss to see how this knowledge might help prevent wars. We have already discussed the formidable institutional obstacles in the way of applying scientific knowledge to the prevention of war. But models stimulate searching questions. At one point in the course of his research, Richardson posed the question of whether an arms race could end without fighting, a question of overwhelming importance today. To answer this question, he designed another type of model of an arms race in which the decisive predominance of one side over the other caused the other to "submit." In the context of the model, this meant to disarm. Whatever answer is deduced from the implications of this model, whether "yes," "no," or "yes under certain conditions," attention is drawn to considerations that otherwise might have remained outside the sphere of attention. P. Smoker (1964) put Richardson's "submissiveness model" to a test using Soviet and American data from the period 1948–1960.

Finally, the advent of computer technology has vastly expanded opportunities for research on systemic models of arms races. The computing laboratory serves as a surrogate for an experimental laboratory. A laboratory in which experiments on actual global processes could be performed does not exist. One shudders to think what might happen if it did. The computer provides opportunities for experimenting on the world in perfect safety. In a very real way, it is an extension of human thought processes which enables humans to engage in "trial and error" in the mind instead of in reality, thus avoiding the possibly disastrous consequences of error.

In global modeling, some aspect of the world is represented as a system in the mathematical sense of postulated interactions between variables defining the state of the system. These interactions are built into the program. The system is put in some initial state and the model is allowed to "run." The trajectories of the system are examined. Experimentation consists of starting from different initial states or changing the parameters of the dynamics or changing the laws of interaction.

One can experiment with "arms races" in this way. The computer laboratory removes the severe limitations on the complexity of the mathematical models that can be investigated "by hand." Recall that Richardson's original model of an arms race was about the simplest conceivable system of differential equations: a pair of linear equations with constant coefficients.[1] Subsequent elaborations did not venture very far. The attempts were rather like those of navigators before the invention of the compass. The linear system of differential equations was the "visible shore." High-speed computers have changed all that. Not only can the number of variables be immensely increased, but also non-linear systems can be investigated. These are not usually amenable to formal analytic treatment.

Members of the Systems Dynamics Group at the Massachusetts Institute of Technology, where global modeling is done, turned their attention to the arms race (Forrester 1984, 1985; Kreutzer 1985). Among the interesting models examined were those in which the adversaries' misperceptions about the levels of each other's arsenals were incorporated. It was shown that under certain conditions, even if the goal of each side was "parity" (not superiority), the arms race might escalate. *Even if the goal of each side were a "build-down,"* the arms race might still escalate (Kreutzer 1985). One can see how this could happen if each side's estimate of the other's destructive potential (instead of knowledge of actual potentials) drove the arms race. Simulations present a clearer picture of *how* this could happen and delineate the conditions under which it would happen.

Simulation has made it possible to extend the investigation of mathematical models of arms races far beyond the limits set on the applicability of analytical methods. In particular, it has become possible to test a great variety of complex models by comparing the trajectories generated by the simulations with observed trajectories. The nuclear arms race between the U.S. and the U.S.S.R., being the longest lasting arms race in recorded history and also producing the richest and most accurate data base, has served as the process examined. An interesting finding was obtained by

M.D. Ward (1984); namely, that although the Richardsonian model of mutual stimulation was not corroborated when the trajectories were defined in terms of military budgets, it *was* well corroborated when the trajectories were defined in terms of military stockpiles. (Recall that Richardson, too, had to replace budgets by another measure when countries went off the gold standard.) The irrelevance of the budgets as the driving force of the nuclear arms race could be expected on commonsense grounds. First, rapid qualitative development of weapons can radically change the cost per amount of destruction. Second, the cost-maximizing practices of the war economy play havoc with the budgets. As Ward (1985, p. 215) points out, " . . . it seems clear that a $1000 Allen wrench will probably work no better than one costing $2." Results of simulation have also suggested that internal political and economic conditions are important input into the dynamics of military budgets, at least in the United States (cf. Cussack and Ward 1981). In this way, by shifting attention away from budgets and focusing it on military stockpiles, simulation has led to a vindication of the Richardsonian mutual stimulation models when the variables are properly chosen.

Simulation also provides ways of examining the dynamics of non-linear systems not amenable to analytic treatment. In these, thresholds often play a vital role. In some contexts thresholds embody the most serious dangers associated with these processes because, from the observed behavior of a system near a threshold, it is often impossible to infer that the system is approaching a critical state. A critical state when reached can completely change the behavior of the system in an irreversible manner. All of these matters can be vividly brought to attention by simulation. Trajectories can be actually seen. The possible futures unroll before one's eyes.

Whether these exercises induce fundamental changes in ways of thinking remains an unanswered question. For example, arms race simulation may warn of impending dangers of an escalating process. In describing the model that underlies the simulation, investigators by force of habit still identify levels of arsenals with "national security." This conceptualization remains as the barrier blocking the fundamental change in our way of thinking that could prevent the drift to catastrophe. If the simulations show that this sort of concern with "security" produces explosive arms races despite apparently reasonable attempts to control the process, questions can be raised about the fundamental assumption. However, the most valuable feature of the approach is in the way it brings to attention the systemic aspects of the process. This framework of thought facilitates the conception of a single global war machine threatening all of humanity and so undermines the legitimacy of what is sold to populations under the respectable and reassuring label of "defense."

The systemic approach to a theory of war and attendant processes has already induced extensive changes in ways of thinking about war. How big an impact these changes can make depends, of course, on how widespread they become and this depends, in turn, on how widespread and accepted are activities subsumed under "peace research."

Thinking Induced by Game-Theoretic Analysis

Let us turn to the changes in ways of thinking that can be expected from the strategic approach to the study of conflict. We have seen how an analysis of the strategic structure of formal games reveals a wide range of contexts in which the concept of "rationality" is no longer unambiguous. Recurrent paradoxes force a conceptual bifurcation of the concept into individual and collective rationality. The paradoxes are resolved only if one views certain decision problems from the point of view of collective rationality. Prisoner's Dilemma and Tragedy of the Commons are examples of such problems. The pressure to model decision problems from the point of view of a single decision maker (self or client) is very strong. We have seen how the conceptual leverage provided by the non-zero-sum game failed to produce a shift of focus from the individually rational to the collectively rational paradigm. Only the opportunity to communicate and bargain entered the conceptual repertoire of strategic thinking. With this a new mode of strategic analysis was hailed: the "rational non-use of force."

Recall the Balance of Power game described by its inventor as a "peace game." The claim is based on the fact that the objective of the game is to conquer the world while avoiding a nuclear war, which is a loss for both sides. The "non-zero-sum" feature is introduced into this game in the same way as the "non-zero-sum" aspect of the struggle for power in the international arena was introduced by T.C. Schelling (1960). The *modality* of thinking in terms of a struggle for power was retained in both cases. Only a new constraint was introduced. Namely, the struggle for power must be conducted "safely," i.e., while avoiding precipitating the final catastrophe.[2]

In contrast, Fisher and Ury (1981) specifically attack the struggle for power paradigm as a barrier to conflict resolution through negotiation. Only when the negotiators of both sides begin to see the problem as "our problem" instead of "my problem" can such negotiation become productive.

Herein lies the educational value of the theory of games carried beyond the two-person zero-sum game paradigm. This paradigm has a powerful grip on people's thinking about "games." It is easy enough to see the relevance of game models in a world where competition dominates the direction of effort. The word "game" has even entered the vocabulary of the business community. One is in the "real estate game" or in the "insurance game" or whatever.

Frequent references to the theory of games in peace research literature have aroused public interest. "What can game theory contribute to the cause of peace?" is a question frequently addressed to peace researchers who mention the theory. The answer to this question should be the following: the paradoxes arising in the analysis of decision situations involving more than one decision maker with interests that are partly in conflict and partly coincident can be resolved only if the concept of collective rationality enters the analysis *essentially*, not merely tangentially in the form of lip service paid to areas of common interest. Once collective rationality advances to the forefront of attention, struggle for power and maneuvering for advantage, lose their salience. This stimulates essential changes in ways of thinking.

Relevance of "Hard" Sciences to Peace Research

The emphasis on technology as the decisive factor in war has been increasing since World War II. It became overwhelming when the defense community turned its attention to space as the theater of future wars. As the technical problems associated with the design of sophisticated and vastly complex weapons systems proliferated, the flow of scientific personnel into weapons research and related fields accelerated. The generosity of governments, especially of the superpowers, in supporting this research has been a major factor in this movement. As this is written (1986), over 70% of research funds provided by the U.S. government goes into war work, and over 40% of American scientists are engaged *directly* in it.

Militarization of science has caused much concern among scientists whose horizons extend beyond opportunities of getting lucrative contracts and who have come to question the concept of "security" based on burgeoning destructive potential. Appeals to governments to stop the arms race on grounds of its potential dangers have so far fallen on deaf ears. However, an opportunity arose to challenge some of the most extravagant warfighting schemes of the American government, in particular, the so-called Strategic Defense Initiative ("Star Wars"). This is a program aimed at the massive militarization of space. The challenge was made in terms that the scientists recruited into the program could understand. If their scientific integrity weighed more than the seductive power of contracts and proximity to the seats of power, some were induced to have second thoughts about participation. A lively discussion developed around "Star Wars" of the sort that scientists working for the defense establishment could not ignore, because their scientific competence was challenged. Here, then, was an opportunity for "non-controversial" peace research, for "hardheaded" investigations of technical feasibility of the proposed weapons systems in space without any reference to matters held to be outside the competence of science, such as political considerations or humanitarian concerns.

The opportunity to challenge the designers of weapons on their own ground, however, is not without pitfalls. Recall the "laws of civilized warfare," which statesmen with genuine humanitarian concerns attempted to establish in the late nineteenth and early twentieth centuries. Outlawing "inhumane" weapons props up the "legitimacy" of war. The relation of the attempts to "humanize" war to the present debate on the feasibility of "Star Wars" is that both obscure the real issue. Prohibition of the dumdum bullet involves a tacit acceptance of the regular bullet; prohibition of a jagged bayonet involves a tacit acceptance of smooth bayonets. Similarly, arguing against "Star Wars" on the grounds that the required technology is not feasible carries an implication (even if unintended) that if the technology *were* feasible, the project would have merit. From the point of view of those who have nothing to gain from the arms race and everything to lose, it can be argued with conviction that it would be much worse if the "Star Wars" project were feasible than if it turned out to be a crackpot's dream. In the latter case, it would be "only" a huge waste of resources and talent, whereas the actual deployment of the new weapons in space would bring the final holocaust that much nearer.

Meeting the nuclear warriors on their own ground in a "dialogue" is beset with similar pitfalls. It involves acceptance, however provisionally, of *their way of thinking*, with its postulated eternal "adversary" around whom everything revolves and with its identification of "security" with death technology and all its adjuncts. On the one hand, the opportunity to utilize scientific expertise to expose the degradation of science *as science* by addiction to power ought to be welcome. On the other hand, the danger of treating seriously the issues that ought to be dismissed as irrelevant has to be kept constantly in mind.

Perhaps the clearest example of this dilemma is research done on the dangers of accidental nuclear war. As the weapons systems become increasingly more complex and dependent on automated responses, attacks by nuclear weapons triggered by some electronic failure become more likely. This danger would become especially severe if either superpower were to adopt a "launch on warning" policy. This policy demands launching a (supposedly) retaliatory attack on the "adversary" on a signal that he might have launched a strike. The compulsion to adopt such a policy stems from the circumstance that the flight time of medium-range missiles in

Europe to their enemy targets is only a few minutes. In this span of time, there is no room for evaluating signals that *may* portend a launched attack. (Many hundreds of such false alarms are received each year.)

Given certain assumptions concerning possible sources of malfunctioning of automated weapons systems and data on the frequency of "false alarms" of various levels of seriousness, it is possible to estimate the probability of an "accidental nuclear war" in a given time span, and from this the expected time of such an occurrence. It is also possible to estimate the sensitivity of these probabilities or expected time of occurrence to various modifications of the weapons systems or of policies. If no one wants an accidental nuclear war, it appears possible to agree on measures that can be expected to reduce the probability of its occurrence. Here it would seem that the scientist-abolitionist and the defense community might find a common ground and join forces to engage in research on ways of reducing the danger of an accidental nuclear war.

The scientist-abolitionist should keep in mind, however, that an important component of the warrior-scientist's aversion to accidental nuclear war is its being *accidental*, therefore outside the sphere of planning and control. His response to the danger of an accidental war is not greater willingness to consider the abolition of nuclear weapons but rather a determination to make them "safer." As they are made safer, they can be made more complex, a prospect that attracts the warrior-scientist. In this sense, the convergence of interests of the scientist-abolitionist and of the warrior-scientist is illusory.

Another area in which "hard" scientific research could become peace research is that of verification of arms control agreements. A seeming last barrier to a comprehensive nuclear test ban agreement between the superpowers has been their inability to agree on verification proceedings. While tests of nuclear weapons in the atmosphere are easily detected by the resulting spread of radiation, tests of underground explosions require more sophisticated methods of detection. Research on improving verification procedures should contribute to the likelihood of a comprehensive test ban treaty. On closer examination, however, it appears that the technical basis of these objections is only a pretext (Paul 1986). In a moment of greater frankness, the United States declared that a comprehensive test ban was simply "not in the national interest of the United States," the modern version of a *raison d'état* argument, which chokes off all further discussion.

Under these circumstances, it would seem that further research on ways of improving verification procedures to supplement a comprehensive test ban agreement would serve little purpose. Nevertheless, to the extent that the United States still on occasion resorts to the "impossibility of detecting violations" argument against a treaty, research of this sort could have some leverage in exposing the hypocrisy of the argument.

The Relevance of the Behavioral and Social Sciences

The relevance of these sciences to the study of conflict and to peace research is obvious. Establishing connections between the findings of these sciences and matters related to war and peace is not always easy, however. It seems natural to view war as a type of human conflict that differs mainly in magnitude and severity from conflicts between persons, social strata, and ethnic or religious groups. All these conflicts have, of course, common features: confrontations between adversaries and conflicting goals. As already indicated, there are ways in which this view of war can be misleading. It can suggest a conception of war as an event generated primarily by animosity between individuals or groups and with it simplistic ideas about how to prevent wars by reducing animosities. Some years ago a serious proposal was made to feed "pacifying" drugs to leaders of nations in order to reduce their pugnacity and so prevent wars. Attention has been called to the relative sterility of research aimed at revealing the causes of wars by standard techniques of processing masses of data in search of correlations among indices.

The qualification "relative" should be emphasized. For one thing, *negative* findings could be instructive by laying to rest various preconceived notions about the causes of wars and especially about the relation between war preparedness and "national security."[3] The weakest feature of the research on the causes of wars is the suggestion that uncovering these "causes" is a principal step in creating means of preventing or stopping wars. The suggestion results from a false analogy between the rationales for medical research and peace research.

The greatest value of research in the behavioral and social sciences as a contribution of peace is that it helps to create what can be called an infrastructure of peace. It helps change people's way of thinking about war and peace—a prerequisite of informed political action, which seems the most promising road to establishing a firm peace on this planet.

As an example, let us examine the relevance of so-called experimental games. We have already considered the uses of global simulations, in particular simulations of arms races which demonstrate how, under certain assumptions regarding the dynamics of those processes, their trajectories can be seen to be determined by the values of certain parameters. The value of these findings is not that they suggest control of arms races by controlling the parameters, but rather that they reveal the systemic properties of the processes that may be beyond anyone's control as long as political leaders think and act within certain frameworks and paradigms.

We have seen how strategic analysis of certain two-person non-zero-sum games and certain n-person games (with more than two players) dramatically brings out the difference between individual and collective rationality and thus puts in question ideas derived from conventional wisdom about what it means to be "rational" in certain kinds of conflict situations (cf. Chapter 14). Experimental games are designed to provide data on how people in simulated situations of this sort actually behave. Their observed behavior certainly differs widely. Consequently, in view of the interest presented by these situations to social psychologists, research consists of varying the conditions under which the games are played or recruiting subjects from different populations. The interest of peace researchers working with experimental games is focused on the strength of thinking habits and on what it takes to modify them. By far the largest number of experiments have been performed on Prisoner's Dilemma. In contrast, only a few experimental studies have been made on "Tragedy of the Commons" situations, which are equally instructive.

The name "Tragedy of the Commons" derives from the situation of English farmers whose cattle grazed on jointly-owned pastures, known as the "Commons." It was in the interest of each farmer to add a cow to his herd. However, if each farmer, pursuing his individual interest, did this, the pasture would be overgrazed, entailing a loss for everyone (Hardin 1968). Today a similar situation exists in commercial fisheries in international waters. If every fishing fleet, pursuing individual interest, uses the most efficient methods of maximizing its catch, the fish population will be depleted, entailing losses for all.

The situation can be simulated in the laboratory by having subjects draw from a common pool amounts of a resource at their discretion. If the pool is not depleted, it is replenished. Otherwise, no more resources can be withdrawn.

J.J. Edney and C.S. Harper (1978) performed an experiment of this sort under three conditions: (a) with only minimal instructions given to the subjects; (b) with an optimal strategy of withdrawal suggested to the subjects; (c) with an opportunity given to the subjects to discuss the situation and to agree on a withdrawal strategy. They found that the performance (as measured by the size of the total "harvest") was not significantly affected when an optimal strategy was suggested but improved markedly when the situation was turned into a cooperative game and the subjects were able to discuss the situation among themselves.

A. Rapoport (in press) performed a similar experiment. The condition allowing discussion was omitted. Only performances with and without full

Table 24–1

Comparison of performance in a Tragedy of the Commons experiment with and without a full explanation of the "social trap." Explanations of the columns and of the entries is given in the text above.

Condition	(1)	(2)	(3)	(4)	(5)
Full explanation	0.58	3.0	6.3	1.7	$6.40
Minimal explanation	0.31	1.9	4.1	1.1	$1.88

explanation of the "social trap" were compared. The rules of the game were deliberately designed to make the individually rational strategies (equilibria of the n-person non-cooperative game) difficult to compute, while the collectively rational strategy was obvious. After each independent withdrawal by each of the players, the remaining resource in the pool was doubled. (In Edney and Harper's experiment, there was a ceiling on replenishment.) The number of rounds to be played—seven—was announced. The obvious collectively rational strategy was to draw nothing from the pool for the first six rounds, thus permitting the initial resource to increase by a factor of 64 and then for each of the n players to draw exactly 1/n of the total amount on the last round.

Fifteen four-person groups, one three-person group and one two-person group participated in the experiment. Only one of these, the two-person group, which received the full explanation and the collectively rational solution to the game, succeeded in harvesting the full amount on the last round. This disappointing result was somewhat offset by the findings that the extreme form of selfish behavior, "take the money and run," was observed only once. Some positive effects of the full explanation were observed. To assess these, we used several measures of "cooperative behavior" relevant to the Tragedy of the Commons situation: (1) fraction of subjects making no withdrawal on the first round; (2) mean number of the round on which first withdrawal was made; (3) mean number of rounds played; (4) mean number of "no withdrawals" per subject; (5) mean size of the "harvest" per group. The results are shown in Table 24–1.

All differences are in the expected direction, and all but one are significant. The results suggest that while it is possible to induce a tendency toward collectively rational behavior even in the absence of an opportunity to come to an agreement, it is extremely difficult to induce full cooperation based on trust alone, even if the advantages of such cooperation are obvious.

Another important lesson displaying the deficiency of conventional wisdom was derived from a simulation experiment suggested by the results of a contest. An invitation was issued by R. Axelrod to submit computer programs for realizing strategies in playing iterated Prisoner's Dilemma. A strategy of this sort consists of an instruction to the computer to choose either C (the cooperative strategy) or D (the defecting strategy) depending on the "history" of the iterated game up to the round in question. In particular, the choice may be independent of this history. For instance, the instruction may be to always choose D or to choose C at random with a given probability. Or the choice may depend only on a finite stretch of the history, e.g., "Choose C if there were four or more CC outcomes among the last 10 outcomes; otherwise D." And so on.

Each submitted program was to be matched with every other, including itself. In each case, the pair of strategies so matched would determine the course of the iterated game, that is, a protocol of outcomes CC, CD, DC, or DD. The iterated game was to last 200 rounds; the protocol would determine the total payoff to each of the "players." The payoff cumulated over all encounters would determine the score achieved by a program. The program receiving the highest score would be declared the winner of the contest.

Fourteen programs were submitted. In addition, the completely random program with equal probabilities of C and D participated in the contest. The highest cumulated score was attained by an extremely simple program called Tit-For-Tat (TFT). This program begins the iterated game with C and thereafter chooses C or D, depending on whether the "co-player" chose C or D on the preceding round.

The results of the contest were publicized and another contest was announced under the same conditions, except that this time the number of iterations would be decided probabilistically with about 150 being the expected number. Besides the scores achieved by the programs submitted in the first contest, the programs themselves were described. Thus, it became known that TFT obtained the highest cumulated score. It could be expected that the participants in the second contest would try to design programs that could "beat" TFT.

This time 62 programs were submitted from six countries. There were computer scientists, psychologists, and game theorists among the participants. Tit-For-Tat was again among the programs, submitted by the same contestant and only by him. It again obtained the highest score.

The most instructive result of this experiment was the fact that TFT did not "beat" a single program in pair-wise encounters. In fact, it cannot do so, because the only way a program can get a higher score playing another program is by making more D choices than the other, since the only instances in which it can get a higher payoff are those when it plays D while the other plays C. But TFT can never play more D's than its co-player, because it plays D *only* when the other has just played D. The reason TFT got the highest cumulated score in the contests is because other programs (perhaps designed to "beat" TFT), *in confrontations with each other*, depressed each other's scores.

The results of this experiment can be said to be an illustration of a principle often neglected in strategic thinking, namely, that at times there is strength in weakness. The principle manifests itself whenever the "strong" destroy each other, leaving the field to the less pugnacious. That TFT is not pugnacious can be seen from the fact that it never "defects" (plays D) first and never "bears a grudge." It retaliates against defection just once, reverting to cooperation as soon as the co-player does.

Recall the observation that intraspecific combats between nonhumans are seldom fatal and that this can be attributed to reproductive advantage conferred on genotypes that have developed comparatively harmless combat weapons or inhibitions against killing their own kind. A "weak" individual of this sort is bound to lose in a confrontation with a "strong" individual, but this very success of the strong can contribute to their ultimate undoing. For if success means reproductive advantage, the strong will become more numerous, and therefore encounters between the strong, in which both lose, will become more frequent. This situation illustrates a principle distinctly brought out in the theory of non-constant-sum games, namely, that the success of a strategy may depend crucially on how many other players use it. We see this in real life. In competing for the consumer's dollar, some business firm may gain an advantage by incorporating some appealing innovation into its product. But this advantage lasts only as long as the innovation is not imitated. If every firm producing the product adopts it, the advantage is lost. The validity of this principle in the context of arms races and proliferation of new war technologies and tactics is obvious.

The results of the Prisoner's Dilemma program contests and the relevant observations of biologists (cf. Maynard Smith and Price 1973) led to simulation experiments in which game-theoretic principles were linked to theoretical biology.

Assume that a population of animals consists of several genotypes, each representing a certain strategy used in intraspecific combats. The outcome of a combat may confer a reproductive success on one or the other of the combatants, on both, or on neither. The "payoffs" can define the structure of a Prisoner's Dilemma game. That is, an encounter between two "weak" individuals confers a moderate reproductive success on both. An encounter between two "strong" individuals impairs moderately the reproductive success of both (both may suffer injuries). An encounter between a "strong" and a "weak" individual confers a large reproductive success on the former and a large reproductive disadvantage on the latter.

In the simulation experiment performed by R. Axelrod (1984), the "individuals" were iterated Prisoner's Dilemma programs. Reproductive success or failure following each encounter was represented by addition to or removal from the population replicates of the programs. Thus, the composition of the programs kept changing. The population "evolved," as it were. The overall success of TFT was manifested in the fact that ultimately this program was the only one that "survived," that is, the entire population eventually consisted only of this genotype.

The simulation experiment turned out to be a realization of an "evolutionarily stable strategy" (Maynard Smith 1982). In theoretical biology, the term "strategy" (borrowed from the terminology of game theory) refers to a "choice of evolutionary direction." Mutations, which can be conceived as impulses propelling the evolution of organisms in one or another direction, have nothing to do with choices in the context of conscious decisions. Nevertheless, the figure of speech is suggestive and provides a conceptual link between apparently widely disparate fields. Moreover, the link between the two fields—theory of evolution and theory of games—reveals the relevance of both to peace research, in that the strategic analysis of the Prisoner's Dilemma game and the demonstration of TFT as an evolutionarily stable strategy reveals a crippling fallacy of conventional strategic thinking: the extension of principles of individual rationality to conflict situations where these principles turn out to be traps.

Data Gathering

The popular image of scientific research pictures laboratories crowded with mysterious apparatus, geniuses making momentous discoveries and speaking unintelligible jargon, above all an activity motivated primarily by a quest for power. However, if research is understood in its basic sense as a quest for *knowledge*, then much research has nothing to do with laboratories, equipment, or sensational discoveries. Nor do the findings of research necessarily contribute to the acquisition of power, as is imagined when research is conceived as a servant of technology. Some research does not even produce "new knowledge." Historical research, for example, does not really "create" new knowledge, the way a naturalist's discovery of a hitherto unknown species or a chemist's discovery of a new element does. Historical research often leads to uncovering some collectively forgotten facts that have been buried in archives or obscure publications. In this way, historical research merely restores knowledge that has been lost. Nor is research of this sort confined to rediscovery of past events. It can deal with the present. The end product of such investigations is the appearance before the eyes of the public of organized factual information. The research consists of digging up this information and organizing it into a coherent picture. With skillful presentation, this research becomes a contribution to peace education. The data gathering necessary for such presentation is a vital part of peace research.

An example of data gathering research is an annual report entitled *World Military and Social Expenditures*. The following is a summary of findings published in the 1985 edition (Sivard 1985).

- The megatonnage of the world's stockpile of nuclear weapons is enough to kill 58 billion people, or to kill every person now living 12 times over.
- In the Third World military spending has increased five-fold since 1960, and the number of countries ruled by military governments has grown from 22 to 57.
- Over 1 billion people live in countries controlled by military governments.
- The U.S. and U.S.S.R., first in military power, rank 14th and 51st, respectively, among all nations in their infant mortality rates.
- The budget of the U.S. Air Force is larger than the total educational budget for 1.2 billion children in Africa, Latin America, and Asia, excluding Japan.
- The Soviet Union in one year spends more on military defense than the governments of all the developing countries spend for education and health care for 3.6 billion people.
- There is one soldier per 43 people in the world, one physician per 1,030 people.
- The developed countries on average spend 5.4 percent of their GNP for military purposes, 0.3 percent for development assistance to poorer countries.
- If the price of an automobile had gone up as much since World War II as the price of sophisticated weapons, the average car today would cost $300,000.
- Only one citizen in four in developing countries has an unrestricted right to vote.
- It costs $590,000 per day to operate one aircraft carrier, and every day in Africa alone 14,000 children die of hunger or hunger-related diseases.

The Question of "Academic Respectability"

The main activity of the Stockholm International Peace Research Institute (SIPRI), one of the earliest of such institutes established under government auspices, is mainly devoted to gathering and publicizing data on the war system. The output consists of series of yearbooks on armaments, effects of weapons, arms trade, and related themes. Concentration on this sort of research has helped establish SIPRI as a source of reliable knowledge. They present a picture of the war system which hardly needs to be supplemented by interpretations or comments. Possibly concentrating on "hard" research, the founders of SIPRI had in mind the need to establish a solid, politically unassailable foundation for the "infrastructure of peace" indispensable in making significant peace research findings applicable.

Aside from this opportunity to confront the war system by simply presenting facts, there is little that academically responsible research can produce that is *directly* applicable in this sense. As we have seen, the relevance of other directions of peace research has to be explicitly established, at times by complex arguments. The development of such arguments is a task of peace education.

Action Research and Investigative Journalism

There are two formats of research activity where the relevance of findings is immediately apparent. For the time being, however, they remain outside the academic mainstream. One format is called "action research"; the other is investigative journalism.

Action research is characterized by the circumstance that the researcher, instead of assuming the role of an outside observer, becomes deliberately involved in the process under investigation. This involvement appears to violate standards of objectivity, and for this reason action research has so far failed to achieve respectable academic stature. An example of action research is the conciliatory activities of the Quakers previously discussed. Note that the title of the book describing these activities contains the word "experiences" (Yarrow 1978). There is no question that the members of the conciliation teams were deeply involved in the processes described. At the same time, however, they took pains to *look at themselves* in their role and to draw lessons from the events. The element of subjectivity is not removable from these self-observations. To the degree that honest self-appraisal can be regarded as a contribution to (self) knowledge, the concept of "research" can be extended to include activities of this sort.

The "findings" of this self-evaluative research are given in the last chapter of *Quaker Experiences in International Conciliation*, entitled "Quaker Conciliation and Peace Research." In particular, participation in the conciliation process induced the Quakers to examine closely the differences in outlook that characterize different approaches to conflict resolution. These

differences needed to be actually experienced during the process of attempted conflict resolution. The Quakers also had to face the challenge of
those who maintained that in some situations, characterized by structural
violence (cf. Chapter 4), confrontation is unavoidable and must be regarded
as a prerequisite to conciliation.

> The most cutting charge of the radical school of peace research is that the
> traditional school is identified by position, class, culture, and ideology with
> the dominant, status-quo oriented elites of the West and therefore the tra-
> ditional claim of objectivity is suspect. The Quaker establishment could be
> similarly criticized as middle class and elitist, a fact only partly corrected by
> the wisdom of Quaker leaders in the past and present who have recognized
> the limitation and tried to overcome it. . . .
> What then is the answer to this challenge, coming as it does both from
> peace researchers and prophetic Quaker voices? (Yarrow 1978, p. 289.)

The discussion that follows in the text can be regarded as a substantial
contribution to the methodology of peace research in which "action research" is incorporated.

Another important example of action research is represented by Alva
Myrdal's book, *The Game of Disarmament* (1976). Myrdal was Sweden's
ambassador to the Geneva Disarmament Conference. The book sheds a
glaring light on the charade, the true significance of which is revealed most
clearly to a frustrated participant. Myrdal appears in that role, representing, as she does, a neutral country with no stake in either world hegemony
or in a partnership with a hegemonial power.

This situation, more than any other, reveals the futility of applying techniques of conciliation or even of creative negotiation in confrontations of
this sort, since the principals of this tragicomedy do not speak with their
own voices. Here, confrontation rather than conciliation is the proper
mode; not, however, a confrontation between the principals but rather
one between the principals and others to whom the "advantages" sought
by either side are meaningless—those who face "annihilation without
representation."

Investigative journalism, like action research, falls outside academic activity. It can be excluded from the realm of scientific research on formal
grounds, because its ethical code prohibits disclosing sources of information—a violation of a cardinal principle of free inquiry. This kind of research is most immediately understood when one says "Watergate." It
amounts to continuing the American tradition of "muckraking," which in
its heyday consisted essentially of exposing corruption in high places and
ruthless abuses of economic and political power against the public interest.

This sort of journalism can flourish only in a country where freedom of the press was never seriously curtailed. Instances of "self-censorship" are frequently cited, and access to mass media, especially to radio and television in America, is incomparably easier for moneyed institutions and organizations (political parties, lobbies, etc.). Still, the difference between limited opportunities to disseminate information and views and no opportunity (as in countries where all channels are monopolized by the authorities) is immense.

The rapid militarization of the U.S. has stimulated investigative reporting on the war system. The findings are frequently published in books, the most natural outlet of penetrating social criticism. *Think Tanks* by P. Dickson (1971), *Project Paperclip: German Scientists and the Cold War* by C.G. Lasby (1971), and *Star Warriors* by W.J. Broad (1985) are typical examples.

Think Tanks describes the work of institutes primarily devoted to war research. The book is a rich source of material illustrating the intellectualization of war, a theme discussed in Chapter 16 of this book.

Project Paperclip tells how German scientists who had worked for the Third Reich were recruited into the American defense community, whereby the regulations excluding the immigration of Nazis into the United States had to be circumvented in one way or another. No doubt many of these scientists were also recruited by the Soviet military establishment. It is well known that German scientists who designed the missiles with which London was attacked toward the close of World War II also aided the development of the weapons for World War III. Such knowledge militates against taking ideological rationales for war preparations seriously.

Star Warriors presents a picture of the lives of young scientists working on the development of so-called third-generation weapons—successors to atomic and hydrogen bombs, in particular weapons to be incorporated in the "Star Wars" system. The book combines descriptions of the fantastically ingenious devices spawned by the Baroque era of weaponry with character sketches of the brilliant young men who live in the monastic world of ideas, dreams, and hard work completely dedicated to inventing ever-more-effective means of mass destruction. It is said that great literature, in depicting "real people" rather than assessing abstractly formulated hypotheses, contributes more to the knowledge of the human psyche than any findings of scientific psychology. Actually, the two kinds of knowledge are not comparable. Both can contribute to enlightenment in different ways. Books like *Star Warriors* occupy a position intermediate between "humanistic" and "scientific" psychology. On the one hand, *Star Warriors* uses the techniques of literature—portraying people in real-life situations instead of in contrived situations. Yet it can be regarded as a contribution to psychological research, since the situations observed by the author are not fictional. In fact, *Star Warriors* is a collection of case studies, a method well established in behavioral science.

Investigative journalism undertaken by Cerf and Beard (1986) has provided some dramatically bizarre evidence of the cost-maximizing practices of the war economy. Their book, in the format of a mail-order catalogue, lists a number of hardware items with descriptions of their distinctive features and their prices. Examples: a toilet seat, priced at $640.09, a plain steel nut (features: circular hole in center, threads, beveled edges, six equal sides, genuine steel construction) priced at $2,043.00, etc. (The nut is offered free with the purchase of the catalogue.) The tone of this report makes it appear to be spoof, but the examples, according to the authors, "are taken from military supply records and the price listed under each item is the actual price it was offered to the Defense Department at . . ." Research findings of this sort can be used to good advantage in peace education.

Investigative journalism has so far been impossible in the Soviet Union. Attempts by Soviet citizens to monitor the compliance of their government with agreed-upon commitments to human rights have been at times severely punished. A foreigner attempting investigative reporting in the military sphere would be sure to be accused of espionage. It is especially gratifying from the standpoint of the peace research community that American society is still sufficiently open to permit investigative reporting on a large scale.

A most significant piece of investigative journalism was carried out by the Defense Department of the United States, unwittingly to be sure, as evidenced by attempts to suppress the publication. This was the gathering and recording of the material in the so-called Pentagon Papers, in which the decision processes that led to the United States involvement in Vietnam are revealed. The attempts to suppress this information were unsuccessful, a reflection of the openness of American society.

Self-Examination Reveals Problems and Suggests Directions

A good view of the problems that arise in peace research can be obtained by making periodic surveys of what has been done. It would be a mistake, however, to try to assess the impact of these studies on policies. Significant direct impacts of the sort that physical science has had on technology will surely not be discernible; not many peace researchers are in positions to advise governments, much less to have their advice accepted. Thus, an assessment of "practical results" would be disappointing. If, however, peace research is regarded as an activity contributing to the creation of an infrastructure of peace, the overall picture looks different. The field has been definitely established and its scope sufficiently well defined to permit a classification of areas and an "epidemiology," the spread and the loci of concentration of the various branches of the field.

One such survey was carried out by Elise Boulding (1972). She has singled out ten areas of fundamental studies and theories:

- *International System:* historical-descriptive, quantitative-descriptive, and theoretical investigations, simulations.
- *Crisis Research:* crisis decisions, tension measurement.
- *Conflict Studies:* history, theory, small-group experiments, causes of war.
- *Attitudes:* attitude survey and scales, images and perceptions, attitude change.
- *Research on the Future:* general studies, models of a disarmed but revolutionary world, transition to and nature of a stabilized world.
- *Integration Studies:* political integration, internaton non-governmental organizations (NGOs), impact of student exchange.
- *Economic Studies:* conversion to a peace economy, economic and technical assistance.
- *International Law:* general studies, definition of aggression, codification of coexistence.
- *Disarmament Studies:* the armament-disarmament spectrum, deterrence, disarmament inspection, UN police force.

Besides these fundamental studies, which fit easily into American academic curricula, Boulding has singled out instances of action research which can be effectively carried out by participants in peace actions; for example, assisting efficacy of protests, studies of participants in protests, studies of nonviolence, its effects on the "targets" of nonviolence and on the participants in nonviolent actions.

Complementary to Boulding's classification by contents of the studies is Hannah Newcombe's classification by method or approach. Newcombe (1984) has singled out four basic approaches.

Traditional Peace Research. This approach centers on areas having an obvious bearing on conflict, conflict resolution, war and peace; for instance, international relations, international law, the ethics of war and peace.

Quantitative-Behavioral Peace Research. This approach is, for the most part, system-oriented. The objects of the investigations are often portions of the international system—nations, blocs, etc., in interaction. Emphasis is on dynamics of behavior. Frequently, mathematical models are constructed from which trajectories of behavior are deduced. Models of arms races and of interactions in crises are common representatives of this format, as are correlation studies. Several samples are found in Singer 1968.

Critical or Radical Peace Research. Investigations of the war system with the view of exposing its most debilitating effects on human populations and the dangers it presents would be subsumed under this category. Investigative journalism, if it adheres to certain standards of rigor, also qualifies as critical peace research.

Policy Proposals Based on Peace Research. Disarmament, peacekeeping and tension-reducing schemes must, to be regarded as feasible, be supported by solid knowledge of political, social, and economic conditions in which these schemes can be implemented. Research designed to generate such knowledge, e.g., research on the economics of converting war industries to peace industries, would be subsumed under this category. Also included are imaginative but presumably possible alternative futures.

Can Peace Research Be Applied?

The author raised this important but apparently controversial issue at the time when peace research was a rapidly growing activity on American campuses (Rapoport 1970). The title of the paper was formulated as a question—the heading of this section. The question was not meant to be rhetorical. Evidently, the author's stance was interpreted by some as unduly pessimistic—even, in the opinion of one (Kent 1971), as "demeaning" of peace research in the sense of minimizing its potential for influencing policy. The discussion was continued by D. R. Wernette (1972), who offered some thoughtful and constructive suggestions for resolving the "conflict" between Rapoport and Kent. The interested reader is referred to the three articles.

Discussions of this sort are to be welcomed. They contribute to the development of self-knowledge in the peace research community, a precondition for an effective transformation of the findings of peace research into materials for building peace education programs. This transformation remains the principal function of peace research. This function can be continually enlarged and reinforced independently of the extent to which these findings can directly influence the present policy makers.

Notes

1. Richardson's differential equation model of an arms race (cf. Chapter 18) is called "linear with constant coefficients," because the variables on the right side appear only in the first degree, and their coefficients are independent of time. These are the simplest systems of differential equations. Their solutions in the form of trajectories can be deduced by elementary methods.
2. In his introduction to G. Sharp's *The Politics of Nonviolent Action*, Schelling welcomes the book as a major contribution to the theory of conflict. He sees it as a sort of complement to a (rational) theory of violent action. In Schelling's opinion, a book on that subject is still to be written.
3. Recent work (Russett 1983) on correlations between arms races and wars has been revealing. Of 99 confrontation crises examined, 82% of the disputes that erupted into war were preceded by an arms race; only 4% that erupted into war were not. It is, of course, important to keep in mind that correlations reveal nothing about the direction of causality. Intention to wage war could well have been the "cause," the arms race the "effect." Most likely, however, "causality" in situations of this sort goes both ways. At any rate, preparations for war have always been rationalized as conducive to the protection of peace. The data belie this.

25

Problems of Peace Education

For centuries in Europe, when the prospect of eternal damnation was a very real concern to practically everyone, the Church performed the function of alleviating this fear. It provided easily understood and easily followed procedures for avoiding hellfire. As long as the Church's authority over these matters was unquestioned, it retained its leadership in defining "spiritual" values. As the hegemony of the Church declined, attention turned to things of this world. The growth of science, discoveries of new lands, the spread of trade and industry, what we call "modernization," removed concerns related to damnation and salvation after death from the focus of attention. Indeed, the prevailing mood of people concerned with matters beyond the immediacies of daily life became increasingly more optimistic, especially during the eighteenth and nineteenth centuries.

The trauma of twentieth-century world wars considerably dampened this optimism, but it was not until well into the second half of this century that a chilling fear of the final holocaust swept over the world. This fear is probably as pervasive as the fear of the impending Last Judgment and eternal damnation was in the Middle Ages. It is as surely founded on almost universally accepted beliefs as the fear of twelfth-century Europeans was founded on beliefs prevalent then. From our modern point of view, the medieval fear appears illusory and ours real, and no matter how we might try to convince ourselves that our fear may also be illusory, we cannot. Not that all of us are convinced of the inevitability of the final holocaust. What we cannot question is that *if* it occurs, it will surely destroy most, perhaps all of us. This knowledge is based on confidence in the validity of physical laws and in the fragility of life, especially of "civilized" life. There is no way of saying which belief was or is firmer: that of our medieval forebears in the impending end of the world or ours in the consequences of a modern war. There is no way of saying whose anxiety was keener. But it does seem that our present malaise resembles that of our forebears in many ways.

In bygone eras, the Church provided a measure of solace. Can a similar solace in the form of hope be provided today, and, if so, by whom and to whom? It is not likely that a genuine faith in "salvation" can be revived except among persons already predisposed to think of the human condition in ways established by rather primitive religious paradigms. There are some who look forward to the final holocaust as the realization of a biblical prophecy, believing they will escape it by being raptured bodily to a cloud, from which they can watch Armageddon in comfort. Not many will be able to take this way out of despair. One aim of peace research is to provide hope rooted in an enlightened view of the human condition.

The Scope of Peace Education

From the time of its inception, university education has been organized into "disciplines." This organization was partly determined by specialization. Pursuit of knowledge in depth makes specialization practically inevitable, since detailed knowledge produces a specialized vocabulary. Specialists in command of each such vocabulary understand each other and form a community. Because of inner cohesion and loss of contact with others for lack of a common vocabulary and a common conceptual repertoire, fractionization of knowledge occurs. The positive connotations of the word "discipline" provide rationalizations for this fractionization. Another source of discipline fixation is rooted in the needs of administrations of educational institutions: to keep track of who belongs where, to have rules for evaluating the competence of educators—in a word, to work within an orderly system.

The limitations of excessive specialization and of dividing up the world of knowledge into "disciplines," each with its standards of expertise, have been long recognized, and various attempts have been made to counter this process by encouraging "interdisciplinary" academic activity in the form of research teams, programs of study, special institutes, and the like. It is easy to tell where such activity has taken off and thrives: namely, where it was organized around a set of clearly recognized problems. Problems have no recognized disciplinary boundaries. Vigorous research and action programs in city planning attract other than architects. Engineers, sociologists, and social workers also participate. Physicians do not suffice for a program in public health. Engineers, specialists in public administration, bacteriologists, and many others must be recruited into it. Effective problem solving demands teamwork across specialties and academic disciplines. Environmental studies are now an established academic "discipline," so called by force of habit, but actually involving many of the traditional disciplines. The success of this integration was assured partly because expertise in the many different areas comprising "environmental science" already existed, partly because of the urgency of the problems whose solution depended on close collaboration between the several kinds of specialists in developing the new "interdisciplinary discipline."

There is no question that the problem raised by the specter of total war is more urgent than those spawned by the degradation of the environment. The difficulty in tackling that problem area is in agreeing on what constitutes expertise relevant to establishing an "interdisciplinary discipline" of peace and conflict studies. Undoubtedly, full use of all established academic disciplines should be made in the organization of peace education programs. Indeed, there is hardly a field of knowledge that cannot be tapped for material relevant to the study of problems to which a peace education program must address itself: economics, history, political science, sociology, psychology, large areas of the natural and biological sciences, philosophy, and religion. The problem is to bring a vast store of knowledge into focus.

What Is and What Ought to Be

One important outcome of peace education programs will be to create an intellectual and occupational home for people to live and work in, in the same way that the world of technology provides a home for people versed in its skills and steeped in its ethos. The question that invariably arises in connection with implementing this goal is whether peace education programs would not involve proselytizing, something that conscientious educators are extremely wary of and often regard as being incompatible with the goals of education. This point leads us to consider the important but often-missed distinction between objectivity and moral neutrality. The two concepts are often linked, usually by practitioners of the natural sciences and by social scientists intent on bestowing "academic respectability" on what might be ethically questionable activities within their disciplines. The idea that objectivity and moral neutrality imply each other arose in the process of drawing a sharp distinction between questions about "what is" and questions about "what ought to be." There is indeed such a distinction, and it is not easy to ascertain when rhetoric obscures it.

Consider the statement "All men are created equal" in the American Declaration of Independence. This statement in the indicative mood appears to be saying something about *what is*. But if it is meant that way, it is obviously false. Men are *not* created equal. What the statement actually means is that men *ought* to be regarded or treated as if they are equal. Many such instances of confusion between "what is" and "what ought to be" can be brought to mind. The pervasiveness of this confusion has led some scientists and educators to declare that science is never in a position to answer questions about what ought to be, only questions about what is. The "objectivity" of science depends on this separation—keeping one's fears and hopes from encroaching upon one's observations and on one's reasoning.

To be objective, however, need not mean to be morally neutral. Moreover, objectivity in determining what is cannot always ignore questions about morals or values, because questions about what is often relate to how people feel, and people's feelings depend on their values, i.e., on their convictions about what ought to be.

Values can be basic or instrumental. We call "instrumental" those values that are believed to facilitate the realization of other values. Ultimately, the chain of instrumental values must lead to some "basic" or "ultimate" values, which need no longer be justified as means to ends. If there are universally shared basic values, surely survival must be among them. By "survival" we cannot mean the survival of some human individuals at the expense of others. It is the survival of the *human race* that must be among the basic values, since no other human values can be served if the human race perishes.

For the first time in the history of humanity, its demise within a foreseeable time appears likely. This is not a prophecy supported by religious belief but a prospect pointed out by scientific study. Dissemination of knowledge necessary to understand this possibility must be a first educational priority. In this context at least, a moral stance cannot be avoided. But then the educator cannot remain neutral between policies if these increase or decrease the likelihood of the extinction of humanity. To the extent that these likelihoods can be evaluated objectively, the educator can remain objective. To the extent that they cannot, he must prefer the instrumental values that enhance the basic value (survival). He cannot remain neutral.

Basic values are not taught. If they are indeed basic, then, by definition, they have been internalized. But a person may not be aware of them. They may be submerged under superstitions, delusions, and compulsions imposed by ideologies. A goal of peace education is to remove obstacles in the way of becoming aware of basic values. It is here that the role of instrumental values (things to be valued because they facilitate the realization of basic values) becomes important. To the extent that learning to recognize instrumental values leads to awareness of basic values, education acquires the status of enlightenment.

"Know-How" and "Know Why"

During the Great Depression in the United States, Robert M. Hutchins, then Chancellor of the University of Chicago, was taunted about his emphasis on the importance of humanistic education in universities. Doctors of philosophy, the critics pointed out, were making a living digging ditches. To this Hutchins is said to have replied, "But at least they know why they have to dig ditches for a living."

A society in which people are taught predominantly "how," while questions about "why" are neglected, can get into serious trouble. While 50 years ago concentration on technical competence at the expense of enlightenment may have been responsible only for cultural impoverishment, today this bias contributes to the mortal dangers of our age. The concentration on preparations for war as the most absorbing preoccupation of a nation speaks for itself. The technological imperative appears as the principal source of this preoccupation. The problems spawned by the preparations projected into the future with due regard for the *extrapolated* growing sophistication of war technology preempt a large part of intellectual energy. All of it is harnessed to solutions of "how" problems: how to plan war, how to fight it, how to come out "ahead." In this preoccupation, "why" questions have no place. The question *why* there should be a war between the United States and the Soviet Union has no answer in the language of technology and therefore is not asked.

The problem of integrating the "how" and the "why" has become acute. In any peace education program, such integration must be a principal goal. Young people must be prepared for a life of work, but they must urgently be helped to become an enlightened generation.

There is a problem with the first task. At this time, a "peace profession" does not exist in the sense of being as clearly recognized as the medical profession, the legal profession, and the numerous technical and business professions with a clear inventory of skills to be mastered. If, however, the creation of an infrastructure of peace with the view of encroaching upon and eventually replacing the infrastructure of war is pursued with energy, competence, and devotion, a peace profession will come into existence, just as all professions came into existence after the "soil" in which they could sprout and grow had been prepared.

The peace educator should not be considered an "idealist" ignorant of the tough and complex problems with which modern policy makers must wrestle, problems of "survival" in a world of competition and power struggles. Sufficiently rich academic programs will include standard courses in the social sciences, the natural sciences, and the humanities to justify their place in post-secondary education along with other programs designed to produce informed men and women capable of independent and critical thinking.

The Road to Enlightenment

"Time-binding" is a term used by A. Korzybski (1921) to refer to the transmission of *accumulated* knowledge to future generations. Human beings are able to do this by virtue of being uniquely able to communicate by symbolic language. The amount of knowledge that can be communicated in this way by word of mouth is limited by the human memory capacity and by the availability of persons who store this knowledge. With the invention of writing, both of these restrictions disappeared. The creation of written texts can be regarded as the foundation of *formal* education, that is, the establishment of times and places reserved for learning and the creation of a teaching profession. This amounted to the *institutionalization* of the learning process.

Like many other institutions, education survived by virtue of becoming adapted to the cultures in which it was embedded, by fulfilling certain functions that contributed to the viability of the cultures. Religious education based on learning a body of literature regarded as sacred is a conspicuous example of how institutionalized education contributed to the survival of a culture by fostering cohesion among its adherents. This sort of education persisted for centuries among the Jews and the Moslems. To be "learned" in the cultures based on Judaism or Islam meant to have extensive and detailed knowledge of what is written in the holy books, the *Torah* or the *Koran*.

In medieval Europe, where the established Church acquired considerable political power, education of this sort was limited mostly to the clergy. In fact, the role of the priest as an intermediary between man and God was for a long time jealously guarded. For this reason, translation of the Scriptures into the vulgate languages was for a long time proscribed. The Reformation crystallized precisely around this issue.

Since, however, the Reformation followed the invention of printing and the attendant spread of literacy, the writings that became available to the general population were no longer confined to the Scriptures. Secular education was born. The criterion of "learnedness," however, was still determined by knowledge of what was written in books.

In a way, the change in the mode of cognition instigated by the scientific revolution was analogous to the change in the basis of faith instigated by the Reformation. In insisting that the Scriptures be available to everyone, the founders of Protestantism maintained that knowledge of "truth"— which was identified with the revealed "truth" of Christian faith—should be arrived at *independently* by every individual without reliance on intermediate human authority (i.e., the priesthood). The basic tenet of scientific cognition is that knowledge of truth, which is identified with knowledge of reality as revealed by direct observation of the external world, can and should be attainable independently by every individual without reliance on any other authority.

The crucial difference between the sort of autonomy fostered by the Reformation and the sort fostered by the scientific revolution was in the view about the source of "true knowledge." For the Protestant of the Reformation, it was still the Word of God as revealed in the Scriptures; for the scientist, it was the criterion of consensus based on independent observation and independently pursued chains of logical deduction.

The emancipation of cognition from established authority, either human or presumably divine, marks the era of Enlightenment. That era, particularly in France, can be regarded as a period of fermenting ideas which dominated the political upheavals initiated by the French Revolution. The common denominator of those ideas was uninhibited challenge of "knowledge" which, upon analysis, turned out to be supported by encrusted dogma, unwarranted generalizations (superstitions), or conventional wisdom—hand-me-down beliefs untested by relevant observations or experience.

In this respect, the Enlightenment was successful. This is not to say that superstition was eradicated from everyone's conception of the world—only that significant inroads were made. There are large superstition-free areas of human activity contributing to making life more bearable and meaningful. For all the criticism that can be leveled at modern medicine or technology, they have indisputable positive aspects. Even though governments claiming legitimacy as establishments of divinely ordained order have not disappeared, the continued existence of such governments has become precarious. Violation of human rights is rampant, but the very fact that they are widely publicized and combated, occasionally successfully, is one of the fruits of enlightenment.

The goal of peace education ought to be to continue the process of enlightenment so that it can be extended into many still superstition-dominated areas of human activity. The most conspicuous superstitions of our age are those that enable the global war machine to grow and flourish. The superstitions are embodied in several robust myths, which are easy to believe because they evoke comforting images or else call attention to events that are real enough but induce unwarranted generalizations.

The most prevalent myth is that the function fulfilled by modern military establishments is "defense." Once one has acquired the habit of examining the possible reference of a word to the real world, it should become clear that modern weapons cannot "defend" anyone or anything. They can only destroy everyone and everything. The association of military might with "defense" stems from another age when an army could keep another army at bay, preventing it from overrunning a country and laying it waste or enslaving its population. In that sense, a military establishment could be said to "defend" a country. As late as World War II, some meaning could be attached to military "defense." For example, the Royal Air Force did defend Britain from German bombers. With the advent of weapons of total destruction, all of them offensive weapons, the function of "defense" can no longer be ascribed to the military establishment. The conclusion is inescapable that the word is used for its still-positive connotations in time when searching questions are being asked about the function of the war system as an institution.

An equally pervasive myth is built around "deterrence"—another shibboleth. This is the back-up myth to which one can resort when the belief in the myth of "defense" has been undermined. The most commonly used illustration of successful deterrence is the 40-year-old peace in Europe. Like any superstition, this one is based on the *post-hoc-ergo-propter-hoc* fallacy. An event is believed to be the cause of another because it preceded it. *Mutatis mutandis*, a condition is believed to have prevented an event if the condition obtained and the event did not occur. By the same token, any invocation, talisman, or ritual can be claimed to be a preventive measure if the feared event does not occur when the measure is taken. Some credence might be given to the deterrence theory if on a number of comparable occasions, a war did not occur when deterrence was practiced but did occur when deterrence was not practiced. Often World War II is cited as an example of a failure to prevent a war by failing to deter the aggressor (Nazi Germany). However, World War I can be cited as a counterexample. In 1914, a heavily armed France was presumably deterring a heavily armed Germany, and a heavily armed Germany was presumably deterring Russia. To argue that World War I occurred because the belligerents did not practice "enough" deterrence is to beg the question.

The myth that war preparations, even war itself, are "good for the economy" deserves special attention. War preparations and most certainly war do not create real wealth. The costs of war production are included in the calculation of the gross national product of a country, but for that very reason, the gross national product is a poor index of the "health" of an economy. If by an economy we mean a system of production and distribution which functions well when desired usable things are produced and needed services are performed in sufficient measure, then war production cannot be said to contribute to the economy, since what it produces is neither consumer goods nor capital goods that produce consumer goods. Nor are the services performed by military personnel of any use to the general population. On the contrary, putting the goods and services produced by a war economy to actual *use* can spell only disaster for the population.

There is no denying that a lagging economy can be stimulated by preparations for war in the sense that governments can see to it that jobs are made available in war industries and that there are opportunities for guaranteed profitable investments (military Keynesianism). But such stimulation is analogous to the "fix" of a drug addict, which gives a momentary "high" but which is followed by a harmful "low." To see the deceptive effects of the stimulation produced by preparations for war, imagine that a government lets the printing presses run and distributes large amounts of cash to the population. Suddenly everyone feels rich. For a while, people may go on shopping sprees, until the supply of goods and services is exhausted. This "fix" does not benefit the economy in the long run, since no *real* wealth is created by printing pieces of paper, which cannot be eaten, lived in, or worn. The mercantile theory was based on just such a fallacy: namely, that precious metals represented significant wealth. The decline of the "great powers" of the sixteenth century, Spain and Portugal, was a consequence of a stubborn belief in an economic superstition.

Polemical Aspects of Peace Education

Education is a process whereby accumulated knowledge is passed on to future generations. There are three components of this process: training, indoctrination, and enlightenment. Training comprises the content of all vocational and of a large part of professional education. It is the least controversial aspect of education for two reasons. (a) The degree to which skills have been acquired can be more or less objectively assessed. Hence the success of an educational system in imparting skills can be evaluated and pragmatic criteria can be applied in developing improvements of methods; and (b) Since opportunities for acquiring skills valued in a society are welcomed by large sectors of the population, sharp controversies concerning the purposes of vocational or professional education are not likely to arise.

The principal beneficiaries of indoctrination are the privileged strata, the elites of a society, since the values transmitted to the young by this process are those that keep the privileged strata in their dominant position. Controversies arise about indoctrination when these dominant values are challenged. Then not only the content of the indoctrination but also the method is attacked. Often those who challenge values inculcated by indoctrination would prefer their own values to be transmitted to future generations. Since, however, they criticize not only the content but also the method by which the values of the incumbent privileged strata are transmitted, the critics must espouse other goals of education.

Dominant values will also be questioned if education fosters habits of independent thinking, habits that are suppressed rather than encouraged by indoctrination. It is this aspect of education, where established values and beliefs that have become dominant in militarized societies are challenged, with which peace educators are most concerned. Modern education has inherited methods for the constant challenge of conventional beliefs that have proved successful. As science became firmly institutionalized in technically advanced societies, the educator acquired powerful tools for combating false beliefs about nature. He could use these tools, because the dominant strata of Western societies, especially after the advent of the Industrial Revolution, welcomed the victory of the natural sciences over religious dogma. A rearguard action was still fought in the nineteenth century by the fundamentalists against the theory of evolution. In America such skirmishes occur even today. But the outcome of these battles was a foregone conclusion.

The weapons used to combat superstition and naive images of the physical world can be used to combat the delusions that have grown up around questions of war and peace. Factual information about the physical and biological effects of weapons of total destruction can help dispel the illusion of "defense." The argument that "deterrence has worked" can be demolished by exposing the *post-hoc-ergo-propter-hoc* fallacy. The most elementary knowledge of economics can refute or at least seriously undermine the conventional wisdom regarding the alleged salubrious effects of war preparations on the economy.

In short, given a modest degree of receptivity of students to reasoned arguments and respect for facts, the chances of enhancing enlightenment by appeal to reason ought to be good. Johann Galtung, in discussing the problem, points out that not only the content but also the form of peace education must be compatible with the idea of peace.

. . . it has in itself to exclude not only direct violence but also structural violence; the days of . . . corporal punishment are more or less gone. But the structural violence is there and it takes the normal forms: a highly vertical division of labor which in this case expresses itself in one-way communication, fragmentation of the receivers of that communication so that they cannot develop horizontal interaction and organize and eventually turn the communication flow the other way. . . . (Galtung 1973, p. 170.)

Recall that to Galtung's way of thinking, any authoritarian structure of organized human activity is suspected of being symptomatic of "structural violence" (cf. Chapter 4). Whether one shares this suspicion or not, it seems reasonable to assume that effective peace education will develop its own evolving format.

The peace educator must expect disharmony with the guardians of traditional military attitudes and loyalties. The content of peace studies programs cannot be confined to "objective" analysis. Like humanistic education, peace education must be at least in part directed toward *sensitizing* students to basic human values. For example, in humanistic education attention of students is directed toward the creative achievements of humanity aside from those related to accumulation of power over nature. An educated person acquires appreciation of beauty, a sympathetic understanding of religious fervor or speculative philosophy, as well as competence imparted by scientific or technical training.

In the same way, peace education should, somewhere along the line, direct students' attention to eloquent and passionate celebrations of life, of love, of peace. Questions about what stands in the way of realizing these values cannot be avoided. As an example, consider the reaction of Herman Kahn to Jonathan Schell's book, *The Fate of the Earth* (1982). Having quoted some passages in which Schell maintains that genuine defense can be achieved only by giving up violence, Kahn replies:

This concept has also been suggested in a Pastoral Letter on War and Peace by the National Conference of Catholic Bishops. Redemption may be an appropriate and correct concern for a church, but it has nothing to do with the policies that the government can—or should—carry out. If there is a "redemption of mankind," it will not occur as a result of a great debate on national security or defense. It is, then, the "nonissue" of least relevance to government policy on nuclear war. (Kahn 1984, p. 24.)

Schell's book is a cry of anguish of a man contemplating the threat of extinction of human life on this planet in consequence of a nuclear war. The propriety of including this book in a course dealing with conflict in the nuclear age can be defended on the same grounds as the propriety of

including personal accounts of victims of torments and humiliations imposed by racist structural violence, by totalitarian repression, and the like.
The intent behind using such accounts is that of widening the range of the
student's experience by making the feelings of other humans in situations
totally outside his experience accessible to him or illuminating his own
personal experiences of torment or humiliation.

Equally legitimate is the inclusion of Kahn's comments. They, too, reveal
an attitude of a person, who, we may assume, is representative of many
persons in similar circumstances. Kahn's posthumously published book,
Thinking About the Unthinkable in the 1980s, begins with listing twelve
"nonissues," as Kahn labels assertions which "however common and sincerely held, are in terms of policymaking basically irrelevant, impractical,
inaccurate, or foolish and should be eliminated from the debate at the
outset." (Kahn 1984, p. 23). Evidently, the prospect of the extinction of
human life as a consequence of military operations is one such "nonissue."
A more direct demonstration of the gulf between the warriors and the
victims is difficult to find.

The difficulties mentioned by Galtung, namely, the incompatibility of
traditional educational methods and those that ought to be adopted by
peace educators, are not insurmountable. In North America, for example,
the educational system is not under complete control of a regime intent
on maintaining the grip of an officially imposed ideology on the population.
New content and new methods can be, and at times have been, introduced.
However, the virtual autonomy of local school boards in shaping curricula
of primary and secondary schools works both ways. It makes innovation
and experimentation possible and so provides opportunities for enriching
curricula and materials designed to prepare children for the world in which
they will live. At the same time, it leaves the content of education at the
mercy of various pressure groups acting out single-purpose hang-ups and
prejudices.

An example of an attack on peace education in the schools is an article
in *Commentary* entitled "The Scandal of 'Peace Education' " (Ryerson
1985). The author first describes what he evidently regards as a menacing
trend—the spread of "peace education," "peace studies," or "nuclear education" promoted by the "largest labor union in America," the 1.7 million-
member National Education Association (NEA) and by Educators for
Social Responsibility (ESR). He goes on to describe a manual for teaching
a unit entitled "Choices" intended for junior high school students and
written for the NEA by the Union of Concerned Scientists. A professor
of psychiatry at Harvard, who, Ryerson reminds the reader, "has made
no secret of his desire to change American defense policy," wrote the
introduction to the manual, in which the pervasive fear of nuclear war

among children is mentioned along with the inadequate response to those fears by parents and teachers ill-equipped to deal with them. Ryerson goes on to challenge the validity of the studies said to show adverse effects of the nuclear arms race on the emotional lives of young people. These fears, if they exist, Ryerson argues, are induced in children by the parents and teachers themselves, as they terrorize the youngsters with lurid images of the effects of nuclear explosions.

Next, a unit of instruction included in the manual is described with the view of exposing half-truths and biases incorporated in it. The manual instructs the teacher to "read one factual and one personal account of the dropping of the atomic bomb on Hiroshima." Ryerson comments, "the 'factual' account gives no background to World War II, and does not even mention who started it. The 'personal' account includes a child's description of the Hiroshima devastation."

Having complained that the description of the bombing of Hiroshima is not accompanied by a "background" (presumably explaining why the bomb had to be dropped), Ryerson proceeds to criticize the background provided in the discussion of the adversarial relationship between the United States and the Soviet Union. Among the explanations of this adversarial relationship is reference to the tendency of Americans to imagine people who are different as enemies, to the selfishness of nations, to the role of competitiveness in the genesis of war, to the role of self-realizable assumptions: assuming that someone is an enemy makes an enemy; assuming that the other is a friend makes a friend.

Ryerson's complaints refer to the very feature of peace education that under favorable circumstances can help change our ways of thinking about war. One *should* acquire the ability of looking at the reality of war dissociated from all rationalization, in this instance at the effects of the atomic bombing of a *city* and of the *people* in it, not of a "target" and of "enemies," those who "started the war." One *should* be able to experience the event as it was experienced by a child, not the way it was written about in operational reports. Further, one *should* be able to think about attitudes of Americans toward people who think differently from them.

The main thrust of Ryerson's attack on peace education in the schools is in the form of a warning against ideological subversion. "One might be tempted to dismiss ESR as a marginal left-wing element in the larger scheme of American education. This would be a serious mistake." A long list of persons "of power and prestige" who support the program follows: George Rathjens of the Massachusetts Institute of Technology, Ernest Boyer, president of the Carnegie Foundation for the Advancement of Teaching, Mary Rutrell, president of NEA, and other names prominent in the worlds of science, education, and religion.

Political Aspects of Peace Education

Political battles cannot be avoided, and in spite of the impressive roster of friends of peace education in the schools, the outcome of that battle, given the variability of the political climate, is far from certain. Political control over at least primary and secondary education in America is a by-product of democracy to be reckoned with, as can be seen from the last paragraph of Ryerson's article.

> The large degree of local control which American communities still enjoy over their schools permits relief from the current disorder by those who would wish to correct it. We—taxpayers and parents—have long assumed that public schools should remain politically neutral. We have assumed that teachers' politics are their private business, not the public's, and so have demanded no political tests for the job; but the other half of the implicit contract has been that teachers, in turn, are not to use their authority over children for indoctrinating them in their own political enthusiasms. Teachers who push "peace education" in the classroom are manifestly violating the terms of their trust. The public is entitled to say that they should either cease the indoctrination, or find another form of employment. (Ryerson 1985.)

All education is political, war education no less than peace education. The reason some aspects of education—like some aspects of science, religion, or art—seem to be "free of politics" is that in some environments there is ideological consensus on particular issues with which those aspects of education (or science or religion or art) are concerned. Recall the assault on genetics in the U.S.S.R. by Lysenko and his cohorts (cf. Chapter 8). Biologists all over the world were repelled by the intrusion of politics into science and by the ideologues' insistence that there is no such thing as "apolitical" science. In principal, the ideologues were right. The infusion of Stalinist politics into biological theory was appalling, not because it was politics, but because it was bad politics—at least politics bad for science. Science thrives in a climate of free discussion where criteria of truth are rooted in the principle of independent reasoning and verification of observations, where care is exercised in relating theoretical constructs to observable events, where difficulties of establishing chains of causality are realized, and so forth. This climate can be maintained only in a certain political environment. We may not realize this because we live in a political environment more rather than less favorable to the practice of science. This is the reason why we are prone to think that science or education is or ought to be "apolitical."

However, if an attack on a scientific discipline or on a religious creed or on education is political, so is the defense of academic, religious, or artistic freedom. This point is now brought home especially clearly in the United States. Seven families in Greenville, Tennessee, sued their county board of education for violating their "right to religious freedom." They objected to several books used as background material in the schools, such as *The Diary of Anne Frank*, which makes it appear that all religions should be tolerated, and *The Wizard of Oz*, which tells children that traits such as courage, intelligence, and compassion are personally developed rather than God-given, and which portrays witches as good. Stories by Margaret Mead, a social anthropologist writing about people in the South Pacific, Isaac Asimov, a science and science fiction writer, and Hans Christian Andersen were also on the list of proscribed authors. A federal judge ruled in favor of the plaintiffs.

Any educator who chooses to resist such pressures *ipso facto* joins the political struggle. There is, therefore, no point in pretending that education can be kept free of politics, least of all peace education. Rather, the peace educator should squarely face the political problems that arise in conse-quence of bringing the quest for peace into the schoolroom. He or she should take advantage of the opportunities provided by the inevitable struggles. The wave of fundamentalist bigotry in the United States during the 1980s can be seen to be aggravated by the change in the political climate, a response to the challenge to U.S. hegemony in world affairs. The peace educator is advised to acquire a solid background in the political aspects of his/her mission on whatever level a peace education program is introduced.

Preparing for Peace

As one looks at the global peace movement, it can be seen to consist of three components: peace research, peace education, and peace activism. Each component has its own specific problems, but those problems are also interlinked. We have already pointed out that the most important "product" of peace research ought to be knowledge that can be used to make peace education effective. The most important function of peace education ought to be the dissemination of knowledge that can be used to make informed peace activism effective. At the same time, experience in peace activism ought to provide grist for the mill of peace education, and problems arising in peace education ought to indicate some directions in peace research.

The motto introducing *To the People of the World: A Baha'i Statement on Peace* (Universal House of Justice 1986) reads "World peace is not only

possible but inevitable. It is the next step in the evolution of this planet."
Many will not be able in all honesty to agree that peace, however desirable
or imperative, is inevitable. However, not even the most convinced pes-
simists will deny that peace is a possibility. If it comes, peace will bring
with it a plethora of complex problems, because humanity has had so little
experience living with it. The function of peace activism is to increase the
likelihood that someday peace will come to this planet. One function of
peace research and peace education is to prepare humanity to live under
conditions of peace. This preparation is tantamount to building an infrastructure of peace—a body of informed and devoted cadres, specialists in
coping with a large variety of problems, presently those associated with
peacemaking and peacekeeping, eventually those that will inevitably arise
in a peaceful world. The cadres will include people learning to think in
new ways and competent in transmitting these skills to future generations.
Those whose concerns are predominantly with war have created a vast and
pervasive infrastructure. To prepare for peace means to create an infrastructure that will encroach on the one built in the course of preparing for
war and will ultimately replace it.

26

Concluding Remarks: Can There Be a Science of Peace?

I want to return now to the question I posed in the preface: Can there be a science of peace? The reader may have gathered that in my opinion there is no definitive answer to this question. There is a science of mechanics, and knowledge of it enables us to build machines to work for us. There is a science of medicine, and knowledge of it enables us to prevent, control, or cure some diseases. There is a science of chemistry, and knowledge of it enables us to produce useful substances not found in nature. However, to think of a "science of peace" as a body of knowledge that can be used to prevent or stop wars is likely to lead to disappointment. Wars are not events in the external world that we can control by virtue of knowing how they occur. *People* make wars. So if knowledge is to be of help in eliminating wars, it must be knowledge of ourselves. To acquire such knowledge is much more difficult than to acquire knowledge about the external world—first, because people often resist the process that leads to self-knowledge; second, because in acquiring self-knowledge we change. By the time we have found out something about ourselves, we have become *ipso facto* different.

The ongoing controversy about whether there can be a "social science" revolves around the same issue. Some deny the existence of a social science by pointing out the indifferent success in predicting, let alone controlling, social events. The only genuine expertise in the social sciences appears to consist of familiarity with the literature, in knowing who said what. Yet knowledge of how people have thought and currently think about the social

and political systems in which they live, about conflict and conflict resolution, about war and peace, about social justice and injustice, constitutes
self-knowledge on the level of humanity. Therefore the content of the
social sciences perceived in this way can be a contribution to real knowledge. There is no need to apply to the content of social sciences the same
yardsticks of objective validity that are routinely applied in the natural
sciences because, in contrast to what people say or write about their natural
environment, what they say or write or even think about their social environment constitutes a substantial part of that environment. It speaks for
itself.

The controversy over whether there is or can be a "science of peace"
should be seen in the light of what is expected from such a science. If one expects peace science to generate knowledge about "how to make or preserve
peace," one will be disappointed, for reasons that were spelled out in
Chapter 24. If one recognizes the paramount importance of self-knowledge
on the level of society or of humanity as a whole as an indispensable
precondition of peace, then anything that contributes to self-knowledge
can be conceived as a contribution to a substantive science of peace. This
book represents an effort to present facts, theories, conjectures, and speculations in the hope that they can serve as evidence of how people have
thought and currently think about conflict and conflict resolution, about
war and peace, and so can serve as a contribution to self-knowledge.

It goes without saying that my own thoughts on these matters have
governed the selection and organization of the material. The predominance
given to the Cold War and to the concomitant chronic confrontation between the superpowers reflects the overwhelming importance I ascribe to
this situation. I cannot avoid wondering how posterity (if there are any)
may regard my views (if they deserve their attention at all). In every age
warnings have sounded of impending doom, proclamations of approaching
"turning points of history," pictures of humanity facing a crucial and irreversible choice, and so forth. Is our situation no different? That is, is it
just another "crisis" like innumerable ones before it, seeming enormous
just because we are in the midst of it but destined to be replaced by other
"crises," which will, in turn, seem to be "final"?

It seems to me that this time it is for real. The reason I think so is because
the impending catastrophe is foreseen not as a consequence of "loss of
faith" or "moral degeneration" or some other condition perceived as a
calamity from the point of view of a particular value orientation. The "end
of humanity" is now foreseen as a consequence of events which had no
precedent that by any stretch of imagination can be regarded as relevant
and yet which are predictable on the basis of the most reliable knowledge
that human beings possess: knowledge of physics.

On this score, therefore (I beg the reader to forgive my vanity), I can reassure myself. If posterity (if any) pay any attention to my views, they will not, I think, dismiss my concern as just another instance of keen anxiety produced by dissolution of accustomed patterns of life and expectations. In other ways, however, some of the arguments I have advanced in support of my political views and priorities may quickly become out of date. In the last forty years, the global political system has changed so radically, often through suddenly perceived salience of unforeseen developments, that any extrapolation of trends entails a risk of consigning one's ideas to the ash heap of intellectual history. I myself have repeatedly emphasized the obsolescence of political and military thinking that seemed sober and mature in the pre-nuclear age. Who knows what may occur within a few years to make the most "progressive" and "enlightened" ideas of today hopelessly obsolete, naive, or misleading?

In his introduction to Heinrich von Treitschke's *Politics*, Arthur James Balfour wrote:

> Political theories, from those of Aristotle downwards, have ever been related, either by harmony or contrast, to the political practice of their day; but of no theories is this more glaringly true than of those expounded in these volumes. They could not have been written before 1870. Nothing quite like them will be written after 1917.

These remarks were published in 1916, in the midst of World War I. Treitschke's ideas about the role of the state and about the nature of war did not die in 1917. They still energized the final spasms of German militarism a quarter of a century later. But they were never again clothed in intellectual respectability.

In this book I have taken issue with similar ideas couched in another language, one adapted to the rhetoric of democracy rather than to the rhetoric of absolutism. I can say, like Balfour, that nothing like what was written by Herman Kahn or Colin S. Gray could have been written before 1945. Dare I predict that nothing like that will ever be written after just a few years? Such is, of course, my hope. But then great portions of this book would become obsolete—a small disappointment, to be sure, compared to the significance of such obsolescence.

On the other hand, I believe that certain ideas developed in this book have proved viable and will continue to be viable. These ideas should, in my opinion, serve as a foundation for a science that embodies both theories of conflict and theories of conflict resolution, a science that could with justification be called a science of peace. The ideas are reviewed in the following summaries.

The Variety of Psychological Concomitants of Conflict

Chapter 5 was devoted to this theme. To associate conflict, in particular war, with psychological states in which hostility dominates the participants is unduly restrictive. Conflicts occur in an immensely wide variety of contexts. Even "war" encompasses phenomena which, except for the common denominator of organized violence, have very little else in common. This is especially true of modern war in which actual fighting may play only a small part. Because people playing different roles in conflicts (which themselves may be very different sorts of phenomena) may be very differently motivated and may feel very differently, insights suggested by individual psychology may be of limited value in constructing theories of conflict. Other approaches, which I have called ideological, strategic, and systemic, are of equal and at times greater importance.

Perception of Social Reality as Part of Social Reality

This peculiarity of social reality has been emphasized throughout this book. Its clearest manifestation is in the role of the self-fulfilling assumption. Actually, this principle is manifested even in experimental physics. The paradox reflected in the apparently dual nature of light as waves and as particles is resolved when particles and waves are defined *operationally*, that is, in terms of concrete experiments that must be performed in order that the one or the other aspect of light is manifested. It turns out that an experiment which in effect asks the question, "Does light consist of waves or of particles?" is impossible to perform. What is possible is to perform two separate experiments, one to answer the question "Does light consist of particles?" the other to answer the question "Does light consist of waves?" The answer to both questions turns out to be "Yes." The dichotomy between the apparently incompatible "natures" of light turns out to be a pseudo-dichotomy, induced by our language doing our thinking for us.

In contrast to our perceptions of physical reality, in which self-fulfilling assumptions play a part only rarely, these assumptions are commonplace in the way we perceive social reality. In assessing others as friends or enemies, self-fulfilling assumptions play a crucial, often decisive role. The most dangerous aspect of the influence of military thought on statesmanship is its inability to appreciate the role of self-fulfilling assumptions. The "adversary" is always *given* as an adversary. The only problem faced by the military professional is how to deal with the adversary. The question of how the adversary got to be an adversary or why he is an adversary may be of intellectual interest, or it may need to be answered in order to justify the role of the military professional. But the possibility that adversaries are *made*, not given, is shut out of consciousness.

The fact that our perceptions of social reality are part of social reality brings out the most important difference between the natural and the social sciences. Whereas only events in the external world are legitimate sources of "hard data" in the natural sciences, what people have said or written constitutes equally "hard data" in the social sciences. Thus a foundation in the form of a hard data base for a genuine science of conflict or peace, which is the obverse side of a science of conflict, can be said to exist.

The Central Role of Language in Shaping Human Affairs

We do not perceive reality directly. Between us and reality is a screen of language. We perceive what is on that screen, that is, what others—and we ourselves—*tell* us about reality. Langauge is by far the most important instrument of communication among human beings, including communication of a human being with him/herself. It is also the principal instrument of cognition and the medium in which attitudes are formed, firmed, or changed. By making it possible to learn without going through trial and error, language has served as a marvelous survival mechanism of our species. But this same property has made it possible for human beings to live in a world of ideas completely isolated from the concrete reality of which they are believed to be reflections. An understanding of this double role of language and how it functions in shaping attitudes and beliefs must be incorporated into a science of peace. In particular, ideological components of large-scale conflicts are rooted in the attitude-forming role of language.

Power Addiction as a Possibly Fatal Disease of Humanity

The human is unquestionably a social animal. However, unlike the most social animals (e.g., social insects), the human did not adapt to the social way of life by developing appropriate instincts. Or, perhaps, if such instincts do exist somewhere in the depths of the human psyche, they are buried deep under a superstructure of culturally conditioned thinking habits and attitudes which play the dominant role in determining human behavior. As a result, the human has become a product of *cultural* evolution. There is no evidence that a process analogous to natural selection governs the evolution of cultures. Thus, the fact that a culture still exists and flourishes is not conclusive evidence that it has "adapted." It may be doomed to extinction without showing any conspicuous symptoms of its impending demise. The same applies to humanity as a whole. A principal survival mechanism of social animals is cooperation. Man is no exception. However, the way social communalities have been traditionally organized, by the establishment of hierarchies and intense competition for vital resouces, has conferred a strong (although always temporary) survival advantage on the possessors of superior power. Consequently, addiction to power often overshadows nurturing and cooperative impulses, which must be inherent in human nature, since we are both mammals who must nurture their young and social animals who must cooperate. Because of the formidable destructive potential controlled by the power-addicted elites of human societies, power addiction is now revealed to be a maladaptation that may lead to the extinction of the human race. Our survival as a species depends on our ability to overcome this addiction.

The Greater Relevance of Systemic Dynamics Compared to Individual Psyches

The idea that the course of history is determined by geniuses or potentates was probably suggested by the prominence of dramatic conquests and individuals invested with absolute power. It is difficult to accept this idea when empires are no longer created by rapid decisive wars and the power of leaders depends in varying degrees on collective consensus, so that it is now inherent in *roles* rather than in persons.

It is more reasonable to suppose that large-scale human events are determined by the dynamics of economic, social, or political systems. For this reason, investigations of system dynamics has become an important component of peace and conflict studies. To the extent that models of systems defined by certain structures and interactions of parts approximate the actual structure, dynamics, and evolution of social, economic, or political systems, the branch of peace science concerned with such models acquires a resemblance to the natural sciences. Here mathematical methods of theory-building can come into their own.

The Relevance of Strategic Analysis

The theory of games and other branches of formal decision theory can define fruitful directions for peace research. They can be included in curricula of peace and conflict studies programs, in the role of a theoretical framework in which the strategic thinking of intellectuals serving the military-industrial-academic establishments can be subjected to a vigorous critique. Especially fruitful are insights derived from the branches of game theory that reach beyond the theory of the two-person zero-sum game— the principal paradigm in which strategic analysis in military contexts is largely implicitly conducted. The assumption of the total opposition of adversaries' interests and the "worst case" scenarios that predominate in military and diplo-military analyses of conflict situations derive directly from the zero-sum model. Exposing the distortions of value systems imposed by that model upon decision makers and power elites is one of the principal tasks of peace education.

Pacifism, Conflict Resolution, and Its Limits

Tolerance, nonviolence, and primacy of cooperative relations between human individuals and groups are values inherent in peace education. That these values can be internalized by almost any human being is an assumption that underlies all forms of peace activity (by definition of such activity). However, how to go about facilitating the internalization of these attitudes is by no means obvious. The efficacy of didactic or proselytizing methods remains in doubt. The position I have assumed in writing this book is that a stable commitment to peace is a consequence of enlightenment and that the intellectual aspect of enlightenment ought to be the cutting edge of the process. To some extent, the emphasis on the creation and dissemination of solid knowledge (rather than attempts to inculcate attitudes directly) will be justified by the fact that peace researchers, peace educators, and those who enroll in peace studies programs are a self-selected population, probably already imbued with the sort of attitudes usually associated with the commitment to peace. The growth of these cadres constitutes the creation of an infrastructure of peace which, in my opinion, ought to be the source of an antidote to the ideational poisons generated by exacerbating destructive conflicts. There is no need to preach to the converted. They ought to be *"armed"* for the inevitable struggle against the infrastructure of war. By the nature of the struggle, the "armament" must consist of superior knowledge, especially self-knowledge on the level of society and of the whole of humanity.

The "know-how" acquired in the process may involve command of techniques, for example, techniques of conciliation and of conflict resolution. However, as even the pacifist Quakers have come to realize (cf. Chapter 23), in some contexts confrontation (rather than conflict resolution) is inevitable. The limits of conflict resolution are set in situations where a common ground between the conflicting parties cannot exist because of totally irreconcilable values. Such are situations where the values of power confront the values of love, peace, or cooperation among human beings. It is important to keep in mind that irreconcilable conflicts of this sort are conceived as conflicts between roles or institutions, not between persons. One can preserve faith in the ultimate conciliation between persons and tolerance of persons regardless of the views they hold, respect for persons regardless of their social roles, and yet remain adamant in conflicts involving the abolition of roles or institutions. Such ought to be, in my opinion, the aim of the struggle waged by the victims against the warriors, a struggle aimed at the abolition of the institution of war and of all the roles that confer legitimacy on that institution. The issue is no less than the survival of the human race.

Bibliography

In the case of older works, the publication date of the edition consulted is preceded by the date of original publication, if known, otherwise by its most recent edition; e.g., Hobbes, T. (1651/1929) *Leviathan*; Cato the Censor (1933) *On Agriculture*.

Adler, M. (1958–1961) *The Idea of Freedom. A Dialectical Examination of the Conceptions of Freedom.* Garden City, N.Y.: Doubleday.

Adorno, T., Frenkel Brunswick, E., Levinson, D., and Sanford, R.N. (1950) *The Authoritarian Personality.* New York: Harper & Bros.

Amos, S. (1880) *Political and Legal Remedies for War.* London: Cassell, Potter, Galpin & Co.

Ardrey, (1967) *The Territorial Imperative.* London: Collins.

Arendt, H. (1958) *The Origins of Totalitarianism.* Cleveland: World Publishing Co.

Aronson, E. (1984) *The Social Animal.* New York: W.H. Freeman.

Auerbach, M.M. (1968) Burke, Edmund, In *International Encyclopedia of the Social Sciences.* D.L. Sills, ed. New York: Macmillan and The Free Press.

Axelrod, R. (1984) *The Evolution of Cooperation.* New York: Basic Books.

Bandura, A. and McDonald, F.J. (1963) Influence of social reinforcement and the behavior of models in shaping children's moral judgments. *Journal of Abnormal and Social Psychology*, No. 67: 274–281.

Banzhaf, J.F. III (1965) Weighted voting doesn't work: A mathematical analysis. *Rutgers Law Review*, No. 19: 317–345.

Barker, R., Dembo, T., and Lewin, K. (1941) *Frustration and Regression in Young Children.* University of Iowa Studies in Child Welfare, Vol. 18. Iowa City: University of Iowa Press.

Bartlett, R.J. (1956) *The Record of American Diplomacy.* New York: Alfred A. Knopf.

Bell, D. (1960) *The End of Ideology*. Glencoe, Ill.: The Free Press.

Bendedict, R. (1946) *The Chrysanthemum and the Sword*. Boston: Houghton Mifflin.

Bentham, J. (1780/1948) *A Fragment on Government and an Introduction to the Principles of Mores and Legislation*. New York: Macmillan.

Bernhardi, F. von (1914) *Germany and the Next War*. New York: Longmans, Green & Co.

Berkowitz, L. (1964) The effects of viewing violence. *Scientific American*, Vol. 210, No. 2: 41–53.

Berkowitz, L. and Green, R. (1966) Film violence and the cue property of target. *Journal of Personality and Social Psychology*, No. 3: 525–530.

Berkowitz, L. and Rawlings, E. (1963) Effects of film violence on inhibition against subsequent aggression. *Journal of Abnormal and Social Psychology*, Vol. 66, No. 5: 405–412.

Blackburn, G.W. (1985) *Education in the Third Reich: Race and History in Nazi Textbooks*. Albany: State University of New York.

Boserup, A. (1985) Non-offensive defence in Europe. In *Defending Europe. Options for Security*. D. Paul, ed. London: Taylor and Francis.

Boulding, E. (1972) Peace research: dialectics and development. *The Journal of Conflict Resolution*, No. 16: 469–475.

Boulding, K.E. (1974) The relations of economic, political and social systems. In *Collected Papers* L.D. Singall, ed. Vol. 4, pp. 151–162. Boulder, Colo.: Associated University Press.

Boulding, K.E. (1978) Future directions in conflict and peace research. *The Journal of Conflict Resolution*, No. 22: 342–354.

Brennan, D.G. (1965) Review of *Strategy and Conscience* by A. Rapoport. *Bulletin of the Atomic Scientists*, No. 21: 25–30.

Brill, A.A., ed. (1938) *The Basic Writings of Sigmund Freud*. New York: Modern Library.

Broad, W.J. (1985) *Star Warriors*. New York: Simon & Schuster.

Brock, P. (1968) *Pacifism in the United States*. Princeton: Princeton University Press.

Buchanan, J. and Tullock, G. (1962) *The Calculus of Consent*. Ann Arbor: University of Michigan Press.

Caldicott, H. (1984) *Missile Envy. The Arms Race & Nuclear War*. Toronto: Bantam Books.

Cato the Censor (1933) *On Agriculture*. New York: Columbia University Press.

Cerf, C. and Beard, H. (1986) *The Pentagon Catalog*. New York: Workman Publishing.

Chase, S. (1938) *Tyranny of Words*. New York: Harcourt Brace & Co.

Chomsky, N. (1968) *Language and Mind*. New York: Harcourt Brace Jovanovich.

Christoffel, K. (1944) *Volk-Bewegung und Reich*. Frankfurt: Diesterweg.

Churchill, W. (1953) *Triumph and Tragedy*. Boston: Houghton Mifflin.

Clark, G. and Sohn, L. (1958) *World Peace Through World Law*. Cambridge, Mass.: Harvard University Press.

Clausewitz, C. von (1832/1966) *On War*. New York: Barnes & Noble.

Craig, P.P. and Jungermann, J. A. (1986) *Nuclear Arms Race*. New York: McGraw-Hill.

Crowley, P.M. (1968) Effect of training upon objectivity of moral judgment in grade school children. *Journal of Personality and Social Psychology*, No. 8: 228–232.

Cusack, T.R. and Ward, M.D. (1981) Military spending in the U.S., U.S.S.R., and China. *The Journal of Conflict Resolution*, No. 25: 429–468.

Czechoslovak Academy of Sciences (1964) *The Universal Peace Organization of King George of Bohemia: A Fifteenth Century Plan for World Peace*. Prague: Czechoslovak Academy of Sciences.

Dana, Sotoku (1978) Sinking of the Tsushima-maru. *In Cries for Peace*. Compiled by the Youth Division of Soka Gakkai. Tokyo: Japan Times.

Darwin, C. (1859/1954) *On the Origin of Species*. Cambridge, Mass.: Harvard University Press.

Deutsch, K.W. (1963) *The Nerves of Government*. New York: The Free Press of Glencoe.

Deutsch, M. (1985) Zhelanie mira (Desire for peace). *Strana i Mir*, No. 8: 12–16 (my translation—A.R.).

Dickson, P. (1971) *Think Tanks*. New York: Atheneum.

Dollard, J., Doob, L., Miller, N., Mowrer, O.H., and Sears, R.R. (1939) *Frustration and Aggression*. New Haven: Yale University Press.

Douhet, G. (1921/1972) *The Command of the Air*. New York: Arno Press.

Dulles, J.F. (1957) *War or Peace*. New York: Macmillan.

Dyson, F. (1984) *Weapons and Hope*. New York: Harper & Row.

Earle, E.M. (1941/1960) Hitler: The Nazi concept of war. In *The Makers of Modern Strategy*. E.M. Earle, ed. Princeton: Princeton University Press.

Eckhardt, W. (1972) *Compassion: Toward a Science of Value*. Oakville, Ontario: CPRI Press.

Edney, J.J. and Harper, C.S. (1978) The effects of information in a resource management problem. A social trap analog. *Human Ecology*, No. 6: 387–395.

Erasmus, D. (1517/1946) *The Complaint of Peace*. New York: Scholars' Facsimile and Reprints.

Etheredge, L.S. (1985) *Can Governments Learn?* New York: Pergamon Press.

Etzioni, A. (1967) The Kennedy Experiment. *Western Political Quarterly*, No. 20: 361–380.

Feschbach, S. (1955) The drive-reducing function of fantasy behavior. *Journal of Abnormal and Social Psychology*, No. 50: 3–12.

Festinger, L. (1957) *A Theory of Cognitive Dissonance*. Stanford, Cal.: Stanford University Press.

Festinger, L. and Carlsmith, J.M. (1959) Cognitive consequences of forced compliance. *Journal of Abnormal and Social Psychology*, No. 58: 203–210.

Fischer, H., ed. (1943) *Hirts Englandkundliches Lesebuch für die Oberstufe an Oberschulen*. Breslau: Ferdinand Hirt.

Fisher, R. and Ury, W. (1981) *Getting to Yes*. Boston: Houghton Mifflin.

Foch, F. (1903/1918) *The Principles of War*. London: Chapman and Hall.

Forrester, J.W. (1984) System dynamics modeling of the arms race. *System Dy-*

namics Group Memo D-3561. Cambridge, Mass.: Massachusetts Institute of Technology.

Forrester, J.W. (1985) Dynamic modeling of the arms race. *System Dynamics Group Memo* D-3732. Cambridge, Mass.: Massachusetts Institute of Technology.

Freeman, D. (1964) Human aggression in anthropological perspective. In *The Natural History of Aggression*. J.D. Carthy and F.J. Ebbing, eds. New York: Academic Press.

Freud, S. (1930/1961) *Civilization and Its Discontents*. New York: W.W. Norton & Co.

Friedenberg, E. (1975) Thoughts on liberty and rancor. *Harpers Magazine*, June.

Galtung, J. (1964) A structural theory of aggression. *Journal of Peace Research*, No. 2: 95–119.

Galtung, J. (1969) Violence, peace and peace research. *Journal of Peace Research*, No. 3: 169–192.

Galtung, J. (1971) A structural theory of imperialism. *Journal of Peace Research*, No. 2: 81–177.

Gerard, R.W. (1958) Concepts and principles of biology. *Behavioral Science*, No. 3: 95–102.

Glossop, R.J. (1983) *Confronting War*. Jefferson, N.C.: McFarland.

Goldwater, B. (1970) *The Conscience of a Majority*. Englewood Cliffs, N.J.: Prentice-Hall.

Goldwater, B. (1976) *The Coming Breakpoint*. New York: Macmillan.

Gray, C.S. (1982) *Strategic Studies and Public Policy*. Lexington: The University of Kentucky Press.

Gray, C.S. (1984) *Nuclear Strategy and Strategic Planning*. Philadelphia: Foreign Policy Research Institute.

Gray, C.S. and Payne, K. (1980) Victory is possible. *Foreign Policy*, No. 39 (Summer): 14–27.

Griftalcon, J. and Weik, M.H. (1954) *A U.N. Charter for Man* (World Community Series). New York: American Federation of World Citizens.

Grotius, H. (1625/1962). *The Law of War and Peace*. Indianapolis: Bobbs-Merrill.

Hall, A.D. and Fagen, R.E. (1956) Definition of a system. *General Systems*, No. 1: 18–28.

Harary, F., Norman, R.Z., and Cartwright, D. (1965) *Structural Models. An Introduction to the Theory of Directed Graphs*. New York: Wiley & Sons.

Hardin, G. (1968) The tragedy of the commons. *Science*, No. 162: 1243–1248.

Harris, M.B. (1974) Mediators between frustration and aggression in a field observation. *Journal of Experimental Social Psychology*, No. 10: 561–571.

Harsanyi, J.C. (1977) *Rational Behavior and Bargaining Equilibrium in Games and Social Situations*. Cambridge: Cambridge University Press.

Hartsborne, H. and May, M.A. (1928) *Studies in the Nature of Character*. Vol. 1: *Studies in Deceit*. New York: Macmillan.

Hayakawa, S.I. and Goodfield, B.A. (1966) Reflections on a visit to Watts. *ETC.: A Review of General Semantics*, Vol. 23, No. 3: 295–326.

Hazlett, B. (1983) Intraspecific negotiations. Mutual gain in exchanges of a limiting resource. *Animal Behavior*, No. 31: 160–163.

Hegel, G.W.F. (1837/1944) *The Philosophy of History*. New York: John Wiley & Sons.

Heider, F. (1958) *The Psychology of Interpersonal Relations*. New York: John Wiley & Sons.

Hentoff, N. (1967) Introduction to *The Essays of A.J. Muste*. N. Hentoff, ed. Indianapolis: Bobbs Merrill Company.

Hitch, C.J. and McKean, R.N. (1965) The criterion problem. In *American National Security*. M. Berkowitz and P.G. Bock, eds. New York: The Free Press.

Hitler, A. (1925/1943) *Mein Kampf*. Boston: Houghton Mifflin.

Hobbes, T. (1651/1929) *Leviathan*. Oxford: Clarendon Press.

Hobe, K. (1979) *Zur ideologischen Begründung des Terrorismus*. Köln: Druckhaus Rudolf Müller (my translations—A.R.).

Hofstadter, D.R. (1985) *Metamagical Themas*. New York: Basic Books.

Hofstadter, R. (1962) *American Political Tradition*. New York: Alfred A. Knopf.

Hokanson, J. and Burgess, M. (1962) The effects of three types of aggression on vascular process. *Journal of Abnormal and Social Psychology*, No. 64: 446–449.

Hornblower, M. (1975) American revolution: myth and realities. *The Washington Post*, July 6.

Horvath, W. and Foster, C.C. (1963) Stochastic models of war alliances. *The Journal of Conflict Resolution*, No. 7: 110–116.

House Document 93–208 (1974) *Inaugural Addresses of the Presidents of the United States*. Washington, D.C.: Government Printing Office.

Hyams, E.S. (1975) *Terrorists and Terrorism*. London: J.M. Dent & Sons.

Iakovlev, N.N. (1974) *Solzhenitsyn's Archipelago of Lies*. Moscow: Novosti Press Agency.

Iakovlev, N.N. (1983) *Siluety Vashingtona*. Moscow: Politizdat.

Isaacs, R. The past and a bit of the future. In *The Theory and Applications of Differential Games*. J.D. Grote, ed. Dordrecht-Holland: D. Reidel Publishing Co.

Jervis, R. (1970) *The Logic of Images in International Relations*. Princeton: Princeton University Press.

Johnson, A.B. (1836/1947) *A Treatise on Language*. Berkeley: University of California Press.

Kahn, H. (1960) *On Thermonuclear War*. Princeton: Princeton University Press.

Kahn, H. (1962) *Thinking about the Unthinkable*. New York: Horizon Press.

Kahn, H. (1965) *On Escalation: Metaphors and Scenarios*. New York: Frederick A. Praeger.

Kahn, H. (1984) *Thinking about the Unthinkable in the 1980s*. New York: Simon & Schuster.

Kant, I. (1784/1891) *Principles of Politics*. Edinburgh: T. and J. Clark.

Kant, I. (1795/1903) *Perpetual Peace. A Philosophical Essay*. London: Swan Sonnenschein & Co.

Kennedy, R. (1969) *Thirteen Days*. New York: W.W. Norton.

Kent, G. (1971) The application of peace studies. *The Journal of Conflict Resolution*, No. 15: 47–53.

Kissinger, H.A. (1957) *Nuclear Weapons and Foreign Policy*. New York: Harper & Row.

Kissinger, H.A. (1973) *A World Restored*. Glouster, Mass.: Peter Smith.

Kohlberg, L. (1963) The development of children's orientation toward a moral order. Part I: Sequence in the development of moral thought. *Vita Humana*, No. 6:11–33.

Kohlberg, L. (1968) Stage and Sequence: *The Cognitive Approach to Moralization*. Chicago: Aldine.

Korzybski, A. (1921) *Manhood of Humanity*. New York: E.P. Dutton & Co.

Korzybski, A. (1933) *Science and Sanity*. Lancaster, Penn.: Science Press.

Kreutzer, D.P. (1985) A personal computer workshop exploring the dynamics of the arms race. *System Dynamics Group Memo* D–3732. Cambridge, Mass.: Massachusetts Institute of Technology.

Kuhn, T. (1962) *The Structure of Scientific Revolutions*. Chicago: University of Chicago Press.

Kuo, Z.Y. (1961) Genesis of the cat's response to the rat. In *Instinct*. Princeton: Von Nostrand.

Lasby, C.G. (1971) *Project Paperclip. German Scientists and the Cold War*. New York: Atheneum.

Lefebvre, V.A. (1982) *The Algebra of Conscience*. Dordrecht-Holland: Reidel Publishing Co.

Lefebvre, V.A. (1987) The fundamental structure of human reflexion. In *The Journal of Social and Biological Structures*.

Leibnitz, G.W. (1768) *Opera Omnia*. Geneva: L. Dutens.

Lenin, V.I. (1905a/1925) Padenie porta Artura (The fall of Port Arthur). In *Sobranie Sochineniy* (*Collected Works*), Vol. VI: pp. 28–32. Moscow: Gosudarstvennoie Izdadel'stvo (my translations—A.R.).

Lenin, V.I. (1905b/1925) Razgrom (Crushing defeat). In *Sobranie Sochineniy* (*Collected Works*), Vol. VI: pp. 204–207. Moscow: Gosudarstvennoie Izdatel'stvo (my translations—A.R.).

Lenin, V.I. (1909/1964) *Materialism and Empiriocriticism*. Moscow: Progress Publishers.

Lenin, V.I. (1916/1964) *Imperialism, the Highest Stage of Capitalism*. In *Collected Works*, Vol. 22: pp. 185–304. Moscow: Progress Publishers.

Levy-Bruhl, H. (1931/1960) Theorie de l'esclavage. In *Slavery in Classical Antiquity: Views and Controversies*. Cambridge, Mass.: Heffer.

Liddell Hart, B.H. (1933) *The Ghost of Napoleon*. London: Faber & Faber.

Liddell Hart, B.H. (1967) *Strategy. The Indirect Approach*. London: Faber & Faber.

Locke, J. (1690/1966) *The Second Treatise on Government*. Oxford: Basil Blackwell.

Lorenz, K. (1966) *On Aggression*. New York: Harcourt, Brace and World.

Luce, R.D. and Raiffa, H. (1957) *Games and Decisions*. New York: John Wiley & Sons.

Machiavelli, N. (1532/1950) *The Prince and the Discourses*. New York: Modern Library.

Mahan, A.T. (1917) *The Interest of America in Sea Power Present and Future.* Boston: Little, Brown & Co.

Malcolmson, R.W. (1985) *Nuclear Fallacies.* Kingston, Ontario: McGill-Queens University Press.

Malthus, T.R. (1798/1966) *An Essay on the Principle of Population.* New York: St. Martin Press.

Mannheim, K. (1929/1949) *Ideology and Utopia. An Introduction to the Sociology of Knowledge.* New York: Harcourt Brace & Co.

Marx, K. (1845–1846/1947) *The German Ideology.* New York: International Publishers.

Marx, K. and Engels, F. (1848/1955). *The Communist Manifesto.* New York: Appleton-Century-Crofts.

Maslow, A. (1943) A theory of human motivation. *Psychological Review*, No. 50: 370–396.

May, A.J. (1963) *The Age of Metternich.* New York: Holt, Rinehart & Winston.

Maynard Smith, J. (1982) *Evolution and the Theory of Games.* Cambridge: Cambridge University Press.

Maynard Smith, J. and Price, G.R. (1973) The logic of animal conflict. *Nature*, No. 246: 15–18.

McDougal, M.S. and Lasswell, H. (1966) The identification and appraisal of diverse systems of public order. In *The Strategy of World Order.* R.A. Falk and S.H. Mendlovitz, eds. Vol. 2: *International Law.* New York: World Law Fund.

McElwee, W. (1974) *The Art of War.* London: Weidenfeld & Nicolson.

Mead, M. (1956) *New Lives for Old.* New York: William Morrow.

Meggitt, M. (1977) *Blood Is Their Argument: Warfare among the Mae Enga.* Palo Alto, Cal.: Mayfield Publishing Co.

Melman, S. (1974) *The Permament War Economy.* New York: Simon & Schuster.

Menashe, L. and Radosh, R. (1967) *Teach-ins, U.S.A.* New York: Frederick A. Praeger.

Midlarsky, I. (1975) *On War: Political Violence in the International Arena.* New York: The Free Press.

Milgram, S. (1963) Behavioral study of obedience. *Journal of Abnormal and Social Psychology*, No. 67: 371–378.

Millard, E.L. (1961) *Freedom in a Federal World.* New York: Oceana Publishing.

Miller, J.G. (1978) *Living Systems.* New York: McGraw-Hill.

Molesworth, W., ed. (1839–1845) *The English Works of Thomas Hobbes.* London: John Bohn.

Morgenthau, H. (1973) *Politics among Nations.* New York: Alfred A. Knopf.

Morison, S.E. and Commager, H.S. (1950) *The Growth of the American Republic.* New York: Oxford University Press.

Morris, C. (1946) *Signs, Language, and Behavior.* New York: Prentice Hall.

Muste, A.J. (1967) *The Essays of A.J. Muste.* N. Hentoff, ed. Indianapolis: Bobbs Merrill Co.

Myrdal, A. (1976) *The Game of Disarmament.* New York: Pantheon Books.

Nash, J.F. (1953) Two-person cooperative games. *Econometrica*, No. 21: 128–140.

National Conference of Catholic Bishops (1983) *The Challenge of Peace*. Washington: United Catholic Conference.

Newcombe, A.G., Barker, J.D., Wert, J., Haven, M., and Hieber, K. (1974) An improved inter-nation tensiometer for the prediction of war. *Peace Research Reviews*, No. 5: 1–52.

Newcombe, H. (1967) Alternative approaches to world government. *Peace Research Reviews*, Vol. 1, No. 1: 1–84.

Newcombe, H. (1974) Alternative approaches to world government II. *Peace Research Reviews*, Vol. 5, No. 3: 1–94.

Newcombe, H. (1984) Survey of Peace Research. *Peace Research Reviews*, Vol. 9, No. 6: 5–95.

Nietzsche, F. (1887/1905) *The Will to Power*. In *Complete Works*, Vol. 14. London: George Allen & Unwin.

Noel-Baker, P. (1958) *The Arms Race: A Programme for World Disarmament?* London: Stevens.

Norton, G.A. and Holling, C.S., eds. (1979) *Pest Management*. Proceedings of an International Conference October 25–29, 1976. Oxford: Pergamon Press.

Osgood, C.E. (1962) *An Alternative to War or Surrender*. Urbana: University of Illinois Press.

Parrington, W. (1927/1958) *Main Currents in American Thought*. New York: Harcourt, Brace & World.

Paul, D.A.L. (1986) Test ban: the excuses just don't wash. *Toronto Globe and Mail*, September 11.

Pavlov, I.P. (1903/1928) *Lectures on Conditioned Reflexes*. New York: International Publishers.

Peckel, E.W. and Deegan, J., Jr. (1982) An axiomated family of power indices for simple n-person games. In *Power, Voting and Voting Power*. M. J. Holler, ed. Würzburg: Physica Verlag.

The Pentagon Papers: The Defense Department History of the United States Decision-making on Vietnam. G. Gold, A.M. Siegal, and S. Abt, eds. Toronto: Bantam Books.

Piaget, J. (1932/1966) *The Moral Judgement of the Child*. New York: The Free Press.

Pierrefeu, J. (1923) *Plutarque a menti*. Paris: Bernard Grasset (my translation—A.R.).

Plato (1875) Meno. In *The Dialogues of Plato*. B. Jowett, ed. Oxford: Clarendon Press.

Plutarch (1841) Cato the Censor. In *Plutarch's Lives*. Longhorne, J. and Longhorne, W., eds. London: J.J. Chidley.

Possony, S.J. and Mantoux, E. (1941) DuPicq and Foch: The French school. In *The Makers of Modern Strategy*. E.E. Earle, ed. Princeton: Princeton University Press.

Poussaint, A. (1971) A Negro psychiatrist explains the Negro psyche. In *Confrontation: Issues of the 70's*. R. Kytle, ed. New York: Random House.

Proceedings of the Lenin Academy of Agricultural Sciences. (1949) Moscow: Foreign Languages Publishing House.

Rapoport, A. (1964) *Strategy and Conscience*. New York: Harper & Row.

Rapoport, A. (1970) Can peace research be applied? *The Journal of Conflict Resolution*, No. 14: 277–286.

Rapoport, A. (1983) *Mathematical Models in the Social and Behavioral Sciences*. New York: John Wiley & Sons.

Rapoport, A. (in press) Experiments in social traps II. Tragedy of the Commons. *The Journal of Conflict Resolution*.

Rapport, D.J. (1986) Macroecology from an economic perspective: Exemplifying the congruity of system ecology with human economics. In *Ecosystem Theory and Applications*. N. Poluvin, ed. New York: John Wiley & Sons.

Rapport, D.J. and Turner, J.E. (1977) Economic models in ecology. *Science*, No. 195: 367–373.

Richardson, L.F. (1960a) *Statistics of Deadly Quarrels*. Chicago: Quadrangle Books.

Richardson, L.F. (1960b) *Arms and Insecurity*. Chicago: Quadrangle Books.

Riechert, S.E. and Hammerstein, P. (1983) Game theory in the ecological context. *Annual Review of Ecology and Systematics*, No. 14: 377–409.

Rogers, C. (1951) *Client-Centered Therapy*. Boston: Houghton Mifflin Co.

Rosenthal, L. (1979) *Endlösung der Judenfrage*. Darmstadt: Darmstädter Blätter (my translation—A.R.).

Rousseau, J.J. (1761/1955) *A Lasting Peace Through the Federation of Europe and the State of War*. New Haven: Whitlock's.

Russett, B. (1983) *The Prisoners of Insecurity*. San Francisco: W.H. Freeman.

Ryerson, A. (1985) The scandal of "peace education." *Commentary*, June: 37–46.

St. Pierre, Castel de, C.I. (1714) *A Project for an Everlasting Peace in Europe First Proposed by Henry IV of France . . . and Now Discussed at Large and Made Practicable*. London: J. Watts.

Schell, J. (1982) *The Fate of the Earth*. New York: Alfred A. Knopf.

Schellenberg, J.A. (1982) *The Science of Conflict*. New York: Oxford University Press.

Schelling, T.C. (1958) The strategy of conflict. Prospectus for a reconstruction of game theory. *The Journal of Conflict Resolution*, No. 2: 203–264.

Schelling, T.C. (1960) *The Strategy of Conflict*. Cambridge, Mass.: Harvard University Press.

Schwartz, K. (1878) *Das Leben des Generals Carl von Clausewitz und der Frau Maria von Clausewitz*. Berlin: Fred Dümmlers Verlag (my translation—A.R.).

Senghaas, D. (1986) *Die Zukunft Europas. Probleme der Friedenserhaltung*. Frankfurt: Suhrkamp Verlag.

Shapiro, E. (1986) First in a series. *Byte the Small Systems Journal*, Vol. 11, No. 3: 299–300.

Shapley, L. and Shubik, M. (1954) A method of evaluating the distribution of power in a committee system. *American Political Science Review*, No. 48: 787–792.

Sharp, G. (1971) *Exploring Nonviolent Alternatives*. Boston: Porter Sargent.

Sharp, G. (1973) *The Politics of Nonviolent Action*. Boston: Porter Sargent.

Sherif, M., Harvey, O.J., White, B.J., Hood, W.R., and Sherif C.W. (1961)

Intergroup Conflict and Cooperation. The Robber's Cave Experiment. Norman, Oklahoma: University of Oklahoma Press.

Simpson, G.G. (1950) *The Meaning of Evolution.* New Haven: Yale University Press.

Singer, J.D., ed. (1968) *Quantitative International Politics.* New York: The Free Press.

Singer, J.D. and Small, M. (1966) The composition and status ordering of the international system 1815–1940. *World Politics*, No. 18, January: 236–282.

Singer, J.D. and Small, M. (1968) Alliance aggregation and the onset of war 1815–1945. In *Quantitative International Politics: Insights and Evidence.* New York: The Free Press.

Sivard, R.L. (1985) *World Military and Social Expenditures 1985.* Washington: World Priorities.

Smith, A. (1759/1966) *The Theory of the Moral Sentiment.* New York: A.M. Kelley.

Smith, A. (1776/1910) *The Wealth of Nations.* New York: E.P. Dutton.

Smith, M.C. (1903) Translator's Introduction to Kant, I., *Perpetual Peace.* London: Swan Sonnenschein.

Smoker, P. (1964) Fear in the arms race: A mathematical study. *Journal of Peace Research*, No. 1: 55–64.

Sokolovskii, V.D., ed. (1963) *Soviet Military Strategy.* Englewood Cliffs, N.J.: Prentice-Hall.

Solzhenitsyn, A. (1975) *The Gulag Archipelago.* New York: Harper & Row.

Sroffa, P. (1951–1955) Introduction. In Ricardo, D., *Works and Correspondence.* P. Sroffa, ed. Cambridge, England: Cambridge University Press.

Tait, C.W. (1965) *What happened to the State Department? The Nation*, September 13.

Thoreau, H. (1937) *The Writings of Thoreau.* H.S. Canby, ed. Boston: Houghton Mifflin.

Tolstoy, L. (1899) *The Kingdom of God Is Within You.* New York: Thomas Y. Crowell.

Tolstoy, L. (1901/1968) Notes for soldiers. In *Tolstoy's Writings on Civil Disobedience and Non-violence.* New York: New American Library.

Tolstoy, L. (1937) A letter to a Hindu. In *The Works of Tolstoy*, Vol. 21: *Reflections and Essays.* London: Oxford University Press.

Tolstoy, L. (1968) Letter to the Peace Conference. In *Tolstoy's Writings on Civil Disobedience and Non-violence.* New York: New American Library.

Treitschke, H. von (1897–98/1916) *Politics.* New York: Macmillan.

Trofimenko, G.A. (1968) *Strategia global'noi voiny (The Strategy of Global War).* Moscow: Mezhdunarodnyie Otnoshenia.

Ulam, A.R. (1968) *Coexistence and Expansion.* New York: Frederick A. Praeger.

Universal House of Justice (1986) *To the Peoples of the World: A Baha'i Statement on Peace.* Ottawa: Association for Baha'i Studies.

U.S. Senate Committee on Foreign Relations. (1954) Document No. 42435, I to V. Washington: U.S. Government Printing Office.

Vagts, A. (1937) *A History of Militarism.* New York: W.W. Norton.

Van Alstyne, R.W. (1960) *The Rising American Empire.* Oxford: Basil Blackwell.

Vattel, E. (1758/1916) *The Law of Nations*. Washington: Carnegie Institution.

Vining, D.R., Jr. (1986) Social versus reproductive success. The central theoretical problem of human sociobiology. *The Behavioral and Brain Sciences*, Vol. 9, No. 1: 167–187.

Voltaire, F. (1771/1935) *Dictionnaire Philosophique*. Paris: Libraire Garnier Frères.

Von Neumann, J. and Morgenstern, O. (1944/1947) *Theory of Games and Economic Behavior*. Princeton: Princeton University Press.

Wagner, D.L., Perkins, R.T., and Taagepera, R. (1975) Complete solution to Richardson's arms race equations. *Journal of Peace Science*, No. 1: 159–172.

Ward, M.D. (1984) Differential paths to parity. A study of the contemporary arms race. *American Political Science Review*, No. 78: 297–313.

Ward, M.D. (1985) Simulating the arms race. *Byte: The Small Systems Journal*, Vol. 10, No. 10: 213–222.

Weaver, R.M. (1948) *Ideas Have Consequences*. Chicago: University of Chicago Press.

Wernette, D.R. (1972) Creating institutions for applying peace research. *The Journal of Conflict Resolution*, No. 16: 531–538.

Wicksteed, P.H. (1933) *The Common Sense of Political Economy*. London: George Routledge.

Wilson, E.O. (1975) *Sociobiology: The New Synthesis*. Cambridge, Mass.: The Belknap Press of Harvard University Press.

Wohlstetter, A. (1976) Is there a strategic arms race? *Foreign Policy*: Part I: No. 15: 3–20; Part II: Rivals but no race. No. 16: 48–81.

Wright, Q. (1942) *A Study of War*. Chicago: University of Chicago Press.

Wright, R. (1936) The ethics of living with Jim Crow. In *Uncle Tom's Children*. Cleveland: World Publishing.

Wrong, D. (1980) *Class Fertility Trends in Western Nations*. New York: Arno.

Wylie, J.C. (1967) *Military Strategy*. New Brunswick, N.J.: Rutgers University Press.

Yarrow, C.H.M. (1978) *Quaker Experiences in International Conciliation*. New Haven, Conn.: Yale University Press.

Yarrow, M.R. and Scott, P.M. (1972) Imitation of nurturant and non-nurturant models. *Journal of Personality and Social Psychology*, No. 23: 259–270.

York, H.F. (1970) A personal view of the arms race. *Bulletin of the Atomic Scientists*, Vol. 26, No. 3: 27–30.

Zinnes, D. (1968) The expression and perception of hostility in a pre-war crisis, 1914. In *Quantitative International Politics*. J.D. Singer, ed. New York: The Free Press.

Name Index

Italicized numbers refer to pages where the author is quoted in the text.

Adams, John Quincy, *218*
Adler, Mortiner, 119, 140–41, 455
Adorno, T., 84
Alexander III (czar), 144
Amos, S., *106–107*, *481*, 488
Andersen, Hans Christian, 583
Ardrey, R., 22, *23–24*
Arendt, Hannah, 163, 165, *167*
Aristotle, 102, 147
Aronson, E., 181
Asimov, I., 583
Axelrod, Robert, 274, 275n, 558, 560

Bach, J.S., 417
Bachman, J.G., 182
Bakunin, Mikhail, *185–86*, 190, 195–96
Balck, Hermann, 533–34, 536
Balfour, Arthur James, *587*
Bandura, A., 45
Banzhaf, J.F. III, 314
Barker, R., 36–37
Bartlett, R.J., 218
Beard, H., 565
Becker, Dr., *167–68*

Beethoven, Ludwig van, 415, 417, 444
Bell, David, 232–33, 236–240
Bentham, Jeremy, 124
Beria, Lavrenti, 215
Berkowitz, L., 35, 39–40, *41–42*
Berkley, George, 114, 145
Bernhardi, F. von, 17, 19, 489
Bethune, M. de, 482
Bismarck, Otto von, 110, 128, 195n
Blackburn, G.W., 65, 66, 72n
Bogdanov, A., 145
Boserup, A., 474, 475
Boulding, Elise, 566
Boulding, Kenneth E., xviii, 206–207, 371, 418
Boycott, C.C., 544
Boyer, E., 581
Brennan, D.G., *336–38*
Broad, W.J., 564–65
Brock, P., 453–54
Bryan, William Jennings, 133
Buchanan, J., 201, 202, *204*–205, 235, 237
Burbank, Luther, 148

Burgess, M., 38, 39
Burke, Edmund, 112

Caldicott, Helen, 478, 479–80, *485*, 532
Calhoun, John C., 112
Calvin, John, 9
Carlsmith, J.M., 86
Carter, J., 172
Cartwright, D., 90
Castro, Fidel, xxv, 250, 257
Cato, *56–57*
Cerf, C., 565
Charlemagne, 115
Charles I (King of England), 426
Chase, Stuart, 93
Che Gueva, 250
Cherkasov, N., 161
Chomsky, N., 12
Christoffel, K., 66
Churchill, Winston, *81*, 82–84
Clark, G., 504–505
Clausewitz, Carl von, 155, 158, 159, 179–*80*, 201, 249–50, 251, 267, 323, 417, 419, 428, 468
Cleveland, Grover, 133
Commager, H.S., 218
Cowper, William, *493–94*
Cowen, J., 417
Craig, P.P., 380
Crowley, P.M., 46
Cusack, T.R., 550

Dana, S., *82*
Darwin, Charles, xix, 15–16, 22; vulgar Darwinism, 16–18
Deborah, 83
Deegan, J. Jr., 315
Debs, Eugen, 231
Delilah, 469
Dembo, T., 36
Descartes, René, 101, 203
Deutsch, M., *150–151*
Deutsch, K.W., 364–65
Dickson, Paul, 169, 564
Disraeli, Benjamin, 67
Dollard, J., 33–34
Dostoyevsky, Feodor, 69, 88
Douhet, Giulio, *250*, 275
Drescher, M., 296

Dubinin, N.P., 148
Dulles, John Foster, 219, *259–60*, 298
DuPicq, 251–*52*
Dyson, Freeman, 484–487, 531, *532–34*, 535–36

Earle, E.M., 268, 270
Eckhardt, William, 84
Edison, Thomas A., 103
Edney, J.J., 556–57
Einstein, Albert, 471, 502, 243, 478
Eisenhower, Dwight, D., 219, 392n
Elizabeth (Empress of Austria), 187
Engels, Friedrich, 58, 79, 128, 199, 254, *488–89*, 496
Erasmus of Rotterdam, xix, 79, 488–89
Etheredge, L.S., 256
Etzioni, Amitai, 522
Euclid, 101

Fagan, R.E., 350
Faraday, Michael, 329
Ferdinand (Bourbon), 499
Ferdinand (Crown Prince), 70, 407
Feschbach, S., 38
Festinger, Leon, 85–86
Fisher, Roger, 514–520, 551
Flood, M.M., 296
Foch, Ferdinand, 251–52
Ford, Gerald, 172
Ford, Henry, 104
Forrester, J.W., 549
Foster, C., 539
Fourier, Charles, 237
Frederick II (King of Prussia), *78–79*, 420
Freeman, Derek, 17–18
Freud, Sigmund, *10–11*, 24, 34, 169
Friedenberg, E., 118

Galileo, 102, 148, 393
Galtung, Johann, 58–*59*, 64, 401, 578–79, 580
Gandhi, Mahatma, xix, 449, 461–64, 532
Genghiz Khan, 275, 362
George (King of Bohemia), 490, 493, 497–98

Gerard, Ralph W., 355–59
Goethe, Johann Wolfgang von, *93*
Glossop, R.J., 196–97
Gogol, N.V., *62*
Goldfield, B.A., *230*, 240
Goldwater, Barry, *111*, 172
Gompers, Samuel, 238
Gorbachev, Mikhail, 217, 222, 340, 391
Gray, Colin S., *221*, *328–29*, 331–*32*, 333–34, *339*, 587
Green, R., 39
Griftalconi, J., 505
Grotius, 491–92
Guibert, Jacques, 251, 322, 335, *416*, 439n

Hall, A.D., 350
Hammerstein, P., 273
Hannibal, 516
Harary, Frank, 90
Hardin, G., 556
Harding, Warren G., *117*
Harper, C.S., 556–57
Harris, M.R., 37
Harrison, Benjamin, *117*
Harsanyi, John C., 299–300
Hartsborne, H., 52
Hayakawa, S.I., *230*–31, 237, 240
Hazlett, B., 20
Hegel, G.W.F., 109–110, 202, 209, 494, 496; and collective freedom, *141*–43
Heider, F., 89
Hellman, Lillian, 22
Henry IV (King of France), 492
Hentoff, N., 450
Heraclitus, 106, 347
Herz, Alice, 234
Herzen, Alexander, *238*
Hitch, C.J., *485*–86
Hitler, Adolf, 94, 268, 387, 419, 534; race mystique of, *65*; war experience of, *80*, 83; scheme of conquest, 270; industrialists' support of, 390
Hobbes, Thomas, 119–*20*, 124, 148, 179, 268, 270, 495
Hofstadter, Douglas, 303n
Hofstadter, R., *133–34*

Holling, C.S., 360
Hokanson, J., 38–39
Hoover, Robert, 133
Hornblower, M., 118
Horvath, William, 539
Hutchins, Robert M., 573
Hyams, G.S., 195–96

Iakovlev, N.N., *116*, 213, 222
Iegoriev, Captain, 225
Isaacs, Rufus, 329–*30*
Isaiah, xix, 451, 488
Ivan the Terrible (czar), 161

Jackson, John, 454–55
Jackson, Andrew, 133
Jaures, J.L., 533
Jefferson, Thomas, 118, 133, 198, 238
Jervis, R., 321–22
Jesus, 9, 321, 443, 467
Jodl, Alfred, 533–34, 536
Johnson, Alexander Bryan, 103
Johnson, Lyndon B., 216
Jomini, A.H., 323
Jones, T.K., 480
Julius II (pope), 107, 401
Jungerman, J.A., 380

Kahn, Herman, 265–*66*, 285, *317–18*, 333–*34*, 335, *337*, 361–62, *579–80*, 587
Kant, Immanuel, 101, 494, *495*–96
Kautsky, Karl, 146, 238
Keith, George, 454
Kekulé, F.A., 330
Kennedy, John F., 82, 83, 84, *133*, 257, 283–85, 521
Kennedy, Robert, 81–*82*, *83*, 84
Kent, G., 567
Kepler, Johannes, 330
Khomeini, Ruholla, 243
Khrushchev, Nikita, 83, 392n
King, Martin Luther, 56, 235, 465, 477
Kingsley, Sydney, 22
Kissinger, Henry, *264*, *501–502*
Koestler, Arthur, *164*
Kohlberg, L., 47–49, 84, 449
Korzybski, Alfred, 91–93, 103, 574

Kreutzer, D.P., 549
Kuhn, T., 100
Kuo, Z.Y., 43
Kurtz, S., xx

Labriola, A., 238
Lansbury, G., 533
Laplace, P., 494
Lasby, C.G., 564
Lasswell, Harold, 507–508
Lefebre, Vladimir, *135*–40, 161
Leibnitz, G.W., 493
Levy-Bruhl, H., 57
Lenin, V.I., 189, 199, 208, 256, 497;
  on the Battle of Tsushima, *224–25*;
  fixation on orthodoxy, *146*, *158–60*, 176, 338; philosophical crusade, 15, 545–46; social revolution and, 144–45
Liddell Hart, J., 267–68, 415–*17*, 419, 439n, *460–61*
Lincoln, Abraham, 117–*18*
Locke, John, 118, 121
Lorenz, Konrad, 4, 6, 8, 13, 23
Louix XIV, 426
Louix XVI, 426
Louis XVIII, 499
Luce, R.D., xxi
Luke, 9
Lunacharsky, A., 175n
Lynch, Charles, 466
Lysenko, Trofim, 147–49, 582

Mach, Ernst, 145
Machiavelli, Niccolo, xix, 154, 160, 169
Madison, James, 199
Mahan, A.T., 250
Malcolmson, R.W., 478
Malthus, Thomas, 15–16
Mannheim, Karl, 97, 99–100, 113
Mantoux, E., 252
Mao Zedong, 189, 190, 249, 250
Marx, Karl (Marxism), 55, 58, 69, 97, 198, 202, 219, 236, 241; Bakunin and, 186; bases of society, 206; class struggle, 128–29; critizue of capitalism, 126–28, 496–97; ideology and, 97–99, 113, 158–159; materialism and idealism, 108–10,

142–45, 208–210; Soviet strategy and, 254
Maslow, Abraham, 10, 11, 121
May, A.J., 499
May, M.A., 52
Maynard Smith, J., 274, 559–60
McCarthy, J., 214
McDonald, F.J., 45
McDougal, M.S., 507–508
McElwee, W., 417–18
McKean, R.N., *485*–86
McKinley, William, 187
Mead, Margaret, *107–108*, 583
Meggitt, M., *78*
Meinhof, Ulrike, 188–*89*
Melman, S., *434–36*
Mendel, Gregor, 148
Metternich, Prince Clemens, 499, 501–502
Michaelangelo, 415
Michurin, I.V., 148
Midlarsky, I., 402–403, 411–12
Milgram, S., 49–51
Millard, E.L., 505
Miller, James G., 357
Millikan, Robert, 320
Mohammed, 63
Molesworth, W., 120
Molière, J.B.P., 5
Moltke, Helmuth, 275, 417–18, 420
Monroe, James, *117*, 199
Morgenstern, Oscar, 306
Morgenthau, Hans, 173, 225–30, 235–36, 238, 239–40
Morison, S.G., 218
Morozov, Pavlik, 139, 151n
Morris, Charles, 91
Morris, R., 118
Morse, J., 217–*218*
Moses, 26
Muelder, Walter, 450
Mussolini, Benito, 94, 419
Muste, A.J., *450–51*, 461
Myrdal, Alva, 386, 563

Napoleon I, 79–80, 179, 242, 250, 274–75, 323, 362, 416, 420, 426, 494, 498, 516
Napoleon III, 157

Nash, John, 306–307, 315–16, 516, 518
Nechaev, Sergei, *185–86*, 190
Newcombe, A., 403, 412–13
Newcombe, H., 503, 505–506, 566–67
Newton, Isaac, 144, 353
Nicholas I (czar), 499
Nicholas II (czar), 224
Nietzsche, Friedrich, 17
Nixon, Richard, *133*, 172
Noel-Baker, P., 386
Norman, R.Z., 90

Oppenheimer, Robert, 478, 532
Origen, 451–*52*
Orwell, George, 154–55, *165–66*, 215
Osgood, Charles E., 520
Otto I, 115n

Packel, E.W., 315
Paine, Thomas, 416
Painlevé, P., 252
Pavlov, Ivan, 43
Paul, D.A.L., 554
Payne, K., *221*
Paynell, T., 94
Penn, William, 454
Perry, Matthew, *218*
Peter the Great (czar), 322
Piaget, J., 45, 47
Pierrefeu, J., *251–52*
Plato, 101, 106, 114, 201
Plotius, 208
Plutarch, *57*
Pontriagin, L.S., 330
Possony, S.J., 251–52
Poussaint, A., *58*
Price, G.R., 274, 559
Pugachev, Yemelian, 52, 185, 195n
Pushkin, Alexander, 195n, 324n

Qaddafi, Muammar, 243

Radosh, R., 235
Raiffa, H., xxi
Rapoport, A., 336, 357, 512, 540, 556, 567

Rapport, D.J., 357
Rathjens, G., 581
Rawlings, E., 39
Razin, Stepan, 185, 195n
Reagan, Ronald, 169–70, 172, 193, 267, 380, 479–80
Remarque, E.M., *80–81*, 83
Ricardo, David, 126, 128
Richardson, Lewis F., 367–77, 383, 410, 512, 539, 549–50, 548, 567n; indices and, 394–96, 399, 406
Riechert, S.E., 273
Robespierre, Maximilien, 494
Rosenthal, L., 168
Robinson, J.P., 182
Rousseau, J.J., 493
Russett, B., 568n
Rutrell, M., 581
Ryerson, A., 580–81, *582*

Sakharov, Andrei, 222
Samson, 469
Saxe, Maurice de, 322
Schell, Jonathan, 579–80
Schellenberg, J.A., xix
Schelling, T.C., 315–*16*, 318–19, 323, 328, 333, 518, 551, 568n
Schiller, Friedrich, 209, *444*
Schwartz, K., 186
Scott, P.M., 44
Semmelweiss, I.P., 542
Senghaas, Dieter, 171–72
Shakespeare, William, *42*
Shapiro, E., *326*
Shapley, L.S., 314
Sharp, Gene, 457, 463, 467, 469, 472, 568n
Shaw, Bernard, 61
Shaw, Irwin, 22
Sherif, M., 506
Shubik, Martin, 314
Simpson, George, 76
Singer, J.D., 399, 401–402, 412, 413n
Sivard, R.L., 561
Small, M., 399, 401–402, 412, 413n
Smith, Adam, *122*, 123, *124*, 125, 201, 204, 363, 390–91
Smith, M.C., 452, 488, 492
Smoker, Paul, 548

Sohn, L., 504
Sokolovskii, V.D., *254–255*
Solzhenitzyn, Alexander, 222
Spencer, Herbert, 121
Spillane, M., *192–193*, 195n
Spinoza, 101
Spock, Benjamin, 235
Sraffa, P., 126
Stalin, J.V., 147–48, 164, 169, 199, *219*, 221, 233, 381, 497; addiction to power of, 160–61; and disarmament, 384–85; excesses of, 212–13, 215, 255
St. Augustine, 452, 457, 483
Stevenson, Adlai, 332
St. Paul, *121*
St. Pierre (Abbe), 492–93
Struve, P.B., 175n
Sully, Duke of (see Bethune, M.)
Surikov, V.I., 54
Suvorov, A.V., 426
Swift, Jonathan, 10, *53*
Szilard, Leo, 478

Tait, C.W., *341*
Tamerlane, 362
Thomson, D., 325
Thoreau, Henry David, *448–49*
Togo, H., 223–24
Tolchin, M., *436–37*
Tolstoy, Leo, xix, 58, 72n, *79–80*, 362–64, 412, 545; pacifism of, *444–51*, 459
Treischke, H. von, xix, *79*, 587
Trofimenko, G.A., 256
Trotsky, Leon, 254
Tuchachevsky, M.N., 255
Tucker, A.W., 296
Tullock, G., 201, 202, *204–*205, 235, 237

Turgenev, I., 58
Turner, J.E., 357
Twain, Mark, 168–69

Ulam, A.R., 218–*19*
Ury, W., 514–20, 551

Vagts, A., 179, 414–15, 418, 521
Van Alstyne, R.W., 218
Vattel, E., 492
Vavilov, N.I., 148
Vidal, Gore, 437
Von Neumann, J., 306
Vyshinsky, A.Y., 384

Wagner, Claus, *17*
Wagner, Richard, 66, 417, 375
Ward, M.D., 550
Washington, George, *117*
Weaver, Richard, *93–94*
Weik, M.H., 505
Wernette, D.R., 567
Westmoreland, W., *169*, 257
Wicksteed, P.H., 202, 301
Wilson, E.O., *26*, 54
Wilson Woodrow, 198
Wohlstetter, A., *378*
Wright, Quincy, xix
Wrong, D., 25
Wylie, J.C., 267–68, 248–49

Yarrow, C.H. Mike, 562–*63*
Yarrow, M.R., 44
Yogi, N., 223
York, M.F., 392n

Zamenhoff, L., 60
Zinnes, D., 405–406, 409, 410, 412

Subject Index

Abhorrence, war and, 79

Abolitionism, 477–88

Acquired freedom of self-determination, 119, 120–21

Action research, 562–63

Aggression, 3–13; cooperation and, 20–22; drives, 7–8; Freud's death-wish hypothesis, 10–11; frustration and, *see* Frustration and aggression; human nature and, 9–10; human potential and, 11–13; instinctive behavior, 6–7; Lorenz and, 4–5, 6, 8, 12; Maslow's list of human needs, 11; as part of being human, 8–9; single word explanations, 5–6; so-called evil, 4–5; sublimation of, 77

Alienation, 208–209

All Quiet on the Western Front (Remarque), 80–81

American Peace Society, 455–56

American Political Traditions (Hofstadter), 133–34

American way of war, 420–22; defense community and, 422–24

Anabaptists, 452–53, 455

Analogies, 353–54; based on identical mathematical structures, 354–55

Anarchists, 187

Apathy, war and, 80–81

Arms races, 366–92; keeping it going, 391–92; mass compulsion and, 389–91; model of, *see* Mathematical model of the arms race; negative feedback and, 366; positive feedback and, 366–67; qualitative, 378–84; suicidal tendencies and, 387–91; systemic inertia and, 386–87; when disarmament was almost within reach, 384–86

Artifacts, 28, 29

Art of war, 415–18

Attitudes, formation of, 52

Attitudinal balance, theory of, 89–90

Attitudinal perspective, *see* We and they

Authority, obedience to, 49–52

Balance of power, 239–43

"Balance of Power" game, 326–27, 551

Bargaining, 304–309; *see also* Cooperative games and strategic bargaining

Battle of Tsushima, 223–25

Bay of Pigs, 256–57

Behavioral perspective, 33–52; conditioning and imitation, 43–44; correlation between different forms of moral behavior, 52; formation of attitude, 52; frustration and aggression, *see* Frustration and aggression; moral development, 44–49; obedience to authority, 49–52; social learning, 44

Believers versus non-believers, 61–63

Bible, 26, 66–67, 77–78; pacifism and, 451, 454–455, 467, 469

Bolsheviks, 144–46, 157–60, 461

Brinkmanship, 298–300

Buddhism, 456

Cabinet wars, 425–26

Calculus of Consent, The (Buchana and Tullock), 201–202

Capitalism, critique of, 126–28, 496–97

Causal connections, 349–50

Characteristic function, 309–11

Chicken, game of, 298–300, 317–18

Christian theology, 9–10, 569; defensive alliance and, 490–91, 497–98; pacifism and, 443–57, 483; Reformation and, 574–75

Churchill, Winston, 81, 83–84

Circumstantial freedom of self-realization, 119–20

Citizen army, 425–28

Civilian defense, 468–73; feasibility of, as a substitute for military defense, 470–73; refusal to obey and, 469–70

Civilization and Its Discontents (Freud), 10–11

Civil rights movement, 233, 235, 464–65, 477

Class struggle, 128–29, 147; as an end in itself, *see* Violence, cult of

Coexistence and Soviet conceptions of a world order, 497–98

Cognitive dissonance, 85–88

Cognitive implications of the systemic world view, 359–62

Cold War, ideological issues of, 196–222; biological analogy and, 203–205; clash of, 210–11; Communist materialism, 208–10; Communist models of societies, present and future, 205–208; democracy, 212–13; economic model of politics and, 200–202; historical role of, in large-scale conflicts, 197–98; intellectual freedom, 213–15; internalized ideologies or hang-ups, 220–22; origins of, 198–200; religion, 211–12; rightists and leftists, 196–97; U.S. support of Soviet hardliners, 215–20

Collective freedom and the cult of struggle, 135–51; freedom conferred by, 140–42; genetics and, 147–49; from ideals to cults, 149–51; Lefebvre and, 135–40; Lenin and, 145–46; Lysenko and, 147–49; materialism and idealism, 142–45; paradigm of struggle as political clout, 147; Soviet versus U.S. ethical system and, 136–40

Collective security, 498–500; League of Nations and, 499–500; preservation of the status quo and, 498–99

Collective will, 155–57

Communism, 450–51; cold war and, *see* Cold war, ideological issues of; constitution and, 164; ideology of, 199–200; intellectual roots of, 161–62; materialism and, 208–10; society based on the love relationship and, 206–208; in the U.S., 230–36; *see also* Marx, Karl (Marxism)

Communist Manifesto, 496–97

Conclusions: can there be a science of peace?, 585–92; central role of language in shaping human affairs, 589; greater relevance of systemic dynamics compared to individual psyches, 590; pacifism, conflict resolution, and its limits, 591–92; perception of social reality as part of social reality, 588–89; power addiction as a possibly fatal disease of humanity, 589–90; relevance of strategic analysis, 590–91; variety of psychological concomitants of conflict, 588

Conditioning, 43

Conflict resolution, 457–58, 510–36; case of the Germanies and, 524–27; civil war in Nigeria and, 527–29; emphasis on the non-zero-sum nature of the game, 518–19; fights, games, and debates, 510–11; Graduated Reciprocation in Tension Reduction (GRIT), 520–23; limits of, 529–36, 591–92; objective criteria, 516–17; reconciliation, 523–29; rules of constructive debate, 511–16; separating the people from the problem, 517–18

Conservatism, 111–13

Constant-sum games, 286–89

Controlled experiments, 349–50

Cooperation and aggression, 20–22

Cooperative games and strategic bargaining, 304–24; characteristic function, 309–11; Chicken, 317–18; games nations play, 321–24; Nash's criteria and, 306–307; n-person, 309, 311–13; power indices, 313–15; randomized threats, 318–21; strategist's conception of the non-constant-sum game, 315–17

Cooperative interdependence, 506–507

Correlation, 396–98; dynamic indicators, 405–10; of war, 399–400; of war-proneness of states, 401–405

Creationist and evolutionist views of the world, 14–15

Cuba, 81–82, 256–57, 283–85

Cultural determinism, 24

Cultural evolution and transformation of functions, 30–31

Death-wish hypothesis, 10–11

Debates, 511; rules for constructive, 511–16

Decisions: momentous risky, 283–86; under certainty, 277; under risk, 278–82; see also Limits of individual rationality

Deduction, 104–105

Defense community, 422–24

Dehumanization, 166–68

De Jure Belli et Pacis (Grotius), 491–92

Democracy and the Cold War, 212–13

Democratized wars, 425–28

Desensitization through habituation, 181–82

Deterrence, 332–35

Disarmament, 384–86; systemic inertia and, 386–87

Doomsday Machine, 317

Drives, 7–8

Dynamic indicators, 405–10

Dynamic view of the world, 14–15, 105–108

Economic model of politics, 200–202

Economy, war, 430–36, domestic economy and, 436–37

Ecstacy, war and, 77–78

Empiricism, 102–104

End of ideology, 223–44; in America, 230–36; Battle of Tsushima and, 223–25; political realism and pragmatism, 236–43; theoretical framework of political realism and, 225–30

End of Ideology, The (Bell), 232–33

Enlightenment, road to, 574–77

Environment, war as a system adapted, to, 429–36

Equilibrium principle, 288–89, 291–94

Erasmus of Rotterdam, 79, 488

Ethical systems, Soviet versus U.S., 136–40

Evil, so-called, 4–5

Evolutionarily stable strategy (ESS), 274

Evolutionary perspective, 14–32; aggression or cooperation, 20–22; evolution independent of genes, 27–30; implications of cultural evolution and transformation of functions, 30–31; natural selection, 15–16; reproductive success, 18–20; sociobiological theory of human aggression, 22–27; static and dynamic views of the world, 14–15; vulgar Darwinism, 16–18

Exchange relationship, societies based on, 204, 206–208

Exploring Nonviolent Alternatives (Sharp), 465–67

Fate of the Earth, The (Schell), 579–80

Fear, 76

Fights, 510

Flexible response strategy, 263–66

Founding fathers, 198–99, 239

Freedom, *see* Collective freedom and the cult of struggle; Individual freedom and the cult of property

Free market, *see* Laissez-faire

Frustration and aggression, 33–35; catharsis and, 38–39; disentangling, 39–42; experiments in, 35–38; names and, 42

Functional cooperation, 506–507

Functionalism, 429–30

Games, 510–11

Games nations play, 321–24

Game theory, 268–75; science of peace and, 590–91; thinking induced by analysis of, 551–52; *see also* Cooperative games and strategic bargaining; Limits of individual rationality

General system theory, 353

Genetic basis of behavior, 22–30; evolution independent of, 27–30; Lysenko affair and, 147–49; sociobiological theory of human aggression, 22–27

Germanies, reconciliation and, 524–27

Ghost of Napoleon, The (Liddell Hart), 415–17

Global modeling, 548–51

God, 117

"Godson, The," 444–45, 446

Graduated Reciprocation in Tension Reduction (GRIT), 520–23

Hegemony, 171–74

Hero worship, war and, 79–80

History of Militarism, A (Vagts), 414–15, 418–20

Homo economicus, 123–24

Human nature, 9–10

Human potentiality, 11–13

Idealism, 108–10, 142–45; war and, 78–79

Ideology, 97–114; constraints of, on strategy, 253; end of, *see* End of ideology; Marx and, 97–99, 108–10, 113; materialism and idealism, 108–10; orientations toward the past, the present, and the future, 110–14; rationalism and empiricism, 101–104; scientific outlook, 104–105; scope of the term, 100–101; static and dynamic views of the world, 105–108; *see also specific ideological issues*

Ideology and Utopia (Mannheim), 97, 99, 100

Imitation, 43–44

Indices, 321, 394–96; constants and, 394; correlation and, *see* Correlation; critique, 410–13; dynamic indicators, 405–10; parameters, trends, and, 393–413; quantification and, 393

Individual freedom and the cult of property, 116–34; class struggle and, 128–29; idea of freedom, 119–21; laissez-faire, *see* Laissez-faire opportunity and, 129–34; ritual of self-praise, 117–18

Induction, 104–105

Inertial properties of large systems, 362–64; disarmament and, 386–87

Infrastructure and peace research, 542–45

Instinctive behavior, 6–7

Intellectual freedom and the Cold War, 213–15

Intellectualization of war, 325–43; "A long and healthy future," 328–31; "Balance of Power" game and, 326–27; catalysts of inquiry, 329–31; deterrence and, 332–35; rationality and, 335–40; strategic studies and public policy, 331–35; technolatry, objectivity, and cost-benefit tally, 340–42

International law, 489–94; early attempts at, 489–92; in the spirit of the enlightenment, 492–94; *see also* World order, conceptions of a

International relations and realism, 238–43

Interrelatedness, 347–48, 350–53; of disciplines concerned with living systems, 358–59

Investigative journalism, 563–65

"Ivan the Fool," 445–46, 449

Joy, war and, 80

Justice as private enterprise, 192–93

Khmer Rouge, 173

"Know-how" and "know why," 573–74

Labor theory of value, 126–28

Laissez-faire, 121–28, 200–201; critique of, and capitalist system, 126–28; as replacement for the mercantile theory, 125–26; Smith and, 122–25

Language, 27–29; behavior and, 91–94; central role of, 589; speakers versus non-speakers, 60–61; unsane, 92–93

Law, disavowal of, 163–64

Law of Nature, 491–92

League of Nations, 499–500, 504

Leftist ideologies, 196–97; new versus old, 230–36

Limits of individual rationality, 276–303; beyond two-person zero-sum games, 291–97; Chicken, 298–300; decisions under certainty, 277; decisions under risk, 278–82; escape from social traps, 300–302; mixed strategies, 289–91; momentous risky decisions, 283–86; Prisoner's Dilemma, 296–98; probability and, 279; two-person antagonistic games, 286–89; utility and, 278, 280–82

Logic of Images in International Relations, The (Jervis), 321–22

Love relationship, societies based on, 206–208, 209

Manifest Destiny, 218

Mass compulsion, 389–91

Massive retaliation, 332–33

Materialism, 108–10, 142–45; Communist, 208–10

Materialism and Empiriocriticism (Lenin), 145–46, 147

Mathematical model of the arms race, 367–73; conditions that determine stability, 371–72; critique of, 373–75; differential equations, 367–73; implications of, 375–77; indices and, 394–96; stable case, 368–70; unstable case, 370–71

Mathematical models, thinking stimulated by, 548–51
Mathematics, 350–53; analogies based on, 354–55
Maximin principle, 287, 288, 291–94
Mennonites, 452, 453
Methodological individualism, 202, 203–204
Militarism, 414–15, 418–20; American Way of war and, 420–22; defense community and, 422–24
Military-industrial complex, 430–36
Mixed-motive games, 292
Moral development, 44–49
Moral neutrality and objectivity, 571–73
Muenster, 452–53
Multiple Independently Targeted Reentry Vehicles (MIRVs), 341–42
Mutual Assured Destruction (MAD), 260–63, 533
Mutual Assured Vulnerability, 339

Names, 42
Nationalism, 68–72
National security, 74–76
Natural freedom of self-determination, 119, 121
Natural selection, 15–16
Nazis, 61, 64, 65–67, 110, 174, 193–94, 338, 530; dehumanization by, 167–68; law, disavowal of, 163–64; rationality, disavowal of, 162
Negative feedback loops, 356, 366
Nerves of Government (Deutsch), 364–65
New Deal, 131–32
New Left, 230–36
Nigeria, reconciliation of the civil war in, 527–29
1984 (Orwell), 154–55, 165–66
Non-constant-sum game, 286; strategist's conception of, 315–17
Non-directive therapy, 512
Non-provocative defense, 473–76
Non-tuism, 202, 210, 272

Nonviolent struggle, 460–61; against oppression, 465–68; civilian defense and, 468–73; civil rights movement and, 464–65; Gandhi and, 461–64
Non-zero-sum games, 326–27, 518–19, 551–52
Normalized Banzhof index, 314
N-person cooperative games, 309; stability of solution to, 311–13
Nuclear war, 73–76; accidental, 553–54; flexible response and, 263–66; intellectualization of, *see* Intellectualization of war; massive retaliatory power and, 259–60; Mutual Assured Destruction and, 260–63
Nuclear Weapons and Foreign Policy (Kissinger), 264

Objectivity and moral neutrality, 571–73
Omnipotence, illusion of, 165–66
On Aggression (Lorenz), 4–5, 6, 8, 13
On Escalation (Kahn), 265–66
On Thermonuclear War (Kahn), 333–35
On War (Clausewitz), 155, 180, 249
Organismic general system theory, 355–58
Orientations toward the past, the present, and the future, 110–14
Origin of the Species, The (Darwin), 16–17

Pacifism, 443–88; abolitionism and, 477–88; limits of, 591–92; non-provocative defense and, 473–76; nonviolent struggle and, *see* Nonviolent struggle; personal, 444–51; political, 457–60; religious, 451–57; "selective," 476–78
Packel-Deegan power index, 314–15
Parameters, trends, and indices, 393–413
Pareto optimality, 295, 518

Past experience, constraint on strategy of, 251–53
Patriotism, 426–27
Peace education, 569–84; attacks on, 580–851; "know-how" and "know why," 573–74; polemical aspects of, 577–81; political aspects of, 582–83; preparing for peace, 583–84; road to Enlightenment, 574–77; scope of, 570–71; what is and what ought to be, 571–73
Peace movement, 212–13
Peace research, 367–73; correlates of war and, 399–405; correlation and, 396–98; problems of, *see* Problems of peace research
Perpetual peace, 492–96
Personality theory, 84–85
Personal pacifism, 444–51
Poisson distribution, 355
Political liberty, 141
Political pacifism, 457–60; concerted action and, 459–60; conflict resolution and, 457–58; injustice and, 458–59
Positive feedback loops, 366–67
Positive peace, 507–508
Power, 152–75; addiction to, 152–55, 589–90; as a commodity, 153–54; dehumanization and, 166–68; hegemony and, 171–74; law, disavowal of, 163–64; omnipotence, illusion of, 165–66; orthodoxy, fixation on, 157–61; over people, 155–57; rationality, disavowal of, 161–62; responsibility, disavowal of, 164–65; technolatry and, 168–70; triumph of, 163–64
Power indices, 313–15
Pragmatism and political realism, 236–43
Predation, 18
Prisoner's Dilemma, 296–97, 551, 556–60; escape from social traps, 300–302; iterated many times, 297–98
Private detectives, 192–93

Probability, 279
Problems of peace research, 537–68; academic respectability, 561–62; action research, 562–63; application of, 567; building an infrastructure, 542–45; changing our way of thinking, 547–58; data gathering, 560–61; game-theoretic analysis, thinking induced by, 551–52; investigations of causes of wars, 539–41; investigative journalism, 563–65; mathematical models, thinking stimulated by, 548–51; medical research analogy, 540–44; relevance of behavioral and social sciences to, 555–60; relevance of "hard" sciences to, 552–55; search for self-knowledge, 546; self-examination and, 565–67; technological fixes, 545–46
Professional fighters, 176–80; Clausewitz and, 179–80; examples of, 176–77; loyalty of, 426; selection of, 177–178; transformation of, 427–28; weapons and, 178
Project Paperclip (Lasby), 564
Property, cult of, 116–34
Psycholinguistics, 91–94
Psychological approach, 73–94, 588; attitudes and, *see* We and they; attitudinal balance, 89–90; behavior and, *see* Behavioral perspective; cognitive dissonance, 85–88; diversity of states associated with war, 77–84; evolution and, *see* Evolutionary perspective; fear and rage, 76; language and behavior, 91–94; national security and, 74–76; personality theory, 84–85; war as a manifestation of aggression, 73–76

Quaker Experiences in International Conciliation (Yarrow), 523–29, 562–63; case of the Germanies, 524–27; civil war in Nigeria, 527–29

Quakers, 452, 453–55, 562–63; reconciliation and, 523–29
Quantification, 393
Quintuple Alliance, 499–500

Racism, 58, 63–67
Rage, 76
Randomized threats, 318–21
Rationalism, 101–104; conception of a world order and, 494–96
Rationality: collective, 274, 295; of a decision, 279–82; disavowal of, 161–62; individual, *see* Limits of individual rationality; of war, 335–40, 418–20
Reactive theories, 33
Realist school of political science: pragmatism and, 236–43; theoretical framework of, 225–30
Red Army, 254–56
Religion, 62–63; Cold War and, 211–12; Enlightenment and, 574–77; pacifism and, 443–57
Reproductive success, 18–20
Responsibility, disavowal of, 161–62
Revolutionary Catechism, The (Nechaev or Bakunin), 185
Rightist ideologies, 196–97
Rising expectations, 37–38
Rote Armee Fraction (RAF), 188–90

Science and Sanity (Korzybski), 92–93
Science of peace, *see* Conclusions: can there be a science of peace?
Scientific outlook, 104–105
Scientific revolutions, 100–101
"Selective pacifism," 476–78
Self-knowledge, search for, 546
Self-praise, American, 117–118, 133–34
Shapley value of a game, 314
Signals, 321
Simulations, global, 548–51
Single word explanations, 5–6

Situational constraint on strategy, 250–51
Socialist Party, 231–32
Social learning, 44
Sociobiological theory of human aggression, 22–27
Sociology of knowledge, 97; *see also* Ideology
Socialty reality, perception of, as part of social reality, 588–89
Spectators of the cult of violence, 180–83
Stability and justice, 501–502
Star Warriors (Broad), 564–65
Static view of the world, 14–15, 105–108
Stationary attrition defense, 474–75
Status inconsistency, 401
Stockholm International Peace Research Institute (SIPRI), 561–62
Strategic bargaining, *see* Cooperative games and strategic bargaining
Strategic Defense Initiative (SDI, Star Wars), 216–17, 271, 391, 473, 552–53
Strategic Studies and Public Policy (Gray), 331–35
Strategy, 247–75; American, 256–58; flexible response, 263–66; general theory of, 267–75; ideological constraints in, 253; massive retaliatory power, 259–60; Mutual Assured Destruction, 260–63; in the nuclear age, 258–66; past experience, constraint of, 251–53; as a philosophy of war, 248–50; prevailing, 266–67; sequential and cumulative, 249–50; situational constraints on, 250–51; Soviet, 253–56; theory of games and, 268–75, 287; *see also specific systemic issues*
Strategy and Conscience (Rapoport), 336–37, 339–40
Strategy of Conflict, The (Schelling), 316
Structural violence, 64–65

Suicide, 387–91
Sully, Duke of, 492–93
Sure-thing principle, 291–94
Systemic view of the world, 347–65; analogies, 353–55; Being, Acting, and Becoming, 357–58; cognitive implications of, 359–62; establishing causal connections, 349–50; inertial properties, of large systems, 362–64; interrelatedness and, 347–48, 350–53, 358–59; legitimizing the biological metaphor, 364–65; mathematical paradigm, 350–53; organismic general system theory, 355–58; science of peace and, 590; systems, 350–51; wholeness and, 347, 350–53; see also specific systemic issues

Tabula rasa model, 11–12
Teach-ins, 233–35, 477
Technolatry, 168–70, 257–58; objectivity, cost-benefit tally and, 340–42
Technological fixes and peace research, 545–46
Television, violence on, 180–83
Tension Ratio (TR), 404–405
Territorial Imperative, The (Ardrey), 22, 23–24
Terrorism, 183–92; anarchists, 187; classification of, 184; features of, 183–84; ideological, 184–92; modern, 187–92; nationalist, 184; Rote Armee Fraction (RAF), 188–90; Russian, 185–86; southern European, 186–87; state, 191–92, 193; worldwide organizations of, 190–91
Theory of games, see Games theory
Thesis-antithesis-synthesis, 109–10
Thinking About the Unthinkable in the 1980s (Kahn), 580
Think Tanks (Dickson), 564
Threat relationship, societies based on, 206–208

Tit-For-Tat (TFT), 273–74, 558–59, 561
Top dog versus underdog, 55–59
Tragedy of the Commons, 551, 556–57
Trends, 395, 397–98; see also Indices
Twain, Mark, 168–69
Two-person antagonistic games, 286–89; beyond, 291–97
Two-valued orientation, 90–94

United Nations, 500–502; new world order and, 503–507
University of Michigan, 234–35
Us and them, see We and they
Utility, 278; expected, 280–82

Values, 572–73
Vicarious experience of violence, 180–83
Vietnam War, 233–36, 477–78
Violence, cult of, 176–94; justice as private enterprise, 192–93; professionals, see Professional fighters; roots of violence-oriented politics, 193–94; spectators, 180–83; terrorism, see Terrorism

War, 73–76; abhorrence and, 79; among the victims, 82–84; apathy and, 80–81; businesslike attitude and, 78; correlates of, 399–400; ecstacy and, 77–78; hero worship and, 79–80; hero worshiped and, 80; intellectualization of, see Intellectualization of war; joy and, 80; at the pinnacle of power, 81–82; strategy and, see Strategy; see also War system
War and Peace (Tolstoy), 79–80, 362–63, 364
War-proneness of states, correlate of, 401–403; militarization of economy and, 403–405
"Warriors and victims," 484–88; conflict resolution and, 530–36

War system, 414–39; adapted to its environment, 429–36; American way of war, 420–22; art of war, 415–18; declining economy and, 436–37; defense community, 422–24; everyman's war and specialist's war, 425–28; as an institution, 425; other adaptations, 438; "rational" and "humane" conduct of war, 418–20; war economy and, 430–36

War toys, 325

Watts riots, 230

Wealth of Nations, The (Smith), 122, 123–24

We and they, 53–72; believers versus non-believers, 61–63; nationalism, 68–72; racism, 63–67; speakers versus non-speakers, 60–61; top dog versus underdog, 55–59

Weapons and Hope (Dyson), 484–87, 531–36

What is and what ought to be, 571–73

Wholeness, 347, 350–53

World Military and Social Expenditure (Sivard), 561

World order, conceptions of a, 489–509; coexistence and Soviet, 497–98; collective security and, 498–500; Communist Manifesto and, 496–97; conditions of "positive peace," 507–509; early attempts to regulate war, 489–92; international law in the spirit of the enlightenment, 492–94; League of Nations and, 499–500; preservation of the status quo and, 498–99; proposed roads toward, 502–507; rationalist, 494–96; United Nations and, 500–502

World Peace through World Law (Clark and Sohn), 504–505

World Restored, A (Kissinger), 501–502

Zero-sum games, 286–89; beyond, 291–97